Jewish City or Inferno of Russian Israel?

A History of the Jews in
Kiev before February 1917

Jews of Russia and Eastern Europe and Their Legacy

Series Editor
Maxim D. Shrayer (Boston College)

Editorial Board
Ilya Altman (Russian Holocaust Center and Russian State University for the Humanities)
Karel Berkhoff (NIOD Institute for War, Holocaust and Genocide Studies)
Jeremy Hicks (Queen Mary University of London)
Brian Horowitz (Tulane University)
Luba Jurgenson (Universite ParisIV—Sorbonne)
Roman Katsman (Bar-Ilan University)
Dov-Ber Kerler (Indiana University)
Vladimir Khazan (Hebrew University of Jerusalem)
Mikhail Krutikov (University of Michigan)
Joanna Beata Michlic (Bristol University)
Alice Nakhimovsky (Colgate University)
Antony Polonsky (Brandeis University)
Jonathan D. Sarna (Brandeis University)
David Shneer (University of Colorado at Boulder)
Anna Shternshis (University of Toronto)
Leona Toker (Hebrew University of Jerusalem)
Mark Tolts (Hebrew University of Jerusalem)

Jewish City or Inferno of Russian Israel?

A History of the Jews in
Kiev before February 1917

Victoria Khiterer

Boston
2017

Library of Congress Cataloging-in-Publication Data:

The bibliographic data for this title is available from the Library of Congress.

© 2016 Academic Studies Press

All rights reserved

ISBN 978-1-61811-476-1(cloth), ISBN 978-1-61811-634-5 (paper)
ISBN 978-1-61811-477-8 (electronic)

Book design by Kryon Publishing
www.kryonpublishing.com

Published by Academic Studies Press in 2016, paperback 2017
28 Montfern Avenue
Brighton, MA 02135, USA
press@academicstudiespress.com
www.academicstudiespress.com

The publisher and the series editor gratefully acknowledge the support of Boston College.

To the memory of
John Doyle Klier

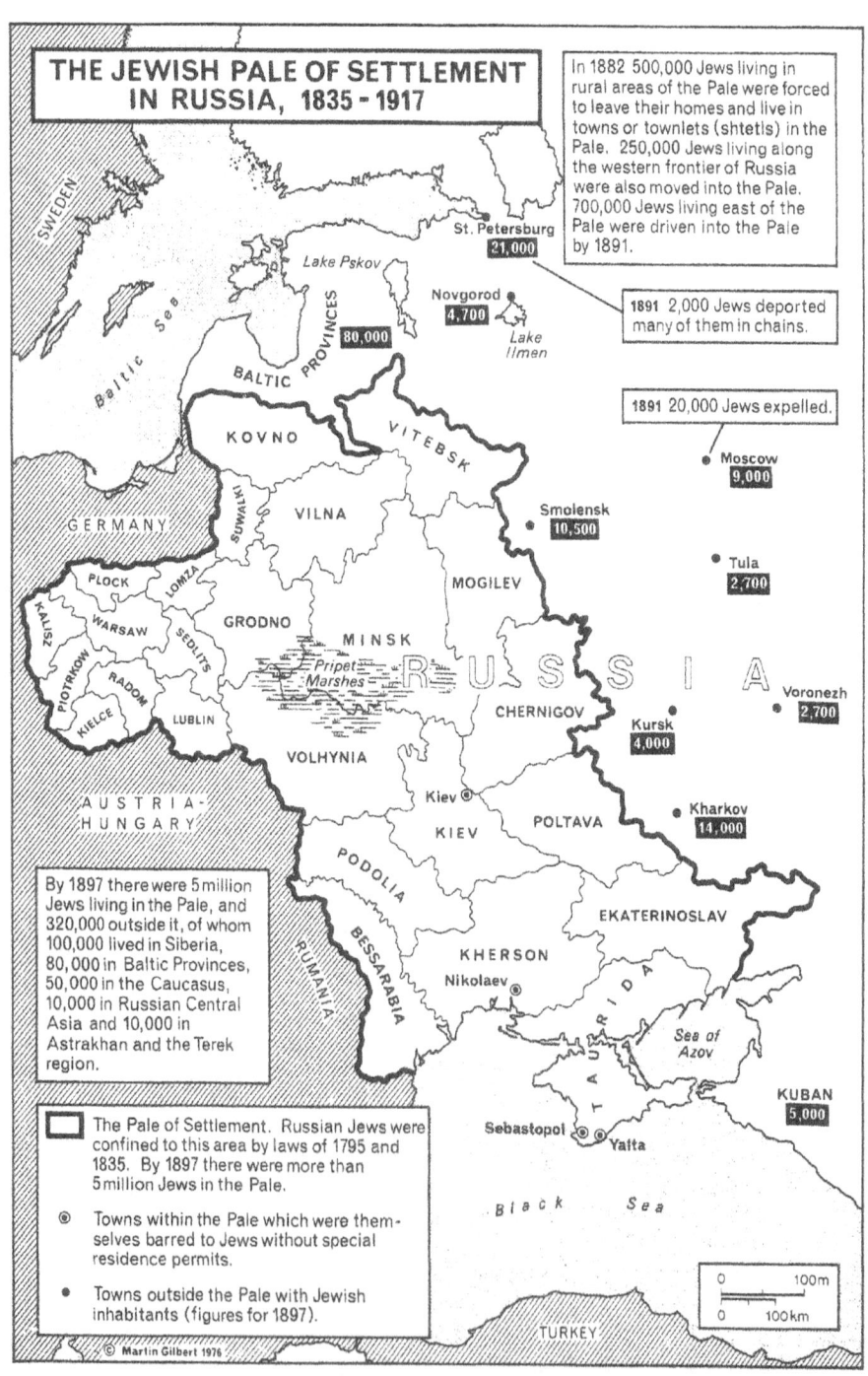

Map 1. The Jewish Pale of Settlement in Russia, 1835–1917. From Sir Martin Gilbert, *The Routledge Atlas of Jewish History*, © **Sir Martin Gilbert (2010),** Routledge, reproduced by permission of Taylor & Francis Books UK.

Map 2. Kiev circa 1900. Courtesy of Indiana University Press. All rights reserved. From Natan M. Meir, *Kiev, Jewish Metropolis, a History, 1859–1914*.

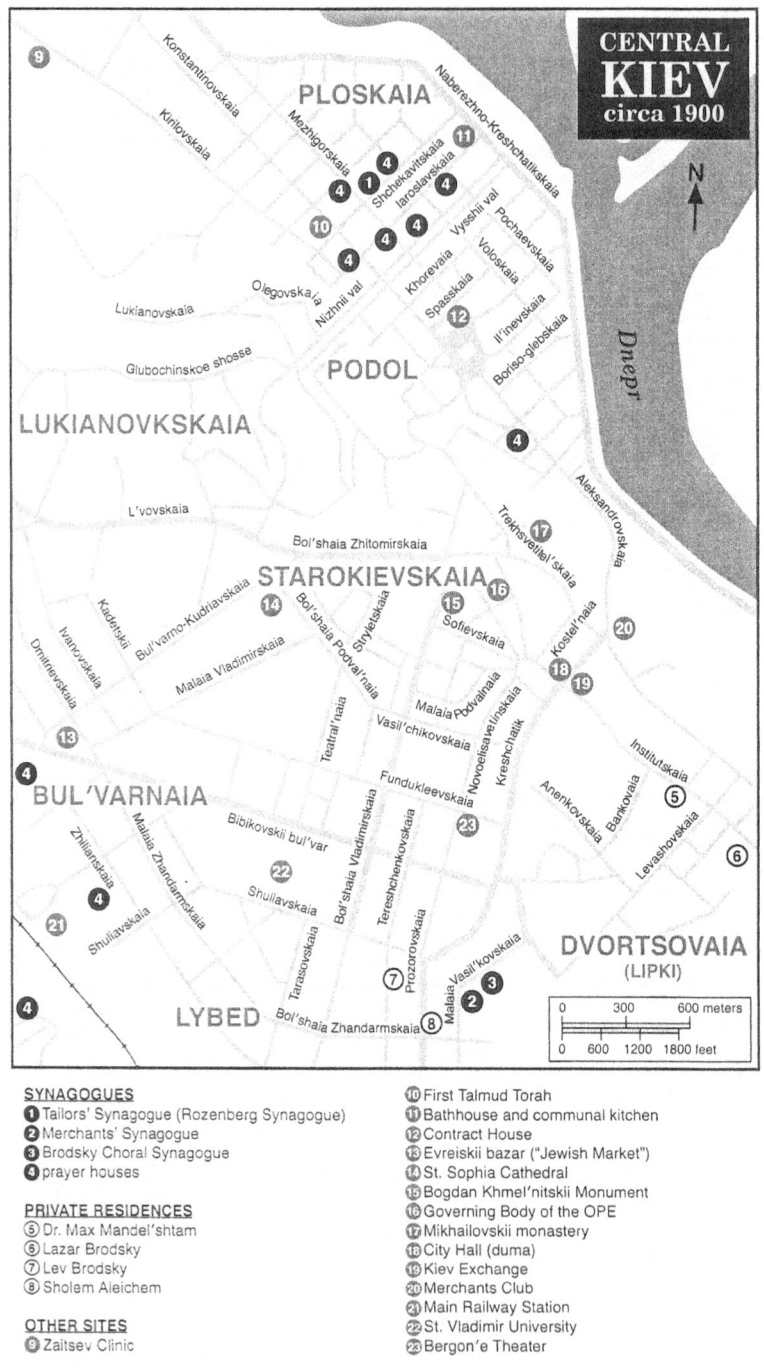

SYNAGOGUES
① Tailors' Synagogue (Rozenberg Synagogue)
② Merchants' Synagogue
③ Brodsky Choral Synagogue
④ prayer houses

PRIVATE RESIDENCES
⑤ Dr. Max Mandel'shtam
⑥ Lazar Brodsky
⑦ Lev Brodsky
⑧ Sholem Aleichem

OTHER SITES
⑨ Zaitsev Clinic
⑩ First Talmud Torah
⑪ Bathhouse and communal kitchen
⑫ Contract House
⑬ Evreiskii bazar ("Jewish Market")
⑭ St. Sophia Cathedral
⑮ Bogdan Khmel'nitskii Monument
⑯ Governing Body of the OPE
⑰ Mikhailovskii monastery
⑱ City Hall (duma)
⑲ Kiev Exchange
⑳ Merchants Club
㉑ Main Railway Station
㉒ St. Vladimir University
㉓ Bergon'e Theater

Central Kiev, c. 1900. *Cartography by Margaret Seiler, based on map in* The YIVO Encyclopedia of Jews in Eastern Europe.

Map 3. Central Kiev circa 1900. Courtesy of Indiana University Press. All rights reserved. From Natan M. Meir, *Kiev, Jewish Metropolis, a History, 1859–1914*.

Contents

Acknowledgments x
Abbreviations xiii
A Note on Dates, Spelling, and Names xiv
List of Tables xiv
List of Illustrations xv
List of Maps xviii

Introduction 1
Chapter One.
The History of Jews in Kiev from the Tenth Century to 1660 21
Chapter Two.
The Jews of Kiev in the Embrace of the Russian Empire (1794–1859) 45
Chapter Three.
The Jewish Right of Residence in Kiev in 1859–1917 87
Chapter Four.
The Kiev Jewish Community and its Leaders 135
Chapter Five.
The Wealth and Poverty of Jews in Kiev 196
Chapter Six.
Jewish Pogroms and the Beilis Affair 259
Chapter Seven.
How Jews Gained Their Education in Kiev 290
Chapter Eight.
Jewish Culture in Kiev 332
Chapter Nine.
Between Tradition and Modernity: Jewish Religious Life in Kiev 387
Conclusion 422

Appendix. Dmitrii Bogrov and the Assassination of Stolypin 428
Bibliography 437
Index 458

Acknowledgments

This book is based on my second doctoral dissertation, defended at Brandeis University in 2008. I really appreciate the generous advice and support of a number of individuals and organizations during my work on the book. First and foremost, I would like to give my heartfelt thanks to my thesis adviser, Professor Antony Polonsky. He brought me to Brandeis as a doctoral student, which allowed me to successfully pursue my academic career in the United States. His lectures, advice, and our scholarly conversations helped me gain a deeper understanding of Western historiography, which has had a major influence on my work. I would also like to thank Professor Polonsky for his intensive review and careful editing of this work, as well as his wife Arlene, to whom I am grateful for her many improvements to the text. Professor Marcus Levitt of the University of Southern California was kind enough to edit several chapters of this work, for which I am very grateful.

The excellent lectures of Brandeis University Professors Jonathan D. Sarna and Benjamin Ravid deepened and widened my knowledge of Jewish history. Professor Sarna's academic support, interest in my work, and personal encouragement gave me confidence in my scholarship and inspired my work on my dissertation and this book.

The thoughtful advice, recommendations, and comments of the late Professor John Doyle Klier helped shape this work. I had the good fortune to meet Professor Klier in 1991 in the Kiev archives at the beginning of my academic career. He had a major influence on my formation as a scholar and helped me many times during my academic career. Professor Klier was the external reader for my first doctoral dissertation in 1996 at the Russian State University of Humanities in Moscow, and he provided comments and corrections for four chapters of my second dissertation before his untimely death in 2007.

I really appreciate all the help and encouragement of Professor Maxim D. Shrayer. Professor Shrayer encouraged me to publish this book with Academic Studies Press and found financial support for its publication. The publication of this book was also supported by a publication grant from Millersville University. I want to give special thanks to the Faculty Grant Committee, the Dean of the School of Humanities and Social Sciences, Dr. Diane Umble, and the Chair of the History Department, Professor Ronald Frankum for their support for the preparation of my book and their encouragement of my work.

I began to gather materials for this book while I was a Eugene and Daymel Shklar Fellow at the Ukrainian Research Institute at Harvard University in the fall of 2002. My conversations with Professor Roman Szporluk and Dr. Lubomyr Hajda guided the formulation of this work's main ideas. My access to Harvard University's libraries, which I had during this scholarship, and later during the years of my association with the Harvard Ukrainian Research Institute (HURI), gave me access to many important sources for this work.

In would like to thank my colleagues Simon Rabinovitch and Natan Meir for their suggestions and advice. Natan Meir's book, *Kiev, Jewish Metropolis: A History, 1859-1914*, and several of his articles became important sources for this text.

My visits to Kiev and YIVO archives and libraries were made possible due to the generous support of a number of American institutions and organizations. I received the Natalie and Mendel Racolin Memorial Fellowship at the YIVO Institute for Jewish Research, two grants from the Tauber Institute for the Study of European Jewry, an IREX (The International Research and Exchanges Board) grant, a Pennsylvania State System of Higher Education Faculty Professional Development Council grant, a Marion and Jasper Whiting Foundation grant, and several grants from Brandeis University. I really appreciate this generous financial support for my research.

The late Mrs. Alla Spektor, who was an archivist at the Center for Studies of the History and Culture of East European Jewry in Kiev, generously helped my research in the Kiev archives. I am very thankful for the advice of Mr. Mikhail Kalnitsky, a senior scholar at the Center, whose works brought to light many unknown aspects of the history of Kiev and its Jewish community. I would like to express my gratitude to the Director of the Center for Studies of the History and Culture of East European Jewry, Leonid Finberg, and to Mr. Kalnitsky for their permission to use illustrations from their collections in this book.

I really appreciate the endless support of my parents, Michael Khiterer and Ludmila Brovarnik, and their encouragement of my education and my work on this book. Finally, I must give my heartfelt thanks to my husband James E. Danaher, who is the indefatigable editor of my writings, and who cheerfully supported me throughout all my trials and tribulations in completing this monograph.

Without this scholarly, financial, moral, and practical support, this work would certainly not have been possible. Thanks to you all!

Abbreviations

CAHJP—The Central Archive for the History of the Jewish People, Jerusalem
DAKO—The State Archive of the Kiev Region
DAMK—The State Archive of the City of Kiev
GARF—The State Archive of the Russian Federation
PSZ—Polnoe sobranie zakonov Rossiiskoi imperii (The Complete Collection of Laws of the Russian Empire)
RGIA, St. Petersburg—Russian State Historical Archive, St. Petersburg
RGVIA—Russian State Military Historical Archive
TsDAKFFD U—The Central State Archive of Film, Photo, Sound Documents of Ukraine
TsDIAK U—The Central State Historical Archive of Ukraine in the City Kiev
YIVO—YIVO Institute for Jewish Research, New York

A Note on Dates, Spelling, and Names

Pre-revolutionary dates in this book are given in the "Old Style." In conformity with academic practice, pre-revolutionary Russian orthography has been modernized. Transliterations follow the Library of Congress method, except where a common usage in English is well-established.

In the text I use "Sholom Aleichem." In notes, I refer to the famed writer with his name as spelled in the title page of the cited work; thus "Sholem Aleichem" also appears.

List of Tables

Table I: Kiev Population According to the 1897 Census 96

Table II: Jewish Population of Largest Cities
According to the 1897 Census 98

Table III: Budget of the Kiev Jewish Community for 1907 144

List of Illustrations

Figure 1.	Kreshchatik Street at the turn of the twentieth century. Postcard.	242
Figure 2.	Proreznaia Street at the turn of the twentieth century. Postcard.	242
Figure 3.	Downtown Kiev, early twentieth century. Postcard.	243
Figure 4.	Podol, Jewish district of Kiev. Postcard.	243
Figure 5.	View of Podol from Truchanov Island. Postcard.	244
Figure 6.	Ester Vons, the author's great-grandmother in Kiev, circa 1905. Courtesy of the author.	244
Figure 7.	Israel Brodsky. Courtesy of the Center for Studies of the History and Culture of East European Jewry.	245
Figure 8.	Lazar Brodsky. Courtesy of the Center for Studies of the History and Culture of East European Jewry.	245
Figure 9.	Lev (Leon) Brodsky. Courtesy of the Center for Studies of the History and Culture of East European Jewry.	246
Figure 10.	The Circus Lover, Solomon Brodsky, 1880s. Courtesy of Lybid' Publishing House.	246
Figure 11.	Brodsky Choral Synagogue. Postcard.	247
Figure 12.	Bessarabskii Market. Postcard.	247
Figure 13.	Kiev Rabbi Evsei Tsukkerman. Courtesy of Mikhail Kalnitsky.	248
Figure 14.	Max Mandelstamm. Courtesy of the Center for Studies of the History and Culture of East European Jewry.	248
Figure 15.	David Margolin. Courtesy of Mikhail Kalnitsky.	249
Figure 16.	Iosif Marshak. Courtesy of the Center for Studies of the History and Culture of East European Jewry.	249

Figure 17. Cover of the book devoted to the 35th anniversary of Marshak Jewelry Company, Kiev, 1913. 250

Figure 18. The persecution of Jews in Russia: scene inside the Arsenal at Kiev (after the pogrom of 1881). *The Illustrated London News*, June 18, 1881. 250

Figure 19. Sholom Aleichem with his family. Courtesy of the Central State Archive of Film, Photo, Sound Documents of Ukraine. 251

Figure 20. Beilis and his counselors. Postcard. 251

Figure 21. Tsar Nicholas II greeted by the Kiev Jewish delegation (from left to right: Kiev Rabbi Iakov Aleshkovskii, Kiev Rabbi Avram Gurevich, and barrister Avraam Gol'denberg), 1911. Courtesy of the Central State Archive of Film, Photo, Sound Documents of Ukraine. 252

Figure 22. Petr A. Stolypin. Courtesy of the Central State Archive of Film, Photo, Sound Documents of Ukraine. 252

Figure 23. Kiev City Theater (now Kiev Opera Theater). Postcard. 253

Figure 24. Mug shots of Dmitrii Bogrov after his shooting of Stolypin. Courtesy of the Central State Historical Archive of Ukraine in the City Kiev. 253

Figure 25. Kiev St. Vladimir University. Postcard. 254

Figure 26. Kiev Polytechnic Institute. Postcard. 254

Figure 27. Boruch Zelikovich (Boris Zacharovich) Shteinberg in a student's uniform of Kiev Polytechnic Institute (on the left) with his mother Bella, daughter Tamara, and brother David. Courtesy of the author. 255

Figure 28. First Kiev Gymnasium. Postcard. 255

Figure 29. Solomon Brodsky Artisan School. Courtesy of the Center for Studies of the History and Culture of East European Jewry. 256

Figure 30. Interior of Solomon Brodsky Artisan School. 256
Courtesy of the Center for Studies of the History
and Culture of East European Jewry.

Figure 31. Report of the Society to Maintain Summer 257
Sanatorium Colonies for the Sick Children of Poor
Jews in the City of Kiev for 1910. Report cover.

Figure 32. Irene Nemirovsky and her cat Kissou. © Fonds 258
Irène Némirovsky/IMEC.

Figure 33. All-Russian Exhibition in Kiev in 1913. Postcard. 258

List of Maps

Map 1. The Jewish Pale of Settlement in Russia, 1835–1917. From Sir Martin Gilbert, *The Routledge Atlas of Jewish History*, © Sir Martin Gilbert (2010), Routledge, reproduced by permission of Taylor & Francis Books UK.

Map 2. Kiev circa 1900. Courtesy of Indiana University Press. All rights reserved. From Natan M. Meir, *Kiev, Jewish Metropolis, a History, 1859–1914*.

Map 3. Central Kiev circa 1900. Courtesy of Indiana University Press. All rights reserved. From Natan M. Meir, *Kiev, Jewish Metropolis, a History, 1859–1914*.

Introduction

> Only serpents slip their skin
> While their souls remain unchanged
> Alas, in us the soul constantly changes
> While the body cannot alter.
> —Nikolai Gumilev

> You cannot understand Russia with logic,
> A common yardstick cannot measure it:
> It is unique—
> You can only believe in Russia.
> —Fedor Ivanovich Tiutchev

My memories of Kiev are mixed: love and nostalgia for my native city, where five generations of my family lived, beginning with my maternal great-great grandparents who settled in the city in the late nineteenth century; and, simultaneously, bitter recollections of my encounters with anti-Semitism, which I faced many times when I lived there. I believe many Kievan Jews have shared my feelings. Kiev, like the Roman God Janus, has always had two faces turned toward Jews: one smiling and beckoning them to the city with far better conditions than in the overcrowded shtetls of the Pale of Settlement, commercial and business opportunities, the possibility of a good education, and a vibrant cultural life; the other face snarling, "Go away, Yids, or you will be killed, you will find your death in Kiev." This was no idle threat. Violence struck Jews many times in the city, beginning in Kievan Rus' and up to the present day. Jews have paid a high price for the right to live in Kiev.

My family was no exception to this rule. My great-great grandparents first achieved financial success in Kiev—they had a store on the city's central street, Kreshchatik, where they sold sterling silver. But their wealth became the cause of their demise. During the civil war in Ukraine (1918–1920), their store was robbed three times; the third time, the pogrom-makers, upset at finding an empty store, killed them. My grandmother told me that her grandparents were killed by *petliurovtsy* (members of the Ukrainian National Army), but neither she, nor her mother, were in Kiev at the time. She heard this story a few years later, from her grandparents' neighbors. Hence my great-great grandparents could have been murdered by any of the various bandits roaming Ukraine in those years.

What was Kiev for the Jews? A Jewish city, with one of the wealthiest and largest Jewish communities in the Russian Empire and a multitude of Jewish organizations and institutions? Or *Yehupets* (i.e., Egypt, as Sholom Aleichem calls the city in his works), the place with the worst Judeophobia and anti-Semitism in Russia, and the most severe persecution of Jews by the authorities?

I know the term *Yehupets* may be new and surprising for Western readers, but it best characterizes one of the city's two faces and its nature and attitude toward Jews. I therefore use this term with the hope that it will be associated with the history of Jews in Kiev in future historical literature. Sholom Aleichem, who lived there for more than a decade, referred to Kiev as *Yehupets*, recalling the biblical account of the brutal enslavement of the Hebrews. Just as the Hebrews had suffered in Egypt under the pharaohs, so Kiev Jews suffered under their local "pharaohs," as policemen were called in Russian slang.[1] In Kiev,

---

1 Hryhorii Hryhoriev, *U staromu Kyievi* (Kiev: Radians'kyi pys'mennyk, 1961), 65.

the police were continuously hunting for illegal Jews, and made weekly night round-ups of them.² (Kiev was outside of the Pale of Settlement, and only certain categories of Jews were officially allowed to live there.) The local authorities required the Jewish community to pay the police to perform this task from the basket tax funds. If the police detected illegal Jews in Kiev, they immediately expelled them from the city. Local officials worked hard to re-categorize some legal Jews as illegal, and thereby expel them. However, the authorities' efforts to decrease Kiev's Jewish population failed, as the desperate poverty of the Pale swept in wave after wave of Jewish migrants. Thus, the Jewish population of Kiev increased steadily, from the beginning of the 1860s to the February 1917 Revolution.

However, we can understand the complexity of the history of Jews in Kiev only in the context of the city's long and complicated history.

A BRIEF OVERVIEW OF KIEV HISTORY

I believe that some old cities change their soul and national character many times during their existence. One such is my native city, Kiev. Kievan Jewry also changed its features many times along with the city.

Kiev is a city with a thousand-year history. The city has been ruled by the Khazars, Normans (i.e., Norsemen), Slavic princes, Tatars, Lithuania, Poland, Russia, Ukraine, the Soviet Union, Nazi Germany, again the Soviet Union, and finally by independent Ukraine. Kiev became the capital of the Kievan Rus' state in the ninth century. In 1240, the Mongols occupied Kiev, and the Kievan Rus' rulers lost their independence. The Mongol occupation led to a degradation of the social, political, economic, and cultural life of the city. In 1362, Kiev was occupied by the Lithuanian State. After the Union of Lublin of Poland and Lithuania in 1569, Kiev became part of the Poland-Lithuanian State, and was the principal city of the Kiev *Voevodstvo* (administrative-territorial unit) from 1470 to 1700. As a result of the Ukrainian war for liberation from Poland, Left Bank Ukraine and Kiev became part of the Russian Empire in 1654. From 1654 to 1700, Kiev was under Hetman

---

2   "Za proshlyi god," *Voskhod* 1 (1897): 43–45; 1 (1898): 49–50; 1 (1899): 35.

(Ukrainian political leader) rule, the Hetman being appointed by the Russian tsar. In the beginning of the eighteenth century, rule by a Russian-appointed governor was established in Kiev. During this period, Kiev was the main city of Kiev province. In 1832, the office of governor-general was established in Kiev, and it became the main city of the southwestern region of the Russian Empire, which included the three provinces of Kiev, Volhynia, and Podolia. All these political transformations were reflected in the changing outlook, character, and spirit of the city. We cannot talk about one Jewish community in Kiev. Instead, there was a sequence of different Jewish communities that were established in different historical periods after the repeated expulsions of Kiev's Jews. Each of these Jewish communities was very different in their origin and character.

According to some Western scholars, Kiev was established sometime between the eighth and the first half of the ninth century by Khazarian Jews, and originally had the typical features of a Central Asian city. Khazarian Jews were Turkic by origin. Thus, the first Jewish community in Kiev was formed by non-Ashkenazic, Khazarian Jews. Omeljan Pritsak believes that these pre-Ashkenazic Jews lived in Kiev and Eastern Europe before their expulsion by the Lithuanian Grand Prince Alexander in 1495.[3] The Ashkenazic Jews, who came from Poland, first settled in Kiev during the fourteenth and fifteenth centuries.

HISTORICAL GOALS, PROBLEMS, AND METHODS

This book describes the history of Jews in Kiev from the foundation of the first Jewish community in the tenth century until the February Revolution of 1917. Kiev's Jewish community was one of the largest in the Russian Empire at the beginning of the twentieth century. In 1913, over eighty thousand Jews lived in Kiev. My work focuses on the social and economic history of Kiev Jewry, and provides biographical sketches

---

3   Omeljan Pritsak, "The Pre-Ashkenazic Jews of Eastern Europe in Relation to the Khazars, the Rus' and the Lithuanians," in *Ukrainian-Jewish Relations in Historical Perspective*, ed. Peter J. Potichnyj and Howard Aster (Edmonton: University of Alberta, 1988), 15–16.

of the most prominent Jewish community leaders, industrialists, and philanthropists. Because of their importance in forming and developing the community, I pay special attention to leading figures among Kiev Jews. This study also describes Kiev's Jewish inhabitants of different social strata: the Jewish wealthy elite, as well as the middle class and poorer Jews who made up the majority of Kiev Jewry—their lifestyles, activities, education, culture, and religious life. My work also details the right of residence of Jews in Kiev as the key issue in the foundation and development of the Kiev Jewish community. Special attention is given to the legal status and activities of Jewish women, and to the life of Jewish children in Kiev.

PREVIOUS SCHOLARSHIP

The few published books and a few dozen articles about Jews in Kiev describe some aspects of their social and economic history. Israel Darevskii's *Le-korot ha-Yehudim be-Kiyov* (*Sources of the History of Jews in Kiev*) is a somewhat superficial work that does not cover many aspects of the history of Kievan Jewry.[4] It is a brief overview of the history of Jews in Kiev, from the eighth century until the beginning of the 1860s. Darevskii mainly describes the legal status of Jews in Kiev, focusing on government orders and restrictions regarding the Jewish population. Ivan Malyshevskii's *Evrei v iuzhnoi Rusi i Kieve v X-XII vekakh* (*Jews in Southern Rus' and Kiev in the Tenth to Twelfth Centuries*) concentrates on the early history of Jews in Kiev, when the city was the capital of the Kievan Rus' state. This work was published in 1878 as one of a series of works of the Kiev Theological Seminary, and is based on medieval Russian chronicles.[5] The famous "Kievan Letter" had not yet been found; however, for Malyshevskii, it was obvious that Jews first came to Kiev from Khazaria.

---

4   Israel Darevskii, *Le-korot ha-Yehudim be-Kiyov* (Berdichev: Publishing House of Y. G. Sheftel, 1902).
5   Ivan Malyshevskii, *Evrei v iuzhnoi Rusi i Kieve v X-XII vekakh* (Kiev: Publishing House of Davidenko, 1878).

The Kievan letter is "the earliest original document in any language containing the name Kiev... [and] also bears the earliest specific reference... to the Jewish community of that city."[6] Norman Golb discovered this Hebrew document in the Cambridge University Library in 1962, among documents recovered from the Cairo *Genizah* by Solomon Schechter in 1896. Due to its great importance, Golb, together with Omeljan Pritsak, wrote an entire monograph about the letter, *Khazarian Hebrew Documents of the Tenth Century*.[7]

Another important work is the historical essay of Mikhail Kulisher, "Evrei v Kieve" ("Jews in Kiev"), published in two volumes of *Evreiskaia starina* in 1913, which provides an overview of the history of Kiev Jewry from the twelfth century until the 1860s.[8] In *History of the Jews*, Simon Dubnov also described various aspects of Jewish life in Kiev during Imperial times: anti-Jewish pogroms, the expulsion of Jews from the city, and the Judeophobia of Kiev's authorities.[9]

Imperial Russian historians of Kiev devoted several pages in their works to the city's Jewish population. Their attitude toward Jews varies from neutral to openly hostile. One of the earliest histories of Kiev, by Maksim Berlinskii, was written in 1798–1799, and mentions Jews several times as merchants and artisans living in the city.[10] The monograph *Kiev v 1654-1855 gg. Istoricheskii ocherk* (*Kiev in 1654-1855. Historical Essay*) by V. S. Ikonnikov also briefly mentions the Jewish inhabitants of Kiev.[11]

Nikolai Zakrevskii devotes more attention to the city's Jewish population in his work *Opisanie Kieva* (*Description of Kiev*), published in Moscow in 1868. The author's ambivalent position toward Jews is

---

6 Norman Golb and Omeljan Pritsak, *Khazarian Hebrew Documents of the Tenth Century* (Ithaca, NY: Cornell University Press, 1982).
7 Ibid.
8 M. Kulisher, "Evrei v Kieve: Istoricheskii ocherk," *Evreiskaia starina* 3 (1911): 351–366; 4 (1912): 417–438.
9 Simon Dubnov, *History of the Jews* (South Brunswick, NJ: Thomas Yoseloff, 1973), 5: 516–521.
10 Maksim Berlinskii, *Istoriia mista Kyieva* (Kiev: Naukova Dumka, 1991).
11 V. S. Ikonnikov, *Kiev v 1654-1855 gg: Istoricheskii ocherk* (Kiev: Publishing House of the Emperor University of St. Vladimir, 1904).

similar to the views of Aleksandr Solzhenitsyn in *Dvesti let vmeste* (*Two Hundred Years Together*).¹² Zakrevskii writes:

> We are far away from any fanaticism, and willingly respect the *human* rights of Jews, but we should say frankly…that the interests of Jews as a consequence of their religion, character, and separate nationality, always were, and will be, opposed to Christians' interests.¹³

Zakrevskii then adds that prohibiting Jews from living in Kiev would be highly beneficial for the city. This is a position typical of many Russian intellectuals at that time: they were ready to recognize the human rights of Jews in theory, but could only tolerate Jews as long as they were living elsewhere.

Statistics detailing the participation of Jews in the economic life of Kiev and Kiev province were provided by *Statisticheskoe opisanie Kievskoi gubernii* (*A Statistical Description of the Kiev Province*). This work was published in St. Petersburg in 1852 under the name of Ivan Funduklei, the governor of Kiev province.¹⁴ It was actually written by the Kiev historian D. P. Zhuravskii, under the sponsorship of Funduklei.¹⁵ *Statisticheskoe opisanie Kievskoi gubernii* shows the dominant role Jews played in trade in Kiev and Kiev province, even during years when Jews were forbidden permanent residence in the city. Jewish merchants came to the Kiev fairs, and also entered into contracts with local shops for the delivery of various goods. Such facts led Funduklei (Zhuravskii) to ask: "Is it good or bad that Jews control all local trade?" His answer is ambiguous: the Jewish merchants were very useful for the southwestern region and very entrepreneurial; however, they were too greedy, using both honest and dishonest means to make a profit. The

---

12 Aleksandr Solzhenitsyn, *Dvesti let vmeste*, vols. 1–2 (Moscow: Russkii Put', 2001–2002).
13 Nikolai Zakrevskii, *Opisanie Kieva* (Moscow: Publishing House of V. Grachev and Co., 1868), 1: 39.
14 Ivan Funduklei, *Statisticheskoe opisanie Kievskoi gubernii* (St. Petersburg: Publishing House of the Ministry of Interior Affairs, 1852).
15 Iu. Iu. Kondufor, ed., *Istoriia Kieva* (Kiev: Naukova Dumka, 1986), 6.

local Christians, according to Funduklei (Zhuravskii), often suffered from cheating by Jewish merchants.[16]

During the 1960s–1980s, Soviet historians published three comprehensive works on the history of Kiev, but these barely mentioned the Jews due to the prohibition against the discussion of Jewish topics under Soviet censorship.[17]

Modern Western historians have published several works that discuss various aspects of the history of Jews in Kiev. John Doyle Klier, in his monograph *Imperial Russia's Jewish Question, 1855–1881*, describes Russian-Ukrainian-Jewish relations in Kiev.[18] His article "*Kievlianin* and Jews: A Decade of Disillusionment, 1864–1873" shows how the discussion of Jewish questions by this major Kiev newspaper changed in tone from "optimistic Judeophilia" to "cynical Judeophobia."[19]

Several recent works by Western scholars reveal certain aspects of the social and economic history of Jews in Imperial Kiev. Natan Meir's *Kiev, Jewish Metropolis: A History, 1859–1914* is an important work that focuses on Jewish communal institutions, conflicts inside the community, the struggle for leadership, as well as Jewish philanthropy, religion, and culture. It also shows the strong anti-Semitism and the persecutions of Jews in Kiev. Meir's article "Jews, Ukrainians, and Russians in Kiev: Intergroup Relations in Late Imperial Associational Life," describes the devastating effect of the October 1905 pogrom on relations between gentiles and Jews in Kiev.[20] His article "From Pork to *Kapores*: Transformation in Religious

---

16 Ivan Funduklei, *Statisticheskoe opisanie Kievskoi gubernii* (St. Petersburg: Publishing House of the Ministry of Interior Affairs, 1852), 3: 370.
17 O. K. Kasimenko, ed., *Istoriia Kieva*, vols. 1–2 (Kiev: Publishing House of the Academy of Sciences of Ukrainian SSR, 1963); V. O. Boichenko, ed., *Istoriia mist i sil Ukrains'koi RSR: Kyiv* (Kiev: Holovna Redaktsiia Ukrains'koi Radians'koi Entsyklopedii AN URSR, 1968); Iu. Iu. Kondufor, ed., *Istoriia Kieva*, vols. 1–3 (Kiev: Naukova Dumka, 1986).
18 John Doyle Klier, *Imperial Russia's Jewish Question, 1855–1881* (Cambridge: Cambridge University Press, 1995), 182–221.
19 John D. Klier, "*Kievlianin* and Jews: A Decade of Disillusionment, 1864–1873," *Harvard Ukrainian Studies* 5, no. 1 (Mar. 1981): 83–101.
20 Natan Meir, *Kiev, Jewish Metropolis: A History, 1859–1914* (Bloomington and Indianapolis: Indiana University Press, 2010); Natan Meir, "Jews, Ukrainians, and Russians in Kiev: Intergroup Relations in Late Imperial Associational Life," *Slavic Review* 65, no. 3 (Fall 2006): 475–501.

Practice among the Jews of Late Imperial Kiev," analyzes the impact of modernization upon the religiosity of Kievan Jews, who "created a variety of Judaism that was compatible with modern urban life and an emerging Russian Jewish identity."[21]

Mikhail Kalnitsky's book *Sinagoga Kievskoi iudeiskoi obschiny, 5656-5756. Istoricheskii ocherk (The Synagogue of the Kiev Jewish Community, 5656-5756. A Historical Study)* is an overview of the history of Kiev's oldest functioning synagogue.[22] His book *Evreiskie adresa Kieva (Jewish Addresses of Kiev)* is a detailed guidebook to Kiev Jewish sites.[23] Kalnitsky is also the author of several books and numerous articles on the history of Kiev, which contain useful information about Kievan Jews.

Robert Weinberg's book *Blood Libel in Late Imperial Russia: The Ritual Murder Trial of Mendel Beilis*, explores the Beilis affair and trial, which took place in Kiev in 1911-1913.[24] The author uses previously unpublished archival documents, transcripts, and evidence from Beilis' trial, publications in the Russian and foreign press, and the personal correspondence of Beilis' contemporaries to paint a vivid picture of this notorious blood libel trial.

Important information about the history of the Kiev Jewish community, anti-Semitism and the persecution of Jews, pogroms, and the Beilis trial is contained in Antony Polonsky's monumental work, *The Jews in Poland and Russia*.[25]

The chapter "Jewish Kiev" in the monograph by Michael Hamm, *Kiev: A Portrait, 1800-1917*, provides a brief survey of the history of Jews in Kiev, and highlights their contribution to the city's economic

---

21 Natan Meir, "From Pork to Kapores: Transformation in Religious Practice among the Jews of Late Imperial Kiev," *The Jewish Quarterly Review* 97, no. 4 (Fall 2007): 616-645.
22 Mikhail Kalnitsky, *Sinagoga Kievskoi iudeiskoi obschiny, 5656-5756. Istoricheskii ocherk* (Kiev: Institut Iudaiki, 1996).
23 Mikhail Kalnitsky, *Evreiskie adresa Kieva* (Kiev: Dukh i Litera, 2012).
24 Robert Weinberg, *Blood Libel in Late Imperial Russia: The Ritual Murder Trial of Mendel Beilis* (Bloomington, IN: Indiana University Press, 2014).
25 Antony Polonsky, *The Jews in Poland and Russia, I: 1350 to 1881; II: 1881 to 1914* (Oxford and Portland, OR: The Littman Library of Jewish Civilization, 2010).

development.²⁶ Daniel R. Brower, in *The Russian City between Tradition and Modernity, 1850–1900*, writes about Kiev as one of the Russian Empire's few merchant cities, where wealth was concentrated "in the hands of a very small urban mercantile and propertied elite."²⁷

Several modern works by Ukrainian historians analyze various aspects of the history of Jews in Kiev: the legal status of Kievan Jews during Imperial times, their business and philanthropic activities, and the history of Kiev synagogues. These modern works also deal with the social and economic history of Kiev Jewry.²⁸

However, all these works are limited by period and topic, and do not cover many important events and developments in the history of Kievan Jews. In fact, a comprehensive history of Jews in Kiev has never been written. There is a specific reason for this: many important archival materials on the history of Jews in Kiev were inaccessible to scholars during Imperial times. After a brief period of research by the Historical-Archaeographical Commission of the Ukrainian Academy of Science from 1919 to 1928, these materials were again hidden in secret departments of Kiev archives until the beginning of the 1990s.

In the present text, I use all available scholarship on the topic, and moreover add to this scholarship by using recently discovered archival documents, many of which I found in Kiev archives and am publishing here for the first time.

PRIMARY SOURCES

Because scholarly literature about Kiev Jewry does not cover many aspects of the topic, I have made significant use of archival materials in this study. When the secret Soviet archives, with their extensive Jewish

---

26 Michael F. Hamm, *Kiev: A Portrait* (Princeton, NJ: Princeton University Press, 1993), 117–134.
27 Daniel R. Brower, *The Russian City between Tradition and Modernity* (Berkeley, Los Angeles, and Oxford: University of California Press, 1990), 69.
28 M. Kalnitsky, *Sinagoga Kievskoi iudeiskoi obshchiny, 5656–5756: Istoricheskii ocherk* (Kiev: Institut Iudaiki, 1996); Victoria Khiterer, *Dokumenty, sobrannye Evreiskoi istoriko-arkheograficheskoi komissiei Vseukrainskoi Akademii Nauk* (Jerusalem: Institut Iudaiki, Gesharim, 1999); M. Kalnitsky, "Pravovoi status evreev Kieva (1859–1917)," *Ievreis'ka istoriia ta kul'tura v Ukraini: Materialy konferentsii. Kyiv 8–9 hrudnia, 1994* (Kiev: Oranta, 1995), 77–81.

historical materials, opened in Kiev in the early 1990s, I was fortunate to be there as a young researcher and doctoral student. I spent eight years as a researcher in the Kiev archives before my emigration from Ukraine to Israel in 1997. Since then, I have returned to conduct research in the Kiev archives every summer. The Kiev archives contain thousands of documents on Jewish history, among which are many hundreds of documents on the history of Jews in Kiev. My first dissertation—defended in 1996 at the Russian State University of Humanities, Moscow, and later published as a monograph—is a detailed description, classification, and analysis of all Jewish sources in the eleven Kiev archives.[29]

The present work is based on my second doctoral dissertation, defended at Brandeis University in 2008. It introduces a wide range of primary sources on Jewish history from the Kiev archives and from the YIVO Archives in New York City. The collections in the Kiev archives contain numerous documents on the history of Jews in Kiev. However, the earliest available relevant documents date from the beginning of the nineteenth century. Unfortunately, the Historical Archive of Ancient Documents in Kiev, where all local historical materials prior to the beginning of the nineteenth century were housed, was blown up and torched during World War II by the retreating Nazis. Only a small part of this archival collection survived and, among these remaining documents, there are very few sources on the history of Jews in Kiev. Thus, I reconstruct the early period of the history of Jews in Kiev mainly on the basis of previously published sources and secondary literature.

The Kiev archives contain rich collections of documents dealing with the social and economic history of Kievan Jews in the nineteenth and early twentieth century. The collection of the Chancellery of the Kiev, Podolia, and Volhynia Governor-General in the Central State Historical Archive of Ukraine in the City of Kiev (TsDIAK U) contains the greatest number of materials about Jews in Kiev. The collection includes hundreds of orders, circulars of the Russian central and local

---

29 Victoria Khiterer, *Dokumenty po evreiskoi istorii XVI–XX vekov v kievskikh arkhivakh* (Kiev: Institut Iudaiki, Gesharim, 2001).

authorities regarding Kievan Jews, and their correspondence on this question. Because local bureaucrats accurately copied every piece of paper that arrived at the Chancellery, this collection gives us a comprehensive picture of the Russian authorities' discussions on the status of Jews in Kiev. Also important for this study are the collections of materials of the Chancellery of the Kiev Military Governor, the Kiev Governor, Kiev Police Department, and Kiev censorship committees, which contain numerous documents about Jewish residence in Kiev, anti-Jewish pogroms, the censorship of Jewish books, and the Beilis affair. The Kiev archives also hold materials about Jewish entrepreneurs and philanthropists, the Kiev Jewish community and its institutions and organizations, Jewish businesses in Kiev, and Jewish interactions with gentiles.

The Tcherikower collection in the YIVO archives has important information about the Kiev Jewish community, its rabbis and religious life, anti-Semitism and anti-Jewish violence. In my monograph, I also use scholarly literature, memoirs, published documentary materials, periodicals, fiction, and other relevant works.

OVERVIEW OF THE HISTORY OF JEWS IN KIEV

A key peculiarity of the history of Jews in Kiev was the repeated interruption of the existence of the Kievan Jewish community. Political leaders expelled Jews from Kiev many times over the centuries. Yet, in spite of the open hostility of the administration and the local population, Kiev, as the most important economic and cultural center in the region, continued to attract Jews. However, Judeophobia and anti-Semitism were worse in the city than in most other places in the Tsarist Empire. The historian Simon Dubnov wrote about the city, "Kiev—this inferno of Russian Israel."[30] I show in my work why such strong tensions existed in relations between the Jewish and gentile populations of Kiev.

The history of Jews in Kiev is possibly longer, and probably more complex, than the history of Jews in any other major city of Eastern

---

30 S. M. Dubnov, *History of the Jews in Russia and Poland*, trans. I. Friedlaender (Philadelphia: The Jewish Publication Society, 1916), 3: 19–20.

Europe. Complications in the history of Jews in Kiev first of all reflect the complications in the history of the city itself.

Kiev has played a special role in Russian history. Russians always call Kiev the "mother of Russian cities." Russian statehood was established in Kiev, and it was the capital of the old Slavic state, Kievan Rus'. Prince Vladimir converted his subjects to Christianity in Kiev in 988. The main Christian Orthodox churches and monasteries—St. Sophia Cathedral and Kiev-Pechersk Lavra (Kiev Cave Monastery)—were built there in the eleventh century. Russian Orthodox faithful have made pilgrimages to these places since they were established. Thus, for Russian Orthodox Christians, Kiev is regarded as one of their main spiritual centers and as a holy place. Tsar Alexander II echoed the words of Metropolitan Dmitry Rostovskii of the seventeenth century when he called Kiev "Jerusalem of the Russian land."[31] The leading Imperial Russian historian of Kiev, Nikolai Zakrevskii, described the holiness of the city and its meaning for Russian history:

> Kiev is the holy treasure of the Russians! This is the place from which the Christian religion spread its benevolent light over the whole Russian sky. This is the cradle of enlightenment for the descendants of the Slavs, which serves as a second Athens for us. Briefly, Kiev, which is famous by its greatness and calamities, is a beauty of the history of our motherland, the best diamond in the crown of our Tsars![32]

This special attitude of Orthodox Christians toward Kiev provoked religious intolerance, and inspired repeated prohibitions against Jewish residence in Kiev over the centuries. Even when Jews were allowed to reside in Kiev at the end of the eighteenth and in the nineteenth century, they were forbidden to settle near holy Christian places—the main churches and monasteries. Thus, one peculiarity of Jewish-Christian relations in Kiev is the strong religious intolerance of the gentile

---

31 Aleksandr Anisimov, *Skorbnoe beschuvstvie* (Kiev: Tabachuk Ltd., 1992), 36.
32 Nikolai Zakrevskii, *Opisanie Kieva* (Moscow: Publishing House of V. Grachev and Co., 1868), cited in Anisimov, *Skorbnoe beschuvstvie*, 36.

population toward Jews, which lasted until the February 1917 Revolution and beyond. The long and complicated history of Kiev, which, as mentioned, in different times belonged to different states, has had a direct impact on the history of Jews there. Changes of political power in Kiev had major consequences, sometimes dire, for the lives of the city's residents and especially for its Jewish ones.

Jews have lived in Kiev for over a thousand years. They first arrived in Kiev from Khazaria in the tenth century, and settled in the Kievan Rus' state. However, as mentioned earlier, the existence of the Jewish community in Kiev has been interrupted many times. The rulers of the Polish-Lithuanian State and the Russian Empire repeatedly expelled Jews from Kiev. Each time, Jews resettled again in Kiev, and the history of the Jewish community restarted largely from scratch. During periods of expulsion of Jews from the city, the authorities attempted to exterminate all traces of Jewish life in Kiev. For example, after the expulsion of the Jews from Kiev by the order of Tsar Nicolas I in 1835, the Kiev synagogue was demolished by order of the local authorities. However, each expulsion of Jews badly affected the city's economic life, compelling authorities to allow Jews to resettle in Kiev.

From 1835 to the February 1917 Revolution, Kiev was legally outside of, but surrounded by, the Pale of Jewish Settlement. Thus, only certain categories of Jews were allowed to live there. This situation created the peculiar structure of Kiev Jewry: the percentage of Jewish intelligentsia (e.g., lawyers, medical doctors, writers, journalists, etc.) in the city was very high, comprising 13 percent of the Jewish population at the turn of the twentieth century.

Why were Jews so attracted to Kiev, despite the bitter hostility of so many of their gentile neighbors? There were several reasons. Kiev was always a large economic and cultural center. There were more opportunities to earn money, establish a business, and trade at Kiev fairs and markets. From the second half of the nineteenth century on, Jews were drawn by the possibility of receiving a higher education in Kiev gymnasiums, institutes, and the university. Kiev, in the words of Dubnov, was located in the "very heart" of the Pale of Settlement. This was particularly significant for Jewish merchants and entrepreneurs, whose businesses depended upon suppliers from the Pale. Kiev is a beautiful city with a mild climate and picturesque landscape, which always drew people there.

The Kiev Jewish community was one of the wealthiest in the Russian Empire; however, according to statistics of the Jewish Colonization Society (EKO), in 1904, ten thousand Jews in Kiev (20 percent of the total population) lived below the poverty line.[33] However, Dubnov has pointed out that the economic situation of Jews in many other Russian cities was even worse than in Kiev.

> In 1897, the number of Jews without definite occupations amounted in certain cities to fifty percent and more. The number of destitute Jews applying for help before the Passover festival reached unheard of proportions, amounting in Odessa, Vilna, Minsk, Kovno, and other cities to forty and even fifty percent of the total Jewish population.[34]

Jewish community leaders established many philanthropic institutions in Kiev, but all the efforts of these institutions were not enough to overcome poverty among the Jews. Jewish magnates in Kiev had much influence over communal affairs, and contributed significantly to the development of the city and local industry. The legal status of Jewish women in Kiev depended upon the status of their husbands, which made them easy targets for expulsion in cases of divorce, the death of their husbands, or even if their husbands were drafted into the army. A significant number of Jews lived in Kiev illegally, due to the great difficulty in obtaining from the authorities permission for legal residence.

The possibility of making a living in Kiev, and the support provided by Jewish institutions and charitable organizations, attracted Jews to

---

33 Gershon Badanes, *S odnogo vola tri shkury: k voprosu o polozhenii evreev v Kieve* (Kiev: Tip. I. M. Rozeta, 1907), 21.
34 S. M. Dubnow, *History of Jews in Russia and Poland from the Earliest Times until the Present Day* (Philadelphia: The Jewish Publication Society of America, 1920), 23–24.

Kiev, and held them there in spite of the open hostility of the local authorities and much of the gentile population. The Jewish population of Kiev grew continuously from 1861 to the February 1917 Revolution. This growth of the Kiev Jewish population created fear among Judeophobes and anti-Semites, who believed that Kiev was being transformed from a Holy Russian Orthodox city into a Jewish city, while Jews simultaneously complained about the increasing hostility toward them from the local authorities and gentile population. Thus was formed the paradoxical and ambivalent character of Kiev as simultaneously a Jewish city and the hostile *Yehupets*.

In addition to religiously inspired hatred, anti-Semitism in Kiev had deep economic, social, and political roots. On April 23, 1881, a major pogrom began in Kiev.[35] One important consequence of the pogrom was that in Kiev, as well as throughout the Tsarist Empire, the position of the older Jewish leaders, who believed in compromise and intercession, was undermined. Lazar Brodsky (1848–1904) was the last classical shtadlan-leader of the Kiev Jewish community. Although during and after the first Russian revolution there was some democratization of Kiev Jewish communal institutions, the Brodsky family was able to preserve its leading role. However, after 1905 the youngest brother of Lazar Brodsky, Leon, acted toward the local authorities not as a shtadlan, but as a rival leader.

The anti-Jewish violence, which occurred in Kiev in October 1905, had a completely different character from the earlier pogrom. This was a political pogrom provoked by the Black Hundreds after the declaration of the October 17th Manifesto.[36] During this pogrom almost all Jewish stores, houses, and apartments in Kiev were looted, one hundred Jews were killed, and 406 wounded.[37] Thus, by the beginning of the twentieth century, the Kiev Jewish population lived in the city under the continuous threat and fear of new pogroms. The crushing of the

---

35 John D. Klier and Shlomo Lambroza, eds., *Pogroms: Anti-Jewish Violence in Modern Russian History* (Cambridge: Cambridge University Press, 1991), 44–61; *Evreiskaia entsiklopediia*, s.v. "Kiev," 9: 523–524.
36 Victoria Khiterer, "The October 1905 Pogrom in Kiev," *East European Jewish Affairs* 22, no. 2 (1992): 21–37.
37 Ibid.

1905 revolution did not end the problems of Kiev Jewry, and, between 1911 and 1913, the city was the scene of the infamous blood libel trial of a manager of a local brick factory, Mendel' Beilis.

These pogroms and the Beilis trial took place against the background of generally hostile official policies towards Kiev Jews for most of the nineteenth and in the beginning of the twentieth century. Kievan Jews first faced the bitter consequences of Russian state Judeophobia during the reign of Nicholas I, who expelled all Jews from the city in 1835 and excluded Kiev from the Pale of Settlement. Several categories of Jews were again allowed to settle in Kiev in 1859–1861, in the relatively liberal early years of the reign of Alexander II. However, in the mid-1860s, new expulsions of Jews from Kiev started, the semi-official newspaper *Kievlianin* began its calls for attacks on Jews, and police units made ongoing round-ups of illegal Jews in the city. Very few Kiev, Podolia, and Volhynia governors-general or Kiev governors regarded Jews in a positive light, wrote benignly about Jews, or saw the Jews' influence on the city as an overall good. Most local authorities were openly hostile toward Jews, and worked in close cooperation with Kiev police to reduce the number of Jewish inhabitants in the city.

The rabid anti-Semitism of the local authorities and of a significant part of the gentile population alienated Kievan Jews. Support for the "selective integration" of the Jews, as described in Benjamin Nathans' *Beyond the Pale: The Jewish Encounter with Late Imperial Russia*,[38] waned much more rapidly in Kiev than in either Odessa or St. Petersburg. Jewish communal leaders in Kiev changed their course from cooperation with the authorities to confrontation, and supported the emigration of Jews earlier than those of other communities.

When Jewish communal leaders discussed the question of Jewish emigration at the conference of the representatives of Jewish communities in St. Petersburg on April 8–27, 1882, they "saw in emigration an impermissible form of protest."[39] At the convention, Max Mandelstamm was the only attendee to publicly support the emigration of Jews from

---

38 Benjamin Nathans, *Beyond the Pale: The Jewish Encounter with Late Imperial Russia* (Berkeley and Los Angeles: University of California Press, 2002).
39 Ibid., 117.

Russia. A prominent Kiev ophthalmologist, Mandelstamm was vice president of the Kiev Jewish community. He later became one of the leaders of the Jewish emigration movement in Russia, and was the founder and first president of the Jewish Emigration Society in Kiev. After Mandelstamm's death, Leon Brodsky, the leader of the Kiev Jewish community, was elected to this position. The society operated in the fifteen provinces of the Pale of Settlement and the Kingdom of Poland.[40] Thus, it was an umbrella organization for the entire Russian Empire, supporting the emigration of Jews to America through the port of Galveston, Texas.

The relations of Kiev Jews with the local gentile population were complicated. Initially, in the wake of the new mood engendered by the "Great Reforms" of the 1860s, there was significant financial cooperation, mutual support, and cultural exchange. For example, the Brodsky family joined their business into a cartel with other rich sugar producers, including the Ukrainians Tereshchenko and Kharitonenko, the Russian Bobrinskii, and the Pole Jaroszyński. When the Russian authorities attempted to restrict Jewish trade and residence in Kiev, the head of the Merchant Guild (*starosta*), Nikolai Ivanovich Chokolov, traveled to St. Petersburg with a petition to the government to remove these restrictions as they were harmful to the local economy—a petition that was ignored by the central authorities.[41]

The Kievan Jewish wealthy elite and middle class put great effort into improving the situation and providing effective aid to poorer Kiev Jews, who often lived illegally, and who made up a significant portion of the Jewish community. My work examines how the Jewish elite negotiated their modern visions of philanthropy and communal institutions with a state that looked upon the innumerable impoverished Jews at best with disdain and suspicion. One strategy adopted by the elite was the "universalization" of care, whereby their philanthropy was also extended to non-Jews. In my discussion of philanthropy, I also examine the politics of power within the Jewish community. My work also shows

---

40 *Programma Evreiskogo emigratsionnogo obshchestva* (Kiev: n.p., 1909), 6.
41 *The Central State Historical Archive of Ukraine in the City Kiev* (TsDIAK U), f. 442, op. 634, d. 528, ll. 64–65.

the legal status and activities of Jewish women, and the lives of Jewish children in Kiev. This sheds further light on the attitude of the elite toward the Jewish poor. In this way, I provide a comprehensive picture of the economic and social life of this community.

Jewish education and religious life in Kiev were under continuous surveillance, and the local authorities imposed strict restrictions upon them. Based on the status of Kiev being outside the Pale of Settlement, for a long time the local authorities did not allow Jews to open either traditional Jewish religious schools or to build synagogues in the city. This situation changed for the better only in the 1890s when Lazar Brodsky, thanks to his connections with the authorities in St. Petersburg, received permission to build a synagogue in downtown Kiev and to open a Jewish artisan school. After this precedent was set, it became easier for the Jewish community to obtain permission to open new Jewish schools and to erect other synagogues in the city.

Before the February 1917 Revolution, Kiev did not have as rich a Jewish cultural life as St. Petersburg or Odessa, which were the Jewish cultural centers of the Russian Empire. However, the prominent Jewish writer Sholom Aleichem, the poet Yehalel (acronym of Yehudah Leib Levin), and the artist Abram Manevich lived in the city. Jewish cultural life in Kiev included public lectures, art exhibits, theatrical and musical performances, and the celebration of Jewish holidays. Jewish writers, poets, and artists contributed to the creation of modern Kievan culture. Kievan Jews who studied and traveled abroad and adopted European culture brought to the city many European technical innovations and influences, including electricity, cinema, public transportation, and modern architectural and artistic styles. Under their influence, Kiev became a more European and modern city.

I show in my work a comprehensive picture of Jewish life in Kiev before the February 1917 Revolution. My book describes the rise and development of the Jewish community in Kiev and its institutions, and shows the roots of the Judeophobia and anti-Semitism of the authorities and the local population. I reveal the city's ambivalent nature toward Jews. Kiev, as a two-faced Janus, turned toward Jews alternately each of its faces: it attracted and expelled them; enriched and impoverished their lives; provided comfortable and modern living conditions while revealing itself to be an intolerant place where Jews were killed, chased away, and accused of ritual murder. How did Jewish communal leaders handle such a complicated situation? What was the response of Kievan Jews to their travails? What did gentiles think about Jews in Kiev? These and other questions are examined in this work.

CHAPTER ONE

The History of Jews in Kiev from the Tenth Century to 1660

FOUNDATION OF THE CITY

Kiev is one of the largest cities in Eastern Europe, and has a current population of about three million. The city is located on the Dnieper, one of the major rivers in Europe, which flows into the Black Sea. Situated on the border of forest and steppe, Kiev has a comparatively mild climate, with pleasantly warm summers and moderately cold winters. The old part of the city is located both on the hills above the Dnieper, and on the alluvial plain along the river. The city is set in a lovely landscape, with hills covered by parks and gardens, making it very green. Its convenient location on a major waterway between northern and southern Europe made Kiev an important commercial hub on the trade route "from the Varangians to the Greeks," i.e., from the Scandinavian countries to Constantinople. Kiev was one of the largest urban centers of medieval Europe. According to Michael Hamm and Petr Tolochko, Kiev had about fifty thousand inhabitants in the year 1200, and "[b]y comparison, Paris had about fifty thousand inhabitants at that time, while London had an estimated population of thirty thousand."[1]

Historians debate the date of Kiev's establishment, the identity of its founders, and the etymology of its name. Some Russian and Ukrainian

---

1 Hamm, *Kiev: A Portrait, 1800–1917*, 3.

scholars believe that Kiev was established by the Slavic tribal leader Kii, his brothers Shchek and Khoriv, and sister Lybid'. This theory is based on the chronicle *Povest' vremennykh let* (Tale of Bygone Years, or the *Primary Chronicle*, as it is often referred to in English sources), written in the second decade of the twelfth century by the learned monk Nestor of the Kiev Caves Monastery, with re-writings over the centuries.[2]

At the beginning of the 1980s, Ukrainian archeologists found in the city's Podol district near the Dnieper River ancient Byzantine coins dating from the end of the fifth to the middle of the sixth century CE. Some of these coins bear the portrait of Byzantine Emperor Justinian I, who ruled from 527 to 565.[3] Archeologists also found in Kiev ruins of houses and remains of pottery and jewelry that they dated to the beginning of the sixth century. On the basis of these discoveries, Soviet scholars concluded that Kiev was established around the end of the fifth to the beginning of the sixth century.

In 1982, Kiev had a splendid celebration of its fifteen hundredth anniversary. Many historical books, special issues of scholarly journals, posters, postcards, and souvenirs were created for this event. However, Western historians have expressed doubts concerning the conclusions of the Ukrainian archeologists. More recent dendrochronological analysis of the remaining log dwellings excavated in the Podol district provides evidence of a settlement only as far back as 887.[4]

The American historians Norman Golb and Omeljan Pritsak have proposed yet another theory about the establishment of Kiev. Their theory is based on tenth-century Hebrew documents from the Cairo *Genizah* (a depository for worn-out and damaged sacred Jewish books), the most famous of which is the so-called Kievan letter. In 1896, the rabbinic scholar and leader of Conservative Judaism, Solomon Schechter (1847–1915), traveled to Egypt and brought to Cambridge University Library a huge collection of Hebrew and Judeo-Arabic manuscripts from the Cairo Genizah.[5] In 1962, Norman Golb discovered in the

---

2 *Povist' mynulykh lit: Litopys* (Kiev: Ukraina, 1996).
3 Iu. V. Pavlenko, *Narys istorii Kyieva* (Kiev: Feniks, 2003), 44–46.
4 Hamm, *Kiev: A Portrait*, 3.
5 Norman Golb and Omeljan Pritsak, *Khazarian Hebrew Documents of the Tenth Century* (Ithaca, NY: Cornell University Press, 1982), 3.

Cambridge University Library, among materials from the Schechter collection, the Kievan letter, a Hebrew document of the tenth century, which mentions the city Kiev and the existence of a Jewish community there.[6] This is the earliest known document in any language that contains the name of the city Kiev. The Kievan Letter describes

> the troublesome affair of this Mar Jacob ben R. Hannukah, who is of the sons of [good people]. He was of the givers and not the takers, until a cruel fate was decreed against him, in that his brother went and took from gentiles; this man Jacob stood surety. His brother went on the road, and then came brigands who slew him and took his money. Then came creditors and took captive this (man) Jacob, they put chains of iron on his neck and fetters about his legs. He stayed there an entire year [...and after-]wards we took him in surety; we paid out sixty [coins] and there ye[t...] remained forty coins; so we sent him among the holy communities that they might take pity of him.
>
> So now, O our masters, raise up your eyes to heaven and do as your goodly custom, for you know how great is the virtue of charity. For charity saves (men) from death...Only be strong and of good courage, and do not put our words behind your backs: and may the Omnipresent bless you and build Jerusalem in our days and redeem you and also u[s] with you...[7]

Eleven men from the Kiev Jewish community signed the letter. Norman Golb suggested that the names of the letter's signatories showed their ethnic origin and the nature of the Judaism they practiced. The majority of the signatories' names are of Hebrew origin, and a few are Khazaric Turkic. Even though this document contains no date, paleographic analysis indicates that the letter was written sometime during the tenth century.[8]

---

6 Ibid., 3–4.
7 Ibid., 13–15.
8 Ibid., 20–21.

Scholars continue to debate how, when, and in what status the Khazars first came to Kiev. Modern Ukrainian historians believe that the Khazars first came to Kiev as merchants in the eighth and ninth centuries, and that the city existed for a few centuries before their arrival. Some Western scholars claim that the Khazars established Kiev in the eighth or first half of the ninth century.

The establishment of Kiev is a key question for understanding Kievan Jewish history. Kiev Jews realized the importance of this question in the beginning of the twentieth century. The son of Kiev Rabbi Boris Gurevich wrote in his brochure *O voprosakh kul'turnoi zhizni evreev* (About Jewish Cultural Life), which was published in Kiev in 1911, that Jews lived in Kiev even before the word "Russia" appeared.[9] Thus, in the Jewish mind, Kiev was always thought of as a city established by Jewish Khazars, and the Jews therefore felt they had a historical right to live in this city without asking for the ruling authorities' permission.

Historians agree that the first Jewish community in Kiev was Khazarian and not Ashkenazic. Thus, to understand the city's character, we must briefly examine the history of the Khazarian state or Kaganate.

The Khazarian Kaganate was originally a Turkic polytheistic state, where some Christians and Jews lived. Scholars divide its history into two periods: the North Caucasian (650–750) and the Volga Kaganate (750–965). During the first period the Khazars attempted, without success, to conquer the southern Caucasus. After "a crushing defeat by the Omeiyad Arabs (737)...[they were forced] to change the direction of their activities."[10]

In the mid-eighth century, the Khazars moved their capital to the Volga, and some of them converted to Judaism. Scholars disagree about what proportion of Khazarian society converted to Judaism. The traditional view is that this affected only the Khazarian elite. However, the Kievan letter and other Hebrew documents in the Solomon Schechter

---

9 B. A. Gurevich, *O voprosakh kul'turnoi zhizni evreev* (Kiev: Kiev Society of Friends of Peace, 1911), 3–5.

10 Omeljan Pritsak, "The Pre-Ashkenazic Jews of Eastern Europe in Relation to the Khazars, the Rus' and the Lithuanians," in *Ukrainian-Jewish Relations in Historical Perspective*, ed. Peter J. Potichnyj and Howard Aster (Edmonton: Canadian Institute of Ukrainian Studies University of Alberta, 1988), 5.

collection demonstrate that Judaism was more widely spread among Khazarian society than was previously thought. Based on these documents, some scholars have claimed that what occurred was "the actual conversion of the Khazars (rather than just their rulers) to Judaism [and] their use of Hebrew…"[11]

Norman Golb and Omeljan Pritsak have argued that the Kievan Rus' state was founded by Khazars in the late eighth or early ninth century. According to Pritsak,

> In the 830s, the religious controversy forced the ruling Khazar kagan to emigrate. He took refuge in one of the trading factories of the international company called *Rus*, where he found an opportunity to exchange the now unrealistic designation "Khazar" for "Rus," after the name of the trading company that sheltered him. This factory was located in the middle course of the Volga, between the future cities Iaroslav and Rostov. In this way, a second kaganate, the "Rus kagan," was established in the Volga basin.[12]

Pritsak writes that Jews came to the region of Kiev from the Khazar Kaganate in the eighth and ninth centuries, and that the Khazars founded Kiev as a stronghold in the first half of the ninth century.[13] The Khazar kagan needed a fortress city to secure his western frontiers. "His solution was to engage Slavic-speaking Avar marines and Altaic Onogurs and to settle them in a system of fortresses. Included were Sarkel on the Don, and Kiev on the Dnieper."[14] By then "the Dnieper was the Khazarian frontier, and it is possible that Kiev was originally a Khazarian military garrison town."[15]

---

11 Golb and Pritsak, *Khazarian Hebrew Documents of the Tenth Century*, 77. An alternative point of view is that the conversion of Khazars to Judaism never took place; see Shaul Stampfer, "Did the Khazars Convert to Judaism?," *Jewish Social Studies: History, Culture, Society* 19, no. 3 (Spring/Summer 2013): 1–72.
12 Pritsak, "The Pre-Ashkenazic Jews of Eastern Europe," 4.
13 Ibid., 7.
14 Ibid., 5.
15 Golb and Pritsak, *Khazarian Hebrew Documents of the Tenth Century*, 44.

This view regarding Kiev's establishment is shared by the Israeli historians Samuel Ettinger and Michael Bogachek (Goldelman).[16] Michael Bogachek writes that Kiev was named after the Khazarian ruler Kuy.[17] According to this view, the Khazars established Kiev, and the first Jewish community was of non-Ashkenazic origin—thereby defining the character of the city. Omeljan Pritsak writes:

> Kiev was originally built according to a central Asian pattern that had become well established by the seventh or eighth century. The three composite parts of a central Asian city were typically: (1) the citadel...; (2) the inner town...; (3) the commercial and industrial suburb...
>
> In Kiev the central Asian pattern had these components: (1) the citadel, Gora; (2) the inner town, *Kopyrev konec*; and the suburb, Podol.[18]

The presence of Jews and Khazars in the city is supported by the toponymy of old Kiev. One of the ancient city gates was called the *Zhidovskie* or "Jewish" gate, and the original inner town of Kiev consisted of only one borough (*konets*), the *Kopyrev konets*, which is thought to have been named after the Khazar tribal group *Kabar/Kapyr*.

An alternate name for Kiev, which also suggests its Jewish connections, is contained in *De Administrando Imperio* of Byzantine Emperor Constantine VII Porphyrogenitus (913–959). He called the city *Sambatas*. According to Pritsak, soon after its foundation Kiev "acquired importance as the trading station *Sambata*."[19] This name seems to be derived from the legendary river *Sambation*, which Jewish literature describes as the border beyond which the ten lost tribes of Israel were exiled.[20] This may be explained by the frontier location of Kiev as a trade center of Khazaria on its northwestern border. Ukrainian historians Petr Tolochko

---

16 Ibid., 20–1; Michael Bogachek (Goldelman), "O diarkhii v drevnei Rusi," *Jews and Slavs* 3 (Jerusalem, 1995): 69–87.
17 Bogachek, "O diarkhii v drevnei Rusi," 76–77.
18 Golb and Pritsak, *Khazarian Hebrew Documents of the Tenth Century*, 56.
19 Pritsak, "The Pre-Ashkenazic Jews of Eastern Europe," 7.
20 Bogachek, "O diarkhii v drevnei Rusi," 77.

and Iurii Pavlenko deny that the Khazars established Kiev; they believe that the city existed from the late fifth century, well before the Khazars appeared there. However, they do concede that a significant number of Khazarian Jews settled in Kiev during the period of the Kievan Rus' state. Pavlenko writes that in old Kiev there was a Jewish district that was located around modern L'viv square, where in ancient times there was a large market.[21] One of the hills on which the old city Kiev was sited was called Khorevitsa. This word, according to Pavlenko and Bogachek, does not have a Slavic etymology, but is derived from the Khazarian-Hebrew word "Horiv or Horev," the biblical name of Mount Sinai.[22] However, other scholars believe that Khorevitsa was derived from Khoriv, the name of one of the legendary founders of Kiev.

JEWS IN THE KIEVAN RUS' STATE (NINTH–THIRTEENTH CENTURIES)

The Varangians—a Germanic-Scandinavian people known in the West as the Vikings, Norsemen, or Normans—conquered Novgorod in 862 and Kiev in 882, establishing the Varangian dynasty of Kievan rulers.[23] The conquest of Kievan Rus', and the establishment in Kiev of the Varangian dynasty, became the basis for the Varangian (or Norman) theory of the creation of the Old Slavic state. This theory was first formulated by German scholars in the eighteenth century.[24] They based their theory on a passage from the *Primary Chronicle*, written by Nestor more than two hundred years after the events in question, which claims that the Slavs themselves invited the Varangians to rule Kievan Rus' at a time of rivalry between several local candidates for the title of Grand Prince. Many modern historians explain this story as Nestor's attempt to legitimize the Varangian dynasty, which ruled Kievan Rus' when he composed his chronicle.[25]

---

21 Iu. V. Pavlenko, *Narys istorii Kyieva* (Kiev: Feniks, 2003), 47.
22 Bogachek, "O diarkhii v drevnei Rusi," 77.
23 Hamm, *Kiev: A Portrait*, 3.
24 Ibid.; Petr Tolochko, *Drevniaia Rus': Ocherki sotsial'no-politicheskoi istorii* (Kiev: Naukova Dumka, 1987), 20.
25 Hamm, *Kiev: A Portrait*, 3; Orest Subtelny, *Ukraine: A History*, 3rd ed. (Toronto: University of Toronto Press, 2000), 25; Tolochko, *Drevniaia Rus'*, 19–22.

However, Nestor's chronicle makes other claims. He writes that Kievan Rus' was founded long before the Varangian conquest by the Slavic Prince Kii, who together with his brothers Shchek and Khoriv and sister Lybid', established the city of Kiev. The chronicle describes how Kii made a visit to the Byzantine emperor, who bestowed upon him great honors. Several later Slavic princes, according to Nestor, also came to the Byzantine Empire for diplomatic visits, or to participate in military campaigns; thus, Kievan Rus' existed a long time before the conquest of the state by the Varangians.[26]

Eighteenth-century German historians emphasized this particular episode in the *Primary Chronicles* in order to show that Slavs were unable to institute their own state. This theory was used in Nazi Germany as evidence of the Slavs' inferiority and of the superiority of the German and Norman "ruling race"—and it can still be found in modern Western historiography. However, it is based only on legends, and on a short passage in the *Primary Chronicle* recorded two centuries after the purported events.

The Varangian conquest changed only the origin of the ruling dynasty; it did not change the political system and other features of Kievan Rus', or its dependence on the Khazarian Kaganate. Orest Subtelny finds that the Varangians rapidly assimilated with the local population of Kievan Rus', and they were "too few in number to bring about important changes in native ways."[27] Hence, Kievan Rus' continued to pay tribute to Khazaria. Only after the victory of Rus'ian Grand Prince Sviatoslav over Khazaria in 965 did this subjection of the Rus' come to an end. The Khazarian Kaganate never fully recovered from this defeat, though it continued to exist until the beginning of the eleventh century.

The new rulers retained the existing Khazarian political system in Kievan Rus' with its diarchy (the division of power between two leaders: a holy ruler—the Grand Prince; and a military ruler—the *voevoda*). In addition, Rus'ian Grand Princes took the Khazarian-style title of *kagan*, which was used by Kievan Rus' rulers of the tenth and eleventh centuries. Metropolitan Illarion addressed the Kievan Rus' rulers Vladimir

---

26 *Povist' mynulykh lit: Litopys*, 12–27.
27 Subtelny, *Ukraine: A History*, 25.

and Iaroslav as "kagan." An inscription on the wall of the St. Sophia Cathedral, which was built in the eleventh century, reads, "God save our Kagan..."[28]

The Arabic traveler Ibn Fadlan, who visited Eastern Europe in 921–922, wrote of the king of the Rus' that he "lived in a high place in their capital, which was called Kyawh (Kiev)."[29] Archeological excavations have confirmed that the palace of the king/prince/kagan (all these titles can be found in different sources) was located on the top of one of Kiev's hills, *Zamkovaia gora* (The Palace Mount), which has retained its name since that time. Ibn Fadlan described the lifestyle of the king of the Rus' as follows:

> One of the customs of the King of the Rus' is that four hundred of the strongest men live permanently with him in the palace ... that they die together with him... These four hundred men sit near and at night sleep near the base of his couch... And he does not have any other business besides sleeping with girls, drinking and giving himself up to amusement.[30]

The king of the Rus' had a co-ruler, whom Ibn Fadlan calls the "caliph," who was commander-in-chief of the army and "substituted for him to his subjects."[31] From this account we can therefore conclude that the king was a holy ruler and the caliph carried out the responsibilities of government. Ibn Fadlan describes the diarchy of the Khazar Kaganate on the Volga River as very similar to the Kievan Rus' system, providing more evidence for the Khazarian origins of Kievan Rus'. Goldelman claims that the diarchy continued to exist in Kievan Rus' until the regency of Vladimir Monomakh (1113–1125), who established the autocracy and accepted the title "Caesar."[32]

---

28 Ibid., 83; Ivan Malyshevskii, *Evrei v iuzhnoi Rusi i Kieve v X–XII vekakh* (Kiev: V. Davidenko Publishing House, 1878), 58.
29 James E. Montgomery, "Ibn Fadlan and the Rusiyyah," *Journal of Arabic and Islamic Studies* 3 (2000): 21.
30 Bogachek, "O diarkhii v drevnei Rusi," 79.
31 Ibid.
32 Ibid.

Legend claims that Prince (Kagan) Vladimir converted the Kievan Rus' population to Greek Orthodox Christianity in 988. According to the *Primary Chronicle*, ambassadors from various countries—a Muslim from Bulgaria, a Catholic from Germany, and a Jew from Khazaria—came to Prince Vladimir in 986 in order to persuade him to choose their religion. The chronicle describes the discussion of Prince Vladimir with the Khazarian delegation:

> And said Vladimir, "What is your Law?" They answered, "Circumcision, do not eat pork and rabbit, and keep the Sabbath." He said, "Where is your land?" They answered, "In Jerusalem." He asked: "Is your land there now?" They said, "God became angry with us and dispersed us in different countries for our sins and gave our land to the Christians." He said, "How can you teach other people, when God rejected you and dispersed you? If God loves you, He would not have dispersed you on to alien lands: you wish us to accept the same fate?"[33]

Most scholars consider this story to be a legend. Prince Vladimir's religious choice was made on the basis of the political interests of the Kievan Rus' state. The Byzantine Empire was a powerful state with which Rus' had trade and cultural connections, and by adopting Greek Orthodox Christianity from Byzantium, Rus' also obtained a strong ally. Furthermore, because the Khazarian Kaganate was in decline after its defeat by Prince Sviatoslav in 965, it is unlikely that Khazaria sent ambassadors to Rus' after that time. Moreover, as the Russian historian Dmitrii Ilovaiskii (1832-1920) pointed out, Prince Vladimir could meet representatives of all these religions among the Khazarian, Bulgarian, Greek, and German merchants in Kiev.[34] This legend rather reflects the religious polemic between the newly converted Kievan Rus' Greek Orthodox Christians and members of other religions in Kiev.

Other evidence of polemical debates between peoples of different faiths in Kiev is found in Nestor's *Primary Chronicle*. He describes how

---

33 Malyshevskii, *Evrei v iuzhnoi Rusi i Kieve v X–XII vekakh*, 1.
34 Ibid., 40.

an eleventh-century abbot of the Kiev Caves Monastery, Theodosius the Blessed, visited Jewish homes at night to debate with the householders. Grand Prince Iziaslav, who was very attached to Theodosius, frequently visited him in the monastery, so Theodosius was clearly an important figure. Why did Theodosius visit Jewish homes for these nocturnal debates? Nestor claims that Theodosius wanted to be killed by the Jews, and thereby become a martyr for the Christian faith.[35] However, historians questioned this claim as early as the nineteenth century. Malyshevskii's explanation is more credible: Theodosius' strange night visits to Jews were an expression of his religious zeal. Malyshevskii assumed that Theodosius attended evening Jewish religious services with the purpose of returning Judaized Christians to the Orthodox faith. Christianity was still a very young religion in Kievan Rus', so perhaps some Kievans were reverting to the Jewish faith of their Khazarian forefathers. However, there is no documentary evidence for the existence of Judaizers until the fifteenth century. Perhaps, therefore, Theodosius' visits to Jews can be explained by his missionary zeal to convert local Jewish residents of Kiev to Christianity.

Additional evidence of the existence of Jews in Kiev is the likely route of a letter from Hasdai Ibn Shaprut (c. 915–970), the first of the Jewish dignitaries to serve the Cordoba caliphs. This letter, which inquired about the Jewish origins of the Khazar state, was sent to the Khazarian Kagan through his coreligionists who lived or traded in the land of Kievan Rus'.[36]

In the eleventh century, a number of Jews from Western Europe settled in Kiev, fleeing persecution during the First Crusade. In the Kiev city wall, completed in 1037, there was a *Zhidovskie* (Jewish) gate that opened onto the Jewish quarter.[37] Members of the Kiev Jewish community had business connected with the prince's court. According to Nikolai Zakrevskii and Ivan Malyshevskii, Grand Prince Iziaslav

---

35　Ibid., 66.
36　Ibid., 42.
37　M. Kulisher, "Evrei v Kieve: Istoricheskii ocherk," *Evreiskaia starina* 3 (1913): 351; P. P. Tolochko, *Istorychna topohrafiia starodavn'oho Kyieva* (Kiev: Naukova Dumka, 1972).

(r. 1068–1078, with interruptions) moved the city market from Podol (the lower part of the city, along the Dnieper River) to the upper town, where the prince's court was located, and where the nobles and Jews lived. Some historians believe that Iziaslav did this in response to a request by Jewish merchants, and that they paid the prince for this favor.[38]

The death of Kievan Prince Sviatopolk II on April 16, 1113 created a power vacuum in the city for a few days. The Kievan boyars invited the prince of Pereiaslav, Vladimir Monomakh, to rule in Kiev; he arrived on April 20, 1113. However, during the anarchy before his arrival, a city mob attacked and looted the prince's court and monasteries, and robbed boyars and Jews.[39] The *Hypatian Codex*[40] states that

> the [Palace] Hill [*Zamkovaia gora*, the prince's residence] and all the monasteries on the hill in the town, and the Zhidove [i.e., Jewish quarter] burned down.[41]

Vasilii Tatishchev and Ivan Malyshevskii propose that the Kievans' attack on the Jews was due to their privileged status during the reign of Prince Sviatopolk II. They explain that Jews monopolized the salt trade in Kiev with the prince's permission. The delivery of salt from Galicia had been interrupted because of a war between the Kiev and Galician rulers. In addition, the Crimean salt trade, by which all salt was delivered to Kiev via the "salt road," was monopolized by Jews.[42] Malyshevskii also claims that the Jews in Kiev were moneylenders and charged very high interest rates of up to 40 percent, selling insolvent debtors into slavery.

---

38 Nikolai Zakrevskii, *Opisanie Kieva* (Moscow: Moskovksoe arkheologicheskoe obshchestvo Publishing House, 1868), 1: 14; Malyshevskii, *Evrei v iuzhnoi Rusi i Kieve v X–XII vekakh*, 72.

39 Tolochko, *Drevniaia Rus'*, 100–101.

40 The *Hypatian Codex* is a compendium of three medieval Russian chronicles: *Primary Chronicle*, *Kiev Chronicle*, and *Halych-Volhynian Chronicle*. The *Hypatian Codex* was discovered at the Hypatian Monastery of Kostroma by the Russian historian Nikolai Karamzin (*Polnoe sobranie russkikh letopisei*, ed. A. A. Shakhmatov, 2, *Ipat'evskaia letopis'*, 2nd ed. [St. Petersburg: M. A. Aleksandrov Publishing House, 1908]).

41 Pritsak, "The Pre-Ashkenazic Jews of Eastern Europe," 12.

42 I. A. Darevskii, *K istorii evreev v Kieve ot poloviny VIII v. do kontsa XIX v.* (Kiev: I. M. Roset Publishing House, 1907), 65.

According to Malyshevskii and Tatishchev, Jews enjoyed their privileged status in Kiev due to the personal patronage of Prince Sviatopolk II, who was very greedy and took from them large sums of money. When Sviatopolk II died, an angry mob took its revenge on all wealthy people and Jews. As Tatishchev writes, during the anti-Jewish violence in 1113,

> The Kievans not only looted the houses of Jews, but beat many of them, because they took advantage of Christians in trade; many of them gathered in the synagogue and organized self-defense until Vladimir [Monomakh] arrived in the city… When Vladimir arrived and suppressed the uprising, the Kievans asked him to reconsider the privileged status of Jews in the city, who had taken over all Christians businesses.[43]

Tatishchev and Malyshevskii claim that Vladimir Monomakh expelled all Jews from Kiev. Jews soon settled again in the city, but they never achieved such a privileged status as in previous times.

Modern historians question the reliability of this explanation of the 1113 events in Kiev. Vasilii Tatishchev (1686–1750), the earliest Russian historian, used old Russian chronicles that were later lost; thus we cannot verify his account. Ivan Malyshevskii, a nineteenth-century Kievan historian, based his claims on the works of Tatishchev and other early historians. He did not always provide accurate references for his sources, making it difficult, if not impossible, to check many of his assertions. For this reason, some modern historians have reconsidered the 1113 events in Kiev. Omeljan Pritsak argues that the 1113 anti-Jewish violence in Kiev cannot be qualified as a Jewish pogrom; it should instead be considered as part of a popular revolution against the local ruling elite.[44] Jews in Kievan Rus', says Pritsak, "were not granted any special privileges (which were unknown in that society) but they were also not subjected to discrimination."[45] But Pritsak's explanation of the 1113 events in Kiev and his evaluation of the social status of Jews in

---

43 Malyshevskii, *Evrei v iuzhnoi Rusi i Kieve v X–XII vekakh*, 109.
44 Ibid.
45 Ibid., 17.

Kievan Rus' pose problems similar to those found in the work of Imperial Russian historians: he does not provide references to the sources on which he bases these conclusions. The fact is that we do not have sufficient reliable information to assess the privileges of Jews in Kievan Rus'. However, we can conclude that the first known anti-Jewish violence in Kiev occurred during a period of political anarchy. In latter periods, the breakdown of governmental authority in the city constituted a potential danger for the Jewish population, and anti-Jewish violence often flared up in times of unrest. Religious intolerance may not have played a role in the 1113 violence because the mob attacked simultaneously the Jews and Christian monasteries. The anti-Jewish violence and the subsequent expulsion of Jews from the city were provoked instead by the sharp competition between Christian and Jewish merchants.

The first Jewish exile from Kiev did not continue for long, and Jews soon settled again in the city. Nikolai Karamzin and Nikolai Zakrevskii tell us that Jewish property in Kiev was severely damaged during the city fire of 1124. The fire continued for two days—July 23 and 24—and burned down almost all the city, including Jewish houses.[46]

In the twelfth century, Kiev was an important trade hub, and Jewish merchants played a significant role in this area. The commercial routes from north to south, from the Varangians to the Greeks, and between east and west, went through Kiev. Jewish twelfth-century sources mention Jewish merchants who visited Kievan Rus'. The well-known Jewish traveler of the second half of the twelfth century, Benjamin of Tudela, wrote about Kiev as a great city. He said that the large Jewish community in Kiev was comprised of long-settled Jewish inhabitants and respected Jewish merchants. The Kiev Jewish community had a large decorated synagogue and many prayer houses. Jews from Kiev studied in the yeshivas of northern France in the twelfth century.[47]

At the end of the twelfth and the beginning of the thirteenth century, the power of Kievan Rus' declined due to the local nobility's constant feuding; it finally collapsed with the Mongol invasion. In 1240, the Mongols "took Kiev by storm, exterminated the population, and

---

46 Darevskii, *K istorii evreev v Kieve*, 69.
47 Ibid., 66.

leveled the city."⁴⁸ The city was largely ruined by the Mongolian invaders and, according to Russian chronicles, the formerly flourishing capital of Kievan Rus' was turned into a village of a few hundred people. Many Kievan Jews fled along with the Christians to other lands, while some hid in the forests and remote villages.⁴⁹ Kiev was under Mongol rule from 1240 to 1320. Very few historical sources survive from this period of Kiev history, which is a "dark period" not only in the history of Jews in Kiev, but also in the history of Kiev itself. After the fall of Kiev, Batu Khan continued his conquest of Eastern Europe and moved with his troops to Hungary. He left Kiev and all southwestern Rus' under the rule of his subordinate Prince Daniil Romanovich. The prince invited more people to settle in the depopulated city. The historian Sergei Solov'ev writes,

> In 1259, Prince Daniil Romanovich invited Germans and Jews, Poles, and other foreigners from everywhere to settle in Russia. Tatar-artisans also came with them. Russian cities then ruined by the Mongol invasion were revived.⁵⁰

JEWS IN KIEV UNDER LITHUANIAN AND POLISH RULE (1320–1654)

Kiev was conquered by the Grand Duchy of Lithuania in 1320. However the Lithuanian rulers failed to control Kiev for long. From the 1320s to 1362, power in Kiev changed hands many times between Lithuanian, Tatar, and local Slavic rulers. Finally in 1362, the Grand Duchy of Lithuania established its authority over Kiev, which lasted until 1569. Under the Union of Lublin in 1569, Poland and Lithuania merged into one state, the Polish-Lithuanian Commonwealth, and Poland, as the stronger partner in this union, took control over all Ukrainian lands. In this way Kiev came under the control of Poland.⁵¹ In the

---

48 Nicholas V. Riasanovsky, *A History of Russia*, 6th ed. (New York: Oxford University Press, 2000), 70–71.
49 Darevskii, *K istorii evreev v Kieve*, 73.
50 Ibid., 74.
51 Hamm, *Kiev: A Portrait*, 7; Iu. V. Pavlenko, *Narys istorii Kyieva* (Kiev: Feniks, 2003), 154–155.

mid-fourteenth century a terrible outbreak of the plague, which had previously struck other Asian and European countries, spread to Kiev. Maksim Berlinskii hypothesizes that the Black Death was brought to Kiev by Tatars, who traded with Crimea. The majority of Kiev's inhabitants perished during this epidemic.[52]

After the Mongolian invasion and the plague, Kiev was reduced to the size of a small provincial town. Between the fourteenth and the seventeenth centuries, the population of Kiev was less than ten thousand, and in the eighteenth century, the city had an estimated population of 15,500. Not until the nineteenth century did Kiev recover the importance it had enjoyed when it was the capital of Kievan Rus'. A Venetian traveler, who visited Kiev in 1474, described the city as "plain and poor."[53] The new Lithuanian and Polish rulers could not protect Kiev from Tatar raids. "From 1450 to 1586...eighty six [Tatar] raids were recorded, and from 1600 to 1647, there were seventy more."[54] Tatars sacked Kiev many times and took the younger and more skillful inhabitants into captivity, later selling them into slavery.

From the end of the fifteenth century, Kiev was granted the right of municipal self-government according to the Magdeburg Law. City residents now elected their city council (the Magistrat)—its head and executives. The Magistrat ran the city and was responsible for the budget, police, local courts, and other municipal affairs. Kiev even had its own armed cavalry unit for self-defense. One of the reasons for the slow growth of the city's population was that the Kiev Magistrate did not allow strangers to settle there or to own real estate.[55]

Under Lithuanian and later Polish rule, Kievan Jews were granted some privileges ensuring their safety and that of their property. Fifteenth-century documents mention Kiev Jewish tax collectors, who were quite wealthy. Jews in Kiev also collected the customs and other tolls. In 1507, King Zygmunt I leased the city's collection of taxes to Shamak Danilovich.[56] In the fifteenth and sixteenth centuries, Kievan Jews actively

---

52 Pavlenko, *Narys istorii Kyieva*, 154–155.
53 Hamm, *Kiev: A Portrait*, 5–10.
54 Ibid.
55 V. S. Ikonnikov, *Kiev v 1654–1855 gg: Istoricheskii ocherk* (Kiev: Kiev Imperial University of St. Vladimir Publishing House, 1904), 63.
56 Kulisher, "Evrei v Kieve: Istoricheskii ocherk," 357–358.

participated in local and international trade. Many of them were intermediaries in trade with the East and the coastal Black Sea region.

At this time, the Kiev Jewish community was famous for its scholars, including the rabbinical scholar and Kabbalist Rabbi Moshe ben Yakov (1449-1520), the author of several Kabbalistic works, commentaries on the Pentateuch, and polemical works against the Karaites. He was expelled from Kiev, along with all other Jews, in 1495. Later Moshe ben Yakov settled in Kaffa (Feodosia), where he became a spiritual leader of the Krimchak community.[57]

The Kiev Jewish scholar Zacharia ben Aharon ha-Kohen and his pupils may have spread ideas of Judaism among some Orthodox Christians in Russia in the late fifteenth century, perhaps contributing to the establishment of the Judaizers sect. Zacharia was very knowledgeable in astronomy and the Kabbalah. He wrote and copied, with his own commentaries, several Hebrew manuscripts on these subjects. In 1471, Zacharia arrived in Novgorod in the retinue of Kievan Prince Mikhailo Olel'kovich.[58] Zacharia, along with a few of his students who arrived with him, converted some local Orthodox Christian priests to the sect of Judaizers. According to Nikolai Karamzin, the people who became "heretics" (i.e., Judaizers) were of an above average intellectual level, educated, and avid readers. Many priests were quite ignorant, and in any religious debate the "heretics" could overcome the Orthodox Christian believers.[59] Zacharia also brought to Novgorod Kabbalistic and astronomical books in Hebrew. Many of the most intellectual among the Novgorod Orthodox clergy were interested in these subjects and were also attracted to the ideas of Judaism; they founded the sect of Judaizers.

---

57 Y. Petrovsky, "Abraham Harkavy or the Lost Chapter of Russian Judaica (Newly Discovered Documents from the Vernadsky Library, Kyiv)," *Jews and Slavs* 5 (1996): 168; *Evreiskaia entsiklopediia*, s.v. "Moisei ben Yakov ben Moisei," 11:213-214.

58 Moshe Taube, "The Kievan Jew Zacharia and the Astronomical Works of the Judaizers," *Jews and Slavs* 3 (1995), 173-174.

59 N. I. Kostomarov, *Russkaia istoriia v zhizneopisaniiakh ee glavneishikh deiatelei* (Moscow: Mysl', 1993), 197-201; Joseph L. Wieczynski, "Hermetism and Cabalism in the Heresy of the Judaizers," *Renaissance Quarterly* 28, no. 1 (Spring 1975): 17-28; N. A. Kazakova and Ia. S. Lur'e, *Antifeodal'nye ereticheskie dvizheniia na Rusi XIV-nachala XVI veka* (Moscow: Academy of Sciences of the USSR, 1955); John D. Klier, "Judaizing without Jews? Novgorod and Moscow, 1480-1505," in *Culture and Identity in Muscovy, 1359-1584*, ed. A. M. Kleimola and G. D. Lenhoff (Moscow: ITZ-Garant, 1997), 336-349.

The members of this sect denied the New Testament, the divinity of Jesus Christ, and the sacredness of icons. However, they did not follow all laws and obligations of traditional Judaism. For example, to protect the secrecy of their conversion, they did not perform circumcision. Like the Marranos, they observed many of the rules of Judaism while pretending to be Orthodox Christians. Judaizers kept their conversion secret because of the severe punishment for people who abandoned the Christian Orthodox faith.

When Prince of Muscovy Ivan III visited Novgorod, he brought with him from Moscow two Orthodox priests, Denis and Aleksei, who were secret Judaizers. They spread their teaching among the Moscow clergy and ruling elite. Their main goal was to appoint their co-believers—members of Judaizing sect—as Orthodox priests. They even converted to their faith Princess Elena, the daughter-in-law of the Muscovite prince. When the Muscovite authorities discovered the Judaizers' sect in 1502, its members were severely punished. Princess Elena and her son were imprisoned for life, while other heretics were condemned and excommunicated. Several of their religious leaders were burned alive in Moscow and Novgorod in 1504; others were imprisoned for life.[60]

Recent scholarship has cast doubt on the Jewish origins of the Judaizers. The Soviet medievalist Ia. S. Lur'e (Jacob Luria) and his collaborators "rejected all suggestions of Jewish influence, to say nothing of real Jews, in the origins of the heresy."[61] In the words of Jacob Luria,

> The apodictic judgment of the [Church] Council of 1490 against the "destroyers of the souls of Orthodox men" [i.e., Judaizers] and the epistle about the observance of the Council's decision of 1504 and all the "slova" and "skazaniia" against heretical teachings were just such propagandistic works designed for a wide audience.[62]

---

60 Klier, "Judaizing without Jews?," 336-349.
61 Ibid.
62 J. Luria (Ia. S. Lur'e), "Problems of Source Criticism (with Reference to Medieval Russian Documents)," *Slavic Review* 27, no. 1 (March 1968): 1-22.

The American historian John V. A. Fine Jr. and the Israeli historian Samuel Ettinger disagree with Lur'e's view, insisting on Jewish influence in the creation of the Judaizing heresy.[63] The controversy is not resolved. As John Klier puts it:

[D]irect sources regarding Judaizers remain ambiguous and as yet no scholar has fully established whether ecclesiastic literature of the times displayed active hostility to Jews as physically present contemporaries rather than remote Biblical characters.[64]

However, what is clear is that some of the churchmen responsible for the repression of heretics were convinced that they were combating Jewish influence, a claim that echoes the earlier assertion that the Khazars tried to convert the Grand Duke of Kiev.[65]

In 1495, the Grand Duke of Lithuania, Alexander Jagiello (r. 1492–1506), expelled the Jews from the whole of the Grand Duchy, including Kiev. This exile was brief, and in 1503 Alexander, who had become by this time the king of Poland (r. 1501–1506), again allowed Jews to settle throughout Lithuania. According to Sergei Bershadskii, Alexander

---

63 John V. A. Fine, "A Review of Current Soviet Books on Russian History," *Kritika* 1, no. 3 (Spring 1965): 10–18; 2, no. 2 (Winter 1966): 35–45; Shmuel Ettinger, "Ha-hashpaah ha-yehudit al ha-tesisah ha-datit ve-mizrahah shel Europa be-sof ha-meah ha-tet-zayin" ("Jewish Influence on the Religious Ferment in Eastern Europe at the End of the Fifteenth Century"), *Yitzhak F. Baer Jubilee Volume* (Jerusalem: ha-hevrah ha-historit ha-yisreelit, 1960); and "Vliianie evreev na eres' zhidovstvuiushchikh v Moskovskoi Rusi," *Jews and Slavs* 4 (1995): 9–27.

64 Klier, "Judaizing without Jews?," 338.

65 There is a great deal of literature on the Judaizing heresy. See E. E. Golubinskii, *Istoriia russkoi tserkvi* (Moscow: Obshchestvo istorii i drevnostei rossiiskikh, 1900–1917), 2; N. A. Kazakova and Ia. S. Lur'e, *Antifeodal'nye ereticheskie dvizheniia*; A. I. Klibanov, *Reformatsionnye dvizheniia v Rossii v XIV–pervoi polovine XVI v.* (Moscow: Academy of Sciences of the USSR, 1960); G. Vernadsky, "The Heresy of the Judaizers and the Policies of Ivan III of Moscow," *Speculum* 8 (October 1933): 436–448; C. J. Halperin, "The Heresy of the Judaizers and the Image of the Jew in Medieval Russia," *CASS* 9 (1975): 141–155; Klier, "Judaizing without Jews?," 336–349; and C. G. De Michelis, *La Valdesia di Novgorod 'Giudaizzanti' e prima riforma* (Turin: Claudiana, 1993). For the view that Jews were involved with the Judaizers, see S. Ettinger, "Vliianie evreev na eres' zhidovstvuiushchikh v moskovskoi Rusi," *Jews and Slavs* 4 (1995): 9–27.

Jagiello wanted to avoid paying his debts to Jewish moneylenders, so he exiled them from Kiev (a subterfuge often used by European rulers). Officially, however, Jews were expelled from Kiev for religious reasons.[66]

When Jews again settled in Kiev at the beginning of the sixteenth century, they lived in the Jewish quarter, which was located beyond the Jewish gate (the district around modern L'viv Street and L'viv Square). In 1522, the Jewish cemetery was founded beyond the Jewish gate.[67] But the situation of Jews in Kiev was unstable in the sixteenth century. Christian merchants often complained to the Polish kings about competition from Jewish merchants. Christian inhabitants also complained that the Kiev *wojewoda* (the governor appointed by the king of Poland) Constantine placed the Jews under the jurisdiction of the royal court. The Kiev Christians insisted that according to the Magdeburg Law, jurisdiction over Jews belonged to the city administration, and that the Kiev *wojewoda* was contravening this law. These complaints were upheld three times: in 1557, 1565, and again in 1578 the king prohibited both Jewish and Christian non-residents of the city from trading in Kiev. Mikhail Kulisher considers these restrictions as an attempt by Kiev's merchants to monopolize trade in the city.[68] Zakrevskii and Darevskii write that the Jews of Kiev were obliged to wear yellow hats outside their houses in the sixteenth century.[69] Zakrevskii also states that Jews were not allowed to buy or sell horses, have Christian servants, or collect taxes and tolls such as customs, salt, and road tolls. They were also prohibited from leasing crown estates and from buying goods and supplies prior to Christians on the roads and at tollgates.[70] Hamm sums up the situation, asserting that "despite the protection of the Polish Kings, Jewish trade and settlement rights remained precarious in Kiev, and the city's Jewish community almost certainly remained small."[71]

---

66 S. A. Bershadskii, *Litovskie evrei* (St. Petersburg: M. M. Stasiulevich Publishing House, 1883), 260.
67 Zakrevskii, *Opisanie Kieva*, 2:317.
68 Kulisher, "Evrei v Kieve: Istoricheskii ocherk," 354–357.
69 Kondufor, ed., *Istoriia Kieva*, 1:214–215, 253; Hamm, *Kiev: A Portrait*, 115; Zakrevskii, *Opisanie Kieva*, 1:315; I. A. Darevskii, *K istorii evreev v Kieve* (Kiev: I. M. Roset Publishing House, 1907), 83.
70 Zakrevskii, *Opisanie Kieva*, 1:315.
71 Hamm, *Kiev: A Portrait*, 117.

The local gentile population's hatred toward Jews was an expression of the religious intolerance that existed in Kiev. The city became a major battlefield between the followers of the Roman Catholic, Uniate (Christians who follow Greek Orthodox rites but recognize the authority of the Pope), and Greek Orthodox religions. Poles were Catholics, while the Ukrainian population was split between the Uniate and Greek Orthodox churches. In addition to the religious struggle, these years were marked by conflict between Poland and Russia, in which the leaders of these two states supported their coreligionists. The Hetman of Ukraine (a Ukrainian Cossack supreme military leader), Petro Konashevych-Sahaidachnyi, was a strong adherent of the Greek Orthodox faith. In 1620, the Orthodox Metropolitan See was restored to Kiev under his patronage. The followers of the Orthodox Church did not have enough power to expel Catholics from Kiev, but they did attempt to expel Jews. Hetman Konashevych-Sahaidachnyi sought permission from the Polish court to ban Jews from settling in Kiev. The Polish king Zygmunt III granted this petition in 1619. Thereafter, Jews were allowed to visit Kiev only one day per visit and were made to stay in the city guesthouse.

In spite of this rule, Jews continued to live in Kiev in the first part of the seventeenth century. They owned houses, shops, and land, and played an important role in Kiev trade. Some historians believe that Jews were not actually expelled from Kiev according to the privilege granted to the city by Zygmunt III in 1619 because the *wojewoda* protected them. He received a sizable profit from the Jewish residents. For example, a Kiev Jew, Leizor, paid 8,000 zloty per year in the 1640s for the rent of taverns belonging to the *wojewoda*.[72] Kulisher has questioned the existence of the original privilege granted by Zygmunt III to Kievans, since there only exist copies that were made much later. He believes that Christian Kievans later fabricated this document in order to get permission from the authorities to expel the Jews from the city.[73]

The uprising of the Cossacks under the rule of Bohdan Khmel'nyts'kyi in 1648-1654 demolished the Kiev Jewish community. In 1649,

---

72 Kulisher, "Evrei v Kieve: Istoricheskii ocherk," 357-358; I. I. Artemenko and H. Ia. Serhiienko, eds., *Istoriia Kyieva*, 1, *Starodavnii i seredn'ovichnyi Kyiv* (Kiev: Naukova Dumka, 1986), 253.
73 Kulisher, "Evrei v Kieve: Istoricheskii ocherk," 355-361.

Khmel'nyts'kyi seized Kiev, and his Cossacks killed all Jews and Poles in the city. The only survivors were those who converted to the Greek Orthodox faith, fled from the city, or hid in the Orthodox monasteries. The Ukrainian Cossacks protected the life and property of all who agreed to convert to the Greek Orthodox faith, which shows the religious character of this war.[74] Usually Ukrainian historians describe the Khmel'nyts'kyi uprising as a Ukrainian war of liberation for independence from Poland. However, the Ukrainian Cossacks in the seventeenth century did not have any idea of national liberation, which is clearly a phenomenon of the nineteenth century. Nevertheless, they were fanatic followers of the Greek Orthodox faith, and regarded anybody who did not belong to their faith as a heretic. Thus the Ukrainian Cossacks' war should be considered as one of the religious wars that shook Europe from the second half of the sixteenth to the mid-seventeenth century; it should be described in the context of events such as the St. Bartholomew's Day Massacre (1572), the Dutch revolt against Catholic Spain (1566-1648), and the Thirty Years War (1618-1648). All of these events, massacres, and wars between Catholics and Protestants, as well as between Catholics and Greek Orthodox, were rooted in the same cause: religious intolerance shared by most Europeans at that time.

In his work *Between Remembrance and Denial*, Joel Raba analyzes the theory, put forward by earlier Ukrainian historians, that viewed Jews as exploiters of Ukrainian peasants and supporters of Polish landlords. The Ukrainian historian Mikhailo Hrushevs'kyi goes even further, suggesting Jewish dominance over towns in Ukraine:

> the Poles failed to gain control of the towns and to give them a Polish character; this was done by the Jews and not only in Galicia and in Podolia, but also in Volhynia and the Kiev area; in places where the Polish element was not powerful enough to

---

74 Victoria Khiterer, *Dokumenty, sobrannye Evreiskoi istoriko-arkheograficheskoi komissiei Vseukrainskoi Akademii Nauk* (Jerusalem: Institut Iudaiki, Gesharim, 1999), 183; *Evreiskie khroniki XVII stoletiia (Epokha "khmel'nichiny")*, ed. and trans. S. Ia. Borovoi (Moscow: Gesharim, 1997), 187-188; Joel Raba, *Between Remembrance and Denial: The Fate of the Jews in the Wars of the Polish Commonwealth during the Mid-Seventeenth Century as Shown in Contemporary Writings and Historical Research* (New York: East European Monographs, 1995), 32-33, 129, 137, 302, 305-307, 314, 380.

push the Russians [Ukrainians] into the background, the Jew became the ruling master of the town and gave it his own character. The Jewish colonization of the towns was one of the special gifts of the Polish rule in the Ukraine.[75]

These claims of Jewish dominance over and exploitation of the local Christian population do not apply in the case of Kiev. The city's Jewish population was quite small between the fifteenth and the first half of the seventeenth century, and did not have any influence over city affairs or power over the peasants.

After the Poles defeated the Ukrainian Cossacks in a number of battles, they forced them to sign the Peace Treaty of Belaia Tserkov' in 1651. According to this treaty, Jews were allowed to reside and own real estate in Kiev, and everywhere in Ukrainian lands. Thus, the Polish king Jan II Kazimierz (r. 1648–1668) restored to the Jews in Ukraine their previous rights, and a number of Jews subsequently settled in Kiev.[76] In 1654, Khmel'nyts'kyi signed an agreement with the Russian tsar, Aleksei Romanov, in Pereiaslav, "which resulted in the union of the Cossack controlled territory of Ukraine with Muscovy," and led to the inhabitants of Kiev swearing allegiance to him.[77] The tsar confirmed the privilege ostensibly given to the Kievans by Zygmunt III, which forbade Jews from settling in Kiev. Nevertheless, Jews continued to reside in the city for a few more years, and were only finally expelled, together with the Armenians and Poles, by the order of Tsar Aleksei Romanov in 1660.[78] This simultaneous expulsion of the adherents of all other faiths clearly shows the Russian authorities' desire to establish the religious purity of Orthodox Christian Kiev.[79] This expulsion

---

75 Raba, *Between Remembrance and Denial*, 289.
76 Darevskii, *K istorii evreev v Kieve*, 90–91; V. F. Kolesnyk, A. P. Kotsur, and N. V. Teres, eds., *Istoriia Kyieva vid kniazhoi doby do suchasnosti: Zbirnyk dokumentiv i materialiv* (Kiev: Knyhy-XXI, 2005), 154.
77 Paul Robert Magocsi, *A History of Ukraine* (Seattle: University of Washington Press, 1998), 213.
78 Darevskii, *K istorii evreev v Kieve*, 90–91; Zakrevskii, *Opisanie Kieva*, 1:592.
79 Like the Jews, Armenians were a persecuted minority in the Russian Empire. Armenians belonged to the Armenian Apostolic Church, which is a part of the Oriental Orthodox communion, and independent from both the Catholic and the Eastern Orthodox churches. The Russian authorities persecuted this Church,

initiated the absence of Jews from Kiev for over a century, a period during which the Russian rulers did not allow Jewish settlement anywhere in their state. A new Jewish community was founded in Kiev only at the end of the eighteenth century.

The early history of Kiev and of its Jewish community illuminates many later developments. Kiev's position on the middle Dnieper and on the western edges of the steppe explains its early commercial and strategic significance. The city lost its economic importance during the Mongol conquest of Kievan Rus', and only in the nineteenth century began again to play the role of a commercial and industrial hub. Because of its location, Kiev was also a crossroads of peoples. Khazarian Jews clearly played an important part in its early history. Kievan Jews, as demonstrated by the words of the son of Kiev Rabbi Boris Gurevich, believed that their ancestors had lived in Kiev even before the creation of the Kievan Rus' state. They thought that Jewish Khazars established Kiev. Jews therefore felt that they had historically justified rights for residence there, more than any other inhabitants of the city. Kiev, in the Jewish mind, was a Jewish city.

From its origins, Kiev was a place where different religious and ethnic groups encountered each other, sometimes peacefully, but also frequently in conflict. The struggle of Poles, Ukrainians, and Russians for political power, as well as for religious and cultural dominance in the city, often provoked violence and created an atmosphere of religious intolerance, which made the Jewish presence in the city particularly complicated. Additionally, Kiev was the ancient capital of the Old Slavic state, the cradle of East Slavic civilization, the "mother of all Russian cities," and a holy city for all Orthodox Christians, from which the Christianization of the Rus' was accomplished. This gave Kiev a special character, in conflict with its multi-ethnic and multi-religious past. This paradoxical character of the city reemerged in the nineteenth century with the development of a major Jewish community.

---

and under Nicholas II they confiscated Armenian Church property. S. Liubosh, *Poslednie Romanovy* (Leningrad: Petrograd Publishing House, 1924), 198–199.

CHAPTER TWO

The Jews of Kiev in the Embrace of the Russian Empire (1794–1859)

> Russia is a Sphinx. Rejoicing, grieving,
> And drenched in black blood,
> It gazes, gazes, gazes at you,
> With hatred and with love!...
>
> Is it our fault if your skeleton cracks
> In our heavy, tender paws?
> —Aleksandr Blok, *Scythians*

THE TSARIST BUREAUCRACY AND THE CITY OF KIEV

When Jews were allowed to settle again in Kiev at the end of the eighteenth century, the city was in a lamentable condition. Years of war and many occupations had led to its decline. Catherine the Great, who visited Kiev from January 29 until April 22, 1787, described it as follows:

> Since my arrival I have been looking for the city; but thus far I have not found anything apart from two fortresses and suburbs; all these ruins are called Kiev, and lead one to reflect on the lost greatness of this ancient capital.[1]

---

1 V. S. Ikonnikov, *Kiev v 1654–1855 gg: Istoricheskii ocherk* (Kiev: Kiev Imperial University of St. Vladimir Publishing House, 1904), 59.

In spite of its poor state, Kiev had been the main city of the Kiev province since the administrative reforms of Peter the Great in 1708, which divided Russia into eight provinces. In 1781, Catherine the Great eliminated the Kiev province and established the Kiev viceroyalty, which comprised several provinces. After her death, Tsar Paul I, who was opposed to most of his mother's reforms, abolished all viceroyalties and, in December 1796, reestablished the Kiev province. By his order of September 9, 1801, the provinces of Kiev, Volhynia, and Podolia were designated as "border territories" ruled by military governors.[2]

In 1832, the office of governor-general was established in Kiev, and it became the main city of the Russian Empire's southwestern region, which included the provinces of Kiev, Volhynia, and Podolia. The governors of these provinces were subordinated to the governor-general; however, all of them were appointed directly by the tsar. The Kiev, Podolia, and Volhynia governors-general were responsible for implementing the policies of the central authorities, who were determined to ensure the incorporation of this area, with its largely Polish and Ukrainian population, into the Russian Empire.[3]

In first half of the nineteenth century, Kiev was the key outpost of the Russian monarchy's struggle against the Polish liberation movement in the southwestern region of the Russian Empire. Before the 1830s, Poles dominated the cultural life of the region. The territories, which were joined to Russia at the end of the eighteenth century as a result of the partitions of Poland, had not yet become fully integrated into the culture of the Russian Empire. The continued menace of new Polish uprisings forced Nicholas I to turn Kiev into a city-fortress and to keep in the city the First Army, which had played a crucial role in the defeat of Napoleon.

According to Daniel Brower, "in the mid nineteen century...the quartering of military garrisons and paying for municipal police"[4] was

---

2   Valentyna Shandra, *Kyivs'ke general-gubernatorstvo (1832–1894): Istoriia stvorennia ta diial'nosti, arkhivnyi kompleks i ioho informatyvnyi potentsial* (Kiev: UDNDIASD, 1994), 5–30; "Impers'ke upravlinnia Ukrainoiu, 1794–1902," *Nashe mynule* 1, no. 6 (1993): 198.
3   Shandra, *Kyivs'ke general-gubernatorstvo (1832–1894)*, 5–30.
4   Daniel R. Brower, *The Russian City between Tradition and Modernity, 1850–1900* (Berkeley and Los Angeles: University of California Press, 1990), 131.

onerous for large Russian cities. Kiev quartered the entire Russian First Army for a long time, which definitely was a major financial burden.

The first governors-general were all military officers, who before their appointment had made their careers in the army. Governor-General Dmitrii Bibikov occupied the position for fifteen years, from 1837 to 1852. He was a hero of the Russian war against Napoleon, and had lost his arm at the battle of Borodino. Bibikov was a typical military officer of Nicholas I's time: a brutal enforcer of iron discipline. Under his rule, by eleven o'clock at night Kiev was as "quiet as a cemetery."[5] "Barrack rules" and corporal punishment for minor offences prevailed.[6] According to Hamm:

> Bibikov cruised about the city with two Cossacks in search of students improperly attired [students were required to wear uniforms] or found to have buttons missing. In January 1843 students were prohibited from appearing in public places after ten o'clock at night, except for theaters, concerts and the major social clubs. Students were forbidden to enter any drinking establishment except for the tavern at the Contract Hall…[7]

Bibikov was especially suspicious of Poles, seeing in every Pole "a potential revolutionary."[8] He also was suspicious of students, who were mostly Poles. Bibikov, who himself did not have a formal education, saw state schools solely as a tool for the Russification of the southwestern region.[9] Bibikov suppressed the Polish and Ukrainian national movements with great brutality, which won him the favor of the tsar. In 1852, he was appointed minister of the interior and remained in office until the death of his patron Nicholas I in 1855. The new tsar, Alexander II, considered Bibikov one of the most odious figures of the previous regime, and rejected his request to continue his service.[10]

---

5 Ikonnikov, *Kiev v 1654–1855 gg*, 190.
6 Hamm, *Kiev: A Portrait, 1800–1917*, 66.
7 Ibid., 66–67.
8 Ibid., 65.
9 Shandra, *Kyivs'ke general-gubernatorstvo (1832–1894)*, 125.
10 Ibid., 125–126.

The tsars regarded Kiev as an important city-fortress in the west of the Russian Empire. During his visit to Kiev in 1706, Peter the Great laid the foundation stone of the Pechersk fortress in a solemn ceremony.[11] Pechersk is situated about three miles away from the Podol, and until the end of the eighteenth century had the status of an independent town (*mestechko Pecherskoe*). This fortress, and other Pechersk fortifications, were expanded and rebuilt many times in the eighteenth and nineteenth centuries. The fortifications were first built during the Great Northern War (1700–1721)—the main battles of which took place on Ukrainian territory—and were later used for the city's defense during the war with Napoleon in 1812. In 1764, the arsenal inside the Pechersk fortress was established as a repair and production facility for the Russian Army. In this way Pechersk became the military district of the city.

One of the main holy places for all Russian Orthodox believers, the Kiev Cave Monastery, established in the eleventh century, is also located in the Pechersk district. According to the Kievan historian Ikonnikov,

> For a long time Kiev was on the one hand a religious center (as it will always remain) and a military city, and, on the other a self-governing magistracy.[12]

At the end of the eighteenth century, Kiev was made up of four districts: Pechersk, Upper city, Podol (aka Lower city), and Plosskaia Sloboda (modern Kurenevka). Podol was the most populous part of the city. The city hall and market were located there. All merchants were Ukrainians, and they established a strict monopoly on trade. The priest Luk'ianov wrote at the end of the eighteenth century that

> The *khokhly* [a nickname for Ukrainians] are tradesmen, they control all trade, and do not allow the *strel'tsy* [members of the

---

11 V. H. Sarbei and P. V. Zamkovyi, eds., *Istoriia Kyieva*, 2, *Kyiv periodu pizn'oho feodalizmu i kapitalizmu* (Kiev: Naukova Dumka, 1986), 80.
12 Ikonnikov, *Kiev v 1654–1855 gg*, 62.

Russian military garrison] to trade in the stores in the Lower City...[13]

These restrictions, which prevented the Russian *strel'tsy* from trading in Podol, can be explained by the division of the settlements of these two national groups in the city: Podol was Ukrainian, Pechersk Russian. In Podol lived the local burghers: merchants and artisans; in Pechersk the vast majority of the population consisted of Russian military. The inhabitants of these districts even spoke different languages: Ukrainian dominated in Podol, and Russian in Pechersk.[14]

The third largest nationality in Kiev was the Poles. According to Hamm, after the transfer of Kiev to Russian rule, "Polish influence in the city diminished, but did not cease...Kiev remained the most important outpost on the Russo-Polish frontier."[15] The vast majority of the nobles in Kiev province in 1812 were Polish (43,677 Polish versus 1,170 Russian). At the same time, the Polish population never exceeded 10 percent of the city's total population.

Poles constituted the Kievan intellectual elite in the eighteenth and the first half of the nineteenth century, and contributed greatly to the establishment of various schools in the city. Polish students predominated in the Kiev First Gymnasium, which opened in 1812. Even the textbooks were in Polish until the 1830s. When, in 1834, the Kiev St. Vladimir University was opened in Kiev, Polish students were, until the 1860s, the largest national group there. One former student later recalled that "Polish was the predominant language" among the students in the university in the mid nineteenth century.[16] Members of the Polish nobility continued to hold many regional offices, speaking Polish among themselves, but using Russian in official business. Russian influence

---

13 Ivan Luchyts′kyi, "Kyiv 1766 roku," *Kyiv—Sviata zemlia: Khronika 2000* 49–50 (2002): 639.
14 Oleksa Andriievs′kyi, "Arkhivna dovidka pro sklad Kyivs′koho 'hromadianstva' u 1782–1798 rokakh," *Kyiv—Sviata zemlia: Khronika 2000* 49–50 (2002): 696.
15 Hamm, *Kiev: A Portrait*, 56. For more on Polish influence in Kiev, see Daniel Beauvois, *Trójkąt ukraiński: Szlachta, carat i lud na Wołyniu, Podolu i Kijowszczyźnie, 1793–1914* (Lublin: Wydawnictwo Uniwersytetu Marii Curie-Skłodowskiej, 2005).
16 Hamm, *Kiev: A Portrait*, 67.

and culture were still weak in the region, and Polish culture dominated. For example, in the 1830s Kievans relied on Polish calendars, published in Berdichev.[17]

According to Hamm, "Poles were the first to challenge authority, and their discontent came to dominate local politics until the insurrection of 1863."[18] The Poles rebelled several times against the Russian government during the nineteenth century, and the Polish population of Kiev sympathized, and some even participated, in these revolts. In 1830–1831, a number of students and some instructors of the Kiev gymnasium joined the insurrection. This uprising was, however, centered in Warsaw, and had only a limited echo in Kiev.

In 1838, the Kiev St. Vladimir University was closed for a year because of some students' participation in the Young Poland (*Młoda Polska*) movement, which began in 1837, and later spread to the army. The authorities were determined to crush this movement, and Nicholas I even personally came to Kiev during the investigation. 251 students out of a total of 274 were expelled from the university, and many were drafted into the army. When the university was reopened a year later in September 1839, new students were admitted, and most of the Polish professors had also been replaced.[19]

JEWS IN KIEV FROM THE END OF THE EIGHTEENTH CENTURY TO 1835

After the three partitions of Poland (1772, 1793, and 1795), Russia acquired, together with Polish lands, a large Jewish population. Jews were allowed to live in Russia within the Pale of Jewish Settlements, which was established for Jews in the 1790s. The Pale continued to exist until the February 1917 Revolution. The borders of the Pale changed over time: some territories were added to the Pale, while others were exempt from it.[20] Kiev was within the Pale of Jewish Settlements from

---

17 Ibid., 61–65.
18 Ibid., 55.
19 Antoni Podraza, ed., *Kraków-Kijów, szkice z dziejów stosunków polsko-ukraińskich* (Kraków: Wydaw, Literackie, 1969), 24–26.
20 Antony Polonsky, *The Jews in Poland and Russia I: 1350 to 1881* (Oxford and Portland, OR: The Littman Library of Jewish Civilization, 2010), 322–323, 335–336.

1794 until 1827. Then, the city was excluded from the Pale by the order of Nicholas I. However, the expulsion of Jews from the city was postponed several times until 1835.[21]

Jews began again to settle in Kiev after a long break (since their expulsion in 1660), sometime around 1781. However, in 1792 an edict ordered the expulsion of Jews from Malorossiia (Little Russia), the territory of modern Ukraine, including Kiev. It is unknown if the Kiev authorities enforced this edict, and if the 73 Jews living in Kiev were ejected from the city. According to the census, almost all the Jews who lived in Kiev in 1792 were craftsmen; twelve of them had come to the city from Belorussia and the rest from Poland. In subsequent years, Jews continued to come to Kiev from Poland, Belorussia, Right Bank Ukraine (west of the Dnieper), and from locations near the city. A law promulgated in 1794 allowed Jews to settle in Kiev and register in the estates of merchants and townspeople (*meshchanskoe*).[22] Maksim Berlinskii, one of the first Kiev historians, wrote in his history of Kiev in 1798–1799 that "since 1794 a significant number of Jews have settled in Kiev, especially in Pechersk, where they engage in different kinds of handiwork, mainly in tailoring."[23] Jews also settled in the Podol district at the end of the eighteenth century. According to the city census of 1795, there were 94 Jews living in Kiev. Kiev State Chamber (*Kievskaia Gosudarstvennaia Palata*) statistics show that in 1797, three Jewish merchants and 563 Jewish townsmen lived in the city.[24] The list made by the city municipality showed that 1,500 Jews lived in Kiev in 1815.[25] We can assume that the actual number of Jews living in Kiev was larger than the official number, because the elders of the Kiev kahal, like other kahals, did not include impoverished Jews in the census so as to

---

21 Kulisher, "Evrei v Kieve," 425; Illia Galant, "Vyselennia zhydiv iz Kyieva roku 1835-ho," in *Zbirnyk prats' Ievreis'koi istorychno-arkheohrafichnoi komisii*, ed. A. Ie. Kryms'kyi (Kiev: All-Ukrainian Academy of Sciences, 1929), 2:153.
22 Mikhail Kulisher, "Evrei v Kieve: Istoricheskii ocherk," *Evreiskaia starina* 4 (St. Petersburg, 1913): 418–419; *Evreiskaia entsiklopediia*, s.v. "Kiev," 9:519.
23 Maksym Berlyns'kyi, *Istoriia mista Kyieva* (Kiev: Naukova Dumka, 1991), 261–262.
24 Hamm, *Kiev: A Portrait*, 118.
25 I. A. Darevskii, *K istorii evreev v Kieve ot poloviny VIII v. do kontsa XIX v.* (Kiev: I. M. Roset Publishing House, 1907), 101.

avoid paying taxes for them. In 1817, the elders of the Kiev kahal were arrested "for the crime of 'hiding souls.'"[26]

The transfer of the Contract Fair from Dubno to Kiev in 1797 helped revive life in the city, and contributed to the rapid rise of the Kiev population from 19,000 in 1797 to about 30,000 in 1800. The traveler E. M. Dolgorukii, who visited Kiev in 1810, mentioned the presence of different kinds of craftsmen in the city, as well as a variety of shops and stores where it was possible to buy all necessities, including luxury goods. He added that these goods had appeared in the city since the transfer of the Contract Fairs to Kiev.[27] These fairs attracted Jews to the city, where they were able to sell their goods, make business contracts, and conduct other business activities. They were held every year in Podol, and many Jewish merchants came to the city from the southwestern region, Odessa, and other places.[28]

The Jewish community in Kiev had two synagogues—one in the Podol district and another in the Pechersk district—and a prayer house. The larger synagogue was in Pechersk on Tripol'skaia Street (in the area of the modern Pechersk Square). It was a large wooden building that was constructed in 1808, following the plans of a locally well-known architect, Andrei Melenskii. This beautiful synagogue burned down in 1829. The synagogue in Podol, which was built in 1815, had two floors: a stone first floor and a wooden second. It was destroyed after the expulsion of Jews from Kiev by the order of Tsar Nicholas I.[29]

The Jewish community in Kiev also had a cemetery, which was established in 1798 in Zverinets.[30] At the same time, a Jewish funeral

---

26 Isaac Levitats, *The Jewish Community in Russia, 1772–1844* (New York: Octagon Books, 1970), 35; Iulii Gessen, *Istoriia evreiskogo naroda v Rossii* (Moscow: Gesharim, 1993), 178–179.
27 Kulisher, "Evrei v Kieve," 422.
28 Ivan Funduklei, *Statisticheskoe opisanie Kievskoi gubernii* (St. Petersburg: The Ministry of the Interior Publishing House, 1852), 1:324–326; 3:559–560, 571; Kulisher, "Evrei v Kieve," 428; M. Kalnitsky, *Podol: Putevoditel'* (Kiev: Ukrreklama, 1996), 29.
29 Darevskii, *K istorii evreev v Kieve*, 102; Mikhail Kalnitsky, *Sinagoga Kievskoi iudeiskoi obshchiny 5656–5756: Istoricheskii ocherk* (Kiev: Institut Iudaiki, 1996), 8; idem, *Podol: Putevoditel'*, 46.
30 Iurii Khodorkovs'kyi, *Ievreis'ki nekropoli Ukrainy* (Kiev: UTOPIK, 1998), 54. It was closed in 1895 because of the shortage of space. In 1894 the Jewish cemetery in Luk'ianovka was opened to replace the Jewish cemetery in Zverinets.

brotherhood (*hevra kadisha*) was established in Kiev. The bylaws of this brotherhood were written in the *pinkas* (chronicle) of the Kiev Jewish community, which was begun in 1793. In the early nineteenth century, the community also had a *mikva* (ritual bath) and a shelter for the homeless.[31]

Unfortunately, there are very few surviving sources that deal with the Kiev Jewish community from the end of the eighteenth century to the expulsion of Jews from Kiev in 1835. The Historical Archive of Ancient Documents was destroyed on September 5, 1943, during the Nazi occupiers' retreat from Kiev. Many unique documents on Ukrainian and Jewish history from the thirteenth to the beginning of the nineteenth century were irretrievably lost.

The earliest known original document about Kiev Jewish history that can be found in current-day Kiev archives is dated January 26, 1806. This is the report of the Board of Kiev Province (*Kievskoe Gubernskoe Pravlenie*) to the Kiev military governor, about the Kiev municipality's decision concerning a petition by two Jewish Kiev burghers, Shimanovich and Abramovich, to recover a debt from the Jew Gershkovich. They complained that, as Gershkovich's guarantors, they were required to reimburse the merchants Tatz and Verednovich, and that their houses had to be sold to cover Gershkovich's debt. The Kiev municipality ruled that Shimanovich and Abramovich could recover the sum of the debt from Gershkovich.[32]

Because of the Christian inhabitants' religious intolerance as well as the competition between Jewish and Christian merchants, relations between the Kiev Jewish community and the city's gentile population were complicated. The religious intolerance of the Christians was sometimes combined with their efforts to convert Jews. Local Christians even kidnapped Jewish children and converted them by force. Salo Baron writes that in 1814, Khaia,

> the thirteen-year-old daughter of Rabbi David Slutsky of the then rapidly growing Jewish community of Kiev was kidnapped

---

The Nazis destroyed Jewish tombstones in the Luk'ianovka cemetery during World War II. After the war, the Soviet Kiev authorities closed the cemetery.

31 Darevskii, *K istorii evreev v Kieve*, 96.
32 TsDIAK U, f. 533, op. 1, d. 1030, ll. 2–3.

one Friday night from her home, held incommunicado from her parents for several months, converted to Christianity, and married off to a Christian husband. She succeeded in smuggling out a few notes to her parents, indicating her chagrin about the separation and her unwillingness to abandon Judaism. Once she escaped from her guardians, but was quickly overtaken.[33]

Rabbi Slutskii accused Serapion, the Kiev and Galich metropolitan, of participating in the kidnapping of his daughter, and demanded that she be returned. The investigation of the case continued for three years. Tsar Alexander I ordered that the case be considered by the Holy Synod. However, Metropolitan Serapion was a member of the Holy Synod. It is thus not surprising that the Holy Synod decided that Metropolitan Serapion was innocent, and Rabbi Slutskii was punished "according to the laws...for his unfair complaint against the Metropolitan to the Holy Synod."[34] Metropolitan Serapion wrote in his diary on April 13, 1817 that Rabbi Slutskii came to him and asked for forgiveness for his false denunciation to the tsar.[35]

Jews had been living in Kiev for over forty years when Nicholas I ordered them expelled in 1835. A number of factors led to this expulsion. One was the hostility of Christian burghers toward Jewish competition. The Kiev municipality, where the majority of members were Christian merchants, petitioned Tsar Paul I in 1801 to expel all Jews from Kiev. Andrei Mikhailovich Fen'sh, the military governor of Kiev, forwarded this petition to the tsar. Like a number of local bureaucrats, he did not agree with the burghers' demands, and noted that he did not see any reason to ban Jews from residing in Kiev. In his words, "among the Christian townspeople there are no such skillful artisans as exist among the Jews and the local Christian merchants do not sell all

---

[33] Salo W. Baron, *The Russian Jews under Tsars and Soviets* (New York: Macmillan Publishing Co., 1976), 25.
[34] From the preparation materials "To the History of the Kiev Jewish Community" by Boris Khandros. Khandros began to work on the manuscript, but drafted only about 30–40 pages before his death. The original file is located in the State Archive of the City of Kiev (DAMK), f. 1 (Kievskii gorodovoi magistrate).
[35] Ibid.

necessary goods and things."³⁶ On this occasion, Paul followed Fen'sh's advice, and in February 1801 issued a decision "to allow Jews to remain in residence in Kiev."³⁷

The members of the Kiev municipality made a new attempt to expel Jews from the city under Tsar Alexander I. In 1808, they submitted petitions to the tsar, in which they cited the old privilege that was ostensibly given to the city by the Polish king Zygmunt III in 1619, which did not allow permanent residence of Jews in the city. They also complained that there were often clashes and quarrels between Christians and Jews, and that these clashes in time would inevitably lead to open violence.³⁸

Darevskii writes that after the abolition of the Kiev municipality in 1835, a list of municipality expenses in connection with petitions to St. Petersburg was found. Among them was mentioned a bribe to the higher authorities to secure permission for the expulsion of Jews from Kiev. Alexander I replied to this petition that Jews had the right to reside in Kiev according to the law, and "if some of them are involved in disorders at their residence and trade, these disorders should be stopped by the administration according to the law."³⁹ Thus, he ruled that Jews be allowed to live in Kiev.

The Kiev municipality tried to get permission to expel the Jews at the accession of each new tsar. The members of the municipality wrote to Nicholas I that the residence of Jews in Kiev was "harmful for city industry," and citing "the privilege of Zygmunt III," insisted on the expulsion of the Jews. They also complained that Jews monopolized all city trade, and did not allow Christians to work in commerce or as artisans. On this occasion, the Kiev municipality's petition was supported by Kiev Civil Governor Bukharin. He gave an additional reason to expel Jews, arguing that it was obscene that Jews lived in a city that contained relics of Christian Orthodox saints.

According to Ilia Galant, this argument had a strong impact on Nicholas I, who, in 1827, ordered that all Jews be expelled from Kiev. Perhaps more important than the desire to preserve the purity of Kiev's

---

36 Kulisher, "Evrei v Kieve," 420.
37 Ibid.
38 Darevskii, *K istorii evreev v Kieve*, 99.
39 Ibid., 100–101.

Orthodox character was Nicholas' intent to turn Kiev into a city-fortress. According to Mikhail Kulisher,

> for several decades there was a struggle between two views on the character of the city of Kiev—whether it should be a trade city or a fortress. At the end of the 1820s, the latter won and defined for a long period the fate and face of Kiev.[40]

The conversion of Kiev into a city-fortress was reflected by the large number of troops that were stationed in the Kiev military garrison. Soldiers constituted almost half of Kiev's population in the 1830s and 1840s. According to Kiev governor Ivan Funduklei, in 1845 there were 64,000 civilian inhabitants in Kiev and over 62,000 military troops that "passed through and stayed in the city."[41]

Some historians claim that Nicholas I seriously considered moving the capital of the Russian Empire from St. Petersburg to Kiev. According to Anatolii Makarov,

> In the summer of 1835, the Chief of Staff of the First Army, General Murav'ev, made a business trip from Kiev to St. Petersburg. The first thing that he heard was that the question of moving the capital to Kiev had finally been resolved. Officials were already looking for appropriate facilities for government offices, which should be moved to the south at the earliest date. Somebody said that the tsar had already discussed this with Kiev governor-general Levashov. In a diary entry, Murav'ev wrote, "When Levashov went last year to St. Petersburg, the tsar said that he wished to make Kiev the third capital. This was told to him personally by the tsar or through the minister of war."[42]

---

40 Kulisher, "Evrei v Kieve," 425.
41 Funduklei, *Statisticheskoe opisanie Kievskoi gubernii*, 1:352–353.
42 Anatolii Makarov, "Gosudarynia, eto samyi divnyi, samyi velichestvennyi, samyi velikolepnyi gorod, kotoryi ia kogda-libo videl," *Fakty*, May 31, 2007.

General Murav'ev's words do not prove that the tsar was really considering moving the capital. Indeed, the statement of Nicholas I that "he wished to make from Kiev the third capital" could mean that he merely wished to make Kiev a city comparable to St. Petersburg and Moscow. Nicholas I definitely considered Kiev to be more important than his predecessors did, and he enhanced the status of the city. This can be shown by the construction of a fortress in the city, the exclusion of Kiev from the Pale of Settlement (so that Jews were not allowed to live there), and the reform of the city administration.

According to Simon Dubnov, "The Kiev expulsion was a beginning of a new system, the narrowing of the internal region of cities, leading Jews to the 'Pale of Settlement.'"[43] Certainly, the Kiev expulsion was the first of many similar expulsions of Jews. In the same year, Jews were expelled from villages and hamlets in Kiev province, as well as from the Baltic region of the Russian Empire—Kurland and Lettland. Two years later, in 1829, Nicholas I ordered that within one year Jews "who are not in the armed forces" should be expelled from the city-fortresses of Sevastopol' and Nikolaev, since they were "inconvenient and harmful."[44] In 1843, he ordered that all Jews be removed from a fifty-*verst* (an old Russian measure of length, one *versta* equals two-thirds of a mile) border zone. This last eviction of Jews was not enforced; however, all Jews, according to the tsar's order, were ultimately expelled from Kiev, Nikolaev, Sevastopol', Kurland, and Lettland. This attitude of the Russian authorities toward Jews showed that they considered them to be internal enemies, potential traitors, or smugglers—too dangerous to live in important strategic places or near the border.

The Russian authorities' use of the privilege supposedly given Kiev by King Zygmunt III as the reason for the expulsion of Jews had an ironic aspect. In 1835, the same year that all Jews were expelled from the city, Kiev was also deprived of its basic privilege of self-government under the Magdeburg Law, which was so prized by its inhabitants. This was part of a series of reforms, which were intended to decrease the

---

43 Simon Dubnov, *History of the Jews* (South Brunswick, NJ: Thomas Yoseloff, 1973), 5:162.
44 Ibid., 161–162.

rights of the city's self-government. In addition, members of the Kiev municipality had completely compromised themselves by the theft and embezzlement of 1,400,000 rubles of city funds, and had been under investigation for this crime since the 1820s. In 1834, by order of the Senate, all members of the Kiev municipality were dismissed from their positions because they were either under investigation or standing trial.[45]

The expulsion of the Jews was a result of the changing status of Kiev. The higher authorities wanted to make Kiev an administrative center and military fortress, and to downplay its commercial role in the southwest. According to the new government plans, Jewish merchants and artisans were not necessary in the city. In addition, the Judeophobia of Nicholas I and his entourage also played a role. Judeophobia had also affected Alexander I in the last years of his reign, as was evident in 1823 when Alexander devoted much attention to a blood libel accusation in the city of Velizh. The Velizh affair continued under Nicholas I, and was widened in scope. On the instructions of Nicholas, the Deputy Minister of National Enlightenment, Dmitrii Bludov, wrote to the Kiev military governor P. F. Zheltukhin on September 29 and December 13, 1828, instructing him to conduct in great secrecy a search among Jews to find the book that prescribes the use of Christian blood for Jewish rituals. This book, he wrote, would most likely be found "in the possession of old rabbis."[46] It would provide important evidence for the Velizh trial. Of course, this mythical book was never found. The Velizh affair ended in 1835 with the acquittal of the accused Jews by the State Council. While Nicholas I approved the State Council's decision, he also noted that he was not convinced that the Jews were innocent.[47]

Thus, along with the view that the Jews were not needed in a Kiev where commerce would not play a large role was the irrational fear and hatred of Jews revealed in the highest circles of the bureaucracy during the Velizh prosecution. But expulsion was not always supported by local officials, who seem to have been more concerned with the

---

45 Kulisher, "Evrei v Kieve," 424; Galant, "Vyselennia zhydiv iz Kyieva roku 1835-ho," 2:153.
46 TsDIAK U, f. 1423, op. 1, d. 5, ll. 77-8.
47 Victoria Khiterer, *Dokumenty, sobrannye Evreiskoi istoriko-arkheograficheskoi komissiei* (Jerusalem: Institut Iudaiki, Gesharim, 1999), 146.

prosperity of Kiev. The law of December 2, 1827 forbade Jews from living in Kiev because their residence there was "opposed to the rights and privileges given to the city of Kiev in different times" and was "harmful to the city and to the state."[48] Jews who did not own real estate were to be evicted from Kiev within one year; Jews who owned real estate would be evicted within two years. Jewish merchants of the first and second guilds could be granted permission to come to Kiev for the Contract Fairs, while other Jews could, with the permission of the local authorities, come temporarily to Kiev on business affairs (i.e., for work on government contracts, but not for trade). In such cases they were not allowed to stay longer than six months.[49]

The process of evicting the Jews from Kiev lasted over seven years. While Jews who did not have real estate in Kiev were expelled in 1828, Jews who were owners of houses, stores, and shops were finally expelled in 1835. Visits of Jews to Kiev were strictly restricted. According to the Ministry of the Interior's order of May 14, 1829, Jewish ship owners were allowed to enter Kiev only if they had documents from their local police certifying that their visit to Kiev was necessary for navigation purposes. The Ministry of the Interior also ordered that Jewish ship owners be carefully watched to ensure that they were not involved in any trade in Kiev.[50]

Temporary permission for Jewish merchants to visit Kiev was issued by the local police and the Kiev civil governor. However, in the years after the law of 1827 was promulgated, the local police did not pursue a consistent policy in allowing Jewish merchants to stay temporarily on business affairs. For instance, Litman Feigin—a Jewish merchant of the first guild and inhabitant of the city of Chernigov—complained to the Kiev military governor that the Kiev police originally gave him permission to stay in Kiev until the end of his contract with the Kiev Commissariat Commission on March 1, 1829, but on January 3, 1829 the police demanded that he immediately leave the city. Feigin wrote that he and his assistants had come to Kiev to deliver a large consignment of fabrics for troops in accordance with his contract. Thus, concluded

---

48 TsDIAK U, f. 533, op. 2, d. 521, ll. 1–2.
49 Kulisher, "Evrei v Kieve," 424.
50 TsDIAK U, f. 533, op. 2, d. 500, ll. 394–395.

Feigin, his temporary residence in Kiev could not be considered harmful; on the contrary, it was in the national interest. As evidence of this, Feigin noted that the military governor of Little Russia had nominated him to receive the golden St. Vladimir medal for his useful service.

In response, the Kiev police, as reported by the police chief, claimed that they had properly expelled the merchant Feigin from Kiev because he had not submitted to their office "permission from his local authorities for entrance to Kiev" and had also not provided information about his assistants.[51] This case reveals how easy it was to contravene the complex regulations, and how arbitrary were the decisions of the lower bureaucracy. During the seven years of the eviction process, gentile merchants frequently asked the authorities to accelerate it. The main motivation for their petitions was a desire to get rid of their competitors. Thus the "foreign subject," optician Yakov Gelman[52] wrote in his denunciation to the Kiev military governor in January 1831,

> The inhabitant of Warsaw, the Jew Leiba Zal'tsfish, came to Kiev and began to sell optical equipment and other goods against the law. This Jew shaved his beard and concealed in his ticket [document for temporary residence in Kiev] his Jewish religion. He intentionally left his real passport, which he received in Warsaw four years ago, in Zhitomir to hide his religion and estate, to use the right for trade in the old Russian cities and at the fairs. So, I would like to inform you that he is a Jew, which can be confirmed by many local Jews...
>
> I would like to ask that you do not allow Zal'tsfish to conduct further trade and, for his defiance of the orders of the Highest Authority, punish him according to the law.[53]

The subsequent police investigation showed that Leon Zal'tsfish was in fact a Jew and lived in Kiev with his Austrian friend, Morits Shifer, and his Polish assistant, Yakob Zeiger. Zal'tsfish, Shifer, and

---

51 TsDIAK U, f. 533, op. 2, d. 444, ll. 1–4.
52 Documents do not mention Yakov Gelman's nationality or religion, but probably he was a Jew converted to Christianity.
53 TsDIAK U, f. 533, op. 2, d. 735, ll. 1–5.

Zeiger explained that they did not hide their religion because they had arrived in Kiev before the December 2, 1827 law was issued that forbade Jewish residence in Kiev.[54] The affair was sent for final decision to the council of Kiev province. Its decision on this case is unknown, but, in any case, by 1835 all Jews had been expelled from Kiev.

The Jews attempted to prevent their expulsion by petitioning and lobbying in the time-honored fashion. After the law was issued on December 2, 1827, Kiev Jews petitioned to be allowed to continue their residence in the city, or if this was not possible, to be permitted to settle in the Kiev suburb on the right bank of the river Lybid'. They wrote in their petition of August 1828 to Nicholas I that their houses, synagogue, and prayer houses in Kiev together had cost about a half million rubles (according to government estimates, Jewish real estate was worth a total of 300,000 rubles). They said that if they were made to sell their houses within a short time, they would only receive a very low price. Many of the Jewish houses were situated on that part of the Pechersk district that was supposed to be included in the expanded territory of the Kiev fortress. In these cases, sale was impossible. While Christian inhabitants of this district would ultimately receive some compensation for their houses when the fortress was expanded, the Jews who had to leave the city would not receive any compensation. The Kiev Jewish community also could not sell the synagogue and their prayer houses, since, according to the law of the Russian Empire, religious buildings could not be reused for any other purpose. Eviction from Kiev therefore meant total bankruptcy for many Jews. The Jews wrote that they were useful inhabitants, and that their trade benefited all Kiev residents because it kept prices low on goods and commodities. They also said that in 1827, the Kiev Jewish community donated 3,000 rubles to the city budget to improve firefighting equipment.[55]

Nicholas I agreed to delay the expulsion of the Jews until February 1, 1831. However, in November 1830, the Polish insurrection erupted in Warsaw and soon spread throughout the western region of the

---

54 Ibid.
55 Galant, "Vyselennia zhydiv iz Kyieva," 153–157. Large fires occurred often in Kiev from the eighteenth to the middle of the nineteenth century when the majority of the city's houses were wooden. One of these fires in 1811 destroyed half of Kiev.

Russian Empire. Kiev, Podolia, and Volhynia Governor-General Vasilii Levashov reported to the tsar that it "was necessary to take into consideration the present political situation in which [the Jews] could prove useful."[56] So the Russian authorities, "[f]earful of complicity between Jews and Poles…granted some temporary concessions. In February 1831, the expulsion from Kiev was postponed for three years."[57]

Some members of the local bureaucracy remained opposed to expulsion. Levashov wrote in his report to the tsar in 1833 that "for his part he did not see any objections in granting permission for Jews to establish a separate Jewish settlement beyond the River Lybid'." In his view:

> the residence of Jews in Kiev is useful, because of their modest and simple lifestyle, Jews are able to sell goods more cheaply than Christians. Therefore we can say decisively that with the eviction of Jews from Kiev, many goods will not only become more expensive, but it will be impossible to find them in Kiev. Because of this, we should follow the interests of the majority of city inhabitants, not just the interests of a few Christian merchants, who anticipate personal profit from the expulsion of the Jews.[58]

However, Nicholas I did not give permission for the Jews to found a settlement along the Lybid' near Kiev, although he did allow another delay in the expulsion until February 1, 1835. Many Kiev Jews hoped for further postponements and begged the tsar for a further delay. Because of this hope, they did not sell their property until the last moment and had to leave everything behind when they were finally forced to leave the city.[59]

When the expulsion of Jews from Kiev had already begun, prices increased for all goods, as predicted by Governor-General Levashov. As a result, he made one final attempt to postpone the eviction of the Jews. He informed the central authorities of the price increases, and

---

56 Dubnov, *History of the Jews*, 162.
57 Ibid.
58 Kulisher, "Evrei v Kieve," 426.
59 Darevskii, *K istorii evreev v Kieve*, 108.

asked for a delay in the expulsion until the acceptance of a new Statute Concerning Jews, which had been drafted and was under consideration by the State Council. Levashov's petition was supported by the Department of Laws, which proposed to submit to the tsar a special memorandum about the subject. Fourteen members of the State Council supported this proposal, but the remaining fifteen members held that any discussion of the question was impossible, since the tsar had personally ordered the expulsion. In any case, the Statute Concerning Jews, promulgated in 1835, included a provision forbidding Jewish residence in Kiev.[60] On February 1, 1835, the last remaining 655 Jews were forcibly expelled from the city, leaving only a few Jewish merchants who had contracts for the construction of the Kiev Fortress and St. Vladimir University.

IN THE FORBIDDEN CITY: JEWS IN KIEV IN 1835–1859

Permanent residence for Jews in Kiev was forbidden from 1835 until Nicholas order was rescinded in 1859. Jews expelled from the city settled in other parts of Kiev province. Many of them settled in Berdichev, moved their businesses there, and injected their capital into the city's economy. This, according to Kulisher, resulted in an increase in the economic activity and prosperity of Berdichev in the 1830s and 1840s.[61] Meanwhile, the price of food and other goods in Kiev increased significantly, and shortages arose. These circumstances caused the Kiev governors-general occasionally to request permission for Jews to visit the city temporarily on business. Thus, on December 29, 1837, Governor-General Bibikov requested that the minister of the interior allow Jewish merchants to bring wood, candles, and straw for the army to Kiev, because the price of these goods had become very high after the expulsion of the Jews. Bibikov justified his request as a temporary measure "made necessary by the financial interests of the state," until he could find a substitute for the Jewish merchants. The minister of the interior gave permission for Jews to sell these goods in Kiev, and prices dropped dramatically.[62]

---

60 Kulisher, "Evrei v Kieve," 427; *Evreiskaia entsiklopediia*, s.v. "Kiev," 9:521.
61 Kulisher, "Evrei v Kieve," 425–427.
62 Galant, "Vyselennia zhydiv iz Kyieva," 194–197.

Jews who visited Kiev on business were restricted to a one- to three-day stay; in exceptional cases they were allowed to stay in the city for five days. In general, in the 1830s all non-residents of Kiev who came to the city had to obtain a permit for temporary residence (*vid na zhitel'stvo*), issued by the policemen who guarded the city gates. Jews could be granted permission tickets if the police believed that their business affairs justified their visit to the city. When the police issued these permits, they took possession of the Jewish merchants' passports, which were sent to the police station. When Jews left the city, they were supposed to show their tickets at the police station in order to get their passports back.[63] However, the "cunning Jews" found means to stay in Kiev for longer periods, as the Kiev governor complained in his report on August 22, 1852 to the Kiev, Podolia, and Volhynia governor-general. The law did not limit the number of visits of Jews to Kiev per year. Therefore,

> Jews came to Kiev, stayed there for three days, then went outside the city gate and on the next day, or even on the same day, arrived at the city again and received permission to stay for three more days. In this way Jews lived in Kiev for weeks and months in contravention of the law…[64]

Jews who came to Kiev on business affairs were forbidden to wear traditional Jewish clothes, since in accordance with the Statute Concerning Jews of 1835, Jews traveling outside the Pale were required to wear "clothes, of the type which are in use in the place of their temporary residence and which are not distinguished from other inhabitants of the same estates."[65] On December 1, 1845, on the basis of this law, Governor-General Bibikov ordered that Jews who arrived in Kiev would be allowed to enter the city only if they wore the same style of

---

63 TsDIAK U, f. 533, op. 2, d. 2, l. 2; Darevskii, *K istorii evreev v Kieve*, 109.
64 TsDIAK U, f. 442, op. 1, d. 9931, l. 2.
65 TsDIAK U, f. 442, op. 770, d. 45, l. 293. Iu. Gessen, "Bor'ba pravitel'stva s evreiskoi odezhdoi v Imperii i Tsarstve Pol'skom," *Perezhitoe* (1910): 10–18; idem, *Evreiskaia entsiklopediia*, s.v. "Russkoe zakonodatel'stvo ob odezhde evreev," 12:46–50; I. Klausner, "Hagezerah al tilboshot hayehudim, 1844–1850," *Gal-Ed* 6 (1982): 11–26; Adam Penkalla, "The Socio-Cultural Integration of the Jewish Population in the Province of Radom, 1815–1862," *Polin* 3 (1988): 220–224.

dress as that worn by the local population, and he instructed the local police to inform Jews of this order. It is hard to say how strictly the city guards and police enforced this law. In 1853, the Russian writer Ivan Aksakov visited Ukraine to study the local fairs. This investigation was financed by St. Petersburg merchants because of the "huge amounts of money in circulation" at the Ukrainian fairs, and their "very important influence on the industrial and commercial development of all Russia."[66] Aksakov described Kiev as a mixed city of scholars, monks, soldiers, and traders, and of Poles, Russians, Ukrainians, and Jews, among whom there were striking differences in dress.[67]

In spite of all the restrictions, a large number of Jews visited Kiev for trade and other business affairs during the period from 1843 to 1859. On January 31, 1854, the Kiev civil governor reported to the Kiev, Podolia, and Volhynia governor-general that in each year since 1846, the Chancellery Publishing House of the Kiev province had printed 36,000 "Jewish tickets" for visits to Kiev.[68] According to Ivan Funduklei, governor of Kiev, Jews constituted 39,000 of the 60,000 people who visited the city in 1845. Only 2,065 Jews came to Kiev in 1845 for the Contract Fair, so the remainder visited Kiev on business affairs throughout the year. The number of Jewish visitors to Kiev was almost twice the number of Christian visitors, and many times larger than the number of Christian pilgrims who visited the Orthodox holy places (in 1845, 7,650 such pilgrims came to Kiev).[69] Certainly, Jewish visitors were very visible in Kiev, since the total civilian population of the city in 1845 was only 64,000 people.[70]

The Kiev Contract Fairs took place in the Podol district at Contract Square annually from January 15 to February 1. Funduklei wrote,

> Every year in the second half of January the merchants with their goods, landlords, nobility, clerks and people of the various estates came to the Kiev Contract fair...There landlords make

---

66 Ivan Aksakov, *Issledovanie o torgovle na ukrainskikh iarmarkakh* (St. Petersburg: Imperial Academy of Sciences Publishing House, 1858), 1.
67 Cited in Hamm, *Kiev: A Portrait*, 76.
68 TsDIAK U, f. 442, op. 85, d. 69, ll. 1–3.
69 Funduklei, *Statisticheskoe opisanie Kievskoi gubernii*, 1:261, 355.
70 Ibid., 352.

agreements and sign contracts of sale, purchase and rent their estates and receive quit-rent, sell their goods: bread, wine, sugar, wood, forest products, etc., pawn and re-pawn their estates, paying money to their creditors for their loans, borrow money from private bankers or settle their debts...Jews came there from the various districts [*uezdy*] of the provinces of Kiev, Volhynia and Podolia to buy for local resale crystal dishes, sugar, tea, fur, and the so-called noble goods of the Russian factories; others from Odessa and Berdichev bring their capital, which they put into circulation mainly as loans to landlords. All these affairs, with many other smaller interests, lead to the signing during the fair of many official documents: contracts, conditions, obligations, agreements, which bring profit to the state budget. Kiev tradesmen also make a good profit during the Contract Fairs, since the sale of all kinds of goods increases enormously at that time and the population of Kiev rises by more than 5,000 people due to the number of visitors.[71]

Funduklei also emphasized the prominent role of Berdichev merchants in the Contract Fairs, many of whom were former Kiev Jews. He wrote that during the seven years from 1843 to 1849, Berdichev merchants brought to the Kiev Contract Fairs goods worth 793,000 rubles, or an average of 113,000 rubles per year.[72] But even more important, according to Funduklei, was the capital brought to the fairs by the Berdichev merchants. With the exception of some funds brought by Odessa merchants, the capital put in circulation in the Kiev fairs came mainly from Berdichev merchants. This money was primarily disbursed as loans to landlords, merchants, and other people to help them make various contracts, purchase estates, pay debts, and establish their own businesses and workshops. During the same years, agreements signed at the fairs amounted annually to 1.5–2.5 million rubles.[73] The Kiev Contract Fairs provided considerable revenue for the city budget

---

71 Ibid., 3:529.
72 Ibid., 559.
73 Ibid., 571.

as well as to the merchants who participated in them, and stimulated the rise of trade and industry in the southwestern region. They also performed the function of a stock exchange and bank, as there was only one bank branch in all of Kiev.

Aksakov describes the participation of Jews in the Ukrainian fairs as follows:

> Like locusts the Jews struck the city, sold goods from stores and shops, from cabins and tents, wholesale and retail, from tables and as peddlers, and at the homes of the inhabitants. But when the Sabbath came, all Jews disappeared and dead silence fell upon the city; trade in the Russian shops continued, but slowly, quietly, without noise. One of the specific features of Jewish trade is that around each Jewish wholesale merchant gathered a hundred small-scale traders, poor Jews, who take the goods from the wholesale store and sell them retail. This reviving retail trade enlarged the amount of cash at the fair; thus fairs where Jews traded always had lots of cash in circulation. Jews always support each other, they have their own bankers, stewards, and carriers. They are in good relations with the Russian merchants...who do not consider Jews as serious competitors for themselves. The Russian merchants say that it is strange that among the Jews there are not many *serious* merchants, perhaps because they are too hasty and greedy. The Jew often sells his goods for a lower price than he paid for them: he always needs cash by the circulation of which he hopes to pay his expenses. [Russian] merchants say that in the time that a ruble of a Russian merchant rotates twice, a ruble of a Jew rotates five times...A visitor, especially one unaccustomed to such events and who does not belong to a commercial estate, is besieged and stunned by Jews surrounding him from all sides with offers of their goods; not a quarter of a hour goes by before a Jew peeps into your room, sneaking through the hall or back door; and you hear the importunate words: "Would you like Holland fabric, foreign goods?" etc. You chase the Jew

away, but he continues to enumerate his goods, without listening to you, and begins to spread out his goods from the box. Often he manages to tempt you and while swearing at him and yourself, you just buy something.[74]

The importunity of Jewish salesmen was provoked by restrictions on the length of Jewish visits to Kiev, Khar'kov, and other cities of Left Bank Ukraine situated outside the Pale of Settlement. If a Jewish merchant did not sell his goods before the end of his stay in the city, the police could expel him and he would lose his money and goods, or have to transport his goods to other places where it was not possible to sell them at as high of a price as in the large cities. Therefore, Jewish merchants attempted to turn their goods into cash as soon as possible.

Aksakov also admitted that

Jews are the most active purchasers, especially of Russian manufactured goods, which they carry throughout the western region, even into Belorussia…Almost all trade in foreign goods via non-maritime routes is carried by either Russian or Austrian Jews.[75]

However, the Contract Fairs that ran for only two weeks in January could hardly begin to satisfy the needs of Kiev's population for food and other commodities throughout the year. Thus, in 1843, the authorities allowed Jews to visit Kiev not only to attend the city fairs, but also to deliver food, goods, and products made by Jews and to purchase various materials. The rules governing their stay in Kiev remained, however, the same. They could stay in Kiev for one to three days, and then only if they brought in provisions, or purchased or transported goods.[76] Jewish merchants therefore came to Kiev at all times of the year to deliver goods.

Because of the large number of Jews who came to Kiev during the Contract Fairs, they were allowed to stay not only in Jewish guesthouses

---

74 Aksakov, *Issledovanie o torgovle*, 36, 327–328.
75 Cited in John Doyle Klier, *Imperial Russia's Jewish Question, 1855–1881* (Cambridge: Cambridge University Press, 1995), 288.
76 Kulisher, "Evrei v Kieve," 4:426–429.

but also in private houses. However, the Kiev governor laid down the rule that only the operators of Jewish guesthouses could rent private houses to Jews. Private houses could be rented in three city districts: Podol, Plosskii (half houses), and Lybedskoi (full houses). The operators of the Jewish guesthouses "must inform the police in advance about leasing additional houses during the fair and the leasing of such dwellings should not continue in any case longer than February 4th of each year. The rent for these houses should be set according to the price of July 27, 1849."[77] Thus, the local administration kept all Jews who arrived for the Contract Fair under close observation, and took care to ensure that none of them stayed in Kiev longer than three days after the end of the fair.

Jews who came to Kiev on business affairs at other times of the year were only allowed to stay in two Jewish guesthouses (*postoialye dvory*), established "to facilitate police observation of Jews who visit Kiev," in the Podol and Lybedskoi districts.[78] The Jewish guesthouses were leased to Christian operators, and produced considerable revenue for the city. For example, Ekaterina Grigor'eva, the wife of a clerk, leased two Jewish guesthouses in Kiev for six years beginning on April 1, 1851 for 4,080 silver rubles annually. Clearly, the Christian operators of the Jewish guesthouses received an income that was considerably more than what they paid for their lease. Soon the two Jewish guesthouses were unable to accommodate all Jewish visitors to the city, and in 1851 two additional Jewish guesthouses were opened, each of which added 350 rubles to the annual city budget. Of this revenue, 450 silver rubles were used for the salary of the five guards posted at the city gates and the Dnieper River port who issued entry permission tickets to arriving Jews; 150 silver rubles were used to print these tickets; and the rest, amounting 3,830 silver rubles, went to city funds.[79]

The Jewish guesthouses had a rather prison-like character. Jewish guests were obligated to return for the night by ten o'clock in the evening, in accordance with the rules of their temporary residence in Kiev. Jews were required to buy their food from the Christian operators

---

77 TsDIAK U, f. 1423, op. 1, d. 21, ll. 47–52.
78 Kulisher, "Evrei v Kieve," 4: 429; TsDIAK U, f. 1423, op. 1, d. 21, ll. 47–52.
79 Ibid.

of the guesthouses. The operators used this monopoly to sell cheap low-quality food to their guests at very high prices, and the authorities ignored complaints about this from Jews. According to the law, the operators were not allowed to let Jews stay in their guesthouses for more than three days. When the day came for the required departure of a Jew as determined by his ticket, the guesthouse servants were supposed to ensure his departure. If a Jew returned to the guesthouse after the hour when he should have already left Kiev, he was supposed to be taken to the police. The police would then send him with an escort to the city gates, where the city guards watched to make sure he really left the city.[80]

The operators of the Jewish guesthouses also had to ensure the validity of Jewish residence permits. If an innkeeper found any Jew staying in Kiev without a permit, he was obligated to report him to the police. The operators of the Jewish guesthouses had the right to stop any Jew on the street and check his permit. If the Jew did not have a permit, then the operator was required to take him to the police station.[81] Because Jews who came to Kiev illegally stayed in private houses and thus reduced guesthouse profits, the guesthouse operators fulfilled this obligation zealously.

Jews who stayed illegally in Kiev always attempted to avoid the Jewish guesthouses with their Christian operators, who in effect acted as police agents. Instead they surreptitiously rented rooms in private houses. The city police established a fine of one silver ruble to be paid by any house owner who allowed a Jew to stay in his house, and who did not inform the police about his arrival in Kiev.[82] However, despite the fine, the practice of illegally renting rooms to Jews in private houses continued. Probably the profit exceeded by many times the possible fines. Ekaterina Grigor'eva, the operator of the first two Jewish guesthouses, complained to the governor in 1852 that

> a significant number of Jews live in Kiev illegally in private apartments and on boats near Kiev. She had demonstrated this

---

80 Darevskii, *K istorii evreev v Kieve*, 110–111; Il'ia Galant, "K istorii kievskogo getto i tsenzury evreiskikh knig (1854–1855)," *Evreiskaia starina* 2 (1913): 276.
81 Darevskii, *K istorii evreev v Kieve*, 110–111.
82 Galant, "K istorii kievskogo getto," 265.

when she went with a police officer of the Lybedskoi district and caught many Jews in the house belonging to Nezhentsova...[83]

Grigor'eva also complained that the police did not allow Jews who had already visited Kiev to come again. These problems, Grigor'eva said, did not allow her to make a profit from leasing the Jewish guesthouses. The investigation into Grigor'eva's complaint showed that some of the Jews who resided in Kiev outside the Jewish guesthouses actually had the permission of the authorities to stay there. Exceptions from the general rules regarding the residence of Jews in Kiev had been made for

> the son of the Grodno second guild merchant Arenshtein with his Jewish assistants, Kremenets first guild merchant Abram Kostlianskii with four servants, who had a contract for construction of the Cadet Military School Building, the Dissecting Room and the embankment road, and Berdichev first guild merchants Aron and Borukh Reikh, who received permission to live in Kiev from the authorities of Kiev Province until the end of their contracts.[84]

We have other evidence that some Jews lived in Kiev on boats and illegally in some city inns. Yekhezkel Kotik describes in his memoirs the kind of hospitality that awaited them in the city:

> In the days of Nicholas I, a Jew was afraid to be seen in the streets of Kiev. Even the sailors on the barges sailing by on the Dnieper from Pinsk to Nikolayev slept aboard ship when they passed Kiev. They did not dare to put up at an inn in town. And if one happened to sleep in an inn, he couldn't even risk looking out of the window. When a Jew came to Kiev to buy merchandise on a Sunday—from a Russian, of course, since there were no Jewish stores in the town—he had to pay the exact amount asked for by the storekeeper then and there.

---

83 TsDIAK U, f. 442, op. 1, d. 9931, l. 2.
84 Ibid., ll. 4–5.

And if he started bargaining, he was asking for trouble. He would immediately be rewarded by a punch in the mouth, and the innocent victim dared not utter a word in protest, since he was, after all, on forbidden territory!...Not much different from the situation nowadays.[85]

In spite of the inherent unpleasantness, illegal stays in city inns or private houses were more attractive to Jews than residence in one of the official Jewish guesthouses, with their terrible living conditions. The Jewish guesthouses had two kinds of rooms—private for wealthy Jews and shared for all others; in the shared rooms ten people slept in one room. Both kinds of rooms were filthy, and the Christian innkeepers were invariably rude to Jews.[86] After many complaints about the appalling conditions of the Jewish guesthouses, the Kiev police made an inspection of the guesthouse in Podol on July 26, 1856. According to the report:

> All rooms occupied by Jews, private as well as general, were extremely dirty: filth on the damp floors, litter, there are buckets full of garbage and because of these the air in the room is permanently noxious and intolerable; there is a great multitude of bedbugs in and near the beds, cobwebs with big spiders on the ceiling and in the corners, the glass in the windows is broken in every room...there are bones, rotten radishes and cucumber peels under the beds and in every corner...This filth appears to be due to the negligence of guesthouse operator Grigor'eva...[87]

When the policemen who inspected the Jewish guesthouse told Grigor'eva that it was very dirty, she replied: "It should be so, because Jews are not people, but pigs…" During the police inspection, when some Jews began to complain that it was very stuffy, Grigor'eva cursed them and "in addition to indecent words, called them scoundrels,

---

85 David Assaf, ed., *Journey to a Nineteenth-Century Shtetl: The Memories of Yekhezkel Kotik* (Detroit: Wayne State University Press, 2002), 354–355.
86 Khiterer, *Dokumenty, sobrannye Evreiskoi*, 157–158.
87 Ibid.

villains and rogues, repeating this many times…" There was the same filth and piles of rotten garbage in the guesthouse courtyard. The guesthouse kitchen was "in a very dirty and disgusting condition, there are no metal dishes, but all food is cooked in grimy clay pots."[88]

Police officer Plekhanov arrested Grigor'eva "for the trouble that she made during the inspection of the Jewish guesthouse." However, Grigor'eva was soon released. She then sent a complaint to the State Senate. The Senate forwarded Grigor'eva's complaint to the governor-general for investigation. He came to the conclusion that "order in the Jewish guesthouses can only be established after the dismissal of Grigor'eva from their operation."[89] Grigor'eva was also accused of using five Christian peasants as servants in the Jewish guesthouses, which was forbidden by law.[90]

While this investigation continued, the time of "Great Reforms" in Russia began, and the new tsar Alexander II, attempting to eliminate the more odious features of the previous reactionary regime, ordered the closure of the Jewish guesthouses in Kiev in 1857.[91] A new law allowed Jews to stay temporarily in the Lybedskoi and Plosskii districts, as well as on a few specific streets in Podol—all of which were distant from the city center. Later, some categories of Jews were allowed to permanently reside in these districts. However, only Jewish merchants of the first guild were allowed to live in all parts of the city before the February 1917 Revolution. According to the lawyer and historian Grigorii Vol'tke, Kiev was the only city in the Russian Empire where the features of the medieval ghetto survived until the beginning of the twentieth century.[92]

THE NON-REALIZED PROJECT TO CREATE IN KIEV A JEWISH PUBLISHING HOUSE AND THE CASE OF ZEIBERLING

Following the expulsion of Jews from Kiev, one of the Russian government's strangest decisions was to make Kiev one of two imperial centers

---
88 Ibid.
89 Ibid.
90 Ibid.
91 Ibid.
92 *Evreiskaia entsiklopediia*, 9:526.

for Jewish publications and their censorship. According to a law of 1836, all censorship of Jewish publications in the Russian Empire was to be concentrated in the Kiev and Vilna Censorship Committees, where the censors of Jewish books were established. According to the same law, all Jewish publishing houses, except in Kiev and Vilna, were closed for the "convenience of observing Jewish publishing houses."[93] However, no Jewish publishing house was ever actually opened in Kiev. The local authorities had many excuses for delaying the opening of a Jewish publishing house, including the lack of a censor of Jewish books, and the lack of an appropriate candidate for the lease of the Jewish publishing house.

Several Jewish converts to Christianity tried to lease the planned Kiev Jewish publishing house. The printer Teofil Gliksberg—a converted Jew and graduate of the Vilna Medical-Surgical Academy, who came from a family of Warsaw publishers—asked for permission to take this lease. In his request, Gliksberg emphasized that the Jewish publishing house should be under the control of a non-Jew. However, the Ministry of National Enlightenment did not agree that a Jewish publishing house should be operated by a Christian. Several other converts attempted to lease this proposed publishing house. An Odessa merchant, the convert Karasik, offered to lease it for 25,000 rubles a year, while a Rovno merchant, the convert S. Borovskii, offered even more money: 28,000 rubles a year.[94]

There were also several Jews who wanted to lease the Kiev Jewish publishing house. The head of the Vilna kahal sought to lease both the Vilna and Kiev Jewish publishing houses. He proposed to pay 10,000 rubles annually for this lease, with the money designated "for Jews who wish to live in Jewish agricultural settlements or for other useful goals."[95] Gertsenshtein, an Odessan Jewish merchant and one of the four founders of the Odessa Jewish school, also attempted to lease the publishing house. In lieu of rent, he proposed to establish and finance

---

93 Dmitry Eliashevich, *Pravitel'stvennaia politika i evreiskaia pechat' v Rossii 1797–1917* (St. Petersburg and Jerusalem: Gesharim, 1999), 179.
94 S. Borovyi, "Nezdiisneni proekty utvoryty v Kyievi ievreis'ku drukarniu (1836–1846)," *Bibliolohichni visti* 4 (1929): 30–31.
95 Ibid.

a Jewish school in Kiev with the same study program as the Odessa Jewish school (one of the first maskilic Jewish schools in Russia, where Jewish and general subjects were taught, including Russian and German). Iosif Gal'perin, a Berdichev Jewish merchant and well-known banker, also offered to lease the Kiev Jewish publishing house.[96]

However, Russian authorities were never satisfied with any of these candidates, whether they were converts, maskilic Jews, or Orthodox Jews. So Sergei Uvarov, the Minister of National Enlightenment, announced that the lease of the Kiev Jewish publishing house would be auctioned off. However this auction never took place.

A few years later, the council of Kiev province allowed the former Ostrog publisher, F. Aisenberg, to open the Jewish publishing house in Kiev. However, the governor-general revoked this permission. Finally, according to a new "Law concerning Jewish publishing houses" of 1845, the authorities decided to permit the opening of a Jewish publishing house not in Kiev, but instead in Zhitomir, where a government rabbinical seminary had also been created. The Zhitomir publishing house was established by the Shapiro brothers on January 27, 1847.[97]

Why did the authorities reject the offers of the other candidates to open a Jewish publishing house in Kiev? Obviously the problem was not the candidates themselves, but the place: the local authorities did not want to see a Jewish publishing house established in Kiev. They had attempted to cleanse the city of Jews, and the presence of a Jewish publishing house would be an excuse for more Jews to visit Kiev. Thus, the local authorities postponed as long as they could the opening of the Jewish publishing house in Kiev on various pretexts, until the higher authorities in St. Petersburg changed the law and opened it instead in Zhitomir.

During this period, the law concerning the censorship of Jewish books came into effect, and in 1837 the Kiev Censorship Committee created the position of censor of Jewish books. At different times, this position was held by converts, maskilic Jews, and Christians. On July 21, 1837 a converted Jewish medical doctor, Y. Lips, was appointed to the position. He was favored by the authorities because of his

---

96 Ibid.
97 Ibid., 32.

denunciations of Jews, and was appointed by order of Tsar Nicholas I. Despite his appointment to the Kiev Censorship Committee, Lips remained in St. Petersburg, where he had served as the censor of Jewish books in 1836–1837.[98] Perhaps Lips was reluctant to leave the Russian capital and move to distant Kiev. He proposed to the authorities that all censorship of Jewish books be carried out in St. Petersburg rather than in Kiev and Vilna. Lips justified his request by claiming that the Vilna Jewish censors made significant errors. He also argued that it was necessary to confiscate and destroy all "harmful" books, in which category he included almost all Jewish books. The Minister of National Enlightenment and the Committee of Ministers rejected his proposal along with his denunciation of the Vilna censors. Lips was dismissed in February 1838 for neglecting his duty, bribery, and extortion of Jews.[99]

In June 1838, the Jew Iosif Zeiberling was appointed as the censor of Jewish books at the Kiev Censorship Committee. He also worked as the learned Jew (i.e., an expert on Jewish questions) in the office of the Kiev, Podolia, and Volhynia governor-general.[100] Zeiberling was one of the first prominent maskilic Jews in the Russian Empire, and his biography deserves special attention.

Zeiberling was a second-generation maskil who was born in Vilna in 1811. His father, Isaac Zeiberling, studied at Vilna University and worked as an assistant to the censor of Jewish books in Vilna. Isaac Zeiberling later practiced as a doctor in the city of Polotsk, where he perished in a fire at his home in 1837. Iosif Zeiberling graduated from the Vilna gymnasium and then studied at the Medical-Surgical Academy in St. Petersburg. However, he did not complete his studies "because of his illness, and was released from the student body."[101] He continued his education later, and "twenty years after his appointment to the position of censor, he received the degree of Doctor of Philosophy from the University of Giessen."[102] Zeiberling had the command of many

---

98 El'iashevich, *Pravitel'stvennaia politika i evreiskaia pechat'*, 538, 717.
99 *Evreiskaia entsiklopediia*, s.v. "Tsenzura," 15:800.
100 Dmitry Eliashevich, *Pravitel'stvennaia politika i evreiskaia pechat'*, 203, 538.
101 TsDIAK U, f. 293, op. 1, d. 46, l. 3.
102 El'iashevich, *Pravitel'stvennaia politika i evreiskaia pechat'*, 190.

languages, including Yiddish, Hebrew, Russian, Latin, German, French, and Polish, and was recommended for the post of censor to the Committee of Ministers by the Minister of National Enlightenment Sergei Uvarov. The Committee of Ministers approved his candidacy, and Zeiberling held the position for fifteen years until 1852.[103]

As a Jewish expert in the office of the governor-general, Zeiberling was involved as a consultant and translator in various Jewish questions and affairs. An unattributed biographical note states:

> At the request of the governor-general of the Kiev province [Bibikov], Zeiberling participated very usefully in very important secret affairs, as well as in all measures which the government undertook regarding Jews at this time. Zeiberling had the chance to show in this position all his abilities and zeal, and his world outlook.[104]

Governor-General Bibikov was certainly well disposed toward Zeiberling. In 1841, after Zeiberling had worked for two years in the governor-general's office, Bibikov recommended him for "personal honorary citizenship," as Zeiberling had requested in a petition. To receive personal honorary citizenship was very important for Jews in Imperial Russia, because it gave them the right to live outside the Pale of Settlement. Bibikov wrote that Zeiberling worked as a translator of Jewish papers in his office, and

> with special success was engaged in some important affairs regarding Jews, and was even involved in the interrogation of Jews accused of political crimes. He fulfilled all of these tasks with zeal, successfully, and without any reward.[105]

Bibikov further explained that Zeiberling, who fulfilled all the obligations of a learned Jew, officially "cannot occupy this state

---

103 Ibid.
104 TsDIAK U, f. 293, op. 1, d. 46, l. 3.
105 Ibid., ll. 1–2.

position, because he did not finish his education at the St. Petersburg Medical-Surgical Academy and does not have a university degree"; for this reason, he did not receive any compensation for his work, undertaking it without remuneration.[106] Accordingly, Bibikov considered it fair that as compensation for his work, Zeiberling should be rewarded with personal honorary citizenship. However, in spite of Bibikov's positive recommendation, personal honorary citizenship was not granted to Zeiberling. The Minister of National Enlightenment, Uvarov, explained in his letter of April 3, 1842 to the Director of the Kiev Educational District that, according to the law, personal honorary citizenship could be given to a Jew for distinguished service only by order of the tsar. Therefore, the Committee of Ministers decided instead to award Zeiberling with a silver medal "For Zeal."[107]

Like the Vilna Jewish censors, Zeiberling did not have the right to give permission for the publication or circulation of Jewish books. He merely submitted his recommendations to the Kiev Censorship Committee, which made the final decision.[108] However, the Censorship Committee paid great attention to his views and recommendations. As a true maskil, Zeiberling believed in the Enlightenment, not only for Jews but also for gentiles who should be educated in Jewish tradition and religious literature. We can see Zeiberling's desire to enlighten gentiles on these matters from his review of the *Talmud Bavli* (Babylonian Talmud) *Tractate Berachot* with a German translation, *Babylonischer Talmud. Tractat Berachoth* was published in Berlin in 1842. A Prussian subject—Pinner, a doctor of philosophy—brought forty-one copies of this book to Russia for sale in 1844, and submitted a copy to the Kiev Censorship Committee. Zeiberling's opinion reads as follows:

1. This publication of the Talmud with a German translation has attracted the attention of all European leading figures and scholars and the especial attention of our Most August Monarch, who gave permission to dedicate this work to His Highest Person.

---

106 Ibid.
107 Ibid., ll. 4–5.
108 El'iashevich, *Pravitel'stvennaia politika i evreiskaia pechat'*, 191.

2. The publication of this enormous work that from ancient times has been inaccessible to Christians, in a new translation, in a language understandable by everybody, satisfies the desire expressed for a long time by all scholars for whom mainly it has been published. The uneducated Jewish masses will without doubt refuse to buy this work because of its high price, their lack of knowledge of German and their superstition.
3. The completeness of this work and the preservation of its original character, give it special value in that Christians and adherents of different faiths can have an exact and complete understanding of the original. I recommend that the circulation of this book be allowed without any limitations...[109]

In 1845, the Kiev Censorship Committee and the Minister of National Enlightenment allowed this work to circulate in Russia. There are some ironic aspects to this story. Before this publication the Russian authorities, and especially Uvarov, had taken many measures to overcome the "harmful" influence of the Talmud on Jews. Uvarov wrote a report to Nicholas I on March 17, 1841 "On the Transformation of the Jews, and on Opinions on this Subject Abroad." Uvarov said that he had contacts

> both in person and in writing with "educated Jews in Germany." From these men he had learned that the major obstacle to the reeducation of their coreligionists in Russia is the self-interest of the rabbis and their erroneous prejudice that the Talmud is essential to the education of every Jew. This is not so, advised his informants. The Talmud is necessary only for future rabbis; other Jews should instead study the Bible and the ethical and moral teachings of Judaism.[110]

Uvarov followed the same principle in his well-known memorandum "On the Education of the Jews" of 1844. It stated that Jewish

---

109 TsDIAK U, f. 293, op. 1, d. 85, l. 4.
110 Michael Stanislawski, *Tsar Nicholas I and the Jews: The Transformation of Jewish Society in Russia 1825–1855* (Philadelphia: The Jewish Publication Society of America, 1983), 64.

state (*kazennye*) schools should direct their activities "against the effects of the Talmud."¹¹¹ Yet a year later in 1845, apparently basing himself on Zeiberling's opinion, Uvarov allowed the circulation of the uncut *Tractate Berachot* with German translation. Moreover, this work was dedicated to Tsar Nicholas I by his permission. Did the Russian authorities change their opinion about the Talmud or did they finally decide to read this "harmful book" themselves? Presumably, when Uvarov banned the study of the Talmud in Jewish state schools, he had only a vague notion about the book and was influenced by his advisers. Furthermore, as later developments were to show, this publication of a major Talmudic tractate did not change the Russian authorities' opinion that the Talmud was the source of the perceived deficiencies in Jewish morality. Their policy to forbid the use of the Talmud in Jewish state schools therefore continued.

Zeiberling worked at the Kiev Censorship Committee until 1852, when he was forced to resign after being denounced. The censor of Jewish books of the Vilna Censorship Committee, the convert V. V. Rozen, claimed that Zeiberling approved for publication the book *Sefer Ein Yaakov*, which "contains statements against Christianity and the government."¹¹² Rozen wrote that Zeiberling intentionally hid the real meaning of this book, and provided in his denunciation several extracts from the book in his own translation. Tsar Nicholas I commented on this denunciation: "Absolutely right." The fate of Zeiberling was sealed. The new Minister of National Enlightenment, Platon Shirinskii-Shikhmatov, following the order of the tsar, instructed Governor-General Bibikov to severely reprimand Zeiberling in the presence of the other Kiev Censorship Committee members and to consider the possibility of replacing him with a more reliable person. Zeiberling was reprimanded on March 10, 1852, and forced to resign. He was replaced by the convert Vladimir Fedorov (Tsvi-Hirsh Grinboim).¹¹³

The accusation against Zeiberling and the statements about the book *Sefer Ein Yaakov* were utterly absurd. *Sefer Ein Yaakov* is a collection

---

111 Ibid., 65.
112 Galant, "K istorii kievskogo getto," 266.
113 El'iashevich, *Pravitel'stvennaia politika i evreiskaia pechat'*, 225–227.

of Talmudic *aggadot* (stories), compiled by the fifteenth-century Talmudist Rabbi Yaakov ibn Chaviv. However the authorities, who understood nothing about Jewish religious literature, always had more trust in converts or gentiles than in Jews. Consequently Zeiberling lost both his job and his right to live in Kiev. Zeiberling attempted to rehabilitate himself and wrote several explanations to the authorities about this book, but these efforts were in vain, and he was not reappointed. In December 1854 Zeiberling wrote a letter of self-justification to the governor-general, explaining that he had made deletions and corrections in 1,245 places on 405 pages in *Sefer Ein Yaakov*. He wrote that many of the quotations that Rozen had characterized as harmful could be found in other Jewish books published with the permission of other censorship committees, and even in textbooks published by the Ministry of National Enlightenment for Jewish schools in 1850.[114] Zeiberling's petition was left unanswered. He wrote again in 1855—this time to the new Minister of National Enlightenment, Avraam Norov—a 177-page explanation of *Sefer Ein Yaakov*, which showed that Rozen intentionally distorted the sense of the book with incorrect translations. Zeiberling's manuscript was forwarded to the convert Vasilii Levinson, Professor of Hebrew of the St. Petersburg Theological Academy. Levinson concluded that he completely agreed with Zeiberling's arguments and that

> Zeiberling's work shows his extraordinary knowledge of Jewish as well as Christian religious literature...He is completely innocent and has suffered for no cause. Meanwhile all other censors, even Christian ones, have allowed the same parts of the book to be published...[115]

Despite Levinson's opinion, the Minister of National Enlightenment ordered that Zeiberling's request be denied.

Zeiberling, who was forty-one years old when he lost his position as censor, decided to start a new career. He enrolled in the merchant estate, and became a merchant of the first guild in the city of Oster.

---

114 Galant, "K istorii kievskogo getto," 274.
115 El'iashevich, *Pravitel'stvennaia politika i evreiskaia pechat'*, 218, 226.

During the Crimean War (1853–1856), he supplied medicine and canvas for the Russian Army. Zeiberling wrote to the new Kiev, Podolia, and Volhynia governor-general, Prince Illarion Vasil'chikov, that his business affairs required his presence in Kiev "as is allowed to other Jewish first guild merchants who have government contracts" until the end of their contracts.[116] Zeiberling received a large government contract for the delivery of one million *arshin* of canvas and "other commissariat items" for the army to the Kiev Commissariat Commission.[117] He was supposed to receive the canvas and other goods from his agents and teamsters, make payments to them, take care of the bookkeeping, sort the arriving goods, and deliver them to the shops of the Kiev Commissariat Commission.[118] Zeiberling's request for permanent residence in Kiev was supported by the Kiev governor Krivtsov and the director of the Kiev Commissariat Commission. However, Governor-General Vasil'chikov did not allow Zeiberling to stay in Kiev until the end of the contract, and required that he obtain his personal permission each time he stayed in the city for more than three days. The governor-general also ordered that Zeiberling stay in one of the Jewish guesthouses, and that the chief of police report each time Zeiberling departed from Kiev.

The writer Leskov characterized Governor-General Vasil'chikov as being "kind, with a soft character." Why was he so harsh toward Zeiberling?[119] Vasil'chikov was not a Judeophobe, and later, in the reign of Alexander II, "he advocated an easing of restrictions upon Jews" and supported the establishment of new Jewish state schools.[120] Because Zeiberling was forced to resign during the administration of Bibikov, we can assume that Vasil'chikov did not know Zeiberling personally, and did not have personal antipathy towards him. Presumably, the harsh attitude of Vasil'chikov toward Zeiberling can be explained by his desire to execute the will of Nicholas I. All governors-general in Russia were appointed by the tsar, and they were loath to

---

116 Galant, "K istorii kievskogo getto," 267.
117 *Arshin* is an old Russian measure of length: one arshin equals 0.71 meters or $2^{1}/_{3}$ feet.
118 Galant, "K istorii kievskogo getto," 268–269.
119 *Dve Rusi: Ukraina Incognita*, 451.
120 Klier, *Imperial Russia's Jewish Question*, 152; Shandra, *Kyivs'ke general-gubernatorstvo (1832–1894)*, 127.

provoke his anger. When Zeiberling was removed from his position in compliance with the will of the tsar, he also became a *persona non-grata* for the governors-general. And Vasil'chikov did everything possible to ensure that Zeiberling did not stay for long in Kiev.

Meanwhile, Zeiberling received an important new government contract. In 1855–1856 he obtained a lease from the Kiev Commissary Commission for the transportation of "commissariat goods and medicine to the army and other places, as required." The Kiev Commissary Commission again asked the governor-general to allow him to reside in Kiev. The director explained in his request that the presence of Zeiberling in Kiev was necessary to fulfill his contract, and that Zeiberling transported goods and medicine from the commission to the army on a daily basis. On December 23, 1854, Zeiberling sent a new petition to the governor-general, requesting permission to reside in Kiev. He wrote that the prohibition against his living in Kiev

> according to the order of Your Highness, struck him not only in his commercial affairs, but also struck him in a moral way, humiliated his honor and the dignity of a person, who perhaps deserves a better fate; a person, who has received some systematic education and who irreproachably toiled for 15 years in state service.[121]

Zeiberling petitioned for permission to live in Kiev until the completion of his contract, to board outside of the Jewish guesthouses, and to rent an apartment for his residence and an office near the Kiev Commissariat Commission. He wrote that he should be at the commission

> on a daily basis, mostly regarding emergency affairs, arranging for delivery to the troops of commodities and medicine, as well as supplying them with canvas, etc. It is impossible to demand that the Commissariat officials or the officers look for him in the other end of the city, among the crowd of Jewish teamsters and workers, and asked whether it was possible that

---

[121] Galant, "K istorii kievskogo getto," 272.

Zeiberling could take care of his significant commercial affairs with the state and keep state goods in this dirty and crowded building [i.e., a Jewish guesthouse].[122]

Vasil'chikov ordered that Zeiberling be allowed to open an office near the Kiev Commissariat Commission, on the condition "that the clerks and salesmen there should be indisputably Christian, and that Zeiberling himself continue to reside in one of the Jewish guesthouses."[123] So no exception to the general rule was made for Zeiberling regarding the residence of Jews in Kiev.

At this time, the old regime of Nicholas I ended in Russia with the death of the tsar, and the period of the "Great Reforms" was beginning. The new government established a position of censor for Jewish publications in St. Petersburg, and Zeiberling was appointed to this position in 1862. In the same year, Zeiberling was appointed "Jewish expert" for the St. Petersburg Educational district. The new government of Alexander II believed that through education they could achieve their goal of assimilating Russian Jews. Thus, they encouraged Jews to study at Jewish state schools as well as general schools, and looked toward the Jewish maskilim as supporters of this policy. This was when the principles of the Haskalah seemed to have triumphed in Russia, and many maskilim—like Zeiberling—were called into service by the authorities.

However, the romance of the Russian government with the maskilim did not last for long. In the 1870s, anti-Jewish sentiment increased among the Russian authorities, in society, and in the press. Ultimately, Zeiberling left Russia forever and settled in Vienna, where he hoped to find the ideals of the Haskalah realized. Zeiberling and his adopted son gave up their Russian citizenship on June 16, 1876. The Russian government nevertheless continued to pay Zeiberling his "subsidy" for his service as censor until 1889.[124]

Zeiberling's fate recalls that of another prominent maskil, Max Lilienthal (1815–1882), who was born in Munich, and who drew up a

---

122 Ibid., 276–267.
123 Ibid., 278.
124 El'iashevich, *Pravitel'stvennaia politika i evreiskaia pechat'*, 640.

project for the establishment of Jewish state schools in Russia to provide a Haskalah-style education. However, in contrast to Zeiberling, Lilienthal quickly realized that even men like Uvarov and Kiselev could not be trusted to have the interests of Jews at heart. Lilienthal discretely left Russia in 1844, just as his Jewish school reform project was beginning to be implemented.[125] Like Lilienthal, Zeiberling attempted to cooperate with the Russian authorities to spread Haskalah ideas among Jews in Russia, and like Lilienthal he was ultimately disillusioned about the real goals of the government. Only Lilienthal was disillusioned much more quickly than Zeiberling.

CONCLUSION: THE MYTH ABOUT JEWISH ISOLATION AND THE POLICY OF NICHOLAS I'S GOVERNMENT TOWARD JEWS

Similar to other European governments, Russian authorities officially supported a policy of rapprochement (*sliyanie*) of Jews with the local population; however, in practice, in 1825-1855, the government policy was Russification and isolation of Jews. The tsarist government narrowed the Pale of Settlement, exempting from this territory the Kurland and Lettland regions and the cities of Kiev, Sevastopol', and Nikolaev, as well as rural areas. Jews were expelled from all of these places. While the government officially announced the course for rapprochement and merging the Jews with the Russian population, in reality the Jews were isolated and concentrated into a smaller Pale. This inconsistency was a typical feature of Nicholas I's regime.

The declaration of the principle of the rapprochement of Russian Jews with the larger society attracted some highly educated Jewish maskilim from abroad. However, these maskilim—who initially believed in the sincerity of the government's attempts to enlighten and modernize Jews—became disillusioned regarding the Russian authorities' real goals, either quickly as was the case with Max Lilienthal or

---

125 Michael Stanislawski wrote that Lilienthal never expressed disappointment about the policy of the Russian government regarding Jews until he left Russia. If Lilienthal had dared do so, he would have finished his life not as a respected Reform rabbi in Cincinnati, but in exile in Siberia (Stanislawski, *Tsar Nicholas I and the Jews*, 88-91).

more gradually as with Iosif Zeiberling. The pogroms of 1881–1882, and the government response to the riots, finally ended all illusions about a better future for Jews in the Russian Empire.

The Russian government often accused Jews of self-isolation and religious fanaticism. However, Jews in Kiev, as shown in archival documents and the memoirs of contemporaries, were far from religious fanatics, had many financial contacts with the local population, maintained good relations with Russian merchants during the fairs, came to Christian homes to sell their goods, and spoke Russian. The Russian authorities expelled from the city Orthodox as well as completely modern enlightened Jews, who were ready to merge with the local population in economic and social ways—even such a prominent follower of the Haskalah in Russia as Iosif Zeiberling.

Russian authorities talked a lot about the parasitic way of life of Jews in Russia, and their involvement in non-productive enterprises. However, Jews in Kiev performed very important city works such as the construction of Kiev St. Vladimir University, the Kiev fortress, and the city fortifications. They built roads, delivered necessary goods and food, worked at the military plant *Arsenal*, and brought supplies and medicine for the troops. Jewish merchants also invested heavily in the local economy.

The Russian authorities' assimilation efforts, based on Enlightenment principles, ran parallel with Nicholas I's superstitious fears about Jews, and his attempts to create Jew-free zones inside the Pale of Settlement. This latter tendency of government policy toward Jews dominated in Kiev. The tsar's order for the expulsion of Jews from Kiev interrupted the existence of the city's Jewish community for twenty-four years (from 1835 to 1859). This decision had a negative impact on the city's economy, and brought much suffering to the Jews. Although Nicholas I's government claimed to be acting in accordance with enlightened values, it was also strongly influenced by medieval fears and attitudes toward Jews. While other European countries in the late eighteenth and nineteenth centuries admitted Jews to civil society, and increased their civil rights in accordance with the national interest, the Russian authorities, contrary to the interests of the state, maintained a policy of isolating Jews and established for them a ghetto in Kiev.

CHAPTER THREE

The Jewish Right of Residence in Kiev in 1859–1917

> The large, beautiful gentle city of Yehupets [Kiev]...is certainly not the kind of city that would seek to have even a token Jewish population. Quite the contrary, it is well known that, from time immemorial Jews have been as welcome to the people of the city as a migraine.[1]
> —Sholom Aleichem

THE READMISSION OF JEWS TO KIEV

The accession of Alexander II initiated the period of the "Great Reforms." The abolition of serfdom and the reform of the legal system opened the way for the development of capitalism in the country. The urban population increased rapidly, with the migration of many thousands of liberated serfs to the cities. Russian industry, which had previously existed in an embryonic state, began to develop at an accelerating pace.

---

1 Cited in Gennady Estraikh, "From Yehupets Jargonists to Kiev Modernists: The Rise of a Yiddish Literary Centre, 1880s–1914," *East European Jewish Affairs* 30, no. 1 (2000): 21.

Kiev grew swiftly, and, by the turn of the twentieth century, had become the fifth largest city in the Russian Empire (after St. Petersburg, Moscow, Warsaw, and Odessa). During the second half of the nineteenth century, the population of Kiev increased dramatically from 71,365 in 1865, to 127,251 in 1874, and to 154,586 in 1884. By 1897, the number of inhabitants had reached 247,723, and had doubled again by 1910 to 527,287.² This growth was mostly the result of migration from Ukrainian villages and towns. The city census of 1874 showed that only 30 percent of Kiev's inhabitants had been born there.³

In 1856, Kiev had 4,873 buildings and houses, including 361 built of stone. By the 1880s, there were 21,120 buildings and houses, including three thousand of stone. In the 1870s, the administrative and commercial center of Kiev moved from the Pechersk district to the Kreshchatik, which a few decades earlier had been "a wooden ravine and creek favored by hunters, trappers, and anyone who could put up a distilling shack."⁴ In 1874–1876, a beautiful city hall was built on Kreshchatik Street. By the beginning of the twentieth century, several new districts were included within the city limits: Solomenka, Protasov Iar, Shuliavka, and Karavaevy Dachi. In 1897, there were seventeen large plants and factories, employing more than 100 workers, and many small enterprises; by 1913, there were 177 enterprises in which 15,000 people were employed. The most important industries were metallurgy and the production of sugar and construction materials. Kiev also became an important commercial center. City trade constituted 35.8 percent of that of the Russian Empire's southwestern region. A stock exchange and eleven different banks and their branches operated in the town.

During this period, Kiev became an important transportation hub. In the 1870s, the Kiev-Odessa and Kiev-Kursk railroads were built, and in the second half of the nineteenth century navigation on the Dnieper was developed. Civic improvements also took place. Between 1870 and 1872, a water main was installed, and in 1894 a sewer system was

---

2   *Kyiv: Entsyklopedychnyi dovidnyk*, ed. A. V. Kudryts'kyi (Kiev: URE, 1981), 18; Hamm, *Kiev: A Portrait*, 42.
3   Iurii Pavlenko, *Narys istorii Kyieva* (Kiev: Feniks, 2003), 255.
4   Hamm, *Kiev: A Portrait*, 28.

constructed. The erection of an electric power station in the beginning of the 1890s made possible the illumination of the city as well as the development of public transportation with the replacement of horse-drawn by electric trams.

Jews played a major role in Kiev's rapid development. Their readmission was initiated by the local authorities, who understood that the city's economy had suffered since the expulsion of the Jews in 1835. The local administration now had the support of the higher authorities for this initiative. On March 30, 1856, Pavel Kiselev, Chairman of the Committee for the Transformation of the Jews, responded to the tsar's call for changes in the Jews' position by suggesting the legislation be revised "with the goal of making [them] useful Russian subjects like the native [*korennoe*] population of the country."[5] Kiselev believed that this process should commence with opening the inner provinces of the empire to Jews, and allowing them to serve in the state bureaucracy. The government consulted local authorities on the question of increasing the rights of Jews. An official letter was sent to the administration in Kiev, requesting its views on the readmission of Jews to the city and on granting them the right to buy real estate there. In two communications in 1856, Lieutenant General Pavel Gesse, the governor of Kiev, gave his response. He wrote:

> If we search for the reasons for the high prices in Kiev of all articles, and especially of food and consumer goods, we must admit that the prices of such goods began to increase after the expulsion of Jews from Kiev in accordance with the law of December 2, 1827...
>
> Therefore, we can conclude that the expulsion of the Jews from Kiev impeded the natural development of trade in the city, and was harmful for the majority of its rather large population...It is impossible to hold that the Jewish population has only vices and is of no value to the state; on the contrary, we have to accept that Jews are wholly devoted to trade, industry and artisan crafts, and that some of them possess significant

---

5 I. A. Darevskii, *K istorii evreev v Kieve ot poloviny VIII v. do kontsa XIX v.* (Kiev: I. M. Roset Publishing House, 1907), 113.

capital. They mostly follow a simple way of life and are satisfied with moderate profits. With their ability to facilitate the circulation of money, and their tireless activity, they will be able more than others, once living and trading in Kiev, to restore and develop trade and industry here, and, by their competition with the Christian merchants, to force prices to fall, bringing to the city and its population great benefits...

Monopoly is, in general, harmful for the natural development of trade, but it is usually advantageous to those who exercise it. Yet the experience of nearly thirty years has proved that the Kiev merchants have not been able to benefit from their own monopoly. Their action in expelling the Jewish merchants has not only harmed their Christian customers but has not even proved beneficial for themselves.[6]

The Christian merchants, who before 1837 had demanded the expulsion of Jews from Kiev, monopolized all trade in the city and did not allow other Christians to become involved. In 1797, 347 Christian merchants lived in Kiev. This number barely increased in the following half century; in 1845 their number was 358, and by 1856 it had fallen to 241.[7] In Gesse's words:

> In Kiev with its large population, the number of people who are members of the merchant estate is as follows: 11 of the first guild, 19 of the second guild, and 211 of the third guild. Many of these have become members of this estate to avoid the military draft. With such a small number of merchants can we expect trade to flourish?[8]

Between 1797 and 1861, the city's population had increased from 19,000 to 65,000. Thus it seemed obvious to the local authorities that

---

6 These responses were published in *Den'* in 1870 and are reprinted. Ibid., 114–117.
7 Mikhail Kulisher, "Evrei v Kieve: Istoricheskii ocherk," *Evreiskaia starina* 4 (1913): 427.
8 Darevskii, *K istorii evreev v Kieve*, 116.

the readmission of Jews was necessary for its further economic development. Illarion Illarionovich Vasil'chikov, the Kiev, Podolia, and Volhynia governor-general, supported Governor Gesse's conclusions, and the question of the readmission of Jews to Kiev was submitted for the consideration of the government.

Neither Vasil'chikov, who was governor-general from 1852 to 1863, nor Gesse, who was governor of Kiev between 1855 and 1864, expressed any opinion on the readmission of Jews to Kiev until the government asked them. On the contrary, Vasil'chikov, as was shown in the previous chapter, expelled Iosif Zeiberling from Kiev without a second thought. This metamorphosis, in which previously conservative officials became liberal in the time of "Great Reforms," occurred not only with Vasil'chikov, but also with higher officials. For example, Dmitrii Bludov, one of the most conservative officials during the reign of Nicholas I, became a liberal in the time of "Great Reforms." As Chairman of the Council of Ministers between 1861 and 1864, he participated in the preparation for the liberation of the serfs, and called for the reduction of censorship.[9] This is a striking example of how high officials faithfully served the reigning tsar, and strictly followed official policies. Those who broke this rule were dismissed.

The issue of the readmission of Jews to Kiev now came before the Russian government. On March 16, 1859, Stepan Stepanovich Lanskoi, the minister of the interior, in his report to the general session of the Council of Ministers, spoke of the need to grant Jews the right of permanent residence in Kiev as an exception to the general rule forbidding Jews from residing permanently outside the Pale of Settlement. Lanskoi also proposed to allow temporary residence in Kiev for all categories of Jews without exception. The Council of Ministers took a more conservative line, and decided to grant Jewish merchants of the first guild and foreign Jewish merchants the right of permanent residence in Kiev with their families and employees.[10] In the same year, the Russian government adopted a law that allowed Jewish merchants of the first guild to enroll in the merchant estates of any city in Russia (i.e., to live there)

---

9 Iu. M. Sokol'skii, *Tsari i ministry* (St. Petersburg: Poligon, 2002), 345.
10 Darevskii, *K istorii evreev v Kieve*, 117.

if they had been enrolled in the first guild for two years before this law was issued, or if they had been enrolled in the first guild for a continuous five years after the acceptance of the law.[11] This law did not have any significant impact on the vast majority of Jews. In their petitions to the government, Jewish representatives claimed that not more than a hundred Jewish merchants of the first guild were to be found in the entire Tsarist Empire, and that due to their financial situation, only twenty of them would be able to move to the inner provinces of the country.[12] The authorities were aware that this law would not affect the status of the vast majority of Russian Jews. In subsequent years, they considered extending the right of residence outside the Pale to other categories of Jews. When Count A. G. Stroganov, the governor-general of Novorossiisk, proposed granting Jews equal rights with the rest of the population in accordance with their appropriate estate status, Lanskoi supported this proposal. In his words:

> [T]he rapprochement of Jews with the native population in education, professions, and in other areas...can only be attained by making them equal in their rights with other subjects of the empire. Therefore, limitations and restrictions in any decrees which are solely applicable to Jews, apart from those relating to religious matters, should be seen as obstacles to their rapprochement with the rest of the population, and as the principal and only reason why they remain in the pitiful situation which we see today.[13]

This was also the view of Vasil'chikov, under whose jurisdiction almost half of the empire's Jewish population lived. In 1861, he submitted a detailed proposal for the abolition of a number of restrictions on Jews. According to Gessen:

---

11 Mikhail Kalnitsky, "Pravovoi status evreev Kieva (1859–1917)," in *Ievreis'ka istoriia ta kul'tura v Ukraini: Materialy konferentsii. Kyiv 8–9 hrudnia, 1994* (Kiev: Institut Iudaiki, 1995), 77–78.
12 Iulii Gessen, *Istoriia evreiskogo naroda v Rossii* (Moscow: Gesharim, 1993), 158.
13 Ibid., 147.

His proposal was motivated by the need to create in the southwestern region a social and economic force to counterbalance the Poles, hostile to the Russians, who were strong because of their education and wealth. If the government gave Jews the opportunity to acquire an education and develop trade and industry, this would impede the revolutionary plans of the Poles. Vasil'chikov also argued against restrictive legislation regarding Jews because of the economic necessities of the region and the well-being of the Jews themselves.[14]

The recommendations of Stroganov, Lanskoi, and Vasil'chikov were not accepted. Bludov, who succeeded Kiselev as head of the Jewish Committee, took the view that equal rights could only be gradually granted to the Jews of Russia. Unlike the Jews of Western Europe who, he claimed, at their governments' first invitations sent their children to general schools and turned to useful occupations, in Russia the government was compelled to struggle against Jewish prejudices and fanaticism. Jews could only be granted equality when true enlightenment spread among them, their internal life was transformed, and they turned to useful occupations.[15]

Tsar Alexander II supported Bludov's point of view that selected categories of "useful" Jews, who made up only a small percentage of the Jewish population, should gradually be given the right of residence outside the Pale. A law of 1861 extended the right to live outside the Pale to Jewish merchants of the second guild, and to graduates of universities and gymnasiums. In 1865, this right was granted to Jewish artisans; in 1867, to retired soldiers.[16] All were allowed to live outside the Pale with members of their families.

On December 11, 1861, the tsar approved the State Council's decree on the permanent and temporary residence of Jews in Kiev.

---

14   Ibid., 157.
15   Ibid.
16   Ibid., 154; *Evreiskaia entsiklopediia*, s.v. "Zhitel'stvo," 7: 595; Irwin Michael Aronson, "Russian Bureaucratic Attitudes Toward Jews, 1881–1894" (PhD diss., Northwestern University, 1973), 29.

The decree gave the right of residence in Kiev to the following categories of Jews:

1. Merchants of the first and second guilds with their stewards [*prikazchiki*] and servants five years after their enrollment in these guilds, and for as long as they remained enrolled;
2. Those serving in the state administration during the period of their service;
3. Those who were involved in the delivery for sale of "vitally important supplies and other merchandise" were allowed to enter the city in order to do so;
4. Those who wished to purchase various materials, to deliver goods they had themselves produced, or who were transporting people and baggage, were allowed to remain in the city for two weeks;
5. Those who came to obtain treatment in Kiev mineral water clinics could remain until the end of their treatment;
6. Students were permitted to remain until the end of their studies;
7. Students of art and craft schools, and workers studying for diplomas, could remain for the period set down in their study arrangements.

In other cases Jews could obtain special permission from the governor-general to remain in Kiev for six weeks, a period that could be extended to half a year. Jews were only to reside in the Lybedskoi and Plosskii districts of the city.[17]

Along with the readmission of certain categories of Jews to Kiev, the government lifted some restrictions on Jewish residence in the cities of Nikolaev, Sevastopol', and Yalta. With the expulsion of the Jews, Nikolaev and Sevastopol' had lost most of their merchants and artisans. To remedy this situation, in 1838 the government had granted various privileges to Christian merchants and artisans, hoping to attract them to these towns. However, as in the case of Kiev, this goal was not achieved. Therefore, in 1859 the authorities allowed Jewish merchants

---

17 Kalnitsky, "Pravovoi status evreev Kieva," 78.

of all three guilds to settle again in Nikolaev and Sevastopol', and other categories of Jews to live there temporarily. In 1860, Jews again received the right to settle in Yalta, from which they had been expelled in 1837.[18] In this way, the new Russian government returned Jews to those cities from which they had been expelled by Nicholas I.

The liberal mood, which made these changes possible, did not last. Its waning in the wake of the Polish insurrections was reflected in Kiev in the fact that Vasil'chikov's successors—Nikolai Nikolaevich Annenkov and Aleksandr Pavlovich Bezak—did not share his opinion on the Jews' positive impact on Kiev's economy. They were both influenced by memories of the role Jews had played in the noble-dominated feudal economy of pre-partition Poland-Lithuania, and by new fears that, in the aftermath of the Polish insurrection, Jews might replace the *szlachta* (Polish nobility) as exploiters of the peasantry. Their concerns were shared by the tsar. In response to Annenkov's observation in 1864 that "the question of the Jews has the highest importance and deserves the special attention of the government," the tsar noted "very true."[19]

In addition, the reforms did not eliminate the Kiev ghetto; it was merely expanded in the 1860s to encompass two city districts. Instead of the revenue (about 5,000 rubles annually) that the city received from the Jewish guesthouses before their closure in 1857, Kiev now received a contribution from special taxes levied on Jews.[20]

Nevertheless, in this new situation the Jewish population of Kiev—which remained outside of the Pale of Settlement until February 1917—grew rapidly. In 1862, a total of 1,411 Jews lived in Kiev; in 1863 there were 3,013; in 1910 over 50 thousand; and in 1913 the official count was 81,256. In 1917, officials estimated 87,240 Jews lived in Kiev (about 15 percent of the city's total population).[21] The Jewish population in Kiev grew so fast that in the 1880s, a Jewish post office was established for correspondence in Yiddish. Many Jews did not know Russian, and they may have also wished to avoid censorship of their

---

18 Gessen, *Istoriia evreiskogo naroda v Rossii*, 154–155.
19 Klier, *Imperial Russia's Jewish Question*, 185.
20 Ibid.
21 *Evreiskaia entsiklopediia*, s.v. "Kiev," 9: 516; *Kratkaia evreiskaia entsiklopediia*, s.v. "Kiev," 4: 253.

correspondence sent through the official post office. In addition, the Jewish post office delivered Russian newspapers from Kiev to Berdichev and Zhitomir. This Jewish post office operated for several years. However, when it was found to be in competition with the government post office, it was closed by the authorities.[22]

By the turn of the twentieth century, Jews were the third largest national group in Kiev, after Russians and Ukrainians. The first all-Russia population census of 1897 provides information about the major ethnic groups in Kiev according to native language (Table I).[23]

Table I: Kiev Population According to the 1897 Census

	Male	Female	Total
Great Russians	71,722	62,556	134,278
Ukrainians	31,721	23,343	55,064
Jews	15,798	14,139	29,937*
Poles	8,571	8,008	16,579
Belorussians	1,709	1,008	2,717

*According to the census, the total number of people of the Jewish faith in Kiev was 31,801.[24] The difference between these two figures reveals that about 6 percent of the city's Jewish population did not claim Yiddish as their native language and were probably native Russian speakers.

KIEV: A "JEWISH" CITY

The rapid growth of Kiev's Jewish population made local Judeophobes very anxious, leading them to claim that Kiev was being transformed into a "Jewish" city. In 1862, shortly after the readmission of Jews, the journal of the Russian Orthodox Church, *Kievskie eparkhial'nye vedomosti* (Kiev Diocese Herald), stated:

> As soon as Jewish merchants of the first two guilds were allowed to live in Kiev with the necessary number of stewards,

---

22 S. G. Iaron, *Kiev v vos'midesiatykh godakh: Vospominaniia starozhila* (Kiev: n. p., 1910), 35–41.
23 Hamm, *Kiev: A Portrait*, 104.
24 *Evreiskaia entsiklopediia*, s.v. "Kiev," 9: 526.

about eight thousand Jews burst into our city.[25] They are allowed to live in the Lybedskoi and Plosskii districts of Kiev, but have also crowded into Podol. Even Jewish cabbies have come to Kiev, though they do not belong to the first and second merchant guilds. It is not enough that Jewish entrepreneurs, who live in Kiev temporarily, trade to the disadvantage of the city's Christian population, which pays all city taxes; a whole crowd of Jew-craftsmen hide in the city courtyards and dart in and out from courtyard to courtyard for jobs. In addition, Jews, who have spuriously claimed that they have converted to the Christian faith, are even trading on the morals of Christians and have opened nine brothels in Podol, on the border of two of the most populous parts of the city, and on a street where children walk to school. The consequences of all this is already noticeable in the moral and economic spheres. We can guess that if the number of Jews in Kiev multiplies during the next twenty-five years, as it has in the last five years, then the image of our city will be completely altered. Our Cathedrals will stand in Jewish squares, without any means of maintenance, because Christians will have been pushed to the city outskirts, and many will have moved to the villages. Half of the churches will be left without parishes, or with parishes which cannot maintain their churches. Christian trade will decline completely and the economic life of the Christian population will be completely destroyed...[26]

This apocalyptic vision did not correspond to reality. The reports of Governor-General Levashov and Kiev Governor Gesse show how Jewish trade benefited the majority of the city's population. However,

---

25 Official statistics show a significantly smaller number of Jewish residents; according to the official data, in 1863 there were 3,013 Jews in Kiev. But the number, 8,000 Jews in Kiev, was also used by the editor of the newspaper *Kievlianin*, Vitalii Shul'gin, in his article on September 21, 1864. Perhaps both these sources exaggerated the number of Jews in Kiev or many Jews lived in Kiev illegally; the latter seems more likely.
26 Cited in Nikolai Zakrevskii, *Opisanie Kieva* (Moscow: Moskovkoe arkheologicheskoe obshchestvo, 1868), 1: 318–319.

if the mass migration of Jews to the city had been allowed to continue unchecked, Kiev's national and religious composition would have changed. When residence in the city was finally allowed for several categories of Jews, many others came to Kiev illegally. The Pale was just outside Kiev, and poverty, unemployment, and backwardness in the shtetls drove into the city many thousands of young and active people seeking a better education and more advantageous economic and social conditions. In these circumstances, the Judeophobes saw Kiev as a city under siege—a Christian island-fortress in the sea of the Jewish Pale—and until the February 1917 Revolution they struggled unceasingly to expel illegal Jews from the city and to prohibit the further immigration of Jews to Kiev.

Kiev had a significantly lower proportion of Jewish inhabitants than cities in the Pale such as Berdichev, Minsk, Odessa, Warsaw, and Vilna. Table II shows the proportion of Jews in these cities according to the census of 1897:

Table II: Jewish Population of Largest Cities According to the 1897 Census

City	Percentage of Jewish population	Jews	Total population
Berdichev	almost 80 percent	41,617	53,351
Minsk	52.3 percent	47,562	90,884
Odessa	34.4 percent	138,935	403,815
Warsaw	32.5 percent	219,128	683,692
Vilna	40.9 percent	63,996	154,532
Kiev	12.8 percent	31,801	247,723
St. Petersburg	1.3 percent	16,649	1,265,000
Moscow[27]	0.78 percent	8,095	1,038,000

Berdichev and Minsk each had a majority Jewish population, but this did not have the dire impact on the Christian economy that was

---

27 In 1892, about 45,000 Jews lived in Moscow; however, after their expulsion in that year only approximately 7,000 remained. *Evrei v Moskve: Sbornik materialov*, comp. Iu. Snopov and A. Klempert (Jerusalem: Gesharim, 2003), 85.

predicted by the Kievan Judeophobes. The question therefore arises: why did the Judeophobes, and, particularly after 1881, the authorities, defend Kiev so energetically from a mass migration of Jews into the city?

One reason was religious. As already mentioned, Kiev was a holy city for Russian Orthodox Christians because of the acceptance there of the Christian faith by Prince Vladimir, and the preservation of relics of Christian Orthodox saints in the Kiev Cave Monastery. The religious factor definitely played an important role in the Russian authorities' opposition to the lifting of restrictions on Jewish residence in Kiev. However, even more significant for the authorities and Judeophobes was the national factor. They refused to allow Kiev to become a city with a majority or even a large minority of Jews.

"Kiev was, is and will be Russian!" was the slogan of the semi-official newspaper *Kievlianin*, which was published from 1864 to 1917.[28] In Imperial Kiev, Russians were the dominant nationality. This dominance was supported by the Russian government, which from the 1860s on followed a policy of Russification in the empire. *Kievlianin* received a sizable government subsidy, and its point of view on the residence of Jews in Kiev is especially revealing as it appears to reflect government policy.

Kievlianin's editor, Vitalii Iakovlevich Shul'gin, shared the concern of the article earlier cited from *Kievskie eparkhial'nye vedomosti* regarding the presence of a large number of illegal Jews in Kiev. Shul'gin's anxiety about the future of Christians in Kiev as well as in the western region of the empire is also evident in his debates with Mikhail Morgulis. Morgulis—then a student in the law school of Kiev St. Vladimir University and later a tireless Jewish publicist—was invited to publish an article in *Kievlianin* in 1865, during the aftermath of the Polish insurrection of 1863-1864; in this article he proposed that Jews be permitted and even encouraged "to purchase land from Polish landlords."[29] In the subsequent issue, Shul'gin replied:

> Yes, Mr. Morgulis, your plan is very good: the Jews to be sure, will dislodge the Polish element from western Russia sooner

---

28   Cited in Klier, *Imperial Russia's Jewish Question*, 182.
29   Ibid., 191.

than we can. Nonetheless, it seems to us that we will not sin against the wishes of Russian society, if we refuse the honor granted to Kiev of being the new Jerusalem, and to western Russia being the second Promised Land. History shows that Poland paid too dearly for this honor.[30]

Even in the relatively liberal 1860s and 1870s, those who feared a "Jewish invasion" of Kiev were also concerned that the authorities were acting too leniently towards illegal Jewish immigrants. Thus Shul'gin criticized the local Kiev authorities and police for their failure to enforce the government's regulations requiring the expulsion of these illegal residents from the city. On September 21, 1864, he wrote in *Kievlianin*:

> Five years ago Jewish merchants of the first guild received the right to settle in Kiev; in one to two years 8,000 Jews have appeared in Kiev, among whom only about twenty are merchants of the first guild...
>
> In December of last year the authorities announced to all [illegal] Jews in Kiev that they were required to leave the city within seven days; the fulfillment of the order *was made the obligation of the homeowners where they lived*! It is obvious that the immediate eviction of eight thousand, mostly poverty-stricken, people could not be accomplished, especially in the middle of winter.
>
> The homeowners, of course, were not eager to get rid of their tenants; the police washed their hands. Three months passed and in March 1864 the expulsion order was renewed, with the same result, the only difference being that embittered Jews imposed a *herem* (anathema) on one [Jewish] homeowner, who had persecuted them severely while simultaneously receiving a large income from turning his house into a Jewish guesthouse.

---

30 *Kievlianin*, Aug. 14, 1865. Cited in Klier, *Imperial Russia's Jewish Question*, 192.

How is this to be understood?
If the law exists, it should be enforced...

What Shul'gin was, however, concerned about was the way the expulsion had been carried out, which undermined an otherwise desirable policy measure. As he wrote on October 13, 1864:

Laws must be obeyed...but not in ways which disrupt the peace and economic order of the city. It was not humane to expel Jews from the city precipitously, in the dead of winter and still less acceptable to rescind expulsion orders at the last possible minute.[31]

The relatively lenient attitude of the local authorities toward the eviction of illegal Jews from Kiev during the 1860s and the first half of the 1870s is also discussed by the historian Darevskii. He writes that in addition to the categories of Jews who received the legal right of residence in Kiev, a large number of Jews illegally settled in the city:

The local authorities did not observe this law rigorously, and if police officers sometimes checked the rights of Jews [for residence in Kiev], they did so only for appearances' sake and for their own "satisfaction" [i.e., to receive bribes].

The punishment for illegal residence in Kiev was also insignificant: the authorities did not institute criminal proceedings against the guilty party, did not evict him by force from the city, did not deprive him of his livelihood and did not prevent him from again appearing in the city.[32]

Why were the Kiev police and administration so lenient toward illegal Jews during the 1860s and 1870s? Why did they arrange the expulsion of illegal Jews in a manner that was likely to fail? Why did they make homeowners—who made a tidy profit from their Jewish

---
31 Cited in Klier, *Imperial Russia's Jewish Question*, 199.
32 Darevskii, *K istorii evreev v Kieve*, 120.

tenants—primarily responsible for the eviction of Jews? Less important than the alleged unwillingness of the central and local authorities to take strong action against Jews living illegally in the city was the perennial Russian curse of bribery. According to Kiev Jewish journalist S. G. Iaron:

> Bribery, which was created by government decrees and their elucidations by the Senate...is the reason for the failure to observe the law which has allowed a large Jewish population to settle in Kiev.[33]

When Jews were readmitted to Kiev in 1861, the local authorities allowed them to settle in only two districts, Lybedskoi and Plosskii, which were far from the Christian holy sites. The Plosskii district was also far from the city center, and regularly suffered from spring floods.[34] In 1886, the authorities permitted Jewish merchants of the first guild who had lived in Kiev more than five years to buy real estate in all parts of the city.[35] Leading Jewish merchants, such as the Brodskys, M. R. Zaks, S. P. Liberman, M. I. Zaitsev, and M. B. Gal'perin, now built mansions in the most prestigious parts of Kiev, above all in the Dvortsovyi district (the modern Pechersk district) near the Mariinskii Palace, the tsar's official residence, and the residence and office of the governor-general.[36] However, until the February 1917 Revolution, the vast majority of the Jewish population was allowed to reside only in the poorer districts of Kiev: Lybedskoi, Plosskii, and Podol.

According to Iaron:

> These three police districts, which contain the majority of the Jewish population, were the ultimate goal of all the aspiring police officers: just as in the old times, for special

---

33 Iaron, *Kiev v vos'midesiatykh godakh*, 36.
34 Kulisher, "Evrei v Kieve," 430–431; Mikhail Kalnitsky, *Sinagoga Kievskoi iudeiskoi obshchiny 5656–5756: Istoricheskii ocherk* (Kiev: Institut Iudaiki, 1996), 11.
35 E. P. Kel'berin, *Desiatiletie Kievskogo evreiskogo khoral'nogo molitvennogo doma: 1898–1907* (Kiev: I. M. Roset Publishing House, 1909), 9.
36 Kalnitsky, "Pravovoi status evreev Kieva," 77–78.

merit an official was appointed *voevoda* [provincial governor], giving him the right to live off the population, so in Kiev, the most "distinguished" police officers, or those who had patronage, were appointed to these areas and especially to the Lybedskoi district...The Jews were aware that it was necessary to give bribes to the police, because this was the only way to receive the right of residence in Kiev; we should not condemn Jews for striving to obtain the right of residence in Kiev, everybody strives to reach his goal by any means at his disposal.

If the law was implemented without too much abuse then the Jewish population of Kiev was satisfied. Jews were offended only by excessively large extortions; these provoked their complaints...Thus one complaint alleged that a *pristav* demanded of Podol Jewish store owners, who had the legal right of residence, a monthly contribution of ten rubles per person. This quit-rent appeared to be too high, and the Jewish store owners sent a petition in which they asked that this *pristav* be replaced by another who would take less money. They did not ask for a *pristav* who did not demand bribes, because they were absolutely sure that such a person did not exist and could not exist; the petitioners claimed only that they would be completely satisfied if the *pristav* would take less money from them, honestly...

That the only salvation was in bribes, we can see from the fact that when a new chief of police was appointed, Jews asked only one question: does he take bribes or not? Upon the answer to this question depended whether they would remain Kiev inhabitants.[37]

The Kiev police were not the only ones receiving "satisfaction" in the form of bribes. Other categories of Kiev officials also participated. For example, from 1865 on Jewish artisans were granted the right to

---

37 Iaron, *Kiev v vos'midesiatykh godakh*, 35–36.

reside in Kiev, provided that they passed a special exam at the Kiev Office for the Control of Handicrafts. According to Iaron:

> The Office for the Control of Handicrafts had a major role in giving Jews the right to reside in Kiev; hundreds of Jews applied there to take their examination for an artisan certificate. The examinations were usually held in the morning from 10 am to noon. A Jew arrived in a dirty apron covered by different colors of paint, a bucket of water and a paintbrush. The members of Handicraft Control asked him, "What is your craft?" "Painter." He paid three rubles and…he instantly became a "painter." A girl came with piece of fabric. "What is your profession?"—"Milliner" "Cut-out the fabric!" The girl paid the money and the "milliner" was certified….
>
> At twelve o'clock the examinations were over, and the examiners went to a restaurant where they stayed until night spending the fees they had collected. And this is repeated day after day: "craftsmen" acquire "the right of residence" and in a short time seek to make a fortune by becoming moneylenders, brokers, and so on, swamping the stock exchange…[38]

We can assume that most of these people were not really artisans, since Jews would do almost anything to live in Kiev and not in the small, overcrowded shtetls. The inundation of Jewish "artisans" to the city was so great that even Jews who had settled earlier in Kiev began to call for a limit on the number of new artisans.

There were other ways to acquire the right of residence in Kiev. One was to suffer from an illness that required treatment in Kiev hospitals or clinics. In this case, Jews were supposed to submit a certificate from a doctor verifying that they needed treatment. Jews paid large sums for such certificates, which allowed them to acquire "first temporary and then subsequently, because of the forgetfulness of the police, permanent rights of residence." Some of the illnesses were clearly

---

38 Ibid., 37.

bogus: one account describes an individual who suffered from a "chronic head cold," which required permanent observation by Kiev doctors.[39]

Another way to obtain the right of residence in Kiev was for the education of one's children. Even at the time it was unclear how this law was supposed to operate. Should children be accepted at the schools or gymnasiums first, and their parents acquire residence rights second? Or did parents first need to have the right of residence in Kiev before they could send their children to local schools? Iaron claims that arguments over this issue began in Kiev before the establishment of the *numerus clausus* for Jews in education. The educational administration ultimately decided that only Jewish children whose parents already had the right of residence in Kiev could be accepted in Kiev schools. Jews responded by acquiring the right of residence as stewards, sent their children to the Kiev schools, and then continued to live in the city because their children were being educated there. (It was more difficult to remain in Kiev as a steward, as this required frequent bribes to the police.)[40] The case of Ms. F. (Iaron does not give her full name) provides evidence that the local administration, educational authorities, and police were basically selling Jews the right of residence in Kiev. She lived in Kiev for an extended period to "supervise the education of her daughter" in a music school. An investigation showed that her daughter was only three years old. The introduction in 1887 of the *numerus clausus* for Jews in schools merely increased bribery by the local authorities and school administrators. According to Iaron, money and influence—rather than ability—played the key role in the admission of Jewish students. For example, for the admission of a child to Kiev St. Vladimir University, Jewish parents paid up to 10,000 rubles. Obviously not many parents could afford this, which resulted in the conversion to Christianity of young Jews who desired to study in Kiev gymnasiums and the local university. In this way, they obtained a place in Kiev schools, but simultaneously deprived themselves of the right to live with their parents, since, in 1889, the Ministry of National

---

39 Ibid.
40 Ibid., 38.

Enlightenment had issued a circular prohibiting converted Jewish children from living with their Jewish parents or guardians.[41]

Iaron held that the police were no guiltier of this situation than the Jews themselves:

> A Jew is not guilty if he has enough money to *buy* the right [of residence], which other nationalities have for free, and a police officer is also not guilty, when, because of poverty, he is forced to *sell* the right on the basis of one or another interpretation of the law. As one columnist wrote about the Jewish question, "If you have any sympathy for our police, then of course you should want the proposed abolition of the Pale of Settlement to fail, but if you want to play a dirty trick on them, you should call for the rapid enactment of this reform."[42]

The large Jewish population in Kiev, as well as its institutions, incensed the anti-Semites. A number of these institutions were established between the 1860s and the turn of the century, including a Jewish hospital, a Jewish market, a Jewish post office, and several synagogues and Jewish schools. Even the Kiev stock exchange only worked five days a week, because so many of its brokers were Jews. In the words of Alfred J. Rieber,

> Jews continued to maintain their overwhelming preponderance among guild merchants in the [Kiev] province. As early as 1871 the [Kiev Exchange] committee ended all restrictions on the right of first-guild merchants to act as brokers. Even more startling for the time was the committee's decision to honor the Jewish Sabbath by transferring one of its bi-weekly sessions from Saturday to Friday.[43]

---

41 Ibid., 38–39.
42 Ibid., 40.
43 Alfred J. Rieber, *Merchants and Entrepreneurs in Imperial Russia* (Chapel Hill: University of North Carolina Press, 1982), 106–107.

At the beginning of the 1870s, Andrei Nikolaevich Murav'ev (1806–1874), a conservative nobleman, wrote in his *Note on the Preservation of the Uniqueness of Kiev* that the Jews

> have swamped the whole city and taken possession not only of the Plosskii district, which was assigned to them, but also of all the best places. They have taken in their hands all industry, and spread their usual net everywhere in the form of taverns, where they corrupt the population. The houses of Jewish magnates, who, in spite of their wealth, have not yet abandoned their *peyses* (sideburns) and Yid customs, now appear on Palace Square across from the Tsar's Park, which has become their favorite place for Sabbath walks, as well as on the commercial Kreshchatik Street. Thus Kiev is gradually being transformed from the Holy center of our Christian Faith into the capital of the Yids; they will soon take it completely under their control along with the whole southwestern region...[44]

Murav'ev also wrote that Kiev was losing its original Orthodox Christian character because the Jews "suck out the last juices from the Christians who are delivered to them as prey" by the excessively humane authorities, who were unable to maintain proper order in the city. In his view, Jewry had become an "ulcer" in the city, an ulcer that was growing from hour to hour.[45]

By the 1890s, Judeophobes were even more certain of the inevitable transformation of Kiev into a "Jewish city." On October 30, 1890, the semi-official St. Petersburg newspaper *Novoe vremia* (New Times) published a report "From the southwestern region" by A. N. Molchanov:

> The highest authorities call on our local administration to "Save Kiev from the Yids." Given the past history of our town, this is a vital necessity.

---

44 Andrei Nikolaevich Murav'ev, "Zapiska o sokhranenii samobytnosti Kieva (Nachalo 1870-kh gg.)," *Yehupets* 5 (1999): 265.
45 Ibid., 264.

Kiev, according to the law, is located outside the Pale, which means that Jews are allowed to settle here only as an "exception to the general rule." Yet, it is enough to walk during business hours on the central street, the Kreshchatik, for your eyes to tell you, "this is a Jewish city." Look at the stores, there are 190 Jewish merchants of the first guild and only twenty Russian; come to the banks and you can see there only Jewish faces; seek out the artisans—there the ringleaders are Jews, and for them a special guild of "vinegar producers" was created. In a short time tens of thousands of Jews have become inhabitants of Kiev; they monopolize trade and industry, and each one of them lives here as an "exception to the general rule."

Molchanov was not exaggerating. Jewish merchants did constitute the vast majority of those in Kiev. Even the story about the creation for Jews of the special guild of "vinegar producers" was true: some Jews did receive the right to live in Kiev as producers of vinegar. Thus,

> [t]he Board of Kiev Province ordered on December 14, 1884 that the Kiev Office for the Control of Handicrafts enroll the burgher Yankel Mokran from Brest in the guild of the producers of vinegar, and, according to article 66 of the Artisan bylaws, ensure that Mokran actually works in this profession.[46]

The mayor (*gorodskoi golova*) of Kiev, Gustav Eisman (presumably a Russified German), was angered by this and other decisions of the Board of Kiev Province and the Office for the Control of Handicrafts, which granted Jews artisan status and thus the right of residence in Kiev. In January 1885, Eisman, in a letter to Governor-General Aleksandr Romanovich Drentel'n, expressed his concern over the large number of Jews who had settled in Kiev with the connivance of these institutions. He also reminded the governor-general that according to

---

46 TsDIAK U, f. 442, op. 534, d. 282, ll. 176–184.

the law, only Jewish artisans who belonged to artisan guilds enjoyed the right of residence beyond the Pale. However,

> [i]n recent times Kiev has become the place of residence for all categories of Jews. In their cherished aspiration to take over this ancient Russian city, which is fighting a difficult historical struggle for its distinctive existence, for its inviolable holiness for all Russian people, Jews have found the means to circumvent the law. Many come to Kiev with passports which do not allow them to live here, and without certificates of qualification as artisans, and obtain here these certificates for the first time. In addition, they have created for themselves crafts that do not fit any existing artisan guilds, and do not even fit the definition of the artisan profession, either according to the law or to common sense.
>
> For example, in 1880, the burgher Peisach Greenstein received from the Office for the Control of Handicrafts a certificate qualifying him as a master of "artificial mineral waters." The Board of Kiev Province, considering this certificate submitted by Greenstein, concluded that the production of artificial mineral waters requires pharmaceutical knowledge, which he did not possess. Therefore, this certificate was issued incorrectly, and by order number 6864 on December 9, 1880, the board directed that it be invalidated, and Greenstein excluded from the rank of artisans.
>
> The Board of Kiev Province allows Jews who are not artisans to enroll in a special, *non-artisan guild*, created particularly for them, and then receive the right to live in Kiev, exploit its Christian population unimpeded, and establish here various businesses without special certificates and without paying taxes, something which harms state and city interests...[47]

Eisman concluded his letter with the assertion that Jewish pavers, construction workers, masons, carpenters, plasterers, cabmen, gardeners,

---

47 Ibid.

factory workers, day laborers, servants, and stewards should not have the right to live in Kiev, since these professions do not fall under the definition of "artisan" according to the law or common sense.[48]

Governor-General Drentel'n's response to this particular letter is unknown. However, in the 1880s and 1900s, in accordance with the more hostile central government policy towards Jews after 1881, the local authorities became less tolerant of the Jews. The local administration continued to grant Jews the right of residence in Kiev in exchange for bribes, but now the expulsions of illegal Jews from the city were larger and occurred more frequently, the categories of Jews allowed to live in the city were narrowed, and the authorities encouraged anti-Jewish violence as well as the deprivation of those limited civil rights the Jews enjoyed.

YEHUPETS

In stark contrast to the views of the anti-Semites, Jews considered Kiev to be a hostile city. Life in Kiev was more difficult for Jews than in many other places in the Russian Empire. All Jews who came to Kiev for more than twenty-four hours needed a document giving them permission to stay in the city. They had to apply for this permission to the governor-general, and if he found a sufficient reason for the visit, he could allow a Jew to stay in Kiev for a few days. The legal status of Jewish men in Kiev did not guarantee the same rights for their families. A Jewish woman, even if her husband had the right to live in Kiev and own real estate there, did not have these rights herself. Genrikh Sliozberg, a lawyer and Jewish activist, describes in his memoirs a case in which a Kiev senior attorney refused in 1888 to approve the deed for a house purchased by the wife of the Jewish lawyer Avraam Moiseevich Gol'denberg. Her husband had the right to own real estate in any part of Kiev. According to the attorney, wives of those Jews who had the right to reside everywhere in the Russian Empire and acquire property there were not themselves entitled to acquire property without restriction. This case was decided against Mrs. Gol'denberg by the State

---

48 Ibid.

Senate, a decision that became the precedent for the legal principle that "a derivative right to reside everywhere in the Russian Empire" did not exist for wives of Jewish men who themselves had this right. Such wives could not purchase real estate, nor could they live outside the Pale of Settlement without their husbands. All subsequent cases were decided according to this precedent.[49] A Jewish woman whose husband was drafted into the army or died, or who divorced her husband, lost her right to live in Kiev. Often, if a Jewish man was unable to pay the taxes necessary to remain enrolled in the first guild of merchants or chose another non-artisan profession, he and his entire family would be expelled from Kiev.

These regulations often led to the separation of families and their financial ruin. For example, on November 5, 1900, Abram Iudelevich Lipman, a student at the Medical School of Kiev St. Vladimir University, wrote a petition to the governor-general in which he claimed that his father had permanently lived in Kiev from 1854. After his father died, his three sisters lost the right of residence in Kiev.

> If they leave Kiev, where they have lived all their lives, for the Pale of Settlement, where they do not have relatives or acquaintances, they will lose the small earnings on which the whole family survives since the death of our father...[50]

The governor-general granted Lipman's request that his sisters be allowed to live in Kiev until his graduation. However, not all such requests were approved. On August 10, 1900, Simkha Shoinskii, a retired soldier who owned a small grocery store in Kiev, requested that the governor-general allow his son Chaim to live with him, since because of his age and illness, Shoinskii was unable to continue to work in his store and could not support himself. He wrote that his son, with his wife and two children, lived in the village Glebovka, Kiev province, where he owned a small store. The governor-general rejected this

---

49 G. B. Sliozberg, *Dela minuvshikh dnei: Zapiski russkogo evreia* (Paris: Imprimerie Pascal, 1933), 1: 236–237.
50 TsDIAK U, f. 442, op. 630, d. 47, l. 73.

request, because he did not "see any reason for the settlement in Kiev of an additional Jewish family. If Chaim Shoinskii needed to look after his father, his father should move to the Pale."[51]

Some Jewish public figures hoped that these brutal decisions were aberrations on the part of the local administration, and that the central government's true policy was more lenient. This was particularly the case in the relatively liberal period after the accession of Alexander II. On August 18, 1868, Baron Evzel' Ginsburg, a well-known Jewish banker and public figure, in a petition to Governor-General Aleksandr Pavlovich Bezak, attacked the vindictiveness of Kiev's local authorities toward Jews, and the expulsion from the city of legal Jewish residents. These acts, he claimed, were at odds with the policy of the central government:

> We have heard here [in St. Petersburg] of the harsh measures taken by the local administration against Jews in Kiev. They have expelled from the city not only illegal residents, but also artisans who are allowed to live in Kiev according to the law; they were evicted to remote and depopulated suburbs, where they are unable to find the means for life by their productive labor. We are convinced that the local administration could not wish to act in this way against the clearly stated policies of the government. However, we have often learned from sad experience, that if in some district a decree is introduced against Jews in general, without mentioning the specific persons involved, the lower executive authorities often go beyond the law and Jews have to bear unbelievable sufferings, as is now the case in Kiev...
>
> I request you to generously allow Jews to live freely in Kiev without restrictions; if not all of them, at least those who have the legal right to do so. They should be allowed to enjoy there that little space and sustenance to which they are now entitled in the capitals and everywhere in the inner provinces [i.e., beyond the Pale of Settlement].

---

51   Ibid., l. 52.

In preventing the violation of the law in this way, Your Excellency will, at the same time, guarantee the success of government measures for the transformation of the Jews and their rapprochement with the native [*korennoe*] population.[52]

In this way, Baron Ginsburg attempted to persuade Governor-General Bezak to follow the government's policy and its laws regarding Jews. Clearly, many abuses were already occurring in this ostensibly liberal period. It seems the governor-general ignored this petition, as no reply to it has been found in the archives.[53]

Jews were often able to mitigate the harshness of the local government's actions with bribery. If a Jew had money but did not have the right of residence in Kiev, the local police could help him obtain this right by an appropriate payment, registering him as a steward (*prikazchik*) of a Jewish merchant (who was allowed by law to have four to six stewards at different times). However, if the Jew was poor and could not pay the bribe, then of course the police and local authorities were unable to help him.

The situation of the Jews in Kiev worsened significantly during the reign of Alexander III (1881–1894) and Nicholas II (1894–1917). In January 1895, the local authorities ordered that within two weeks all Kiev Jews had to renew their certificates of residence in the city, threatening with expulsion those who did not renew on time. This gave local officials ample opportunity to abuse their power by delaying the renewal of Jews' residential certificates.[54]

The local administration's hostility toward Jews, the deprivation of their civil rights, the night round-ups of Jews, the anti-Semitism of a significant part of the city population, and the anti-Jewish pogroms are well reflected in the contemporary Yiddish literature. It was these conditions that led Sholom Aleichem (pseudonym of Sholom Yakov Rabinovitz, 1859–1916) to create the image of Kiev as a hostile city, which he called

---

52 TsDIAK U, f. 442, op. 45, d. 564, ll. 218–220.
53 At least his reply is not present in the archive file with the Ginsburg petition. Usually, if an official replied to a petition, his answer is kept in the same file.
54 Kalnitsky, "Pravovoi status evreev Kieva," 79–80.

Yehupets (Egypt), in his works. The writer knew Kiev quite well: he first visited the city illegally in 1879, and returned to the city in 1887, living there with interruptions for almost twenty years. He finally left the city for good after the October 1905 pogrom. He writes how, apart from the few categories of Jews who had the right of residence in Kiev,

> [a]ll other Jews sneak around there as if they are contraband, and live there in great fear "by the grace" of yardmen, police officers and the district superintendent of police. This continues only until the first night round-up, when the soldiers and policemen invade the Jewish guesthouses in the middle of the night. In their language, they call it "making a revision." If they find contraband, in other words Jews "without the right of residence," they herd them like cattle to the police station, and send them out of the city with great pomp, deporting them under guard, together with thieves, to the place of their registration.[55]

In his autobiographical novel *Funem Yarid* (From the Fair), Sholom Aleichem describes his own experience of such a round-up:

> The author of this story, on his first visit to the great holy city of Kiev, had the honor and pleasure, together with a few other Jews, to tremble in the attic of the guesthouse of Alter Kanever. It happened on a dark winter night. Because the "revision" [round-up of Jews] happened suddenly, men barely had time to pull on their underwear and women their underskirts. The "revision" fortunately did not last long; otherwise we would have been completely frozen in the attic. When the owner of the guesthouse, Alter Kanever, an honorable man with a white beard, told the people that the police had gone, everyone rejoiced. He told them, "Jews, feel as at home, come out from the straw! The devils are gone, come down from the attic…"

---

55 Sholom Aleichem, *Sobranie sochinenii* (Moscow: Khudozhestvennaia literatura, 1974), 6: 284.

The happiness, however, was spoiled by the fact that the owner of the guesthouse imposed upon his tenants something like a contribution—one and a half rubles per person to cover his expenses [i.e., bribe to the police] for the "revision."[56]

This experience was clearly traumatic, and Sholom Aleichem returned to this topic in his novel *Menakhem-Mendl*. The main character of the novel, Menakhem-Mendl, like Sholom Aleichem, "wheeled and dealed on the Kiev stock exchange, at which he was a failure, losing a great deal of money before turning exclusively to writing."[57] In the second volume, Menakhem-Mendl visits Kiev as a journalist during the Beilis trial in 1911. Little had changed in the way Jews were treated. Menakhem-Mendl did not have the right to live in Kiev, but this did not stop him from going there.

> And in truth, quite a few Jews travel every day to Yehupetz without a permit—and what happens to them? Are they killed? And so I went, I arrived in Yehupetz toward evening. It was already pitch dark outside, damp and cold, but I was actually happy it was dark. Why do I need anyone to see me? Not because I am afraid, what do I have to be afraid of? Did I steal something? Or murder someone? It's just I hate to have anything to do with the police.[58]

Menakhem-Mendl took a cab and went to Podol to his friend, who was also staying in Kiev illegally. They had gone to sleep, when

> suddenly from the apartment next door we heard a noise, a familiar noise to me which sounded like trouble. I am, thank God, very experienced in these matters and have a keen sense

---

56 Ibid., 284–285.
57 Sholem Aleichem, *The Further Adventures of Menachem-Mendl (New York–Warsaw–Vienna–Yehupetz)*, trans. Aliza Shevrin (New York: Syracuse University Press, 2001), viii.
58 Ibid., 163.

of hearing. I said to him, "I think it's a house search." He said, "I think so too." I said, "What shall we do? We need to hide." He said, "I think so too." He was terrified and we spoke very quietly so as not to be heard. "Where can we hide?" I said. "That's not a problem. I have an attic and a cellar," he said. "Which do you prefer?" I said, "It's all the same to me, so long as we don't have to march to Kasrilevka in a prison-gang the night before the holiday, God forbid."...

To make a long story short, we spent the whole night in fear and terror, may such a night never return! We finally lived to see daylight and as soon as it was light enough, I grabbed my belongings and prepared to leave, but my friend wouldn't let me, saying in Hebrew:

"What's your hurry? Don't worry, it's nothing. I've been living here almost half a year and on this street there have been no more than three or four of these searches. Believe me, we make more of a fuss over it than it is worth. It's just bad when a search happens at night, one is frightened, you think who knows what, but in the morning, when you come through it in one piece, you feel a little ashamed of yourself!" That's the way he spoke to me, wishing to convince me to stay. But I refused. I was adamant and stated that if he were to give me a roomful of gold, I would not spend another night there!

So we parted and I went as fast as I could to Slobodka, which is part of Tchernigover province,[59] where Jews can live freely wherever they wish, except in the villages.[60]

Sholom Aleichem's account is remarkably true to life. Numerous articles in such newspapers as *Kievlianin* (Kievan), *Kievskie vesti* (Kiev

---

59 Nikol'skaia Slobodka was a suburb of Kiev, but part of Chernigov province, which was located inside the Pale where Jews were allowed to live. Nikol'skaia Slobodka was separated from the city of Kiev by the Dnieper River; Kiev is situated on the right bank of the river, Nikol'skaia Slobodka on the left. Many Jews who had business affairs in Kiev, but who did not have the right of residence in the city, settled in Nikol'skaia Slobodka, constituting a large percentage of the inhabitants.
60 Sholem Aleichem, *The Further Adventures of Menachem-Mendl*, 165–166.

Herald), *Sovremennoe slovo* (Modern Word), *Odesskie novosti* (Odessa News), *Smolenskii vestnik* (Smolensk Herald), and others describe the periodic night raids conducted by the Kiev police in the last peaceful years before World War I.

Some elderly Jews still remember their grandparents' stories about how they hid under the bed from the Kiev police during these round-ups. Kiev policemen were known to break into the bedrooms of Jewish women at night to check their "documents."[61] Legal Jewish inhabitants of Kiev also suffered. Police searched their apartments at night to find illegal visitors. G. Vol'tke writes:

> Nowhere were the police as cruel as in Kiev. Kiev was famous for night round-ups of Jews, where the police searched apartments and houses on many streets to find and immediately expel Jews who did not have the right to stay in Kiev.[62]

On January 28, 1905, the governor of Kiev, in a letter to the governor-general, explained the need for the night round-ups:

> [T]he night roundups of Jews are necessary to enforce the law... Checking the right of residence of Jews in daytime does not achieve its goal, because illegal Jews at that time cannot be located in a particular apartment and it is impossible to find them.[63]

The governor felt that the authorities had shown their benevolence by allowing Jews to come to Kiev for visits of less than twenty-four hours without permission of the authorities. In the governor's view

> to extend this term to two weeks, as requested by the hotel owners, or to seven days, as proposed by the police, is....

---

61 S. M. Dubnov, *History of the Jews* (South Brunswick, NJ: Thomas Yoseloff, 1973), 5: 553, 768; B. A. Gurevich, *O voprosakh kulturnoi zhizni evreev* (Kiev: Kievskoe obshchestvo druzei mira, 1911), 1-12.
62 *Evreiskaia entsiklopediia*, s.v. "Kiev," 9: 526.
63 TsDIAK U, f. 442, op. 634, d. 528, ll. 14-15.

unnecessary and against the law. Any exemption from the rule in this case could result in the *de facto* abolition of the law restricting Jewish residence.[64]

Gershon Badanes, one of the leaders of the Kiev Jewish community, argued that these night round-ups of Jews were, in effect, paid for by the Jewish community:

> The Kiev governor applied to the governor-general for a temporary increase in the local police, justifying his request on the grounds of the inundation of Kiev by illegal Jews, which imposed and increased the workload on the police.[65]

This request was approved, and the Kiev Jewish community was obliged to pay annually 14,550 rubles in additional taxes to finance the extra police, in addition to the fifteen thousand rubles they were already paying annually to the city budget. These taxes were very hard on the poorer sections of the Kiev Jewish community. In 1904, according to statistics of the Jewish Colonization Society (EKO), ten thousand Jews in Kiev (20 percent of the Jewish population) lived below the poverty line.[66]

Even some Christian inhabitants complained about the night round-ups and expulsions of Jews from Kiev. They argued that the local authorities neglected their economic interests, as well as the economic interests of the city and region, when they "hunted" illegal Jews and expelled them from the city. As a result, Christian house owners in Kiev sent several petitions in 1881 and 1882 to the minister of the interior and the governor-general, requesting an end to the expulsion of Jews from Kiev.[67] This was a period when tsarist policy towards the Jews had become significantly more repressive. In their petition of

---

64 Ibid.
65 Gershon Badanes, *S odnogo vola tri shkury* (Kiev: I. M. Roset Publishing House, 1907), 11.
66 Ibid., 21.
67 TsDIAK U, f. 442, op. 534, d. 245, ll. 1–20.

July 24, 1881, twenty-one Kiev Christian house owners wrote to the minister of the interior the following:

> Since the Jewish pogrom in Kiev on April 26 and 27 [1881], from which [Christian] house owners also suffered, the local police have begun to expel Jews from Kiev. Many families have already left the city, apartments and commercial facilities remain empty, nobody wants to rent them; because of the decrease in competition, goods and food will certainly become more expensive. A rise in all prices was noticeable after the pogrom, when Jews for a period were afraid to again begin trading. This order of the police for the expulsion of Jews from Kiev is inhumane and outdated and will have negative consequences for homeowners. Our houses and commercial facilities stand empty, all profits from them have ceased, which makes more difficult the situation of the many among us who have taken loans, and makes it impossible to pay state and city taxes. In our opinion, as a consequence, state and city interests will suffer. Therefore, we request your Excellency to order a halt to the expulsion of Jews from Kiev. Even if there are some merchants who sympathize with this expulsion, their motive is solely that of getting rid of competitors.[68]

We do not know whether Nikolai Pavlovich Ignat'ev, the minister of the interior, responded to this petition. However, we do know Governor-General Aleksandr Romanovich Drentel'n's response to a similar petition from Evdokiia Pilipeeva, the widow of a professor of the Kiev Theological Seminary. On December 23, 1881, she claimed that the payments for the lease of her house to the Jew Yankel Aleksandrov were the only source of income for herself and her sick son, and requested that Aleksandrov be allowed to remain until the end of his lease the following spring. Governor-General Drentel'n commented on this petition, "What scoundrels these Jews are! As if the non-payment

---

68 Ibid., l. 5.

of rent for three months could cause everything to collapse," implying that the petition had been initiated by the Jewish leaseholder. However, the number of petitions made by Christian homeowners, and the number of names and signatures on them, are both so great that they leave little doubt that they were genuine.

The governors-general and the local administration did not accede to these requests, and continued to cleanse Kiev of legal and illegal Jewish residents. In 1882, in accordance with an order of Governor-General Drentel'n, all Jews were expelled from Podol.[69] This expulsion was initiated by the mayor, who claimed in his letter of January 9, 1882 to the governor-general that, according to the law, Jews were allowed to settle only in the Plosskii and Lybedskoi districts of Kiev. Governor-General Vasil'chikov had allowed Jews to live in Podol in 1862 as a temporary arrangement following a flood in the Plosskii district. Since that year, they had continued to live in Podol illegally.[70] In fact, many Jews with the legal right of residence in Kiev had relocated to Podol because of the annual spring floods in the Plosskii district. They were now moved back to the Plosskii district, while Jews without the right of residence were expelled and compelled to return to the towns where they were officially registered. After this expulsion, many houses in Podol remained empty. The homeowners continued to complain that their profits had diminished, and such complaints seem to have eventually persuaded the local administration to again allow Jews to settle in the Podol district.

Other pretexts were also used to expel Jews. The local authorities constantly revised downward the list of professions allowed to live outside the Pale, and excluded from residence in the city ever more categories of Jews such as butchers, masons, carpenters, and other workers since, according to Russian law, they could not be classified either as merchants or as artisans.

On March 17, 1898, the Kiev Provincial Board issued an order restricting the number of Jewish *mohels* (circumcisers) and cantors to

---

69 Ibid., l. 20.
70 Ibid., ll. 13–15.

one for each prayer house, and limiting the total number of gravediggers and persons who assisted at funerals and at Jewish cemeteries to "not more than thirty."[71] All "surplus" Jews in these professions were to be expelled. Two large expulsions of Jews from Kiev thereafter took place, one in 1886 involving more than 2,000 Jewish families, and another in the spring of 1910 when 1,200 Jewish families were banished.[72] In addition to these large expulsions, the local administration and police continuously expelled from the city illegal Jews who were detained during the round-ups. *Kievlianin* wrote on January 6, 1907:

> Last October [1906] the police checked the hotels in some city districts where Jews live and discovered that Jews without the right of residence in Kiev were living there.
>
> On October 13 they found scores of Jews who do not have the right of residence in the hotel *Metropol'* belonging to the Jewess Berenfus, and in the hotel *Marsel'* belonging to the Jew Faier.
>
> The owners of the hotels Faier and Berenfus were fined three thousand rubles each by the former Kiev Governor, Lieutenant General A. P. Veretnikov.
>
> The Lybedskoi district Superintendent of Police Mr. Rapota was dismissed....
>
> On December 16 [1906] the Assistant of the Chief of Kiev Police Mashir again ordered a search in the hotel *Metropol'*, now under the ownership of the townspeople [*meshchane*] Zeilik Raiskii and Abram Komissarov, and found that Jews who did not have the right of residence in Kiev, continued to live in the hotel. It was revealed that in order to circumvent the law, those Jews who did not have the right of residence in Kiev checked out and then checked back in again every day. The police informed Governor P. G. Kurlov of this violation of the order of June 15, 1904 issued by the Head of the Region

---

71 TsDIAK U, f. 442, op. 532, d. 304, ll. 207–215.
72 Dubnov, *History of the Jews*, 5: 553, 768.

[i.e., the governor-general]. On December 15 [1906] Governor Kurlov ordered that the owners of the hotel *Metropol'* Zeilik Raiskii and Abram Komissarov should together be responsible for paying a fine of three thousand rubles. Should this cause them to become bankrupt, they should be imprisoned for three months. The execution of this order was entrusted to the Chief of the Kiev Police.

On March 24, 1910 the newspaper *Sovremennoe slovo* reported:

According to a dispatch from Kiev of March 23, in the morning the police conducted a round-up of stewards and salesmen in the workshops and haberdashery and other shops belonging to Jews, with the purpose of detaining those who did not have the right of residence. Seven stores on the Central Duma Square were searched, and 37 men and 33 women were detained. The detained were escorted to the police station where their documents were checked. The illegal Jews were immediately expelled from the city.

Three days later the newspaper *Smolenskii vestnik* wrote:

These persecutions of Jews, according to a report from Kiev, have inspired a new form of fraud. Many impostors wearing a badge reading "Agent of Kiev Criminal Investigation Department (Police)" have recently detained Jews in hotels and on the street, in preparation for taking them to the police station, ostensibly for the purpose of checking their right of residence. The majority of the intimidated Jews paid bribes on the way to the police station. In cases where bribes were not offered, the impostors eventually fled.

All these round-ups of Jews in Kiev were only a prelude to the large expulsion of Jews from Kiev already mentioned, which was scheduled for April 15, 1910. The newspaper *Odesskie novosti* wrote on March 30, 1910,

The local merchants are very anxious regarding the persecution of the Jews. Nikolai Ivanovich Chokolov,[73] the Head [*starosta*] of the Kiev Merchant Guild, sent telegrams to F. F. Trepov, the Head of the Region [the governor-general], who is now in St. Petersburg, to Petr A. Stolypin, the Prime Minister and to V. N. Kokovtsev, the Minister of Finance, in which he, in the name of the Kiev merchant estate, requested the suspension of the expulsion of Jews from Kiev scheduled for April 15th.

However, the petitions of the Kiev merchants and the Jews only resulted in delaying the expulsion for two weeks. This time the Kiev authorities and police decided to carry out the expulsion "in a humane way," as Vitalii Shul'gin had advocated almost a half century earlier. According to the order:

Between May 1st and 5th Jews who do not have children will be evicted from Kiev; between the 5th and 10th of May— families that have one or two children, May 10–15th—families with three children, and so on. The final date for the expulsion of [illegal] Jews from Kiev is June 1st [1910].[74]

Unlike the prior expulsion, which had been criticized by Shul'gin, this one took place in the spring and summer, giving families with children a few more days before they were compelled to leave the city. This did not prevent subsequent complaints from both Jews and Christians concerning the negative consequences of these measures for the economic development of the city and region. Chokolov even went to St. Petersburg to personally submit to the Minister of Trade and

---

73 Nikolai Ivanovich Chokolov (1845–after 1917) was an honorary hereditary citizen of Kiev, member of the City Duma (1883–1910), one of the founders of the Society for the Spread of Commercial Education and the Society of Literacy, owner of a publishing house, and a philanthropist. He donated 9,000 rubles for the development of a new district of Kiev, which was named Chokolovka after him, as was Chokolovskii Boulevard.

74 *Kievskie vesti*, April 30, 1910.

Industry a petition dated November 28, 1910 by members of the merchant estate. According to the petition:

> Noticing in recent times the instability of trade in Kiev, compared with the general improvement and increase of trade in other places, we, the merchants of Kiev, have investigated the reasons for these phenomena.
>
> One of the most important reasons is the restrictive measures imposed in recent times by the administration on Jews, who wish to trade in Kiev permanently or come there on commercial business for a short time.
>
> Kiev is the center of commercial and industrial life in the southwestern region. As is well known, a significant part of the trade and industry in the southwestern provinces is in the hands of Jews, who have the right of residence and trade in these provinces. On account of this, the commercial interests of Kiev are strongly connected with the commercial interests of the Jewish population of the region, and any difficulties which Jews have in trading in Kiev have an adverse effect on the situation in commerce and industry in the whole region. The artificial obstacles created for Jews, who need to visit Kiev for a short time for their commercial affairs, exercise a particularly unfavorable influence on the commercial life of our city...
>
> [I]n recent times the visits of Jews from other towns to Kiev have been made difficult by the punctilious implementation of the many formalities required for them to receive permission to come to Kiev for short periods. Thus a Jew is required to submit a special petition to the Governor requesting permission to allow him to stay in Kiev. The insistence for such petitions goes beyond what is required by law...
>
> Even more hardship and inconvenience is caused by the system of night round-ups and evictions with transit passes.[75]

In addition, Jewish merchants, who do not possess the

---

75 A transit pass indicated the person's ultimate destination. Usually, illegal Jews from Kiev were sent to the places of their registration.

above-mentioned permission for residence from the Governor, are frequently deported together with groups of convicts. These measures can hardly be considered necessary.

Industrialists and merchants are seriously alarmed by the fact that the administration does not now recognize the right to trade of whole categories of people who have long enjoyed this right. Thus the administration does not allow the widows and children of Jewish merchants, who were enrolled in the first-guild merchant estate for more than fifteen years, to trade, and insists on the eviction from Kiev of Jews who were enrolled in the first guild for ten years or more, and then transferred to the second guild.

Similarly harmful is the order prohibiting Jewish merchants, who have been enrolled in the first guild for less than five years and live in Plosskii and Lybedskoi districts and trade in other districts, to continue their commerce outside these districts. This order, which has driven Jewish merchants from familiar places, has not only ruined them, but has also seriously affected the interests of people who have business connections with them...

This petition is being simultaneously submitted to the Minister of the Interior and the Minister of Finance.[76]

The only response to this petition came from the Ministry of the Interior, which stated bluntly "take no action." Consequently, the Kiev merchants' hopes that the authorities would stop the expulsions and night round-ups and create normal conditions for the development of commerce in the city were dashed. It is clear that the Kiev administration acted according to the government's orders. The Kiev merchants argued in their petition that the economic interests of the city and region were suffering from the persecution of Jews. However, the authorities willingly sacrificed the financial interests of the region and state to their anti-Jewish obsession.

---

76 TsDIAK U, f. 442, op. 634, d. 528, ll. 64–65.

The views expressed in the petition were in sharp contrast to the official opinion both in St. Petersburg and in Kiev. The governor-general, in his undated *Note regarding the question about the right of residence of Jews in Kiev*, filed under 1893, wrote that "the right of residence of Jews in Kiev has been narrowed as much as possible to weaken the annually increasing influx of Jews to Kiev."[77] In order to implement this policy, the Kiev authorities deprived additional categories of Jews the right of residence. Thus, while the law of 1861 allowed Jewish merchants of the first and second guild to live in Kiev, the governor-general in his *Note* claimed that only Jewish merchants who were enrolled in the *Kiev* first guild were allowed to live in Kiev, while Jewish merchants who were enrolled in the first guild in other places had only the right of temporary residence in Kiev.[78] As is clear from the petition of the Kiev Merchant Estate of 1910 discussed above, Jewish merchants of the second guild were also expelled from Kiev.

In 1891, the governor-general proposed in a report to the minister of the interior the prohibition of Jews from living in dachas in the countryside near Kiev, as the residence of Jews in villages was forbidden by the law of May 3, 1882. The governor-general wrote in his report,

> The number of Jews living in dachas has increased every year and in 1891 there were 204 such families, coming from different, even distant, provinces. They do this because of their desire to avoid the restrictions [on residence] and to obtain the possibility of making use of the advantages which Kiev offers in commercial and industrial affairs.[79]

At the beginning of the twentieth century, the local authorities and official press further justified the need for night round-ups of illegal

---

77 TsDIAK U, f. 442, op. 623, d. 408, ll. 26–33.
78 Ibid.
79 TsDIAK U, f. 442, op. 543, d. 377, l. 9.

Jews in Kiev because of the allegedly large number of revolutionaries among them. *Kievlianin* wrote on August 17, 1906:

> On the night of August 16 in Podol, in the Podol'skii and Plosskii police districts, the officers searched a number of houses for people who do not have the right of residence in Kiev.
>
> 83 Jews without the right of residence were found in the Podol'skii district and 56 in the Plosskii district. All were detained, and yesterday they were identified. Among the 83 people, 35 were sent for identification to the police station in Demievka, Slobodka and to the Kiev District Police Administration [*uezdnoe pravlenie*]. Eight people detained in the Plosskii District were also sent there, and two Jewish women were released after they were identified. Two were arrested, because they possessed illegal literature.
>
> In the house on 19 Mezhigorskaia Street, in a separate room in the apartment of Yankel Altman, Iosif Mendelev Kordeman, 20 years old, and Gersh-Beier Kremenetskii, 21 years old, were detained; they had in their possession two revolvers and 28 bullets and a large dagger.
>
> In house number 35 on Nizhnii Val Street, Ios' Sheikman was arrested; in his house illegal literature was found.
>
> The discovery of weapons led the police to search the apartments more thoroughly: in the search three illegal iron bomb shells were found, each three *vershoks*[80] in diameter.
>
> Among those detained were 89 people from other towns, who were sent to the city police for eviction from Kiev. Persons who do not have passports will be sent to their place of registration with groups of convicts, and all who have passports will receive transit passes, and are obliged to leave Kiev on their own and return to their places of registration.

---

80 *Vershok* is an old Russian unit of measure equal to 1.75 inches (4.445 centimeters).

The police in Kiev were quite busy checking the Jews' rights of residence, catching revolutionaries, and protecting Kiev from illegal Jews. However, their work was not particularly effective. The police deported thousands of Jews from Kiev, but in their place came new thousands of illegal Jewish inhabitants, including many revolutionaries who desperately struggled against the tsarist regime that condemned Jews to inequality and humiliation. According to an article, "The Explosion of the Bomb," in *Kievlianin* on December 23, 1906:

> Yesterday, December 22, just after 6:00 pm, in Podol on Voloshinskii Street number 29, in the house of Vinarskii, there was an appalling explosion of a bomb. The hotel *Kupecheskaia*, which belongs to the Jewess Kesselman, is located on the second and third floors of this house.
>
> The explosion occurred on the third floor in room number 1. This room was occupied from the night of December 20th by Feiga Khaimovna Kaplan, 19 years old, who came from Odessa and who claims to be a milliner.
>
> A few days before her arrival at the hotel, a young man, Tama Lezerov Abramovich, came and stayed there for one night. When Kaplan arrived Abramovich came to her and they talked for a long time....Nobody saw anything suspicious. Other people of both sexes also visited Kaplan on those days.
>
> Last night Abramovich and another unknown person sat as usual in Kaplan's room. Just after 6:00 pm three muffled shots were heard from the room and then suddenly an explosion of terrible power occurred; the doors and windows in the room were blown out of their frames, and blue fire appeared. In nearby rooms, windows were also blown out, mirrors broken and plaster and goods dislodged. In the hallway of the third floor near room number 1 the maid Varvara Belovolova, 20 years old, lay groaning on the floor. Two peasants rushed out of room number 2; one of them covered a large cut on his

face with his hand. Rooms 1 and 2 were totally destroyed. Nobody was in the rooms and there was no trace of blood...

On the threshold of room 1, about 40 bullets for a Browning revolver were found. The outside of the building was not destroyed, but windows on two floors were blown out and windows were even blown out on nearby houses.

At the moment of the explosion, in the excitement, a young woman ran away from the hotel door. People shouted, "Catch her! Catch her!" A peasant passing on the street seized the woman who screamed, "I did not do this, let me go!" She was detained by the police and sent to the Plosskii police station where she was identified as Feiga Kaplan. She had received three minor wounds from the explosion.

When she was searched, the police found a Browning revolver with bullets. She refused to give the names of the men who were in her hotel room and said that she knew nothing.

The physician bandaged her wounds...

The maid Belovolova became deaf in one ear and was injured by the explosion in her head, right arm and leg. She remembers nothing.

The police officers made a thorough search of the hotel.

People said that after the explosion they saw two men running away along the street.

On December 24, 1906, *Kievlianin* demanded action:

Thus Kiev received a bomb before the holidays, brought from either Odessa or from Minsk. We do not yet know for whom it was intended, but of course it was not intended either to blow up the small Jewish hotel, or to blow up the bomb's owner Feiga Kaplan and her friend Leizer Abramovich.

We must arm ourselves against such fiends with redoubled passion and energy. The hotel must be closed and its owners should be expelled from Kiev. They should have searched the suitcases of the unknown riff-raff to whom they gave lodging and taken the necessary measures for their supervision and not provided rooms for keeping bombs and organizing conspiracies for murder. The owners of hotels and furnished rooms should constantly bear in mind that they now have a big responsibility: they must watch their tenants with redoubled attention so that they will not be blown up together with them. This is no time for standing on ceremony. Strangers are especially dangerous.

Kievlianin's call was answered: the owner of the hotel was punished even more severely than the newspaper demanded. On December 30, 1906, the paper reported:

According to the order of V. A. Sukhomlinov, the Kiev, Podolia and Volhynia Governor-General, the *Kupecheskaia* hotel was closed, and the owner of the hotel the Jewess, Kesselman, was imprisoned for three months.

A military tribunal sentenced Feiga Kaplan to be deprived of all rights and property, and sent her to "eternal" hard labor (*katorga*).[81] She later admitted that she had planned to assassinate the governor-general. However the premature explosion of the bomb destroyed her plan.[82] Kaplan spent eleven years in hard labor in Siberia where she partially lost her sight, and was released only after the February 1917 Revolution. She became a socialist revolutionary during her years of hard labor and, like other socialist revolutionaries, she believed that the Bolsheviks betrayed the revolution by dissolving the Constituent Assembly in January 1918. On August 30, 1918, she made an attempt on the life of Vladimir Lenin, shooting him twice at close range. He was

---

81 *Kievlianin*, December 30, 1906.
82 V. M. Lytvyn, ed., *Politychnyi teror i teroryzm v Ukraini XIX–XX st. Istorychni narysy* (Kiev: Naukova Dumka, 2002), 88.

seriously wounded but survived. After a short interrogation, Kaplan was shot by the Bolsheviks on September 3, 1918.[83]

The Russian authorities drove many Jews to revolution through their policy of persecution and restrictions, night round-ups and expulsions, and by humiliating them and depriving them of their civil rights. Because the persecution of Jews in Kiev was more severe than in other places in the Russian Empire, Jewish youth there participated even more actively in the revolutionary movement than in other places. At the beginning of the twentieth century, 48.2 percent of the people convicted of political crimes in the Kiev Judicial District were Jews. Jews also comprised the majority of members of anarchist organizations in Kiev.[84]

Yet, in spite of the difficulties, Jews continued to flock to Kiev. In his autobiography, Sholom Aleichem writes:

> Where can a homeless young man go, who dreams of achieving something in his life? Of course, to the big city. The big city is the foundation of all life, a magnetic center for everybody who is looking for business, work, profession or position. A newly married man who has spent his wife's dowry; a husband who is disgusted with his wife; a man, who quarreled with his father-in-law or mother-in-law or with his parents; a merchant who broke with his companions—where will all of them go? To the big city. Somebody heard that in the [Kiev] stock exchange they make cheese pies from snow and fill sacks with

---

83 Some historians doubt the role of Kaplan in the attempted assassination of Lenin due to her near-blindness; others think that several people participated in the shooting. But after her arrest, Kaplan took the guilt upon herself and, as in her first arrest, she refused to give the names of her accomplices. She made the following statement during her interrogation: "My name is Fania Kaplan...Today I shot at Lenin. I did it on my own. I will not say from whom I obtained my revolver. I will give no details...I had resolved to kill Lenin long ago...I consider him a traitor to the Revolution...I favored the Constituent Assembly and I am still for it" (V. K. Vinogradov, ed. and comp., *Delo Fani Kaplan ili kto strelial v Lenina: Sbornik dokumentov* [Moscow: X-History, 2003], 17–18).

84 S. A. Stepanov, *Zagadki ubiistva Stolypina* (Moscow: Progress-Akademiia, 1995), 124.

gold. What can you do? You go, of course, to the big city to look for happiness. The big city has a magnetic power that pulls you up and doesn't let you go. It sucks you in like a swamp. You hope to find in the city everything that you are looking for.

In the region, where our hero lived, this big city was the renowned city of Kiev.[85]

CONCLUSION

Kiev was, in the eyes of anti-Semites, a city dominated by Jews, and, simultaneously, in the eyes of Jews, a hostile place, *Yehupets*. While anti-Semites worried about the future Jewish dominance of the city, Jews saw Kiev as the city with an administration increasingly hostile towards them, and with one of the most restrictive sets of regulations in the empire. According to Simon Dubnov, "no place in the empire could vie as regards hostility to the Jews with the city of Kiev—the inferno of Russian Israel."[86]

During the period from the legal return of Jews to Kiev in 1859 to the February 1917 Revolution, only limited numbers of Jews in certain restricted categories—merchants, university graduates, high school students, and artisans—enjoyed the legal right to live in the city. Inevitably, given Kiev's position in the heart of the southwestern region with its large and impoverished Jewish population, other classes of Jews sought to establish themselves there. In the relatively liberal 1860s and 1870s, they managed in many cases to do so, often facilitated by bribery. The policy of rapprochement meant that until 1881, regulations were implemented more leniently. However, from the 1880s on, the Kiev administration, encouraged by the central authorities, took an unremittingly harsh line with illegal Jewish residents, organizing night raids and frequently expelling those without the right to remain in the city. The essence of government policy was now that the Jews were a harmful element that needed to be controlled strictly to prevent their oppression

---

85 Sholom Aleichem, *Sobranie sochinenii*, 6: 283.
86 Cited in Hamm, *Kiev: A Portrait*, 133.

of the surrounding population. The growing revolutionary crisis, for which Jews were held at least partly responsible, intensified official hostility toward them at the turn of the century. All Kiev, Podolia, and Volhynia governors-general after Vasil'chikov (1852–1863), and all Kiev governors after Gesse (1855–1864), pursued a Judeophobic policy. They frequently described Jews as exploitative, hostile, and harmful in their reports to the tsar. Governor-General Aleksandr Mikhailovich Dondukov-Korsakov (1869–1878) went so far as to describe Jews as "virtually the most important problem confronting the government."[87]

Unlike the situation between 1793 and 1835, local Christian merchants in the late nineteenth to the early twentieth century largely opposed both the expulsion of Jews and the punitive policy pursued towards the Jewish community. They now saw the Jewish presence as essential to the city's prosperity. In their view, the restrictive measures against Jewish residence in Kiev destabilized normal economic life and commerce in the city and region. Many Christian inhabitants of Kiev petitioned the local authorities and the governor-general to end the evictions of Jews from Kiev, and to ease the restrictive measures toward them. Public opinion in the city was now generally on the side of the Jews for pragmatic economic as well as compassionate reasons.

However, neither Jewish nor Christian appeals to the government against the brutality of the Kiev administration toward Jews achieved the desired results; they never stopped the expulsions, and new restrictions were frequently imposed. The argument that the local administration was not executing government policy toward the Jews was used by Baron Evzel' Ginsburg in his petition in 1868, quoted above. He must not have realized that this policy ultimately originated in St. Petersburg. The governors-general were appointed by the tsar and none dared challenge the official policy.

Despite the hostility of both the local and central authorities, nothing apparently could thwart the desire of Jews to live in Kiev and enjoy the benefits of life in the big city. At the beginning of the twentieth century, Kiev had the largest Jewish population of cities outside

---

87 Klier, *Imperial Russia's Jewish Question*, 201.

the Pale of Settlement. The restrictions on Jewish residence in Kiev remained in place until the February 1917 Revolution. On August 15, 1915, Nikolai Shcherbatov, the minister of the interior, published a circular expanding the Pale of Settlement due to the emergency created by the war. During World War I, Germany occupied Russia's western provinces, and tens of thousands of Jewish refugees and displaced persons moved to the inner provinces. The circular allowed Jews to live in all cities of the Russian Empire, except the capitals (St. Petersburg and Moscow) and the cities that were under the jurisdiction of the Military and Imperial Court Ministries. Even then, the commanders of the Kiev Military District refused to allow all categories of Jews to settle in Kiev on the grounds of the "overpopulation of the city by refugees."[88] Only after the February 1917 Revolution, when the Provisional Government abolished all national and religious restrictions, did all Jews finally receive the right to reside in Kiev.

---

88 Kalnitsky, "Pravovoi status evreev Kieva," 80–81.

CHAPTER FOUR

The Kiev Jewish Community and its Leaders

> The police officer called the whole station together and gave them a speech: "We must finish off Benya Krik," he said "because when you have His Majesty the Tsar you cannot have a King also."
> —Isaac Babel' "The King"[1]

Kiev was always very attractive for Jews. There were many factors that made the city so desirable. At the beginning of the twentieth century, Kiev was the fifth largest city in the Russian Empire; in 1910, its population was 527,000.[2] It was an important political, economic, and cultural center. There one's chances to find work were better than in the overpopulated shtetls that had chronic high unemployment. A university, polytechnic and commercial institutes, and many gymnasiums were located in Kiev. Thus, Jewish youth who wanted to receive a better education went to Kiev to study. For rich Jewish merchants, it was important to live in the city, as it was one of the Russian Empire's most significant trade and industrial centers. There they could develop their businesses and make important trade contacts. Kiev was not part

---

1 Isaac Babel', *Sochineniia* (Moscow: Khudozhestvennaia literatura, 1991), 1: 121.
2 Hamm, *Kiev. A Portrait, 1800–1917*, 42.

of the Pale of Settlement, but the Pale's territory began just outside the city. Hence, Kiev Jews could maintain close connections with Jews in nearby areas. Also Kiev was, and is, a beautiful city with a pictorial landscape and a mild climate.

Additionally, Kiev's Jews had a strong emotional attachment to their city. According to Alexandra Fanny Brodsky, descendant of the famous dynasty of "Sugar Kings,"

> industrialists with means [i.e., the Brodsky family] did not leave Russia in the face of persecution and many obstacles hindering normal activity. The reasons for this were complex...They loved the city, the countryside, the proximity of the extended family, their friends; in short it was home. The anti-semitic stirrings backed by the Government did not impede the rapprochement between Jews and the liberal-minded and educated section of the population. The spontaneous love of their homeland appears to have kept the family there...[3]

The Kiev Jewish community was one of the largest in the Tsarist Empire from the late nineteenth to the early twentieth century. In spite of the restrictive measures imposed by the authorities, and the frequent expulsion of Jews who had settled illegally in Kiev, the Jewish population grew steadily and reached 87,240 people—or 15 percent of the city's total population—in 1917.[4]

Kiev was a merchant city, where merchants dominated the city duma and community organizations. Wealthy Jewish merchants also led the Kiev Jewish community and most local Jewish organizations. The Brodsky family had the most prominent role in Jewish communal life. Israel Brodsky and his two sons, Lazar and Lev (Leon), led the Kiev Jewish community from the mid-1860s to October 1917. They were

---

[3] Alexandra Fanny Brodsky, *Smoke Signals: From Eminence to Exile* (London and New York: Radcliffe Press, 1997), 16.
[4] Victoria Khiterer, "Jewish Life in Kyiv at the Turn of the Twentieth Century," *Ukraina Moderna* 10 (2006): 75.

the real kings on the Jewish street. Due to their wealth and connections with the authorities, the Brodskys had a major influence on Jewish life in the city. They helped many Jews receive the right of residence in Kiev. Through their connections, the Brodskys obtained permission for the construction of two major synagogues in downtown Kiev, and for the opening of the first Jewish school in the city. They financed these institutions and participated in almost all Kiev Jewish charitable organizations and initiatives.

Officially, the Jewish Community Board, the kahal, did not exist in Kiev or anywhere else in the Russian Empire after its abolishment by law in 1844. The government of Nicholas I eliminated structures of Jewish self-government, hoping to put an end to "Jewish isolation" and to push Jews toward assimilation and "merging" with the gentile population.[5] However, in many cities and towns, Jewish communal structures went underground or functioned behind the names of various charitable institutions.

An unofficial communal body dominated by the Brodskys began operating in the 1860s, and in 1906 was recognized by the municipality as the "Representation for Jewish Welfare."[6] A number of Kiev Jewish philanthropic organizations attempted to help poor Jews by providing various kinds of financial aid and by granting small loans to individual Jewish artisans for the establishment of businesses. However, they were unable to significantly reduce Jewish poverty in the city.

The leaders of the Kiev Jewish community put much effort into protecting all Kievan Jews from further expulsions and persecutions. The skillful *shtadlan* diplomacy of the leader of Kiev's Jewish community, Lazar Brodsky, was quite successful. During his presidency (from the 1890s until his death in 1904), he was able to prevent major Jewish expulsions from the city and anti-Jewish violence. However, after his death, when his brother Leon became leader of the community, state anti-Semitism and anti-Jewish violence increased not only in Kiev, but throughout the entire Russian Empire. Jewish communal leaders now

---

[5] Isaac Levitats, *The Jewish Community in Russia, 1844–1917* (New York: Octagon Books, 1970).
[6] Meir, *Kiev, Jewish Metropolis*, 82–83.

abandoned their belief that they could cooperate with the local authorities and turned their efforts towards the support of Jewish emigration from Imperial Russia.

The Jewish elite also tried to improve its position by contributing to the general welfare. Jews were involved in the development of public transportation (Margolin's tram company) and free health care. The Kiev Jewish hospital, subsidized by the Jewish community, provided free treatment to both the Jewish and gentile populations. While this sometimes mitigated anti-Jewish hostility, ironically it also created resentment of the Jewish community's wealth and resources.

THE KAHAL IS ABOLISHED, YET THE KAHAL EXISTS: JEWISH COMMUNAL INSTITUTIONS IN KIEV

We do not know much about the establishment of Jewish communal structures in Kiev after the readmission of Jews to the city, nor about their functioning until the 1890s, because the few surviving Jewish community documents from this period do not address this question. Virtually all the material located in Kiev archives and in the press dealing with Jewish communal institutions relates either to the late nineteenth or the beginning of the twentieth century. There is a specific reason for this lack of information. As noted, the kahal was officially abolished by law in Russia on December 19, 1844.[7] However, as Michael Stanislawski writes:

> Most Jewish historians have correctly observed that to a large extent the abolition of the kahal was a paper reform since the kahal in fact persisted in its previous form at least until the last years of the nineteenth century...
>
> While the essential structure of the kahal remained intact even after its formal abolition, its function and status within Russian-Jewish society were significantly altered after 1844.[8]

---

7 Michael Stanislawski, *Tsar Nicholas I and the Jews: The Transformation of Jewish Society in Russia 1825–1855* (Philadelphia: The Jewish Publication Society of America, 1983), 124.
8 Ibid., 126–127.

The new Kiev kahal, or Community Board, was probably formed as soon as Jews resettled in the city in the 1860s. Like other kahals, it had no legal status and therefore could not publicize its activities, which were often camouflaged as the actions of various charitable institutions. The secret, underground existence of the kahal during this period makes it very hard to find any materials about its work, since it preferred not to leave any evidence of its existence for the authorities to uncover.

Documents produced by Kiev Jewish communal institutions came only occasionally to state organizations and their archives, usually when community members made appeals to the authorities. Kahal members intentionally avoided using the term "kahal," or even calling themselves representatives of the community. Instead they called themselves "a group of educated Jews" or the "educated section of the community." However the structure, activities, and leadership of the Kiev Jewish communal institutions can be sketched in spite of the limited documentary sources.

The end of the nineteenth and the beginning of the twentieth century were the peak years in the development of Jewish communal structures in Kiev. The community had twenty-two synagogues and prayer houses, two Talmud-Torahs, a Jewish orphanage, several Jewish schools, two Jewish hospitals, and many philanthropic organizations. The communal institutions were very active and played an important role in the lives of Jews in Kiev.[9]

In the second half of the 1880s and the beginning of the 1890s, the Kiev Jewish community had an unofficial Advisory Board with thirty-six members. Two different sources mention this number. On October 30, 1890, the anti-Semitic author Molchanov, who was cited in the previous chapter, wrote in the St. Petersburg newspaper, *Novoe vremia*, in a report "From the Southwestern region," that "unofficially, but quite openly there exists [in Kiev] a Jewish communal body...which has its presidents, secretaries, orators, judges. This communal body consists of thirty-six members." He also mentioned the names of several of the

---

9 Khiterer, "Jewish Life in Kyiv at the Turn of the Twentieth Century," 74–94.

members.¹⁰ More indirect evidence of the existence of the Jewish Community Board is provided by E. P. Kel'berin, the secretary of the Economic Board of the Kiev Choral Synagogue, in his brochure *Desiatiletie Kievskogo evreiskogo khoral'nogo molitvennogo doma* (Ten Years of the Kiev Jewish Choral Synagogue):

> At the beginning of 1886 the educated part of the Jewish population of Kiev, thirty-six people in number, led by Lazar I. Brodsky, presented a petition requesting permission to open a temporary choral prayer house in the Starokievskii district of Kiev.¹¹

Obviously in 1886, by which time many hundreds of Jews had graduated from Kiev St. Vladimir University, the educated part of Kiev's Jewish population was not limited to thirty-six people. Bearing in mind that Lazar Brodsky is known from other sources to have been the president of the Kiev Jewish community from the second half of the 1880s until his death in 1904, it becomes clear that Kel'berin was talking about the Jewish Community Board.

The selection of thirty-six as the number of Community Board members seems not to have been accidental. This is a sacred number according to Jewish tradition. "Thirty-six Just Men" (*Lamed vav tsaddikim*) in each generation are mentioned in the Babylonian Talmud and in Jewish mystical literature. In the Kiev Jewish community there was a high percentage of hasidim, among whom this legend was especially popular. It is likely that for the members of the Community Board, it was a compliment to be compared to the *lamedvavniks*, whose mission was "at times of great peril, particularly of antisemitic violence...to rescue their fellow Jews from danger."¹²

Natan Meir has identified the Jewish Community Board with the Jewish Welfare Committee, which was legal and recognized by the

---

10 TsDIAK U, f. 442, op. 528, d. 450, ll. 1–4.
11 E. P. Kel'berin, *Desiatiletie Kievskogo evreiskogo khoral'nogo molitvennogo doma: 1898–1907* (Kiev: I. M. Roset Publishing House, 1909), 7.
12 *The New Encyclopedia of Judaism*, s.v. "Lamed vav tsaddikim," 467–468.

tsarist authorities. In his view, the Jewish Welfare Committee served as the governing body of the Kiev Jewish community and "at least in its first years, was a self-selected group of merchants and businessmen."[13] This committee originally (before 1906) had nine unelected members, and "most ordinary Kiev Jews did not even know who sat on it."[14] Perhaps the different number of members of the Community Board and the Jewish Welfare Committee suggests that we should not completely equate these two bodies.[15] Most likely, the Jewish Welfare Committee was the "visible" part of the communal structure, enjoying a legal status as a charitable body. However, the larger part of the communal structure—responsible for questions concerning Jewish religious life—could not be legalized, and was kept hidden from the authorities.

There were other reasons for the double structure. Officers of the Kiev kahal who performed traditional functions, such as *dayanim* (judges), kosher supervisors, and spiritual rabbis, would have been out of place in the Jewish Welfare Committee. At the same time, a modern welfare committee was clearly necessary to provide aid to poorer Jews on a legal and more professional basis than traditional charitable methods made possible.

The presidency of the Kiev Jewish community was held by the Brodsky family for almost the entire period from the readmission of Jews to Kiev in the 1860s until 1917. In their turn, members of this family took the leading position in the community—in particular, Israel Brodsky and his two sons, Lazar Brodsky and Lev (Leon) Brodsky.[16] The vice president of the Kiev Jewish community, Max Emilievich (Emmanuil) Mandelstamm, was also a prominent figure among Russian Jews. He was one of the founders of the Palestinophile and later Zionist movements in the late Russian Empire.

The other members of the board of the Kiev Jewish community were wealthy Kievan Jews, among them the banker Leon Ashkenazi

---

13 Meir, *Kiev, Jewish Metropolis*, 73.
14 Ibid., 69, 71.
15 Ibid., 140–141; TsDIAK U, f. 442, op. 528, d. 450, ll. 1–4.
16 TsDIAK U, f. 442, op. 528, d. 450, ll. 1–4; S. Iu. Witte, *Izbrannye vospominaniia, 1849–1911* (Moscow: Mysl', 1991), 117–118.

and the lawyer Avraam Moiseevich Gol'denberg. In 1874, Israel Brodsky invited Gol'denberg to take the position of secretary and legal adviser in his Aleksandrovskii sugar plants. Gol'denberg accepted this offer and moved to Kiev. In 1884, he became manager of the Aleksandrovskii factory. In 1897, he was elected chairman of the Economic Board of the Kiev Choral Synagogue and held this position for at least ten years.[17] Another distinguished figure in the community was Iona Zaitsev (1828–1907), the owner of several factories in Kiev, who in 1896 financed the Jewish Surgical Hospital in Kiev.[18]

The process of democratization and the legalization of various public organizations and institutions during the 1905 Revolution brought changes to the Kiev communal institutions. The Jewish Welfare Committee increased its membership from nine to twenty-four after the first actual elections to the board in November 1906, in which about one hundred electors from the city's synagogues and communal institutions participated.[19] After these elections, the Jewish Welfare Committee, now renamed the Representative Board for Jewish Welfare, seems to have become the representative organ of the Kiev Jewish community; the Community Board is no longer mentioned in any sources. Thus, the Kiev kahal was able to legalize itself, while at the same time decreasing the number of its members. By now many Kievan Jews had become more indifferent to religious life, and for them the number thirty-six had lost its mystical connotation. Whereas wealthy merchants had dominated the old Community Board, the new representatives came from more diverse socio-economic backgrounds: among them were merchants, lawyers, an engineer, and two artisans.[20] Half of the members (twelve of twenty-four) of the Jewish Welfare Committee were selected from Jews who had previously been invited by the city council to be representatives of the Jewish community when the distribution of the basket tax (*korobochnyi sbor*, the tax on kosher meat),

---

17 Kel'berin, *Desiatiletie Kievskogo evreiskogo khoral'nogo molitvennogo doma: 1898–1907*, 3.
18 Maryna Vynohradova and Mykhailo Kal'nytskyi, "Bezkoshtovna khirurhichna likarnia I. M. Zaitseva," *Zvit pamiatok istorii ta kul'tury Ukrainy* 1 (1999): 188–189.
19 Meir, "The Jews in Kiev, 1859–1914," 141.
20 Ibid., 142.

which was the source of the Jewish communal budget, was decided by the city council. Leon Brodsky remained the head of the Jewish Welfare Committee. Wealthy merchants still dominated, while artisans, who constituted the majority of working Jews, were represented by only two members. However, the Jews of Kiev seem to have been satisfied with the results of this first election. Certainly, there were no public complaints or protests reported in the local press. On the contrary, a member of the Kiev Community Board, Gershon Badanes, who was not a magnate himself, wrote:

> First of all we should bear in mind that even though wealthy people do not have absolutely perfect notions about public affairs, essentially they are doing a great public service and are honestly attempting to comprehend the people's needs. They show a clear desire to aid and give relief to the people in their calamities, and without their participation none of these public works would be possible.[21]

Gershon Badanes probably expressed the opinion of the limited Jewish electorate. Its members were convinced that without the resources of the Jewish elite and their influence with the authorities, it would be impossible to conduct any public business. As a result, the democratization of the Kiev Jewish community during the first Russian revolution was only partial.

The Kiev Jewish community was one of the wealthiest in the Russian Empire. In 1907, it had at its disposal 144,000 rubles collected in the previous year from the basket tax. The newly elected representatives increased the price of kosher meat and were able collect 187,000 rubles for 1907. "By 1908 this sum reached 260,000 rubles."[22] The Kiev Jewish Community Board did not have the right to decide how this money should be used; its budget was supervised by the city administration. The city council selected representatives from local Jews who,

---

21 Gershon Badanes, *Evreiskie obshchestvennye dela v Kieve* (Kiev: Sliusarevskii Publishing House, 1910), 16.
22 Ibid., 143.

under the chairmanship of a gentile member of the city council, set the community budget.[23]

Badanes gives the budget of the Kiev Jewish community for 1907 (Table III) as follows:[24]

Table III: Budget of the Kiev Jewish Community for 1907

Revenue	144,000 rubles
Payment to the city	15,009 rubles
To finance the police (From January 1 to April 19)	4,784 rubles
For the Jewish Hospital	45,400 rubles
Travel expenses of the Medical Inspector of Kiev Province	600 rubles
For the creation of a morgue at the Jewish Hospital	2,000 rubles
For the reinforcement of the ravine near the Jewish Hospital	4,500 rubles
Subsidy for Zaitsev's Surgical Hospital	3,000 rubles
For the Obstetric Hospital for poor women in Podol	1,500 rubles
Boiarka Sanatorium for tuberculosis patients	1,000 rubles
Aid for drug purchase for poor ambulatory patients	1,000 rubles
For the care and education of orphans and poor children	15,000 rubles
For the Brodsky two-grade school	6,000 rubles
For daycare for children of the working class	2,000 rubles
For tuition payment for study at middle schools [i.e., gymnasiums, vocational schools, etc.]	3,000 rubles
Kiev Department of the Society for Spreading Enlightenment among Jews [OPE]	4,000 rubles
To Dr. Iampol'skii for the teaching of Judaism	400 rubles
Subsidy for old people who have lost the ability to work	5,000 rubles

---

23 Gershon Badanes, *S odnogo vola tri shkury: K voprosu o polozhenii evreev v Kieve* (Kiev: I. M. Roset Publishing House, 1907), 14.
24 Ibid.

Subsidy for fuel during winter	1,000 rubles
Subsidy for Passover	500 rubles
Subsidy for two low-cost dining halls	1,500 rubles
For the Society for Aid to Poor Artisans and Workers	4,000 rubles
For maintenance of the Luk'ianovskii Cemetery	8,400 rubles
For the salary of kosher supervisors	12,000 rubles
Salary for two state rabbis	2,400 rubles
For printing two metrical books	16 rubles
Total	144,000 rubles[25]

As can be seen from these figures, a significant part of the community's budget (about 20 percent) went to city taxes and to finance the police. Between 1901 and 1906, the community was required to pay 14,550 rubles annually towards the costs of policing the city. On February 21, 1905, the tsar ordered that proceeds from the basket tax should be used for this purpose only until April 19, 1906. However, this term was extended for an additional year at the request of the governor of Kiev. As a consequence, the community's budget for 1907 included a provision for the payment to the police only until April 19, 1907. The payment was then extended again until January 1, 1908, and the community was now charged an additional 9,766 rubles on top of the original sum of 14,550 rubles. This onerous charge remained in place until the February 1917 Revolution. The community leaders deemed the charge to be illegal, and waged a long and unsuccessful struggle with the authorities for its abolition. In a petition to the governor-general, the Jewish Welfare Committee asked that charges from the communal budget to finance the Kiev police be ended. These charges, the committee asserted, were "illegal and manifestly unjust with regard to the entire Jewish population of Kiev, violating the principle of equality of this population with the other citizens of the city."[27] Meir states:

---

25 Ibid., 14–15.
26 Ibid.
27 Meir, *Kiev, Jewish Metropolis*, 282.

The petitioners noted that Jews paid the same municipal taxes as their non-Jewish neighbors and did not receive any special benefits from the city; indeed, the city council had refused to provide any assistance to the victims of the 1905 pogrom.[28]

In their petition of September 1905 to the governor-general, two Kiev Jewish industrialists and community leaders, Leon Brodsky and David Margolin, proposed an even more radical resolution to this problem. They asked that the basket tax be abolished and replaced by a universal income tax, which would be fairer for all categories of city residents.[29] However, the authorities rejected this proposal, and Leon Brodsky took his struggle for the abolition of the basket tax to the Convention of Jewish Communal Leaders in Kovno in 1909, as described below.[30]

Apart from city and police taxes as well as traditional expenses for religious needs, the principal expenses of the community derived from its social work. This had three main aspects: healthcare, education, and financial aid for poorer Jews. The way the resources of the community were spent aroused some criticism. According to Meir:

> A Jewish communal leader from Warsaw visited Kiev in 1908 or 1909 and commented that, while the generosity of Kiev's Jews was admirable, the funds were not being put to the best use; Warsaw's Jewish institutions were run more cheaply.[31]

However, from this criticism it is unclear specifically what the Warsaw communal leader had in mind. Certainly, the salaries of the two rabbis took up only a small percentage of the community's budget. Apart from the contributions to the city, the remaining money was spent on aid to the Jewish population. The most expensive Kiev Jewish institution was the Jewish hospital, on which the community spent

---

28 Ibid.
29 TsDIAK U, f. 442, op. 658, d. 97, ll. 93–94.
30 "Otchet o soveshchanii evreiskikh obshchestvennykh deiatelei, proiskhodivshem v Kovno 19–22 noiabria 1909 goda," *Evreiskii mir* (November–December, 1909): 44.
31 Meir, *Kiev, Jewish Metropolis*, 293.

about one third of its revenue, 45,400 rubles. This provided less than half of the hospital's budget; the total budget for 1908 was 96,127 rubles. The difference was covered by private donations.[32] The Jewish hospital was a source of communal pride, although there was criticism regarding the large sums spent on it. In 1908, Lev Shtammer, a Kiev Jew, published a brochure in which he accused community leaders of inefficient use of their resources. He claimed that the leaders generously financed their "favorite institution," the Jewish hospital, while

> Jews in Russia in general, and in Kiev particularly, are in a calamitous situation and are dying from starvation. To find a solution for their position requires very complicated, laborious and expensive work, and this work is not visible to everybody and therefore not gratifying. To create a model hospital is much easier and you can receive lots of gratitude: here it is possible to give charity for a *grosh* [half a kopeck] and make the noise of a whole ruble…[33]

This was an exaggeration. Even if all the funds that the Kiev Jewish community spent on the Jewish hospital had instead been used for financial aid to poor Jews, this would not have been enough to provide sufficient help to all the needy Jews in Kiev, not to mention the entire Russian Empire. Meanwhile, the Jewish hospital, which provided free medical aid to Jews and gentiles from throughout the Kiev region, was the only medical institution accessible to poor Jewish people.

Because of the unrelenting anti-Semitism in Kiev, philanthropy and the network of Jewish social institutions played a key role in Jewish life. According to Badanes, special Jewish institutions were necessary in Kiev because local schools, hospitals, and clinics accepted Jews "only with major limitations and restrictions."[34] By order of the wife of Governor-General Dragomirov, Jews were not accepted at Red Cross clinics. Kiev Jews, Badanes noted, "could not count on the aid of the

---

32 P. T. Neishtube, *Otchet po Kievskoi evreiskoi bol'nitse za 1908 god* (Kiev: n.p., 1910), 26.
33 Lev Shtammer, *Na sud obshchestvennogo mneniia* (Kiev: n.p., 1908), 10.
34 Badanes, *S odnogo vola tri shkury*, 20.

non-Jewish population…[and could rely] only on themselves and their own means."³⁵

The creation of the Jewish hospital in Kiev was a Brodsky family affair. The hospital opened in 1862, but did not have its own building until 1885. In its early years, the community was still quite small and was able to provide only very modest means for its support. As a consequence, the hospital initially rented small and unsuitable facilities. The construction of its own premises became possible only as a result of private donations from Jewish businessmen, the largest from the Brodsky family. In 1885, the hospital's surgery department opened, financed by Israel Brodsky. In all, he donated 165,000 rubles to the Jewish hospital, mostly for the construction of its various buildings.³⁶ After his death, his sons Lazar and Leon continued to serve as patrons of the hospital; several new buildings were built and new departments opened. They also gave money for the support and modernization of the hospital, and Leon Brodsky donated 100,000 rubles for the construction of a Jewish clinic. In 1892, the hospital board elected them as trustees in recognition of their contributions.³⁷

The Jewish community partially funded patient treatment, medicine, the salaries of doctors and nurses, and other hospital needs. The hospital provided free medical treatment for needy Jewish, as well as gentile, patients, and was "spending more than double per patient what other hospitals spent."³⁸ The best Kiev physicians—such as Professor K. G. Tritshel' and the ophthalmologist Max Mandelstamm—worked there. It offered better quality treatment than any other hospital or clinic in Kiev, which created resentment among anti-Semites. Molchanov, a correspondent of *Novoe vremia*, wrote in his above-cited report that "Kiev has an excellent Jewish hospital whose lavish resources are envied to no avail by the lousy local Christian hospital."³⁹

---

35 Ibid.
36 *Zhurnaly zasedanii Soveta Kievskoi evreiskoi bol'nitsy za 1895 god* (Kiev: n.p., 1902), 17.
37 P. T. Neishtube, *Istoricheskaia zapiska v pamiat' 50-letiia sushchestvovaniia Kievskoi evreiskoi bol'nitsy 1862–1912* (Kiev: n.p., 1912).
38 Ibid.; Meir, *Kiev, Jewish Metropolis*, 294.
39 A. N. Molchanov, "Iz Iugo-Zapadnogo kraia," *Novoe vremia*, October 30, 1890, no. 5270.

The Jewish hospital had such a good reputation that many Christian patients chose it for treatment. When there was a cholera epidemic in Kiev in 1892–1893, the Jewish hospital treated more Christian cholera patients than Jewish patients (in 1892, there were 182 cholera patients: 101 Christians and 81 Jews; in 1893, there were 231 cholera patients: 147 Christians and 84 Jews).[40] In 1901, the Jewish hospital treated in all 2,712 patients: 2,258 Jews and 324 gentiles. The patients came to the hospital from the city of Kiev, and from the Kiev, Podolia, Volhynia, and other provinces of the empire. Among the hospital's gentile patients, almost half were women in childbirth. In 1901, among the patients of the obstetric department there were 300 Jewish and 156 Christian women.[41] At the turn of the twentieth century, the vast majority of women in Russia (98 percent) gave birth to children without any medical aid. Annually, about 100,000 women in Russia died from complications due to childbirth. In the Kiev area, the Jewish hospital was the only place where poor women could receive free medical care in childbirth.[42]

The Kiev Jewish community also subsidized Zaitsev's Surgical Hospital, which was established in Podol in 1893. This hospital leased a house until 1897, when the industrialist Iona Zaitsev financed the construction of its own building. Iona Zaitsev and his son Mark were owners of the brick factory in Kiev where Mendel' Beilis, who was accused in 1911 of a ritual murder, was manager. Mark Zaitsev financed the construction of a new building for the hospital in 1912. This hospital functioned until 1991, although in Soviet times it was converted into a maternity home. The first director of the hospital was a prominent doctor, a professor of surgery at the Kiev Clinical Institute, G. B. Bykhovskii, who led the hospital for twenty-five years. Like the other Jewish hospital in Kiev, Zaitsev's Surgical Hospital provided free treatment for all patients.[43]

---

40 *Zhurnaly zasedanii Soveta Kievskoi evreiskoi bol'nitsy za 1895 god* (Kiev: n.p., 1902), 18.
41 Ibid., 3, 5, 7.
42 P. T. Neishtube, *Istoricheskaia zapiska v pamiat' 50-letiia sushchestvovaniia Kievskoi evreiskoi bol'nitsy 1862–1912* (Kiev: n.p., 1912).
43 Vynohradova and Kal'nytskyi, "Bezkoshtovna khirurhichna likarnia I. M. Zaitseva," 188–189; S. Iu. Karamash, "Novi arkhivni dokumenty pro Kyivs'ku likarniu Zaitseva," *Likars'ka sprava* 7–9 (1996): 205–207.

Critics of the Jewish communal administration claimed that it did not spend enough money on Jewish education and did not equally distribute money among the various Jewish schools. Thus in 1908, according to Meir,

> Fourteen community schools received 4,260 rubles, ten percent of their annual budget, while the Brodsky School alone was allocated 6,000 rubles—almost a third of its budget. Critics complained that the community schools were poorly run and in terrible condition.[44]

However, this criticism is not wholly justified. While we do not have full information about the budget of the Kiev Jewish community for 1908, the community budget for 1907 provided 30,400 rubles (about 21 percent of all community revenue) for Jewish education, including a subsidy for the Society for Spreading Enlightenment among Jews in Russia (OPE).[45] Badanes argues that problem was not the distribution of money for Jewish schools, but internal debates and disagreements among members of the School Committee:

> In the School Committee there were permanent frictions and continuous debates between different ideological streams and directions, from which, of course, the oversight and education of the children suffered. For the same reason there was permanent chaos in providing financing to the schools; some schools almost disintegrated before they received their assigned money.[46]

An important part of the Kiev Jewish Welfare Committee's work was to provide financial aid to poor sick Jews who had temporarily lost their ability to work. The committee had a special office where needy Jews came for charity. Among these were a large number of Jews from

---

44 Meir, *Kiev, Jewish Metropolis*, 293–294.
45 Badanes, *S odnogo vola tri shkury*, 14–15.
46 Badanes, *Evreiskie obshchestvennye dela v Kieve*, 12.

the entire Kiev province who came to the city for medical treatment. Although they could receive free medical treatment in the Jewish hospital, they still needed money to stay in the city and for transportation back to their hometowns. Many Jews who came to Kiev to look for work or to study also applied for charity, as well as retired soldiers and other needy Kiev Jews. The Welfare Committee gave thousands of rubles in financial aid to poor Jews, and while this sum increased every year, it was never enough to provide aid to all the needy. In 1907, the Jewish Welfare Committee gave for this purpose 7,879 rubles; in 1909, 8,500 rubles; and in 1910, 12,000 rubles.[47]

However not only needy, sick, and unemployed people came to the office of the Welfare Committee; professional Jewish beggars also came and demanded money. The beggars frequently caused scandals and disturbances.[48] On the whole, given the scarcity of resources, dispensing charity was a painful task. Badanes wrote:

> It is necessary to have a great deal of fortitude, persistence and patience to be a Jewish public figure in Russia. It is necessary to have iron nerves to see every day the bloody tears, to listen to the hysterical keening, moans and wailing of those suffering from poverty and persecution, the gritting of teeth and cursing of fate from desperate and perishing people.
>
> It is necessary to have considerable spiritual power to refuse to aid so many people, to give to the majority only half of the required aid, and very seldom to satisfy the needy completely.[49]

In spite of all the difficulties of philanthropic work, many wealthy Jews in Russia took leading roles in Jewish communal life, and contributed large amounts to charitable relief. According to Steven Zipperstein, Jewish grandees "wielded an enormous influence over Jewish communal

---

47 Ibid., 14–15.
48 Ibid., 25.
49 Ibid., 28–29.

life in Russia."⁵⁰ Even though the traditional policies of *shtadlanut* were in crisis at the turn of the twentieth century in Russia, the role of the grandees was still quite significant in communal affairs, especially before the 1905 Revolution. However, Jewish magnates could not overcome the policy of state anti-Semitism with its numerous restrictions on Jews, and they could not stop anti-Jewish violence or mass Jewish emigration.⁵¹ In the case of the Brodsky family, they did not try to achieve impossible goals or solve all problems. As community leaders, they focused their work on improving the socio-economic condition of Jews in Kiev and preventing the expulsion of Jews from the city. Leon Brodsky also supported Jewish emigration from the Russian Empire. Some of their efforts were successful, some not, but the "Sugar Kings" led the Kiev community for many years.

THE BRODSKY "SUGAR KINGS": JEWISH INDUSTRIALISTS, PHILANTHROPISTS, AND COMMUNITY LEADERS

After the revolution in Russia, there was a popular jingle that went, "Tea Wissotzky's, Sugar Brodsky's, Russia Trotsky's." The Brodskys were among the wealthiest Jewish industrialists and most prominent philanthropists in late Imperial Russia. However, in spite of the family's almost legendary status, no comprehensive scholarly work has been written about them. Information about the Brodsky family is dispersed among various memoirs and archival and published sources, which I use here to piece together the history of the dynasty.

The progenitor of the Brodsky family was Meir Shor, who descended from a family of well-known rabbinical scholars and authors.

---

50 Steven J. Zipperstein, "The Politics of Relief: The Transformation of Russian Jewish Communal Life during the First World War," *Studies in Contemporary Jewry: An Annual*, 4, *The Jews and the European Crisis 1914-1921*, ed. Jonathan Frankel (New York: Oxford University Press, 1988), 26.

51 John D. Klier, "Krug Gintsburgov i politika shtadlanuta v imperatorskoi Rossii," *Vestnik Evreiskogo Universiteta v Moskve* 3, no. 10 (1995): 38-39; Eli Lederhendler, *The Road to Modern Jewish Politics: Political Tradition and Political Reconstruction in the Jewish Community of Tsarist Russia* (New York: Oxford University Press, 2001), 19-20.

His father, Alexander-Chaim Shor, was a grandson of Rabbi Alexander Sender Shor, author of the religious treatise *Tevuot Shor* on *shekhita* (kosher butchering) and *kashrut*, first published in 1733 and republished many times. Meir Shor came to Russia from the border city of Brody in Galicia (Austria) at the beginning of the nineteenth century. He settled in the shtetl Zlatopol' of Kiev province and changed his family name to Brodsky after his native city.[52] He had five sons: Abram (Abraham), Isaac, Israel, Joseph (Iosif), and Solomon (Zalman). Meir gave each of his sons a gift of 500 rubles to go into business when they married, and all did well and became rich. The source of their wealth was the sugar industry, which was rapidly developing in Russia at the time. The Brodsky family came to own a number of sugar plants in southwestern Russia, where they introduced various technical innovations. At the end of the nineteenth and the beginning of the twentieth century, the Brodsky family combined their business into a cartel with other rich sugar industrialists, including the Ukrainians Tereshchenko and Kharitonenko, the Russian Bobrinskii and the Pole Jaroszyński. This cartel "eventually came to control most of the empire's sugar production" and made Kiev the "sugar capital" of Imperial Russia.[53]

In the shtetl of Zlatopol', where they built a hospital and almshouse, the Brodsky brothers were famous for their charity. Their aptitude for business and philanthropy appeared in full measure when they moved from the shtetl to large cities after a new law in 1859 allowed Jewish merchants of the first guild to live in any city of the Russian Empire. Branches of the Brodsky family settled in Kiev and Odessa, where they expanded their business interests.[54]

The most distinguished representative of the Brodsky family's Odessa branch was Abram Brodsky, the oldest son of Meir Shor. He was not involved in the sugar industry, but made his fortune as a collector of the basket tax. (Fifty years later, as mentioned above, his nephew

---

52 Victoria Khiterer, "The Brodsky Sugar Kings: Jewish Industrialists, Philanthropists and Community Leaders of Late Imperial Russia," *Jews and Slavs* 19 (2008): 25.
53 Hamm, *Kiev: A Portrait, 1800–1917*, 84.
54 M. Kalnitsky, "Pravovoi status evreev Kieva (1859-1917)," in *Ievreis'ka istoriia ta kul'tura v Ukraini: Materialy konferentsii. Kyiv 8–9 hrudnia, 1994* (Kiev: Institut Iudaiki, 1995), 77; V. V. Kovalinskii, *Metsenaty Kieva* (Kiev: Kii, 1998), 204–245.

Leon Brodsky agitated for the elimination of this tax.) Abram Brodsky was famous for his charity. He financed the construction of an orphanage in Odessa and gave money for the establishment of two Jewish agricultural colonies in South Russia. Brodsky was rewarded for his generous philanthropic activity with the title Hereditary Honorary Citizen of the Russian Empire and a gold medal "For Zeal" ("*Za userdie*").[55]

All the Brodsky brothers were ambitious and dreamt of perpetuating their names in history. This sometimes caused problems. For example, Abram Brodsky offered 15,000 rubles for the construction of a Jewish hospital in Kiev on the condition that it be named after him. Kiev, Podolia, and Volhynia Governor-General Nikolai Nikolaevich Annenkov rejected this offer, and Brodsky refused to give money for the project.[56] Nevertheless, a Jewish hospital was subsequently built with donations from the Kiev branch of the Brodsky family.

The Brodsky brothers did not limit their activities to business and philanthropy, but also took part in local affairs. They gained influence by participating in local representative bodies and public institutions, and by leading Jewish societies and organizations. Abram Brodsky was famous for his public activity. He was the first president of the Odessa branch of the Society for Spreading Enlightenment among Jews in Russia (OPE), a member of the Odessa City Duma and City Council (*Gorodskaia Uprava*), and a *shtadlan* (representative) of the Odessa Jewish community. According to Patricia Herlihy, "Avram Brodskii… was one of the six men who formed the executive committee heading the city's government in 1873."[57] Russian legislation limited Jews to one third of the seats in a City Duma. In the Odessa City Duma, they constituted twenty-four of seventy-two members, although "their influence far exceeded their numbers."[58] The most influential among the Jewish deputies was Abram Brodsky. Steven Zipperstein writes:

---

55 I. Kotler, *Ocherki po istorii evreev Odessy* (Jerusalem: Noy, 1996), 157; *Evreiskaia entsiklopediia*, s.v. "Brodskie," 5: 22; Kovalinskii, *Metsenaty Kieva*, 204–245.
56 Kovalinskii, *Metsenaty Kieva*, 207–208.
57 Patricia Herlihy, *Odessa: A History 1794–1914* (Cambridge: Harvard University Press, 1986), 253.
58 Steven Zipperstein, *The Jews of Odessa: A Cultural History, 1794–1881* (Stanford, CA: Stanford University Press, 1986), 132.

The relative apathy of non-Jewish members and the organizational skills of the Jewish ones, especially of the financier Abram Brodskii, ensured them a leading role in municipal deliberations. So influential was Brodskii that the local British Consul held him personally responsible for a controversy that in 1873 threatened to lead to the liquidation of a partly British-owned waterworks firm.[59]

During the pogrom of 1871 in Odessa, Brodsky was a member of a Jewish delegation that visited Novorossiiskii Governor-General Pavel Kotsebue, who refused to talk to them. However, after their visit Kotsebue gave the order to stop the pogrom in the city.[60] The work of Abram Brodsky as a *shtadlan* of the Jewish community was not always successful, but he worked diligently to improve the conditions of life of his coreligionists and to protect them from harm.

Although the Brodsky brothers settled in different cities, their Jewish communal leadership and philanthropic and public activities had many similar features. Several members of the Brodsky family played prominent roles in the history of the Kiev Jewish community. The founder of the Kiev branch was Israel Brodsky (1823–1888), the first among the Brodsky brothers to become involved in the sugar industry. In 1846, twenty-three-year-old Israel established his first sugar refinery in the village of Lebedin near the shtetl of Zlatopol', where he lived. Originally, his business partner was a local landowner, Petr Lopukhin, a great-nephew of Prince Grigorii Potemkin. They conducted a business together for eight years, after which Brodsky became its sole owner.

Subsequently, Brodsky became a partner of the sugar magnate and landowner Aleksei Alekseevich Bobrinskii (1800–1868). Count Bobrinskii was a well-known inventor of agricultural implements and author of books promoting commerce in Russia.[61] Bobrinskii and Brodsky introduced the latest technologies in sugar refining. Their

---

59 Ibid., 132–133.
60 Ibid., 122–123.
61 Kovalinskii, *Metsenaty Kieva*, 206; Khiterer, "The Brodsky Sugar Kings," 27.

business was very successful, and Israel bought additional sugar refineries in Ukraine. He also created an efficient system of sugar trading in Russia and abroad.

The main Brodsky sugar refineries were in the southwestern region, but Israel also had a plant in Odessa, where he lived from 1860 to 1865. He then moved to Kiev, where he enrolled in the merchant estate, which allowed him to live there. Later his brothers Solomon (Zalman), Isaac, and Joseph (Iosif) also settled in Kiev, where they originally conducted jointly their sugar refinery business. "When this enterprise began to yield ever larger returns," recounted Alexandra Fanny Brodsky, "Israel eased out his two brothers. This business remained the main source of his eventual multi-million fortune. Joseph and Solomon continued to run other joint holdings..."[62]

Count Sergei Iul'evich Witte, later Chairman of the Council of Ministers of the Russian Empire, who lived in Kiev between 1880 and 1888 when he served as manager and director of the Southwestern Railroad, met Israel Brodsky frequently. He described him in his memoirs:

> At the time that I lived in Kiev, [Israel] Brodsky was the most important of the Jews. He looked much like a very venerable old man, whose appearance reminded one of a Biblical patriarch; but he did not look Jewish. He was enormously rich....I talked with him many times, and we had business conversations, and he always impressed me as being very wise, although almost uneducated.[63]

Witte had a more negative view of Israel's brother, Abram:

> I also met his brother when I worked in Odessa. The brother was very rich, but not quite as rich as the Kievan Brodsky. In contrast to the Kievan Brodsky, the Odessa Brodsky made a repulsive impression: without going into his morals, one can

---

62 Alexandra Fanny Brodsky, *Smoke Signals: From Eminence to Exile* (London: Radcliffe Press, 1997), 4.
63 Witte, *Izbrannye vospominaniia, 1849–1911*, 117–118.

say that his physiognomy, his mannerisms, even his speech were entirely Jewish.[64]

Thus, even such a liberal Russian politician as Count Witte had a positive attitude only toward completely acculturated Jews—those who did not irritate him by their Jewish appearance, accent, and manners.

The sons of Israel Brodsky, Lazar (1848-1904) and Leon (Lev, 1852-1923), inherited their father's businesses, and played prominent roles in the life of the Kiev Jewish community. At the beginning of the twentieth century, the brothers owned six companies. Their holdings included ten sugar-beet processing and three sugar refinery plants. In the 1890s, the Brodskys produced one quarter of all sugar in the Russian Empire.[65] Lazar Brodsky also owned major shareholdings in banks, and was the head of the municipal water supply company, a leading shareholder of a steamship company, and one of the richest merchants not only of Kiev but of the entire empire. He was the brightest figure and the most successful businessman in the Brodsky family.

Lazar and Leon Brodsky financed the construction of a number of public buildings in Kiev, many of them still in use. In the 1890s, they built two synagogues in downtown Kiev: the Choral Synagogue and the Merchant Synagogue. Jews in Kiev had striven for many years for permission to build a synagogue. From the 1860s on they had repeatedly asked for permission, but had been consistently rejected. The explanation was always the same: Kiev was located beyond the Pale of Jewish Settlement, it was a holy city for Orthodox Christians, and the construction of a synagogue would desecrate it. Kiev Jews were only allowed to have small prayer houses inside private homes. However, in 1895, permission was given to open a synagogue in the Plosskaia part (now Podol district) of Kiev, where poor Jews lived. The precedent of opening a synagogue in Kiev was thus established, but the local authorities still rejected the request for the construction of a synagogue in the city center. The wealthy Jews who lived downtown and in Pechersk district

---

64 Sidney Harcave, ed. and trans., *The Memoirs of Count Witte* (Armonk, NY: M. E. Sharpe, Inc., 1990), 87.
65 Kovalinskii, *Metsenaty Kieva*, 206.

could not walk to synagogue on Sabbath and Jewish holidays because it was located too far away. Furthermore, they were not eager to pray together with their poorer coreligionists. They wished to have a modern synagogue with a choir, like the choral synagogues in St. Petersburg, Moscow, and Odessa. Beginning in 1886, a group of wealthy Kiev Jews, led by Lazar Brodsky, repeatedly submitted petitions for the construction downtown of a choral synagogue "for educated Jews." However, the Kiev Provincial Administration rejected all of their requests.[66]

Permission to build a synagogue downtown was finally obtained after great difficulties in 1897 with the help of Lazar Brodsky's connections with the authorities. The Russian Senate decided to allow a synagogue to be built in downtown Kiev as Brodsky's private prayer house, and on September 18, 1897, Brodsky received permission from the Kiev Provincial Administration to build a synagogue on his own land. He allocated 95,000 rubles for its construction. "Lazar's eagerness to make the synagogue beautiful knew no bounds," wrote Alexandra Fanny Brodsky in her memoirs.[67] According to the original plan, the synagogue would have had three floors with a choir level on the top floor. However, the local authorities—who wished to make the synagogue in downtown Kiev as modest and invisible as possible—rejected this plan. They demanded that the synagogue look like a residential building. Finally, a compromise was struck, and a two-floor building designed by the architect Georgii Shleifer was accepted. Lev Ginzburg's construction company built the synagogue in less than a year.

On August 24, 1898, the Choral Synagogue was solemnly dedicated. However, the celebration of its opening was marred for Kiev Jews by the fact that their beloved Rabbi Evsei Tsukkerman was dismissed by the governor-general, apparently because of his sermon at the opening ceremony.[68] According to Lev Shtammer, Governor-General Fedor Fedorovich Trepov (the younger) attended the opening ceremony, dismissed

---

66 Kel'berin, *Desiatiletie Kievskogo evreiskogo khoral'nogo molitvennogo doma: 1898–1907*, 6–15.
67 Brodsky, *Smoke Signals*, 10.
68 Kel'berin, *Desiatiletie Kievskogo evreiskogo khoral'nogo molitvennogo doma: 1898–1907*, 21.

Rabbi Tsukkerman on the spot, and drove him out of the synagogue.[69] He was able to do so because Tsukkerman was a state rabbi, and was therefore subordinate to the state official. Owing to censorship, Tsukkerman's speech at the opening ceremony was never published. Tsukkerman had been the state rabbi of Kiev since the 1860s. Sholom Aleichem met the Kiev rabbi during his first visit to the city and left his recollection in his autobiographical novel *From the Fair*.[70] He compared the Kiev rabbi to

> the crown rabbis of the smaller towns he had known... Compared to them, the Kiev crown rabbi was a magnate...He was a giant. A good-looking man. His one flaw was he had... red hair[71] [people with red hair were often teased in Russia, because clowns had red hair] and was phlegmatic. He spoke slowly, moved slowly, thought slowly. A man without fire. People like him live to be a hundred. They're in no rush to die—they have plenty of time.[72]

But it seems unlikely that Tsukkerman's sermon alone provoked the governor-general's action. Perhaps it was in part the local administration's revenge for the imposition from above of permission to construct the synagogue in downtown. Rabbi Tsukkerman had actively supported Brodsky in the struggle for the right to build the synagogue. Tsukkerman and Brodsky had complained earlier to the Senate that the local authorities would not allow them to build a private prayer house on Brodsky's land. The Senate supported their request, and the synagogue was built. But perhaps this complaint caused Tsukkerman to lose his position.

The following year, Lev Brodsky financed construction of the Merchant Synagogue designed by the architect Vladimir Nikolaev, near the Choral Synagogue. These buildings still exist, and the Brodsky Choral Synagogue has been restored to its original purpose (it was used

---

69 Shtammer, *Na sud*, 14.
70 Curt Leviant, ed. and trans., *From the Fair: The Autobiography of Sholom Aleichem* (New York: Viking Penguin Inc., 1985), 262–263.
71 Sholom Aleichem, *Sobranie sochinenii* (Moscow: Khudozhestvennaia literatura, 1974), 6: 291–292.
72 Ibid.; Leviant, ed. and trans., *From the Fair*, 262–263.

as a puppet theater during Soviet times). The building of the former Merchant Synagogue is now a movie theater. Lazar Brodsky also financed the construction of many other buildings in Kiev, including the Bessarabskii Market, the Kiev Polytechnic Institute, the Bacteriology Institute, the Jewish State School (with an arts and crafts department that was named after his brother Solomon), a steam mill, and several large residential buildings.[73]

Both Jewish and anti-Semitic observers, some with irony, some with open anger and sarcasm, referred to Lazar Brodsky as the "Jewish King." Genrikh Sliozberg wrote in his memoirs:

> Lazar Izraelevich Brodsky was very influential in Kiev and in the entire southwestern region, [so that] all recognized him as the King and the master of the sugar industry of the Kiev district...Brodsky had private contacts with the majority of the governors-general...He had especially good relations with [Governor-]General Dragomirov, during whose rule the number of round-ups, checking and expulsions of Jews somewhat decreased.[74]

This influence on local authorities infuriated anti-Semites. Molchanov wrote in his article "From the Southwestern Region" in *Novoe vremia*,

> Lazar Brodsky, a golden idol, is recognized as the King of Kiev Jews and has despotic control there of the honor and credit, of the right of residence and even in some sense the right to live of the local Jews. He is one of the main Kiev bankers, the head of the city water-supply system, a large stockholder of the shipping company, the biggest of the local sugar industrialists and merchants. Without his protection, a Jew cannot receive credit at the bank, cannot get a good job, won't be admitted to the hospital; and, as shown by experience, if somebody dares

---

73 Kovalinskii, *Metsenaty Kieva*, 204–245.
74 G. B. Sliozberg, *Dela minuvshikh dnei: Zapiski russkogo evreia* (Paris: Imprimerie Pascal, 1933), 1: 282–283.

to go against Brodsky he will finish in a bad way....[Molchanov claims elsewhere in the article that Jews who did not please Brodsky had disappeared from the city.]⁷⁵

As always, anti-Semites exaggerated the power of Jews, but Lazar Brodsky certainly had significant influence over local affairs. For example, during his first visit to Kiev the young Sholom Aleichem, searching for a job, visited Rabbi Tsukkerman and received a recommendation letter to Herman Markovich Baratz,[76] "one of the lawyers in town, a Jewish intellectual who advised the governor-general." Baratz told him, "I'm angry at the crown rabbi. Day after day he keeps sending me young men. What can I do for them? What do I know? Who am I? What am I? I'm not Brodsky!"[77]

As a leader, Lazar Brodsky always attempted to solve problems in Jewish communal life through negotiation (the traditional practice of *shtadlanut*). During the pogroms of 1881–1882, he led a delegation of Kiev Jews to St. Petersburg, who attempted to persuade high officials to legalize Jewish emigration from the country. Jonathan Frankel writes that "a five-man delegation from Kiev, headed by Lazar Brodsky, went to St. Petersburg in August [1881]" to obtain governmental permission to legalize organized Jewish emigration.

> The group went with the strong backing of [Kiev, Podolia, and Volhynia Governor-General] Count [Alexander Mikhailovich] Dondukov-Korsakov. But, according to [Avraham Shalom] Friedberg's report, [Minister of the Interior Count Nicholai] Ignatev, on hearing the delegation's request, "jumped up and swore that as long as he were there such a policy would never

---

75 Molchanov, "Iz Iugo-Zapadnogo kraia."
76 Herman (Hirsh) Markovich Baratz (1835–1922) was an adviser on Jewish affairs to the Kiev, Podolia, and Volhynia governor-general; from 1871 to 1881, he served as censor of Jewish books. He published several works on the history of ancient Russian law; his chief work concerned the influence of the Bible and Talmudic sources on ancient Russian literature (*Encyclopedia Judaica*, 2nd ed., CD-ROM ed., s.v. "Baratz, Herman [Hirsh] Markovich").
77 Leviant, ed. and trans., *From the Fair*, 264.

be allowed." The meeting with the tsar, which Ignatev had promised to arrange, failed to materialize.[78]

At this moment, the effort of the Kiev Jewish delegation to legalize Jewish emigration from the country failed. However, in less than half a year, Minister of the Interior Ignat'ev completely changed his mind regarding Jewish emigration, at least of the non-organized kind. Ignat'ev told Dr. Orshanskii in January 1882, "The western border [of the Russian Empire] is open for Jews. Jews already use this right and their emigration has in no way been hindered."[79] Ignat'ev seemed to be expressing a basic change of government policy toward Russian Jews from one that aimed at assimilating the Jews into one of isolating them and driving them out of the country. However, when pressed on this point by the established integrationist leaders of Russian Jewry, Horace Guenzburg and Leo Bakst, he retreated somewhat. Indeed, according to an Austrian diplomat writing to Vienna on July 24, 1881, the tsar had asked Guenzburg and his associate A. I. Zak to use their influence to prevent emigration.[80] Unlike the St. Petersburg integrationists, the Kievan Jewish delegation, in their support for organized Jewish emigration, reflected their conviction that Judeophobia in Kiev was stronger than in other places in the empire.

The old methods of *shtadlanut*, used by Lazar Brodsky, in many cases worked well in his negotiations with local authorities. In the early 1890s, when Governor-General Aleksei Ignat'ev ordered the expulsion of a large number of poor Jews from Kiev, Lazar Brodsky offered to buy the practically worthless shares of Ignat'ev's unprofitable brewery for

---

78 Jonathan Frankel, *Prophecy and Politics: Socialism, Nationalism, and the Russian Jews, 1862–1917* (Cambridge: Cambridge University Press, 1981), 62.
79 S. M. Dubnov, *Noveishaia istoriia evreiskogo naroda: Ot Frantsuzskoi revoliutsii do nashikh dnei* (Moscow: Gesharim, 2002), 3: 110.
80 A. Orbach, "The Pogroms of 1881–1882: The Response from St Petersburg Jewry," *The Carl Beck Papers in Russian and East European Studies*, no. 308 (Pittsburgh, PA: University of Pittsburgh, 1984), 24–28; N. M. Gelber, "The Pogroms in Russia" (in Yiddish), in *Historishe Shriftn* (Vilna: Kultur lige, 1937), 2, 487; Hans Rogger, "Government Policy on Jewish Emigration," *Jewish Policies and Right-Wing Politics in Imperial Russia* (Berkeley and Los Angeles: University of California Press, 1986), 178–179.

300,000 rubles, if "the expulsion of poor Jews from Kiev were stopped, together with the agitation for a pogrom."[81] The governor-general accepted his offer. Before he offered the deal, Lazar Brodsky had consulted with Baron Rothschild in Paris, who was a friend of his brother Leon.[82] Rothschild approved of Lazar's plan.

Genrikh Sliozberg wrote, "Kiev Jews are much more worried about changes in the mood of the Kiev governor-general than about the orders of the Ministry of the Interior," because it was the governor-general who decided to increase or decrease police persecution of Jews.[83] According to the journalist A. E. Kaufman,

> Kiev police beat all records by their persecution and oppression of Jews. The highest officers of the local police—it was no secret to anybody in Kiev—received a large bribe at New Year's, which was gathered as a special tax by the representatives of the Jewish community. Jews paid for the right to reside in Kiev in general and paid additionally for the right to reside in particular districts of the city.[84]

Thus Brodsky, as leader of the Kiev Jewish community, often bribed the authorities as the only way to save Kiev Jews from expulsion. This tactic worked well during his leadership. Before he became president of the community and after his death, mass expulsions of Jews from Kiev took place, but this did not happen under his leadership.[85] He used similar methods to neutralize influential anti-Semites. A good example is his relations with Dmitrii Ivanovich Pikhno (1850–1913), professor of political economy at Kiev St. Vladimir University,

---

81 Brodsky, *Smoke Signals*, 12.
82 Ibid.
83 Sliozberg, *Dela minuvshikh dnei*, 1: 281.
84 A. E. Kaufman, *Druz'ia i vragi evreev: D. I. Pikhno* (St. Petersburg: Knigoizdatel'stvo Pravda, 1907), 18.
85 In 1886, more than 2,000 Jewish families were expelled from Kiev, and in the spring of 1910, 1,200 Jewish families were banished from the city (S. M. Dubnov, *History of the Jews* [South Brunswick, NJ: Thomas Yoseloff, 1973], 5: 553, 768). According to the census of 1897, the total number of Jews in Kiev was 31,801, hence a significant percentage of the Kiev Jewish population was expelled in these two events.

and from 1878 on journalist and editor of *Kievlianin*. Since the mid-1860s, the newspaper had published a number of Judeophobic articles, which blamed the Jews for exploiting the local population, opposed increasing Jewish legal rights, and contained numerous attacks against Jews.[86] Pikhno recounted as fact a story about a Berdichev Jewish woman who gave birth to a piglet, and how local Jews did not know what to do with it—either to bury it, or throw it into a cesspit. He claimed that all Jews were "parasites," called them "Jerusalem nobles," and complained about the "Yids' invasion" of the southwestern region and Kiev. He proposed the expulsion of Jews from state schools and from the city, and specifically demanded the "expulsion of Mr. Brodsky from Kiev."[87]

However, Brodsky found a way to pacify even such a rabid Judeophobe as Pikhno. The official version is that Brodsky and Pikhno, improbably, became close friends. Certainly a strange metamorphosis occurred, as Pikhno and *Kievlianin* became best friends of the Jews. Kaufman writes that from the beginning of this friendship in the 1890s, *Kievlianin* published such philo-Semitic articles, and showed so much compassion towards persecuted Jews, that these articles could easily have been published in the Jewish press. The new *Kievlianin* condemned the persecution of Jews by the local government, expressed indignation at anti-Jewish pogroms and the Dreyfus Affair, and demanded the abolition of restrictive laws against Jews and the end of expulsions of Jews from Kiev.[88] Pikhno was apparently richly rewarded for his articles supporting the Jews. Kaufman reports that "when Pikhno bought property, Brodsky participated in these purchases. One of Brodsky's properties in Podolia was transferred to Pikhno."[89] Lazar Brodsky also built the Kiev

---

[86] John D. Klier, "*Kievlianin* and the Jews: A Decade of Disillusionment, 1864–1873," *Harvard Ukrainian Studies* 5, no. 1 (1981): 92–101; V. G., *Russkie gazety po otnosheniiu k nekotorym iz sovremennykh voprosov*, part I, *"Kievlianin" po evreiskomu voprosu* (Kiev: n.p., 1880): 1–19. *Kievlianin* was established in 1864 by professor of history of Kiev St. Vladimir University, Vitalii Iakovlevich Shul'gin (1822–1878). After his death in 1878, Shul'gin's friend and colleague Dmitrii Pikhno took all his rights, including control of the newspaper, and also married Shul'gin's widow and later his daughter.

[87] V. G., *Russkie gazety po otnosheniiu k nekotorym iz sovremennykh voprosov*, 5–18.

[88] Kaufman, *Druz'ia i vragi evreev*, 10–28.

[89] Ibid., 31.

Bacteriological Institute on Pikhno's suggestion, and Pikhno was repeatedly elected to the institute's board with Brodsky's support.

Pikhno's idyllic relationship with the Jews lasted until Brodsky's death in 1904. Deprived of Jewish financial support, Pikhno reverted to his original anti-Semitic views and attacked Jews even more furiously than before. During the Russo-Japanese War, *Kievlianin* declared all Jews to be traitors and enemies of Russia, and later wrote that Japan had won the war because it was financed by Jewish money.[90]

During the Kiev pogrom of October 1905, the Black Hundreds "patriotic" processions came to the *Kievlianin* publishing house, where they gave a noisy greeting to editor Pikhno, who blessed the crowd for their "heroic deeds." Then the crowd went on to enthusiastically fulfill its "patriotic duty" of attacking Jews.[91] The pogrom continued for three days; about one hundred Jews were killed, over four hundred were wounded, and most Jewish property in the city was destroyed. These riots occurred with the connivance of the local authorities, and a number of policemen and soldiers took part in the pillaging and murder of Jews.[92] After the pogrom, Pikhno expressed his satisfaction that the Jews had received a good lesson and had become more "calm." The Russian authorities appreciated Pikhno's new "patriotic" feelings. He was appointed a member of the State Council (*Gosudarstvennyi Sovet*), and even was considered for appointment as prime minister (i.e., chairman of the Council of Ministers) of Russia in 1906.

Pikhno then underwent yet another metamorphosis, telling a correspondent of a foreign newspaper that "I am not an anti-Semite," and that people were mistaken in considering him an enemy of the Jews. He said that Jews had even elected him to public positions (i.e., as board member of the Kiev Bacteriological Institute, where he was elected a life member, as requested by Lazar Brodsky in his will).[93]

---

90 Ibid., 28–29.
91 Ibid., 8–9.
92 John D. Klier and Shlomo Lambroza, eds., *Pogroms: Anti-Jewish Violence in Modern Russian History* (Cambridge: Cambridge University Press, 1992), 231; Victoria Khiterer, "The October 1905 Pogrom in Kiev," *East European Jewish Affairs* 22, no. 2 (1992): 21–37.
93 Kaufman, *Druz'ia i vragi evreev*, 7–8.

Lazar and Leon Brodsky were famous for their generous philanthropic activity not only towards Jews, but also for all Kiev citizens. Such actions drew criticism from some members of the Jewish community. Badanes complained that Lazar Brodsky spent money on Kiev's gentile population, while many Jews lived in poverty.[94] Contemporaries, as well as some modern scholars, have also criticized the anti-democratic methods of the Jewish magnates in Russia, including the Brodsky family. Molchanov wrote that "the Jewish crowd is sick and tired of Jewish moneybags with their despotism and demands for royal honors and sheep-like obedience."[95] He also criticized the way Lazar Brodsky distributed charity among the poor:

> There is a great comedy in this charity. Each Wednesday on Kreshchatik Street a crowd of Jewish beggars gathers, they wait in the rain and snow for several hours. Finally they are allowed to come into the Jewish palace and there the Jewish King Brodsky himself distributes charity by the *grosh*, believing the honor of seeing him is worth a ruble.[96]

However, the leadership style of Brodsky and other Jewish grandees, as well as the nature of their relations with the authorities, was a product of their time. Russian grandees of the same period exhibited a similar pattern of behavior with respect to their poor coreligionists, although the Jewish magnates were usually more generous. Alexandra Fanny Brodsky admitted that "All the wealthy branches of the Brodsky family emulated the lavish life-style of the Russian landowners."[97] In an autocratic country, Jewish community leaders adopted authoritarian methods in managing communal affairs. Following the 1905 Revolution, power in the Kiev Jewish community was transferred to the elected Representative Board for Jewish Welfare. But, as has been shown, the influence and power of the Brodsky family as communal leaders still

---

94 Badanes, *S odnogo vola tri shkury*, 20.
95 Molchanov, "Iz Iugo-Zapadnogo kraia."
96 Ibid.
97 Brodsky, *Smoke Signals*, 4.

remained significant. Nevertheless, the successful conduct of communal affairs by the Jewish elite, including the Brodsky family, depended primarily upon the political situation and only secondarily upon their personal inclinations.

Despite their close cooperation and warm family relations, the brothers Lazar and Leon Brodsky were quite different in their styles of dealing with people. According to Alexandra Fanny Brodsky, "Leon displayed a loathsome ruthlessness in his dealing with staff, some of whom were related to him."[98] She also recollected that their cousin Alexander Brodsky urged both brothers "to pay higher wages to their employees, pointing out that people worked better if they were not troubled by constant worries about meeting their family's needs."[99] Others also complained about the low salaries and difficult working conditions at the Brodsky enterprises. A worker at Lazar Brodsky's steam mill in Kiev wrote in his memoirs:

> Like the adult porters I successfully carried sacks weighing five *puds* each.[100] The conditions of work were difficult: unbelievable dust, we did not receive any special work clothes, we had to carry the sacks up planks over bridges that were untrustworthy and broke all the time, the workers fell and were injured. The required work norms were high, for filling them completely a porter received seventy-five kopecks a day for working twelve hours [this was the normal pay for an unskilled laborer]. The attitude of our overseers was unbearable, including beatings…
>
> Gradually we began to express our dissatisfaction, and this led to an organized protest to the mill managers. The mill representative came to us and said: "You are still under-age porters; we gave you the job because we counted on you being an example of good discipline, but you are not! You dare to

---

98 Ibid., 14.
99 Ibid.
100 A *pud* is an old Russian measure of weight: one *pud* is a bit more than thirty-six pounds; thus five *puds* is over 180 pounds.

organize a protest. Do you know what will happen to you if we call the police? We'll fire you so that the other workers don't follow your example." About ten young porters were then thrown out onto the street.

I was the main instigator of this protest and the workers expressed their sympathy for me, and facetiously said: "You see—our owner's name is Lazar, your name is also Lazar, so why don't you tell him: 'Why did Lazar fire Lazar, it is not good, probably he will be ashamed and take you back and increase your pay.'" Everybody laughed and said, yes, wait for mercy from the bloodsucker![101]

The author of this account was Lazar Kaganovich, who came to Kiev as a young boy and later became a dedicated communist and leader of the Communist Party of the Soviet Union. As an important member of the Soviet government, Kaganovich was one of the most faithful of Stalin's henchman.[102]

The conditions of work at the Brodsky plants and factories were certainly as difficult as at other plants and factories in the Russian Empire. The long working hours, low wages, and absence of safety precautions were reasons for strikes at many enterprises in the beginning of the twentieth century. The Brodsky enterprises were no exception.

However, in the context of the time, the "old capitalists" still came out as relatively kind and generous, considering their philanthropy and attempts to provide aid to the sick and the poor. The charity of Lazar and Leon Brodsky helped many.

In particular, they felt a certain *noblesse oblige* to aid struggling Jewish intelligentsia. The Brodskys, like other wealthy Jewish families, "created around themselves a circle of 'learned wise men who were otherwise unemployable' but still could serve as teachers, secretaries, accountants and cashiers."[103] Thus the Hebrew poet Yehalel, who was

---

101 Lazar' Kaganovich, *Pamiatnye zapiski: Moi 20 vek* (Moscow: Vagrius, 1996), 60–61.
102 Ibid., 5.
103 Gennady Estraikh, "From Yehupets Jargonists to Kiev Modernists: The Rise of a Yiddish Literary Centre, 1880s–1914," *East European Jewish Affairs* 30, no. 1

one of the first members of the early Zionist movement *Hovevei Zion*, in 1870 was employed as a cashier at the Brodsky sugar mill and as a tutor and secretary by the Brodsky family. Later, Yehalel became an adviser to Leon Brodsky. He worked for the Brodsky family until the Soviet authorities closed their businesses in 1918.[104] In *From the Fair*, Sholom Aleichem describes his meeting with Yehalel at the Brodsky steam mill.[105] The historian Il'ia Galant was also employed as a secretary by the Brodsky family before the revolution.[106] The Brodsky family funded the education of gifted young people, of whom some subsequently became prominent cultural figures. Moshe (Mikhail) Milner (1886–1953)—a Jewish composer who wrote music for the Hebrew theater "*Habima*" and the State Jewish Theater (GOSET), and was the musical director of the Jewish Voice Ensemble "*Evokans*"—began his career as a *hazan*[107] at the Brodsky synagogue in Kiev. The financial support of the Brodsky family enabled him to study at the St. Petersburg Conservatory.[108] The patronage of the Brodsky family helped many talented people and allowed them to contribute to Jewish cultural life.

Lazar Brodsky was awarded the French Order of the Legion of Honor in 1900 and the Russian medals of Stanislav, Anna, and St. Vladimir for his philanthropic activity. He held the title of Commercial Adviser, and was vice president of the Kiev Stock Exchange Committee. According to Alfred Rieber,

> The committee also enjoyed cordial relations with the Kiev intellectual community, the local branch of the Russian Technological Society, the university, and the Agricultural Society. Their mutual cooperation flowered in the Kiev Polytechnical

---

(Summer 2000): 22.
104 Khiterer, "The Brodsky Sugar Kings," 33.
105 Sholom Aleichem, *Sobranie sochinenii*, 6 (Moscow: Khudozhestvennaia literatura, 1974), 287–288; Leviant, ed. and trans., *From the Fair*, 257–259.
106 Victoria Khiterer, *Dokumenty, sobrannye Evreiskoi istoriko-arkheograficheskoi komissiei Vseukrainskoi Akademii Nauk* (Jerusalem: Institut Iudaiki, Gesharim, 1999), 14.
107 Hazan—the official of a synagogue who conducts the liturgical part of the service and sings or chants the prayers intended to be performed as solos.
108 Khiterer, "The Brodsky Sugar Kings," 33.

Institute. On the initiative of the enormously wealthy Jewish sugar-beet industrialist Lazar I. Brodsky and his brother Lev, a conference of Kiev university professors, engineers, and representatives of industry launched a campaign to found the institute. Half the original capital was raised by Brodskii and N. A. Tereshchenko, a Ukrainian sugar magnate, patron of the arts, and future minister in the provisional government.[109]

The Kiev Polytechnic Institute, which was founded in 1898, became the second school of higher education in the city after Kiev St. Vladimir University.

It is astonishing how much Lazar Brodsky achieved in his comparatively short life of fifty-six years. He died suddenly in Basel on September 19, 1904 while he was visiting his daughter Maria, who lived there with her husband Jules Dreyfus. Lazar Brodsky was buried in the Luk'ianovskii cemetery in Kiev.[110]

After his death, control over family business affairs was transferred to his brother Leon (Lev). However, Leon lacked the inclination for systematic work on business problems. At an early age, Leon had made an unsuccessful attempt to establish an independent business in Odessa,

> but after a time unwise business transactions caused him to lose 1,000,000 rubles. His father forced him to sell his house and he moved into three small back rooms of his father's house in Kiev until he was able to restore his financial position. In due course he re-established his independence...[111]

Various memoirs refer to Leon Brodsky as a womanizer; his first two wives died young and, until he remarried later in life, he reportedly became embroiled in various scandalous affairs with women. One story unraveled quite dramatically for him as reported by *Kievlianin*:

---

109 Alfred J. Rieber, *Merchants and Entrepreneurs in Imperial Russia* (Chapel Hill: University of North Carolina Press, 1982), 106–107.
110 Kovalinskii, *Metsenaty Kieva*, 234–235; Khiterer, "The Brodsky Sugar Kings," 33.
111 Brodsky, *Smoke Signals*, 5.

On May 8 [1899] around 7 p.m. in the front room of the Kiev Nobles' Club, a former governess and French subject, De La Ruse, a 30-year-old woman, lay in wait for Lev Izraelevich Brodsky, who was leaving the Club, and suddenly splashed his face with sulfuric acid from a perfume bottle. L. I. Brodsky's left eye and the left side of his face were badly burned. The crime was inspired by personal revenge of a romantic nature. The culprit did not try to escape and was detained by the police.[112]

Leon Brodsky was also an avid gambler. According to Count Witte, he spent most of the year at casino resorts. Witte recalled that he often met him in Biarritz,

> where he spends part of the year because the card playing there is heavy. Just recently I was visited by someone who had just returned from Nice. When I asked who was there from Russia, he told me that he had seen Lev Brodskii lose 600,000 francs there in the course of a week.[113]

Brodsky also led a bohemian way of life in Kiev. In one of his penthouses, he opened his own casino "Concordia."[114] He was a fervent admirer of the theater, and bought the Russian Dramatic Theater building in Kiev, which was often called Solovtsov's Theater after the name of its director.[115] The building, which was constructed in 1898, is now the Ukrainian Drama Theater of Ivan Franko.[116]

Like his brother Lazar, Leon Brodsky was a generous philanthropist. He was among the founding benefactors of the first public library in Kiev and of the Museum of Arts and Industry. During World War I, he contributed to a committee that provided aid for injured soldiers. According to Solomon Ansky, during the war Leon Brodsky sent wagonloads of flour and sugar to the Galician Jewish population, which was

---

112 *Kievlianin*, May 10, 1899, no. 128.
113 Harcave, ed. and trans., *The Memoirs of Count Witte*, 87.
114 Khiterer, "The Brodsky Sugar Kings," 34.
115 Kovalinskii, *Metsenaty Kieva*, 235–236; Brodsky, *Smoke Signals*, 14.
116 Kovalinskii, *Metsenaty Kieva*, 236.

suffering pogroms, famine, and expulsions under Russian military occupation.[117] Brodsky was a member of various philanthropic organizations, and was awarded several Russian medals as well as the Order of the French Legion of Honor for this activity. He was also an honorary trustee of the Kiev Jewish hospital, to which he donated hundreds of thousands of rubles. Together with his brother Lazar, he gave 460,000 rubles for the establishment of the Jewish State Artisan School in Kiev, and, as already mentioned, he built the Merchant Synagogue in downtown Kiev.

In spite of his unconventional lifestyle, Leon Brodsky was very ambitious and attempted to take a prominent position in the Kiev Jewish community as well as in the world of Russian Jewry. In 1912, Leon sold his shares in the Aleksandrovskii Sugar Refining Corporation, and devoted all his time to Jewish public affairs.[118] After Lazar's death, he served as chairman of the Kiev Jewish Welfare Committee, and he represented the Kiev Jewish community at the Convention of Jewish Communal Leaders in Kovno in 1909.[119] Leon also led such important organizations as the Kiev department of the Society for Spreading Enlightenment among Jews in Russia (OPE) and the Jewish Emigration Society. "One wag had commented only half-jokingly at an OPE meeting in 1905, 'That's why we voted for Brodsky as chairman, so we would always have money!'"[120]

However, during the process of democratization of Kiev Jewish institutions in 1906, Dr. Max Mandelstamm was elected chairman of the Kiev department of the OPE instead of Leon Brodsky. Mandelstamm was not as wealthy as Brodsky, who thereupon stopped contributing to the society. Within a year the Kiev department of the OPE indeed faced major financial difficulties. According to Meir,

> Not surprisingly, the lack of funding proved to be a serious problem: the 1907 annual report repeated over and again that

---

117 S. Ansky, *The Dybbuk and Other Writings*, ed. David G. Roskies (New York: Schocken Books, 1992), 173.
118 Mikhail Kalnitsky, "Sakharnye koroli," *Vedomosti*, January 30, 2006.
119 "Otchet o soveshchanii evreiskikh obshchestvennykh deiatelei, proiskhodivshem v Kovno 19–22 noiabria 1909 goda," 44.
120 Meir, *Kiev, Jewish Metropolis*, 303.

many important activities had to be put on hold "in view of limited resources." The OPE was already facing criticism from the community for its lack of accomplishments. Even a member of the Society's own Adult Education Commission, L. E. Dynin, wrote in the newspaper *Khronika evreiskoi zhizni* (Chronicle of Jewish Life) that the society was good at promising things but not delivering on them.[121]

As a result, in 1909 the board of the Kiev branch of the OPE recommended that Leon Brodsky and Baron V. G. Ginsburg again be elected to the board. Both were elected, however Ginsburg declined the position.[122] According to Meir, Brodsky quickly improved the financial situation of the Kiev branch of the OPE:

Though the society's programs were apparently not affected, its fiscal standing improved dramatically, as did—perhaps more significantly—its standing among Kiev's Jewish haute bourgeoisie.[123]

Brodsky was now placed in charge of a new Finance Committee, and was also made honorary chairman of the Library Commission and the Board of Trustees of the model *heder*, which the OPE had set up. The financial situation improved greatly due to his contributions and those he induced others to make. One major fundraising initiative was a gala concert of Jewish folk music followed by a ball, which raised over five thousand rubles. He also gave interest-bearing securities to the OPE, which further increased its income.[124]

As leader of the Kiev Jewish community, Leon Brodsky advocated active opposition to the existing regime. Whereas Lazar had carefully avoided political struggle and preferred to use negotiation with the authorities to solve all problems, Leon used other methods. The situation of the Jews in the Russian Empire was drastically changing for the

---

121 Ibid.
122 Ibid., 304.
123 Ibid.
124 Ibid., 305.

worse at the turn of the twentieth century. Anti-Semitism was acquiring an ever more violent character. The wave of anti-Jewish pogroms of 1905-1906, the Beilis affair, the activity of anti-Semitic organizations, and increased state anti-Semitism did not leave Jewish leaders many possibilities for negotiation with the authorities. The previous methods of *shtadlanut* did not work anymore. These developments, even more than Leon Brodsky's personal inclinations, dictated his policies as the Kiev Jewish community's leader.

During the 1905 Revolution, Leon Brodsky still hoped for the liberalization of the political regime in the country and the removal of restrictive laws against Jews. He attempted to draw the attention of Russian public opinion to the question of Jewish civil rights, and to refute attacks on Jews by the anti-Semitic press. When on May 28, 1905, the newspaper *Rizhskii vestnik* (Riga Herald) published an anti-Semitic article "Regarding Equal Rights for Jews" by Mikhail Dragomirov, who had been the Kiev, Podolia, and Volhynia governor-general between 1898 and 1903, Brodsky wrote an open letter from Paris on June 9, 1905 to the publishing house of the newspaper. This letter was never published, but was forwarded by the publisher to the chancellery of the Kiev, Podolia, and Volhynia governor-general and placed in its archives. Brodsky wrote:

> General Dragomirov is indignant that Jews strive for equal rights with other members of the population in access to secondary and higher education; he claims that the percentage quota for Jews of 5-7 percent exactly corresponds to the percentage of Jews in the entire population. He is surprised that Jews are not satisfied with this norm and considers this a manifestation of their impudence. I think that the method of calculating percentages of the entire population should not be used in this case, because it is well known that a significant part of the Russian population, regrettably, still lives in ignorance and does not have any education. If we compare the number of literate people among the Russian and Jewish peoples then it becomes obvious that the quota of 5-7 percent

is very unfair and is one of the significant ways that Jews are persecuted in Russia.

Dragomirov notes that Jews occupy the majority of positions in financial and commercial companies; however this fact cannot be used as an accusation against Jews. It merely proves that Jews are more capable in financial and commercial affairs than Russians.

Regarding the cases mentioned by General Dragomirov where Jews ostensibly refused to fulfill their duties during the current mobilization, I cannot check the instances he provides. However, from the beginning of the [Russo-Japanese] war about 30,000 Jews and 200,000 Russians have been killed in combat, so the percentage of Jewish victims versus their percentage of the entire population was significantly larger than Christians.

Finally, regarding the main idea that the Jews do not deserve civil rights because they do not recognize their civil obligations, this idea is amazing in its lack of logic; even though it is true that Jews evade military service, we cannot, based on this fact, make groundless accusations against all Jews, who live under restrictive laws. Jews neglect their civil duties because they are aware of their exceptional treatment under Russian law.

This can be proved by the example of Western European countries, where there are no restrictive laws against Jews; none of these states complain that Jews neglect their civic duties; there they fulfill their duties equally with the native populations and, if necessary, sacrifice their lives like other citizens.

It is hardly possible to demand the expression of civic feelings by Russian Jews when the laws restrict and persecute them…[125]

Although Leon Brodsky's open letter was never published, his point of view was well known to other Jewish public figures. One of

---

125 TsDIAK U, f. 442, op. 855, d. 26, l. 35.

Leon Brodsky's critics, the Zionist and Hebrew writer Eliezer Friedmann, wrote that Brodsky was

> a man "frozen in the period of the Haskalah" who is unfamiliar with progressive currents in Jewry. He knows nothing about self-emancipation, continuing to believe that European civilization will bring the Jews a better future through equal rights and economic freedom.[126]

However, this critique misrepresents Brodsky's point of view. In contrast to Jewish public figures of the Haskalah period, Brodsky did not anticipate equal rights for Jews until the liberalization of the Russian Empire's political regime. However, for a while Brodsky believed that a better future for Jews in Russia was possible, which led him to reject Zionism. In addition, as we have seen, prestige played an important part in his conflict with Max Mandelstamm over their respective roles in the OPE. When the first Russian revolution was suppressed, with much attendant anti-Jewish violence, Brodsky's hopes were dashed. He abandoned the idea of the assimilation of Jews into Russian culture and emphasized the importance of preserving Jewish national identity. From this point forward, Brodsky directed most of his efforts toward supporting the emigration of Jews to America, but he remained skeptical of the Zionist project.

Before the bloody anti-Jewish pogroms of October 1905, Leon Brodsky still believed in the possibility of the liberalization of the autocratic Russian state and the granting of equal rights to Jews. Like many other residents of Kiev, he enthusiastically welcomed the Tsar's Manifesto of October 17, 1905, which promised freedom of speech and assembly as well as the establishment of a State Duma. In fact, many people considered this manifesto to be the first Russian constitution. The stepson of Dmitrii Pikhno, Vasilii Shul'gin, described the day of the declaration of the manifesto in Kiev—October 18—as follows:

---

126 *Kiever vort*, January 6, 1910, no. 5, cited in Natan Meir, "From Pork to Kapores: Transformations in Religious Practice among the Jews of Late Imperial Kiev," *Jewish Quarterly Review* 97, no. 4 (Fall 2007): 616–645.

Something unbelievable was going on in the city. Seemingly everybody who could walk came onto the streets. At least all of the Jews. However, it seemed that there were more Jews than there really were because of their provocative behavior. They did not hide their jubilation.[127]

Leon Brodsky and another prominent Kiev Jewish industrialist and philanthropist, David Margolin, were members of the Board of Trustees of the Kiev Second Commercial School, which had a significant number of Jewish students. On the day of the declaration of the October Manifesto, Brodsky and Margolin gathered many students of the First and Second Commercial Schools, as well as students from the Women's Commercial School of Volodkevich, and organized a "liberation" trip for them on the Dnieper River. According to a well-known anti-Semite, Aleksei Shmakov, Brodsky and Margolin invited the students onto Margolin's ship "to celebrate the Constitution." As Shmakov described it, the Russian national flag on the ship was torn down and a red flag raised. Then everybody sang the *Marseillaise* and gave speeches. After the trip, the students were taken to Margolin's dacha on an island in the river. A subsequent government investigation verified that these events occurred, but did not note whether or not Brodsky or Margolin were on the ship. That night, by the time the ship returned to Kiev, an anti-Jewish pogrom—provoked by this behavior, according to Shmakov—had already begun in the city. Margolin's and Brodsky's homes were ransacked, supposedly in revenge.[128] Given the timing of the pogrom, this is clearly an ex post facto justification. Moreover, the mansions of other wealthy Kiev Jews such as Landau, Zaitsev, Leon's cousin Alexander Brodsky, and Baron Ginsburg, none of whom are known to have taken part in any celebrations, were also pillaged.[129] Shmakov further complained that in spite of their "liberation trip," "the pious Jews"—Margolin and Brodsky—were allowed to remain

---
127 V. V. Shul'gin, *Gody-dni-1920* (Moscow: Novosti, 1990), 340–341.
128 A. S. Shmakov, *Pogrom evreev v Kieve: Ocherk* (Moscow: Imperatorskii Moskovskii universitet Publishing House, 1908), 73–74.
129 *Kievlianin*, October 20, 1905, no. 290.

trustees [of the school] and used their position "to dismiss almost all 'Black Hundreds' teachers."¹³⁰

Brodsky's confrontations with the authorities became even sharper after the defeat of the 1905 Revolution. He participated in the Convention of Jewish Communal Leaders in Kovno on November 19–22, 1909, and was elected a member of the presidium. The basket tax was discussed at length. The Russian Jewish press had been complaining since the 1890s that the basket tax was unfair to the poor and should be replaced by an income tax.¹³¹ Brodsky saw an additional reason for abolishing the basket tax in the way that the tax money was used. He argued that

> [t]he basket tax should be eliminated, not only because it is unfair to the poor, but also because it is often used for anti-Jewish purposes. The Kiev [Jewish] community, for example, gives 15,000 rubles [from the tax] annually to the city Duma for financing the police, so that the police can…expel Jews from Kiev.¹³²

Some participants at this convention attempted to defend the basket tax on Orthodox religious grounds. They said that liquidation of the tax would undermine the spirit of Judaism. Brodsky's reply was that

> [i]t is not the Kovno Convention that keeps this spirit alive. You don't need to worry about the spirit of Judaism; it is as eternal as the Sun.¹³³

Leon Brodsky's eloquence, sharp mind, generosity, and ambition made him a natural leader. In 1912, after the death of Max Mandelstamm, the founder and first leader of the Emigration Society, Brodsky was elected to succeed him as president. This society, with its Central Committee in Kiev and in cooperation with American and European

---

130 Shmakov, *Pogrom evreev v Kieve*, 73–74.
131 B. Bogrov, "K voprosu o zamene korobochnogo sbora," *Voskhod* (1894), 2: 1–13.
132 "Otchet o soveshchanii evreiskikh obshchestvennykh deiatelei," 44.
133 Ibid.

Jewish organizations, assisted the emigration of Jews from throughout the Russian Empire to America through the port of Galveston, Texas. It had a number of local committees and representatives in various cities and shtetls in the Pale of Settlement. By 1913 these representatives numbered 324.[134] They and the local committees were responsible for the selection of candidates, helping them to obtain the necessary emigration documents, giving them information about emigration to Galveston, and organizing a preliminary medical exam for them (in preparation for the final medical exam given upon arrival in the United States). The Jewish Emigration Society in Kiev and its local departments paid up to 50 percent of travel expenses to America, which made emigration feasible even for poor Jewish families.

The Galveston Project was intended to open a new gateway to America, and to encourage Jewish immigration to the American West, as an alternative to northeastern American port cities where many immigrants lived in overcrowded and slum conditions. Between 1901 and 1913, over half a million Jewish immigrants came to the United States. Most settled in New York, Boston, Philadelphia, and Baltimore, and many had problems finding work and accommodations. A scholar of Jewish emigration, Iakov Leshchinskii, wrote in 1909 that two thirds of the Russian Jews who immigrated to the United States were unemployed for an average of one year. The majority of Russian Jews who found jobs in America worked in sweatshops, where labor conditions were very hard.[135] Jewish immigrants created ghetto colonies, which, in the opinion of an opponent of immigration, "were hotbeds of disease, sedition, and moral depravity."[136] The US Congress considered restricting Jewish immigration at the beginning of the twentieth century. The US administration also attempted to spread immigrants around the country, as did Jewish and state government organizations, but without much success. It became obvious that immigrants who

---

134 *Otchet o deiatel'nosti Evreiskogo emigratsionnogo obshchestva za 1913 god* (Kiev: Rabotnik, 1914), 40.
135 Iakov Leshchinskii, "K psikhologii evreiskogo emigranta," *Evreiskii mir* (November –December 1909): 42–50.
136 Bernard Marinbach, *Galveston: Ellis Island of the West* (Albany: State University of New York Press, 1983), 4.

were already settled in northeastern American cities were not inclined to move elsewhere. Thus was born the idea for the Galveston Movement to redirect Jewish immigration to the western states, which badly needed laborers.

Leon Brodsky was a generous contributor to the Galveston Project, and donated significant sums to the Emigration Society in Kiev from the moment of its establishment in 1909. The necessity for large-scale emigration of Jews from Russia was obvious to him. In spite of their wealth, even the Brodsky family did not feel safe in Tsarist Russia. According to the memoirs of Alexandra Fanny Brodsky, some members of the family discussed the possibility of immigrating to California. However, all their capital was invested in Russian industry, and the tight restrictions on the export of currency from the Russian Empire kept them in the country.[137]

As the president of the Emigration Society, Leon Brodsky coordinated its work with the other Jewish organizations involved in the Galveston Project. In the summer of 1913, he went to London where he discussed the Galveston Project with its other supporters—the American and British Jewish philanthropists Jacob Schiff and Leopold de Rothschild, as well as the English Jewish author and president of the Jewish Territorial Organization, Israel Zangwill. During this meeting, a difference of opinion arose between Brodsky and the other leaders about the future of Jews in America. Brodsky asserted:

> I want these emigrants…to become not only good citizens of the country that gave them refuge, but also to remain good Jews.[138]

For this reason Brodsky considered it necessary for all Jewish immigrants to be concentrated in one state, and not to be dispersed throughout the United States. He proposed to accomplish this by

---

[137] "Report of L. I. Brodsky to the General Meeting of the Members Jewish Emigration Society, November 3, 1913," *Otchet o deiatel'nosti Evreiskogo emigratsionnogo obshchestva za 1913 god* (Kiev: Rabotnik, 1914), 77–80; Brodsky, *Smoke Signals*, 5–16.

[138] "Report of L. I. Brodsky to the General Meeting of the Members Jewish Emigration Society, November 3, 1913," 77–80.

creating Jewish agricultural settlements in one of the locations where Jewish immigrants were concentrated.[139] His plan for creating such settlements was not unique at the time. In 1900, the Jewish Colonization Association and the Baron de Hirsch Fund had joined together "to establish a credit institution for the establishment and maintenance of agricultural and industrial homesteads, known as the Jewish Agricultural and Industrial Aid Society."[140] Like the members of this society, Brodsky dreamed of settling Jews on the land. He proposed the creation of agricultural settlements where Jews could live according to their traditions and resist assimilation, and saw this as an alternative to condemning Jewish immigrants to work in urban sweatshops.

However, this plan was utopian. Most Jewish immigrants in the United States were town-dwellers and had neither the inclination nor the skills for agricultural work. In addition, the US government opposed the creation of areas for territorially compact immigrant settlement. Brodsky's proposal was also unacceptable to the other leaders of the Galveston Movement.

There were other points of disagreement. Brodsky believed that the Jewish Emigration Society should help the poorest Jews first, because they were perishing in Russia.[141] In contrast, the American representatives of the project demanded that the Russian Emigration Society not send destitute Jews to Galveston because the local US Immigration Service often rejected them. They required that each immigrant who arrived in Galveston be carrying at least ten dollars. In fact, however, the great majority of emigrants sent to America by the Kiev Emigration Society were poor or very poor, and some of them came literally barefoot to Galveston. 23 percent of the emigrants were from cities that were district centers, and only 16.3 percent from large cities. Almost two thirds of these emigrants (60.7 percent) were inhabitants of shtetls, reflecting the impoverishment and unemployment in the shtetls.[142]

---

139 Ibid.
140 Marinbach, *Galveston*, 3.
141 "Report of L. I. Brodsky to the General Meeting of the Members Jewish Emigration Society, November 3, 1913," 77–80.
142 Iakov Leshchinskii, *Gal'vestonskaia emigratsiia i emigratsionnaia politika* (Kiev: Rabotnik, 1912), 32.

The Galveston Movement came to an end mainly because of the termination of financial support by Jewish philanthropists on the European side. The Rothschild brothers, who were dissatisfied with the modest results of the Galveston immigration, ended their support in 1913. The £20,000 ($100,000) that the Rothschilds had donated to the Galveston Project had now been spent. After the refusal of the Rothschilds to continue financing the project, Israel Zangwill, the president of the Jewish Territorial Organization, sent a request for 100,000 rubles ($50,000) to Leon Brodsky as president of the Jewish Emigration Society in Kiev. However, Brodsky disagreed with the other leaders of the Galveston Movement about its goals. He believed that the movement, in its existing form, supported the assimilation of Jews in America. He refused to give money for its continuation unless there was a change in the operation. The American side of the Galveston Movement still had money, but US law made it illegal for Americans to finance immigration to the United States on the European end.[143]

In spite of all the difficulties of the Galveston Project, immigration to Galveston saved ten thousand Russian Jews from poverty, pogroms, the atrocities of World War I, and the civil war in Russia. For the majority of Jews who came to America through Galveston, the project was successful, and the Galveston Movement helped create vibrant Jewish communities throughout the American West.

Leon Brodsky left Kiev forever after the death of his son Michael in September 1918. He immigrated with his family to Paris and died there in 1923.[144] The other members of the Brodsky family were not as prominent in business and public affairs as Abram, Israel, Lazar, and Leon. However, they were also wealthy, and owned several breweries and smaller sugar refineries.[145]

The influence and power of the Brodsky "Sugar Kings" were limited by the fact of their Jewishness. During times of turmoil, the Brodskys' social status and wealth did not protect them from pogroms

---

143 Ibid., 150–151, 173; "Report of L. I. Brodsky to the General Meeting of the Members Jewish Emigration Society, November 3, 1913," 77–80.
144 Kovalinskii, *Metsenaty Kieva*, 239.
145 Brodsky, *Smoke Signals*, 5–16.

and persecution. Their mansions were ransacked during the Kiev pogroms of 1881 and 1905, and two members of the family were severely beaten during the 1905 pogrom. Alexandra Fanny Brodsky writes that Gregory, the son of Alexander Brodsky (cousin of Lazar and Leon), attempted to stop an attack on his neighbor and relative Alexander de Ginzburg who was being severely beaten by a group of hooligans. The rioters abandoned their previous victim and beat Gregory "about the head with an iron chair, clearly intent on killing him."[146] Gregory's youngest brothers Joseph and Michael came to his rescue, and began to shoot at the pogromists. However, they inadvertently wounded a policeman in the crowd and were imprisoned for several months, but were finally acquitted after two trials.[147]

The activities of the Brodsky dynasty played a significant role in the developing sugar industry in Russia. The Brodskys introduced many innovations that made more efficient the production of sugar in their factories, and at the same time earned for them millions of rubles. The Brodskys generously shared their profits with local Jewish communities, spending a good part of their money on communal needs and investing large sums on various city projects and services. Only the increasing hostility of the local administration and escalating anti-Jewish violence compelled Leon Brodsky to change his strategy of communal leadership from one of negotiation to one of confrontation with the authorities.

Even with all the limitations on their power and their authoritarian methods of rule, the Brodskys were prominent Jewish leaders and philanthropists. They lived in complicated and difficult times, and they simply could not solve the growing problems that faced Kievan Jews and all of Russian Jewry. However, they did what was possible under the circumstances to aid their fellow Jews and save them from even worse calamities. Their wealth and personal connections with Russian authorities did sometimes allow them to solve problems. Nevertheless, during periods of violence and pogroms the Brodsky "Sugar Kings" themselves became victims. Such was the power and powerlessness of the Jewish "Sugar Kings." The Brodskys contributed so much

---

146 Ibid., 11.
147 TsDIAK U, f. 317, op. 1, d. 5125. ll. 2–13; Brodsky, *Smoke Signals*, 11.

to the Jewish communities as well as to the entire population of the cities where they lived that people still enjoy the fruits of their labor: the synagogues, schools, hospitals, markets and buildings that they constructed.

When World War I began, Brodsky family members demonstrated their patriotism by supporting the Russian Army. Leon Brodsky's son, Michael, went to the front. Leon and Lazar's cousin, Alexander Brodsky, and his wife, Eugenia, "turned the reception hall of their home in Sadovaia [Street in Kiev] into a military hospital. [Their daughter] Nina abandoned her art to become a nurse in a field hospital... [Her brother] Gregory, who was at Cambridge, enlisted in the British Army."[148]

After the February 1917 Revolution, the Brodsky family provided significant financial assistance to the Provisional Government. When the government issued state bonds, the so-called "Liberty Loan" of April 1917, different branches of the Brodsky family bought two million rubles worth.[149] However, after the Bolsheviks took power in October 1917, the family lost everything: the Soviet authorities confiscated all of their enterprises and property. Under Bolshevik threat to their lives as "capitalists," most Brodsky family members immigrated to various European countries. While the history of the Brodsky family did not end at this point, the eminence of the Brodsky "Sugar Kings" disappeared forever.

MAX MANDELSTAMM: PALESTINOPHILE, ZIONIST, AND COMMUNITY LEADER

The vice president of the Kiev Jewish community, Max Emmanuil Mandelstamm (1839–1912), was one of the most prominent Palestinophile and Zionist leaders in late Imperial Russia. Mandelstamm had tremendous energy, successfully combining various high profile activities and simultaneously holding several positions. He was a prominent ophthalmologist and he established one of the best ophthalmology clinics in Russia. In addition, he was one of the founders of the Palestinophile movement in the Russian Empire, and was later one of the leaders of the

---

148 Brodsky, *Smoke Signals*, 16.
149 *Russkaia volia*, April 23, 1917.

Zionist, Territorial, and Jewish emigration movements. He was also the first president of the Emigration Society in Kiev.

Mandelstamm was born in Žagarė, Lithuania, into a renowned family of maskilim. His father, Ezekiel Mandelstamm, was a well-educated merchant who wrote a biblical lexicon *The Book of Names* (1862). Max Mandelstamm's uncle, Leon Iosifovich Mandelstamm, was a "Jewish expert" at the Ministry of National Enlightenment, and the author of several novels, Jewish textbooks, Russian-Jewish dictionaries, and articles about Jewish education. Several members of the family became Russian and Jewish authors and scholars.[150] The prominence of the Mandelstamm family was even recognized by the head of the Kiev Province Gendarmerie Administration, General Vasilii Dement'evich Novitskii. On June 23, 1900, in a letter to the director of the police department, he wrote:

> The Mandelstamm family is very large, has seven brothers, all with distinguished abilities and higher education, the above mentioned [Max Mandelstamm] is the eldest of them, the most influential among the brothers. Only one of them, Iosif Mandelstamm, has converted to Christianity...[151]

Max Mandelstamm, like many maskilim of his generation, received two educations: traditional Jewish education in the *heder*, and general education first in a Vilna gymnasium, and thereafter in Dorpat (Tartu) and Khar'kov Universities. In 1864–1868, he studied ophthalmology at Berlin University. After successfully defending his doctoral dissertation in the St. Petersburg Medical-Surgical Academy in 1868, Mandelstamm was appointed in 1869 as an assistant professor at Kiev St. Vladimir University.[152]

---

150 Victoria Khiterer, "Max Mandelstamm, Palestinophile and Zionist Leader," *The American Association for Polish-Jewish Studies (AAPJS), New Views*, http://www.aapjstudies.org/manager/external/ckfinder/userfiles/files/Mandelstamm.pdf
151 TsDIAK U, f. 1423, op. 1, d. 10, l. 3.
152 Khiterer, "Max Mandelstamm, Palestinophile and Zionist Leader."

In the same year he opened a private ophthalmology clinic that soon became the best in the southwestern region of the Russian Empire. Simon Dubnov wrote in his memoirs *Kniga zhizni* (The Book of Life) that Mandelstamm successfully helped him with his vision problems after other ophthalmologists had failed. Mandelstamm's clinic often treated over a hundred patients daily. Many ophthalmologists came to Mandelstamm for consultation, especially for training in eye surgery. In 1896, during an ophthalmology convention in Kiev, whole sections of the convention observed the treatment of patients and operations performed by Mandelstamm at his clinic each morning.

Mandelstamm promoted the development of ophthalmologic treatment in Russia. Between 1888 and 1893, he published a five-volume monograph about eye diseases. He also published many articles in the Russian and German press on ophthalmic problems.[153] Mandelstamm taught at Kiev St. Vladimir University for twelve years, and during the last four years of his academic career he was the head of the University Ophthalmology Clinic. However, Mandelstamm left his academic career after the university board refused to ratify his promotion to full professor, despite the fact that the members of the medical faculty had voted three times in favor of his promotion. Mandelstamm was denied this promotion because he was a Jew, and declined the proposed compromise that he could be given his promotion if he converted to Christianity.[154] The end of his academic career coincided with the first wave of mass anti-Jewish pogroms in the Russian Empire in 1881–1882. These pogroms came as a great shock to Russian Jewish intelligentsia. According to Kiev Rabbi Dr. Petr Iampol'skii, they affected Mandelstamm deeply:

> Max Emelianovich, as a real European man and a gentleman by nature, could not tolerate nor be reconciled with brutal physical violence toward Jews. From this moment and until the end of his life, he became the mortal enemy of the *golus*

---

153 S. M. Dubnov, *Kniga zhizni* (St. Petersburg: Peterburgskoe vostokovedenie, 1998), 136; *Pamiati Maksa Emilievicha Mande'lshtamma: rechi, statii i nekrologi* (Kiev: n.p., 1912), 60.
154 *Pamiati Maksa Emilievicha Mande'lshtamma*, 60.

[Jewish exile from the land of Israel] and the disgraceful *golus* situation of the people of Israel.[155]

A similar explanation of Mandelstamm's evolving political views was given by Simon Dubnov, who had a long conversation with Mandelstamm during his visit to Kiev in 1887:

> He [Mandelstamm] talked with hatred about the Russian government and with bitterness toward the Russian people, even toward the Russian intelligentsia. He admitted that these feelings first arose when he was an eyewitness to the Kiev pogrom in 1881; then he was invited to Ignat'ev's "Provincial Commission," where the same people who allowed the street pogroms were creating a legislative pogrom. Mandelstamm was by then an adherent of the territorialist ideas of Pinsker and saw the salvation of the Jews in their emigration from Russia.[156]

Mandelstamm was the head of the Committee to Aid the Victims of Pogroms, and at a conference of representatives of Jewish communities in St. Petersburg in 1881, he supported the emigration of Jews from Russia as the only possible solution to their problems. From that time onward, the emigration of Jews from Russia became central to his outlook on public affairs.[157] He was also one of three founders of the Palestinophile movement in Russia. Rabbi Iampol'skii wrote:

> On the first day of the Jewish New Year (the beginning of September 1882) in Odessa in the apartment of Dr. Pinsker, the first Palestinophile group in Russia was founded. It was established by three people: Dr. Pinsker, Dr. Mandelstamm,

---

155 Dr. P. Iampol'skii, *Pamiati doktora Maksa Emilievicha Mandel'shtama: Slovo, proiznesennoe v Kievskoi khoral'noi sinagoge v subbotu, 7-go aprelia 1912 goda, vo vremia panikhidy po pokoinom M. E. Mandel'shtame* (Kiev: n.p., 1912), 12.
156 Dubnov, *Kniga zhizni*, 136. Provincial commissions were created after the anti-Jewish pogroms of 1881 to investigate "the harmful economic activity of Jews." Count N. Ignat'ev was the minister of the interior at that time.
157 Khiterer, "Max Mandelstamm, Palestinophile and Zionist Leader."

who came from Kiev to Odessa especially for this meeting, and our famous writer-nationalist M. L. Lilienblum.[158]

At the beginning of the 1880s, Mandelstamm established in Kiev the "Brotherhood of the Lovers of Zion" ("*Hovevei Zion*"), which collected and sent money to Jewish colonists in Palestine. The secretary of this society was the Hebrew poet Yehalel who, as mentioned above, was employed by the Brodsky family. Kiev authorities shut down the society after it was discovered by the police.[159]

Mandelstamm also later became one of the leaders of the Zionist and Territorial movements in Russia. He took part in all of the first seven international Zionist congresses, and was elected to the Zionist Action Committee, the highest institution of the World Zionist Organization in the interim between congresses.[160] He was a close friend of the Zionist movement's founder, Theodor Herzl, who lovingly depicted him in his 1903 novel *Altneuland* (Old-new-land) as the elderly president of a utopian Jewish state in Palestine in 1923 ("an ophthalmologist from Russia, Dr. Eichenstamm").[161]

The leadership of Mandelstamm in the Russian Zionist movement was well known to the authorities. They asked Mandelstamm to write a note about Zionism for the Department of Police of the Russian Ministry of the Interior in 1900. Before 1903, the Zionist movement was legal in Russia, and the authorities had not yet determined their attitude toward it. Thus, Mandelstamm, characterized by the chief of the Kiev provincial police as a "very clever university educated man" with great influence among Russian and foreign Jews,[162] was selected as the most competent person to write a description of the movement. In this note, on whose contents he consulted with Herzl, Mandelstamm attempted to gain the Russian authorities' support for Zionism by

---

158 Iampol'skii, *Pamiati doktora Maksa Emilievicha Mandel'shtama*, 12.
159 TsDIAK U, f. 442, op. 538, d. 52, ll. 13–15, Letter from the Vice-Governor of Kiev to the Kiev, Podolia, and Volhynia Governor-General, June 6, 1885.
160 Khiterer, *Dokumenty, sobrannye*, 211; Khiterer, "Max Mandelstamm, Palestinophile and Zionist Leader."
161 Marinbach, *Galveston*, 7.
162 TsDIAK U, f. 1423, op. 1, d. 10, l. 3.

convincing them that the movement would be to Russia's economic advantage. The resettlement of Jews in Palestine, he claimed, would have great benefits, particularly to Russia, "which could use Jews as the creators of new Asian markets for [Russian] industry."[163]

The Russian authorities hardened their attitude toward Zionism in 1903, and the minister of the interior, Viacheslav Pleve, banned the movement in Russia. Paradoxically, the reason for this was their disappointment in the small number of Jewish emigrants from Russia. Pleve wrote in his circular of June 24, 1903 that Zionists, instead of promoting the resettlement of Jews to Palestine "in order to create there an independent Jewish state, postponed this mission to the distant future and instead directed their activity toward the development and strengthening of the national Jewish idea...in the places where Jews currently live."[164]

After the prohibition of the Zionist movement in Russia, all Zionist leaders, including Mandelstamm, were placed under police surveillance. For years the Kiev police secretly intercepted and transcribed all of Mandelstamm's personal correspondence. These transcripts show that Mandelstamm considered the Russian monarchy to be backward and barbaric, and hoped that Japan would defeat Russia during the Russo-Japanese War. The police reported that he wrote in a letter to his brother Dr. Leon Mandelstamm in Poltava that if Russia won the war,

> the country will have to suffer more moral degradation and the people who live there will suffocate under the yoke of the Christian Orthodox religion. We Jews will especially perish then....I made a bet with many people [regarding who will win the war], and if I win, I will take a bath in champagne for many weeks; if I lose, woe is me, I will perish.[165]

---

163 Aleksandr Lokshin, "V poiskakh modus vivendi: Sionistskoe dvizhenie i tsarskoe pravitel'stvo v kontse XIX–nachale XX vekov," in *Rossiiskii sionizm: istoriia i kul'tura. Materialy nauchnoi konferentsii* (Moscow: Sefer, 2002), 75.
164 TsDIAK U, f. 1423, op. 1, d. 10, ll. 10–11.
165 Ibid., l. 215.

Jewish immigration to Palestine at the turn of the twentieth century met with significant obstacles because of opposition by the Ottoman Empire, which ruled Palestine and did not recognize the right of Jews to settle there. Thus, "Uganda" emerged as an alternative destination for Jewish emigration, as a place where a large Jewish settlement could be established.[166] Under the Uganda Plan, the British government proposed that the Zionist organization establish an autonomous Jewish colony in British East Africa (now Kenya). Herzl introduced the Uganda Plan to the Sixth Zionist Congress in August 1903, which provoked a sharp disagreement among the delegates. Debates about the Uganda Plan continued after Herzl's death in 1904. At the Seventh Zionist Congress in Basel in 1905, a majority of the delegates, including the Russian Zionists, voted against the Uganda Plan. A small group of proponents of the Uganda Plan "led by Israel Zangwill, Dr. Mandelstamm, and Dr. David Jochelmann, now abandoned the conference. They met separately in Basel and established the Jewish Territorial Organization (ITO) of which Zangwill became president."[167] Mandelstamm became president of the Russian branch of the organization with its headquarters in Kiev.[168]

However, with time, it became obvious to all that the Uganda Plan was unrealistic. A special commission sent to East Africa by the Sixth Zionist Congress found the location unsuitable for a large Jewish settlement. The Jewish Territorial Organization now sought alternative places for Jewish emigration and for the creation of Jewish settlements, and simultaneously supported greatly-increased Jewish emigration to America.

The turbulence of life in the Russian Empire at the beginning of the twentieth century—the increased level of violence, simmering revolution, anti-Jewish pogroms, and difficult economic conditions—led to a rapid increase in Jewish emigration. To support the emigration of Jews to Galveston, Mandelstamm founded and led in 1909–1912 the

---

166 "Uganda" as understood at the time was not identical with the country that today bears that name, but was identified with an area in British-ruled East Africa.
167 Marinbach, *Galveston*, 6.
168 Ibid., 7.

Jewish Emigration Society in Kiev, the activity of which has already been described. The emigration movement was one area where Zionists and non-Zionists were able to cooperate in the face of an increasingly desperate situation.[169]

For forty-five years, Mandelstamm successfully combined energetic political and public activity with his professional work. However, he wrote very little about his Zionist views or on the Jewish question generally. It seems that he did not believe that Zionist propaganda addressed to Russified Jews would be effective. Thus, he consciously rejected theoretical work in favor of practical efforts. In an open letter to the editor of *Illiustrirovannyi sionistskii al'manakh* (Illustrated Zionist Almanac), Mandelstamm wrote that he refused to cooperate with the periodical, since he did not believe that it could change the mentality and awaken the national feelings of Jewish people. In this open letter, he said that the "[Russified] Jew, who considers himself an intellectual, does not read Jewish journals and newspapers, nor Jewish books."[170] Assimilation had made rapid progress among educated Russian Jews so that during the last third of the nineteenth century, "the Russian-Jewish intelligentsia has taken a big step forward in their denial of all things Jewish." As a result, the realization of Zionist plans depended rather on the Jewish masses, who were "tied together by the cement of tradition and suffering." Mandelstamm expressed his hope that the Russian Jewish intelligentsia would later join the Zionist movement, after it had achieved success in Palestine. He concluded that there was no reader to whom *Illiustrirovannyi sionistskii al'manakh* could be addressed. The Jewish masses did not read Russian Jewish periodicals due to their lack of knowledge of the Russian language; at the same time, the vast majority of the Russian Jewish intelligentsia did not have any interest in Jewish topics.[171]

Mandelstamm's other principal article, "The Quintessence of Zionism," has the subtitle "A Letter by a Zionist to His Daughter." In it,

---

169 *Programma Evreiskogo emigratsionnogo obshchestva* (Kiev: Rabotnik, 1909), 6.
170 M. Mandel'shtam, "Otkrytoe pis'mo," *Illiustrirovannyi sionistskii al'manakh* (1902–1903): 44.
171 Ibid., 44–47.

he contrasted cosmopolitanism with nationalism, arguing that by serving one's own nationality it is possible to serve all mankind. Jews should devote themselves to work for their own nationality and remove the Jewish people from the ghetto where they are degraded physically and morally.[172]

Mandelstamm was a charismatic figure with a talent for attracting people and earning their respect and love. Rabbi Iampol'skii, in his funeral eulogy for Mandelstamm on April 7, 1912, observed:

> Dr. Mandelstamm was not only popular; he had the respect of all classes of Jews: Orthodox and liberals, conservatives, capitalists and progressives, rich and poor, old and young; first of all, all of them sincerely loved him.[173]

The general love and popularity he evoked, Iampol'skii claimed, lay in his willingness to help all Jews irrespective of their social status. Genrikh Sliozberg wrote of the "major influence" Mandelstamm exercised over the Kiev Jewish community.[174]

Mandelstamm took pride in his scholarship and in his role in the Zionist movement. In his open letter, he described himself as "one of the leaders of Zionism."[175] In a letter to his brother Leon on May 31, 1904, he wrote: "Recently I was elected as president of the Ophthalmology Society and I delivered a brilliant speech in the university clinic."[176] He often expressed his thoughts in the high-flown language typical of the late nineteenth century. By the second decade of the twentieth century, this had an archaic ring to the younger generation. Sergei Kablukov, a friend of the Russian poet Osip Mandel'shtam (who was a distant relative of Max Mandelstamm), writes in his diary of a conversation he and the poet had with Max Mandelstamm in 1910, in

---

172 M. Mandel'shtam, "Sushchnost' sionizma: Pis'mo sionista k docheri," in *Byt' evreem v Rossii: Materialy po istorii russkogo evreistva. 1880–1890*, comp. Nelli Portnova (Jerusalem: The Hebrew University of Jerusalem, 1999), 272–274.
173 Iampol'skii, *Pamiati doktora Maksa Emilievicha Mandel'shtama*, 15.
174 Sliozberg, *Dela minuvshikh dnei*, 1: 284.
175 Mandel'shtam, "Otkrytoe pis'mo," 44.
176 TsDIAK U, f. 1423, op. 1, d. 10, l. 9.

which they discussed modern literature. Kablukov and Osip Mandel'shtam

> defended new literary styles and schools. Dr. Mandelstamm was very backward and conservative on this question. He referred to the writings of the famous [Zionist writer and critic] Nordau and called his feuilletons "pearls."[177]

However, Kablukov's comments on Mandelstamm's literary tastes should be read in light of the fact that neither Kablukov nor Osip Mandel'shtam, a Christian convert, had any interest in the Jewish national movement. This made it difficult for them to evaluate either Mandelstamm's personality or his ideas.

Mandelstamm made a much more favorable impression on Nahum Sokolow (1859–1936), a journalist and president of the World Zionist Organization, who was also a generation younger than Mandelstamm. Sokolow wrote,

> Many were struck that a Russian Jew could be such a gentlemen with such noble manners and could speak such exquisite German! Yes, the German language of Mandelstamm had a solemn, even an oracular character…His speeches had a romantic cast and he possessed at the same time the soul of a poet and of a child. He lived in Western Europe for long time [during the years when he studied at Berlin University]…and became an adopted son of the German Enlightenment. All his life he resembled more a German Professor than a Russian Jew.[178]

Mandelstamm, as vice president of the Kiev Jewish community, provided aid to the needy Jewish population and assistance to the victims of pogroms, and also attempted to develop a system of Jewish education. He did not see a viable future for Jews in Tsarist Russia, and

---

177 Leonid Katsis, *Osip Mandel'shtam: Muskus iudeistva* (Jerusalem: Gesharim, 2002), 478–479.
178 *Pamiati Maksa Emilievicha Mande'lshtamma*, 120.

devoted much effort to facilitating Jewish emigration. Although he did not write any major theoretical works on the Jewish national question, his practical work for the liberation of Jews from the "country of pogroms" gave thousands of them a chance for new and much happier lives in America.

CONCLUSION

All available primary sources about Kiev's Jewish communal structures date from the end of the nineteenth to the early twentieth century. In its initial period, the Kiev Community Board was a self-selected group of businessmen and merchants.[179] At this time, the Jewish Welfare Committee was the legally recognized part of a larger communal structure, the Kiev kahal, which existed unofficially until the 1905 Revolution. After the first election of the Jewish Welfare Committee in 1906, this institution appears to have become the sole communal body.

Even after this election, the Jewish communal body in Kiev remained dependent upon the city administration in its financial affairs. The city council selected representatives from local Jews, who under the chairmanship of a gentile member of the city council formulated the budget of the Jewish communal body. Some Kiev Jews criticized the way these resources were used. However, as we have seen, the authorities took one fifth of the community revenue for the city budget and to finance the local police, and the remaining money was insufficient to satisfy all the needs of the Jewish poor—even though the Kiev Jewish community was one of the wealthiest in the Russian Empire. Certainly the leaders of the community made great efforts to help not only the city's Jewish population, but also poor Jews who came to Kiev for medical, legal, or other reasons. Additionally, some Kiev Jewish institutions, such as the Jewish hospital, provided aid not only for Jews but also for gentiles.

The democratization of Kiev Jewish communal life, which took place during the revolutionary years (1905–1907), was only partial, and

---

179 Meir, "The Jews in Kiev," 90.

the community's leadership remained in the hands of the Jewish tycoons, above all the Brodsky family. However, most Kievan Jews were satisfied with this leadership, and expected the community to be led by wealthy Jews who had influence with the authorities. The Brodsky brothers, Lazar and Leon, ruled in an authoritarian manner. Yet their methods produced results, particularly before 1905. Lazar Brodsky successfully prevented the expulsion of Jews from Kiev. He used the traditional methods of *shtadlanut*: negotiation with the local authorities and, if necessary, bribery.

However, after the suppression of the 1905 Revolution, the reactionary political regime was re-established, and the newly elected Kiev Jewish representative institutions faced new challenges, including increasing state and popular anti-Semitism and anti-Jewish violence, which they were unable to overcome. The previous methods of *shtadlanut* no longer worked in the deteriorating political situation. The Kiev Jewish leaders therefore were forced into a policy of confrontation with the local authorities and support for Jewish emigration.

Jewish communal life in Kiev at the turn of the twentieth century had some internal conflicts and encountered various external obstacles. However, in spite of growing state anti-Semitism and persecution, this period witnessed the peak of the development of the community and its institutions. Never again was Jewish communal life as vibrant, nor did it have as great of an impact on the everyday life of Kiev's Jews.

CHAPTER FIVE

The Wealth and Poverty of Jews in Kiev

> If the statistics are right, the Jews constitute but one per cent of the human race. It suggests a nebulous dim puff of star-dust lost in the blaze of the Milky Way. Properly the Jew ought hardly to be heard of; but he is heard of, has always been heard of. He is as prominent on the planet as any other people, and his commercial importance is extravagantly out of proportion to the smallness of his bulk. His contributions to the world's list of great names in literature, science, art, music, finance, medicine, and abstruse learning are also away out of proportion to the weakness of his numbers. He has made a marvelous fight in this world, in all the ages; and has done it with his hands tied behind him.
> —Mark Twain, "Concerning the Jews," *Harper's Magazine*, March, 1898

THE MODERNIZATION OF KIEV

Kiev was one of the most modern, flourishing, and wealthy cities of late Imperial Russia. In the words of the Russian economist Andrei Pavlovich Subbotin, who wrote a description of Kiev after he visited the city in the summer of 1887,

> In terms of its revenue, Kiev is the sixth city in the Russian Empire...The arrangement of the city could be improved, but Kiev stands out strikingly from the run of provincial cities: the wide and rather clean streets, fine buildings, the system of water-borne plumbing, the horse-drawn trams, the well-preserved monuments, ravines, fences, and so on; 90 percent of all streets are paved and partially turned into highways; the roadways are not worse than in St. Petersburg, and in its level of services and utilities Kiev surpasses even Moscow. The city is illuminated by 2,415 street lamps, of which 1,343 are gas and 1,072 kerosene...
>
> In general over the last ten years, the improvements of the city's arrangements have been more marked than even those in the capitals...
>
> The city has very great commercial significance; large commercial contracts for sugar, bread and other products are signed here; and there are many wholesale storehouses, large stores, and commercial connections with the main Russian and foreign centers.[1]

The city's amenities were even more developed at the beginning of the twentieth century. By that time most of Kiev "had plumbing and sewer systems, electric lighting, telephone connections, and electric

---

1   A. P. Subbotin, *V cherte evreiskoi osedlosti. Otryvki iz ekonomicheskikh issledovanii v zapadnoi i iugozapadnoi Rossii za leto 1887 g.* (St. Petersburg: "Ekonomicheskii zhurnal" Publishing house, 1890), 2: 166–168.

transportation and was one of the most comfortable cities of the Russian Empire."²

Financial magnates, industrialists, merchants, and bankers dominated the work of the city council and city duma (the executive and legislative branches of the local government).

> Among the eighty deputies of the city duma only twelve actually participated in its work, who, according to a contemporary, "seized power in the duma and council...performed all work in the twenty paid city commissions, and simultaneously occupied several positions in the city council and in private enterprises, mainly in the banks with many thousands rubles of funds."³

A narrow circle of the Jewish elite participated in the work of local representative institutions. Lazar and Leon Brodsky occupied in turn the position as head of the city council's Jewish Welfare Committee. Kiev State Rabbi Evsei Tsukkerman was a member of the city duma. Because of the prohibition against Jews joining many of the commissions, the Jewish elite did not play a significant role in the work of the city council and duma. However, the role of the Jewish elite in the life of the Kiev Jewish community was quite similar to the role of the Christian elite in the municipal government. Both ruled by authoritarian methods and typically applied few democratic principles. Still, they were quite efficient in securing the city's economic development. Due to their efforts, governing skill, money, and connections, Kiev became a European metropolis, a comfortable and beautiful city.

JEWS IN THE ECONOMY OF KIEV

At the end of the 1880s, factories and plants owned by Jews accounted for 25 percent of the gross revenue of all factories and plants in Kiev.

---

2 O. K. Kasimenko, ed., *Istoriia Kieva* (Kiev: Ukrainian Academy of Arts and Sciences Publishing House, 1963), 1: 482.
3 Ibid., 480.

According to the census of 1897, 42.3 percent of Kiev's Jews were employed in industry and crafts; 26.6 percent were in trade.[4]

Kiev Jewish merchants, though not as large a percentage as in other cities inside the Pale, still made up a significant proportion of all tradesmen. According to Subbotin, in 1869 among the forty-four Kiev merchants of the first guild, there were thirty-two Jews and twelve gentiles; among the 438 merchants of the second guild, there were four Jews and 434 gentiles. By 1884, this proportion of Jewish merchants had changed drastically: among 193 Kiev merchants of the first guild there were seven Jews and 186 gentiles; among 1,719 merchants of second guild there were 829 Jews and 890 gentiles. Subbotin explained that the Jews, who in previous years had dominated the first guild, had almost all moved to the second guild when Jewish merchants of the second guild received the right of residence in Kiev, since second guild merchants paid lower taxes. Certainly, a number of Jews who were involved only in small trade, or who did not participate in trade at all, had enrolled as first guild merchants to gain the right of residence in Kiev.[5]

The percentage of Jewish merchants of the first and second guilds combined increased from 7.3 percent in 1869 to 43.7 percent in 1884. In 1897, Jewish merchants comprised 44 percent, and in 1910 over 42 percent of all Kiev merchants. Although the percentage of Jewish merchants decreased, their number increased significantly in these thirteen years, from 2,238 to 4,896. Many Jewish merchants were involved in grain, sugar, and other agricultural trades, as well as in the alcohol, tobacco, garment, and fabric industries.[6] According to Subbotin, "Jews very actively participate in the grain trade in the region; they purchase grain from landlords and peasants and sell it to export companies, and participate in the transportation of grain abroad."[7] In 1887, according to the *Gosudarstvennaia Palata* (State Chamber),[8] the turnover of trade in Kiev was about 42 million rubles, of which Jewish merchants were

---

4 *Evreiskaia entsiklopediia*, s.v. "Kiev," 9: 527–528.
5 A. P. Subbotin, *V cherte*, 166–168.
6 Ibid., 172–174; *Evreiskaia entsiklopediia*, "Kiev," 9: 527–528.
7 A. P. Subbotin, *V cherte evreiskoi osedlosti*, 173.
8 National organization for gathering statistics and for government auditing.

responsible for 45.2 percent. The average turnover of Jewish tradesman was larger than that of gentiles; however, the average profit of the gentile merchants was 30 percent higher than that of the Jews. Ivan Aksakov first described this phenomenon in the 1850s as one of the peculiarities of Jewish trade. He wrote that Jews sold their goods at lower prices because they always needed cash. According to Subbotin, Kiev Jewish businessmen and merchants were less wealthy than their gentile counterparts:

> Kiev has many large Jewish companies that all are smaller than the comparable Russian and European companies. Thus all large sugar industrialists are gentiles with the exception only of Mr. Brodsky; similarly Russians and Germans are the majority among the largest exporters.[9]

Subbotin noted that Kiev had more merchants than "any other city in the Pale, even Odessa had less."[10] This severe competition compelled Jewish traders to sell their goods for less.

Many Kiev Jewish traders were women. According to one study, over three quarters of those engaged in trade were women.[11] Jewish women in Kiev were engaged in retail trade or were owners of small shops, while all the Jewish owners of large trading companies in Kiev were men.

One important element of the city's commercial life was the Jewish market (*Evbaz*). It had developed spontaneously around 1850 on the road that runs from the city to Galicia and Volhynia. When Jews were expelled from Kiev in 1835, the prices of all goods in the city increased significantly. This angered residents and threatened to provoke a confrontation with the authorities. As a result, the local administration allowed Jews who had permission to come to the city for a few days to sell goods to also trade there. In the summer of 1854, this market was

---

9 A. P. Subbotin, *V cherte evreiskoi osedlosti*, 170.
10 Ibid.
11 ChaeRan Y. Freeze, *Jewish Marriage and Divorce in Imperial Russia* (Hanover, NH: Brandeis University Press, 2002), 66.

given legal status "in order to allow city inhabitants to purchase necessary everyday food."[12]

Officially this market was called the *Galitskii* market because it was located on Galitskii Road, later renamed Galitskii Square. But Kievans have always called it *Evbaz*, which is shorthand for *Evreiskii bazar* (Jewish Bazaar), due to the large number of Jewish traders there. Nikolai Zakrevskii wrote in 1868 that the Jewish market was comparatively small. However, it grew significantly when in 1870 the Kiev railway station was built in its vicinity.[13] The Jewish market became popular with Kiev's middle class and poor inhabitants because of the low price of goods there. It was a flea market where food, inexpensive goods, and secondhand clothes were sold. Dmytro Malakov wrote that in spite of its name, the majority of stallholders at the market were gentiles: peasants from nearby villages and secondhand dealers. Only 25 percent of stallholders at the market in 1914 were Jewish.[14] However, Jews monopolized almost all the trade in meat at the market. There was a special place where *shokhetim* (kosher butchers) slaughtered poultry purchased at the market by Jewish buyers.[15]

From the first half of the nineteenth century until the present, Kiev has been the most expensive city in the region. This phenomenon was commented on by Governor-General Bibikov, Kiev Governor Gesse, and other local officials.[16] Subbotin noted in 1887 that the cost of living in Kiev was quite high, and that "middle class people who have a modest income complained about this particularly."[17] The poor had an even harder time making ends meet. For such people the Jewish market was the best place to purchase goods and food. (A similar

---

12 Aleksandr Anisimov, *Kiev i kievliane. Ia vyzovu liuboe iz stoletii...*(Kiev: Kurch', 2002), 1: 215; Dmytro Malakov, *Tut buv Ievbaz, a potim ploshcha Peremohy. Istoryko-informatsiinyi fotoal'bom* (Kiev: Amadei, 2004), 10-11.
13 Dmytro Malakov, *Tut buv Ievbaz*, 10-11.
14 Ibid., 17.
15 Ibid., 17-18.
16 Illia Galant, "Vyselennia zhydiv iz Kyieva," 194-197; I. A. Darevskii, *K istorii evreev v Kieve*, 114-117.
17 A. P. Subbotin, *V cherte evreiskoi osedlosti*, 173.

situation exists today, when the poorer residents purchase all their food and other necessities at the numerous flea markets in Kiev.)

The historian Nikolai Pavlovich Poletika described the Jewish market in his memoirs:

> The Bazaar was called Jewish in common parlance, because many shops and stores there belonged to Jews. This was a district of Jewish poor people. The shop fronts opened onto the pavement, which surrounded the Market Square in a semi-circle...There were small shops, where it was rarely possible to find more than one salesman. The stalls covered the square: there were tents with an overhang and open tables, where rags and old clothes and all kinds of odds and ends, from nails and locks to small pies made of offal were sold. All of these did not cost much.[18]

The *Evbaz* also had another important function for poorer people: it was their main source of information about world events. According to the Russian writer Mikhail Bulgakov, who lived in Kiev before 1919 and visited the city in the early 1920s,

> Kievans, let's talk honestly about them, don't read newspapers, because they are absolutely certain that the newspapers contain only "lies." However, people cannot live without information; they find this information at the *Evbaz*, where old women sell candelabra.[19]

According to Bulgakov, the market was the main source of various fantastic rumors that circulated in the city.[20]

On occasion, the market shared the fate of Kiev's Jews. Despite the fact that it was a place where poor people—including many

---

18 N. P. Poletika, *Vidennoe i perezhitoe (Iz vospominanii)* (Jerusalem: Biblioteka—Aliia, 1990), 21–22.
19 Aleksandr Anisimov, *Kiev i kievliane. Ia vyzovu liuboe iz stoletii...*, 1: 215.
20 Ibid.

gentiles—bought and sold, it was completely destroyed during the October 1905 pogrom. Nikolai Poletika, who was then a child of nine, watched the pogrom with his twin brother and grandmother from the window of their apartment.

> We saw how the pogrom-makers carried away clothes, cloth, shoes, and fancy goods, how they quarreled with each other and snatched loot from each other. A very fat woman with a copper face...was breathing hard, dragging a child's bed and a stylish woman's wide brimmed hat with a bouquet of flowers and feathers. A ragged tramp in a new black frock coat was busily carrying several boxes with shoes. Another ragamuffin with a shaggy beard was carrying a box of shorts and a wall clock. Some people in *poddevkas* [a man's light, tight-fitting coat, worn by the poorer people] picked up goods carelessly thrown out of the looted shops onto the pavement. The police participated in the pillage, taking the most tempting "trophies." The rioters broke into houses and dragged from them not only property, but also people whom they beat bloody and forced to read a [Christian] prayer or display the tsar's portrait. Corpses of murdered people remained in the apartments.[21]

The Jewish market existed in Kiev for more than a hundred years. However, after the massacre of the Kiev Jews in Babi Yar in 1941, only gentiles traded there. After World War II, this district acquired a criminal reputation. There, stolen goods were sold and criminals often robbed people; in the houses around the market the police sometimes found dead bodies. The small houses near the market, which were built in the mid-to-late nineteenth century, after a century had turned into slums or *klopovniki* (bedbug infested places), as Kievans called them. Consequently, in 1952 the local administration closed the market and the entire district underwent large-scale reconstruction.[22]

---

21 N. P. Poletika, *Vidennoe i perezhitoe (Iz vospominanii)* (Jerusalem: Biblioteka—Aliia, 1990), 21–22.
22 Aleksandr Anisimov, *Kiev i kievliane. Ia vyzovu liuboe iz stoletii...*, 1: 217.

THE KIEV JEWISH BUSINESS ELITE

The Kiev Jewish business elite made a major contribution to the development and character of the city. Their generous philanthropic activity benefited the entire city population, as well as the Jewish community. Besides the Brodsky family (described in the previous chapter), there were a number of wealthy Jewish businessmen in Kiev. I will focus on the biographies and enterprises of three of the most prominent: David Semenovich Margolin, Lev Borisovich [Leiba Berkovich] Ginzburg, and Iosif Abramovich Marshak.

David Margolin was an industrial tycoon, a commercial adviser to the local authorities, and a generous philanthropist. He was granted the official title of "Commercial Adviser"[23] and was a merchant of the first guild. He was also a member of the Loan Committee of the Kiev Department of the State Bank for Commercial and Industrial Loans. He was granted numerous Russian and foreign awards for his business and philanthropic activity.[24]

He was born in 1850 somewhere outside Kiev (surviving documents do not contain information about the place of his birth or his early years). Information about his family's economic status is contradictory. David Margolin's official record of service, which was compiled in 1916, described his parents as belonging to "the merchant estate." However, his great-grandson, the pianist Gary Graffman, wrote that he was

> born poor, began to work for a steamship company when he was only twelve, and he did not waste any time. Before too

---

23 Commercial Adviser was an honorary title, established in 1800 in Russia, which was equal to the VIII class of "The Table of Ranks" and gave the hereditary noble rank. (*Rossiiskaia gosudarstvennost' v terminakh. IX–nachalo XX veka. Dictionary* [Moscow: Kraft+, 2001], 225).
24 Margolin's awards included the Golden Alexander medal, the Romanian Crown medal, the Bulgarian St. Alexander medal of the 4th degree, the St. Stanislav medals of the 2nd and 3rd degree, and the St. Anna medal of the 2nd degree for non-Christians. The State Archive of the City of Kiev (DAMK), f. 153, op. 1, d. 309, ll. 1–19.

many years had passed he owned the company, became responsible for most of the huge steamships that plied the wide Dnieper River with passengers and goods.[25]

If the account of his great-grandson is correct, we can assume that David Margolin probably invented for official use his merchant provenance, which looked more impressive than descent from a poor family. According to Genrikh Sliozberg, Margolin "was a self-made man." He went on to observe:

> He had studied classical Jewish texts in his younger years and his Jewish knowledge marked him all his life. Nobody could attract people to himself as did Margolin.[26]

Probably this ability to attract people helped Margolin make the necessary business contacts in Kiev for the establishment of his own companies. His business activity began in Kiev in 1868, which coincided with a period of rapid industrial and commercial development, and a need for significantly improved city services and utilities.[27] Margolin established plants for machine tools, iron founding, cable production, and other materials needed for construction. Together with the Brodsky family, he founded sugar production companies, and also owned two shipping companies on the Dnieper River. When he established "The Second Shipping Company on the Dnieper River" he began to order his ships not from abroad, as was previously done, but from Russian shipyards, which gave an impetus to the development of the Russian shipbuilding industry. According to Iaron:

> [Margolin] significantly increased the Dnieper fleet and made passenger as well as cargo transportation less expensive. A

---

25 Gary Graffman, *I Really Should Be Practicing* (Garden City, NY: Doubleday & Company, Inc., 1981), 15.
26 G. B. Sliozberg, *Dela minuvshikh dnei. Zapiski russkogo evreia* (Paris: Imprimerie Pascal, 1933), 1: 284.
27 S. G. Iaron, *Kiev v vos'midesiatykh godakh. Vospominaniia starozhila* (Kiev: Petr Barskii, 1910), 189–190.

man of unique intelligence and inexhaustible energy, David Semenovich gradually connected his name with all commercial enterprises that appeared in the southwestern region for the last thirty years.[28]

Margolin also contributed to the development of the city's public transportation. Kiev was the first city in the Russian Empire where electric trams were introduced, in 1892.[29] A Belgian tram manufacturer, who participated in this project, presented Margolin with a private tramcar in gratitude. David Margolin's granddaughter, Nadia Graffman, recalled that this car was "all red velvet inside, and even possessed a little icebox, but where could you go? It was on rails..."[30]

Probably Margolin would not have agreed with this statement. He used this tram for his trips around Kiev and, as mentioned above, lent it to Grand Prince Petr Nikolaevich and Count Ignat'ev, the governor of Kiev, during the All-Russian Exhibition in the city in 1913.

Margolin was the owner of the tram company and co-owner of the gas, water, and electric companies, in addition to many others. "[E]verywhere he successfully combined his personal commercial interests with general state usefulness and local needs."[31] He was a member of all Kiev philanthropic organizations, and gave charity to needy people, whether Jew or gentile. Sliozberg wrote that Margolin had a uniquely kind heart: nobody gave more to the needy than he. He made a large donation for the establishment in Kiev of commercial and trade schools, and financed the artisan school and a Talmud-Torah (a religious Jewish school). Because of his generous philanthropic activity and personal qualities, he was highly respected.[32]

---

28 Ibid.
29 Aleksandr Anisimov, *Kiev i kievliane*, 1: 272, 277; *Kyiv. Entsyklopedychnyi dovidnyk*, s.v. "Tramvai," 604–605.
30 Gary Graffman, *I Really Should Be Practicing* (Garden City, NY: Doubleday & Company, Inc, 1981), 15.
31 Ibid.
32 G. B. Sliozberg, *Dela minuvshikh dnei. Zapiski russkogo evreia* (Paris: Imprimerie Pascal, 1933), 1: 284; S. G. Iaron, *Kiev v vos'midesiatykh godakh. Vospominaniia starozhila* (Kiev: Petr Barskii Publishing House, 1910), 189–190.

As one of the leading entrepreneurs in Kiev, the southwestern region, and the entire Russian Empire, Margolin was frequently sought out for advice on economic and financial questions by the Kiev provincial administration. He was also invited to St. Petersburg as the official representative of local trade and industry. Yet he never forgot his coreligionists and always defended the interests of Jews to imperial and local officials.[33]

David Margolin's wife, Rozaliia Isaakovna (née Tsuker), was also involved in various charitable activities. According to the president of the Ukrainian Academy of Arts and Sciences in the United States, professor Michael Vetukhiv, she was

> a gentle cultured woman, constantly engaged in charitable works. With her assistance the first baby health clinic was opened in Kiev. Their son Arnold Margolin, well known lawyer, diplomat and politician of the Ukrainian People's Republic, derived from both his parents a special quality of good will and warmth. He had, too, his father's drive and initiative and his mother's gentleness.[34]

Arnold Margolin recalls in his memoirs that Judaism was scrupulously observed in his parents' household, which attempted to combine traditional religious values with those of the haskalah. During his childhood, Arnold Margolin often attended synagogue with his father. The Margolin family lived a comfortable life. They had a large apartment in Kiev with a spacious drawing room decorated with costly furniture, a piano, and a telephone. They also had a dacha on one of the islands in the Dnieper, where the family would arrive in the summer "on their little boat *Lilliput*."[35]

Gary Graffman, the great-grandson of David Margolin, reports that

---

33 Sliozberg, *Dela minuvshikh dnei. Zapiski russkogo evreia*, 1: 284.
34 The Annals of the Ukrainian Academy of Arts and Sciences in the US, 7:1, 2 (23–24) (1959): 1671.
35 Gary Graffman, *I Really Should Be Practicing*, 14–15.

Even though he enjoyed the good life, my great-grandfather David Semyonovich Margolin was by no means a playboy. He was widely known for his social welfare work, and whenever a poor Jew of Kiev needed intercession with the governmental authorities for one reason or another, it was he who was called upon to act as the go-between. His wife Rosalie was constantly engaged in charitable activities, and opened the first child-care center in the area. Between them they occupied a position of eminence and respect in the city of Kiev. They were included by the Tsar himself on his rounds, when he visited the city, coming every now and then to inspect the streetcars, the public utilities and the shipyards. The memory of this honor paid her family never did impress my mother much, however. "Nicholas the Second," she once drawled in a pitying voice. "He was such a *stupid* man." Not that she ever met him: I believe that her opinion was formed solely as a result of political events. In truth, I am surprised that she does not entertain warmer feelings toward the last of the Romanovs, as a large diamond ring that he presented to her grandfather is still in the family.[36]

This view of the tsar was held not only by Gary Graffman's mother Nadia, but was also shared by her father Arnold Margolin. While still young, he became a socialist and an advocate of victims of persecution and pogroms. As mentioned in chapter four, on the day of the promulgation of the Manifesto of October 17, 1905, David Margolin and Leon Brodsky organized for students of Kiev commercial schools a trip on a Margolin boat "to celebrate the Constitution."[37]

During the October 1905 pogrom in Kiev, rioters led by a policeman broke into Arnold Margolin's apartment, which was located far away from the area where the pogrom was being systematically carried out, intending to kill him. They looted the apartment. Arnold had been

---

36 Ibid., 17.
37 A. S. Shmakov, *Pogrom evreev v Kieve. Ocherk* (Moscow: Tip. Imp. moskov. univ., 1908), 73–74.

included on a list of people to be robbed and killed for his liberal political views. This was the Black Hundreds' revenge for his liberalism and criticism of the regime. He was a member of the Union for the Achievement of Equal Rights for the Jewish People in Russia and of the Union of Unions. His legal defense of peasants who had seized land from their landlords and of pogrom victims had also earned him the antipathy of the authorities. During these trials, Margolin had attempted to prove that the pogroms had been organized and encouraged by local officials.[38]

Arnold Margolin and his family survived the Kiev pogrom by hiding, probably in the apartment of a Christian neighbor or a hotel. David Margolin, in his claim for damages to the governor-general, wrote on October 20, 1905 that the apartment of his son Arnold at number 6 Malo-Zhitomirskaia Street was looted by a "crowd accompanied by a policeman." Even more shocking was that the policeman had brought the crowd to Margolin's apartment. The owner of the house, G. Moskalev, attempted to pacify the rioters by telling them that Arnold Margolin had left Kiev. However, the policeman replied, "Margolin is not here, but here is his apartment."[39] Then, according to an eyewitness—Arnold Margolin's cook, Ksenia—the policeman was the first to destroy property in the apartment: he took a hammer and broke the mirrors. The crowd, inspired by his example, began to break the windows and threw all of the furniture, including the piano, wardrobe, and mirrors, from the third floor. In his claim, David Margolin wrote that the apartment was "totally destroyed." This petition was written on the third day of the pogrom when looting, pillaging, and the murder of Jews still continued in the city. Accordingly, he concluded:

> It is my duty to inform Your Excellency that today the pogrom took even more violent forms, and if decisive measures are not

---

38 Victoria Khiterer, "Arnold Davidovich Margolin: Ukrainian-Jewish Jurist, Statesman and Diplomat," *Revolutionary Russia* 18, no. 2 (December 2005): 147–148.
39 TsDIAK U, f. 442, op. 855, d. 391, part. 1, l. 179.

taken immediately, then it is difficult even to predict what terrible consequences may follow.[40]

As was usual during pogroms in Russia, measures were taken only on the third day. When the authorities gave the order to shoot the rioters, the crowd of the pogrom-makers dissolved within a few hours.

The wealthy Jews of Kiev, as well as the poor, were bitter at being left defenseless in the face of a wild mob, which was directed to their dwellings by the police. None of the titles and ranks received by them for their entrepreneurial activities, nor the state awards and expensive presents from the authorities, could compensate for the absence of equal rights or for the everyday humiliations. This explains why, in spite of being presented with a large diamond ring "from the Cabinet of His Imperial Majesty…for his work as a member of the Board of the Shipping Society on Dnieper River and its tributaries,"[41] David Margolin and his family did not harbor "warmer feelings toward the last of the Romanovs."

David Margolin was a member of the delegation of the Kiev Jewish community that congratulated the tsar on the three hundredth anniversary of the accession of the Romanov dynasty in 1913, for which the tsar thanked him in person.[42] Because of his business interests, as well as the interests of the Kiev Jewish community, he felt it necessary to maintain connections with the high authorities, but it is doubtful that he harbored many illusions about the possibility of improving the status of Jews in the Russian Empire under the tsarist regime.

After the declaration of the autonomy and later the independence of the Ukrainian People's Republic, David Margolin, like his son Arnold, worked with the new Ukrainian government. On January 21, 1918, David Margolin was appointed a member of the Financial-Economic Council. In March 1918, he was also appointed to the Barter

---

40 Ibid.
41 DAMK, f. 153, op. 1, d. 309, l. 4.
42 Ibid., ll. 10–11.

Commission with the Central Powers.[43] After the defeat of the Ukrainian national movement, he emigrated and died in the mid-1920s.

Another important figure in the Kiev Jewish elite was the developer Lev Borisovich [Leiba Berkovich] Ginzburg (1858–c. 1926). From 1895 to 1905 the population of Kiev doubled, reaching 450,000 inhabitants.[44] Such rapid population growth, as well as the significant capital available in the city, created a building boom at the turn of the twentieth century. Kiev transformed from a provincial city into a real European center with tall buildings, theaters, modern offices, and apartments.

This decade was the golden age of Ginzburg's construction company. Ginzburg moved to Kiev after graduation from the Vitebsk district (*uezdnoe*) school when he was nineteen years old. He began work as a contractor with Lazar' Chernoiarov, but soon established his own company. Ginzburg's company erected many beautiful buildings in the city. Some were built in the art nouveau style and were designed by the most prominent Kievan architect of the time, Vladislav Gorodetskii.[45] Ginzburg's company built the Museum of Antiquities and Art, the Choral Synagogue, the Karaite religious building (the Karaim Kenassa), the Catholic cathedral, the South Russian factory, the Opera, the Operetta, the Solovtsov Theater (the Russian Dramatic Theater), the polytechnic institute, and many other notable buildings. Contracts for construction were awarded by auction and granted to the lowest bidder. Ginzburg's company won many of the most prestigious Kiev construction projects because it built better and at a lower cost than other companies.[46]

Ginzburg owned the tallest building in the entire Russian Empire, the twelve-story "Kiev Skyscraper," which included ninety-four apartments and several stores. Ginzburg's private two-story mansion was built in the Moorish style in its courtyard. Over twenty janitors

---

43 V. F. Verstiuk and O. D. Boiko, comps., *Ukrains'ka Tsentral'na Rada. Dokumenty i materialy* (Kiev: Naukova dumka, 1997), 2: 132, 201.
44 *Kyiv. Entsyklopedychnyi dovidnyk*, 32; M. Kalnitsky, "Zolotoe desiatiletie Gintsburga," *Art. City. Construction.* 1 (1995): 38–40.
45 Dmytro Malakov, *Arkhitektor Horodets'kyi* (Kiev: Kyi, 1999), 80.
46 M. Kalnitsky, "Zolotoe desiatiletie Gintsburga," 38–40.

(*dvorniks*) served in the building, cleaning the front and back stairways, walls and carpets, the courtyard and stained-glass windows. They received a salary for their work and rent-free accommodation in the building.[47]

The majority of the buildings constructed by Ginzburg are still used by Kievans in their original functions. Only the skyscraper and the Ginzburg mansion did not survive—they were destroyed by Soviet partisans during the Nazi occupation of Kiev in September 1941.[48]

Lev Ginzburg was a well-known philanthropist. He gave money to Jewish and general philanthropic organizations in Kiev, and was a trustee of the Kiev Jewish hospital and the Kiev women's gymnasium named after Kiev governor Ivan Funduklei. Mikhail Kalnitsky wrote that various organizations willingly elected Ginzburg as a member of their boards of trustees, and subsequently did not have problems with repair and construction work that was carried out for free by Ginzburg's company.[49] Ginzburg was a merchant of the first guild. He was awarded the title of "Commercial Adviser," and received several state awards, including the order of Saint Anna.

The Russian economic crisis at the beginning of the twentieth century put an end to the "golden age" of the Ginzburg construction company. In 1904, the company was not able to pay its suppliers on time, and it was placed under administration. The company overcame that crisis, but the scale of its construction works never again reached that of the previous decade.

After the October Revolution, the Bolsheviks confiscated Ginzburg's company. We do not know much about his last years. In 1926 poet Osip Mandel'shtam wrote in his essay "Kiev" that Kievans honored the memory of "the well-known contractor Ginzburg, fabulous house owner, who died impoverished in the Kiev hospital."[50]

Among Kiev's jewelers at the turn of the twentieth century, the most prominent was Iosif Abramovich Marshak, whose jewelry

---

47 Aleksandr Anisimov, *Kiev i kievliane*, 1: 55.
48 Ibid., 51.
49 Kalnitsky, "Zolotoe desiatiletie Gintsburga," 38–40.
50 Ibid.

company produced many examples of decorative arts that brought the company international prestige and awards. Marshak was born the eldest of six children into a poor Jewish family in the shtetl of Ignatovka in the province of Kiev, where, according to the census of 1897, there lived 1,093 people of whom 926 were Jews.[51] Even in his childhood he showed artistic talent and dreamed of owning his own jewelry workshop.

At the age of fourteen Marshak moved to Kiev and began work as an apprentice at one of the local jewelers' workshops. He was certified as a master jeweler by the Kiev Office for the Control of Handicrafts, and with a small initial capital of a hundred rubles—probably his wife's dowry—opened a jeweler's workshop.[52] In 1878, he established his own jewelry company. At first it was located in the Podol, but a year later Marshak moved his business to the main street of Kiev, renting two rooms at number 4 Kreshchatik from Célestin Verle, a Swiss immigrant watchmaker. Thirteen years later, in 1891, Marshak opened a jewelry factory on the same street. In 1908, he purchased Verle's watch business and opened a watch shop at his factory. Marshak's factory and jewelry store occupied several buildings, Kreshchatik Street numbers 2, 3, 4, 5, and 8. In 1913, the business had 126 employees. The working schedule of the factory was adjusted to the religious needs of Jews as well as Christians. In accordance with the regulations of the city duma, Marshak's factory did not work on Sundays or on Christian religious holidays. In addition, the factory did not work on Saturdays, nine days at Pesach, three days at Rosh Hashana, Yom Kippur, four days on Sukkoth, one day at Purim and at Tisha be-Av.[53]

The workday at Marshak's lasted from eight in the morning to six in the evening, with an obligatory one-and-a-half-hour break for lunch. Underage employees (up to seventeen years old) worked only until 3:00 p.m. Marshak was a pioneer of the employment of women in jewelry production. Women workers more successfully performed some less

---

51 *Evreiskaia entsiklopediia*, s.v. "Ignatovka," 8:13.
52 Zhanna Arustamian, "Ukrainskii Faberzhe," *Evreiskoe slovo* 20, no. 143 (May 21–27, 2003): 8.
53 Vitalii Kovalyns'kyi, *Kyivs'ki miniatiury* (Kiev: Litopys, 2002), 1: 155.

strenuous operations that required greater attention to detail. The factory maintained strict discipline; employees were fined for late arrival or for bad behavior toward their co-workers, and the fines were subtracted from their salaries. Workers earned three to ten rubles per day depending on their qualifications. Marshak included in the business his younger brother Israel, who was the assistant director of the factory, and his wife Liia Faivishevna (Elizaveta Fedorovna), who had her own office at the factory. When Marshak's sons Vladimir and Alexander grew up they also joined their father's business.[54]

The secret of the great success of Marshak's company was its sensitivity to new artistic trends, its use of the best materials, new technology, effective organization of production, and the involvement of the best artists and artisans in the production process. Together with the artists from his company, Marshak attended jewelry exhibitions in Moscow and St. Petersburg. In 1890, he traveled to Europe to study the art of jewelry making. He also visited the World Exhibition in Paris and several industrial cities in Germany. Following this trip, he introduced new equipment and materials as well as better work organization.[55] He invited artists from St. Petersburg and Paris to work with his company, and imported gold from Hamburg, Berlin, and Paris, silver from Moscow, and platinum from St. Petersburg.[56]

Marshak's company was particularly adept in the casting of silver and platinum. It produced beautiful silver vases, dishes, jewelry with precious stones, jewel boxes, models of Kiev buildings and ships, watches, and medals. The company also made jewelry to order for wealthy Kievans. One such commission came from S. Mogilevtsev, who ordered a silver model of the Kiev Pedagogical Museum (now Teacher's House) in order to present it to the tsarevich Alexei (the next in line to the throne in Russia) during the tsar's visit to Kiev in 1911. Marshak's company was preeminent among the ninety-two jewelry companies in Kiev, and competed successfully with the jewelry companies of Moscow and St. Petersburg. Its products were sold not only in

---

54 Zhanna Arustamian, "Ukrainskii Faberzhe," 8.
55 Ibid.
56 Ibid.

his own store but also in Moscow, St. Petersburg, and Warsaw. They won awards at international exhibitions in Chicago, Paris, Kiev, and St. Petersburg.[57]

Marshak, who was one of Kiev's wealthiest Jews, actively participated in the community; he was a generous philanthropist and financed a *heder*.[58] In 1913, in honor of the thirty-fifth anniversary of his factory, he donated 5,000 rubles to the fund for disabled and retired factory workers. In the same year, he established at his own expense a school for artisans at his factory.

On August 27, 1911, in his petition to the governor-general to be made an official court supplier, Marshak described the history of his company:

> Your Excellency has known me a long time. I am proud that my company, which has grown and developed under your administration, has become one of the leading elements in the Russian art-jewelry industry at the present time.
>
> I will allow myself to recount to Your Excellency the history of my company. It was established in Kiev in 1878 as a small workshop and developed gradually without rapid leaps. I continuously took care to maintain a conscientious attitude to the progress of the business, as a result of which my company now enjoys the esteem and confidence of all estates of society in the southwestern region, in all of Russia and abroad.
>
> At the time of the Holy Coronation of His Imperial Majesty on May 14, 1896 I was favored with many orders from different institutions in Kiev and in our region. During the visit of His Imperial Majesty to Kiev in 1896 I received orders for almost all the presents to the Tsar, and artistic works of my factory were praised by many high-ranking persons.
>
> For its products, my company has received many awards at World Exhibitions: a medal with honorable diploma at

---

57 TsDIAK U, f. 442, op. 641, d. 35, part I, ll. 964–965; S. G. Iaron, *Kiev v vos'midesiatykh godakh*, 189–190.
58 *Rossiiskaia evreiskaia entsiklopediia*. s.v. "Marshak Iosif Abramovich," 2:255.

Chicago 1893, a golden medal at Antwerp 1894, a medal at Paris 1900, and the Grand-Prize at Liège in 1905. In addition my company received the main prize at Kiev in 1897 and at St. Petersburg in 1902.

I have received praise from many different governmental institutions and private companies. In addition, the local press has noted the contribution of my company to the economy of the southwestern region…

I allow myself to add to this that on the twenty-fifth anniversary of my company the High Authorities recommended me for the title of hereditary honored citizen, which I was awarded by the Highest Grace.

I was also chosen by the Kiev City Administration to be a member of the Representatives on the Affairs of Jewish Charity under the Kiev City Board. I am also a trustee of the Kiev Jewish Hospital, a deputy appraiser of the committee to evaluate its activity and a deputy of the Kiev Assay Administration.

Because of all the foregoing, I dare humbly to submit to Your Excellency this petition to His Imperial Majesty, the request of a faithful subject, who has worked continuously for thirty-four years for the benefit and progress of the art so dear to him, to grant me most graciously the high title of Court Supplier and allow me to display the State Coat of Arms. These distinctions will be for me the highest award in my life for my many years of outstanding work and the best adornment of one of the premier jewelry factories in Russia. This will be the best heritage which I could leave to my five sons, three of whom work in my business in the hope that they will be able to preserve all that their father has achieved during his long working life.[59]

The title of Court Supplier and the right to display the State Coat of Arms of the Russian Empire guaranteed the quality of product.

---

59 TsDIAK U, f. 442, op. 641, d. 35, part I, ll. 964–965.

These awards would have increased the prestige of Marshak's company and its products in Russian and foreign markets. Unfortunately, there is no answer to this petition in the archives, so we do not know if the Russian authorities fulfilled his request.

Among the customers of the Marshak Jewelry Company were not only Kiev Jewish organizations but also Russian nationalist and anti-Semitic bodies such as the Kiev branch of the Union of the Russian People. Perhaps the leaders of this organization made an exception to their hatred of Jews in order to present to the tsar a gift of the highest quality.

Marshak enjoyed great prestige among his fellow jewelers. When in 1913 Kiev jewelers created a professional organization, the Diamond Club, its thirteen-member board unanimously elected Marshak as president. In 1918, Marshak wrote a will in which he divided his estate between his five sons and three daughters. He also left one million rubles for the school at the factory and for other philanthropic purposes.[60]

He died at the age of sixty-four on August 22, 1918. His will was only partially carried out: his children inherited only the money that he had deposited in foreign banks, since the Bolsheviks nationalized his jewelry factory. His sons Alexander and Vladimir, who worked with their father, immigrated to France and opened a jewelry store in Paris. However, they were unable to reestablish the jewelry factory.

There are many similar features in the biographies and paths to business success of the wealthiest Jewish entrepreneurs in Kiev. Men like David Margolin, Lev Ginzburg, and Iosif Marshak achieved tremendous financial success in one generation. For the Brodsky family it took two generations. Margolin, Ginzburg, and Marshak each came to Kiev at a young age without any significant means, and only through their talent, ability, and financial genius were they able to establish their companies.

The activity of Kiev's Jewish industrialists and philanthropists changed the appearance of the city, improved the quality of life there,

---

60 Vitalii Kovalyns'kyi, *Kyivs'ki miniatiury*, 1: 160.

and benefited all its inhabitants. However, the flourishing of Kiev's economy and various businesses continued for only a short time. The normal economic life of the city was first interrupted by World War I and then destroyed by the revolution and ensuing civil war. Jewish entrepreneurs, like their non-Jewish counterparts, lost all their property. Thus, most Jewish businessmen acquired and then lost all their capital in one or two generations.

JEWISH POVERTY IN KIEV

Why was a significant percentage of the Jewish population poor in such a wealthy city as Kiev, about which people said that it was possible to "make cheese pies from snow and fill sacks with gold"?[61] According to the statistics of the Jewish Colonization Society (EKO), in 1904 ten thousand Jews in Kiev (20 percent of the Jewish population) lived below the poverty level.[62]

In her memoirs, Golda Meir left a fine account of how poor families in Kiev lived. She wrote that her parents were newcomers to Kiev: her father Moshe Yitzhak Mabovitch was from Ukraine, and her mother Blume was from Pinsk. They moved to Kiev a few years before 1898, when Golda was born. Her father obtained the right of residence in Kiev as an artisan-carpenter. She recalled that

> In Kiev father found work for the government, making furniture for school libraries, and even got an advance. With this money, plus money my parents borrowed, he built a little carpentry shop of his own, and it seemed as though all would be well. But in the end the job fell through. Perhaps, as he said, it was because he was Jewish, and Kiev was noted for its anti-Semitism. At all events, very soon there was no job, no money, and debts that had to be paid somehow. It was a crisis that was to recur throughout my childhood.

---

61 Sholom Aleichem, *Sobranie sochinenii*, 6: 283.
62 Gershon Badanes, *S odnogo vola tri shkury* (Kiev: I. M. Roset Publishing House, 1907), 21.

My father began desperately to look for work everywhere; he would be out all day and much of the night, and when he came home in the bitter dark of a Russian winter, there was rarely enough food in the house to make him a meal. Bread and salt herring had to do.

But my mother had other troubles. Four little boys and a girl all fell ill: two of them died before they were a year old, two of them went within one month...Then, right after the last of the babies had died, a well-to-do family who lived near us offered my mother a job as wet nurse to their new baby. They made one condition: my parents and Sheyna [Golda's older sister] were to move from their miserable, damp little room to a larger, lighter, airier one, and a nurse was to come teach my poor young mother the rudiments of child care. So it was thanks to this "foster child" that Sheyna's life improved and that I was born into relative order, cleanliness and health. Our benefactors saw to it that my mother always had enough to eat, and soon my parents had three children, Sheyna, Zipke and me.[63]

However, her mother's work as a wet nurse could not provide enough means for the entire family. Golda Meir wrote,

I remember all too clearly how poor we were. There was never enough of anything, not food, not warm clothing, not heat at home. I was always a little too cold outside and little too empty inside. Even now, from that very distant past, I can summon up with no effort at all, almost intact, the picture of myself sitting in tears in the kitchen, watching my mother feed some of the gruel that rightfully belong to me to my younger sister, Zipke. Gruel was a great luxury in our home in those days, and I bitterly resented having to share any of it, even with the baby...I knew only that life was hard and that there was no

---

63 Golda Meir, *My Life* (New York: A Dell Book, 1975), 14–15.

justice anywhere. I am glad that no one told me then that my older sister, Sheyna, often fainted from hunger in school.[64]

Perhaps under continued threats of pogroms and having lost their hope of improving their financial situation in Kiev, Golda Meir's parents moved to Pinsk in 1903.

Golda Meir's father was right that anti-Semitism was a significant obstacle for Jews searching for work in Kiev. Many gentile business-owners did not hire any Jews. Some local anti-Semites attempted to boycott Jewish merchandise. Löwe wrote, "In Kiev, for instance, the 'Union of Archangel Michael' [a Russian nationalist and chauvinist group] organized…an exhibition with the purpose of not admitting boots produced by Jews."[65]

Many factors contributed to the poverty of Kievan Jews, including anti-Semitism, the poor professional qualifications of many Jewish artisans, serious chronic illnesses, large families, the high rate of unemployment in the city, and the illegal status of many Jews, which made it impossible to obtain well-paid employment. Various Jewish philanthropic organizations and wealthy Jews attempted to improve this situation by donating to the needy, purchasing tools for artisans, and sponsoring low-cost dining halls for poor Jews; however, these measures could only scratch the surface.

In addition to the Jewish Welfare Committee, whose work is described in a previous chapter, there were a number of other Jewish philanthropic organizations in Kiev. Some were organizations of the traditional type, such as the Society for the Welfare of Poor Jews in Kiev (*Gmilus-Hesed*, literally "bestowing kindness"), which sought to provide charity in accordance with long-established Jewish norms. Little remains of their records, and they were less significant in Kiev than institutions that had a more modern approach to the dispensing of charity. At the turn of the twentieth century, more modern Jewish

---

64 Ibid., 12.
65 Heinz-Dietrich Löwe, *The Tsars and the Jews: Reform, Reaction, and Antisemitism in Imperial Russia, 1772–1917* (Chur, Switzerland: Harwood Academic Publishers, 1993), 293.

philanthropic organizations were established in the city: the Kiev Society for the Care of Poor Jewish Artisans and Workers, the Kiev Jewish Branch of the Society for the Protection of Women, the Society to Maintain Summer Sanatorium Colonies for the Sick Children of Poor Jews in the City of Kiev, and the Kiev Department of the Jewish Society for Aid to the Victims of the War.

THE KIEV SOCIETY FOR THE CARE OF POOR JEWISH ARTISANS AND WORKERS

The Kiev Society for the Care of Poor Jewish Artisans and Workers operated for a quarter of a century as a department of the Jewish Welfare Committee, but became an independent entity in 1906. One of the reasons for this split was the society's desire to democratize its work and involve Jewish workers and artisans in its management. The organizers thought that the participation of artisans in the society's work would make it possible to understand better the needs of their co-workers.

The board of the society reported that in the first year of its independent activity, 138 artisans were enrolled and six were elected to the board. The following year, the number of artisans on the board increased to ten.[66] Evsei Tsukkerman, the former rabbi of Kiev, was elected chairman of the society. After his summary dismissal from his position as state rabbi by the local authorities, Tsukkerman continued to occupy important positions in the Kiev community and in Jewish philanthropic organizations. The society's board included the jeweler Iosif Marshak, the secretary of the Economic Board of the Kiev Choral Synagogue Izrail' P. Kel'berin, and Baron Vladimir Goratsievich Ginsburg, among others. The number of board members remained constant at thirty-six from 1906 to 1913. In the previous chapter it was noted that the board of the Kiev Jewish community also had thirty-six members. There was little overlap in the governing boards of these two institutions. However, the choice of the number thirty-six for the

---

66 *Otchet Obshchestva popecheniia o bednykh remeslennikakh i rabochikh evreiakh g. Kieva za 1907 g.* (Kiev: Kaplun Brother Publishing House, 1908), IV.

membership of the boards shows the attachment of Kiev's Jews to this sacred number.

The original funding for the society came from the remaining resources of the Committee for the Aid of the Victims of the [October 1905] Pogrom, the basket tax, membership payments, and private donations from the Brodsky family and Baron Vladimir Goratsievich Ginsburg. The total amount available to the society in 1906 was 33,286 rubles. The society's board complained about its limited means in its 1906 annual report, and argued that if it were to be successful in aiding the many needy Jewish artisans, it would have to obtain more support from the wealthy section of Kiev Jewry. In 1906, the society was able to provide help to 822 of 1,220 artisans who applied for assistance, or only 67 percent of requests. 1906 was an especially hard year for Kiev's Jewish artisans: many lost all their property during the October 1905 pogrom, and other local Jews, impoverished by the pogrom, were unable to purchase their goods.[67] In subsequent years the percentage of requests satisfied was higher, but due to the society's limited resources, and also because the society did not regard all requests as meritorious, it never reached 100 percent. Often the society could not even find the petitioner at the provided address, which meant either that the request was bogus, or more likely, that by the time it was considered, the applicant had died or been forced to leave Kiev.

The goals of the society, as stated in the first article of its bylaws, were ambitious: "The improvement of the financial, intellectual and moral condition of Jewish artisans in Kiev."[68] The society was to provide aid to artisans searching for work, to purchase materials and tools they required, and to help them sell their products. The society was also to provide food and clothing to poor artisans, give grants and loans in critical situations, give aid to sick artisans, and provide funds to bury the dead. The society was to take care of old artisans and orphans, and to spread general and professional knowledge among artisans.[69]

---

67 *Otchet Obshchestva popecheniia o bednykh remeslennikakh i rabochikh evreiakh g. Kieva za 1906 g.* (Kiev: Kaplun Brothers Publishing House, 1907), I–IV.
68 *Ustav Obshchestva popecheniia o bednykh remeslennikakh i rabochikh g. Kieva* (Kiev: Kaplun Brothers Publishing House, 1907), 1.
69 Ibid., 1–2.

The society accomplished most of its goals, except for finding work for artisans and supporting them in selling their products—these were beyond its power. In the first year of its independent existence, the society established an information bureau to place artisans into open positions, but nobody came to the bureau with job offers and it was closed in the same year. The society attributed this to the high unemployment in Kiev, as well as the low professional level of Jewish artisans.

Certainly at the beginning of the twentieth century, the situation of Jewish vocational training in Kiev was lamentable, which was a reflection partly of the low status of artisans in traditional Jewish society. The Kiev artisan school did not accept Jewish students; the Brodsky artisan school accepted only boys and taught them only to be either machinists or locksmiths. Vocational education for Jewish girls did not exist at all.[70] In 1907, in order to improve the training of Jewish artisans, the society's board decided to open a professional school for Jewish girls and a tailoring school for Jewish youth of both sexes. However, subsequent annual reports show that these goals were not accomplished. The artisan school's opening was planned for 1911. The society obtained permission in 1908 from the Ministry of Commerce and Industry to open a Jewish artisan school with a two-year program, but a shortage of resources seems to have prevented its establishment.[71] In 1913, the society did make a modest grant of two hundred rubles towards the foundation of Marshak's artisan school.[72]

The society's board focused its main attention on providing materials and tools to Jewish artisans, considering this assistance to be the most productive.[73] The society's loan department provided loans to a significant number of Jewish artisans. For example, in 1907 artisans received loans totaling 36,128 rubles. Even though the sums were comparatively modest—a maximum of fifty rubles—these loans helped many to purchase

---

70 *Otchet Obshchestva popecheniia o bednykh remeslennikakh i rabochikh evreiakh g. Kieva za 1907 g.* (Kiev: Kaplun Brother Publishing House, 1908), VII.
71 Ibid., VIII.
72 *Otchet Obshchestva popecheniia o bednykh remeslennikakh i rabochikh evreiakh g. Kieva za 1913 g.* (Kiev: Glezer Publishing House, 1914), XII.
73 *Otchet Obshchestva popecheniia o bednykh remeslennikakh i rabochikh evreiakh g. Kieva za 1910 g.* (Kiev: Glezer Publishing House, 1911), V.

sewing machines or other tools and to start their own businesses.[74] In the following years, the maximum loan was increased to 125 rubles per person.[75] This was a significant amount of money, if we remember that Marshak established his jeweler's workshop with one hundred rubles.

The society also provided financial assistance to poor, sick artisans and their widows and orphans. It had a legal department, which gave advice to Jewish workers and artisans on administrative, civil, and criminal matters, including the right of residence in Kiev, work injuries, the draft for military service, and other problems. According to the society's report for 1908, this legal department worked very effectively.[76]

The last published report of the society's committee, which appeared in 1913, admitted with some bitterness:

> Overcoming poverty among Jewish artisans is only possible by improving their professional skills.... The efforts of the Society's Committee are not sufficient for this purpose. Serious financial support is needed from the Kiev Jewish community.[77]

Although the Kiev Society for the Care of Poor Jewish Artisans and Workers had to abandon some of its goals and could not fully accomplish others because of a shortage of money, its work benefited hundreds of poor artisans, helping many to establish small workshops and businesses with loans and financial assistance.

THE KIEV JEWISH DEPARTMENT OF THE SOCIETY FOR THE PROTECTION OF WOMEN

The traditional image of the Jewish woman as a housewife in late Imperial Russia is well known from the writings of popular authors of

---

74 *Otchet Obshchestva popecheniia o bednykh remeslennikakh i rabochikh evreiakh g. Kieva za 1907 g.* (Kiev: Glezer Publishing House, 1908), IX.
75 *Otchet Obshchestva popecheniia o bednykh remeslennikakh i rabochikh evreiakh g. Kieva za 1910 g.* (Kiev: Glezer Publishing House, 1911), VI.
76 *Otchet Obshchestva popecheniia o bednykh remeslennikakh i rabochikh evreiakh g. Kieva za 1908 g.* (Kiev: Brothers Kaplun Publishing House, 1909), V–VI.
77 *Otchet Obshchestva popecheniia o bednykh remeslennikakh i rabochikh evreiakh g. Kieva za 1913 g.*, XIV.

the early twentieth century. In addition, historical literature and memoirs describe Jewish women as breadwinners—maintaining stalls in the shtetl marketplace—while their husbands devoted themselves to religious study. While it is true that Jewish women in shtetls did not participate in the official structures of the community, recent scholarship has substantially modified this picture.[78] At the same time, it is clear that the lives of the women of the Jewish elite in the empire's larger towns were very different. There, emancipated Jewish women participated actively in philanthropic institutions and proto-feminist movements, and established Jewish women's organizations.

The published reports and programs of these organizations show that more than two dozen Jewish women's organizations functioned in the Russian Empire at the beginning of the twentieth century.[79] Most were located in large cities and provincial administrative centers. The majority had primarily philanthropic goals, and provided support for poor Jewish girls and women. Among the most important were the two Jewish departments of the Russian Society for the Protection of Women; the first department was established in St. Petersburg, probably in 1902, and the second in Kiev in 1913. The Society for the Protection of Women was founded in Russia in 1899.[80] It was headed in turn by two princesses, Evgeniia Ol'denburgskaia, a first cousin of the tsar, and Elena Saksen-Al'tenburgskaia.[81] Richard Stites writes that the society

> was well staffed by titled patricians and by wealthy philanthropists like Baron [Goratsii] Gintsburg, Countess Panina, and the Tereshchenkos of Kiev, as well as representatives of the

---

78 ChaeRan Freeze, Paula Hyman, and Antony Polonsky, eds. "Jewish Women in Eastern Europe" *Polin* 18 (2005): 3–188.
79 V. E. Kel'ner and D. A. El'iashevich, comps., *Literatura o evreiakh na russkom iazyke 1890–1947. Bibliograficheskii ukazatel'* (St. Petersburg: Akademicheskii Proekt, 1995), 394–395.
80 Robin Bisha, Jehanne M. Gheith, Christine Holden, and William G. Wagner, comps. and eds., *Russian Women, 1698–1917: Experience and Expression, An Anthology of Sources* (Bloomington and Indianapolis: Indiana University Press, 2002), XXVII.
81 Richard Stites, *The Women's Liberation Movement in Russia: Feminism, Nihilism, and Bolshevism 1860–1930* (Princeton: Princeton University Press, 1978), 192.

intelligentsia, the world of culture, the professions, and a number of feminists.[82]

The society's headquarters was located in St. Petersburg, and it had local branches in Aleksandrovsk, Vilna, Kiev, Minsk, Odessa, Riga, Sevastopol', Rostov-on-Don, and Khar'kov.[83]

One important goal of the Russian Society for the Protection of Women was to combat prostitution and trafficking of women (white slavery).[84] The society had a department to combat prostitution with a dormitory where women could stay for five kopecks a day. It gave women legal and employment assistance and provided medical and financial aid.[85] The society was supposed to support all women who asked for help. However, like the other Russian feminist organization, the Union of Equality for Women (*Soiuz ravnopraviia zhenshchin*) established in 1905, it ignored the specific national and religious needs of Jewish and other non-Russian women. According to Martha Bohachevsky-Chomiak, "Russian women considered the demand for national rights extraneous, illicit, divisive and ill-timed."[86]

As a result, many Jewish women activists felt the need for the establishment of specifically Jewish organizations, which could address the problems of Jewish women. Initially, as was the case with the St. Petersburg Jewish branch of the Russian Society for the Protection of Women, these were often linked with existing Russian bodies. In the first place, it was very difficult to obtain permission from the authorities to establish a Jewish organization in the Russian Empire; it was far easier to create Jewish departments of already existing all-Russian organizations. In addition, it was believed that the international connections of the Russian body would help Jewish women accomplish their goals.

---

82 Ibid.
83 Norma Corigilano Noonan and Carol Nechemias, eds., *Encyclopedia of Russian Women's Movements* (Westport, CT: Greenwood Press, 2001), 58.
84 Ibid., 58–60.
85 Ibid.
86 Martha Bohachevsky-Chomiak, *Feminists Despite Themselves: Women in Ukrainian Community Life, 1884–1939* (Edmonton: Canadian Institute of Ukrainian Studies University of Alberta Edmonton, 1988), 40.

The exact year of the establishment of the St. Petersburg Jewish Department of the Society for the Protection of Women is unknown. However, it was established not later than 1902: the organization's report for 1907 mentions the existence of its dormitory since 1902.

Certain peculiarities of the life of Jewish women in Russia dictated the special aims of the Jewish departments. A key question in Jewish life in the Russian Empire was the rules governing the right of Jews to stay and live outside the Pale of Settlement. St. Petersburg and Kiev were outside the Pale, which seriously affected Jewish women in those cities. This question dominated the work of the Jewish departments. The Kiev Jewish department hired experienced lawyers to defend the rights of Jewish women. The women also received legal help from the organization in cases of divorce, separation, and abuse. Unlike the Russian department of the society, the Jewish departments never mention in their reports any measures to fight prostitution. The Jewish departments seem rather to have used their means to provide legal, educational, and financial help to needy Jewish women.

Both Jewish departments of the Society for the Protection of Women paid a great deal of attention to the question of Jewish education. The St. Petersburg and Kiev departments had different approaches to this issue. The St. Petersburg department had a more bohemian character, which was reflected in its activity. The president of the department was Baron Goratsii Osipovich Gintsburg, a Jewish philanthropist, banker, and public figure, and the vice president was Baroness Roza Sigizmundovna Gintsburg.[87] Baron Gintsburg was chosen as the department's president because he had good contacts with the high authorities, which were crucial for its establishment.

The St. Petersburg Jewish department of the Society for the Protection of Women focused its activity on the education of Jewish girls, organizing Saturday sessions where girls studied literature, Russian, German, Hebrew, mathematics, needlework, music, and dancing. These Saturday sessions were attended by 451 Jewish girls and women in the 1906–1907 academic year. Among those participating in

---

87 *Otchet Otdela popecheniia o evreiskikh devushkakh g. St. Peterburga za 1907 god* (St. Petersburg: n.p., 1908), 3.

these sessions were working Jewish women (tailors, housekeepers, clerks, masseurs, bakers, midwives, stenographers) as well as students at gymnasiums and Jewish professional schools.[88]

Many young Jewish women also attempted to obtain professional training. The St. Petersburg Jewish department stated in its 1907 annual report that many young Jewish women were not satisfied with their work in tailoring workshops and

> sought the life of a member of the intelligentsia, even though this meant they were often hungry. To achieve this goal Jewish girls spend as little time at tailoring as possible, hoping merely to earn what they need in order to sustain a meager existence. They devote all their free time to studying in order to become midwives, masseuses or teachers.[89]

The St. Petersburg Jewish department also provided evening courses for women who wanted to prepare for the examination that would enable them to enter the fourth class of the gymnasium.[90] Its employment agency attempted, not very successfully, to find jobs for Jewish women. In 1907, due to the shortage of job openings for women, the agency could not find jobs even for those who had attended the Saturday sessions on a regular basis.[91]

The Kiev Jewish department was opened in 1914, after a long struggle with the local authorities. The effort to establish this department began in 1911. At the beginning of 1912, the general convention of the Kiev Section of the Society for the Protection of Women approved a proposal to create a Jewish department. However, this decision was not approved by the Russian society's board on the grounds that "there is no need to open an autonomous Kiev Jewish department."[92] This

---

88 Ibid., 6–7.
89 Ibid., 17.
90 Ibid., 6, 10–11.
91 Ibid., 16–18.
92 *Otchet za 1914 god Otdela popecheniia o evreiskikh devushkakh i zhenshchinakh g. Kieva pri Kievskom otdelenii Rossiiskogo obshchestva zashchity zhenshchin* (Kiev: n.p., 1915), 3–4.

decision was made after consultation with the governor-general.[93] The local authorities resisted the registration of any new Jewish organizations in Kiev, especially those intended to defend the legal rights of Jews. The local administration correctly suspected that these organizations would resist the expulsion of Jews from Kiev.

Fortunately for the Jewish women of Kiev, the head of the Russian society, Princess Elena Al'tenburgskaia, came to Kiev in the fall of 1913 to attend the opening ceremony of the Kiev Conservatory. The Jewish women of Kiev presented to her their request to open a Kiev Jewish department. The princess claimed that she

> was unpleasantly surprised when she heard about the previous failure of this project. She said that she was not informed about this proposal, and she would now strongly support the idea of establishing this department.[94]

Princess Al'tenburgskaia kept her promise, and a few months later, in December 1913, the organizing committee received a letter from the St. Petersburg department conveying the permission of Governor-General Fedor Fedorovich Trepov to establish the Kiev Jewish department of the society.[95]

This department was opened in February 1914, and the wives of Kiev's rich Jewish businessmen and public figures became members of the board. Among them were A. F. Brodskaia and R. E. Margolina. E. D. Goldenberg was elected president of the department.[96] Soon after its establishment, the Kiev Jewish department created a dormitory and provided low-cost meals for needy Jewish women. Poor Jewish women who came temporarily to Kiev could stay at the dormitory very inexpensively. The Kiev Jewish department received permission from the local administration to accommodate in their dormitory for seven days Jewish women who came temporarily to Kiev. In general, Jews who did

---

93 Ibid.
94 Ibid.
95 Ibid., 4–5.
96 Ibid., 6.

not have the right to live outside the Pale of Settlement were allowed to stay in Kiev for only three days.[97]

During World War I, the wives, mothers, and relatives of Jewish soldiers often applied to the Kiev Jewish department for help in finding their relatives in Kiev military hospitals. Many of them came to Kiev from other cities and towns and stayed in the dormitory where they received food, assistance in the search for their relatives, and, if necessary, money for train tickets to return home. Jewish women who came to Kiev for medical consultation, or as refugees from the front line, also stayed temporarily in the dormitory.[98]

The activities of the Kiev Jewish department had a more practical and pragmatic character than those of the St. Petersburg Jewish department. The women who ran it organized sewing workshops where women could be trained as seamstresses. The Kiev department also established an employment agency for Jewish women and provided medical and legal aid. The work of the employment agency, like that of the St. Petersburg Jewish department, was not very successful. Women were hired last and fired first during World War I, when unemployment had generally increased. The Kiev Jewish department's 1914 report mentions a lack of work opportunities for women in general, and specifically for work of the type sought by members of the intelligentsia.[99] According to its report, "many women of intelligent professions: students, teachers, students of conservatory, and so on" were working in the sewing workshops of the Kiev Jewish section.[100] Poverty and unemployment had compelled them to take up physical labor. Men in many families were mobilized into the Russian Army during World War I, and women had to find some way to support themselves and their families.

The women who applied to the Kiev Jewish department for assistance in finding jobs were mostly well educated. Among them were graduates of law schools, of the historical-philological faculties of universities, and of commercial schools, dentists, students of "Higher

---

97 Ibid., 9–10.
98 Ibid., 9–14.
99 Ibid., 27–32.
100 Ibid., 24.

Courses for Women," and so on. The majority were at least graduates of gymnasiums. Jewish women searched for jobs as teachers, governesses, saleswomen, housekeepers, clerks, tailors, and similar positions. The activities of the department in seeking employment for Jewish women were further complicated by the fact that many applicants did not have the legal right to reside in Kiev.[101]

Often the department aided Jewish teenage girls who got into trouble. The department's 1914 report describes several such cases. For example, in November 1914, a woman came to the department from Podol and brought with her a thirteen-year-old mother with a four-month-old child. The story of this girl was as follows: she had been orphaned and served as a maid for a Jewish family. The head of the household seduced her, and when he found out that she was pregnant and that he could face criminal charges, he fled together with his family, abandoning the girl. When her child was born, a woman took her to Kiev and compelled her to beg for alms and hand over the money. But the girl did not collect enough money. So the woman applied to the Kiev Jewish department with a request to support the girl and her baby. The members of the department took the girl and her baby away from the woman, and provided care for them.[102]

Another case was that of a Jewish teenage girl who had run away from home:

> In the family of a wealthy Jewish merchant in the shtetl Belaia Tserkov' an unexpected and scandalous event occurred: their youngest daughter, fifteen-year-old Sonia, fled from home with a troupe of actors of the *Miniature* theater. Sonia took several hundred rubles from the cash box of her father's shop, where she had worked.[103]

The actors promised to make Sonia an actress, but they deceived her and took her money. Sonia was left in Kiev without the right of

---
101 Ibid., 27–32.
102 Ibid., 20.
103 Ibid., 38.

residence, completely destitute and unemployed. When she was brought to the Kiev Jewish department, its members summoned her parents so that they could take her home. But Sonia,

> categorically refused to go home and claimed that if they forced her to go home she would commit suicide. She produced some poison and attempted to swallow it, but a member of the department took the poison away from her with great difficulty.[104]

Later Sonia explained that she had run away from home "not for a romantic reason, but in an attempt to find a better life, because according to her words, she had a very bad life at home."[105] The members of the department persuaded Sonia's parents to leave her in the care of the organization. They applied to the governor-general and obtained the temporary right of residence for her in Kiev, where she became a student of the Kiev Dentistry School.[106]

The Kiev Jewish department had an agreement with some of Kiev's best lawyers to defend the rights of Jewish women in court. The principal issue was the right of residence in Kiev. During World War I, the wives of mobilized Jewish soldiers were often expelled from the city by the police. According to Russian law, the wives of Jews who had the right to settle outside the Pale had the right to live there only together with their husbands. The lawyers also attempted to help Jewish women who were refugees from the front to receive the right to stay in Kiev. In addition, they gave legal help to women in cases of divorce, domestic violence, and other family problems.[107]

The Kiev and St. Petersburg Jewish departments' budgets were derived from private donations and membership fees. Eventually, the sewing workshops of the Kiev Jewish departments also produced a profit. In 1914, the workshop received a contract to sew uniforms for the army, for which the Kiev Jewish department received over 3,000

---

104 Ibid., 21.
105 Ibid.
106 Ibid., 39.
107 Ibid., 33–38.

rubles. The sewing workshops employed a number of Kiev Jewish women as well as female refugees from Poland.[108]

Both Jewish departments organized celebrations of Jewish holidays, with concerts and refreshments. They devoted part of their budgets to the philanthropic support of poor Jewish girls and women.[109] Both worked within the limits of the law and did not attempt to change the existing order or struggle for woman's suffrage.

In 1914, the Russian Society for the Protection of Women as well as its Jewish departments published what turned out to be their last annual reports.[110] These organizations disappeared during World War I after the rapid downturn in the country's economic situation resulted in drastically reduced donations. At the same time, this organization and its sections, originally created to solve the problems of hundreds of women in a particular city, could not cope with the flood of thousands and later hundreds of thousands of displaced women who needed help during the war.

The Jewish departments of the Russian Society for the Protection of Women were transitional organizations, which performed functions beyond traditional Jewish charity institutions, but did not reach the development of the later western suffragist and modern feminist organizations. However, they provided Jewish women with employment, legal and medical assistance, dormitories, and a variety of courses. Their activities went beyond those of traditional Jewish charity societies, which limited their work to distributing help to needy Jewish people.

The fact that Kiev was one of only two large cities in the Russia Empire to support such an organization (there is no indication of their existence elsewhere) reflects the self-confidence and modern thinking of the women of the Kiev Jewish elite. At the same time, the precariousness of Jewish life in Kiev is revealed in their concern for the right of Jewish women to work and live outside the Pale of Settlement. This

---

108 Ibid., 15–16.
109 *Otchet Otdela popecheniia o evreiskikh devushkakh g. St. Peterburga za 1907 god*, 1–19; *Otchet za 1914 god Otdela popecheniia o evreiskikh devushkakh i zhenshchinakh g. Kieva pri Kievskom otdelenii Rossiiskogo obshchestva zashchity zhenshchin*, 3–40.
110 Noonan and Nechemias, eds., *Encyclopedia of Russian Women's Movements*, 61.

led to the politicization of their aims, especially in Kiev. The lawyers who worked in these organizations explained to women their rights and helped defend them. Thus, these organizations prepared Jewish women for the next step in their emancipation: their struggle for political and social rights, and for their equal status in family and society.

THE SOCIETY TO MAINTAIN SUMMER SANATORIUM COLONIES FOR THE SICK CHILDREN OF THE POOR JEWISH POPULATION IN KIEV

Children in poor Jewish families often lived in terrible conditions. Many of them had only one parent, or were orphans and lived with their relatives. Others had parents, brothers, and sisters with tuberculosis. They lived in slums or in small, overcrowded apartments or houses. Many did not even have their own beds and slept with two or three siblings in one bed. Others did not have beds at all and slept on the floor.[111] In these conditions, contagious diseases often struck several family members simultaneously. Such were the living conditions of the poor in the Plosskii district, which constituted 54.5 percent of the entire area of Kiev, and included the modern districts of Kurenevka, Priorka, and Pushcha Voditsa. Only 15.6 percent of the Plosskii district was in residential use, and the area also contained many industrial plants, including a brewery, yeast and match factories, a brickyard, and other workshops. The district did not possess plumbing and sewage systems and suffered from floods every spring.[112] Everybody who could afford to live somewhere else moved away. However, poor Jewish families did not have many choices. Their residence was limited to the Plosskii, Podol, and Lybedskoi districts of Kiev.

The populations that lived in Kiev's poor districts had the highest mortality rate. The death rate was especially high among children. Of the 7,174 people who died in Kiev in 1911, children younger than one year old constituted 23.5 percent, and from one to ten years old

---

111 G. R. Rubinshtein and Iu. M. Malis, comps., *Otchet Obshchestva detskikh sanatornykh kolonii dlia bol'nykh detei neimushchego evreiskogo naseleniia g. Kieva po soderzhaniiu sanatornykh kolonii v Boiarke za 1910 god* (Kiev: Pol'skii Printing House, 1911), 10–11.
112 Kasimenko, ed., *Istoriia Kieva*, 1: 467.

18.6 percent. In the same year, 1,244 people died in Kiev from epidemic diseases including 836 from tuberculosis.[113]

The Kiev Jewish community attempted to provide aid to the sick children of poor Jewish families. To achieve this goal, the Society to Maintain Summer Sanatorium Colonies for the Sick Children of the Poor Jewish Population in Kiev was created in 1906. Its president was Leon Brodsky; the two vice presidents were V. Iu. Frenkel' and Dr. G. R. Rubinshtein; the secretary was Dr. V. M. Varshavskii. Its board had fourteen members, including A. F. Brodskaia and A. G. Zaitseva, the wives of two leading magnates, and four medical doctors.[114]

In the summer of the same year, the society opened a sanatorium for thirty children in the Pushcha Voditsa suburb of Kiev. According to the society's annual report, Pushcha Voditsa was not the best location for the sanatorium because it was very damp, but "the acquisition of land in Boiarka or any other rural area was absolutely prohibited" for Jews.[115] In 1910, the sanatorium's capacity was increased to 125 children per session (there were two sessions every summer, each lasting six weeks). Originally, because it could not obtain permission to purchase land in the countryside, the sanatorium did not have its own facilities and rented peasants' houses. Conditions were primitive due to the absence of water and sewage systems in these houses.[116] Subsequently, in 1911 or 1912, the society received permission to open a sanatorium in Boiarka. It is unknown how the society finally got this permission, since all previous attempts to obtain land for a sanatorium had been rejected. In the summer of 1912, the sanatorium in Boiarka accepted 130 Jewish children.[117] However, the number of children who needed sanatorium treatment was more than ten times greater. In 1912, the sanatorium received over 1,400 applications. Consequently, the board

---

113 Ibid., 481.
114 *Otchet Obshchestva detskikh sanatornykh kolonii dlia bol'nykh detei neimushchego evreiskogo naseleniia g. Kieva po soderzhaniiu sanatornykh kolonii v Boiarke za 1910 god*, 3.
115 Ibid.
116 Ibid., 4–5.
117 G. R. Rubinshtein and Iu. M. Malis, comps., *Otchet Obshchestva detskikh sanatornykh kolonii dlia bol'nykh detei neimushchego evreiskogo naseleniia g. Kieva po soderzhaniiu sanatornykh kolonii v Boiarke za 1912 god* (Kiev: K. Kruglianskii Heirs Publishing House, 1913), 5.

decided to build a second sanatorium in Pushcha Voditsa for two hundred children, with all necessary medical and domestic facilities, including electricity. Money for the construction of the second sanatorium was donated by a number of wealthy Kiev Jews.

A special commission of eight doctors selected children for admission to the sanatorium on the basis of their physical condition. Each child was examined by two or, in difficult cases, three physicians. Highest priority was given to children from families suffering from tuberculosis. In 1912, 147 children were accepted into the sanatorium from such families. Next priority was given to orphans and children with one parent; of these 76 were accepted. The remaining places were given to children who were recuperating after long illnesses (pneumonia, measles, typhoid, etc.) or had serious chronic conditions. Most of them stayed in the sanatorium for one six-week session, but those in need of the most care spent the entire summer there.

The annual report of the society provides information about how these children lived outside the sanatorium. Only six of them had an adequate dinner every day at home, sixty-eight had a poor dinner, and twenty-four never had dinner. Others had dinner "when their relatives made some money."[118]

Most of the children who were accepted to the sanatorium in 1912 were from the Plosskii (110 children) and the Lybedskoi (eighty-five children) districts of Kiev, two of the three districts where poor Jews were allowed to live. Other children were from the Jewish market district and other districts and suburbs of the city. Fifty-six children were accepted from homes where the family lived in a single room that also served as a kitchen; ninety-nine lived in dwellings with one room and a kitchen; forty-seven in dwellings with two rooms and a kitchen; and six in dwellings with three rooms and a kitchen. Thirty-three children came from families that did not have an apartment of their own and rented a corner of a room.

> On average in these families eight people live in one room; large (three-room) apartments have the highest concentration of inhabitants; 9.75 people per room.

---

118 Ibid.

In these conditions the majority of the children sleep and eat where and how it is possible. Only twenty children sleep on single permanent beds, fifty-five always sleep on the floor, and the remainder sleep together with adults in the same generally movable beds.[119]

Thus, most of the children who were accepted to the sanatorium from families with tuberculosis were in constant danger of catching this disease from their relatives. Tuberculosis in Imperial Russia was above all a social disease that mostly struck the poor. Although the cause of tuberculosis is infection, this contagious disease spread through sneezing and coughing, and was caught mainly by poor people in overcrowded apartments who were unable to observe basic rules of hygiene or to isolate the infected person. Malnutrition—and the weak immunity that resulted from it—was another reason why so many poor people became infected. Tuberculosis reached epidemic proportions in Kiev in the early twentieth century; the majority of people who died from epidemic disease in the city in 1911 died from tuberculosis (836 of 1,244 people).

For sick Jewish children, the summer sanatorium was only a temporary escape from the nightmare of life in poverty. However, during their short stay in the sanatorium, many were able to recuperate and strengthen their immune systems. The society took care of all aspects of life for the children, including their transportation, medical treatment, nutrition, education, and recreation.

To avoid expense and inconvenience for the parents, the society provided transportation of the children to the sanatorium. The sanatorium staff picked up the children in Kiev and transported them to the facility in two specially-reserved railway cars. When the children arrived at the sanatorium, they were placed in five buildings: two for boys, two for girls, and one for smaller children. All children were from five to fourteen years old. They received medical treatment, if necessary, from the three physicians and one dentist. The sanatorium hired as tutors young girls—students of the Froebel Institute, who were well trained for their duties. Summer work in the sanatorium was good

---

119 Ibid., 8–9.

practice for them. Under the supervision of the *frebelichki* (as students of the Froebel Institute were called), the children also played lively games.[120]

Many children grew better and gained weight in the sanatorium. The fresh air and excellent nourishment helped many to recuperate. The annual reports of the society for 1910 and 1912 (these are the only surviving reports) state that during these two summers there was only one case of serious illness among the children in the sanatorium, when a child contracted measles. This child was isolated from the others and the spread of the disease was prevented.

The 1910 annual report states that children received five meals a day, which included dairy products and meat.[121] As a result, the average weight gain for a child was four to six pounds per session. Some of them gained as much as 20 percent of their original weight.

Nevertheless, six weeks in the sanatorium could not change the whole course of the children's lives, since they soon returned to families who lived in poverty. However, they returned having regained their health, and with knowledge of the existence of a better life. Sanatorium places were highly sought after. According to the 1912 report, many children who came to the sanatorium in that year had been there before. In addition, the society received more than ten times as many applications as places in the sanatorium. The second sanatorium was intended to provide an additional two hundred places. We do not know if it was actually built, as the society's 1913 report has not been found. Since this would normally have been published in 1914, it may not have been produced because of the outbreak of war. World War I and the subsequent civil war brought the work of the society to an end.

The accomplishments of the Society to Maintain Summer Sanatorium Colonies for the Sick Children of the Poor Jewish Population in Kiev perhaps served as an inspiration to other Jewish communities in Russia. In 1908, two years after the summer sanatorium for poor

---

120 *Otchet Obshchestva detskikh sanatornykh kolonii dlia bol'nykh detei neimushchego evreiskogo naseleniia g. Kieva po soderzhaniiu sanatornykh kolonii v Boiarke za 1910 god*, 5.
121 Ibid., 6.

Jewish children was opened in Kiev, the Vilna Jewish community created its Society of Jewish Children's Colonies, which ran summer camps for poor Jewish children in accordance with similar principles as the Kiev sanatorium.[122]

THE KIEV DEPARTMENT OF THE JEWISH COMMITTEE OF AID TO THE VICTIMS OF THE WAR

World War I interrupted the normal work of the Kiev Jewish philanthropic organizations. Kiev was comparatively close to the front, and the city overflowed with tens of thousands of refugees from the war zone. Among them were many Jews who were living in Kiev illegally. The commanders of the Kiev military district (during World War I the city was under martial law) refused to allow all categories of Jews to reside in the city even when, in accordance with the circular issued on August 15, 1915 by Nikolai Shcherbatov, the minister of the interior, residential restrictions were temporarily suspended for Jews in other places because of the military situation. As a result, thousands of illegal Jewish refugees lived in Kiev without any means of support and without the right to work. In these new conditions, the Kiev Jewish community and philanthropic organizations directed their main efforts to supporting these Jewish refugees.

In Kiev, as well as in other large cities of the Russian Empire, the Kiev Department of the Jewish Committee of Aid to the Victims of the War (EKOPO) was created. Among the founders of the Kiev committee were the Jewish entrepreneurs Lev Ginzburg and Iosif Marshak, as well as two other merchants of the first guild D. G. Levenshtein and H. S. Rubinchik, the lawyer M. S. Mazor, and B. E. Vashenboim. It is possible that the names of wealthy Jewish entrepreneurs and merchants were listed as founders of the committee in its bylaws to facilitate its approval by the authorities.

The initiative for the creation of the local Kiev Department of the Jewish Committee of Aid to the Victims of the War came from the Kiev Department of the Society for the Protection of the Health of the Jewish Population (OZE). This body called a meeting of the representatives of

---

122 Iakov Leshchinskii, *Vilenskaia evreiskaia obshchina. Ee uchrezhdeniia i finansy* (Kiev: Idisher Folksfarlag, n.d.), 28–29.

all Jewish organizations in Kiev on September 6, 1914, at which it was decided to create the Kiev department of EKOPO.[123] Like the other departments, the Kiev department provided financial assistance to Jewish refugees, distributed provisions among them, registered Jewish refugees who passed through Kiev, opened public dining halls, shelters, dormitories, employment bureaus, hospitals, clinics, and storage places, and subsidized food shops.[124] The Kiev department coordinated the activities of the local branches of the Jewish Committee of Aid to the Victims of the War, and had thirty-nine members. The Kiev department's resources came from membership dues, the basket tax, private donations, and revenue from benefit concerts. In the case of its liquidation, all its property, according to its bylaws, was to be transferred to the Society for the Care of Poor Jewish Artisans and Workers.[125]

The Kiev Department of the Jewish Committee of Aid to the Victims of the War continued to work after the February 1917 Revolution; however, in 1919 the Soviet authorities closed it and transferred its assets to the People's Commissariat of Social Security.[126]

CONCLUSION

Jewish wealth and poverty existed side by side in Kiev, in spite of all efforts of the wealthiest members of the Kiev Jewish community to help their less fortunate coreligionists. The cycle of poverty was very hard to break, especially because it was linked with the fact that many Jews were living illegally in Kiev, making it difficult for them to obtain employment. Most legal Jewish residents were compelled by law to live in the poorest districts of the city. They lived in overcrowded apartments without plumbing or water-borne sewage, resulting in poor hygiene and the spread of infectious diseases. Health problems, as well as the lack of qualifications of many Jewish inhabitants in the poor districts, made it very challenging for them to escape poverty.

---

123   E. I. Melamed and M. S. Kupovetskii, eds., *Dokumenty po istorii i kul'ture evreev v arkhivakh Kieva. Putevoditel'* (Kiev: Dukh i Litera, 2006), 412–413.
124   Ibid.; *Ustav Obshchestva dlia okazaniia pomoshchi evreiskomu naseleniiu postradavshemu ot voennykh deistvii.* (Kiev: El'nik Publishing house, 1915), 2.
125   *Ustav Obshchestva dlia okazaniia pomoshchi*, 8.
126   *Dokumenty po istorii i kul'ture evreev v arkhivakh Kieva*, 412.

The Kiev Society for the Care of Poor Jewish Artisans and Workers recognized these problems, but did not have the means to solve them. For example, the society was aware of the problems caused by the poor vocational training of Kiev Jewish artisans, because the general artisan school did not accept Jewish students. However, it lacked the resources to establish a school of its own.

Among the philanthropists who provided financial aid to the various Jewish charities in Kiev, we repeatedly encounter the names of Lev Brodsky, David Margolin, Iosif Marshak, Lev Ginzburg, and a few dozen others. At the turn of the twentieth century, over five thousand Jewish merchants lived in Kiev, but only a few hundred of them actively participated in the work of the philanthropic institutions. Others may nevertheless have made personal donations.

In spite of their limited resources, the Kiev Jewish charitable organizations gave considerable aid to the poor Jewish population and helped some Jews escape poverty and establish their own businesses. They provided legal aid and defended the rights of Jews to reside in Kiev. In addition, for needy Jewish women they established a dormitory, ran low-cost dining halls, and employed some of them in sewing workshops. During World War I, the Kiev Department of the Jewish Committee of Aid to the Victims of the War provided shelter and distributed food and clothing to Jewish refugees. The Society to Maintain Summer Sanatorium Colonies for the Sick Children of the Poor Jewish Population in Kiev set up a modern children's sanatorium, which employed medical doctors as well as professional educators.

Jewish charities that worked in Kiev at the beginning of the twentieth century typically attempted to analyze the reasons for the poverty of the Jewish population and, based on this analysis, devised solutions to these problems. The work of charitable organizations can never be completely successful, especially in conditions of limited means and legal restrictions. However, Kiev Jewish charitable organizations were able to satisfy many of the needs of Jewish workers and artisans and provide aid to various categories of the Jewish poor, including women and children. To paraphrase Mark Twain, we can say that these organizations did a fine job in conditions of severe legal restrictions with their hands tied behind their backs.

Figure 1. Kreshchatik Street at the turn of the twentieth century. Postcard.

Figure 2. Proreznaia Street at the turn of the twentieth century. Postcard.

Figure 3. Downtown Kiev, early twentieth century. Postcard.

Figure 4. Podol, Jewish district of Kiev. Postcard.

Figure 5. View of Podol from Truchanov Island. Postcard.

Figure 6. Ester Vons, the author's great-grandmother in Kiev, circa 1905. Courtesy of the author.

Figure 7. Israel Brodsky. Courtesy of the Center for Studies of the History and Culture of East European Jewry.

Figure 8. Lazar Brodsky. Courtesy of the Center for Studies of the History and Culture of East European Jewry.

Figure 9. Lev (Leon) Brodsky. Courtesy of the Center for Studies of the History and Culture of East European Jewry.

Figure 10. The Circus Lover, Solomon Brodsky, 1880s. Courtesy of Lybid' Publishing House.

Figure 11. Brodsky Choral Synagogue. Postcard.

Figure 12. Bessarabskii Market. Postcard.

Figure 13. Kiev Rabbi Evsei Tsukkerman. Courtesy of Mikhail Kalnitsky.

Figure 14. Max Mandelstamm. Courtesy of the Center for Studies of the History and Culture of East European Jewry.

Figure 15. David Margolin.
Courtesy of Mikhail Kalnitsky.

Figure 16. Iosif Marshak.
Courtesy of the Center
for Studies of the History
and Culture of East
European Jewry.

Figure 17. Cover of the book devoted to the 35th anniversary of Marshak Jewelry Company, Kiev, 1913.

Figure 18. The persecution of Jews in Russia: scene inside the Arsenal at Kiev (after the pogrom of 1881). *The Illustrated London News*, June 18, 1881.

Figure 19. Sholom Aleichem with his family. Courtesy of the Central State Archive of Film, Photo, Sound Documents of Ukraine.

Figure 20. Beilis and his counselors. Postcard.

Figure 21. Tsar Nicholas II greeted by the Kiev Jewish delegation (from left to right: Kiev Rabbi Iakov Aleshkovskii, Kiev Rabbi Avram Gurevich, and barrister Avraam Gol'denberg), 1911. Courtesy of the Central State Archive of Film, Photo, Sound Documents of Ukraine.

Figure 22. Petr A. Stolypin. Courtesy of the Central State Archive of Film, Photo, Sound Documents of Ukraine.

Figure 23. Kiev City Theater (now Kiev Opera Theater). Postcard.

Figure 24. Mug shots of Dmitrii Bogrov after his shooting of Stolypin. Courtesy of the Central State Historical Archive of Ukraine in the City Kiev.

Figure 25. Kiev St. Vladimir University. Postcard.

Figure 26. Kiev Polytechnic Institute. Postcard.

Figure 27. Boruch Zelikovich (Boris Zacharovich) Shteinberg in a student's uniform of Kiev Polytechnic Institute (on the left) with his mother Bella, daughter Tamara, and brother David. Courtesy of the author.

Figure 28. First Kiev Gymnasium. Postcard.

Figure 29. Solomon Brodsky Artisan School. Courtesy of the Center for Studies of the History and Culture of East European Jewry.

Figure 30. Interior of Solomon Brodsky Artisan School. Courtesy of the Center for Studies of the History and Culture of East European Jewry.

Vor *Gott* muss man sich
beugen, weil er so *gross* ist, vor
dem *Kinde*, weil es so *klein* ist.

Rosegger.

ОТЧЕТЪ

Общества лѣтнихъ санаторныхъ колоній для больныхъ дѣтей неимущаго еврейскаго населенія г. Кіева

по содержанію
санаторной колоніи въ Бояркѣ

за 1910 годъ

(4-й годъ)

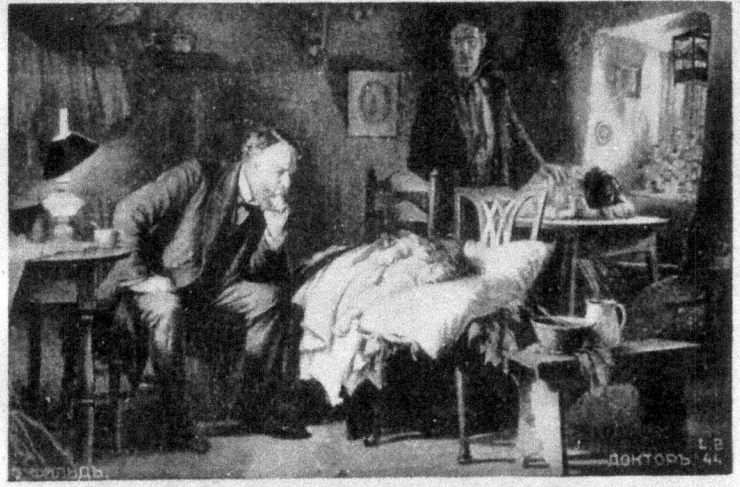

СОСТАВЛЕННЫЙ
Г. Р. Рубинштейномъ и Ю. М. Маписомъ.

КІЕВЪ.
ПОЛЬСКАЯ ТИПОГРАФІЯ, КРЕЩАТИКЪ 38.
1911.

Figure 31. Report of the Society to Maintain Summer Sanatorium Colonies for the Sick Children of Poor Jews in the City of Kiev for 1910. Report cover.

Figure 32. Irene Nemirovsky and her cat Kissou. © Fonds Irène Némirovsky/IMEC.

Figure 33. All-Russian Exhibition in Kiev in 1913. Postcard.

CHAPTER SIX

Jewish Pogroms and the Beilis Affair

> A pogrom...is a system of ruling, however a peculiar system...
> —Barrister E. E. Shik, Simferopol' pogrom trial, 1905[1]

THE POGROMS OF 1881 AND 1905 IN KIEV

In the late nineteenth and early twentieth centuries, the level of violence increased in Russian society in general and against Jews in particular. The assassination of Tsar Alexander II by the People's Will, revolutionary terror, and government repression created an increasingly intolerant atmosphere. The monarchical regime was in deep crisis and hunted for enemies, both real and imagined. Jews were convenient scapegoats: due to the widespread Judeophobic mood, many gentiles believed that Jews were guilty of causing all of Russia's economic and political difficulties. The final two Russian tsars, Alexander III and Nicholas II, implemented a policy of state anti-Semitism, which deprived Jews of basic civil rights. State propaganda represented Jews

---

1 *Rechi po pogromnym delam.* With an introduction by V. G. Korolenko (Kiev: S. G. Sliusarevskii Publishing House, 1908), 37–40.

as internal enemies of the country. In such an atmosphere of hatred and intolerance, mass waves of Jewish pogroms occurred in Russia.

Before 1881, Jews suffered many forms of discrimination and oppression in the Russian Empire, but open violence against them occurred infrequently. Previously, there were just a few Jewish pogroms in Russia: three of them in Odessa in 1821, 1859, and 1871, and one in Akkerman in 1862.[2] The first wave of mass pogroms began in mid-April 1881, six weeks after the assassination of Tsar Alexander II on March 1. The first pogrom broke out in the city Elizavetgrad (now Kirovograd) of Kherson province on April 15–17, 1881.[3] Pogroms soon spread to all of the southwestern provinces of the Russian Empire. According to Antony Polonsky,

> Of 259 pogroms, 219 took place in villages, four in Jewish agricultural colonies and only thirty-six in cities and small towns. The violence continued intermittently until March 1882, with outbreaks occurring in Balta and Podolia. In the final pogrom, which occurred in Nizhnii Novgorod on 7 June 1884 and was accompanied by a ritual murder accusation, ten Jews were hacked to death with axes. Altogether perhaps forty-five Jews lost their lives in these events, thirty-five in 1881–82 and another ten in Nizhnii Novgorod in 1884. Many more were injured and there was also considerable material damage. It was certainly the worst outbreak of anti-Jewish violence in Europe since the Haydamak revolts of the late 1760s.[4]

Most historians believe that the pogroms of 1881–1882 were largely spontaneous, but occurred with the connivance of the authorities.[5]

---

2   John D. Klier, "The Pogrom Paradigm in Russian History," in *Pogroms: Anti-Jewish Violence in Modern Russian History*, ed. John D. Klier and Shlomo Lambroza (Cambridge: Cambridge University Press, 1992), 17–20.

3   S. M. Dubnow, *History of the Jews in Russia and Poland from the Earliest Times until the Present Day*, trans. I. Friedlaender (Jersey City, NJ: Ktav Publishing House, Inc., 1975), 2: 250.

4   Antony Polonsky, *The Jews in Poland and Russia, II: 1881 to 1914* (Oxford and Portland, OR: The Littman Library of Jewish Civilization, 2010), 5.

5   Hans Rogger, *Jewish Policies and Right-Wing Politics in Imperial Russia* (Berkeley and Los Angeles: University of California Press, 1986), 113–175; Klier and

Originally the Russian government thought these pogroms were provoked by the revolutionary agitation of radical groups such as the People's Will. But later, the authorities blamed the Jews. The authorities and conservative press claimed that these pogroms were a response to Jewish "domination" and "exploitation."[6] According to Kiev, Podolia, and Volhynia Governor-General Aleksandr Romanovich Drentel'n, the main reason for the 1881–1882 pogroms was the "deep hatred of the common people [*narod*], the Great Russian and even more the Little Russian, for the ruthless and deceptive business practices of the Jews who victimize a trusting people, seek easy gain, and evade their taxes and public duties."[7] However, the vast majority of Russian Jews lived in poverty, while just a small number of Jews became industrial tycoons during the development of capitalism in the Russian Empire, like David Margolin and the Brodsky "Sugar Kings."

Kiev was one of the places where violence erupted in 1881. Anti-Jewish violence in Kiev began on April 23, 1881, just one week after the pogrom in Elizavetgrad. On this day, twenty people were injured in street fights[8] and local Judeophobes attacked Jewish passers-by, possibly as a prelude to a pogrom.[9] It is likely that the rioters were testing the reaction of the local authorities before initiating violence against Jews on a large scale. They were trying to see if beating Jews would be allowed, or if the local police would defend them. The local authorities arrested the rioters, and in this way prevented a large pogrom in the city. In addition, they issued a warning to Jews to stay home and keep their stores closed.

However, this did not prevent large-scale anti-Jewish rioting in the town just three days later, on April 26. According to Dubnov:

> One day before that fateful Sunday [April 26, 1881], the Jews were warned by the police not to leave their houses, nor to

---

Lambroza, eds., *Pogroms: Anti-Jewish Violence in Modern Russian History*, 39–98; John Doyle Klier, *Russian, Jews and the Pogroms of 1881–1882* (Cambridge, UK: Cambridge University Press, 2011).
6   Dubnow, *History of the Jews in Russia and Poland*, 2: 260–261.
7   Polonsky, *The Jews in Poland and Russia, II: 1881 to 1914*, 6.
8   TsDIAK U, f. 274, op. 1, d. 238, l. 5.
9   Dubnow, *History of the Jews in Russia and Poland*, 2: 252.

open their stores on the morrow. The Jews were nonplussed. They failed to understand why in the capital of the governor-general, with its numerous troops, which at a hint from their commander, were able to nip in the bud disorders of any kind, peaceful citizens should be told to hide themselves from an impending attack, instead of taking measures to forestall the attack itself.[10]

The anonymous author of the article "Persecution of Jews in Russia" in *The Illustrated London News* on June 18, 1881 wrote that Kiev is an administrative city "and has a powerful garrison and a strong police force." So it is obvious that authorities could have done more to prevent the pogrom in the city.

The head of the Kiev Province Gendarmerie Administration, General Vasilii Dement'evich Novitskii, wrote in his memoirs,

> The three day pogrom in Kiev and its spread to districts [*uezdy*] of Kiev province definitely occurred because of the attitude of Kiev Governor-General A. R. Drentel'n, who hated Jews to the depth of his soul, who gave complete freedom to the activities of the unrestrained mob of hooligans and the Dnieper "barefoot brigade," who openly destroyed Jewish property, shops, stalls and bazaars, even before his eyes and in the presence of troops.[11]

Drentel'n clearly expressed to Novitskii his point of view on the Jewish pogrom in Kiev: "let's beat them [Jews] well; it is necessary to put down their impudence and greed."[12] Novitskii also disliked Jews, and believed that the pogrom was the justified revenge of the Russian people against the Jews for their exploitation of Christians. But he was quite nervous about the situation, since he had received an encrypted

---

10 Ibid.
11 V. D. Novitskii, *Iz vospominanii zhandarma* (repr. of 1929 ed., Moscow: Moscow University, 1991), 156.
12 Ibid.

telegram from the minister of the interior, Count Mikhail Tarielovich Loris-Melikov, in which he demanded that anti-Jewish disorders in the city be suppressed. Loris-Melikov demanded that Novitskii report to him every two hours by telegram about the situation in Kiev, and that he take measures to stop the disorders. Accordingly, Novitskii attempted to influence Drentel'n through his close friend Petr Semenovich Vannovskii, the commander of the Kiev military garrison, who was later to hold the position of minister of war. Vannovskii responded by telling Novitskii that he should be aware of Drentel'n's hatred of "Yids." On the same day, April 26, 1881, they both attended a meeting with Drentel'n and the commanders of local military units, at which an order was issued that troops called to Kiev because of anti-Jewish riots should not use weapons against the pogrom-makers. According to Novitskii, Drentel'n said "if somebody dares to use his bayonet, or the stock of his gun, or if the Cossacks use the lash, he would prosecute anybody who disobeyed his order."[13] Thus the troops in the city were completely paralyzed.

Meanwhile, the anti-Jewish riots in Kiev took on a larger dimension. On Sunday, April 26, 1881, Jews followed the advice of the police to lay low. However, according to Dubnov,

> This…did not prevent the numerous bands of rioters from assembling on the streets and embarking upon their criminal activities. The Pogrom started in Podol, a part of the town densely populated by Jews.[14]

Dubnov provides an eyewitness account of the pogrom, without mentioning the name of the witness:

> At twelve o'clock noon, the air suddenly resounded with wild shouts, whistling, jeering, hooting and laughing. An immense crowd of young boys, artisans and laborers was on the march.

---

13   Ibid., 157.
14   Dubnow, *History of Jews in Russia and Poland*, 2: 252.

The whole city was obstructed by the "bare-footed brigade."[15] The destruction of Jewish houses began. Windowpanes and doors began to fly about, and shortly thereafter the mob, having gained access to the houses and stores, began to throw upon the streets absolutely everything that fell into their hands. Clouds of feathers began to whirl in the air. The din of broken windowpanes and frames, the crying, shouting, and despair on the one hand, and the terrible yelling and jeering on the other, completed the picture which reminded many of those who had participated in the last Russo-Turkish war [1877–1878] of the manner in which the Bashi-buzuks[16] had attacked Bulgarian villages. Soon afterwards the mob threw itself upon the Jewish synagogue, which despite its strong bars, locks and shutters, was wrecked in a moment. One should have seen the fury with which the riff-raff fell upon the [Torah] scrolls, of which there were many in the synagogue. The scrolls were torn to shreds, trampled in the dirt, and destroyed with incredible passion. The streets were soon crammed with the trophies of destruction. Everywhere fragments of dishes, furniture, household utensils, and other articles lay scattered about. Barely two hours after the beginning of the pogrom, most of the "bare-footed brigade" were transformed into well-dressed gentlemen, many of them having grown excessively stout in the meantime. The reason for this sudden change was simple enough. Those that had looted the stores of ready-made clothes put on three or four suits, and not yet satisfied, took under their arms all they could lay their hands on. Others drove off in vehicles, carrying with them bags filled with loot…Christians saved themselves from the ruinous operations of the crowd by placing holy icons in their windows and painting crosses on the gates of their houses.[17]

---

15 The Russian nickname for a crowd of tramps.
16 The name of the Turkish irregular troops noted for their ferocity.
17 Dubnow, *History of Jews in Russia and Poland*, 2: 253.

A similar picture of the pogrom is given by Nikolai Ivanovich Petrov, professor at the Kiev Theological Academy,[18] in a letter to his brother Ivan on April 29, 1881. Petrov describes the Kiev pogrom of 1881 as a great spectacle, and does not express any compassion for its victims, since he believed that Jews deserved this treatment because of their exploitation of Russians. However, his account of events is revealing, as it contains many significant details that he observed as an eyewitness:

> I write you under the fresh impression of these events, the like of which I have never seen before, nor am likely to see again.
>
> Even before Easter, rumors spread that on Easter there would be a drubbing of Yids in Kiev, as well as other rumors that the privileged classes would be attacked...Some attacks on Yids were made on April 23. On Sunday April 26, an all-out pogrom against the Yids began. It started in the suburb Demievka and then spread to our Podol, where most of the Jewish population lives. Our Podol is divided into two police districts: Plosskii and Podol'skii. There are entire streets in Plosskii district, where it is hardly possible to find a home, stall or store that has not been robbed. By noon groups of hooligans went from there to Podol'skii district, they beat Yids in two markets and at about one o'clock they attacked the best street on Podol—Aleksandrovskaia and the nearby streets...I counted later over 40 completely ruined stores on Aleksandrovskaia Street alone...On the evening and night of April 26–27 even Cossacks stole Jewish property.
>
> Later it become known, that simultaneously with the pogrom in Podol, Yids were beaten in the other parts of the city, far from Podol, on Zhitnii, Evreiskii (Galitskii) and Bessarabskii markets,

---

18 Nikolai Ivanovich Petrov (1840–1921) taught the history of Russian and foreign literature at Kiev Theological Academy. He is the author of a number of works on the history of Ukrainian literature in the eighteenth and nineteenth centuries. From 1919 on Petrov was a member of the Ukrainian Academy of Arts and Sciences. He was the godfather of the renowned Russian writer Mikhail Bulgakov.

on Bol'shaia Zhitomirskaia and Vasil'kovskaia Streets and elsewhere. People say that up to five thousand rioters participated in the pogrom. The pogrom-makers themselves said that many of them came from Moscow specifically to beat Jews, that others are coming to support them, that this is only the beginning and that the final reckoning will be on May 9, St. Nicholas Day...

On the following morning disorders continued at their previous intensity and continued all day. The crowd was smaller, but more drunk and brutal. In Novoe Stroenie troops fired a salvo at the rioters, and people say that they killed some of them as well as some spectators. In several places fires broke out.

April 28 was already quiet everywhere. Six cannons were put on Kreshchatik as a precaution and everywhere troops stood guard and police made arrests...

I saw myself that the crowd of pogrom-makers had leaders; sometimes they were intellectuals, who directed the crowd's activity. Now rumors are circulating that several disguised students of the University and gymnasiums were among the arrested rioters, and on one street a secret publishing house was discovered on April 27, where fake government manifestos were printed authorizing the robbing of Yids...[19]

Petrov's account of the rioters' organized actions is corroborated by an article in *The Illustrated London News*:

The work of destruction was done by no single mob, but by bands of thirty to a hundred men, mostly under the age of thirty, and armed with choppers, hammers and bludgeons... According to the Kiev correspondence of the *Moscow Gazette* these bands seemed to have been under the control of some organization. A crowd of people would be promenading along a thoroughfare. Suddenly a whistle would be heard, and in a

---

19 TsDIAK U, f. 1423, op. 1, d. 28, ll. 1–4.

moment men would issue from the crowd and form themselves into a band, and an attack would be made upon a house. When the work of destruction was over, another whistle would be heard, and the band would then disperse and mingle with the crowd again. Nearly all the largest and finest shops in Kiev and the principal storehouses in the bazaar belonged to the Jews. None were left unmolested...The authorities seemed paralyzed...On the fifth day cannons were placed in the principal streets and military began to fire on the crowds. The police also began to exert themselves, and 1,400 people were arrested. On the seventh day the riots were reported at an end. Fifteen thousand troops had then arrived at Kiev from various points to protect the city.

The total number of people arrested in Kiev was 1,783, including seventy-three women, and afterwards gangs of prisoners continued daily to arrive from outlying districts, being driven in by Cossacks...The number of persons killed was six, three Jews and three Russians; 187 persons were injured, including three Cossacks, three soldiers, two gendarmes and nine women...More than 500 shops and 500 houses were looted. Upwards of 20,000 Jews fled from Kiev to Berdichev... Three thousand families remaining behind at Kiev were placed for shelter in the Arsenal, but it is not to the credit of the Russian authorities that for forty-eight hours they were without medical succor or food. In the end some compassionate Russians exerted themselves, and subscriptions were freely given by the educated classes to furnish them with the necessaries of life.[20]

All evidence shows that the pogrom crowds had leaders who coordinated their activities, and that the authorities did nothing to stop the pogrom in Kiev for at least the first two days. Furthermore, Kiev, Podolia, and Volhynia Governor-General Drentel'n personally

---

20 "Persecution of Jews in Russia," *Illustrated London News*, June 18, 1881.

encouraged the pogrom, and threatened his troops with prosecution if they used their weapons or even whips against the rioters. The Cossacks, who were supposed to protect the Jews, instead participated in the pogrom and stole Jewish property. Thus, Kiev Jews could not count anymore on the protection of the authorities and many fled to Berdichev. Probably, only in Berdichev, with a majority Jewish population (according to the census of 1897, almost 80 percent of the city's residents were Jews), did they feel safe during the wave of pogroms in 1881, which spread throughout all the southwestern provinces of Russia.

The Kiev pogrom of 1881 was the largest in terms of the number of rioters and amount of the losses incurred.[21] Major General P. I. Kutaisov, who came to Kiev to investigate the disorders, concluded that measures for the suppression of the riot were not taken in time nor efficiently, which explained the large scale of the disturbances. As a result of the investigation, Kiev Governor Gesse was found guilty of negligence for not stopping the riots. He was dismissed from his position and forced to retire. According to Novitskii, Drentel'n, who petitioned for the dismissal of Gesse, was much guiltier than Gesse.[22]

The wave of pogroms of 1881–1882 created deep disillusionment among Russian Jews. Before the riots, maskilim believed in the possibility of "merging" with Russian society and acquiring equal rights with other subjects of the empire; the pogroms dashed these illusions. An appeal entitled "To Jewish Society from Jewish students of St. Petersburg University" clearly expressed disillusionment with the possibility of improving the situation of Jews in Russia, and called for emigration from the country. There is no date on the appeal, but the content suggests that it was written not long after the pogroms of 1881. It states:

> Brothers, consider our current situation and what we can anticipate here in Russia. Previously we thought that even though we lived under conditions that humiliated our dignity, at least our lives and property were protected; now we realize

---

21 *Evreiskaia entsiklopediia*, s.v. "Pogromy v Rossii," 12: 612.
22 Novitskii, *Iz vospominanii zhandarma*, 158.

that this is not the case: recent events compel us to rethink our position and have destroyed any hope for a better future here in Russia. There are people, who for their own selfish reasons persuade us to stay here, saying that soon everything will change for the better; that all our calamities are caused by the power now held by a person who does not like us [presumably Ignat'ev, the minister of the interior]; and as soon as he is replaced our situation will improve. But should we believe such statements? We don't think so! First of all, no minister can help us, if all [Christian] people are against us…Second, even if pogroms end in Russia, should we wish the same life that we had until the present?

You, brothers, remember the time when hostility toward us was explained by our alienation and isolation. They told us: "You should merge with the native population—and all animosity will disappear." The government opened for us the doors of the gymnasiums and universities, gave us the vestiges of some rights, and invited us to make a step toward rapprochement. We naïvely accepted the hand held out to us and from our side did everything that we could, we sacrificed for the sake of this our national peculiarities, we were happy with Russian successes, we mourned Russian calamities, and we lived a Russian life. But when Russian society saw that we wished seriously to merge with them, then in this society the old prejudices revived. "The Yid is coming"[23]—rang out the well-known slogan, warning Russian society away from rapprochement with us, who ostensibly want to converge only to "destroy society from above and below, from above by nihilism, and from below by exploitation."[24] Is it possible, brothers, to anticipate a normal life in such a society, which

---

23 In 1880, the editor of the newspaper *Novoe vremia*, Aleksei Suvorin, published in his newspaper the article "Zhyd idet" ("The Yid Is Coming"), which revealed the change in state policy toward Jews in Russia from a policy of merging to one of isolation and further discrimination.
24 Quoted from "Zhyd idet" ("The Yid Is Coming").

today beckons you and tomorrow pushes you away? Is it possible to believe such a society, even though it again reaches out its hand to us?...

We should move away from Russia everybody who can and wants to search for a new fatherland; we need to create for them our own place, where they can be rightful owners, where they can live in prosperity from their agricultural labor, without concern about the future. In America or Palestine there is so much free land that all three million Russian Jews can settle there...

Jewish youth have decisively rallied under the banner of the emigration of our brothers. We cannot wait, because the dramatic development of events can bring new calamities and poverty to those of our brothers who until now have avoided the bitter fate of many of our coreligionists![25]

This call of the Jewish students for emigration resonated well with young Jews in Russia. While the leaders of the Kiev Jewish community conducted unsuccessful negotiations with Russian authorities on the legalization of organized Jewish emigration from Russia (as described in chapter four), Jewish young people, without permission of the authorities, created their own emigration organizations. In 1881–1882, Jewish youth in Kiev and Vilna established the Russian-Jewish emigration society "Am Olam."[26] Alexander Harkavy wrote in his memoirs *Chapters from My Life*:

> Our group was founded in February 1882 [in Vilna]. Its first act was to suggest to a larger group—the Am Olam already established in Kiev—to take us in under its flag. We found this desirable because the Kiev group had already exchanged letters with the Hebrew Emigrant Aid Society in New York,

---

25 TsDIAK U, f. 1423, op. 1, d. 7, ll. 9–15.
26 TsDIAK U, f. 274, op. 1, d. 252, ll. 16–18; Alexander Harkavy, *"Chapters from My Life": The East European Jewish Experience in America. A Century of Memories, 1882–1982*, ed. Uri D. Herscher (Cincinnati: American Jewish Archives, 1983), 54.

and had received its promise to help it achieve its aims once it arrived in America. The Kiev group willingly received our suggestion, and our two groups merged. The name Am Olam devolved also upon us.[27]

Am Olam's goal, according to its program, was "the emigration of Jews from Russia in the largest number possible and the renaissance of Jewish people in a new land."[28] Their practical program was to support emigration of Russian Jews to America.

Despite Minister of the Interior Ignat'ev's statement that the western border was open for Jews, in practice Russian authorities created various obstacles to Jewish emigration. They ordered the closure of all Jewish emigration organizations in Russia in the 1880s and 1890s. Soon after its establishment, Am Olam was closed by the police, but nothing could stop the emigration of Jews from Russia, "the country of pogroms."[29] New Jewish emigration organizations appeared that provided advice and financial and legal support to Jews who wanted to leave the country.

At the end of the nineteenth and the beginning of the twentieth century, Jews in Kiev lived under the continuous threat and fear of new pogroms. Golda Meir describes in her memoirs how her family awaited a pogrom in Kiev. She did not provide the date of these events, but it would have been before her family moved to Pinsk in 1903. She writes:

> I must have been very young, maybe only three and a half or four. We lived then on the first floor of a small house in Kiev, and I can still recall distinctly hearing about a pogrom that was to descend on us. I didn't know then of course what a pogrom was, but I knew it had something to do with being Jewish and with the rabble that used to surge through town, brandishing knives and huge sticks, screaming "Christ killers" as they

---

27 Harkavy, *"Chapters from My Life,"* 54.
28 TsDIAK U, f. 274, op. 1, d. 252, ll. 16–17.
29 Ibid.

looked for the Jews, and who were now going to do terrible things to me and to my family.

I can remember how I stood on the stairs that led to the second floor, where another Jewish family lived, holding hands with their little daughter and watching our fathers trying to barricade the entrance with boards of wood. That pogrom never materialized, but to this day I remember how scared I was and how angry that all my father could do to protect me was to nail a few planks together while we waited for the hooligans to come. And, above all, I remember being aware that this was happening to me because I was Jewish, which made me different from most of the other children in the yard. It was the feeling that I was to know again many times during my life—the fear, the frustration, the consciousness of being different and the profound instinctive belief that if one wanted to survive, one had to take effective action about it personally.[30]

The threats of pogroms in the Russian Empire became even more immediate for Jews after the Kishinev pogrom on April 6–7, 1903. In this pogrom, forty-nine Jews were killed and 424 wounded, and approximately 700 Jewish houses and 600 stores were destroyed.[31] Just ten days later, many Kiev Jews fled from the city in panic, under the influence of rumors that it was their turn to be beaten. This threat looked very real after the massacre of Jews in Kishinev. Many Kiev Jews must have also recalled the pogrom of 1881, which followed a week after a pogrom in Elizavetgrad. They therefore decided after the Kishinev pogrom not to tempt fate and to leave the city. On April 22, 1903, the newspaper *Kievlianin* wrote,

> Last week anxious rumors [about a pogrom] spread among the Jews in Kiev. Many Jewish families rushed to leave Kiev under the influence of these rumors. On April 16 and 17 the piers

---

30 Golda Meir, *My Life* (New York: Dell Publishing Co., Inc., 1975), 11–12.
31 Edward H. Judge, *Easter in Kishinev: Anatomy of Pogrom* (New York: New York University Press, 1992), 62–86.

were overflowing with Jews, and hundreds of families gathered there, mainly children and women. There was a great shortage of seats on the trains and ships. The trains were overcrowded by Jews and their belongings...

Many Jewish families left Demievka and the other suburbs [of Kiev] and rapidly moved to the shtetls and to the provincial cities of the Kiev province. This included the majority of the poorest part of the population, artisans and petty traders. Wealthier [Jews] temporarily moved to hotels. On Sunday the alert was lifted. People who moved to hotels returned back to their apartments. Several thousand Jews had moved out from Kiev.

Of course, the anti-Semitic mood was not shared by all gentiles in Kiev. Many Kiev gentiles felt compassion for Jews, and tried to help them overcome the injustice of the authorities and the limitations imposed on them by Russian law. Philo-Semitism was widespread in Kiev, present in diverse circles of the population—from janitors, who hid Jews during the October 1905 pogroms, to professors at the local universities. However, anti-Semitism was also widespread among all strata of society.

The pogrom in Kiev in October 1905 had a completely different character from the pogrom in 1881. This was a political pogrom. The October 1905 pogroms occurred at the peak of the first Russian revolution, immediately after the declaration of the October 17th Manifesto, which promised to liberalize the country's political regime. About 690 pogroms took place in 660 cities, towns, and villages between October 18–29, 1905.[32] Most of these pogroms occurred on the territory of modern Ukraine, where the vast majority of the Jewish population lived. Polonsky writes, "Nearly 87 percent (575) of all pogroms took place in the southern provinces of Chernigov, Poltava, Ekaterinoslav, Kherson, Podolia, Kiev, and Bessarabia."[33] During these pogroms, 3,100 Jews were killed, 2,000 Jews were seriously injured, and more

---

32 *Evreiskaia entsiklopedia*, s.v. "Pogromy v Rossii," 12: 618.
33 Polonsky, *The Jews in Poland and Russia, II: 1881 to 1914*, 57.

than 15,000 were wounded.³⁴ This was the largest wave of anti-Jewish violence in the Russian Empire.

The October 1905 pogrom in Kiev began with the suppression of a large political meeting downtown. On October 18, 1905, the tsar's October Manifesto, which had been issued the previous day, was published, and many people came to the meeting to celebrate the first Russian constitution, as they called it. The Manifesto announced civil liberties and promised to call an election of the State Duma, which meant a transformation of Russia's political system from an absolute into a constitutional monarchy. Jews, as the most oppressed people of the Russian Empire, appreciated even more the promised liberalization of the regime. According to Vasilii Shul'gin, all Jews came out into the streets that day to celebrate the Manifesto. However, the celebration of the Manifesto turned into a bloody massacre; in many places, peaceful meetings and demonstrations were attacked by troops. In Kiev troops fired on the meeting in Duma Square and soon thereafter a pogrom began. In the evening groups of hooligans fell upon passers-by and beat them mercilessly. Pogroms against Jews began in different parts of the city. Pogrom-makers, who beat Jews on the street and in their homes, told their victims that they beat them for "the Constitution, the revolution and the desire of Yids for equal rights."³⁵

Senator Evgenii Fedorovich Turau wrote,

> Within a few hours of the start of the disorders the pogrom against the Jews had become outright robbery, merciless and terrifying in its consequences. The instigators and leaders of the pogrom were, in most cases, people from the crowd or ruffians, but it turned out that those who incited others to join the pogrom were small traders (competitors of the Jews), janitors, some homeowners, the owners of craft workshops and... the lower ranks of the police.³⁶

---

34 Shlomo Lambroza, "The Pogroms of 1903–1906," in *Pogroms: Anti-Jewish Violence in Modern Russian History*, 231.
35 TsDIAK U, f. 442, op. 85, d. 391, ll. 260–261.
36 *Kievskii i odesskii pogromy v otchetakh senatorov Turau i Kuzminskogo* (St. Petersburg: Letopisets, 1907), 41–43.

On the first day, October 18, 1905, the pogrom continued until late at night and stopped only when the mob apparently became tired and went home to rest. But it broke out again the next morning and continued for two more days.[37]

On the morning of October 19, crowds began sacking Jewish shops in several parts of the city:

> Groups of ruffians several hundred-strong fell in a frenzy on the shops owned by Jews, breaking into them, smashing the fittings, and throwing goods and wares into the street, where they were partly destroyed, and partly looted. As soon as they had finished with one shop, they moved on to the next...[38]

In the windows and doors of shops belonging to Christians, the owners put up icons and portraits of the tsar with national flags. These shops were not touched. Around midday on Kreshchatik, Duma Square, Proreznaia Street, and other streets, the roadways were littered with scattered bolts, unrolled lengths of material, and fragments of furniture and crockery. The area of Kreshchatik near Tsarskaia Square was completely covered with bed feathers. The pogrom was also going on in other parts of the city: wherever there were Jewish shops and stalls, everything was wrecked with the same bitterness and fury; in the Pecherskii and Plosskii districts, the sacking and looting of Jewish homes began.[39]

The entire Jewish population of Kiev suffered from the pogrom. The mob was interested neither in the social position nor in the political views of its victims; it destroyed all Jewish property that crossed its path. On October 19, 1905 in Lipki, in the presence of the army and police, houses that belonged to rich Jews—Baron Ginsburg, Gal'perin, Aleksandr and Leon Brodsky, and others—were sacked. On the same day, pogrom-makers began sacking the Brodsky Jewish artisan school even though the school headmaster had, on the previous day, alerted

---

37 Ibid.
38 TsDIAK U, f. 442, op. 855, d. 391, ll. 265–269.
39 Ibid.

the Kiev chief of police, Viacheslav Tsikhotskii, that there were plans to attack it.⁴⁰

The local authorities could easily have taken steps to prevent the pogrom in Kiev, or at least to stop it in the beginning. Because of the revolutionary situation, Kiev had been placed under martial law on October 14, 1905.⁴¹ There was in Kiev a "30,000-strong garrison, nine or ten police stations, the governor-general's office, the governor's office and a mass of the other authorities."⁴²

> The city administration put up a notice appealing to the population to preserve public order, but the robberies continued blatantly, and at every attempt at self-defense to protect property from being stolen, the patrols fired volleys at the balconies and the houses, from which single shots had been fired at the robbers.⁴³

Military patrols sometimes participated in the robbery, or sometimes just stood by and protected the robbers. When people appealed to them for help, they said they had not received orders to chase bandits.⁴⁴

The pogrom-makers whipped up "patriotic" demonstrations, which usually began near churches, beat Jews that they found on their way, and robbed Jewish property. Orthodox priests often led these processions. In one such demonstration, the tsar's portrait was carried in front, and behind it rioters carried a big platter with stolen Jewish property. The leaders of the Kiev Black Hundreds seriously discussed preparation of a "St. Bartholomew's Night" for the Jews, "to immediately get rid of these unwelcome guests of the Russian people." Kiev police and troops actively participated in the theft and destruction of Jewish property.

Jewish self-defense units could not stop the pogrom in Kiev because their resistance to pogrom-makers was suppressed by troops that fired

---

40 TsDIAK, f. 316, op. 1, d. 382, ll. 3–5.
41 *Kievskii i odesskii pogromy v otchetakh senatorov Turau i Kuzminskogo*, 23–25.
42 TsDIAK U, f. 442, op. 855, d. 391, ll. 265–269.
43 TsDIAK U, f. 442, op. 855, d. 391, part 2, l. 38.
44 Ibid.

on them on the order of their commanders. "On Mariinsko-Blagoveshchenskaia Street, a group of students shot at a crowd about to attack a Jewish house...Shots were fired from several houses."[45] But these shots gave the military the justification needed to implement their instructions for dealing with revolutionaries, and to open fire on the houses from which the shots had come. When the pogromists broke into a house where there were Jews, they often fired shots as a provocation, making the Jews a target for the soldiers' bullets. The self-defense units in Kiev, as in other places during the October 1905 pogroms, were annihilated by the troops.[46]

Many Christians hid their Jewish neighbors during pogroms, at the risk of their own lives and those of their family. If the pogrom mob found Jews hiding in an apartment of Christians, they spared neither the Christians nor the Jews. Hryhorii Hryhoriev wrote in his memoirs: "In one apartment on our street they found an old Jewish woman in a large trunk. They cut both her throat and that of the Christian owner of the apartment."[47] Toward Christians who tried to offer resistance to the pogromists and to defend Jews, the Black Hundreds were as merciless as to the Jews themselves. Vasilii Karavaevskii, who worked as a janitor in the house of the merchant Brazhnikov, refused to allow the mob, which had already sacked several Jewish apartments, to enter a courtyard where a Jewish family lived. The mob murdered him. No more pogromists appeared on L'vov Street, perhaps afraid of being held responsible for the murder of a Christian.[48]

For three days the local authorities did nothing to stop the riots in Kiev. During this pogrom, almost all Jewish stores, houses, and apartments were robbed. According to police, 1,800 Jewish houses and stores were ransacked, (however, not all Jews made claims for their lost and damaged property), one hundred Jews were killed, and 406 wounded.[49]

---

45 Ibid.
46 Victoria Khiterer, "The October 1905 Pogrom in Kiev," *East European Jewish Affairs* 22, no. 2 (1992): 33.
47 Hryhorii Hryhoriev, *U staromu Kyievi* (Kiev: Radians'kyi pys'mennyk, 1961), 21.
48 *Kievlianin*, Oct. 27, 1905.
49 Khiterer, "The October 1905 Pogrom in Kiev," 21–37.

After the pogrom, some Kiev gentiles felt it necessary to dissociate themselves from the violence and express their opposition to the actions of the authorities, police, and troops during the pogrom. On October 31, 1905, the newspaper *Kievskie otkliki* (Kiev Review) published a "Letter to Officers" that stated:

> Depressed by a number of irrefutable eye-witness testimonies concerning the events of October 18, 19, and 20 in the streets of Kiev, which constituted an inhumane picture of sacking, pillage and violence, and the cruel and totally unjustified inaction and connivance of the military and the police, we...wish to express our profound sympathy to the victims and our indignation regarding those who forgot their duty as human beings, citizens and officers to their long-suffering country... We demand an impartial investigation of the military and the police during these sad days.

The letter was signed by thirty-four artillery officers, sappers, and army doctors. For publishing this letter, all the signatories were sentenced by the Kiev military district court to terms of imprisonment varying from one month to a year and four months. In the words of the judge, this letter, "wherein was expressed a collective protest against the actions of the military, might be conducive to inciting public opinion against the authorities."[50]

A similar protest against the inaction and connivance of the military and police toward the rioters, and against the participation of troops in the pillage of Jewish property, was expressed by 116 Kiev gentile women, whose appeal was published in the *Kievskaia gazeta* on November 1, 1905. They also demanded an investigation of the actions of the Kiev authorities during the pogrom.

Senator Turau, who conducted the investigation of the Kiev pogrom, stated that "to put an end to the pogrom...would have been possible without special exertion."[51] In accordance with the powers

---

50 TsDIAK U, f. 315, op. 2, d. 22, ll. 30, 130.
51 *Kievskii i odesskii pogromy v otchetakh senatorov Turau i Kuzminskogo*, 50–52.

invested in him, Turau "sent to trial, with suspension of duty, the chief of Kiev police Colonel Tsikhotskii, the police officer Liashchenko of the Podol police district and his assistant Pirozhkov, charging them with criminal dereliction of duty with especially serious consequences."[52]

The case against the three never went to trial: the judicial investigation was stopped from above and in 1907 Tsikhotskii was reinstated to his post.[53] This was typical of the protective attitude that the supreme authorities in St. Petersburg demonstrated toward the perpetrators of pogroms. People who protested against pogroms were invariably punished far more severely than the pogromists themselves.

THE BEILIS TRIAL

The crushing of the revolution in 1905 brought the wave of pogroms to an end. However, in the new reactionary climate, Jews faced new threats and their situation throughout Russia deteriorated alarmingly. The worsening situation of the Jews inevitably had an impact on their situation in Kiev. This had now become one of the centers of Russian anti-Semitism and in 1911, the Black Hundreds, with the support of the local and high authorities, organized a ritual murder trial. They accused a local Jew, Mendel' Beilis, of killing a Christian boy, Andriusha Iushchinskii, in order to use his blood in the ritual preparation of matzos for Passover.[54]

In fact, in March 1911, a group of criminals killed the Christian boy, who "knew too much" about them and had threatened to denounce them to the police. The Black Hundreds used this murder to initiate the most famous blood-libel trial in Russian history: the Beilis affair, which

---

52 Ibid., 78–82.
53 A. E. Kaufman, *Druz'ia i vragi evreev: D. I. Pikhno* (St. Petersburg: Knigoizdatel'stvo Pravda, 1907), 18–19.
54 A. S. Tager, *Tsarskaia Rossiia i delo Beilisa: Issledovaniia i materialy* (Moscow: OGIZ, 1933; 2nd ed., Moscow: OGIZ, 1934; repr. Moscow: Gesharim, 1995); Maurice Samuel, *Blood Accusation: The Strange History of the Beilis Case* (Philadelphia: Jewish Publication Society of America, 1966); Hans Rogger, "The Beilis Case: Anti-Semitism and Politics in the Reign of Nicholas II," in *Jewish Policies and Right-Wing Politics in Imperial Russia* (Berkeley and Los Angeles: University of California Press, 1996), 40–55; Polonsky, *The Jews in Poland and Russia, II: 1881–1914*, 72; Robert Weinberg, *Blood Libel in Late Imperial Russia: The Ritual Murder Trial of Mendel Beilis* (Bloomington, IN: Indiana University Press, 2014).

continued from 1911 to 1913. The authorities investigated a common criminal case as a ritual murder on the initiative of the Kiev Russian nationalist organization the "Two-Headed Eagle." Members of the Black Hundreds pointed at Beilis as the possible murderer of Iushchinskii. In their publications about ritual murders, the Black Hundreds appealed to Christians to save their children, who might be sacrificed by Jews on the eve of Passover, and created a hysterical mood. The Russian government supported this medieval accusation and sent special investigators from St. Petersburg to Kiev. The original Kiev detectives were suspended for not steering their investigation toward a ritual murder case. Subsequently, in July 1911, a Jew, Mendel' Beilis, the manager of a brick factory near the murder site, was arrested and charged. The accusation was directed not just against Beilis, but put under suspicion all Jews. The Beilis affair resonated strongly among the public and divided society, much like the earlier Dreyfus affair in France.[55]

Investigation of the Beilis affair as a ritual murder was supported by the minister of justice, Ivan Grigor'evich Shcheglovitov, and the minister of the interior, Nikolai Alekseevich Maklakov.[56] Shcheglovitov and Maklakov perhaps pursued the case because of their desire to support the tsar, "a convinced anti-Semite who believed in Jewish ritual murder, even if it was not clear that Beilis was guilty."[57]

In spite of all the efforts of the Black Hundreds and the authorities to prepare well for the ritual murder trial, "the evidence against Beilis was critically weak."[58] The prosecution, lacking sufficient evidence, and trying to avoid losing altogether, split the indictment into two questions: whether the murder of Andriusha Iushchinskii was ritual, and whether Beilis was guilty of committing it. The jury answered positively to the first question: seven-to-five the jury members judged the murder as ritual. On the second question, about Beilis' involvement in the murder, the vote of the jury was "reportedly split evenly, six-to-six."[59]

---

55 Stepanov, *Chernaia sotnia v Rossii 1905–1914*, 265–319.
56 Polonsky, *The Jews in Poland and Russia, II: 1881–1914*, 72; Weinberg, *Blood Libel in Late Imperial Russia*, 1–43.
57 Polonsky, *The Jews in Poland and Russia*, II, 73.
58 Weinberg, *Blood Libel in Late Imperial Russia*, 43.
59 Ibid., 65.

According to Russian law "a tied vote went in favor of the defendant," so Beilis was acquitted and released.[60] Both sides, liberals and conservatives, proclaimed victory. The liberals celebrated the acquittal of Beilis, while conservatives were happy that the case was judged a ritual murder. The Black Hundred newspaper *Dvuglavyi orel* (Two-Headed Eagle) stated on October 30, 1913, "One Jew is Acquitted, All Kikes Are Found Guilty."[61]

Nicholas II supported the blood libel accusation, even after the acquittal of Beilis by the jury. The tsar told a member of his entourage, "It is certain that there was a ritual murder. But I am happy that Beilis has been acquitted, for he is innocent."[62] Polonsky notes that Shcheglovitov also celebrated with the head of the Union of the Russian People and the Metropolitan of Kiev "that the jury had found that a ritual murder had, in fact, taken place" and they "sent telegrams of congratulation to the Kiev 'heroes.'"[63]

The Black Hundreds, which failed to prove the guilt of Beilis in the ritual murder, took their revenge on one of Beilis' lawyers, Arnold Margolin. When the affair began, Margolin was still a young lawyer, thirty-four years old, but he was already noted for his defense of pogrom victims. He understood very well that the accusation against Mendel' Beilis had been organized by high Russian authorities with the support of local Black Hundreds organizations. He did not believe that there had been an objective and unprejudiced approach toward the case, and thought that only by finding the real murderers of the Christian child would the Jewish people be cleared of the accusation of his ritual murder. He was therefore inspired to make his own private investigation, together with the journalist Stepan Ivanovich Brazul-Brushkovskii. The latter organized a meeting of Margolin with Vera Cheberiak, who claimed she knew who killed the boy. Margolin agreed to this meeting but, by the time it was over, had become

---

60 Ibid.
61 Ibid., 67.
62 A. I. Spiridovich, *Les Dernières Années de la cour de Tzarskoié-Sélo*, trans. M. Jeanson (Paris: Payot, 1928–1929), 2: 447.
63 Polonsky, *The Jews in Poland and Russia*, II, 74.

convinced that Cheberiak was not just a witness to the murder but was, in fact, personally involved in it. When Cheberiak realized that Margolin understood her real role in the murder, she tried to protect herself by making accusations against Margolin and Brazul-Brushkovskii, claiming that the two had offered her a sizable bribe if she would take responsibility for the murder.[64]

Russian laws did not permit the defense to participate in pre-trial investigations and, because of this, Margolin was dismissed from his position as Beilis' lawyer on August 31, 1912, and was disbarred by the Kiev Chamber of Justice in December 1913. However, at the time of his private investigations, Margolin had not yet been officially assigned as Beilis' attorney, so he denied violating the law. Ultimately, his right to practice law was restored after the February 1917 Revolution.[65]

THE BLACK HUNDREDS

The October 1905 pogroms were the first demonstration of the political strength of the Black Hundreds. However, their plans regarding Jews were more radical than just the suppression of Jewish revolutionaries. After the October 1905 pogroms, leaders of the Black Hundreds were not satisfied and developed further plans to annihilate the Jews. The newspaper *Kievskie novosti* (Kiev News) published a note titled "The Headquarters of the Black Hundreds" on November 3, 1905. The article said:

> We have received information about the agitation activity of the leaders of the Black Hundreds, who hold their meetings in the restaurant of A. K. Sack at 45 Aleksandrovskaia Street [Kiev]…They discuss at these meetings the "suppression of sedition and annihilation of the neighbors—enemies [Jews] that aspired to gain rights in the alien state." They admit that the tactic of pogroms is not rational at this time, because

---

64 Victoria Khiterer, "Arnol'd Davidovich Margolin—zashchitnik Beilisa," *Vestnik Evreiskogo Universiteta v Moskve* 3, no. 7 (1994): 156–162.
65 Khiterer, "Arnold Davidovich Margolin: Ukrainian-Jewish Jurist, Statesman and Diplomat," *Revolutionary Russia* 18, no. 2 (Dec. 2005): 148–149.

not only Jews, but Russians also suffer from pogroms...They think that the most perfect and rational solution is the organization of a Saint Bartholomew night, which will immediately rid the Russian people of their unwelcome guests.

The Black Hundreds made one more attempt to foment a large pogrom in Kiev during the Beilis affair, soon after the arrest of Mendel' Beilis. However, this time their scheme was not supported by the authorities. Michael F. Hamm explains that during the Beilis affair,

> Kiev's Two Headed Eagle, led by Vladimir Golubov [a twenty-year-old student of Kiev University and the son of a professor at the Kiev Theological Academy[66]] and a priest, Fedor Sinkevich [the head of the organization], demanded that all Jews be expelled from the city and openly agitated for a pogrom. But with Nicholas II coming in the fall [1911] to unveil a statue of Alexander II, neither city nor state officials wanted disorders, and Golubov was dissuaded out of fear that a pogrom would force Nicholas to cancel his visit.[67]

Because the Black Hundreds acted with complete impunity and with the support of the Russian authorities, they became more and more bold. The Russian press wrote that the Black Hundreds terrorized the population in many cities of the empire (e.g., Kiev, Gomel', Iaroslavl', Ekaterinoslav). They attacked and injured Jews on the city streets just because of their Jewishness, and threatened liberals. Usually, members of the Black Hundreds were neither arrested nor punished.

A rare exception was a case in 1910, when the police detained a few members of the Union of Active Struggle with Revolution after they

---

66 S. A. Stepanov, *Chernaia sotnia v Rossii 1905–1914*, 271–272.
67 Michael F. Hamm, *Kiev: A Portrait, 1800–1917* (Princeton: Princeton University Press, 1993), 132.

made an attack on the streets of Nikol'skaia Slobodka (a suburb of Kiev located in the Chernigov province) and badly wounded several people. An armed detachment of 150–200 people from the Union of Active Struggle with Revolution surrounded the police station where the arrested rioters were jailed, demanding their release. The local police called for support from the Kiev police. Mounted police arrived from Kiev and the Union members retreated to a teahouse. When the police attempted to arrest them, they shot at the police, jumped from the windows, and ran away. Some of them were detained and arrested.[68] However, after a few days, by the order of the governor of the Chernigov province, Nikolai Matveevich Rodionov, all detained members of this Black Hundreds organization were released, and the chief of the Nikol'skaia Slobodka police and his assistant were fired "for professional tactlessness."[69]

What was the attitude of the Russian government and Prime Minister Stolypin toward the activities of the Black Hundreds? As prime minister of the Russian Empire, Stolypin did nothing to stop pogrom-makers, nor did he even attempt to stop the murders of liberals and Jews by the Black Hundreds. Stolypin did not ban any anti-Semitic organization in Russia. But in a circular published in 1910, he did prohibit all Ukrainian and Jewish national organizations in the Russian Empire as "promoting the rise of national self-consciousness."[70]

The years of the Stolypin government were the years when the Black Hundreds flourished in Russia. Stolypin's promotion of Russian nationalist and chauvinist ideas and the suppression of the national movements of all other nationalities in the Russian Empire fit well with the ideology of Russian nationalistic organizations. The later disagreement between Stolypin and the leader of the Union of Russian People, Alexander Ivanovich Dubrovin, only concerned the methods

---

68 *Bessarabskaia zhizn'*, September 3, 1908.
69 *Sovremennoe slovo*, September 10, 1908.
70 Khiterer, *Dokumenty, sobrannye Evreiskoi istoriko-arkheograficheskoi komissiei Vseukrainskoi Akademii Nauk*, 293–294.

for suppressing revolutionary and national minority movements. While the government preferred to use official measures to muzzle these movements, the Union of Russian People and other Black Hundreds organizations frequently employed assassinations and violence against their political enemies and Jews. The leaders of the Black Hundreds organizations criticized the government for its weakness and reluctance to use more radical and violent measures. However, despite this criticism, the Black Hundreds always supported the Russian monarchy, and never challenged the power of the authorities. They always stated that they had the same goals as the government: the preservation of the monarchy and the unity of Russia.[71] A number of high officials joined Russian nationalist and chauvinist organizations. The government always relied upon their faithful supporters. Nicholas II called on all Russian people to unite around the Union of Russian People. He expressed his gratitude to all Russians who joined the organization.[72]

Because of these close connections between members of the ultra-chauvinist organizations and the government, for many it was unclear where the Black Hundreds organizations ended and where the government began. The French ambassador to the Russian Empire, Georges Louis, wrote: "The Black Hundreds are ruling the country and the government obeys them because it knows the Emperor is inclined to sympathize with them."[73]

Russian authorities relied upon the support of right-wing organizations in their struggle against the revolutionary and Jewish national movements. During the tsar's visit to Kiev in 1911, an anti-Semitic brochure "Velikie dni torzhestva v Kieve! Poseshchenie Vysochaishei sem'i! Angel'skii privet!" (The Great Days of the Celebration in Kiev! The Visit of the Tsar's Family! The Angel's Greetings!) written by the favorite of the tsar's family, Grigorii Rasputin, was widely

---

71 Rogger, *Jewish Policies and Right-Wing Politics in Imperial Russia*, 212–232.
72 TsDIAK U, f. 838, op. 4, d. 5, l. 1.
73 Walter Laqueur, *Black Hundred: The Rise of the Extreme Right in Russia* (New York: HarperCollins Publishers, 1993), 19.

disseminated in the city. Rasputin was also in Kiev during the visit. He wrote in the brochure:

> Look at the *Soiuzniks* [i.e., the members of Union of the Russian People], they go like Great Saints!...These organizations [i.e., the Black Hundreds] are needed very much for Jews; they are very scared of them. When they go about in the Kiev streets, Yids whisper and tremble; they are less afraid of the army, because discipline does not allow military people do what they want. The Union of Russian People doesn't have that discipline. We need now to establish more departments of the Union of Russian People and not quarrel; then the Jews will not dare ask for equal rights.[74]

Black Hundreds organizations did not have any constructive program or ideas regarding how to overcome the deep political crises of the Russian monarchy and avoid the approaching revolution. As ultra-conservative organizations, they resisted all necessary political reforms, which might have peacefully transformed the regime. By means of assassinations, street violence, and terror against revolutionaries, liberals, and national minorities, they further destabilized the country.

Prime Minister Sergei Iul'evich Witte, as a liberal, was totally opposed to the goals and methods of the Black Hundreds. He wrote in his memoirs:

> the Black Hundreds movement had a huge role in the Russian revolution and anarchy...This political party is patriotic...But its patriotism is instinctual; its patriotism is not based on intellect and nobility, but on passions. The majority of its leaders are political rascals, dirty people in their thoughts and feelings, who do not have any viable and honest political ideas and all their efforts are directed to the instigation of the basest passions of the wild mob. This party, under the supervision of the

---

74 Grigorii Rasputin, *Velikie dni torzhestva v Kieve! Poseshchenie Vysochaishei sem'i! Angel'skii privet!* (St. Petersburg: M. P. Frolova Publishing House, 1911), 5.

two-headed eagle [i.e., the Russian monarchy], can produce terrible pogroms and troubles, but cannot create anything except a negative and destructive influence on political life.[75]

The Black Hundred organizations disappeared in Russia along with the collapse of the monarchy that financed them, although their anti-Semitic ideology was inherited by the Whites in the civil war. Subsequently, their former members continued to promote ultra-nationalistic and chauvinistic ideas in emigration. Later, many actively supported the Nazi regime in Germany.

CONCLUSION

Anti-Semitism in the beginning of the twentieth century took more violent forms in Russia than elsewhere. Kiev became the most notorious place for state and popular anti-Semitism in the Tsarist Empire. The Kiev Jewish population faced two large pogroms in the city in 1881 and 1905, as well as the Beilis affair, and lived under the continuous threat of new pogroms. Because of the deteriorating political situation and increased violence, Kievan Jews began searching for new solutions to improve their situation earlier than Jews in other communities of the Russian Empire. After the pogroms of 1881, many young Jews in Russia were disappointed in their prospects, and organized the immigration movement to America. One of the first Jewish immigration organizations, Am Olam, was created in Kiev. Kiev community leaders also made unsuccessful attempts to legalize organized Jewish emigration from the Russian Empire.

Anti-Jewish violence in Kiev threatened the lives of all Jews, regardless of their financial and social situations. During pogroms the mansions of wealthy Jews were robbed, as were the houses and apartments of the poorest. Wealthy Jews were beaten by pogrom-makers, along with the poorest Jews. The local authorities never protected Jews during pogroms, and in the course of the pogrom of

---

75 Witte, *Izbrannye vospominaniia*, 432.

1905 they openly encouraged the rioters. The official investigations of the authorities' activities during the pogroms found them guilty of inaction and criminal negligence. Jewish self-defense units could not protect the Jewish population during the 1905 pogrom because self-defense units were illegal in the Russian Empire, and they were fired upon by the troops. Later, investigations showed that a number of troops and policemen participated in the pillaging of Jewish property.

The Kiev Jewish population lost all hope that the authorities would do anything to protect them from rioters. Thus, rumors about a forthcoming pogrom were enough to compel many Jews to flee Kiev in a great panic, as happened in 1903.

The Beilis affair further inflamed the situation in Kiev. The local Black Hundreds organization, which insisted upon the ritual character of Iushchinskii's murder, repeatedly called for a Jewish pogrom. The authorities would allow, or not, new pogroms in the city depending upon their political needs. Thus, a pogrom was allowed in Kiev in October 1905 to suppress the revolutionary movement, in which many Jews actively participated. But the authorities dissuaded the Black Hundreds organizations from a pogrom after the assassination of Stolypin, or during the Beilis affair. In this way, the authorities kept the local anti-Semitic organizations under a modicum of control, unleashing them against Jews and revolutionaries only when deemed necessary. The tsar and Stolypin encouraged and financed the Black Hundreds movement in Russia, and both of them regarded members of the Black Hundreds as great supporters of the monarchy. During Stolypin's rule, the Black Hundreds and their press flourished in Russia due to generous government subsidies.

Public opinion among the Kiev gentile population regarding their Jewish neighbors was sharply divided. While some openly protested anti-Jewish pogroms and attempted save Jews from the riots even at the risk of their own lives, others joined the Black Hundreds and participated in anti-Jewish violence, demanding the expulsion of all Jews from the city.

The collapse of the monarchy in Russia meant for Jews the end of the state system of oppression, persecution, and denial of civil rights. Thus Jews in Kiev joyfully greeted the February 1917 Revolution. Jewish parties and organizations demonstrated in the central streets of Kiev with supportive slogans and posters in Yiddish and Hebrew.[76] Thus, in the history of the Jews of Kiev there began a new era.

---

76 The Central State Archive of Film, Photo, Sound Documents of Ukraine (TsDA-KFFU), Document # 4-7077.

CHAPTER SEVEN

How Jews Gained Their Education in Kiev

> If upon a cage of an elephant you see a sign reading: "buffalo," do not believe your eyes.
>
> —Kozma Prutkov[1]

THE EDUCATION OF NATIONAL MINORITIES IN THE RUSSIAN EMPIRE

The tsarist government followed a policy of Russification of national minorities from the 1830s on, and encouraged them to send their children to Russian state schools. The pressure from the imperial machine was felt more or less by all ethnic minorities in Russia.

Polish schools on the Right Bank Ukraine were closed after the Polish uprising of 1830–1831.[2] Starting in 1885, the authorities made Russian the official language of teaching in the people's (*narodnyi*) schools in the Kingdom of Poland. Russian authorities did not consider

---

1 Kozma Prutkov is a fictional author invented by the nineteenth-century Russian writer Aleksey Konstantinovich Tolstoy and his cousins, the three Zhemchuzhnikov brothers, Alexei, Vladimir, and Alexander.
2 Paul Robert Magocsi, *A History of Ukraine* (Seattle: University of Washington Press, 1998), 373.

Ukrainian to be a literary language, and prohibited all attempts to establish education in Ukrainian. A few timid efforts to teach in Ukrainian were made in Sunday schools in 1859 and the early 1860s. However, the authorities closed these schools and punished their organizers. In 1905, under the influence of the Ukrainian national movement, "some professors of Kiev University began to lecture in Ukrainian, but this was prohibited in 1910."[3] German schools operated in the Russian Empire until World War I, but all signs of German national spirit were eradicated from these schools long before they were finally closed. In the late nineteenth century, Russian officials insisted that all subjects in these schools, even lessons in German, should be taught in Russian. However, due to the reluctance of German teachers and students to switch to Russian, some of these schools continued to teach in their native language until the government circular of December 24, 1914, which prohibited teaching in German.[4]

The Russian government's policy toward Jewish education changed dramatically several times during the nineteenth and early twentieth century. According to Michael Stanislawski, the Russian government actively intervened in the traditional Jewish educational system. According to the law of 1844, Jewish state schools were established in many cities and towns of the Pale of Settlement, and all traditional religious Jewish schools (heders) were put under the Ministry of National Enlightenment. The Russian government planned to transform Jewish society through this new educational system, and achieve the rapprochement of Jews with the gentile population.[5] Thus, the Russian language became a requirement of the curriculum in Jewish state schools. From 1864 on, the government required that all private

---

3 *Encyclopedia of Ukraine* (Toronto, Buffalo, and London: University of Toronto Press, 1985), s.v. "Education," 1: 796–797.
4 E. V. Cherkaz'ianova, "Istoriia shkoly rossiiskikh nemtsev XIX–nachala XX veka v terminakh I poniatiiakh," *Vestnik Cheliabinskogo gosudarstvennogo universiteta* 18, no. 119 (2008): 42, 44.
5 Michael Stanislawski, *Tsar Nicholas I and the Jews: The Transformation of Jewish Society in Russia, 1825–1855* (Philadelphia: The Jewish Publication Society of America, 1983), 44.

Jewish teachers (melameds) pass a proficiency exam in Russian.[6] In this way Jewish state schools became a tool for the Russification of the Jewish population.

The imperial authorities allowed Jews to establish state and private Jewish schools in the Pale of Settlement, and beyond the Pale beginning in the 1860s. Jewish schools were opened in many cities beyond the Pale, even in the Russian capitals, St. Petersburg and Moscow.[7] A private school for poor Jewish children was established in St. Petersburg by Lazar and Anna Berman in 1867. In 1873, their daughter Sara Berman "received permission to open a private school for Jewish girls in St. Petersburg."[8] In Moscow, a Talmud-Torah was established in 1872, and the Alexandrovskii Jewish artisan school was opened in 1880.[9]

However, what was allowed in St. Petersburg and Moscow was often not permitted in Kiev. The city was an exception to the rule, in ways almost always detrimental to local Jews. The authorities' negative attitude toward the growth of the Jewish population resulted in ongoing prohibitions against the opening of any kind of Jewish institution: synagogues, schools, and cultural and philanthropic organizations. The authorities were afraid, with considerable justification, that these Jewish institutions and organizations would attract even more Jews to Kiev.

JEWISH SCHOOLS IN KIEV

For many years the government did not allow Jewish schools to be established in Kiev or allow melameds to work there. With the establishment of the percentage quota for Jews in gymnasiums and universities in 1887, even more obstacles arose for Jews seeking an education in

---

6   Pesakh Marek, "Bor'ba dvukh vospitanii," in *Evrei v Rossiiskoi imperii XVIII–XIX vekov. Sbornik trudov evreiskikh istorikov* (Moscow and Jerusalem: Jewish University in Moscow, Gesharim, 1995), 573.
7   S. Vermel', "K istorii Aleksandrovsogo Remeslennogo Uchilishcha v Moskve," in *Evrei v Moskve. Sbornik Materialov*, comp. Y. Snopov and A. Klempert (Jerusalem and Moscow: Gesharim, 2003), 264–265.
8   Eliyana R. Adler, *In Her Hands: The Education of Jewish Girls in Tsarist Russia* (Detroit: Wayne State University Press, 2011), 54; *Evreiskaia Encyclopedia*, s.v. "Sankt-Peterburg," 13: 945.
9   Vermel', "K istorii Aleksandrovsogo Remeslennogo Uchilishcha," 264–265.

Kiev. These obstacles left the majority of Jewish children without any formal education whatsoever. The absence of Jewish schools in Kiev, which was one of the major concerns of the Jewish community, was completely satisfactory to the authorities. The administration accurately judged that if the Jews had fewer options to educate their children, then a smaller Jewish community would remain in the city. Because the authorities were trying to minimize the number of Jews in Kiev, they repeatedly rejected the Jewish community's requests to establish a Jewish school, and they closed underground Jewish schools as soon as they were detected.

The struggle for Jewish education in Kiev continued from the creation of a new Jewish community in the 1860s until the turn of the twentieth century. Throughout this period, the authorities permitted neither the operation of Jewish schools, nor teaching by melameds in Kiev. Still, Jewish schools and melameds managed to covertly operate in the city. The vast majority of Kievan Jews in the 1860s–1870s were more than reluctant to send their children to the general schools because they believed in traditional Jewish values, and Russian education was based on Orthodox Christian ideals. Jewish parents were concerned that after education in Russian state schools, their children would become heretics and abandon their Jewish faith. The language barrier was also a serious obstacle, especially for children of poorer Jews who typically knew little Russian. Furthermore, the number of Russian state schools in Kiev was too few for the city's population. Thus, even before the introduction of the *numerus clausus* (percentage quota) for Jews, it was difficult for all city inhabitants to obtain places for their children in one of the Kiev Russian schools.[10]

Jews had to teach their children, at least the boys. Literacy is a requirement of Judaism, without which religious Jews cannot fulfill the commandments of Judaism: to read religious books and pray in Hebrew. Jews therefore ignored the authorities' ban, which from their point of view undermined the basis of Jewish life—traditional Jewish education. Well-to-do parents invited melameds to teach their children. Izrail'

---

10 TsDIAK U, f. 442, op. 535, d.280, ll. 1–3.

Beniaminovich Grinshtein complained in his petition of March 15, 1879 representing the Kiev Jewish community to the chancellery of the Kiev, Podolia, and Volhynia governor-general that the Kiev police often arrested melameds and detained them at the police station until their pupils' parents came and offered bribes to release them.[11] Grinshtein asked that the work of melameds in Kiev be legalized; his request was of course rejected.

Poor Jews could not afford to pay melameds, so the Kiev Jewish community opened and financed a Talmud-Torah for their children and orphans. But, if private lessons with melameds could be easily concealed from the authorities, the work of a Talmud-Torah with sixty-eight students was hard to keep secret. The Director of Administration of the Kiev Educational District wrote in a confidential report to the Kiev, Podolia, and Volhynia governor-general, Count Aleksandr Mikhailovich Dondukov-Korsakov,

> The inspector of national schools of the first district of Kiev province, Chechet, reported to me on April 29th [1874], that as he visited on April 26th Kiev municipal parish schools, he discovered in the Plosskii district of the city, on Kirilovskaia Street in Bazilevskaia's house, a people's school that was unknown to him. Entering this school he saw there sixty-eight Jewish boys and three teachers of Jewish subjects. The students, located in three separate rooms, were engaged in reading the Bible and other Jewish books. Considering the similar uniforms of the students, and the quite comfortable furniture of the school, Chechet assumes that this school has good financial means.
>
> On his question: who, when, and with whose permission this school was opened, the teachers answered that it was opened by the Jewish Trusteeship, financed by the Jewish community, has operated since January 1873; however they knew nothing regarding permission about its opening.

---

11   Ibid., f.442, op. 829, d. 51, ll. 1–4.

The inspector instructed one of the teachers to deliver from the Trusteeship information about who allowed this school to open. The next day Inspector Chechet received from the teacher the bylaws of the "Kiev Jewish Orphanage," which was not approved by any authorities. Following the teacher, Kiev Rabbi Tsukkerman came to Chechet, and explained that the Jewish Community did not yet have sufficient funds for the establishment of the shelter for Jewish orphans, left after soldiers died in the cholera epidemic, and had not yet had the opportunity to petition about the formal opening of the orphanage. However, the Jewish community did not want to leave without care orphans wandering on the streets, and found it necessary before receiving official permission for the orphanage to temporarily settle and teach the Jewish orphans, who do not speak or understand anything in Russian.

Due to this, I asked the Kiev Governor to order closure of the school, and charge those guilty of its opening according to the law. However, I have not received an answer to my appeal until the present.

Now the assistant of the Kiev Rabbi, Wolf Bronshtein, has appealed to me with a petition regarding permission for him to open in Kiev a boarding school or private school for Jewish children…[12]

The Director of Administration of the Kiev Educational District asked in his letter the opinion of the Kiev, Podolia, and Volhynia governor-general regarding the request of Wolf Bronshtein.

Governor-General Dondukov-Korsakov demanded from Kiev Governor Nikolai Pavlovich Gesse an explanation as to why he had for several months delayed closure of the illegal Jewish school. The governor's response shows his lenient attitude toward the existing Jewish orphanage. The governor explained that he gave an order to the Kiev police to investigate this case and

---

12 TsDIAK U, f. 442, op. 53, d. 356, ll. 1–2.

during the interrogation, Kiev Rabbi Tsukkerman claimed that the school in Bazilevskaia's house did not exist, but that the Kiev Jewish community considered opening the school, and in the case of its opening, the community intended to elect as trustees of the school the first guild merchant Gersh Fainberg and Mordko Markovich, and the teachers Lander and Kelerman. During further interrogation, Tsukkerman, Fainberg, Markovich, and Lander, and also the clerk's wife Bazilevskaia claimed that there was no school in Bazilevskaia's house, but, from the beginning of the spring, the Jewish community was afraid of a flood, and gathered the orphans left by soldiers and artisans who had passed away. The orphans lived on the allowance of various Jews, mostly in Obolon' [district], and were settled temporarily in the house of the clerk's wife Bazilevskaia who was living there with the Jew Lander, who was taking care already of another eight orphans. Over sixty orphans were placed there, and so that they would not spend their time in vain, the community entrusted Lander to take care of the orphans and he gave them the Bible to read.[13]

The Plosskii district policeman Strel'bitskii confirmed that no Jewish school was operating in Bazilevskaia's house, and the case was directed to the investigator of the Plosskii district for further research. The Kiev governor also recommended the approval of Bronshtein's request for permission to open in Kiev a boarding or private school for Jewish children. The governor and the chief of police considered that if "Jews, according to article 284 volume XIV of the statute about passports, have the right to live in Kiev with restrictions…[so] it is necessary to give them the possibility of teaching their children."[14]

Kiev Jewish merchants and artisans also asked in their petition of April 16, 1877 to the Kiev, Podolia, and Volhynia governor-general that they be allowed to open a private Jewish school, which would be subsidized by the community. They wrote,

---

13   Ibid., ll. 6–8.
14   Ibid., l. 8.

We, artisans, need very much such a school, in which our children from six to ten years old can study the Holy Scripture and the Russian language. Due to the absence of such a school, our children remain without any moral or religious education, which makes us concerned about their behavior as adults.[15]

Despite the petition of the Kiev Jewish community and the support of their request by Governor Gesse, a Jewish school was not opened in Kiev until many years later. Governor-General Dondukov-Korsakov rejected all such requests by the Jewish community and wrote in his letter to the chief of police on April 19, 1877:

Kiev has schools of the Ministry of National Enlightenment, where Jewish children can study, so I ask you to tell to the above-mentioned Jews that their request could not be satisfied.[16]

On October 20, 1881, the former rabbi of the city Nikolaev, Mark Osipovich Kogan, who moved to Kiev in 1880 for the education of his five children in the university and secondary schools, petitioned the Director of Administration of the Kiev Educational District with a request to allow him to open a private school for Jewish boys. The director passed this question on to the Board of Trustees of the Kiev Educational District. The Board of Trustees, according to Rabbi Kogan, postponed a decision, claiming that "opening such a school in Kiev will be opposed to the views and desires of the high authorities."[17] Then, on September 25, 1882, Kogan sent a petition directly to Kiev, Podolia, and Volhynia Governor-General Aleksandr Romanovich Drentel'n. He explained to the governor-general why the opening of the private Jewish school was absolutely necessary. Kogan wrote:

Kiev has a very significant Jewish population…Meanwhile, over one thousand Jewish boys are deprived of any education,

---

15 Ibid., l. 12.
16 Ibid., l. 13.
17 Ibid., f. 442, op. 535, d. 280, ll. 1–3.

which is necessary for any inhabitant of Russia. Jewish boys should study general courses as well as receive basic knowledge of the Jewish Holy Scripture, and reading and translation of everyday Jewish prayers. The cause of such an abnormal and unusual phenomenon among Jews of only one city Kiev is quite clearly due to the following circumstances. From one side, it is impossible to increase even a little the number of Jewish students in the few general elementary and middle schools due to the large number of local Christians. From the other side, this is a direct result of the absence in Kiev of at least one legal Jewish elementary school. This is especially a problem now, when the few melameds who lived in Kiev and taught Jewish children without restriction, were ordered by the Kiev municipal police to leave the city. Thus almost all of the large number of Jewish children in Kiev, the number of which increases every year, grow up without any knowledge about religion and faith, and without any knowledge of the most necessary general subjects such as Russian language, arithmetic and the history of their country, the Russian Empire. Such an upbringing for Jewish children of the city Kiev is very destructive and harmful generally and for the local population particularly...

...private Jewish schools have been opened with the permission of the authorities for a long time even in the Russian capitals, St. Petersburg and Moscow.[18]

Rabbi Kogan's well-grounded explanation did not change the minds of the local authorities; his request was summarily rejected as were all prior petitions.

The authorities responded likewise to the petition of Kiev Jewish women to allow them to open in Kiev a boarding school for Jewish girls who had working parents and who therefore spent daytime hours without adult supervision, and also for orphaned Jewish girls. The wives

---

18 Ibid.

of the wealthiest Kiev Jews, whose husbands held leading positions in the Kiev Jewish community—Berta and Eva Brodskaia, Sofia Mandelstamm, Elka and Maria Rozenberg, and others—signed the petition and submitted it to the Kiev governor in December 1885. The Kiev governor recommended to the Kiev, Podolia, and Volhynia governor-general in his letter of December 31, 1885 that this request be declined. He doubted that the petitioners had the means to finance the boarding school, which

> would give them a reason later to ask for financing of this school from the basket tax, and the bylaws allowed the school to accept children of Jewish non-residents of Kiev, which would give their parents the legal right to live in Kiev.[19]

Kiev, Podolia, and Volhynia Governor-General Drentel'n agreed with the Kiev governor, and refused the Jewish women's request on the basis that this school "will promote further isolation of Jews."[20] The Russian government's struggle against the isolation of Jews and desire to merge them with the gentile population was the official policy before 1881. Then, the government changed their official course to the isolation and increased persecution of Jews. However, for a while the Kiev and higher authorities still used the old doctrines to deny the opening of a boarding school for Jewish girls as well as other Jewish schools. The local authorities' negative attitude toward the establishment of Jewish schools in Kiev was consistent with the stream of government policy toward Jewish education in the 1880s. A circular of the Ministry of National Enlightenment on March 30, 1888, No 5035, stated: "... establishment of Jewish schools outside of the Pale of Settlement cannot be allowed, especially when there are enough general elementary schools."[21]

A few years later, on May 11, 1890, Rabbi Evsei Tsukkerman and two people in charge of the care of Jewish orphans in Kiev, the merchant Leon Ashkenazi and the hereditary honorable Kiev citizen Saul Levin,

---

19 Ibid., f. 442, op. 539, d. 11, ll. 1–2.
20 Ibid., l. 3.
21 TsDIAK U, f. 707, op. 175, d. 39, l. 41.

again appealed with a petition to the Kiev, Podolia, and Volhynia governor-general asking for permission to open two Jewish elementary schools in the Lybedskoi and Plosskii districts for "teaching Holy Scripture and Russian grammar to Jewish children." They wrote,

> Because Jewish home teachers [melameds] don't have the right to teach and live in Kiev, and also because Your Highness ordered that an end be put to any not completely legal teaching, the children of the Kiev Jewish population are in a desperate situation regarding the possibility of studying Jewish religious law,…and also because private education at home is inaccessible for the majority of the population. Thus, almost all Kiev Jewish children are deprived of the chance of receiving at least an elementary religious-moral education, so the sum of 3,000 rubles annually allocated from the basket tax is used only for teaching poor Jewish orphans artisan skills, the religious-moral side of their education is completely neglected, so these children, as all the others, remained illiterate and without any religious education.[22]

Kiev Governor Lev Pavlovich Tomara wrote to the Kiev, Podolia, and Volhynia governor-general on May 24, 1890 regarding this petition the following:

> This petition should not be satisfied, because first of all there does not exist a law that allows Jewish schools to open outside of the Pale of Settlement, and second because the opening of such schools will be the cause for Jews from other towns to settle in Kiev for the education of their children in these schools, and so it can become a cause for an influx of Jews to Kiev, which already has a significant Jewish population. Then, little by little, will be opened still more new Jewish schools, because the existing ones will be too crowded and modern

---

22 Ibid., f. 442, op. 53, d. 356, l. 19.

Kiev will have no distinction as to the places where Jews are allowed to live.[23]

Kiev, Podolia, and Volhynia Governor-General Aleksei Pavlovich Ignat'ev supported the Kiev governor's position and rejected the Kiev Jews' request regarding the opening of two Jewish schools in Kiev.[24]

Education in Russian schools became less available to Jews after the introduction of the percentage quota for Jewish children in gymnasiums and universities in 1887. However, this did not change the authorities' attitude toward the establishment of Jewish schools in Kiev. They therefore deprived the majority of Jewish children any chance of receiving a formal education. The abnormality of this situation was realized even by the director of the Kiev Educational District. He wrote to the Kiev, Podolia, and Volhynia governor-general on March 31, 1894 that Jews were not allowed to open heders or have melameds in Kiev, and that in the city

> permanently live a significant Jewish population for whose children the secondary schools are inaccessible due to the percentage quota; the elementary schools also restrict as much as possible an excessive influx of the Jewish element due to its harmful influence on the schools. Thus, in the current year, Jewish students constituted in all thirty-eight parish schools not more than sixty students, and only three Jewish students enrolled in the Kiev City School.[25]

The director of the Kiev Educational District asked the governor-general to grant the Jewish citizens' repeated requests to open an elementary school in Kiev financed by the Jewish community. However, the governor-general rejected this request because

---

23 Ibid., l. 17.
24 Ibid., ll. 20–21.
25 Ibid., f. 442, op. 624, d. 249, l. 1–2.

only Jewish merchants of the first guild and persons with higher education have the right of permanent residence in Kiev, all other Jews who live in Kiev (artisans, retired soldiers and others) for whom the opening of the school is important have only the right of temporary residence in Kiev. The establishment of this school will strengthen the settlement of those Jews in Kiev and even provoke the further undesirable influx of others.[26]

The governor-general's concern was well grounded, since the parents of Jewish students had the right of temporary residence in Kiev for the education of their children. This so-called temporary residence sometimes continued for many years, as in the case of Iudka Ianovskii, who had already lived in Kiev for fifteen years when in 1899 the police checked why his "temporary" residence had lasted so long. As reported by the Kiev governor to the governor-general on October 8, 1899,

The Jew Ianovskii…lived in Kiev since 1884 for the education of his eleven children, who are from twenty-six to five years old…At this time 139 Jewish families live in Kiev according to the right for the education of their children.[27]

Because Jewish families were quite large, we can estimate that in 1899 according to "the right for the education of their children" more than a thousand Jews "temporarily" lived legally in Kiev. However, this temporary residence, as shown in the Ianovskii case, could last for decades depending upon the number of children. The local authorities attempted to limit the increase of the Kiev Jewish population by repeatedly banning the establishment of Jewish schools in Kiev. Thus, the governor-general was correct when he stated that the Jewish schools would cause many Jewish families to move to Kiev from the Pale "for the education of their children."

---

26 Ibid., l. 3.
27 Ibid., f. 442, op. 629, d. 408, l. 7.

Jewish families who received the right of temporary residence in Kiev for the education of their children sent them to study in Russian gymnasiums, commercial and artisan schools, Kiev St. Vladimir University, the Kiev Polytechnic Institute, and the music school.[28] However, beginning in 1887, the percentage quota limited the entrance of Jews into Russian schools. Thus, the local authorities could be sure that the number of Jewish students and their parents temporarily residing in Kiev would remain limited.

But Kiev Jews needed to teach their children, and in spite of all bans, illegal Jewish schools again and again were opened in the city. For example, on November 18, 1897, the Kiev, Podolia, and Volhynia governor-general received a denunciation from two Kiev Jews about the operation of an illegal Jewish school "with six departments" on Iaroslavskii Street, 23 and 24.[29] After this revelation, the school was closed.

Sometimes, to receive permission for the opening of a school, Kievan Jews offered compromises and proposed to accept not only Jewish, but also Christian children. However, if Jews asked about the opening of a general school, this immediately raised questions regarding the language of teaching and curriculum. By the beginning of the twentieth century, when Kievan Jewry was more or less Russified, such a combination of students became possible. For example, the honorary hereditary citizen of Kiev, Gerts Grigorievich Balakhovskii, asked the authorities in 1900 for permission to open a Jewish agricultural teaching farm. His request was denied, as were all other petitions regarding the establishment of Jewish schools in Kiev. Then, four years later, Balakhovskii asked for permission to open in Kiev an agricultural farm for the education of Jewish children, whose parents had the right of residence in the city, and also for orphans of other religions, "especially the children of fallen warriors in the Far East" (i.e., in the Russo-Japanese War).[30]

According to the the bylaws of the proposed school, healthy thirteen-to-fifteen-year-old boys were to be accepted. Well-off families were

---

28 Ibid., ll. 8–20.
29 Ibid., f. 442, op. 847, d. 288, ll. 1–2.
30 Ibid., f. 442, op. 633, d. 40, l. 6.

supposed to pay for the education of their children. Children from poor families and orphans were exempt from tuition payment. Christian orphans and Jewish children, whose parents or guardians had the right of residence in Kiev, were accepted to the school. To be accepted, it was necessary to provide a diploma showing two years in Russian people's schools or in Jewish state schools, or to pass a placement exam equal to the curriculum of these schools. This, of course, made the teaching farm inaccessible to many Jewish children who had not received an elementary education. At the farm, the students were to study the Russian language, arithmetic, drawing, agriculture, stock-breeding (the farm had its own cattle), the production of medicinal herbs, and carpentry and locksmith crafts. This school was planned as a general school where all subjects were taught in Russian. The term of education was supposed to be three years. The farm was intended to be located on land belonging to Balakhovskii in the Plossko-Luk'ianovskii district of Kiev. Balakhovskii and other philanthropists promised to provide the necessary financing for the farm.

Finally, on October 29, 1905, five years after Balakhovskii's original petition, the Kiev, Podolia, and Volhynia governor-general gave permission for the teaching agricultural farm to open as a general educational institution for Christian and Jewish children.[31] This teaching farm was supposed to realize the Jewish dream of working the land, which, as mentioned earlier, was quite popular at the turn of the twentieth century, and to give vocational training to Jewish and gentile children. Because documents about the actual operation of the farm have not survived, it is unknown how long it worked or how successful it was.

The dreadful situation of Jewish education in the city was finally improved by the "King of Kiev Jews," Lazar Brodsky. When Brodsky applied to the authorities with the request to open a Jewish state elementary school in Kiev in 1901, he received permission. It is unclear why the local authorities changed their minds regarding Jewish schools in Kiev. Probably, Brodsky's connections in St. Petersburg played a significant role, or perhaps he bribed some key local official. Maybe, in

---

31 Ibid., l. 5.

the eyes of the local authorities, his request was more significant than those of other Jewish petitioners—after all, Brodsky was one of the most prominent industrialists in the region, and a generous philanthropist for many city organizations and institutions. In any case, when Brodsky asked to open a Jewish school, the authorities completely changed their tune. The administrator of the Chancellery of the Kiev, Podolia, and Volhynia governor-general wrote to the governor-general on November 17, 1901,

> Kiev is located beyond the Pale of the Jewish Settlement, however a large number of Jews live here and they need to give an education to their children. The law does not instruct us to, but also does not forbid, the opening of Jewish state schools in Kiev. On the other hand, the law's intent does not allow an influx of Jews into Kiev.
>
> Therefore, I assume it would be right to allow [the opening of a Jewish school in Kiev], but with the condition that this school will accept only the children of parents (or even orphans living with their relatives and guardians), who have the right of residence in Kiev.
>
> This condition is consistent with the request of Mr. Brodsky, who proposes to open the school for the poorest part of the Jewish population of Kiev.[32]

The Kiev governor supported this request, and Brodsky received permission to open a two-grade Jewish state school financed by the Jewish community. The question then arose about the right of residence in Kiev for the school's teachers. The governor-general decided that that the school's teachers could reside in the city during their work there. However, after the Jewish community received permission to open the school, it still took three more years to complete its construction. Even though the Jewish school had the status of a state school, it was built and financed by Kiev Jews. Lazar and Lev Brodsky donated

---

32 Ibid., f. 442, op. 631, d. 410, l. 1.

300,000 rubles for the school's construction. The Jewish community provided 6,000 rubles a year from the basket tax for the school budget, the founders covered the other expenses, and the students paid twenty rubles a year. The school was named after the late brother of Lazar and Lev Brodsky, Solomon, and its inauguration was on November 7, 1904. The school reported to the Ministry of National Enlightenment and employed a principal, eight teachers of general subjects, and several arts and crafts teachers. Students could therefore learn a profession along with their elementary education.[33] Students studied Russian and Hebrew languages, Russian and Jewish history, Judaism, arithmetic, geography, and natural science. They could receive optional vocational education in the arts and crafts department. The school was designed for three hundred students, and the arts and crafts department could accept one hundred more.[34] Lev Brodsky, who took care of the school after the death of his brother Lazar, asked the authorities in 1905 to establish two inspector positions at the school, and gave for this purpose 1,000 rubles per year. Although a school of its size and status was not supposed to have inspectors, Kiev, Podolia, and Volhynia Governor-General Sukhomlinov gave permission for these positions to be established. The inspectors received the right of residence in Kiev for the term of their work at the school.[35]

Less than a year after its opening, the Brodsky Jewish State School became a special target for rioters during the October 1905 pogrom in Kiev. Senator Evgenii Fedorovich Turau wrote in his report regarding the Kiev pogrom:

> During October 19th and 20th the wealthy Brodsky Jewish School, belonging to the Ministry of National Enlightenment, was completely looted. On the eve of this, on the evening of October 18th, the principal of the school, Shiperovich, found

---

33 Ibid., f. 442, op. 631, d. 410, l. 7.
34 Mikhail Kalnitsky and Boris Khandros, "Gde uchilis' kievskie evrei," *Interesnyi Kiev*, February 5, 2006, http://www.interesniy.kiev.ua/old/population/obrazovanie/learningevrei.
35 TsDIAK U, f. 442, op. 658, d. 209, ll. 1–2.

out that tram workers were going to loot the school, and informed [the chief of Kiev police] Tsikhotskii about this, asking for protection. In response Tsikhotskii promised to send police and guards. The next day, when the pogrom already had begun, Shiperovich repeatedly asked Tsikhotskii for protection. Tsikhotskii promised to send the guards, but did not fulfill his promise and the school, which did not have any protection, was looted and destroyed. Shiperovich, with his family, was hidden by the director of the people's school Lubenets, who learned about the looting on October 19, and wrote to colonel Tsikhotskii an urgent official report, asking for protection, and pointing out that the school belongs to the state. The chief of police received the report, but did not make any orders regarding this. When Lubenets visited the school on the morning of October 20th, he found the robbers inside, who still were stealing the last remaining valuable items from the school, for example the door handles, etc.[36]

Probably Tsikhotskii did not worry much about the property of the Jewish state school, since he knew that the Jews were paying for everything. For over three years this was the only Jewish school in Kiev. The school operated in Kiev at least until 1918 (the exact date of its closure is unknown) although the building still stands. The number of teachers increased to eleven in 1913, and the school had a new principal, Meier-Iakov Itskovich Kiperman.[37]

Along with the opening of the first Jewish school at Kiev, in 1903 the authorities allowed Kiev Jews to open a branch of the Society for Spreading Enlightenment among Jews in Russia (OPE). Although it opened later than other branches of the OPE, the Kiev branch soon became one of the organization's largest. The first meeting of the Kiev OPE took place on December 23, 1903. Lazar Brodsky was elected as

---

36 Ibid., f. 316, op. 1, d. 382-V, ll. 3–8.
37 Ibid., f. 274, op. 4, d. 254, l. 24.

chairman, and Max Mandelstamm as vice president.[38] The Kiev OPE was active throughout the Kiev, Podolia, and Volhynia provinces, however the wealthy donors preferred that most of their money be spent locally in Kiev.[39]

The opening of the first Jewish state school in Kiev created a precedent, making it easier for Jews to receive permission for the foundation of new Jewish schools in the city. In 1907, the Kiev, Podolia, and Volhynia governor-general permitted the Kiev OPE to open four private Jewish schools in Kiev—two for boys and two for girls.[40] In addition to these schools, in 1908 the Kiev OPE financed Jewish schools in Kiev province and funded in Kiev a Jewish kindergarten, a Jewish Saturday school, as well as a Jewish library.[41]

Thus, the local government finally became reconciled with the existence in Kiev of all kinds of Jewish schools and teachers in the first decade of the twentieth century, after Lazar Brodsky broke the ice with the establishment of his school. Thereafter, the authorities even allowed heders and melameds in Kiev. Several heders operated in Kiev during the 1910s, one of which was financed by the jeweler Iosif Marshak. In 1911, David Margolin opened in Kiev a Talmud-Torah for poor Jewish children and orphans, which he built and financed himself. The school had the capacity for three to four hundred students and was located on Konstantinovsky Street in Podol, the district were the poor Kievan Jews lived.[42]

The number of Jewish schools and teachers grew so rapidly in Kiev that in 1911 the Jewish teachers unified into a professional organization, the Society for Aid to Jewish Teachers and Melameds Living

---

38 Brian Horowitz, *Jewish Philanthropy and Enlightenment in Late-Tsarist Russia* (Seattle and London: University of Washington Press, 2009), 192, 196; Irina Sergeeva and Ol'ga Gorshikhina, "Deiatel'nost' Kievskogo otdeleniia Obschestva dlia rasprostraneniia prosveshcheniia mezhdu evreiami v Rossii v kontse XIX–nachale XX veka," in *Istoriia evreev v Rossii, Problemy Istochnikovedeniia i istoriographii. Sbornik nauchnykh trudov*, ed. D. A. Eliashevich (St. Petersburg: Peterburgskii Evreiskii Universitet, 1993), 125–126.
39 Ibid.
40 TsDIAK U, f. 442, op. 660, d. 208, ll. 1, 3–4.
41 Sergeeva and Gorshikhina, "Deiatel'nost' Kievskogo otdeleniia," 126.
42 Kalnitsky and Khandros, "Gde uchilis' kievskie evrei."

in Kiev and the Pale of Settlement. The society's board was located in Kiev. This organization provided financial support to "Jewish teachers of state and private schools and melameds" if they became unemployed or ill, and aid to their families in the event of their death. According to its bylaws published in 1911, the society was also supposed to organize pedagogical courses for Jewish teachers in the summer, publish a pedagogical journal, organize lectures and libraries for the teachers, and support the organization of Jewish schools, heders, and kindergartens. The society was financed by membership dues and donations, as well as by the lectures, concerts, and plays that it organized.[43]

In the beginning of the twentieth century, primarily poor Jews were attracted to traditional Jewish religious schools. Upper and middle class Jews looked for more modern schools for their children, where they could receive both Jewish and general education. In response to this demand, the A. Kozarinskii and B. Shumer private Jewish gymnasiums opened in Kiev during World War I.[44] Jewish gymnasiums taught the same subjects as Russian gymnasiums, plus courses in Judaism, Jewish history, and Hebrew. The Jewish gymnasiums and schools were also an alternative for Jewish children who were rejected by Russian state schools due to the percentage quota.

Kievan Jews struggled with the local and high authorities to establish all kinds of Jewish religious, educational, and cultural institutions. It was almost as difficult for Kievan Jews to receive permission to open a Jewish library as it was for them to get schools approved. Kievan Jews first asked for permission to open a library in 1898, but the Kiev, Podolia, and Volhynia governor-general rejected their petition. The Poles and Germans also applied to the local authorities with similar requests, which were denied. The Kiev governor and the Kiev, Podolia, and Volhynia governor-general, due to the "specifics of the local region and the goals of the government, aimed at the Russification of the local population," decided "not to allow the opening of such [Jewish, Polish,

---

43 TsDIAK U, f. 442, op. 636, d. 647, part VII, l. 642.
44 Kalnitsky and Khandros, "Gde uchilis' kievskie evrei."

and German] libraries, which will promote the isolation of the various nationalities of the local population."[45]

The Kiev state rabbi, Solomon Kalmanovich Lur'e, repeatedly petitioned the local authorities from 1904 to 1907 to open a Jewish private library in the city. The local authorities rejected his petitions several times, giving various explanations. Initially, in 1904, the Kiev governor and Governor-General Nikolai Vasilievich Kleigel justified their rejection by claiming that a Jewish library would promote the isolation of the Jewish population.[46] Lur'e appealed this decision to the State Senate. It is notable that the Senate was more supportive of Lur'e's request than the local administration. The Senate found that the rejection of the petition was "not well grounded." The only legal reason to deny any person permission to open a private library was the political unreliability of the person.[47] As the state rabbi of Kiev, Lur'e, was of course by definition a wholly reliable figure.

Nevertheless, even after this decision by the Senate, the Kiev authorities continued to stubbornly ban the establishment of a Jewish library. Kiev, Podolia, and Volhynia Governor-General Vladimir Aleksandrovich Sukhomlinov wrote to the minister of the interior on January 9, 1907,

> I consider the opening in Kiev of a Jewish library, especially in our turbulent times, undesirable, because nobody can guarantee that this library won't turn into a storage for revolutionary publications and socialist literature and serve the goals of revolutionary propaganda, because of the obviously defined political direction of the majority of Jewish youth, which appeared in the organization of the Bund and their well-known aspiration to circumvent the law. It will be absolutely impossible to control in the library the existence of publications illegal and harmful for circulation among the people, because we don't have Russian officials who know the Jewish language [i.e.,

---

45 TsDIAK U, f.442, op. 848, d. 137, ll. 1–2.
46 Ibid., f.442, op. 634, d. 633, ll. 1–3.
47 Ibid., l. 14.

Yiddish and Hebrew]. The Senate statement about the absence of information regarding the political unreliability of Rabbi Lur'e cannot be considered in this case. Rabbi Lur'e took only the initiative to petition regarding the opening of the library, which would be opened on the collective means of the Jews and ruled by a specially elected board. According to the plan, Rabbi Lur'e will not participate at all in the management of library affairs and his personal political reliability or unreliability does not matter in this case. Therefore, the only reason the Senate considered Lur'e's complaint well supported, vanished.[48]

Existing documents don't reveal the authorities' final decision regarding Lur'e's petition to open a Jewish library in Kiev. The discussion of this question by the authorities was postponed for so long that Lur'e resigned from his position in 1906.[49] Unfortunately, this was a rather typical situation. In 1905, A. Izraelitin (most likely a pseudonym) wrote in the article "Russian-Jewish Public Libraries" that it was difficult to obtain permission for the opening of Jewish libraries: the bureaucratic process was slow, and therefore the only option was to open unofficial Jewish libraries. So there were "many unofficial [Jewish] libraries."[50]

There were several Jewish libraries in Kiev that worked semi-legally at various Jewish organizations and institutions. The Jewish hospital had a Jewish library, which opened before 1905.[51] The Kiev literary group *Iudaika* (Judaica), which operated for twenty-five years, had its own library that it transferred to the Kiev OPE after its establishment.[52] Based on this library, the Kiev OPE opened its own in 1906, and its collection increased rapidly: by December 31, 1906, the library already had 2,907 books and was receiving thirty-three periodicals; by 1913, there

---

48 Ibid., ll. 11–12.
49 YIVO, RG 81, folder 703, doc. 60668. Address of Kiev City Rabbi S. A. Lur'e to congregation Kiev Jewish Prayer houses, October 8, 1906.
50 A. Izraelitin, "Russko-evreiskie obshchedostupnye biblioteki," *Knizhki Voskhoda* (May 1905): 133.
51 Ibid., 129.
52 Sergeeva and Gorshikhina, "Deiatel'nost' Kievskogo otdeleniia," 132.

were 10,791 volumes of books and periodicals in Hebrew, Yiddish, and Russian.[53] This was the largest Jewish library in Kiev, and it soon became quite popular among the Kievan Jews. During the first four months of its operation, 1,806 people visited the library.[54] Unlike most other OPE libraries, the Kiev library was completely free of charge.[55] The decision of the Kiev OPE to make the library free for the public was against the policy of the Library Department of the OPE, which stated,

> In the interest of the development of library affairs, the department considers it necessary to introduce at least some obligatory insignificant payment for reading. The payment will force the readers to have a more serious attitude toward their participation in library affairs. The payment will release the libraries from the philanthropic charitable character that humiliate the person who uses it and the institution that provides it.[56]

This statement shows the rather astonishing attitude toward philanthropy and charity of some leaders of the OPE's Library Department. Nevertheless, the leaders of the Kiev OPE followed their own independent policy on this question. The Jewish library developed so successfully in Kiev that in 1908 the Kiev OPE leaders considered opening a second branch in Podol.[57]

In spite of all difficulties and obstacles, the Kiev Jewish community ultimately won the struggle for Jewish education. By January 1, 1917, the state Jewish school of Solomon Brodsky (421 students), eleven private elementary Jewish schools (1,206 boys and 522 girls), twenty-nine heders (669 boys), two Jewish private gymnasiums, and several Jewish libraries were operating in Kiev.[58] Neither before nor after did the Kiev Jewish community have so many schools. This was "the golden age" of

---

53 Ibid.
54 Ibid.
55 Jeffrey Veidlinger, *Jewish Public Culture in the Late Russian Empire* (Bloomington and Indianapolis: Indiana University Press, 2009), 51.
56 Izraelitin, "Russko-evreiskie obshchedostupnye biblioteki," 134.
57 Sergeeva and Gorshikhina, "Deiatel'nost' Kievskogo otdeleniia," 127.
58 O. K. Kasimenko, ed., *Istoriia Kieva* I: 584–585.

Jewish education in Kiev. However, nobody could guarantee the Jewish schools, students, and teachers their safety in the event of pogroms and violence in the city. Also, many of their students would have probably preferred to study in the general schools if there had not been a percentage quota.

The achievements of the Kiev Jewish community look especially significant compared with the even more unfortunate situation of other national minorities in Kiev. None of them were allowed to open their national schools in the city. Just like the Jews, the Poles opened underground schools in Kiev, but they were closed by the Russian authorities in 1910-1911. The Kiev governor even issued a special circular on December 31, 1911 regarding the unacceptability of the existence of secret Polish schools.[59] The Ukrainians—the second most populous national group in Kiev after Russians—were not allowed to have any national schools. This situation of the education of national minorities in Kiev was quite typical for the entire Russian Empire.

The Russian authorities showed a somewhat more lenient attitude toward Jewish schools at the beginning of the twentieth century because they considered them a lesser evil than the education of Jewish children in Russian schools. They realized that Jews needed to somehow teach their children, and that the establishment of Jewish schools would divert Jewish students from the general schools. They therefore allowed Kiev and other Jewish communities to open Jewish private and state schools, which they had prohibited for more than forty years. The establishment of numerous Jewish schools in Kiev at the beginning of the twentieth century became possible not only due to the Jewish community's strong efforts, but also because of the Russian authorities' changed policy toward Jewish education.

KIEV JEWISH STUDENTS IN GENERAL SCHOOLS

Young Russian Jews at the turn of the twentieth century had a strong desire for higher education, preferably in universities, or at least in professional schools. Usually, this increased interest in higher education

---

59 TsDIAK U, f. 442, op. 861, d. 9, ll. 38-40; f. 442, op. 642, d. 70.

is explained by the assimilation or acculturation processes among Russian Jews. However, there are deeper roots for their quest. In late Imperial Russia, a university or professional school diploma was the primary means of deliverance for Jews from the Pale of Settlement. The laws of the Russian Empire allowed Jews to settle outside the Pale if they were graduates from universities or professional schools, or if they were students of gymnasiums or universities. Thus, the efforts of Jewish youth to receive a diploma were motivated not only by their wish to acquire knowledge, but also by a desire to receive the right to live outside the Pale of Settlement. However the *numerus clausus*, which was established in 1887 for Jewish students in Russian universities and gymnasiums, was a great obstacle.

The Russian government's attitude toward the education of Jewish students in Russian gymnasiums and universities completely reversed during the nineteenth century. From the early 1800s to the beginning of the 1880s, the Russian government followed a policy of merging the Jewish population with the "native" Russian people, and of the acculturation of Jews to Russian culture. Because of this policy, Russian officials encouraged Jews to receive education in Russian gymnasiums and universities. Often, Jewish students of these schools received state scholarships.

The first Jewish students were accepted to Kiev St. Vladimir University in the 1840s. In 1842, three Jewish students studied at the university; by 1848, their number increased to twenty-seven.[60] In those years, Jews were not allowed to live in Kiev or stay in the city more than a few days for business affairs; the government therefore made an exception for Jewish students. This shows the importance that the government gave to Russian state education of Jews as a tool for their assimilation.

In the late 1850s and the beginning of the 1860s, when some categories of Jews were allowed to settle in Kiev, the number of Jewish students continuously increased at the Kiev St. Vladimir University. However, the Kiev Jewish community was still small and could not

---

60 A. E. Ivanov, *Evreiskoe studenchestvo v Rossiiskoi imperii nachala XX veka* (Moscow: Novyi khronograph, 2007), 30.

provide financial aid to Jewish students, who were very poor and had great difficulties paying their tuition. The director of the Kiev Educational District in 1858–1861, Nikolai Ivanovich Pirogov, well known for his Judeophilia, attempted to help the Jewish students of Kiev St. Vladimir University. Pirogov maintained good connections with the Odessa Jewish community, as he had promoted the education of Jews there in 1856–1858 when he was the director of the Odessa Educational District. Pirogov wrote in 1861 to one of the leaders of Odessa Jewish community, Abram Markovich Brodsky, that

> Jewish students of Kiev St. Vladimir University live in great poverty, some of them may be excluded from the university, as they cannot pay their tuition and the Kievan Jews aren't wealthy enough to provide support to their coreligionists.[61]

Pirogov expressed his hope that the Odessa Jewish community would help the Jewish students of Kiev St. Vladimir University. However, the answer of Brodsky, who was an ardent supporter of the assimilation of Jews, perhaps surprised Pirogov. Brodsky wrote,

> According to the demands of our time, the well-to-do people should help the poor without distinction of their faith. Therefore it is preferable that the Jewish community makes the donation for poor students in general, not only for Jewish students. This can be a first step toward the elimination of exclusiveness, which was and is a barrier for Russian Jews merging with the Russian people.
> The majority of Jews…are able to wish and do good deeds for all their fellow citizens without distinction of their religion.[62]

Brodsky also expressed to Pirogov his readiness to provide means for two poor students of Kiev St. Vladimir University, one Christian

---

61 Aleksandr De-Ribas, *Staraia Odessa. Istoricheskie ocherki i vospominaniia* (Moscow: Kraft, 2005), 210.
62 Ibid.

and one Jewish, giving each of them two hundred rubles a year for five years.

Pirogov considered the Brodsky letter to be a *profession de foi*. On his initiative, the Brodsky letter was published in Kiev and Odessa newspapers, causing a public outpouring of support for students. Many donations for poor students arrived from different strata of the Odessa population, including Jews, Russians, and foreigners, with the note "without distinction of religion."[63] However, this euphoric mood of brotherhood in the early 1860s soon transformed into traditional Judeophobia and later into state anti-Semitism as new restrictions, including the *numerus clausus*, were imposed upon Jews in Russia.

The national distinctions between Kiev students did not disappear either in the 1860s or a decade later. *Kievlianin* published an article in 1876 that emphasized these distinctions:

> The Poles were slim and gracious, dandies with their cocked hats, thin, turned-up mustaches, and self-assured gait. The Jews, sharp-featured, moved quickly and stuck close together. They spoke quietly, but with animated gestures. Some, from wealthy homes of Odessa, wore massive golden chains. Their distinct Russian accent made you uncomfortable. The Little Russians [i.e., Ukrainians] were hefty, well-built, strongly featured people who spoke in loud, animated national speech. They laughed loudly, were a bit rude, even cynical. There were only a few Russians, and they kept to the background. Poles predominated, then Little Russians, then Jews.[64]

After the pogroms of 1881–1882, government policy toward Jews changed from assimilation to isolation and encouraging Jewish emigration. This was immediately reflected in the attitude of Russian educational institutions toward the acceptance of Jewish students. In 1883–1885, several universities in the Russian Empire set a quota limiting the number of Jewish students. On December 5, 1886 and June

---

63 Ibid.
64 Cited in Hamm, *Kiev: A Portrait*, 67, 246.

28, 1887, the Council of Ministers issued circulars, which standardized the percentage quota for the admission of Jews to universities and gymnasiums that were under the supervision of the Ministry of National Enlightenment. The circulars set a quota limiting enrollment of Jews in universities and gymnasiums to no more than 10 percent in the Pale of Settlement, 5 percent outside the Pale, and 3 percent in St. Petersburg and Moscow.[65] These circulars were given the force of law in 1908.[66]

Along with the establishment of the Jewish *numerus clausus*, in 1887 the Russian government issued circulars that were supposed to put in place an obstacle for "socially undesirable" elements and "to keep 'cook's sons' [as the lowest classes were called] out of gymnasiums."[67] The introduction of the percentage quota for Jewish students was motivated by the desire to keep the "right" proportions of Jewish and non-Jewish students. Proponents claimed that

> the flood of Jews was depriving non-Jews of educational opportunities; that Jewish students were exercising a negative moral influence on their Christian counterparts; that Jewish students were supporting the revolutionary movement; and that the disproportionate Jewish presence in higher education threatened to shift the balance of power among technical and professional elites into the hands of a non-Russian, non-Christian minority whose loyalty to the Tsarist state appeared at best doubtful.[68]

At the same time, Russian authorities were reluctant to allow the creation of Jewish national schools, especially beyond the Pale. Minister of National Enlightenment Aleksandr Nikolaich Shvarts wrote in 1908, "It is necessary consistently to decline all requests of non-Russian people for any isolation and nationalization of the schools. The united

---

65 Benjamin Pinkus, *The Jews of the Soviet Union: The History of a National Minority* (Cambridge: Cambridge University Press, 1988), 24.
66 *Evreiskaia entsiklopediia*, s.v. "Prosveshchenie," 13: 55.
67 Nicholas V. Riasanovsky, *A History of Russia*, 7th ed. (New York: Oxford University Press, 2000), 437.
68 Benjamin Nathans, *Beyond the Pale: The Jewish Encounter with Late Imperial Russia* (Berkeley and Los Angeles: University of California Press, 2002), 259–260.

Russian school on all its levels should be the leading basis for all non-Russian people of the empire without exception."[69] Thus, Jewish people were not allowed to open Jewish schools, and their right to send their children to Russian state schools was very limited due to the percentage quota. In this way, the Russian administration deprived the vast majority of Jews the right to any formal education. Kievan Jewish youth especially felt the negative impact of these policies.

The percentage quota was imposed by special circulars, not by laws, and had some exceptions and variations from place to place, and sometimes changed from year to year. During the 1904–1905 academic year, the percentage quota for Jews was increased from 10 to 15 percent in the Pale, from 5 to 7 percent outside the Pale, and from 3 to 5 percent in the capitals "as a special privilege due to the birth of the heir Cesarevitch."[70]

Kiev St. Vladimir University, which was outside the Pale, had a 10 percent maximum acceptance allowance for Jewish students.[71] However, the actual percentage was considerably higher than the prescribed quota. In the 1890–1891 academic year, 2,000 students studied at Kiev St. Vladimir University, including 361 Jews (18 percent). A note on the list of students states that in 1890, sixty-seven Jews were accepted to the university according to the percentage quota, and forty-three Jewish students above the quota following orders from the Minister of National Enlightenment and the director of the Kiev Educational District. Among the 361 Jewish students, 289 studied in the medical department, sixty-four in the department of law, and eight in the physics-mathematics department (two specialized in natural sciences, and six in mathematics). Jews did not study in the historical-philological department, because this specialization was not practical for them.[72] If a Jew planned to make a career as a university professor in Imperial Russia, he would need to convert to Christianity. Russian

---

69 Ibid., 76.
70 Ibid., 65.
71 Ivanov, *Evreiskoe studenchestvo v Rossiiskoi imperii*, 59; Nathans, *Beyond the Pale*, 296.
72 TsDIAK U, f. 442, op. 840, d. 211, l. 7.

schools did not hire Jewish teachers. Jews tried to acquire professions more practical for them, such as medical doctor or lawyer. University education was almost exclusively limited to men. In 1907, Kiev St. Vladimir University accepted its first female students (twenty of about 4,000), including six Jewish women.

The Kiev Women's Higher Courses were popular among Jewish female students, where they always constituted above 16 percent of all students. The Kiev courses were opened in 1878, and at first offered a two-year program that was expanded to four years in 1881. There were two departments: historical-philological and physics-mathematical, where 357 women studied in 1881 (compared with 1,270 male students at Kiev St. Vladimir University the same year). Jewish women also studied in 1881 at the Women's Higher Courses that opened in Moscow, St. Petersburg, and Kazan'.[73] The majority of women who graduated from these courses worked as teachers. Some of them continued their education abroad. The Kiev courses were closed in 1889, due to a decreased number of students. Society was not yet ready to accept emancipated women, and opponents of women's education scared away young girls from higher education with the image of the educated woman as a bluestocking who has lost her interest in family duties and motherhood. The decreased number of students was also driven by the fact that the Kiev courses were quite expensive and offered a difficult program, especially in the physics-mathematics department.[74] The Kiev courses were opened again in 1906, and operated until 1920 when they were reorganized by Soviet authorities into pedagogical courses for both genders.[75] The number of students enrolled in the courses increased to 4,021 in 1915, and 4,919 in 1917. There were four departments: historical-philological, physics-mathematical, law, and economic-commercial.[76]

---

73 Nathans, *Beyond the Pale*, 222–224; Kateryna Kobchenko, "*Zhinochyi Universitet Sviatoi Ol'gy.*" *Istoriia Kyivskykh vyshchykh zhinochykh kursiv* (Kyiv: Kyivs'kyi natsional'nyi universitet imeni Tarasa Shevchenka, 2007), 70.
74 Kobchenko, "*Zhinochyi Universitet Sviatoi Ol'gy,*" 63–66.
75 Ibid., 241–242.
76 Ibid., 135.

To avoid the percentage quota, wealthy Russian Jewish families sent their children abroad to study in universities. But the majority of young Jews who desired a university education had to find a way to receive their diploma in Russia. Even graduation from a gymnasium with a gold medal (the award received by students with excellent grades, similar to *summa cum laude*) did not guarantee acceptance to a university. If the number of Jewish students in the university had already reached the percentage quota, the school could not accept more no matter their educational excellence. There were even suicides of young Jewish men who despaired of breaking into the Russian state school system. Vladimir Ze'ev Jabotinsky wrote about this situation in 1912,

> every Jewish child [in Russia] grows up with the understanding that a diploma is the only path toward elementary human rights…They [government policies] compel tens of thousands to dream about this school, adapt their psyche to its demands, train themselves on its discipline even outside of the school—therefore it [school] is the only path for deliverance from the terrible torture of the depravation of their civil rights.[77]

Many young Jews pursued independent studies and took tests as "externs." However, most externs repeatedly failed their equivalency examinations for diplomas from the gymnasiums and universities. Without teachers and formal instruction, it was quite difficult to acquire the full range of knowledge required to pass the examinations of these educational institutions. The vast majority of externs were from poor Jewish families that could not afford to pay for the education of their children in private schools or by tutors. Many Jewish externs came to the large cities from shtetls. According to Jabotinsky's description of externs in his novel *Piatero* (*The Five*), they were terribly provincial, spoke Russian poorly, and the examinations for the sixth

---

[77] Vladimir Jabotinsky, *Fel'etony* (Berlin: S. D. Sal'tsman Verlag, 1922), 74.

and eighth grade gymnasiums were an insurmountable obstacle for many of them.[78]

To understand the plight of the poor externs, it is important to note that to graduate from the Russian gymnasium was a very hard task even for regular students. Less than one third of students who studied in the gymnasiums graduated. Largely this was due to the very complicated gymnasium program that devoted up to 40 percent of total class time to learning Latin and Greek. This so-called "classical education" was made mandatory by the Ministry of National Enlightenment for all supervised gymnasiums.[79]

For the brightest of the poorer Jewish youth, being an extern was the only possible way to receive a higher education. According to a survey of Jewish students at Kiev St. Vladimir University in 1910, 38 percent of them "reported having received their gymnasium diplomas as externs."[80] Jews constituted a large percentage of the externs, and the government continued to strive to prevent a significant number of Jews from receiving gymnasium diplomas by establishing a percentage quota for Jewish externs in 1909.[81]

Some professional and private schools were exempted from the *numerus clausus*, but many of these required a gymnasium diploma for enrollment. All state gymnasiums had a percentage quota for Jews, so not many of them could study there. But some young Jews found creative solutions for this problem. A scandal in 1906 revealed that over 600 Jewish students in Kiev dentistry schools (about 80 percent of their entire student body) had fake gymnasium diplomas, or had diplomas from private schools that did not have gymnasium credentials. Fifty-seven Jewish students had diplomas from gymnasiums that had never existed. The Ministry of the Interior investigated this case, and ordered the expulsion of all Kiev Jewish students with fake diplomas. Jewish dentistry students in their third to fifth semesters with diplomas from private schools that did not have gymnasium credentials were allowed to finish

---

78 Jabotinsky, *Piatero* (Moscow: Nezavisimaia gazeta Publishing House, 2002), 33.
79 Riasanovsky, *A History of Russia*, 437.
80 Nathans, *Beyond the Pale*, 275.
81 *Evreiskaia entsiklopediia*, s.v. "Prosveshchenie," 13: 56.

their studies, but they also had to pass the exam for the sixth grade state gymnasium within five years of their graduation from the dentistry school.

Most of the expelled Jewish students, according to the newspaper *Kievlianin*, disappeared from Kiev after the "dentistry scandal." They left because most of them had the right of residence in the city only as students of these schools. Also, after expulsion from the schools, most of the former students were eligible to be drafted into the Russian Army.[82] It is perhaps therefore understandable why these young Jews tried to enter the Kiev dentistry schools by illicit means. Not only were they motivated by a desire to obtain a good profession, but they also wanted to receive the right to live outside the Pale of Settlement and to avoid military service.

Commercial schools in Russia were under the supervision of the Ministry of Finance, and for a while did not have restrictions on the number of Jewish students. The absence of a percentage quota made them very popular among Jews. The Russian-Jewish writer Isaac Babel, and the prominent Jewish actor and director of GOSET (State Jewish Theater, established in Soviet times) Solomon Mikhoels, studied in the Kiev Commercial Institute. Often wealthy Jewish merchants were among the trustees of these commercial schools and gave them generous donations. According to Benjamin Nathans, "Jewish donors contributed over four-fifth of the 280,000 ruble start-up funds for Kiev's two commercial schools."[83] This allowed the Jewish trustees to control the administration and teachers' attitude toward Jews. Nathans says that the private and public educational institutions, which did not report to the Ministry of National Enlightenment, were heaven for Jews. However, the Russian government soon realized this, and began to pressure these institutions to establish a percentage quota for Jews by threatening to deprive the schools of their accreditation. By the end of the 1911–1912 academic year, Minister of National Enlightenment Lev Aristidovich Kasso "imposed a five percent quota on Kiev's two commercial schools," where nearly 60 percent of the students were Jewish.[84]

---

82 *Kievlianin*, 1906, № 282, 286, 300.
83 Nathans, *Beyond the Pale*, 299.
84 Ibid., 289–299.

Among Kiev gentiles, there were many who felt compassion for Jews and attempted to help them overcome the injustice of the authorities and the limitations that were imposed by Russian law. For example, the Russian writer Konstantin Paustovskii (1892–1968) wrote in his autobiographical novel *Dalekie gody* (*Distant Years*) that before final examinations in the First Kiev Gymnasium, reputedly the best gymnasium in the city, students of his class held a secret meeting:

> To this meeting were invited all students of my class, except the Jews. The Jews should know nothing about this meeting.
>
> We decided at the meeting that the best Russian and Polish students must intentionally receive in the examination *chetverku* [the equivalent of grade "B"] in at least one course so that they did not receive gold medals. [The gold medal gave the right to be accepted to the university without entrance examinations.] We decided to give all the gold medals to Jews. They were not accepted to the university without these medals.
>
> We swore to keep this decision a secret. To the honor of our class, we did not reveal this secret either then, or later, when we had already become students of the university. Now I am breaking this oath, because almost none of my gymnasium friends are alive anymore. The majority of them died in the many wars experienced by my generation. Only a few have survived.[85]

A similar situation happened during the studies in a Kiev gymnasium of the Pole Volodymyr Miiakovs'kyi (1888–1972), one of the founders of the Ukrainian Free Academy of Arts and Science in the United States. His aunt, Katerina Liatoshinskaia, recalled in a letter:

> Miiakovs'kyi was an excellent student in the final year of the gymnasium, but suddenly he, the first student in the class, began obviously to slow down his achievements. His parents

---

85 Konstantin Paustovskii, *Dalekie gody* (Moscow: Ast Astrel', 2005), 325.

found out that he intentionally did this so that he would not receive a gold medal. He wanted to help his friend and classmate, who was Jewish, to receive a gold medal, without which he would not be accepted to the university.[86]

Miiakovs'kyi was four years older than Paustovskii, so they could not have been in the same class. Thus the philo-Semitism of gentile students of Kiev gymnasiums appears to have been a tradition that was transferred from the older to the younger students. While the Russian government attempted to strictly enforce the percentage quota for Jews in gymnasiums and universities, many students and professors tried to make sure that Jews still had access to education in these institutions.

Because gymnasium and university education gave Jewish youth in Russia residence rights outside the Pale of Settlement, the government opposed any attempt to abolish or increase the percentage quota. In 1905, under the influence of the revolutionary changes in the country, universities received the rights of autonomy and self-government. Academic boards accepted students based on their grades, without a percentage quota, during the three years from 1905 to 1907. The result of this policy was a rapid increase in the number of Jewish students. In 1906, Jews constituted 28 percent of students at Kiev St. Vladimir University, and 40 percent at the mechanical department of the Kiev Polytechnic Institute. In 1907, 240 Christian and 159 Jewish students were accepted to the Kiev Polytechnic Institute. In general, Jewish students constituted 23 percent of all students at the institute. According to rules approved by the institute's academic board, students were accepted to the Kiev Polytechnic Institute on the basis of equal competition and without national or religious discrimination.[87]

This situation aroused dissatisfaction among Russian nationalists, who feared that this policy would lead to Jewish domination of the country's professional and intellectual life. They called for a restoration

---

86 Larysa Zales'ka-Onyshkevich, "Volodymyr Miiakovs'kyi," in *125 rokiv kyivs'koi ukrains'koi akademichnoi tradytsii 1861–1986: Zbirnyk*, ed. Marko Antonovych (New York: The Ukrainian Academy of Arts and Sciences in the US, Inc., 1993), 518.

87 TsDIAK U, f. 442, op. 857, d. 383.

of the percentage quota for Jews for the sake of Russian "national self-protection."[88] In 1907, after the suppression of the first Russian revolution, the government reestablished the percentage quota for Jews. In the same year, Prime Minister Petr Stolypin gave the order to the director of the Kiev Polytechnic Institute to expel one hundred Jewish students and replace them with Russians. The director of the institute proposed instead to accept more Christian students without expulsion of the Jews. But Stolypin continued to demand the expulsion of the Jewish students. The director of the institute, Vladimir Fedorovich Timofeev, three of four deans of the institution's departments, and several professors resigned in protest. Kiev, Podolia, and Volhynia Governor-General Sukhomlinov wrote a telegram to Prime Minister Stolypin, explaining that the resignation of the administration of the Kiev Polytechnic Institute was a public protest against the government's policy.[89]

The position of the Kiev Polytechnic Institute's administration and professors was not an anomaly. A significant part of the Russian academy was quite liberal, and had a very negative attitude toward the *numerus clausus*. According to Minister of National Enlightenment Petr Mikhailovich Kaufman (1906–1908), the councils of all institutions of higher education were "unanimous and persistent" in their desire "to open the doors of the higher school for all who received a secondary education, in spite of their nationality."[90] On September 2, 1905, the Academic Council of Moscow University sent a petition to Minister of National Enlightenment Vladimir Gavrilovich Glazov about the abolition of the percentage quota.

Minister of National Enlightenment Count Ivan Ivanovich Tolstoy,[91] during his brief time in this position (November 1905–April 1906), was, according to his own words,

---

88 *Kievlianin*, September 15, 1906, No 255.
89 TsDIAK U, f. 442, op. 857, d. 383.
90 Ivanov, *Evreiskoe studenchestvo v Rossiiskoi imperii*, 66.
91 Count Ivan Ivanovich Tolstoy (1958–1916), Russian numismatist, archeologist, vice president of the Academy of Arts, Minister of National Enlightenment, mayor of St. Petersburg/Petrograd in 1912–1916, supporter of equal rights of Jews in Russia, and the author of several works regarding the legal status of Jews in Russia.

an opponent of the existing system of Russification through the schools, and on the Jewish question—a supporter of complete equality for this persecuted nation in all rights with other citizens of Russia,…and an advocate of the immediate abolition of the percentage quota for enrollment to educational institutions.[92]

On January 20, 1906, by Tolstoy's initiative, the Council of Ministers discussed the abolition of the percentage quota for Jewish students. Ten out of thirteen ministers—including Tolstoy and the chairman of the Council of Ministers, Witte—voted to abolish the restriction; three voted to retain it. The Council of Ministers sent their resolution to the tsar for his consideration. They emphasized in their note to the tsar that Jews see in the *numerus clausus*, which was not established by law but by special circulars, "administrative arbitrariness." They said that the percentage quota often was a cause of student disturbances:

> The Jewish youth, embittered by such obvious inequality, joined and supported the revolutionary parties; and at the same time the institutions of higher education, as shown by later events, restricted from the influx of Jews, were not sealed off from revolutionary propaganda.[93]

In his resolution regarding the decision of the Council of Ministers, Nicholas II wrote, "The Jewish question should be thoroughly considered, when I find it necessary."[94] Unfortunately, Tsar Nicholas II never found it necessary. After the suppression of the first Russian revolution, Nicholas II fired the liberal ministers, including Witte and Tolstoy, who had supported the abolition of the percentage quota. They were replaced by more conservative ministers who enforced the policy of restrictions and persecution of the Jewish population. Thus, the percentage quota,

---

92 Ivanov, *Evreiskoe studenchestvo v Rossiiskoi imperii*, 68.
93 *Vospominaniia I. I. Tolstogo*, 146–147. Cited in Ivanov, *Evreiskoe studenchestvo v Rossiiskoi imperii*, 69.
94 Ivanov, *Evreiskoe studenchestvo v Rossiiskoi imperii*, 69.

which was spontaneously breached during the revolutionary years by many universities, was again reestablished. Furthermore, the quota was made law in 1908, and was extended to previously exempt institutions and schools that did not report to the Ministry of National Enlightenment, as well as to Jewish externs. Due to this policy, the number of Jewish students at the universities decreased by half from 4,266 (13 percent of all university students in Russia) in 1905 to 2,133 (6 percent) in 1914. The total number of Jewish students in Russian state higher education institutions was 4,440 in the 1913–1914 academic year, or 7.6 percent of the entire student population.[95]

The struggle over the percentage quota for Jewish students continued in the Russian Empire until the February 1917 Revolution and the abdication of the tsar. It was one of the most sensitive issues related to Jewish civil rights. The abolition of the percentage quota would result in the opening of some social prospects for young educated Jews. Conservative tsarist authorities always opposed the lifting of this restriction.

Nevertheless, most Kiev Jewish students remained nationally conscious and rejected assimilation and conversion as the way to solve their national problems. As shown by surveys of Jewish students in Kiev in 1909 and 1910 as well as in Moscow in 1913, Kiev Jewish students were less assimilated and more nationally aware than their Moscow counterparts, and a larger percentage of Kievan Jewish students knew Jewish languages.[96]

These surveys provide valuable information about the students' ages, financial situations, and political and cultural interests. The Kiev 1909 and Moscow 1913 surveys were conducted under the supervision of the Jewish demographer D. E. Sheinis. The Kiev 1910 survey was conducted at the initiative of the Jewish students of the Kiev Commercial Institute with financial support from the Kiev OPE.[97]

---

95   Ibid., 73.
96   D. E. Sheinis, *Evreiskoe studenchestvo v tsifrakh (Po dannym perepisi 1909 g. v Kievskom universitete i Politekhnicheskom institute)* (Kiev: Shenfel'd Publishing House, 1911), 3–59; *K kharakteristike evreiskogo studenchestva (Po dannym ankety sredi evreiskogo studenchestva g. Kieva v noiabre 1910 goda)* (Kiev: Shenfel'd Publishing House, 1913); *Evreiskoe studenchestvo v Moskve. Po dannym ankety 1913 g.* (Moscow: n.p., 1913).
97   Ivanov, *Evreiskoe studenchestvo v Rossiiskoi imperii*, 11.

The Kiev survey of 1909 compiled data on Jewish students of the Kiev St. Vladimir University and the Kiev Polytechnic Institute. The survey showed that the Kiev Jewish students were quite young: more that 65 percent were between seventeen and twenty-four years old, and only 2.2 percent were over thirty years old. In spite of their young age, 20 percent of the Jewish students were already married. Only 32 percent of Kiev Jewish students claimed that they were completely healthy, 35 percent claimed weak health, and 33 percent unsatisfactory health. The most common illnesses among them were myopia, neurasthenia (a popular diagnosis at the time, characterized by hysteria, fatigue, anxiety, headache, and depression), and headaches. 36 percent of Jewish students were dependent on their relatives, the same number lived by their own means, and the rest on the combination of these two kinds of financial resources. The most popular job among Jewish students was tutoring. 78 percent of Kiev Jewish students stated that they could speak Yiddish and 57 percent claimed that they could read Hebrew. About 60 percent of Jewish students said that they sympathized with Jewish national development, 20 percent sympathized with the assimilation of Jews, and 20 percent were indifferent to both. Among the 455 Jewish students who answered the question about their political sympathy, 176 said that they did not sympathize with any political movements, 115 sympathized with social-democrats, 44 with the Bund, 66 with Zionists, and the rest with other political parties.[98]

The Moscow survey of Jewish students, taken in 1913, showed a higher level of assimilation among local Jews. 30 percent of Moscow Jewish students did not know Yiddish. Only 16 percent of Moscow Jewish students read the Jewish press. 60 percent of Moscow Jewish students had a negative attitude toward assimilation, whereas 22 percent had a positive attitude. Moscow Jewish students showed less interest in involvement in various political organizations than Jewish students in Kiev. Only 16 percent of Moscow Jewish students reported that they sympathized with Zionists, 7 percent sympathized with the Bund, and

---

98 Sheinis, *Evreiskoe studenchestvo v tsifrakh*, 3–59.

an even lower percentage of students said that they sympathized with other political movements.[99]

These surveys show the regional and temporal influences of the Russian political situation on Jewish students. The first survey in Kiev was taken just a few years after the first Russian revolution, when political passions were still fresh, as were the memories of the huge wave of anti-Jewish pogroms in 1905-1906. Many Kiev students personally participated more or less in the revolutionary events and were victims or witnesses of the anti-Jewish riots. The second survey in Moscow was taken in the last peaceful year before World War I. The Moscow Jewish students were children during the first Russian revolution, and Moscow Jews had not experienced bloody pogroms. Consequently, they were much less interested and less involved in political life and movements. The survey shows the absurdity of the Russian nationalist press' accusations of Jewish students having innate inclinations toward revolutionary activity.

Russian authorities were responsible for the policy of state anti-Semitism, which included many restrictions and limitations on Jews. The hope of many young Jews to obtain the right to live outside the Pale of Settlement forced them into Russian gymnasiums and universities, and this stimulated their wish to break the *numerus clausus*. This situation created a deep desire among Russian Jews for a university education. However, not only Jewish students but also Russian students, intellectuals, and educators protested the percentage quota, which they considered a relic, unfair and harmful for the country's future.

The question of the percentage quota for Jews created divisions within the Russian government. During the first Russian revolution, when several liberals were appointed to high governmental positions, the majority of them supported the abolition of this restriction, which they viewed first of all as harmful to state interests. The *numerus clausus* radicalized Jewish youth, continuously creating new enemies of the tsarist regime. However, Tsar Nicholas II, in opposition to public opinion and

---

99 Artur Klempert, "Palestinofil'stvo i sionizm v dorevolutsionnoi Moskve," in *Rossiiskii sionizm: istoria i kul'tura. Materialy nauchnoi konferentsii* (Moscow: Sefer, 2002), 146.

the majority view of his government, repeatedly refused until the collapse of the monarchy to abolish this most odious restriction.

CONCLUSION

The Russian authorities did not allow any Jewish schools, synagogues, or other Jewish institutions in Kiev for a long time because they wanted to keep the Jewish community as small as possible in this holy Christian Orthodox city. However the Jewish population grew rapidly in the city. The authorities' plan to keep the Kiev Jewish community small by prohibiting all Jewish institutions therefore failed. But the situation of Kievan Jews was unique. It was perhaps the only large Jewish community in the Russian Empire that was deprived of the right for Jewish education. This contradicted Russian law, which allowed Jews to have Jewish schools within and beyond the Pale.

The ban on Jewish schools in Kiev, which the authorities maintained for forty years, created a peculiar situation in which Jewish education went underground. There were illegal Talmud-Torahs, heders, and melameds throughout the city. Deprived of official Jewish schools, the Jewish elite sent their children to Russian schools. However, just as the Russification desired by the tsarist authorities succeeded among wealthy Jewish circles, the Russian government completely reversed their policy. The percentage quota raised a high barrier against the influx of Jews into secondary schools and universities. Hence, in the late nineteenth century, Kievan Jews were deprived of the right for either Jewish or general education.

The authorities eventually recognized the abnormality of this situation, and the Kiev Jewish community finally received permission to open Jewish schools, synagogues, and other institutions at the turn of the twentieth century. Perhaps the authorities, who recognized the need to provide Jews at least some access to education, decided that it was better to allow Jewish schools than to have an influx of Jews into Russian schools.

The editor of the pro-government newspaper *Novoe vremia*, Aleksei Suvorin, published in 1880 an article entitled "The Yid Is Coming," warning that Russian education opens a way for Jewish superiority in

Russian intellectual life.[100] The Kievan state-sponsored newspaper *Kievlianin* stated that Russian education made Jews only superficially Russian and cleared the path for the domination of aliens over the Russian intelligentsia.[101] *Kievlianin* wrote on November 5, 1880, "We must take care that in the future there is always a compact majority of the native race in the educated ranks of Russian society, and not aliens, be they the Jerusalem nobility, Baltic barons or Georgian princes."[102]

Even though various kinds of Jewish schools opened in Kiev in the early twentieth century, many Jewish youth desired either university or Russian vocational school diplomas, since these diplomas gave Jews the right to live outside the Pale of Settlement. Jews in Kiev, as well as throughout the Tsarist Empire, used all possible means to circumvent the obstacles that the authorities placed in the path of their education, and to break through the percentage quota for admission to Russian schools and universities. Heated debates about the percentage quota divided Russian society. Conservatives supported the percentage quota for Jewish students, justifying it as a necessary protection for the Russian people from Jewish domination and competition. Liberals struggled together with Jews for the abolition of the percentage quota, considering this restriction harmful not only for Jews, but for the entire Russian society.

---

100 Klier, *Imperial Russia's Jewish Question 1855–1881*, 403–404.
101 Ibid., 405.
102 Ibid.

CHAPTER EIGHT

Jewish Culture in Kiev

> And for a long time still I am destined by a wondrous power to walk hand in hand with my strange heroes, to view the whole of hugely rushing life, to view it through laughter visible to the world and tears invisible and unknown to it!
> —Nikolai Gogol, *Dead Souls*[1]

NATIONAL IDENTITY AND THE CULTURE OF KIEV JEWS

Mikhail Bulgakov ended his feuilleton "Kiev, the City" with the section "Scholarship, Literature and Arts." All cultural life of the city is neatly characterized by one word, "No."[2] The author clarifies his "nyet" (no) by stating he could find no words to describe the ugly bust of Karl Marx in the central square of the newly-soviet Kiev (the essay was written in 1923). Bulgakov did not write anything else about

---

1. Translated by Richard Pevear and Larissa Volokhonsky (New York: Everyman's Library, 2004). Cited in Amelia Glaser, "Sholem Aleichem, Gogol Show Two Views of Shtetl Jews," *Jewish Journal*, March 10, 2009 http://www.jewishjournal.com/arts/article/sholem_aleichem_gogol_show_two_views_of_shtetl_jews_20090311/.
2. M. A. Bulgakov, *Povesti, rasskazy, fel'etony* (Moscow: Sovetskii Pisatel', 1988), 85.

cultural or scholarly life in his native city. When Bulgakov wrote his feuilleton, he was living in Moscow. He seems to have already acquired the haughty attitude toward cultural life in the provinces typical of the educated elite living in the Russian capitals (Moscow and St. Petersburg/Petrograd).

The Russian Jewish press shared this contemptuous attitude toward provincial cultural life. The weekly *Evreiskii mir* (Jewish World) divided all news into that from the Russian capitals, St. Petersburg and Moscow, and that from the provinces. Not only Kiev, but even Odessa—with Mendele Moicher Sforim (Sholem Abramovich) and Hayim Nachman Bialik among other prominent writers—were included under the humble category *provintsiia*, i.e., the provinces.[3]

While the Russian Jewish periodical considered Jewish cultural life in Kiev as merely provincial, Russian nationalists utterly denied the existence of any other meaningful culture in Kiev except the Russian. The Russian philosopher Petr Struve wrote that it was impossible to participate in cultural life in Kiev without knowledge of the Russian language. He stated that Russian culture dominated in Kiev, Mogilev, Tiflis (Tbilisi), and Tashkent, "because this culture is an inherent, powerful fact in all parts of the empire, except the Kingdoms of Poland and Finland."[4] However, Struve did not mention that this "fact" had not appeared spontaneously, but was due to forced Russification and the suppression of national minorities.

"Kiev was, is, and shall be Russian!" was the slogan of the state-sponsored newspaper *Kievlianin*, which had been published in the city since 1864.[5] All state schools and universities in Kiev taught in Russian. The wealthy Kiev Jewish elite, educated in Russian gymnasiums and universities, became strong supporters of assimilation to Russian or European culture and considered Jewish and Ukrainian culture to be inferior. Zvi Gitelman wrote, "Jews apparently felt no

---

3   *Evreiskii mir*, February 24, 1911, 8: 15.
4   P. V. Struve, cited in Vladimir Jabotinsky, *Izbrannoe* (Jerusalem and St. Petersburg: Biblioteka-Aliia, 1992), 140–141.
5   John Doyle Klier, *Imperial Russia's Jewish Question 1855–1881* (Cambridge and New York: Cambridge University Press, 1995), 182.

strong affinity for Ukrainians...Consciously or unconsciously adopting the view of imperial Russian officialdom, Jews and others thought of Ukraine as 'Little Russia.'"[6]

Certainly there were some exceptions: a few populist Jewish authors supported Ukrainian literature. Zionist leader Vladimir Ze'ev Jabotinsky (1880–1940), for example, wrote in 1911 in an article "Urok iubileia Shevchenko" (The Lesson of Shevchenko's Jubilee) about the Ukrainian roots of Taras Shevchenko's creativity and the great potential of the Ukrainian national movement and culture.[7] The Yiddish poet David Hofshtein recalled that in the years of political reaction in the Russian Empire, when the authorities had not allowed celebrations in honor of Shevchenko, Sholom Aleichem went to the city Kanev to put flowers on Shevchenko's grave.[8] Some Jewish nationalists also supported the Ukrainian national movement. However, there were significantly more Jewish intellectuals who contributed to Russian and Jewish cultures than to Ukrainian.

The Jewish elite in Kiev, which adopted the lifestyle of the Russian nobility and wealthy merchants, rarely interacted with their poor coreligionists who lived in the Podol and Plosskii districts. Irene Nemirovsky, whose father was "an important Russian [Jewish] banker," belonged to one such assimilated Jewish family. She was born in Kiev in 1903 and lived there until the age of ten, when her parents moved to St. Petersburg. Nemirovsky recalled Kiev in her memoirs:

> The Ukrainian city...was, in the eyes of the Jews living there, formed of three distinct regions, as one sees in old pictures: the damned down below caught between the shades and flames

---

6   Zvi Gitelman, "Native Land, Promised Land, Golden Land: Jewish Emigration from Russia and Ukraine," in *Cultures and Nations of Central and Eastern Europe: Essays in Honor of Roman Szporluk*, ed. Zvi Gitelman, Lubomyr Hajda, John-Paul Himka, and Roman Szporluk (Cambridge, MA: Ukrainian Research Institute of Harvard University, 2000), 146–147.
7   Volodymyr Jabotinsky, *Vybranni statti z natsional'nogo putannia* (Kyiv: Respublikans'ka asotsiatsiia ukrainoznavstva, 1991), 71–79.
8   Marietta Shaginian, *Taras Shevchenko* (Moscow: Khudozhestvennaia literatura, 1964), 26.

of Hades; mortals in the center, illuminated by a pale and tranquil light; and up above, the realm of the chosen.⁹

Irene and her parents certainly belonged among the "chosen" who lived in the best district of the city, Pechersk. The author of Nemirovsky's biography, Jonathan Weiss, wrote:

> From her perch high in the city, Irene observed Jews of the *Podol*, the neighborhood on the banks of the river Dnieper, with its narrow streets, small shops, and modest homes. She found this community of small shopkeepers strange and, in all, repugnant. "A group of people with children who rolled in the mud, who spoke only Yiddish, who wore tattered shirts and enormous caps on narrow necks with long black forelocks," she wrote...Irene—like most of the assimilated Jews in Kiev—wanted to set herself apart from other Jews by adopting wholeheartedly the culture and even the prejudices of the country in which she was born. Social accessibility and religious observance could not coexist.¹⁰

The Kiev Jewish elite bitterly resented the definition of Kiev cultural life as provincial. They felt far superior to Jews from the shtetls and other cities of the Pale and, of course, to their poor coreligionists in Kiev. Because the authorities allowed them to live in all districts of the city, wealthy Kiev Jews felt especially privileged compared to other Jews. The Kiev Jewish elite were certain that they were living an authentic European lifestyle. They enjoyed theaters and concerts, gambling in casinos, and traveled to the best European resorts. Wealthy Jewish families spent the cold seasons in Nice, Monte Carlo, and Biarritz, with these "cold seasons" sometimes lasting most of a year.¹¹

---

9 Jonathan Weiss, *Irene Nemirovsky: Her Life and Works* (Stanford: Stanford University Press, 2007), 9.
10 Ibid., 10.
11 Oliver Philipponnat and Patrick Lienhardt, *The Life of Irene Nemirovsky* (New York and Toronto: Alfred A. Knopf, 2010), 14-15; Kovalinskii, *Metsenaty Kieva*, 236.

Probably they would not have returned to the Russian Empire at all if it was not for their businesses. Ukraine and Kiev were their Eldorado, the source of their wealth, which they could not earn elsewhere.[12]

Irene Nemirovsky, who originally had two names—"Irma for the synagogue, and Irina, after the Tsar's niece"[13]—told the story of her family. Her mother, Anna Margoulis, was from a family of the Kiev Jewish elite and was "brought up by her parents with a veneration for French culture."[14] Her father, Leonid Nemirovsky, was from Odessa. "And yet, despite his undeniable material success, Leonid would always be a pariah among the Kiev bourgeoisie" because he was a newcomer to the city. Leonid was merely tolerated by his wife's parents and even by his wife herself.[15] The Kiev Jewish elite were confident in their superiority and held their shtetl coreligionists in utter contempt. They believed that there was very little in common between them. Kievan Jews considered themselves doubly chosen by their religion and by the authorities who allowed them to live in this wonderful city.

However, even with the Russification of the Kiev Jewish elite and the suppression of Jewish culture by the authorities, Jewish cultural life remained active in Kiev at the turn of the twentieth century. Certainly, it was not as rich as in St. Petersburg, Moscow, or Odessa, but interesting writers, poets, musicians, and thinkers lived in or visited the city. And, as previously mentioned, due to its exception from the rules that restricted the Pale, Kiev had a high concentration of Jewish intelligentsia; a university diploma gave the right of residence in the city.

SHOLOM ALEICHEM

Among the Jewish authors who lived in Kiev, the most prominent was Sholom Aleichem (pseudonym of Sholom Yakov Rabinovitz, 1859–1916). Sholom Aleichem knew Kiev quite well: he first visited the city illegally in 1879 and returned to the city in 1887 and lived there, with interruptions, for almost twenty years. Sholom Aleichem received the right to

---

12 Philipponnat and Lienhardt, *The Life of Irene Nemirovsky*, 29.
13 Ibid., 12.
14 Ibid., 28.
15 Ibid.

live in Kiev not as a renowned Jewish writer, but as a merchant. Later, when he lost his fortune, he obtained the right of residence in the city for his children to go to school. Jewish children who studied in Kiev gymnasiums and universities were "a real treasure" to their parents, since they were allowed to live in the city for the duration of their education.[16]

In his younger years, Sholom Aleichem attempted to combine his literary work with speculation on the Kiev stock market, but his investments were unsuccessful. He had to leave Kiev in 1890 for three years in order to hide from his creditors. During those years, Sholom Aleichem stayed in Odessa and Czernowitz (now Chernovtsy), and traveled to Paris and Vienna. In 1893, he returned to Kiev after his mother-in-law used the inheritance left by her late husband to settle his debts.[17] Sholom Aleichem lived in Kiev for the next twelve years, finally leaving the city for good after the October 1905 pogrom.

Literary critics often compare Sholom Aleichem to the Russian author Nikolai Vasilievich Gogol (1809–1852). Both were born in provincial towns in Ukraine and moved to large cities where they became well-known writers. The influence of Gogol on the writing of Sholom Aleichem has long been recognized by Russian and Western scholars.[18] Both writers employed the motif of laughing through tears. However, the reasons for laughing and for crying were quite different in Russian and Jewish societies. Gogol's humor is acrid and sarcastic, and he does not show much mercy toward his naïve, rude, greedy, and fawning characters. His laughter has the taste of bitterness as he writes about Russian society's imperfections. Sholom Aleichem's humor is gentler; the author clearly has more compassion for his characters. Jewish tears were mostly provoked by the hostile gentile environment, anti-Semitism, and government persecution. The Jewish tears were also more visible to the world because Jews were not ashamed of showing them. They were a reproach to the gentile world for its hostility and

---

16 Sholom Aleichem, *Krovavaia shutka* (Leningrad: Lira, 1990), 262–263.
17 Leonid Shkol'nik, "Sholom Aleichem: 'Serdtse vlozhil ia v knigi svoi...,'" *Evreiskii zhurnal*, March 2, 2009, http://www.jjew.ru/index.php?cnt=6194.
18 Ibid.; Ruth Wisse, *The Modern Jewish Canon* (Chicago: University of Chicago Press, 2003); David Roskies, *A Bridge of Longing: The Lost Art of Yiddish Storytelling* (Cambridge, MA: Harvard University Press, 1995).

mistreatment. This approach of laughing through tears appeared in the early works of Sholom Aleichem, but is even more obvious in his descriptions of the life of Jews in Kiev.

In spite of the hostility of the local authorities and the cruelty of the police, Kievan Jews loved their city and Sholom Aleichem was no exception. He wrote to his niece, the wife of a Kiev lawyer, after his travel to Europe:

> How pitiful now Kiev looks after shining Paris and clean Berlin! And nevertheless, if I have to choose one of these three cities, I'll choose only Kiev, even though it does not smell so sweet and is not so comfortable.[19]

Sholom Aleichem's Kievan years were his most productive. There he wrote the most famous of his novels *Tevye der Milkhiger* (Tevye the Milkman) and *Menakhem-Mendl*. Kiev is depicted as Yehupets in several of his novels. Tevye the dairyman delivers his goods to the Yehupets market and the unlucky Menakhem-Mendl, like Sholom Aleichem in his younger years, unsuccessfully attempts to make a fortune on the Yehupets stock market. Sholom Aleichem continued to describe the life of Kievan Jews in his works after he left the city forever in 1905. He depicted Kiev in his autobiographical novel *Funem Yarid* (*From the Fair*) and in the novel *The Bloody Hoax*, written in 1912–1913 under the impressions of the Beilis trial. Literary critic and essayist Maurice Friedberg wrote that Sholom Aleichem's novels are "a wondrously realistic social history."[20] Friedberg said that part of the novel *The Bloody Hoax* is "quite literally, a chronicle of a current event."[21] Sholom Aleichem wrote about this work that "it is a completely new novel about Jewish life in Kiev. It is completely humorous and sensational. The novel embraces political events which shook Jewry like an earthquake."[22] The plot of the novel concerns two

---

19 Mikhail Kalnitsky, "Vmesto Berlina i Parizha ia vybral by Kiev," *Gazeta po Kievski*, March 2, 2009.
20 Sholom Aleichem, *The Bloody Hoax* (Bloomington and Indianapolis: Indiana University Press, 1991), IX.
21 Ibid., XI.
22 Sholom Aleichem, *Krovavaia shutka*, 261.

young men—a Russian noblemen, Grigorii Popov, and a Jew, Hersh Rabinovitch—who temporarily, for one year, swap their identities. While Rabinovitch enjoys the privileged life of a wealthy Russian nobleman, Popov becomes all too well acquainted with the myriad hardships of Jewish life in Russia; he is denied entrance to the university and then is accused of the ritual murder of a Christian boy. The story has a relatively happy ending: Grigorii Popov's father goes to the court where his son is being tried and states that "Hersh Rabinovitch" is really his son, a Russian nobleman. The absurd accusation of ritual murder collapses, and Popov and Rabinovitch receive a minor punishment "for the hoax of assuming a false identity."[23] Sholom Aleichem finished writing his novel before the end of the Beilis trial; the novel was completed on January 7, 1913, while the trial continued until October. The novel, which suggests the utter absurdity of the accusation against Beilis, was very popular among Jewish readers. It was serialized in the Warsaw Yiddish newspaper *Haynt* (Today) in 1912–1913. The publication of chapter forty-eight of the novel caused the confiscation of the newspaper. The authorities did not like the chapter's objective discussion of blood libels against Jews before the start of Beilis' trial.[24]

Despite the prosecution's efforts to prove Beilis guilty of ritual murder, the accusation collapsed due to its absurdity, as did the blood libel charge in Sholom Aleichem's novel. Beilis was acquitted and released on October 29 (November 10), 1913. In December, Sholom Aleichem wrote to Beilis from his self-imposed exile in Berlin:

Dear Friend Menachem Mendel' Beilis,

I did not write you thus far because there was too much excitement around you. That you cost me my health along with that of other Jews it is even not necessary to explain; you should understand well that I rejoice along with you…

Please accept my congratulations. Let's pray to God that you are the last and that the world does not hear anymore libels against Jews…

---
23 Ibid., 373.
24 Ibid., 264–266.

I asked my publisher in Warsaw to send you all of my books of stories, all sixteen volumes, written in Yiddish, as a present. I will be glad if you, when you rest, glance at them, forget your former misfortunes, and perhaps laugh sometimes or more likely drop a tear...

And also, I would not be a Jew if I did not give you some advice, what should you do regarding America, etc. But you probably have enough advice without mine. You should make up your own mind...I do not know if you know anything about me, I am your compatriot, I lived for twenty years in a row in Kiev and my name is Sholom Aleichem.[25]

Beilis was delighted to receive this letter and replied:

If you have doubts whether I know you, I would like to tell you that not only my eldest children but even my six-year-old daughter knows you and often cries out "Let's read Sholom Aleichem!"...

As you can see, your hope has come true even before I have totally recovered. Among all the works of the different authors which I received, and among all the other gifts, I give special place to your world-famous works, and I consider myself a completely happy man now that I have been given such a present.[26]

The real-life bloody hoax was still on the mind of the writer several months later. Sholom Aleichem wrote from Nervi, Italy to his relatives on February 21, 1914,

My Dear,
A professor of Kiev University lives in the room next to me and I am full of fear, because he is here with an eight- or nine-year-old boy. What if he kills the boy, inflicts thirteen wounds, and

---
25 Ibid., 268–269.
26 Ibid.

claims that I performed this "ritual"? I pray to God every day to keep the boy healthy. There is hope that they will go to Rapallo. When I heard about this I deliberately began to praise this Rapallo at the table in Russian to Dr. Zak to the utmost extent.[27]

From our current point of view, this letter may look like a joke. What could Sholom Aleichem fear while he was in Italy for treatment? This was not Russia, where the officials, as well as a good part of the gentile population, believed that Jews committed ritual murders. However, perhaps Sholom Aleichem's letter was not entirely in jest. The atmosphere in Russian society, especially among Jews, was quite unsettled during and immediately after the Beilis trial. Vladimir Jabotinsky wrote that in the atmosphere of persecution in which the Jews lived, he would not be surprised if one of them went insane and admitted that he committed a ritual murder, or even really committed it.[28]

The Beilis trial also deeply disturbed the Russian intelligentsia. Many Russian intellectuals saw the medieval accusation of ritual murders against Jews as a great shame and disgrace for Russia. They believed that in the twentieth century and in a civilized country, Jews should not be accused of such a preposterous crime. Maxim Gor'kii wrote in a letter to the well-known Russian socialist Georgii Valentinovich Plekhanov, "The Beilis trial so agitated my nerves that I never have been in such a condition before. When I read the report of [the newspaper] *Kievskaia Mysl'* I was almost weeping from shame and wrath."[29] During the Beilis trial, Gor'kii stayed on Capri where he wrote to E. P. Ladyzhnikov that he was so upset about the trial that he had started to take valerian (an herbal tranquilizer).[30] In this hysterical atmosphere, many Russian Jews shared Sholom Aleichem's apparent fear of new blood libels being made.

But in spite of the persecution of Jews in Kiev, Sholom Aleichem dreamed of returning to the city and would probably have done so if not for his illness. He was sick with tuberculosis, and on his doctors' recommendation he stayed for a while in Italy. He was very upset that,

---

27 Ibid.
28 Vladimir Jabotinsky, *Fel'etony* (Berlin: S. D. Zal'tsman Publishing House, 1922), 15.
29 Sholom Aleichem, *Krovavaia shutka*, 256.
30 Ibid.

due to his illness, he could not attend the 1908 celebration of the twenty-fifth anniversary of his literary work in Kiev. This anniversary was celebrated in many Jewish communities throughout Imperial Russia, but Sholom Aleichem found a special meaning in the celebration in Kiev. He wrote to his friend Naum Solomonovich Syrkin[31] that the congratulations that he received from Kiev

> moved me to tears. This is from Kiev. Kiev is my city. It is impossible to go everywhere for the celebration of the anniversary, but that I cannot go to Kiev makes me depressed.[32]

Sholom Aleichem's love for Kiev was not reciprocated, at least not on the part of the local authorities who kept the writer under police surveillance. The author had come to the attention of the police in 1903 for his correspondence with the publishers Vladimir Chertkov and Pavel Alexandrovich Bulanzhe regarding the publication of *Skazki dlia vzroslykh* (Fairytales for Adults) by Leo Tolstoy in an anthology, the revenue of which was intended to aid victims of the 1903 Gomel pogrom. Leo Tolstoy had been excommunicated from the Christian Orthodox church in 1901 and was considered a dangerous "heretic," so he and his followers' correspondence were intercepted and read by the police. Thus, Sholom Aleichem also came under the Russian authorities' suspicion. The director of the police department of the Ministry of the Interior informed the director of the Kiev police department about Sholom Aleichem's correspondence with "P. A. Bulanzhe, a follower of the false prophet Count L. N. Tolstoy," and ordered him "to check who is the author [of the correspondence], his activities and contacts."[33]

However, the local authorities were not only suspicious of Sholom Aleichem's contacts; the censor often banned his writings, such as the novel about revolutionaries *Der Mabul* (The Deluge), and the satiric pamphlet *Peace and Consent: The Story about How Uncle Pinia and Aunt*

---

31 Naum Solomonovich (Nachman) Syrkin (1868–1924), a leader of Socialist Zionism and a writer.
32 Sholom Aleichem, *Sobranie sochinenii* (Moscow: Khudozhestvennaia literatura, 1988), I: 19.
33 TsDIAK U, f. 275, op. 1, d. 231, ll. 1, 3.

*Reizl Live, Quarrel and Reconcile.*³⁴ They even considered images of Sholom Aleichem to be dangerous. On February 6, 1914, the Podolia governor ordered that portraits of Sholom Aleichem and other Jewish writers, poets, and politicians be confiscated from all stores in the cities of Litin and Letichev. This initiative surprised the Kiev, Podolia, and Volhynia governor-general, who rescinded the order.³⁵ However, the Podolia governor continued to insist that confiscation of the portraits of Jewish political and cultural figures was the correct decision because "such images shown in public places inflame one part of the population against the other."³⁶

The local administration prohibited any kind of official celebration of the twenty-fifth anniversary of Sholom Aleichem's literary work, especially if the events were planned in Yiddish. However, Jews found ways around the ban. In the city Kovel' of Volhynia province, when the authorities forbade an official celebration of Sholom Aleichem's anniversary, local Jews held a "family celebration," to which, according to a police report, forty Jews showed up by special invitation. They were "primarily local Jews, belonging to the higher circle of society, as, for example, State Rabbi Brik and merchants. They read the works of Sholom Aleichem and played music."³⁷

In Kiev, representatives of the Jewish community—the renowned jeweler Iosif Abramovich Marshak and the medical doctor Evgenii L'vovich Sklovskii—used a cunning method to get around the prohibition. They petitioned the Kiev governor to allow them to conduct literary readings, the revenue of which would be sent for the treatment of Sholom Aleichem, who, by the advice of doctors, had gone to Italy and was in great financial need. The authorities allowed the readings on the condition that they would be only in Russian.³⁸

---

34 Ibid., f. 442, op. 862, d. 324, l. 95. Circular of the Main Censorship Department from August 21, 1912; f. 295, op. 1, d. 3, l. 12. Circular of the Main Censorship Department from August 23, 1905.
35 Ibid., f. 442, op. 864, d. 66, l. 1.
36 Ibid., ll. 2, 4.
37 Ibid., f. 1598, op. 1, d. 127, ll. 221–226.
38 Ibid., f. 442, op. 858, d. 2, part 2, l. 93.

These ridiculous restrictions and the success of Jews in circumventing them are of course reminiscent of Sholom Aleichem's own stories. The life of Jews in the Russian Empire continuously gave the author plenty of original plots, for laughter through tears. Sometimes, it is even difficult to say where reality ends and the author's imagination begins. Sholom Aleichem's real-life experiences often overlapped with the imagined stories of his characters.

Sholom Aleichem spent his last two years in America. He loved Kiev, and as his health declined he asked to be buried in the Kiev cemetery where his father's grave was located. However, Sholom Aleichem died on May 13, 1916 in New York City, and due to World War I it was impossible to fulfill his request.[39] He was buried in Queens, New York.

The adventures of Sholom Aleichem in Kiev, however, did not end with his death. Like the characters from his novel *The Wandering Stars*, his monument meandered around his beloved city. The statue of Sholom Aleichem was erected originally in downtown Kiev near the Bessarabskii Market in 1997. But a few years later, due to re-planning of the city streets, it was moved to Rognedinskaia Street. Then, in 2005, the monument suddenly disappeared. Rumors spread that it had been stolen by anti-Semites. However, the reality was more mundane; without any notice the local authorities had removed the memorial for restoration in preparation for the 2005 Eurovision Song Contest.[40]

In honor of the 150th anniversary of the birth of the author, on March 2, 2009, a Sholom Aleichem museum was opened in Kiev on Bol'shaia Vasilkovskaia Street. However, just one month before the opening of the museum, on February 3, 2009, an apartment building where Sholom Aleichem lived on the same street was torn down in spite of numerous protests. It seems that the adventures of Sholom Aleichem in Kiev continue even without the author.[41]

---

39 Sholom Aleichem, *Sobranie sochinenii*, I: 19.
40 "Pamiatnik Sholom Aleikhemu ne ukrali, a zabrali na rekonstruktsiiu," *Podrobnosti*, May 2, 2005, http://podrobnosti.ua/society/2005/05/02/209129.html.
41 "V Kieve otkryli muzei Sholom Aleikhema," *Korrespondent*, March 2, 2009, http://korrespondent.net/showbiz/759809; "V tsentre Kieva razrushili dom v kotorom zhil Sholom Alejhem," *Korrespondent*, February 4, 2009, http://korrespondent.net/video/ukraine/732131.

OTHER KIEV JEWISH WRITERS AND INTELLECTUALS

The global fame of Sholom Aleichem overshadowed other Jewish writers and intellectuals from Kiev who were not nearly as well known, but whose contributions to Jewish culture were nevertheless quite significant. Some of the older Jewish intellectuals of Kiev, whom Sholom Aleichem called *khakhme Kiev* (Sages of Kiev), were Jewish maskilim, "the product of the Jewish Enlightenment, Haskalah."[42] Among them were the Hebrew poet Isaak Kaminer (1834–1901) and the Yiddish poet and composer Mark Varshavskii (1848–1907). Both had graduated from Russian universities. Kaminer was a physician and Varshavskii a lawyer, professions that gave them an income, but they devoted their free time to literature. Kaminer's early poetry was influenced by both the Haskalah and socialism. After the pogroms of 1881–1882, Kaminer became a Palestinophile, a "follower of *Ḥibat Tsiyon* and subsequently was one of the most ardent admirers of Theodor Herzl."[43] Kaminer expressed his Zionist views in his poems. His collected works were published posthumously in 1905.

Varshavskii composed melodies and lyrics of Yiddish songs, which he often sang to his friends. Varshavskii decided to publish his songs after much encouragement from Sholom Aleichem. The first edition of *Yidishe folkslider mit notn* (Yiddish Folk Songs with Musical Notes) was published in Kiev with Sholom Aleichem's introduction in 1901. Many of Varshavskii's songs became popular among Yiddish speakers in Russia and abroad; the best known is *Der alef-beyz* or *Afn pripetshik* (*The Alphabet* or *On the Hearth*).[44]

At the turn of the twentieth century, the Hebrew poet Yehalel (acronym of Yehudah Leib Levin), the writer Yitskhok Yoel Linetskii, and the writer and Jewish public figure Gershon Badanes (the pen name

---

42 Gennady Estraikh, *In Harness: Yiddish Writer's Romance with Communism* (Syracuse, NY: Syracuse University Press, 2005), 8.
43 *The YIVO Encyclopedia of Jews in Eastern Europe*, s.v. "Kaminer, Yitsḥak," http://www.yivoencyclopedia.org/article.aspx/Kaminer__Yitshak.
44 Estraikh, *In Harness*, 8; *The YIVO Encyclopedia of Jews in Eastern Europe*, s.v. "Varshavski, Mark," http://www.yivoencyclopedia.org/article.aspx/Varshavski__Mark.

of Grigorii Gurevich) lived in Kiev. They were not as significant for Russian Jewish culture as Mendele Moicher Sforim, Hayim Nachman Bialik, or Sholom Aleichem, but their presence in the city, especially after the departure of Sholom Aleichem, preserved Jewish literary life there.

Yehalel's (1844–1925) work reflects his evolution from a maskil, to a socialist, and after the pogroms of 1881–1882, to a Palestinophile and Zionist. His early maskilic publications provoked the wrath of Orthodox Jews, while his later pro-socialist and pro-Zionist works made him *persona non grata* for the Kiev authorities. After the publication in 1865 of his first article "Hashkafah 'al matsav ha-haskalah ba-'ir Minsk" (An Observation on the State of Haskalah in the Town of Minsk) in the Hebrew newspaper *Ha-Melits* (The Advocate), the Hasidim in Minsk were so outraged that he had to leave town temporarily. In 1871, Yehalel moved to Kiev, where he worked for the Brodsky family as a tutor and secretary, and published his poetry. His Hebrew lyric poems became very popular and Yehalel was dubbed the "King of Poets" by Adam ha-Kohen (Avraham Dov Lebensohn).[45]

In the 1870s, Yehalel was involved in the socialist movement and published articles in Jewish periodicals against the exploitation of workers and in favor of educating the Jewish masses. However, after the pogroms of 1881, he, like other maskilim, was bitterly disappointed regarding the prospects for Jews in Russia and became a vocal proponent of the Palestinophile and then Zionist movements. Yehalel was one of the founders of the Palestinophile "Agudat Tsiyon" (Zionist Society) in Kiev in 1883. He was expelled from Kiev for his political activities in 1887. He moved to the shtetl Tomashpol, where he worked at one of the Brodsky plants and continued to write poetry. Yehalel returned to Kiev only in 1918, where he spent his last years in poverty. He died almost forgotten in 1925.[46]

---

45 *The YIVO Encyclopedia of Jews in Eastern Europe*, s.v. "Levin, Yehudah Leib," http://www.yivoencyclopedia.org/article.aspx/Levin__Yehudah__Leib__poet.
46 Joseph Klausner, *Historyah shel ha-sifrut ha-'ivrit ha-ḥadashah* (Jerusalem: Hotsa'at-Sefarim Aḥi'asaf, 1958), 6: 118–187; Getzel Kressel, *Leksikon ha-sifrut ha-'ivrit ba-dorot ha-aḥaronim* (Merḥavyah, Israel: Sifriyat Po'alim, 1967), 2: 199–202; Meyer Waxman, *A History of Jewish Literature* (New York: Bloch, 1936), 3: 258–260.

We can find many similarities in the biographies and social and political views of Yehalel and the Yiddish writer Yitskhok Yoel Linetskii (1839–1915), who chose Yiddish for his creative works as the language of the Jewish masses. Linetskii was born to a devout Hasidic family in the provincial city of Vinnitsa. His father, a Hasidic rabbi, compelled Yitskhok to get married at the age of fourteen, but when he saw that Yitskhok and his wife were interested in Haskalah ideas he forced his son to divorce his first wife and marry a deaf, mentally handicapped girl. A few years later Yitskhok rebelled against his father, divorced his second wife, and moved to Zhitomir and later to Kiev. He married a third time and "and over the next few years supported his family through writing, teaching, editing, peddling, petty trading, and entertaining in cabarets in towns and villages throughout southern Russia."[47] Linetskii's fame and popularity can be attributed to his fictitious autobiography *Dos Poylishe Yingl* (*The Polish Boy*; in later editions, *The Hasidic Boy*). The novel was first published in the Yiddish weekly *Kol Mevaser* (The Herald) in 1868 and then as a separate edition in 1869. The novel was a satire on Hasidic ignorance, fanaticism, and superstitious beliefs, which the author had experienced in his childhood and youth. Even though the characters depicted in the novel are stereotypical, the novel's vivid language as well as its humor made it very popular; it was republished many times.[48] Sholom Aleichem called Linetskii "one of the three giants" of Yiddish literature and "our foremost Yiddish satirist."[49] Thereafter, Linetskii published other novels and stories; however, his later works never matched his initial success with *Dos Poylishe Yingl*.

Linetskii, like Yehalel, switched from maskilic views to Palestinophilic after the pogroms of 1881–1882. He wrote a number of articles in Yiddish in support of the "Hibat Tsiyon" (Love of Zion) movement. He moved to Odessa in 1882 where he continued his literary work,

---

47 *The YIVO Encyclopedia of Jews in Eastern Europe*, s.v. "Linetski, Yitskhok Yoyel," http://www.yivoencyclopedia.org/article.aspx/Linetski__Yitskhok__Yoyel.
48 N[okhem] Shtif, *Di Eltere Yidishe Literatur, Literarishe Khrestomatye* (Kiev: Kultur-Lige, 1929); *Literaturnaia Entsiklopedia*, s.v. "Linetski Yitskhak Yoyel," http://www.surbor.su/enicinfo.php?id=15643.
49 *The YIVO Encyclopedia of Jews in Eastern Europe*, s.v. "Linetski, Yitskhok Yoyel," http://www.yivoencyclopedia.org/article.aspx/Linetski__Yitskhok__Yoyel.

mostly doing translations into Yiddish in his later years. He outlived his fame and died in anonymity in 1915.[50]

After the pogroms of 1881–1882, many Jewish intellectuals rethought their maskilic and populist views and turned to Jewish nationalism. The Jewish publicist and public figure Gershon Badanes (1852 or 1854–1932) belonged to this generation of Jewish intellectuals. Badanes was born in Mogilev to a wealthy Jewish merchant family. He moved to Kiev in his youth, where he studied law as an "external" student at Kiev St. Vladimir University and was involved in the revolutionary movement. In 1873 he fled to Germany under the threat of arrest. Badanes continued his revolutionary activities abroad: he joined the Jewish socialist group of Aron Liberman in Berlin, which published and delivered illegal socialist literature to Russia. For this activity Badanes was arrested and expelled to Great Britain. Then he moved to Paris and joined the Russian People's Will group. However, he broke with them in 1881 due to their justification of anti-Jewish pogroms. Badanes returned to Russia in 1883 and was arrested for his participation in the People's Will. However, he was released in sixteen months and settled in Kiev, where he served as the Danish consul until 1918.[51] How he acquired this position is unknown, but it gave him the right to live in the city. Badanes became an important Jewish public figure in Kiev, and he published several brochures and articles in the local press about Kievan Jewish life. In his works, he described the difficult financial situation of the majority of Kiev's Jews and the local authorities' discriminatory policies against them.[52]

His essays *Notes of an Apostate* were published in three issues of the Russian Jewish journal *Voskhod* (Dawn) in 1884. In his essays, he

---

50 Ibid.
51 N. Portnova, comp., *Byt' evreem v Rossii. Materialy po istorii russkogo evreistva. 1880–1890* (Jerusalem: The Hebrew University of Jerusalem, 1999), 27–28; Zsuzsa Hetényi, *In a Maelstrom: The History of Russian-Jewish Prose (1860–1940)* (Budapest: Central European University Press, 2008), 97.
52 Badanes, *S odnogo vola tri shkury*; Badanes, *Evreiskie obshchestvennye dela v Kieve*; Badanes, "Kievskaia evreiskaia obshchina v 1913 g.," *Vestnik evreiskoi obshchiny* 3 (March 1914): 34; Badanes, "Kievskaia evreiskaia obshchina na Vserossiiskoi Vystavke 1913 g. v Kieve," *Vestnik evreiskoi obshchiny* 4 (October 1913): 18–25.

attempted to explain why assimilation was so attractive for many Jews of his generation who grew up in provincial cities and shtetls. Russian culture opened for them a new and unknown world of modern ideas and culture. Acculturation and assimilation became the goal of many young Jewish intellectuals in the 1860s and 1870s, who abandoned their national traditions and "became apostates" of their own people. A national awakening came for many of them after the pogroms of 1881–1882, which demonstrated that assimilation would not save them from the wrath of anti-Semites. In addition, they felt that assimilation might provoke even stronger hatred toward Russified Jewish intellectuals, including those who occupied respected positions in Russian society. Badanes became an adherent of the Palestinophile movement after the pogroms; however, he understood that the movement could not immediately organize mass Jewish emigration from Russia. Hence, he attempted to improve the situation of Jews in Kiev and to combat the unrelenting anti-Semitism of the local authorities. However, state anti-Semitism increased with time and Badanes' publications became more and more pessimistic. He emigrated from Kiev during the civil war and Simon Dubnov wrote that he often met with "the already old and sick Gurevich [Badanes]" in Berlin.[53]

The persecution of Jews in Kiev was harsher than in other parts of the Russian Empire and the anti-Semitism of the local population more acute. Because of this, some Kievan Jewish intellectuals strongly advocated the emigration of Jews from Russia. The leader of the Palestinophile and Zionist movement and the vice president of the Kiev Jewish community was Max Mandelstamm, who believed, along with many other Jewish intellectuals, that the emigration of Jews was the only possible solution to the Jewish question in Russia.[54] The pogroms of 1881–1882 shattered the previous ideals of the maskilim about merging with the Russian people and of hope for equality for the Jews of Russia.

---

53 S. M. Dubnov, *Kniga zhizni. Vospominaniia i razmyshlenia. Materialy dlia istorii moego vremeni* (St. Petersburg: Peterburgskoe Vostokovedenie, 1998), 317.
54 Victoria Khiterer, "Max Mandelstamm, Palestinophile and Zionist Leader," *The American Association for Polish-Jewish Studies (AAPJS). New Views*, http://www.aapjstudies.org/index.php?id=141.

The loss of hope for a better future pushed talented Jewish youth away from the country. This included the poet David Edelstadt (1866–1892). Edelstadt began to write poetry in Russian and Yiddish at the age of nine, and after a few years his poetry was being published in local newspapers. Edelstadt was born in Kaluga and lived in Kiev from 1880 to 1882. However, even in such a short time, the young Edelstadt acquired many admirers of his talent. Among them was Max Mandelstamm, who personally began to help Edelstadt prepare for entrance examinations to Kiev St. Vladimir University. Nonetheless, Edelstadt and his older brother, who also lived in Kiev, decided to emigrate after the 1881 Kiev pogrom, which they witnessed. They both joined the Am Olam movement and left for America in 1882.[55]

Edelstadt's literary talent flourished in America; he published many poems, articles, and essays in Russian and Yiddish. However, his literary work did not provide sufficient income, and he was forced to combine his literary activity with hard physical labor in sweatshops and factories. Dissatisfaction with the miserable working and living conditions induced Edelstadt to join the anarchist movement. He participated in the first Jewish anarchist group in New York, the *Pionire der Frayhayt* (Pioneers of Liberty). At twenty-four, Edelstadt became the third chief editor of the anarchist weekly *Freie Arbeiter Stimme* (Free Voice of Labor). Hard labor and tuberculosis, which he contracted in his youth, undermined Edelstadt's health; he died at the age of twenty-six.[56]

At the turn of the twentieth century, a new generation of Jewish intellectuals came onto the political stage. They were completely dissatisfied with the previous methods that had failed to solve Jewish problems in Russia. In their opinion, neither petitions calling for equal rights nor assimilation, acculturation, or emigration could solve these problems. They believed that Jews deserved equal rights and that the government was obligated to grant them. Boris Gurevich, the son of the Kiev state rabbi, in his book *O voprosah kul'turnoi zhizni evreev*

---

55 *Electronnaia Evreiskaia Entsiklopedia*, s.v. "Edelstadt, David," http://eleven.co.il/article/14984; YIVO Archives, RG 517, Box 1 (there is no continuous numeration of the documents in the box).

56 Ibid.

(Regarding Questions of the Cultural Life of Jews), described what he viewed as the main change in the younger generation of Jews. He wrote that a feeling of national dignity had awoken among them, that they didn't want to continue begging for fundamental human rights, and that they deserved the same dignity as any other people.

Boris (Buzia) Gurevich was one of the brightest representatives of the young generation of Kievan Jews in the early twentieth century. The popular Russian singer and author of popular songs and poems, Alexander Vertinsky (1889–1957), left a very interesting memoir about him. They studied together in the Kiev fourth gymnasium. Vertinsky wrote about this period in his memoirs *Dorogoi Dlinnoiu* (On a Long Road):

> The pride and sensation of our gymnasium was Buzia Gurevich, the son of the Kiev rabbi. He was a real child prodigy; at least I had never met anyone like him. When he was in the first grade he already wrote essays for students in the upper grades. When he studied in the fourth grade he made presentations on literary disputes and impressed everybody by his erudition. He participated in discussions after the lectures of academics, wrote poems, was a member of philosophical societies, delivered brilliant speeches on the "literary trials" of the time, and put the theosophical ladies into raptures. He could talk incessantly at any time and on any topic, even when he did not know in advance the topic of the discussion. All Kiev Jews and our entire gymnasium were proud of him. People predicted a great future for him. Nobody had the courage to debate with him, and he was thoroughly self-sufficient, but was also a good fellow.
>
> I could always come to his house to eat a full meal. However, it was necessary to do so when Buzia's parents were not home: they did not like me, because they supposed that I was a free-thinker and low-achiever, and had a bad influence on their son. But Buzia courageously took the remnants of breakfast and lunch from the buffet in the dining room and always fed me. He even gave me his shirts...He had unquestioned authority among our youth. I don't know what role he would

have played in my fate if he had not disappeared from my view in the heat of his Kievan successes. I did not worry about his future. Thus I was very surprised when many years later I met Buzia Gurevich in Paris in the position of a modest employee of the script department of the movie studio "Gaumont."[57]

Being employed in the script department of the world's oldest movie studio in Paris was not a bad career for an emigrant, considering the fate of many Russian nobles who were forced to become taxi drivers and waiters after the revolution. Perhaps, Vertinsky was contrasting his own remarkable career with the more common fate of his child prodigy friend.

Gurevich graduated with honors from the law school of Kiev St. Vladimir University and then worked at Freiburg University in Germany in 1913–1914. He was expelled from Germany at the beginning of World War I and returned to Kiev. In 1917, Gurevich joined the People's Freedom Party (also called the Constitutional Democratic Party, abbreviated and commonly called the Kadets). After the February 1917 Revolution he become a representative of the State Duma for propaganda in the army. In 1919, he worked for several newspapers of Denikin's volunteer army. Together with the lawyer Oskar Gruzenberg, he prepared an agreement between the Congress of Jewish Representatives and General Anton Ivanovich Denikin about methods for preventing pogroms. After the defeat of the White movement, Gurevich emigrated from Russia to Constantinople (Istanbul), and later he moved to Paris, where Vertinsky met him.[58] In the late 1930s, Gurevich emigrated to the United States, where he continued his literary work, and actively participated in Jewish public organizations in America. Gurevich founded and led the Union for the Defense of Human Rights and was nominated for the Nobel Peace Prize in 1957. He died from a heart attack in New York in 1964.[59]

---

57 Alexander Vertinsky, *Dorogoi Dlinnoiu* (Moscow: Pravda, 1990), 22–23.
58 A. I. Serkov, *Russkoe masonstvo 1731–2000. Entsiklopedicheskii slovar'* (Moscow: Rosspen, 2001), 283–284.
59 E. S. Kovaleva, "Russkie philosophy-masony: predvaritel'nyi spisok personalii," *Sofiia: Rukopisnyi zhurnal Obschestva revnitelei russkoi filosofii* 7 (2005): 4.

In his youth Boris Gurevich was one of the rising Kievan Jewish intellectuals. In his early twenties, his ambitious political-philosophical brochure, *O voprosah kul'turnoi zhizni evreev* (Regarding Questions of the Cultural Life of Jews), raised questions about discrimination against Jews in Russia.[60] Gurevich wrote:

> From birth until death the life of the Russian Jew is a continuous path of humiliation, disgrace, struggle...At night police search for Jews in Kiev, where Jews lived even before the Russian state was created...and they make night round-ups of Jews who live in Kiev without special permission and break into women's bedrooms...They take revenge upon Jews by round-ups, expulsion, and lawlessness. Why? "Jewish revolutionaries make revolution for the enslavement of the Russian people"—this is the peculiar assertion of the "extreme right." Let us analyze this statement. The majority of Jews have an inclination toward conservatism. If Jews were not oppressed by their lack of rights, if they did not have such a hard life, as if they were slaves and debtors of every policeman, they would be, as a whole, quiet petite bourgeoisie who support order in the country first of all...
>
> People who do not know Jewish life and traditions created the senseless legend about "ritual murders" and keep innocent people in prison and at the same time accuse Hasidim (about half of Jewry...) of the use of blood and threaten them with pogroms! The general practice of certain kinds of newspapers is to spread lies and slanders against Jews in the country, humiliating them—under these conditions peace in the country does not exist and is impossible...Jews should not ask for human rights, their rights as citizens—Russia must give them these rights to redeem its shameful sin![61]

---

60 B. A. Gurevich, *O voprosah kul'turnoi zhizni evreev* (Kiev: Kievskoe obshchestvo druzei mira, 1911), 1–12.
61 Ibid.

Immediately after its publication, the police confiscated all copies of this brochure and began a criminal investigation against Gurevich.[62] The surviving documents do not show how the investigation ended, but in 1913 Gurevich left for Germany.

While Gurevich's works are practically unheard of today, the Russian Jewish thinker Lev Shestov (Shvartsman, 1866–1938) is well known for his contributions to Russian philosophical thought. Shestov was a scion of a wealthy Kievan merchant family. He received both Jewish and general education, but at a young age chose assimilation with Russian culture.[63] However, Shestov later turned to Jewish themes, using images from the Old Testament in his works. In his youth, Shestov left Kiev for Moscow; however, Jewish life and anti-Semitism in Kiev, and in particular the Beilis trial, had a deep influence upon him. Shestov's friend, Aron Shteinberg, claimed that Shestov turned toward his Jewish roots and culture after the Beilis trial. Shteinberg wrote that "already from the time of the Beilis trial [1911–1913], something occurred in Lev Isakievich's [Shestov's] consciousness which forced him to look back into his own 'Beginnings and Ends' and view himself as a continuation of Jerusalem's spiritual genealogy."[64] The Russian religious philosopher Nikolai Berdyaev and other thinkers also recognized that Shestov's works were "strongly influenced by Judaism."[65]

Shestov's major work *Afiny i Ierusalim* (Athens and Jerusalem) shows the dichotomy between Greek and Jewish civilizations based on the differences in their religion and philosophy. Shestov thought that the Greek logical philosophy was opposed to a "free search for personal values." He questioned logic from the standpoint of religious existentialism. Shestov wrote that "the ancient Jews find their primary place

---

62 TsDIAK U, f. 295, op. 1, d. 438 (About the opening of the criminal investigation against the author of the brochure "Regarding Questions of the Cultural Life of Jews" ["O voprosah kul'turnoi zhizni evreev"], B .A. Gurevich, 1913), ll. 251, 291.
63 Brian Horowitz, *Empire Jews: Jewish Nationalism and Acculturation in 19th and Early 20th-Century Russia* (Bloomington: Slavica Publishers, Indiana University, 2009), 233–234.
64 Ibid., 244.
65 Ibid.

juxtaposed between Athens and Jerusalem, the struggle of faith against rational logic."[66]

THE WAR OF JEWISH LANGUAGES IN KIEV

A group of talented Jewish literary youth gathered in Kiev in the early twentieth century. Among them were the future founders of the *Kultur-Lige* (Culture League) Moshe Litvakov, Yekhezkel Dobrushin, Nakhman Meisel, and David Bergelson.[67] Young Yiddish poets and writers met in Kiev either at the OPE library or at the salon of Rakhil Isaevna, who provided her house for meetings. Some of them, such as David Hofshtein and Osher Shvartsman, had first tried to write their poetry in Hebrew, Russian, or Ukrainian before switching to Yiddish.[68] In 1909, they created the publishing house "Kunst-verlag" (Arts Publisher) in Kiev, which specialized in Yiddish literature.[69] According to Hillel Kazovsky, "A little later, this circle grew into the 'Kyiv Group' that became a noticeable phenomenon in the history of new Jewish literature in Yiddish."[70] Gennady Estraikh has noted that many of the young Jewish writers were "equally fluent in Yiddish, Hebrew, and Russian."[71] However Yiddish was their choice because it was the vernacular language of most Jews to whom they addressed their works. Even though they lived in Kiev, they mostly wrote about the life of shtetl Jews. "Kiev Yiddish prose and poetry was populated by young Jewish shtetl-dwellers, villagers, or recent urbanites..."[72] The young Yiddish writers held populist and socialist principles. They therefore chose to write about the life of the Jewish masses, which was intended to be of more direct interest to their readers. This interest in provincial life put Yiddish writers somewhat apart from the mainstream modernist urban literature of the time.

While the populist Jewish writers promoted Yiddish literature in Kiev, Zionists believed that Yiddish literature and language should be

---

66 Ibid., 248.
67 Estraikh, *In Harness*, 31.
68 Ibid., 14–15.
69 Hillel Kazovsky, *The Book Design of Kultur-Lige Artists* (Kiev: Dukh i Litera, 2011), 6.
70 Ibid.
71 Estraikh, *In Harness*, 16.
72 Ibid.

abandoned in favor of Hebrew. A lecture by Vladimir (Ze'ev) Jabotinsky about Jewish languages in Kiev in February 1911 provoked heated debate. He denied the right of Yiddish to exist "on the Jewish street." A report about Jabotinsky's lecture was published in the Jewish weekly *Evreiskii mir* on February 24, 1911:

> Kiev.
> Jabotinsky's Lecture about Jewish Languages
> On February 7th at the Jewish Literary Society, and by invitation of its Committee, V. E. Jabotinsky presented a lecture about Jewish languages.
>
> The debate concerning languages, the orator said, regards the hegemony of the language of Jewish national culture. One may guess that national Jewish values can be created either in the ancient Jewish language (as he called Hebrew), in Jewish (Yiddish), or in Russian...
>
> Perhaps when the epoch of democratization and decentralization begins in Russia, then Jews along with other national minorities will receive the opportunity to use the Jewish language, if it is still alive by that time...However it [Yiddish] will never become the language of Jewish national culture. Among the two languages which contend with each other for first place in our national school, the victory will go to the ancient Jewish language...
>
> The Jewish nation, according to the lecturer's opinion, can only be considered as integral and indissoluble when the ancient Jewish language is recognized as the language of culture and education. Only the language of the prophets can be the clasp which is able to link the numerous Jewish "leftover bits" dispersed around the world; only the ancient Jewish language was and will be the language of Jewish cultural values, Jewish spirit and poetry...
>
> "It is not a problem," Mr. Jabotinsky said, "that a simple Jew or a Jewish intellectual may cry when he listens to a Jewish [Yiddish] song: the tears are only water!"

Jabotinsky then attacked the "jargon" (as he called Yiddish) and, promising nevertheless to defend it at all times in the face of the "external [i.e., gentile] world." He declared that the war of languages is an eternal struggle "on the Jewish street." He concluded his speech with the exclamation: "So I hereby acknowledge full rights only for the Hebrew language in Jewish life, and declare all others illegal!"

THE JEWISH PRESS IN KIEV

Jewish periodicals in Kiev were published in several languages, including Russian, Yiddish, and Hebrew. Each language targeted its own audience: Russian for the assimilated Jewish elite, Yiddish for the Jewish masses, and Hebrew for nationally conscious, well-educated Jews. However, there were only a few periodicals in Hebrew and they did not last long. For example, on July 29, 1906, Leizer Fridman received permission from the Kiev Deputy Governor to publish a newspaper in the "ancient Jewish language" (i.e., Hebrew) called *Ha-tsofe u-mabit* (The Observer and Spectator).[73] According to its program, the newspaper was "designed for the intelligent reader." It was supposed to publish "political, economic and pedagogical articles."[74] However, after publication of a few issues, the newspaper went out of business due to lack of readers. Fridman revived the newspaper in 1912–1913 under the shorter name *Ha-tsofe* (The Observer), but again its publication did not continue for long.[75]

On the other hand, the Yiddish press in Kiev had a considerably larger audience. The periodicals *Folk shtime* (People's Voice), *Das folk* (The People), *Kiever tagblat* (Kiev Daily Paper), *Yudishe naye leben* (New Jewish Life), *Kiever wort* (Kiev Word), and others published the news of everyday Jewish life in Kiev and in other cities and shtetls of the Russian Empire. The papers also offered information about Jewish emigration, letters to the editor, digests of the Russian press, and

---

73 TsDIAK U, f. 295, op. 1, d. 34, l. 1.
74 Ibid.
75 Meir, *Kiev, Jewish Metropolis*, 165.

Yiddish stories and poetry.⁷⁶ These Yiddish periodicals were designed for the Jewish masses and were quite popular among Jewish workers, artisans, and petty traders. However, most Yiddish periodicals in Kiev were also short-lived. Some could not withstand the intense competition—for example, *Yudishe naye leben*, which closed after its third issue in 1912.⁷⁷

But most Jewish periodicals in Kiev that had even a modicum of success were sooner or later shut down by the authorities for "anti-government propaganda" or for the "unacceptable" editorial focus of their articles. Such large fines were sometimes imposed upon the editors that they were unable to pay them. The editors therefore faced a dilemma: whether to publish the truth about the persecution of Jews in Kiev and Russia, in which case the periodical would likely be fined or closed, or to become utterly obedient to the authorities and not publish anything "inflammatory." Such "toothless" newspapers were uninteresting and soon had to close due to lack of readership. Even taking a moderate position would not always protect a Yiddish periodical. Thus, during the Russian Revolution of 1905, the authorities "temporarily stopped" publication of the Yiddish newspaper *Dos Folk* until the end of martial law in Kiev and Kiev province.⁷⁸

It was hard to obtain permission to publish a Jewish periodical in Kiev. The request had to be approved by the local authorities, the Kiev Censorship Committee, and the Ministry of Internal Affairs in St. Petersburg. This bureaucratic process took a long time. An editor first needed to provide the periodical's program to the authorities; the authorities and censorship committee then evaluated the program and checked the "loyalty" of the petitioner. Sometimes the authorities rejected such requests without explanation. For example, in October 1889, Abel Karasik asked for permission to publish a literary-scholarly journal *Der morgen shtern* (The Morning Star) in Kiev. Seven months

---

76 TsDIAK U, f. 295, op. 1, d. 35, ll.1–4; d. 125, l. 1; d. 139, ll. 85–86, 111–118; d. 189, ll. 38, 97; d. 232, l. 1; d. 438, ll. 86–87, 210–213, 222–223.
77 Ibid., d.438, l. 203.
78 Ibid., d. 35, l. 4.

later, on February 28, 1890, the Ministry of Internal Affairs rejected his request without comment.[79]

A few Russian Jewish periodicals were published in Kiev in the early twentieth century. However, just like the Kiev Yiddish and Hebrew papers, they did not survive for long. Their audience was quite limited, and some of them disappeared because they could not compete with the Russian press. Other Russian Jewish periodicals were closed by the authorities for political reasons. For example, in 1902–1903, *Illiustrirovannyi sionistskii al'manakh* (The Illustrated Zionist Almanac) was published in Russian in Kiev. The periodical was shut down by the authorities after the Zionist movement was banned in Russia.

The Russian Jewish journal *Vestnik evreiskoi obshchiny* (Jewish Community Herald) was published in Kiev in 1913. This periodical, which was focused mainly on Jewish community affairs and philanthropy, also failed to attract a significant audience.

The Russian Jewish intelligentsia were more interested in global questions of Jewish life in Russia than in local Jewish communal institutions and philanthropy. Jewish community leaders could not solve the most important problem in Jewish life—the denial of civil rights to Jews. They could not stop the persecution of Jews in Russia or protect them from violence and state anti-Semitism. The Jewish intelligentsia hoped to obtain equal civil rights as the country liberalized, and for this reason many educated Jews supported the liberal movement and read the liberal press.

The Kiev Russian liberal press constantly published articles relating to Jewish issues. There were many pieces about the persecution and expulsion of Jews from Kiev, the deprivation of the civil rights of Jews, anti-Semitism, and anti-Jewish violence. The local liberal press' attention to the Jewish question was determined by readers' interest in Jewish topics. Among the readers were many intellectual Jews and liberal gentiles who felt compassion toward the oppressed Jewish people. Many Kiev Jews worked as editors and correspondents in Kiev's Russian liberal periodicals. Anti-Semites complained that the

---

79 Ibid., f. 294, op. 1, d. 186, l. 67.

liberal press was in the hands of the Jews in Kiev. The Russian liberal newspapers *Zaria* (Dawn), *Kievskie otkliki* (Kiev Comments), *Kievskaia mysl'* (Kievan Thought), and *Kievskie vesti* (Kiev Herald) were in open opposition to the government. The first two were edited by the lawyer Lev Abramovich Kupernik (1845–1905).[80] Kupernik converted to Orthodox Christianity at a young age to marry a Christian girl. However, after his conversion, Kupernik continued to defend the rights of Jews in court and in his publications. Kupernik became a renowned lawyer after the Kutaisi affair in 1879. He proved the innocence of nine Jews accused of ritual murder who were arrested in the Georgian town Sachkheri (near Kutaisi); all of them were acquitted. Thereafter, Kupernik participated as the advocate in various political trials and in trials related to the Kishinev and Gomel pogroms. He published newspaper and journal articles defending the victims of pogroms, and strove for the abolition of capital punishment for political prisoners in Russia.[81] The authorities closed Kupernik's newspaper *Zaria* for its anti-government focus, and Kupernik was forced to leave Kiev for a few years to avoid arrest.[82]

The authorities often fined liberal editors for their publications, and temporarily or permanently shut down liberal newspapers. However, the government persecution of the liberal press only increased its popularity. On June 5, 1908, the chairman of the Kiev Temporary Committee on Publication Affairs wrote in a secret letter to the Main Department on Publication Affairs that the "government opposition" newspapers *Kievskaia mysl'* and *Kievskie vesti* were very popular among "Jews, youth and semi-intelligentsia, many of whom are clerks."[83]

Conservative newspapers in Kiev also paid a lot of attention to the Jewish question, publishing mostly anti-Semitic articles that depicted the Jews as a threat to the holiness of the city, as exploiters and religious fanatics. They demanded that more Jews be expelled from the city, and

---

80 TsDIAK U, f. 294, op. 1, 151, l. 224; Grigorii Spektor, "Vsekh Plevak Sopernik," *Evreiskoie Slovo* 38 (261), (2005), http://www.e-slovo.ru/261/6pol1.htm.
81 Spektor, "Vsekh Plevak Sopernik."
82 Ibid.
83 TsDIAK U, f. 295, op. 1, d. 139, ll. 117–118.

that they be forbidden to open synagogues, schools, and other Jewish organizations. The government-subsidized newspaper *Kievlianin* and the Kiev Black Hundreds newspaper *Dvuglavyi orel* (Two-Headed Eagle) took an especially aggressive and intolerant position toward Jews. *Dvuglavyi orel* accused Jews of the "ritual murder of Andrisha Iuschinskii," and repeatedly published anti-Semitic materials. *Kievlianin*'s position on the Jewish question was not so consistent. During the Beilis trial, the editor of *Kievlianin*, Vasilii Shul'gin, a well-known Russian nationalist and anti-Semite, published an article in defense of Beilis. Shul'gin wrote,

> one need only have common sense to understand that the accusation against Beilis is babble that any lawyer will demolish easily. We should feel sorry for the Kiev Office of the Public Prosecutor and for all Russian justice, as they will be judged by the entire world for this pathetic mess.[84]

The police confiscated this issue of *Kievlianin*, the first such case of censorship in the newspaper's fifty years of existence. Copies sold before the confiscation were quickly resold for ten to twenty rubles each, a hundred times the original price. As punishment for his article, Shul'gin was sentenced to three months in prison, although Tsar Nicholas II pardoned him.[85] Shul'gin explained many years later that he was sure that the ritual murder trial concocted by the government would fail and that he did not want to be associated with it.[86]

KIEV JEWISH HISTORIANS

Jewish scholarly organizations did not exist in Kiev before the February 1917 Revolution. The local authorities, who barely tolerated the presence of Jews in Kiev, prohibited the opening of any Jewish scholarly society in the city. However, the Jewish historians Israel Darevskii, Herman Baratz, and Il'ia Galant lived and worked in Kiev in the second half of the nineteenth to the early twentieth century. All of them

---

84 Victoria Khiterer, "Vasilii Shul'gin and the Jewish Question: An Assessment of Shul'gin's Antisemitism," *On the Jewish Street* 1, no. 2, (2011): 10.
85 Ibid.
86 Ibid.

developed a strong interest in the history of Jews in Kiev, and published monographs and articles on aspects of their history.

Although Israel Darevskii's *Le-korot ha-Yehudim be-Kiyov* (To the History of Jews in Kiev) is not a serious scholarly work, it was the first attempt to write a history of the Jews in Kiev. It was published in Hebrew in Berdichev in 1902, and then in Russian in Kiev in 1907.[87] This book devotes only twenty-five pages of 120 to modern history, from the end of the eighteenth to the second half of the nineteenth century. Darevskii did not write anything about the history of Jews in Kiev in the late nineteenth century, probably to ease the book's passage through the censorship.

Herman (Hirsh) Markovich Baratz (1835–1922) belonged to the first generation of Russian Jewish intelligentsia and shared the views of many other maskilim. He was born in the city of Dubno, Volhynia province, graduated from the rabbinical seminary in Zhitomir in 1859, and ten years later from the law school of Kiev St. Vladimir University. In 1863, Baratz was appointed as the adviser on Jewish affairs to the Kiev, Podolia, and Volhynia governor-general. From 1871 to 1881, he also served as the censor of Jewish books. As the adviser to the governor-general and censor of Jewish books, Baratz bitterly attacked Hasidism and Hasidic books. In his *Note on Hasidism* to the governor-general, Baratz wrote that Hasidism has a negative influence on the intellectual life of its followers:

> A Hasid does not care about the general success of all of mankind or the success of his coreligionists: he always remains happy about himself and his prophet—tsaddik. And the latter indulges the isolation of his followers for his own interest and supports their intellectual immobility, understanding...that his entire well-being is based only upon the Hasidim's deep ignorance...
>
> For the successful spread of education among Jews in the above mentioned three provinces [Kiev, Podolia, and Volhynia] it is absolutely necessary to annihilate or at least to weaken the influence of the tsaddikim. As long as these ignorant idols of

---

87 Israel Darevskii, *Le-korot ha-Yehudim be-Kiyov* (Berdichev: Publishing House of Y. G. Sheftel, 1902); Darevskii, *K istorii evreev v Kieve. Ot poloviny VIII v. do kontsa XIX v.*

the blind crowd exist, infiltrating Jewish public and private life, any improvements and innovations appropriate to the times will go very slowly, or even be completely stymied.[88]

Baratz wrote in his *Note on Hasidism* that it represents a brief overview of his articles on this topic published in the Russian Jewish journals *Razsvet* (Dawn) and *Sion* (Zion).[89] Baratz had begun to publish articles in the Russian and Russian Jewish press in the 1860s. He also wrote some popular articles on the Jewish question for the periodicals *Den'* (The Day), *Ha-Karmel* (Mount Carmel), and *Severnaya pchela* (Northern Bee).[90]

We know quite a bit about Baratz's personality from Sholom Aleichem's autobiographical novel *From the Fair*. Searching for a job in Kiev, Sholom Aleichem met with Baratz on the recommendation of Kiev Rabbi Tsukkerman in 1879. He visited Baratz at the governor-general's office:

> He [Sholom Aleichem] imagined that this Jewish adviser would be like a professor, bemedaled like a general.
>
> A rill of shivers ran down his spine as he rang the doorbell and was admitted into a room lined with sacred texts and secular books. His teeth chattered. A few minutes later, a man with sparse side-whiskers dashed into the room. He was extremely myopic and seemed to be in a dither. Could this be the Jewish adviser to the Governor-General? If not for the bare chin, Sholom would have sworn that he was a Hebrew teacher or a Talmud instructor. This Jewish adviser spit when he spoke and seemed to be quite scatterbrained. Sholom later discovered that all kinds of stories and anecdotes circulated about him in Kiev. For example, he was never able to find his own house until he saw his nameplate: HERMAN MARKOVICH BARATZ.[91]

---

88 YIVO, RG 80, folder 723, l. 61691.
89 Ibid., l. 61688.
90 *Jewish Encyclopedia*, s.v. "Baratz, Herman (Hirsh) Markovich." http://www.jewishencyclopedia.com/view.jsp?artid=271&letter=B; *Rossiiskaia evreiskaia entsiklopedia*, s.v. "Baratz, Herman," http://www.rujen.ru/index.php.
91 Sholom Aleichem, *From the Fair*, 263.

Sholom Aleichem may have penned such a comic and deprecating description of Baratz because Sholom Aleichem was not received in a very friendly manner. The scene continues:

> This morning Baratz happened to be in quite a daze, and ill-tempered too. He was in a hurry to get somewhere: he gesticulated and spit and sprayed as he spoke. After reading the crown rabbi's letter recommending the young man to him, the Jewish adviser clapped his hands to his head and began to pace back and forth in the room. He muttered and spit and pled for mercy. "Leave me alone. I don't know anything and I'm not going to do anything."...
>
> Brokenhearted and dispirited, Sholom slipped out of the Jewish adviser's office. As he reached the last step he heard someone calling him back. The very same Baratz. He had come to conclusion that although he himself could not do anything for Sholom, he could give him a letter of recommendation to a friend and colleague named Kupernik.[92]
>
> "I want you to know that Kupernik can do quite bit for you. A lot, in fact! Kupernik is nothing to sneeze at! With a letter of recommendation from him you can break through brick walls, move the greatest people!"[93]

As he outlived the writer by six years, Baratz presumably read this characterization. What might he have thought recalling their meeting? Probably something like: you never know who among all these young shtetl Jews, desperately searching for a job and the right of residence in Kiev, will later become a prominent writer!

The anti-Jewish pogroms of 1881–1882 were a major shock for Baratz and other maskilim. In 1881, Baratz resigned as censor of Jewish books and returned to his law practice and scholarly work. But he continued to be involved in Jewish public affairs. In the same year, together with Max Mandelstamm, he represented the Jews of Kiev

---

92 Lev Abramovich Kupernik (1845–1905), prominent lawyer and journalist.
93 Sholom Aleichem, *From the Fair*, 264.

province before the commission investigating the causes of the pogroms in southern Russia. Baratz immigrated to Paris after the revolution and died there in 1922.

Baratz published many articles and several brochures on the history and legal status of Jews in Kievan Rus', and about the influence of the Hebrew Bible and the Midrash on medieval Russian literature. His book *O bibleisko-agadicheskom elemente v povestiakh i skazaniiakh nachal'noi russkoi letopisi* (About Biblical-Haggadic Elements in the Tales and Legends of the Old Russian Chronicles) was published by Kiev St. Vladimir University in 1907.[94] His son, Lev Hermanovich Baratz, formerly a professor of the Kiev Commercial Institute, published two volumes of his father's works as *Sobranie trudov po voprosu o evreiskom elemente v pamiatnikakh drevnerusskoi pis'mennosti* (Collection of Works Regarding Jewish Elements in the Monuments of Old Russian Literature) in 1924–1927.[95]

Baratz wrote that Jewish religious books had a strong influence on ancient Russian chronicles and legends. The modern researcher of the history of Jews in medieval Russia, Alexander Pereswetoff-Morath, comes to much the same conclusion in his book *A Grin without a Cat*.[96] However, while Pereswetoff-Morath believes that this impact on Old Russian literature came directly from Jewish texts, Baratz held that among the monks at the Kiev Cave Monastery there were Jewish converts to Orthodox Christianity, such as the monk Nikita (1078–1108). Baratz thought that Nikita was originally from Kiev and as a teenager had been kidnapped by Christians, converted to Christianity, and then rose in the monastic hierarchy. "Nobody could compete with Nikita in knowledge of the Old Testament and Jewish books," states the chronicle. Baratz assumed that Nikita was from a Jewish family and received

---

94 G. M. Baratz, *O bibleisko-agadicheskom elemente v povestiakh i skazaniiakh nachal'noi russkoi letopisi* (Kiev: St. Vladimir University Publishing House, 1907).
95 G. M. Baratz, *Sobranie trudov po voprosu o evreiskom elemente v pamiatnikakh drevnerusskoi pis'mennosti* (Berlin and Paris: Impr. D'Art Voltaire, 1924–1927), I–II.
96 Alexander Pereswetoff-Morath, *A Grin without a Cat*, 1: *Adversus Iudaeos Texts in the Literature of Medieval Russia (988–1504)*; 2: *Jews and Christians in Medieval Russia—Assessing the Sources* (Lund: Lund Slavonic Monographs, 2002).

a traditional Jewish religious education before he was kidnapped. As he grew up in the monastery, Nikita "fell into heresy" and did not want to recognize the New Testament (i.e., he made an attempt to return to Judaism). However, the monks did not allow him to change his faith. Under pressure, Nikita repented, was later appointed bishop of Novgorod, and subsequently canonized as an Orthodox Christian saint.[97]

While Baratz was interested in the history of Jews in Kievan Rus', another Kiev Jewish historian, Il'ia Vladimirovich Galant (1868–1939), was the first to write specifically about the history of Jews in Ukraine. Galant was born in the Ukrainian provincial city Nezhin where he received a traditional Jewish religious education. Then "he studied under the supervision of the professors of the Nezhin Historical-Philological Institute" but never officially become a student there. Perhaps the obstacle preventing his matriculation was either the quota for Jewish students or his inability to afford the tuition. Galant devoted several years to self-education in the institute's library and was later accepted as a member of the Nezhin Historical-Philological Society. However, life in the provincial city soon became too boring for the young and ambitious man and he moved to Kiev in the early 1890s. There, Galant was fortunate enough to become the personal secretary of the children of the wealthiest Jewish family in Russia, Baron Vladimir Goratsievich Ginsburg.[98] Perhaps this position was just a formality, but it gave Galant the right to live in the city and opened the doors to the Kiev Jewish elite. Soon the young provincial man without a formal education began to teach Jewish history and law in several Kiev schools. At the same time, Galant began to publish articles about the history of Jews in Ukraine in the Russian and Jewish journals *Kievskaia starina* (Kiev Olden Times), *Voskhod*, and *Budushchnost'* (The Future), as well as in separate booklets. Galant focused his research on the history of Jews in Ukraine, which he considered a special field in Jewish history. His interest in the

---

97   German Baratz, "Povesti i skazania drevnerusskoi pismennosti, imeiushchie otnoshenie k evreiam i evreistvu," *Kievskaia Starina* (1906): 4–13.
98   Vladimir Goratsevich Ginsburg married Lazar Brodsky's daughter, Klara, in 1898 and settled in Kiev.

history of Jews in Ukraine may be explained by the availability of local historical sources and by Galant's self-identification as a Ukrainian Jew.

The Kiev banker Baron Vladimir Ginsburg, who had hired Galant, also financed Semen An-sky's (pseudonym of Shloyme Rapoport) famous Jewish ethnographical expedition to the Pale of Settlement in 1911–1914. The expedition was named in memory of his late father Horace Ginsburg. The expedition visited many shtetls and towns in Ukraine and collected about seven hundred Jewish artifacts and over a hundred historical documents, took about two thousand photographs, and recorded Jewish folktales, legends, songs, and melodies. The materials of the expedition become the basis for the Museum of the Jewish Historical Ethnographic Society, which was opened in Petrograd in May 1917.[99]

JEWISH ARTISTS

Many Jewish artists studied in the Kiev Art School, established in 1900, and at the Art Studio of Aleksandra Ekster. Art schools did not have a quota limiting the number of Jewish students, so they attracted many gifted Jewish youth. The well-known Jewish artists Abram Manevich, Aleksandr Tyshler, Mark Epshtein, Zinovii Tolkachev, Isaac Rabinovich, and many others studied there. Hillel Kazovsky noted that Kiev Jewish artists were inspired by the aesthetic, national, and cultural ideas of the Kiev Yiddish writers.[100] Many of these artists illustrated their works. The Jewish artists and Yiddish writers joined the *Kultur-Lige* (Culture League) when the organization was established in Kiev in 1918.[101]

Abram Manevich (1881–1942) is the best known among this group of Kiev Jewish artists. He was born in the Belorussian shtetl Mstislavl' and came to Kiev in 1900 with the sole desire of becoming an artist. He studied in the Kiev Art School, from which he graduated in 1905, and

---

99 A. Kantsedicas and I. Sergeeva, *The Jewish Artistic Heritage: Album by Semen An-sky* (Moscow: Mosty Kul'tury, 2001), 41–47; *The YIVO Encyclopedia of Jews in Eastern Europe*, s.v. "An-ski Ethnographic Expedition and Museum," http://www.yivoencyclopedia.org/article.aspx/An-ski__Ethnographic__Expedition__and__Museum.
100 Kazovsky, *The Book Design*, 6.
101 *Kultur-Lige* promoted the development of Yiddish education and culture, including literature, theater, art, and music. *The YIVO Encyclopedia of Jews in Eastern Europe*, s.v. "Kultur-lige" http://www.yivoencyclopedia.org/article.aspx/Kultur-lige.

then in the Munich Academy of Arts in 1905–1907.[102] An art critic wrote that in the early twentieth century, Manevich's "creative works synthesized all of the new forms of art, giving them his own meaning."[103] Manevich produced many paintings in a modernist style, depicting landscapes and city scenes. The artist devoted many works to Kiev landscapes, and some of his works nostalgically return to Jewish shtetls, such as *Vinnytsia: The Yerusalimka District* and *Ghetto*.[104] From 1910 to 1915, Manevich lived in Switzerland, Italy, Great Britain, and France. He received international recognition after a successful exhibition at the Durand-Ruel Gallery in Paris in 1913. However, he declined offers to move to London or New York and returned to Kiev in 1915.[105] After the revolution, Manevich, along with the well-known Ukrainian artists Aleksandr Murashko, Fedor Krichevski, and Georgii Narbut, was elected as a professor of landscape art at the newly created Ukrainian Academy of Arts.[106] However, after his only son Boris was killed during the civil war in Ukraine in 1919, Manevich immigrated to the United States in 1921 with his wife and daughter. Manevich successfully continued his career in America with personal exhibitions in New York, Philadelphia, Chicago, Baltimore, Boston, Montreal, and Toronto. He died in New York in 1942. In 1928 the Russian Marxist thinker and the first Soviet Commissar of Enlightenment, Anatolii Vasilievich Lunacharsky (1875–1933), wrote that Manevich's art has "very deep Jewish roots. It is difficult to define these Jewish features. Manevich likes very much typical Jewish subjects: old semi-ruined synagogues… and small houses on hunchback shtetl streets…"[107]

JEWS IN HIGH AND POPULAR CULTURE IN KIEV

Jewish musicians and actors made significant contributions to the cultural life of Kiev, while Jewish merchants sponsored many cultural initiatives.

---

102 *Internet Encyclopedia of Ukraine*, s.v. Marko Robert Stech, "Manevich, Abram." http://www.encyclopediaofukraine.com.
103 Ol'ga Zhbankova, "Mag i charodei farb," http:judaica.kiev.ua/eg9/eg941.htm.
104 Marko Robert Stech, "Manevich, Abram."
105 Ibid.
106 Zhbankova, "Mag i charodei farb."
107 Ibid.

In the mid-nineteenth century, a local branch of the Imperial Russian Music Society opened in Kiev; it held concerts of classical music and aided gifted youth in receiving music education. The members of the society were professional musicians as well as music lovers. Among its members were Jewish merchants, including the Brodskys and Iohim Horowitz (1828-1906), the grandfather of one of the greatest pianists of the twentieth century—Vladimir Horowitz (1903-1989). Iohim Horowitz was a merchant of the first guild and owner of a trading firm in Podol. In 1874, he was elected one of the five directors of the Kiev Imperial Russian Music Society. However, his election was not approved in St. Petersburg, and he left the society the same year. He continued to patronize gifted Jewish youth, and provided money for scholarships for Jewish students of the Kiev music school.[108] According to a report of the Kiev Imperial Russian Music Society, 895 students studied in the Kiev music school in the 1912-1913 academic year, of which 445 were Jewish.[109] In 1913, the Kiev music school was transformed into the Kiev Conservatory. It prepared many famous musicians including Vladimir Horowitz. Vladimir began his professional music career in Kiev, where he gave his first concerts in the early 1920s. In 1925, he emigrated from the Soviet Union.

The acting and musical professions were quite popular among Kiev Jews, since they gave the temporary right of residence in the city during the performance season. Usually, if the troupe was successful, the right of residence could be extended for subsequent seasons. Jewish theaters and performances by Jewish troupes were forbidden in Russia between 1883 and 1905.[110] In 1905, Nicholas II lifted this prohibition. But even thereafter impresarios needed to obtain permission for their performances from the local administration. In practice it was quite difficult to obtain such permission. Jeffrey Veidlinger wrote that performances in Yiddish were forbidden in 1908 in Vilna, Siedlce, and Kiev. "A request to establish a Yiddish theater in Bialystok was dismissed out of

---

108 Iurii Zilberman and Iuia Smilianskaia, "Kievskaia uvertiura Vladimira Gorovitsa," *Yehupets* 6: (2000): 277-279; Iurii Zilberman and Iuia Smilianskaia, *Kievskaia simfonia Vladimira Gorovitsa* (Kiev: Fond Volodymyra Gorovytsia, 2002), 40-43.
109 Zilberman and Smilianskaia, "Kievskaia uvertiura Vladimira Gorovitsa," 283.
110 *Kratkaia evreiskaia entsiklopediia*, s.v. "Teatr," 8: 795-798.

hand in December 1908."[111] But in the same year, the Yiddish Theater opened in Odessa. Its founder was the well-known Yiddish playwright, Peretz Hirshbein. The Kaminska Yiddish troupe performed in St. Petersburg in 1908 and 1909 and "the theater was full every evening."[112] Thus, permission for performances by Yiddish troupes was dependent upon the local authorities' arbitrary decisions.

Sometimes Jewish troupes called themselves "Jewish German," and claimed to the authorities that they were performing in German, while they actually performed in Yiddish. For a while this ruse was effective. For example, in 1906 the "Jewish German" troupe of the impresario Semen Novikov received permission from the Kiev governor to perform twenty plays in German at the Chateau de Fleurs (Castle of Flowers) Theater in Kiev. The governor imposed only one condition: that all these "plays be performed exclusively in German without use of the Jewish jargon, and that, as soon as this condition is broken even once, further performances shall immediately be cancelled."[113] However, this condition was preposterous: neither the actors nor their audience—common Jewish people—understood much German. Therefore, the Jewish German troupes performed in Yiddish as usual. This ploy was soon discovered by the authorities, who subsequently forbade performances by Jewish German troupes in Kiev and the southwestern region. Kiev, Podolia, and Volhynia Governor-General V. A. Sukhomlinov[114] wrote in a circular to the governors reporting to him on July 26, 1908:

> I have been informed that the so-called Jewish German troupes, which are constituted exclusively of Jews who don't know German, cannot perform plays in German and use the Jewish jargon [i.e., Yiddish] instead.

---

111 Veidlinger, *Jewish Public Culture*, 181; Antony Polonsky, *The Jews in Poland and Russia, II: 1881 to 1914* (Oxford and Portland, OR: The Littman Library of Jewish Civilization, 2010), 399.
112 Ibid., 183.
113 TsDIAK U, f. 442, op. 636, d. 415, ll. 1–2.
114 Vladimir Aleksandrovich Sukhomlinov (1848–1926) was the Kiev, Podolia, and Volhynia governor-general in 1905–1908 and the Military Minister of Russia in 1909–1915.

Considering that the performance of theatrical plays in the Jewish language is absolutely intolerable in the southwestern region, I would like to ask Your Highness to warn the troupes' entrepreneurs, who already have my permission to put on performances in your province, that beginning with the coming winter theater season I consider it necessary to completely ban performances of German Jewish troupes in the region, and won't issue permission for any more such performances.

The people who received my permission previously can use them only until the beginning of September of this year.[115]

One of these Jewish German troupes came to Kiev in the summer of 1908. This was the well-known troupe of Abram (Avraham) Fishzon, which came at the invitation of an entrepreneur, Mr. Prikhod'ko, who rented the Summer Park "Hermitage" on Trukhanov Island to perform in the park's outdoor theater.[116] Fishzon also signed a contract for performances with the Bergon'e Theater (now the Russian Dramatic Theater) in downtown Kiev, where his troupe was supposed to perform the play *Di Shkhite* (The Slaughter) by Jacob Gordin.[117] Abram Fishzon was a pioneer of Yiddish professional theater in Russia. He had performed with the "Father of Yiddish Theater," Abraham Goldfaden, in 1876–1883. After the ban on Yiddish theater in Russia in 1883, they rechristened their troupe "German." However, Goldfaden soon left for America. Fishzon continued to tour cities and shtetls in Russia with his "German" troupe. It was rumored that Fishzon was so rich that he could bribe the authorities, who closed their eyes to the fact that his troupe really performed in Yiddish. But the Kiev authorities were a special case. Kiev, Podolia, and Volhynia Governor-General Sukhomlinov was a notorious anti-Semite, and before taking this government position, he had been chairman of the Kiev department of the

---

115 TsDIAK U, f. 442, op. 860, d. 67, l. 30.
116 Trukhanov Island, located in the middle of the Dnieper River, was and is the favorite place of Kievans during the summer season.
117 TsDIAK U, f. 442, op. 858, d. 2, part 1, l. 152.

monarchical Black Hundreds organization, *Russkoe Sobranie* (The Russian Assembly).[118]

Fishzon's troupe did not anticipate any trouble during their tour in Kiev. They came to Kiev in the beginning of July 1908, and were supposed to stay there for at least a month. Fishzon received advanced permission from the Kiev governor, and the troupe's repertoire was approved by the censors.[119] But, on July 24, 1908 (before the official prohibition of Yiddish performances by the governor-general), a policeman came to the theater before the performance, and demanded that the play be performed in German. Fishzon immediately sent a telegram to the governor-general in which he reported this incident, and said that he had to cancel the performance and refund the tickets. He begged the governor-general to allow his forty-person troupe to continue performances in Yiddish because otherwise they would be "doomed to starve to death."[120] Fishzon also sent the governor-general a copy of a long telegram that he had sent to Tsar Nicholas II on August 23, 1904, in which he had explained why performances in German were impossible: neither the Jewish actors nor the audience knew the language. Fishzon claimed that the local administration's demand that Jewish theaters perform in German was unrealistic and would leave the Jewish actors destitute.[121] It is unclear if Fishzon's telegram had any influence on Nicholas II's decision to lift the restriction on Yiddish performances in 1905, but it definitely did not have any influence on the governor-general.

Sukhomlinov wrote to the Kiev governor on July 25, 1908, stating that because nobody had yet rescinded the law of August 17, 1883 that prohibited performances in Yiddish, he forbade Fishzon from performing in the southwestern region.[122] The Kiev governor tried to justify the permission previously given to Fishzon's troupe. In his letter to the governor-general on July 31, 1908, he said that the performance of Yiddish plays was allowed in St. Petersburg and that he had asked for

---

118 "Kievskoe Russkoe Sobranie," *Khronos*, ed. Viacheslav Rumiantsev, http://www.hrono.info/organ/rossiya/kiev__ru__sobr.html.
119 TsDIAK U, f. 442, op. 858, d. 2, part 1, ll. 143–144.
120 Ibid.
121 Ibid., ll. 140, 142.
122 Ibid., l. 145.

instructions regarding this question from the Main Administration of Press Affairs. The Kiev governor received a telegram from its chairman on July 17, 1908, which stated that "plays in the Jewish jargon [Yiddish] are allowed to be performed on the stage using censored scripts."[123] However, neither Fishzon's petition nor the Kiev governor's explanation changed the opinion of the governor-general. He stated that the Kiev governor's permission was not sufficient; Fishzon must have his, the Governor-General's, permission for performances, which he denied.[124] Fishzon's explanations as to why Jewish troupes could not perform in German encouraged Sukhomlinov to ban performances of all Jewish German troupes in the southwestern region. The complexity of laws in Imperial Russia, and the numerous government circulars that often contradicted each other, gave local administrations ample justification for this kind of arbitrary decision. They could allow or deny the rights of Jewish people at any time, citing one law or another.

Jewish actors played in numerous Kiev Russian theaters and in the "Russko-Malorusskoi" (i.e., Ukrainian) troupe.[125] Jews also belonged to opera and operetta troupes that performed in the Kiev City, Bergon'e, Chateau de Fleurs, Hermitage, and Olympus theaters. Most Jewish actors had the right to temporary residence permits in Kiev, and many stayed for several theatrical seasons in row.[126] Jewish performers also came to Kiev as members of foreign troupes. For example, eight Jewish singers came to Kiev in 1908 with the Italian opera company of Julia Castellano.[127] Unlike those in local Jewish troupes, Jewish actors in Russian and foreign troupes easily received permission to stay in the city during their performances. The situation was the same with Jewish musicians, as long as they performed in Russian or in other non-Jewish orchestras. These musicians could obtain the right to live in the city, but Jewish culture was not welcome by the authorities in Kiev.[128]

---

123 Ibid., l. 138.
124 Ibid., ll. 145–146.
125 Ibid., f. 442, op. 630, d. 47, ll. 32–33.
126 Ibid., f. 442, op. 857, d. 246, ll. 1–3; op. 633, d. 44, ll. 27–28; op. 634, d. 48, ll. 1–37; op. 637, d.139, ll. 1–31; op. 638, d. 54, ll. 38–40.
127 Ibid., f. 442, op. 638, d. 54, l. 3.
128 Ibid., ll. 9–10, 33, 36.

Even the Jewish actors and musicians who performed in non-Jewish troupes and orchestras and who were granted temporary residence in Kiev were only allowed to live in remote poor districts like Lybedskoi and Plosskii, despite the fact that most of the theaters were downtown. On such conditions, the Kiev governor allowed twenty-two Jewish actors who performed in Bergon'e Theater's operetta troupe to temporarily live in the city in 1908.[129] Since there was no public transportation in these districts, it was costly and inconvenient for the Jewish actors to come to the theater every day. The Jewish actors were allowed to perform in one of the most prestigious Kiev theaters located downtown near Kreshchatik Street, providing entertainment for the city's elite; but after their performances they had to go to remote dirty city districts.

A historian of Yiddish theater, Bernhard Gorin, has noted that the Jewish intelligentsia in Russia "would go to the Russian or Polish theater and would never allow themselves to be found patronizing the Yiddish theater."[130] The Russified Jewish elite unquestionably considered Russian culture superior to Yiddish. But in the case of Kiev, local Jews did not have an alternative, since Yiddish performances, lectures, and concerts of Jewish music were not allowed. The authorities forced the Jewish intelligentsia toward further assimilation, and they did not care at all about the cultural needs of the poor Jews who did not understand Russian. Thus, the ban on Yiddish culture in the city deprived the poor Jews of cultural life.

The Jewish acculturated elite often attended Kiev Russian theaters. The sugar tycoon Leon Brodsky was so obsessed with the Russian theater that he purchased a theater building and leased it to Solovtsov's troupe, after which it was called Solovtsov's Theater. The building, which was constructed in 1898, is now the Ukrainian Drama Theater of Ivan Franko.[131] The theater presented many Russian and foreign plays, and was very popular among the Russian and Jewish elite. However, modern foreign plays often irritated the Orthodox clergy. They did not have the power to ban performances outright, but they bitterly

---

129 Ibid., 39.
130 Veidlinger, *Jewish Public Culture*, 182.
131 Kovalinskii, *Metsenaty Kieva*, 236.

denounced plays to the authorities. Kiev and Galich Metropolitan Flavian complained in a letter of September 5, 1906 to Kiev, Podolia, and Volhynia Governor-General Sukhomlinov about two new plays that were performed in Solovtsov's Theater: *The Joy of All Who Sorrow* (an Orthodox Christian honorific for Mary, the mother of Jesus) by Hiermann, and *The Miracle of Saint Anthony* by Maurice Maeterlinck.[132] The metropolitan had not seen the plays himself, but had heard about them from others. He claimed that the use of such titles for the plays was tantamount to committing blasphemy. The metropolitan said that while some Christians exited the theater in protest, "Jews, the worst enemies of Christ-God incarnate and of Christianity, loudly applauded the actors. Perhaps they made this demonstration because some Christians were leaving the theater."[133] The governor-general replied that he had banned both of these plays, and ordered that no blasphemous plays be performed in the future.[134]

Kiev's acculturated Jews loved not only theaters but also the circus, and often attended performances. A cartoon published in the 1880s depicts Solomon Brodsky (the brother of Leon and Lazar) as a "circus lover." The reason for Solomon's love of the circus was the gymnast Elvira, also shown in the cartoon. The unnamed cartoonist draws Brodsky offering Elvira his burning heart in one hand and 5,000 rubles in the other.[135]

Some of Kiev's circuses had permanent buildings, while others either rented theaters or set up temporary facilities. The Jewish contractor Kaplun specialized in the construction of such temporary circus facilities. He received permission from the city administration to build a circus downtown by his own means, with the agreement that he receive 25 percent of the circus' daily profit. After the end of the performance season, Kaplun dismantled the circus building and sold the leftover materials.[136] Sometimes, if several circuses simultaneously

---

132 Maurice Maeterlinck (1862–1949), a Belgian Symbolist poet, playwright, and essayist whose dramas are the outstanding works of Symbolist theatre. Maeterlinck was awarded the Nobel Prize for Literature in 1911.
133 YIVO, RG 80, folder 727, l. 62011.
134 Ibid., l. 62012.
135 O. V. Pataleev, *Staryi Kyiv. Zi spogadiv Starogo Grishnyka* (Kyiv: Lybid', 2008), 186.
136 Ibid., 183.

arrived in Kiev, some of them could not withstand the competition, and the performers, who could not cover the rent of the facilities, fled with their impresario without paying. Among the circus performers were many Jews.

Especially popular in Kiev was Albert Salamonskii's circus. Albert Salamonskii (1839–1913) was the owner and director of circuses in Moscow, Odessa, Riga, and Kiev. He was from a Jewish family of circus performers and began his career in Germany in 1862 as a circus equestrian; he then directed a circus in Berlin from 1873 to 1879. However, he decided that there were better prospects and less competition for the circus arts in Russia, and in 1879 he moved to Odessa and the next year to Moscow. In both cities, Salamonskii constructed new circus buildings that are still in use today. The circus in Odessa had a capacity of 4,000 and was built according to the latest architectural standards. It was heated by steam, had large stables, and a sewage system. The Salamonskii Circus specialized in pantomime. In January 1880, his Odessa troupe performed the pantomime "Julius Caesar in the Roman Arena," where the producer and performer in the title role was Salamonskii himself. Ol'ga Razina wrote that this pantomime was the most grandiose show seen in Odessa in all the years of circus performances.[137] After four months in Odessa, the Salamonskii Circus took "Julius Caesar" on tour to Berlin and Moscow. Salamonskii decided to settle down in Moscow and built the circus on Tsvetnoy Boulevard. The construction of the circus was rapid, and on October 12, 1880, the circus opened its doors to the public. The circus was exceedingly popular from its opening day. Salamonskii never rested on his laurels and attempted to monopolize the entire circus business in Russia. He "competed with the Italian Gaetano Chiniselli for the monopoly of circus in Russia. This standoff ended when Chiniselli died in 1881. Salamonskii settled in Moscow, leaving Saint Petersburg to Chiniselli's son, Andrea."[138]

However, in a few years new competitors appeared in Moscow in the form of the Nikitin brothers, who established their circus in 1886

---

137 Ol'ga Razina, "Tsirk, tsirk, tsirk…," *Odesski Vestnik*, May 12, 2009, 205-206.
138 Gérard Régnier (Jean Clair), ed., *The Great Parade: Portrait of the Great Artist as Clown* (New Haven: Yale University Press, 2004), 367.

near Salamonskii's. The competition between the two circuses was fierce. The Nikitin brothers appealed to the nationalistic feelings of the audience and emphasized that their circus was Russian, unlike the Jew Salamonskii's foreign circus. However, Salamonskii's circus survived and remained very popular due to its innovative programs. The circus historian Iu. A. Dmitrieva wrote that Salamonskii always tried to surprise and amaze the public. Among his sensational shows included the 1885 Magic Malevskii Show, which featured colored water fountains appearing on stage and creating figures. He also invited black musicians and gymnasts from a "remote island." In 1886, Miss Paula, "the Water Queen," spent several minutes in an aquarium among crocodiles and snakes. A group of bicyclists and "Texas Cowboys," inspired by the Wild West Show of Buffalo Bill (William F. Cody), was a great success.[139]

In the 1880s, Salamonskii opened a branch of his circus in Kiev, which like his other circuses was very popular. Salamonskii rented the building of the first stationary circus, Bergon'e. Aleksandr Pantaleev wrote that the program of Salamonskii's circus in Kiev was always notable for its originality and novelty, and attracted a sizeable audience.[140] After Salamonskii's death in 1913, his company was led by his widow Lina Shtern, who also became the director of the Moscow circus.

Jewish clowns, musicians, and gymnasts performed in other circuses that visited Kiev. The troupe of the famous animal trainer Vladimir Durov, which came from Moscow to Kiev in 1903, included thirteen Jewish musicians. The troupe's impresario Lev Ehrenburg asked the Kiev, Podolia, and Volhynia governor-general for permission for the thirteen Jewish musicians to stay in the city during the performance season, and his request was granted.[141]

Jewish youth who studied abroad often brought back Western innovations and influences to Russia. Sergei Andreevich Frenkel', who

---

139 Iu. A. Dmitrieva, *Tsuirk v Rossiii. Malen'kaia entsiklopedia. Tsirk*, 2nd ed. (Moscow: Sovetskaia entiklopedia, 1979), 165–169.
140 Pataleev, *Staryi Kyiv*, 183.
141 TsDIAK U, f. 442, op. 633, d. 44, l. 7.

studied in Belgian universities and became an electrical engineer, established an enterprise for the electrification of plants and factories in Kiev. In 1906, he founded the first company for showing movies in Kiev, and set up his own movie theater, *Luks* (Luxury), with 300 seats. Four years later, he transformed this company into the Joint-Stock Cinematograph Society "Sergei Andreevich Frenkel'," which had branches over all Russia "from Feodosiia to Tomsk and from Vil'no to Tashkent."[142] Each branch had a large collection of movies, including foreign films. These films were provided by foreign companies, and included exclusive rights to show them in Russia. His company's advertisements often stated that Frenkel' had a monopoly to show movies in Russia.[143] His company showed many foreign and Russian movies: comedies and dramas, love stories and thrillers. Frenkel' was personally acquainted with movie stars. In one photo he is seen with the famous French actor, Max Linder.[144]

Movies with Jewish themes were popular among Jewish audiences. For example, Frenkel''s company and the movie theater *Carmen* in the city Belaia Tserkov signed a contract in 1914 to show a series of films about Jewish life.[145] There was no shortage of such pictures. Three movies were shot about the Beilis affair, one documentary and two fictional pieces: *The Kiev Mystery or the Beilis Trial* (1913) directed by Iosif Soifer, and *Vera Chibiriak* (subtitled *The Blood Libel*, 1917) directed by Nikolai Breshko-Breshkovskii.[146] There were also films based on biblical stories—*Zhizn' Moiseia* (The Life of Moses), *Zhertvoprinoshenie Avraama* (The Sacrifice of Abraham), and *David and Saul*. There were many fictional films on modern Jewish life, which were usually tragedies such as *Rakhil'* (Rachel), *Tragediia evreiskoi kursistki* (The Tragedy of the Jewess Student), *Gore Sary* (The Grief of Sara), and *Kaznennyi zhizn'iu* (Executed by Life) with the subtitle *A Terrible Tragedy from the Life of Kiev Jews*.

---

142 Mikhail Kalnitsky, "Kino: Made in Kiev," *Vlast' Deneg*, no. 308 (May 2011), http://www.vd.net.ua/rubrics-7/15965/.
143 Ibid.
144 Yurii Morozov and Tatiana Derevianko, *Evreiskie kinematografisty Ukrainy, 1910–1945* (Kiev: Dukh i Litera, 2004), 19.
145 Ibid., 18–19.
146 Ibid., 58–61.

This last film was made at the Kiev movie studio *Svetoten'* (Chiaroscuro) in 1914, and unfortunately has not survived. The film's abstract says that it was a movie about Jewish youth, their struggle against old prejudices, and their search for new ideals. The film showed the conflict between the younger and older generations of Jews.[147] *Kaznennyi zhizn'iu* was shot by the leading director of *Svetoten'*, Iosif Abramovich Soifer, who also performed in the film. Soifer was a student of the renowned theatrical director Vsevolod Emilevich Meyerhold (1874–1940). Soifer began his career in 1907 in the Moscow Art Theater, but in 1910 he moved to Kiev to work in Solovtsov's Theater, and then began his career as a film director. During his Kiev years, 1910–1916, he made a series of pictures centered on Jewish themes.

Jewish movie directors and screenwriters made film adaptations of Jewish and world literary classics. In 1915, Soifer shot *Unizhennye i oskorblennye* (Humiliated and Insulted), based on the Dostoevsky novel. In the same year, Soifer made the movie *Rabyni roskoshi i mody* (Slaves of Luxury and Fashion). The script was written by Grigorii Naumovich Breitman, who was the editor of the Kiev newspaper *Poslednie novosti* (The Latest News). It was based on Emil Zola's *Au Bonheur des Dames* (The Ladies' Delight) combined with scandalous details exposed in Russian trial testimony concerning prostitution.[148]

The last Jewish film made by Soifer at *Svetoten'* was *Smert' na postoialom dvore* (Death at the Coach Inn) in 1916. Soifer then moved to Moscow. He returned to Ukraine for short time in 1918–1919, and in the early 1920s immigrated to Berlin and then to Paris. He continued his work as a film and theater director, but never returned to Jewish themes. When World War II began, he took the pseudonym Joseph Ossipoff. He survived the Nazi occupation of France, although he was arrested. In 1973, he visited the Soviet Union as a guest of the Moscow Film Festival.[149]

Jewish movie directors and the companies that showed their movies often ran into trouble with the authorities, who frequently

---

147 Ibid., 61–62.
148 Ibid., 62–63.
149 Ibid., 62–63, 67.

banned the showing of Jewish movies for a variety of reasons. *The Kiev Mystery or the Beilis Trial* (1913) was banned after its first screening. In a secret circular to the chiefs of police of Kiev province on October 17, 1913, the Kiev governor ordered: "do not allow on any pretext the showing of cinematograph pictures related to the Beilis affair. In the case of requests to show such pictures, they should be turned down without citing the order of the Minister."[150] Although the Kiev governor did not mention the title or name of the minister in question, we can assume that the order was given by Minister of the Interior Nikolai Alekseevich Maklakov, since other orders from that minister regarding the Beilis affair are located in the same archival folder. The producers of the movie *The Kiev Mystery or the Beilis Trial* successfully marketed the picture for screening in Western Europe and the United States after its ban in Russia.[151] Based on a decision of the synod, the censor also banned movies of biblical stories. The Black Hundreds and the Union of Russian People closely monitored enforcement of this decision.[152]

In spite of strict censorship, there were many movies focused on Jewish themes that had success among the public: both comedies and tragedies showing various aspects of Jewish life in Russia and abroad. These movies raised many pressing questions that were widely discussed in Jewish society: life in the Pale of the Settlement and beyond the Pale in the movies *L'Haim* (For Life) and *Tragediia evreiskoi kursistki* (The Tragedy of the Jewess Student); the problems of intermarriage and conversion in *Zhidovka-vykrestka* (The Converted Jewess) and *Rakhil* (Rachel); the conflict between generations and the struggle with old traditions in *Gore Sary* (The Grief of Sara) and *Kaznennyi zhizn'iu* (Executed by Life); Jewish prostitution in *Bog mesti* (The God of Vengeance), based on a play by Sholom Ash. Movies also depicted Jewish emigration from Russia and Jewish life abroad: *Za okeanom* (Beyond the Ocean), *Zhizn' evreev v Palestine* (The Life of Jews in Palestine), and *Zhizn' evreev v Amerike* (The Life of Jews in America).

---

150 TsDIAK U, f. 278, op. 1, d. 187, l. 134.
151 Mikhail Kalnitsky, "Kino: Made in Kiev," http://www.vd.net.ua/rubrics-7/15965/.
152 Morozov and Derevianko, *Evreiskie kinematografisty Ukrainy*, 26.

Jewish themes became fashionable, and Jewish movies attracted not only Jews but also the gentile public. For example, the movie *L'Haim* was successfully shown in cities where Jews comprised only a small minority.[153] The producers of Jewish-themed movies were both Jews and gentiles. For example, the movie *Za okeanom* was made by the Russian producer Dmitrii Ivanovich Kharitonov in Khar'kov in 1912. He based his film on a play by Jacob Gordin, and invited actors of Jewish theaters to perform in the movie.[154] Interest in movies overall, and in Jewish movies in particular, was so great in Russia that starting in 1907, the semimonthly trade journal *Cine-Phono* was published in Moscow, which covered the latest cinematographic news. The publisher was the Jew Samuil Viktorovich Lur'ie.[155]

THE ALL-RUSSIAN EXHIBITION OF 1913 IN KIEV

Even if Kiev could not match the highbrow culture of St. Petersburg and Moscow, Kiev industrialists and merchants were very proud of their achievements. This led to the idea of organizing an All-Russian Exhibition in Kiev. The editor of *Kievlianin*, Dmitrii Pikhno, proposed the exhibition in 1908. It took five years to raise the funds and prepare the exhibition, which had twenty-four departments representing industry, agriculture, sports, and science. There were over a hundred pavilions, some quite luxurious, and several decorative ponds with swans, classical statues, and illuminated fountains. The area of the exhibition was so large that visitors with children usually preferred to take the tram, which carried people around the pavilions. The Jewish industrialist, philanthropist, and tram company owner, David Semenovich Margolin, was a member of the committee for the preparation of the exhibition. For the convenience of visitors, he built tram rail lines through the exhibition and provided tram cars. However this was not a purely philanthropic initiative; the ride on the tram cost eight kopeks, earning a nifty profit for Margolin.[156]

---

153 Ibid., 27.
154 Ibid., 29–30.
155 Ibid., 71.
156 Aleksandr Anisimov, *Kiev i kievliane. Ia vyzovu liuboe iz stoletii…*(Kiev: Telegraph, 2003), II: 109–111.

The All-Russian Exhibition (May 29–October 15, 1913) as well as the All-Russian Olympic Games (August 20–30, 1913) in Kiev drew the attention of the entire Russian Empire. Over one million visitors attended the exhibition, while the population of Kiev was about half a million at that time.[157]

Many Kiev Jewish organizations participated in the exhibition, "some under pressure, others by their own initiative."[158] The exhibition was a prestigious project for the city, but it was supposed to be self-financing. Expenses for the construction of the exhibition pavilions were paid for by the organizations that used them; for this reason the city administration put pressure on Jewish community institutions to participate. The reluctance of some to sponsor or share pavilions could be explained by their reluctance to incur the expense, as well as by their anger about the Beilis affair that started in 1911 and the subsequent trial (September 25–October 28, 1913), which occurred simultaneously with the exhibition. According to Badanes, in other circumstances the Jews of Kiev and the southwestern region would have gladly provided examples of their production for the exhibition, and illustrated the spiritual and material life of Jews in these regions.

> But the present circumstances of Jewish life, the atmosphere of hostility and persecution, do not allow the communities and institutions of the region to devote much attention to this peaceful competition of various groups and their public organizations and institutions. Thus Jews have had a quite restrained attitude toward the exhibition.[159]

Nevertheless, several Kiev Jewish organizations did participate: the Jewish Charity Organization of the Kiev City Administration, the Boarding House for Jewish Children, Jewish Inexpensive Dining, the

---

157 Mikhail Kalnitsky, *V dolgakh i v shelkakh*, http://www.oldkiev.info/Delovoy__KIEV/Vserossiyskaya__vistavka.html.
158 Gershon Badanes, "Kievskaia Evreiskaia obshchina na vserossiiskoi vystavke 1913 g. v Kieve," *Vestnik evreiskoi obshchiny* 2 (1913): 29–42; 4 (1913): 18–25.
159 Badanes, "Kievskaia Evreiskaia obshchina na vserossiiskoi vystavke," 2 (1913): 29.

society "Drop of Milk," Jewish kindergartens, the Kiev Jewish hospital, the Brodsky Artisan School, the maternity hospital on Podol, the Zaitsev Surgical Hospital, and the Jewish sanatorium in Boiarka. There were also some Jewish names and names of Jewish enterprises represented in three of the exhibition departments: philanthropy, educational, and trade-industry. Jewish organizations provided pictures, tables, and posters for the exhibition, illustrating the work of Kiev Jewish philanthropic institutions that provided aid to the poor and sick.

Descriptions of the exhibition's other materials bring to light some features of Kiev Jewish society that are not revealed by other sources. For example, exhibition data indicates that seventy girls and no boys lived in the boarding house for children of the poorest Jews. The boarding house was originally designed for children of both genders. However, even the poorest Jewish families preferred to keep their boys at home, while girls seemingly had less value. Among the girls who lived in the boarding house were some with chronic illnesses (heart disease, tuberculosis, etc.). Poor Jewish families, which could not afford to provide medical aid for their sick girls, had handed them over to the boarding house.

Emphasizing the variety of Kiev Jewish philanthropic organizations, Badanes noted that many of them provided aid to the Jewish and gentile populations. In 1912 the society "Drop of Milk" gave free milk to 5,900 children—47 percent were Jewish and the other 53 percent gentile. The Kiev Jewish hospital, as well as other Jewish philanthropic organizations that were established and financed by Jewish merchants and from the basket tax, provided treatment not only for Jews but also for many gentiles.

Badanes did not approve of such charity. He said that while twenty-five or even fifteen years earlier it made some sense to provide aid to gentiles, now this was no longer true. After the bloody Kiev pogrom of 1905, and especially during the Beilis affair, tensions between the Jewish and gentile populations were heightened.[160] Some leaders of the Kiev Jewish community, such as Badanes, were pessimistic that

---

160 Natan Meir, "Jews, Ukrainians, and Russians in Kiev," *Slavic Review* 65, no. 3 (Fall 2006): 491.

Jewish philanthropy directed toward the gentile population would improve Jewish-gentile relations. Badanes bitterly noted that "in the city, where the libel about the use of the blood of Christian children by Jews again appeared...Jewish doctors used Jewish money to treat 396 Christian children in 1911 and 389 in 1912."[161]

Jewish educational institutions were represented at the exhibition by the Brodsky Artisan School and two Jewish kindergartens. The Jewish kindergartens exhibition was made quite carelessly: some children's clay works disintegrated, their drawings faded, and all was covered by dust. Badanes said that whoever prepared this exhibition had perhaps spent a couple hours on it and then forgot all about it. The exhibit of the Brodsky Artisan School was far more professional. It showed pictures of teachers, students, and the school museum, as well as student works. Badanes wrote that the school and its museum had grandiose facilities and were quite fancy. The people who had founded the school and its museum had traveled to Berlin, Vienna, Paris, and London to research museums and European schools, and embodied their experiences in this splendid school.

However, the Brodsky Artisan School's exhibit was the exception to the rule. The Kiev Jewish community generally emphasized in their exhibits not wealth but poverty, so as not to provoke the jealousy of gentiles. The Kiev Jews also highlighted their philanthropic activities and support for the poor Jewish and gentile population. Large Jewish businesses were not represented at the All-Russian Exhibition. This appears to have been intentional on the part of Jewish community leaders; they considered this appropriate due to the growing animosity of the gentile population during the Beilis affair.

CONCLUSION

In spite of the arrogance of St. Petersburg and Moscow intellectuals, Kiev had an active and varied cultural life. Kievans could find culture for all tastes: from highbrow philosophy, modern art, and classical music to popular culture: movies, theatrical performances, circuses,

---

161 Badanes, "Kievskaia Evreiskaia obshchina na vserossiiskoi Vystavke," 2 (1913): 42.

exhibitions, and sporting competitions. Kievan Jews enjoyed the diversity of urban culture and made many valuable contributions to it. Among Kievan Jews there were many actors, singers, and musicians in particular, because these professions gave them the right to temporary or permanent residence in the city. Kievan cultural life was nourished by generous donations from wealthy Jewish merchants. The brothers Lazar and Lev Brodsky, as well as David Margolin and Vladimir Ginsburg, donated many thousands of rubles for the promotion of Russian and Jewish culture in Kiev. They helped many Jewish writers, poets, artists, and historians receive the right to live in the city and financially supported them.

Certainly the strong anti-Semitism of the authorities and much of the gentile population, the pogroms of 1881 and 1905, and the Beilis affair created a very tense situation for Kievan Jews. The authorities continuously tried to suppress Jewish culture in the city, banning Jewish newspapers, theaters, and literature readings. State anti-Semitism and anti-Jewish violence in Kiev was reflected in the works of Jewish Kievan writers and artists; many of them left the city forever after the pogroms.

However, for many Kievan Jews the benefits of life in a large modern city outweighed their fear of anti-Semitism. Jews enjoyed, with other city inhabitants, the atmosphere of modernity in Kiev, which was totally absent in humble shtetls. With their works, Jewish writers, poets, and artists contributed to the creation of modern Kievan culture. Kievan Jews who studied and traveled abroad brought many European innovations and influences to the city, including electricity, cinema, public transportation, and modern architectural and artistic styles. Under their influence, Kiev became a more European and modern city.

Kievan Jews were diverse in their cultural tastes. The Russified Kiev Jewish elite preferred either Russian or European culture, while Jewish populist authors promoted Yiddish culture. Kiev, in the beginning of the twentieth century, became an arena of heated debates between Yiddishists and Hebraists. The diversity of the political and cultural views of Kiev Jewish intellectuals, and their debates about the future of Jews, were fruitful for the formation of modern Jewish national ideology and consciousness.

Many different national cultures were represented in Kiev: Russian, Ukrainian, Jewish, Polish, Czech, and German. There was a place for each of them in the city's cultural mosaic. In spite of all the efforts of the Imperial Russian authorities to Russify the city, Kiev always remained a multi-national and multi-cultural metropolis.

CHAPTER NINE

Between Tradition and Modernity: Jewish Religious Life in Kiev

> "That is Ilya, the rabbi's son," Mordkhe wheezed, turning the bloody flesh of his inflamed eyelids to me, "the damned son, the worst son, the disobedient son!"
> —Isaac Babel, "The Rabbi"[1]

JEWISH PRAYER HOUSES AND SYNAGOGUES IN KIEV

Jews in Kiev suffered from religious intolerance and government persecution. As described in chapter two, the thirteen-year-old daughter of Kiev Rabbi David Slutskii, Khaia, was kidnapped and forcibly converted to Orthodox Christianity. The first two synagogues that Jews built in Kiev in the early nineteenth century were destroyed: one by fire, and the other by the order of the local authorities after the expulsion of Jews from Kiev in 1835.

A few hundred Jews remained in Kiev in the years when Jews were officially not allowed to live there: soldiers of the Kiev garrison, army suppliers, and some workers and artisans. In 1849, the Kiev governor asked Kiev, Podolia, and Volhynia Governor-General Dmitrii Bibikov

---

1 Isaac Babel, *The Complete Works of Isaac Babel*, ed. Natalie Babel, trans. Peter Constantine (New York and London: W. W. Norton & Company, 2002), 236.

for permission to open a prayer house for eighty Jewish soldiers serving in the Kiev Arsenal. Bibikov replied that because Jews did not have the right of permanent residence in Kiev, the establishment of a special prayer house for Jews could not be allowed; however, their officers could provide a place for Jewish soldiers to pray.[2] As a result, five small prayer houses for Jewish soldiers functioned in Kiev during the mid-1850s, reporting to the Ministry of War.[3]

In 1859, a few categories of Jews were allowed to settle in Kiev and a Jewish community was reestablished in the city. On November 1, 1860, several Jewish merchants of the first guild applied to the authorities to open in Kiev a new prayer house with a ritual bath (*mikva*). The new Kiev, Podolia, and Volhynia governor-general, Count Illarion Vasil'chikov, was about to agree, but some gentile inhabitants of Kiev protested furiously against the construction of a Jewish prayer house in the holy Orthodox Christian city. It was therefore not allowed.[4]

Kiev Jews were only permitted to have small prayer houses inside private homes. Even the number of such prayer houses was limited by the authorities. Russian law allowed one *Beit-Hamedrash* (a house of study) for every thirty Jewish houses, and one *Beit-Hakneset* (synagogue) for every eighty Jewish houses. However, this provision only applied within the Pale of Settlement. Outside the Pale, synagogues and Jewish prayer houses could only be opened with permission from the Ministry of the Interior.[5] It was difficult to obtain this permission, especially in such a holy Orthodox Christian city as Kiev.

Jews tried to gain permission for construction of a synagogue in Kiev for almost thirty years. The fledgling Jewish community first sent a petition in 1866 for permission to build a synagogue in Kiev, which was not granted until 1895. During this period, they applied many times and their petitions were always rejected or ignored. In 1893, the minister of the interior, Ivan Nikolayevich Durnovo, decreed, "Jews

---

2 TsDIAK U, f. 442, op. 82, d. 385, ll. 1–2.
3 Mikhail Kalnitsky, *Sinagoga Kievskoi Iudeiskoi obschiny, 5656–5756. Istoricheskiy ocherk* (Kiev: Institut Iudaiki, 1996), 8–9.
4 Mikhail Kalnitsky, *Evreiskie adresa Kieva* (Kiev: Dukh i Litera, 2012), 32–33.
5 Kalnitsky, *Sinagoga Kievskoi Iudeiskoi obschiny, 5656–5756*, 12.

should not be allowed to build a permanent Jewish choral prayer house in the central part of Kiev, nor in any other city district."[6] There were already twelve Jewish prayer houses in Kiev, located in private houses and apartments. However, twelve small prayer houses were not nearly enough for the almost fifteen thousand Jews in Kiev. On November 8, 1894, the Kiev state rabbi, Evsei Tsukkerman, sent a petition on behalf of the Kiev Jewish community to the Kiev, Podolia, and Volhynia governor-general, Count Aleksei Ignat'ev, with a request to open a new prayer house in Kiev. Tsukkerman wrote in his petition,

> This is already the second year in which our children, and all Jewish youth who study in the local educational institutions, are not able to attend any prayer house and do not hear God's words, because the local legal Jewish prayer houses, located in rented apartments, are too crowded and inconvenient, and the local Jewish youth do not have the possibility of attending them.[7]

Governor-General Ignat'ev rejected this petition. He wrote to the Kiev governor on March 8, 1894 that he considered the request of the Kiev Jewish community unjustified.[8] The Kiev authorities thought that Kiev would be less attractive to Jews if there were fewer prayer houses there. However, new Jewish migrants continued to move to the city. They needed to gather somewhere to pray, so they opened illegal prayer houses that the authorities routinely closed.[9] The Jews who established these illegal public prayer houses faced criminal charges. An exception was not even made for the wealthiest Jews. The Kiev millionaires Lazar and Lev Brodsky, and the merchant of the first guild Iona Zaitsev, set up private prayer houses in their homes solely for members of their families. However, in 1902 the authorities questioned the

---

6   Ibid.
7   The Central Archives for the History of the Jewish People, Jerusalem (CAHJP), HM2/9894.20, l. 4.
8   Ibid., l. 6.
9   TsDIAK U, f. 442, op. 628, d. 102, ll. 7–8, 15; f. 442, op. 632, d. 482, ll. 1, 5–6, 17–18.

legality of these private prayer houses and decided to close them.[10] They initiated criminal proceedings against the seventy-five-year-old Iona Zaitsev, a hereditary honorary citizen of Kiev, for having an illegal prayer house in his home.[11] Zaitsev wrote in his petition to the governor-general on August 26, 1903 that he needed the private prayer house because his old age and poor health did not allow him to attend a public prayer house. Eventually, Zaitsev and the brothers Brodsky were allowed to keep their private prayer houses on the condition that they would only be used by members of their families. Governor-General Ignat'ev wrote in his resolution of Zaitsev's petition that if other Jews attended Zaitsev's private prayer house, he would face prosecution.[12]

The Kiev Jewish community was quite wealthy and could afford to build real synagogues in the city, but it was impossible to obtain permission. The Jews therefore had to circumvent the authorities. A wealthy Kiev Jew, Gabriel-Yakov Rozenberg, built a synagogue claiming, during construction, that it was a private house, albeit of a rather unusual design. When the synagogue was ready in 1895, he pretended that he suddenly decided to use the building as a synagogue. The authorities allowed this synagogue, which was in the Plosskaia part of the city where poor Jewish craftsmen lived. The synagogue received the official name of "Jewish Craftsmen's Prayer House # 10" (all Jewish prayer houses in Kiev were given official numbers).[13] The synagogue was built in an elaborate Moorish style by the architect Nikolai Gardenin and is still in use today.[14]

This synagogue was far from downtown Kiev where the wealthy Jews lived, and they could not reach it by foot on Sabbath and during Jewish holidays. Thus, they continued to petition the authorities for permission to build a choral synagogue in downtown Kiev. Finally, Lazar Brodsky received authorization and built the Choral Synagogue at 13 Malovasilkovskaya Street, which was opened in 1898. (The

---

10 Ibid., f. 442, op. 632, d. 482, ll. 1, 5–6.
11 Ibid., ll. 18–19.
12 Ibid., l. 17.
13 Kalnitsky, *Sinagoga Kievskoi Iudeiskoi obschiny*, 13–17.
14 Kalnitsky, *Evreiskie adresa Kieva*, 133–134.

construction of the synagogue is described in chapter four.) One year later, Lazar's brother Lev built the Merchant Synagogue on the same street. Then, in 1909–1910, one more synagogue was built by the Galitskii Jewish Society near the Jewish market. All other Jewish prayer houses in Kiev were located in private homes.[15]

Ironically, just as Kiev Jews were finally allowed to build their synagogues, the interest of Jews in religious life decreased in Kiev, as well as in the other large cities of the Russian Empire. The secretary of the board of the Kiev Choral Synagogue complained in a report in 1907 about the significant decrease in the synagogue's revenue: "without any doubt this shows the indifference of society towards this institution."[16] The Hebrew press reported in 1893 that Jewish students in Kiev "usually spent their Sabbath morning in Kiev cafés," not in the prayer houses.[17] In many ways the indifference of young Jews toward religion was the result of the secularization and forced assimilation of Jews, and the suppression of Jewish education and religious life in the city.

KIEV RABBIS

The local authorities intervened many times in the election of Kiev state rabbis until they completely undermined the prestige of this position.[18] In the 1860s–1890s, Kievan Jews still considered state rabbis to be religious experts and *shtadlans* in negotiations with the authorities. Later, because the authorities imposed upon them state rabbis who they did not respect, Kievan Jews lost interest in this institution.

In December 1862, Kiev Governor Pavel Gesse, on the recommendation of the Kiev chief of police, Fedor Ivensen, appointed Boruch Roisen as the Kiev state rabbi. Roisen came from Berdichev and was the son of a merchant. He had received his education in a Jewish school. However, the Kiev Jewish community refused to accept him as their rabbi. In their letter to Ivensen, Jewish community leaders wrote:

---

15 Ibid.; Vitaliy Kovalinsky, *Metsenaty Kyieva* (Kyiv: Kiy, 1998), 215.
16 [E. P. Kel'berin], *Desiatiletie Kievskogo Evreiskogo Horal'nogo molitvennogo doma. 1898–1907* (Kiev: I. M. Roset Publishing House, 1909), 29.
17 Meir, *Kiev, Jewish Metropolis*, 94.
18 *Kievskaia Mysl'*, September 1, 1911.

a rabbi should represent our spiritual interests and, because of this, the post should be held by a person respected by the society for which he works and he should be elected by the society. We do not have any respect for or trust in the merchant son Roisen. Because of this he cannot be our spiritual representative.[19]

The 1860s were a comparatively liberal time in Russia, the period of the "Great Reforms," when the authorities took public opinion into account to a certain extent. Accordingly, Roisen was dismissed and the Jewish community was allowed in March 1863 to elect a Kiev state rabbi, Evsei Avramovich Tsukkerman. His candidacy was proposed by the Jewish community. He was quite young, only twenty-two years old, but the Kiev Jewish community was itself young. Many Jews who moved to Kiev after the lifting of the ban on Jewish settlement were young and ambitious, and perhaps they wanted as their rabbi a person of their generation who could better understand their needs and interests. Tsukkerman, like all Kiev Jews at this time, was a newcomer; he was born in Starokonstantinov of Volhynia province, graduated from the Zhitomir Rabbinical Seminary in 1862, and came to the big city to make his career. His candidacy for the position of the Kiev state rabbi also pleased the authorities, since the Zhitomir Rabbinical Seminary had a reputation as a stronghold of the Haskalah and its alumni usually shared the government's ideas about the need to integrate Jews into Russian society. Tsukkerman was certainly a master of *shtadlanut* and compromise and, for quite a while, maintained good relations with both the Kiev Jewish elite and the authorities. This enabled him to hold his position for thirty-five years. Tsukkerman was frequently reelected and the authorities approved his reelections. During his tenure, Tsukkerman tried to establish new Jewish religious institutions in the city: synagogues, prayer houses, and religious schools. Chapter seven describes how Tsukkerman attempted to defend the existence of a Talmud-Torah disguised as an orphanage in the city. Tsukkerman petitioned the authorities many times to open a synagogue or at least an additional prayer house.

---

19 Kalnitsky, *Evreiskie adresa Kieva*, 34–35.

However, each time his initiative was rejected by the local administration. Tsukkerman was a classic maskil who believed in the traditional methods of *shtadlanut* and avoided open conflict with the authorities.

The government considered state rabbis as their agents who should promote state policies among the Jewish masses. For this reason, the authorities paid special attention to the elections of state rabbis to make sure only candidates loyal to them would be elected. According to government rules, the chief of police or his assistant was personally required to observe the elections.[20]

Elections of state rabbis and members of the boards of the prayer houses were held every three years. They were neither democratic nor direct. The synagogues and prayer houses elected representatives who then elected the state rabbi. This election was then subject to the authorities' approval. Only adult men twenty-five years and older, who paid a designated amount to the prayer house, could participate in the elections. According to the rules approved by the Ministry of the Interior in 1877, the Kiev Jewish electors were required to pay no less than ten rubles a year to their prayer houses, and had to legally reside in the city. By comparison, St. Petersburg Jewish electors were supposed to pay no less than twenty-five rubles a year.[21] In practice, the Jewish electorate in Kiev was even more exclusive: only Jewish merchants of the first guild and people with higher education were allowed to participate in the election.

Jewish artisans, who constituted the majority of the Jewish population in Kiev, were deprived of the right to vote. By the end of the nineteenth century, they began to struggle for their elective rights. On August 18, 1893, Jewish artisans sent a petition to the Kiev, Podolia, and Volhynia governor-general, in which they complained of anti-democratic practices in the state rabbi elections and asked for the right to participate. The Kiev province administration denied this request and the election of the state rabbi on October 6, 1893 was conducted according to the previous rules. Tsukkerman, who was the only candidate, was elected by a large majority (seventy-four votes in his favor and four

---

20 TsDIAK U, f. 442, op. 626, d. 506, ll. 18–23.
21 Ibid.

opposed) and was again approved by the local administration.²² In 1897, Tsukkerman was once again reelected for a new term. By now the number of electors had almost doubled (139 electors versus 78 in the previous election). However, there is no information about the social status of the electorate from this vote. Perhaps, taking into account the dissatisfaction of the Jewish artisans, the authorities had allowed some new categories of Jews (merchants of the second guild and Jewish artisans) to participate. Tsukkerman received 132 votes in favor and seven opposed.²³

For his long work as the Kiev state rabbi, Tsukkerman was granted the title of hereditary honorary citizen of Kiev in 1894.²⁴ This honor meant a lot for Kievan Jews, because it granted the right of permanent residence in the city not only for the person so honored, but also for the members of his family. But neither his previous achievement nor his exalted title could protect Tsukkerman from ultimately experiencing the authorities' wrath. Tsukkerman was summarily dismissed from his position by Fedor Fedorovich Trepov, the Kiev, Podolia, and Volhynia governor-general, after his speech at the opening ceremony of the Kiev Choral Synagogue on August 24, 1898.²⁵ (More details about this dismissal are provided in chapter four.) With the advent of the state policy of anti-Semitism in the 1880s, the previous methods of *shtadlanut* were no longer effective. It was no longer possible to negotiate agreements with the authorities. Even such a master of compromise as Tsukkerman was powerless in this new situation.

After Tsukkerman was sacked, new elections for the state rabbi were scheduled in Kiev. These took place on December 12, 1898, but the results were annulled because the representatives of one of the Kiev rabbinical districts, Demievka, did not participate. New elections took place on April 14, 1899, in which sixty-six electors voted.

These two elections were unique in that many candidates ran for the position of Kiev state rabbi. Ten candidates competed in the election of December 1898; by April 1899, only four candidates remained.

---

22 CAHJP, HM2/9894.15, ll. 2–15.
23 Kalnitsky, *Evreiskie adresa Kieva*, 35.
24 CAHJP, HM2/9894.12, l. 10.
25 [E. P. Kel'berin], *Desiatiletie Kievskogo Evreiskogo Horal'nogo molitvennogo doma. 1898–1907* (Kiev: I. M. Roset Printing House, 1909), 21.

In both elections, the majority of votes was received by Petr Abramovich Iampol'skii, whose candidacy was approved by the authorities. Iampol'skii was born in 1850, and was a graduate of the Imperial Military-Medical Academy. As a physician, Iampol'skii participated in the Russo-Turkish War of 1877–1878. After the war, he continued to serve in the army as a medical doctor. Iampol'skii retired from the army in 1888 and was elected as the state rabbi of Rostov-on-Don in the same year.[26] He was reelected twice and subsequently served as Kiev state rabbi between 1899 and 1902. According to the historian Azriel Shohat, "Iampol'skii may have been the first Palestinophile (member of Hovevei Zion) to be elected Crown rabbi."[27] Meir points out that Iampol'skii "[c]haracteristically for the older generation of Hovevei Zion…envisioned a synthesis between nationalism and religion that would attract Russian Jewish youth back to their roots and to their faith."[28] Iampol'skii delivered a series of lectures at the Brodsky Choral Synagogue, entitled *Spiritual Conversations*.[29] He told his audience that "if they wished to come to the aid of their nation, they had to learn about its history, religion and culture—and there could be no better teacher than the synagogue."[30] However, Iampol'skii's exhortations left the Kiev Jewish community indifferent. According to the community member Lev Shtammer, the Kiev Jewish community was quite unhappy with their new state rabbi, and that Iampol'skii "did more harm to the Jewish community in the three years of his service than Tsukkerman did in thirty-three years."[31] Iampol'skii charged high fees from poor Jews for his ritual services. In three years he registered over three hundred illegitimate children. When parents had even the slightest problem with their documents, Iampol'skii registered their children as illegitimate. Iampol'skii also published an article in the newspaper *Khronika Voskhoda* (Chronicle of Dawn, issue 34, 1899), in

---

26 *Kievlianin*, April 15, 1899.
27 Azriel Shohat, *Mosad ha-rabanut mi-ta'am be-Rusya* (Haifa: University of Haifa, 1975), 121, cited in Meir, *Kiev, Jewish Metropolis*, 271.
28 Ibid.
29 Ibid.
30 Ibid.
31 Shtammer, *Na sud obshchestvennogo mneniia*, 15.

which he defended the basket tax and talked about its fair use by the city administration. Shtammer called Iampol'skii's article a betrayal of the interests of the Kiev Jewish community, since the city administration used the money from the basket tax to finance the city police, which often made rounds-ups of Jews in Kiev.[32] The administration also used 3,000 rubles from the basket tax in 1899 to finance a public feast in honor of the opening of a new harbor in Kiev, while many Jews in Kiev lived in appalling poverty.[33] Due to his unpopularity among Kiev Jews, Iampol'skii served as the Kiev state rabbi for only one term.

In 1903, Solomon Arkad'evich (Kalmanovich) Lur'e was elected to the position of Kiev city rabbi. Lur'e had run for the position of Kiev state rabbi in 1899, but received only five votes (white balls) in favor and sixty-one (black balls) opposed.[34] In 1903, the electoral system was changed to allow all parishioners of Jewish prayer houses to participate.[35] Perhaps this helped Lur'e—who presented himself as the defender of the interests of poor Jews—to be elected. The Jewish public figure Avraam Gol'denberg commented:

> The vast majority of our intelligentsia do not belong to prayer houses. The same is true of our financial elite: most of our wealthy people have prayer houses in their homes. Because of this the parishioners of the prayer houses, and consequently their representatives for the election of rabbis, come from the lower class of uneducated people who more easily come under the influence of various election agitation tricks. Mr. Lur'e used this to displace Mr. Iampol'skii and become the rabbi. This has set against him the wealthier representatives of our community.[36]

---

32 Ibid., 18–19.
33 Ibid., 16–17.
34 *Kievlianin*, April 15, 1899.
35 Meir, *Kiev, Jewish Metropolis*, 272.
36 Kalnitsky, *Evreiskie adresa Kieva*, 40.

Gol'denberg was the *gabai* (warden) of the Kiev Choral Synagogue, and lawyer and advisor of Lazar Brodsky. Thus, he expressed the opinion of the Kiev Jewish elite, which was quite unhappy with the election of Lur'e. For the Jewish elite, Lur'e was too populist and radical in his political views. They worried that the new rabbi would undermine their authority. These fears were justified. The election of Lur'e showed that the Jewish elite had lost control over the Jewish masses. The period of the absolute authority of the "Jewish Kings" was in the past.

Lur'e was born in 1858 and belonged to the second generation of maskilim. He studied at a gymnasium and then at the St. Petersburg Institute of Railroad Engineers, and had worked as an engineer in Simferopol. In his political views, Lur'e was a populist and Palestinophile. He was well known for his literary works and had published poetry and prose in *Rassvet* (Dawn), *Voskhod*, *Russkii evrei* (Russian Jew), and other Russian Jewish and Hebrew periodicals. Lur'e was also the author of a book about the Jewish scientist and writer Chaim Zelig Slonimskii, a brochure *Budushchee v proshedshem. Palestinofil'stvo i obshchechelovecheskaia kul'tura* (Future in the Past. The Palestinophile Movement and World Culture, 1883), and had translated Heinrich Heine's poems into Hebrew.[37] During his Kiev years, he met Sholom Aleichem. (Lur'e was one of six people in the writer's circle of visitors according to a police report.[38]) According to Shtammer, common Kievan Jews respected Lur'e, "not as a religious authority, but as an honest man and a real defender of their interests."[39] However, the wealthy Jewish elite hated Lur'e, according to Shtammer, because he refused to kowtow to them. In fact, Lur'e not only refused to coordinate his work with the communal authorities; he had to effrontery to repeatedly denounce them to other members of the community and to government officials. Lur'e wrote in his appeal to parishioners of the Kiev prayer houses that

> A group of impostors has taken control over Jewish public money [i.e., the basket tax] and spends it without control! In the

---

37 *Evreiskaia Entsiklopedia*, s.v. "Lur'e, Solomon," 10: 388.
38 YIVO, RG 80, folder 728, doc. 62038.
39 Shtammer, *Na sud obshchestvennogo mneniia*, 20–21.

last few years the Kiev city rabbi [i.e., Lur'e himself] from time to time has raised his voice to unmask this cabal. The public began to listen to the rabbi's voice, and now the time is ripe to legally snatch this public pie from their sticky hands.[40]

The Kiev Jewish community faced enough problems in these years without Lur'e's agitation: the first Russian revolution increased anti-Semitism and violence, resulting in the pogrom of October 1905 during which one hundred Jews were killed, hundreds injured, and most Jewish property was stolen or destroyed. In these difficult times, instead of uniting the community, Lur'e incited poor Jews against the community elite and denounced the Jewish communal authorities to the government. The community leaders therefore did everything possible to remove Lur'e from the position of the Kiev state rabbi.

According to Shtammer and Lur'e, the Jewish elite proposed to the authorities to divide the Kiev rabbinate into two rabbinical districts, in this way depriving Lur'e of the position of Kiev state rabbi.[41] The Kiev Provincial Administration supported this request, perhaps because the government also disliked Lur'e's populist commotion and his instigation of the common Jews against the community's authorities. They may have been worried that the revolution on the Jewish street could turn into a revolt against all authority. Thus the fate of Lur'e was sealed; Kiev was divided into two rabbinical districts in 1906 and Lur'e resigned in protest. He tried to overturn this decision, sent complaints to the Senate, and appealed to the parishioners for help, but all was in vain.[42] The division of Kiev into two rabbinical districts further undermined the prestige of state rabbis among Kievan Jews. Eight of the fourteen Jewish prayer houses in Kiev protested against the new rabbinic organization.[43] However, the authorities did not reverse their decision.

---

40 YIVO, RG 80, folder 703, doc. 60668.
41 Ibid.; Shtammer, *Na sud obshchestvennogo mneniia*, 20–21.
42 Ibid.
43 YIVO, RG 80, folder 703, doc. 60668.

In this way, two rabbinical districts were established in Kiev 1906. The first rabbinical district included two elite city districts where wealthy Jews lived: the Pechersk and Dvortsovaia areas, as well as Lybedskaia and Bul'varnaia and the city suburbs Demievka, Shulyavka, and Solomenka, and also for a while Boiarka. The second rabbinical district included the city's districts where poor Jews lived: Podol and Ploskaia, as well as the Luk'ianovka and Starokievskaia areas of the city.

In the 1906 state rabbi elections in the first rabbinical district, the Kerch City Rabbi Aron Rabinovich received the majority of votes, but the authorities selected another candidate for the position, Avram Borisovich Gurevich, who received fewer votes. (Rabinovich received fifty-nine votes in favor and forty-two against; Gurevich received fifty-six in favor and forty-four opposed). The authorities preferred Gurevich because of his loyalty to the government. The Kiev police had information that Rabinovich belonged to a "radical Zionist party."[44] Kiev Vice-Governor Nikolai Nikolaevich Chikhachev wrote in his report to Kiev, Podolia, and Volhynia Governor-General Sukhomlinov that he had

> very complimentary information [about Gurevich]. The chief of the Kiev police…recommended the approval of Gurevich as a long-time Kiev resident, who was personally known to him, as a person with high morals, absolutely loyal and has great respect among the population. Professor [of Kiev St. Vladimir University K. G.] Tritshel personally recommended his former assistant Gurevich to the Provincial Administration as a very intelligent person, who sympathizes with the needs of poor Jews. It speaks well for Gurevich that he works as a doctor in a state position at the Kiev Mariinskii Community of Nurses and has received the state award "The Sign of the Red Cross."[45]

Several Kiev state rabbis elected after the forced resignation of Tsukkerman had secular professions: Iampol'skii and Gurevich were

---

44 TsDIAK U, f. 442, op. 637, d. 94, l. 3.
45 Ibid.; Kiev Mariinskii Community of Nurses was a clinic and hospital that provided free treatment for the poor.

medical doctors; Lur'e was an engineer. Gurevich, in addition to his position as a medical doctor at the Kiev Mariinskii Community of Nurses, was also the owner of a private mineral spa clinic, which cooperated with various Kiev hospitals.[46] What motivated them to become state rabbis? Perhaps the prestige of the position, closeness to the authorities, and the possibility of influencing Jewish public affairs.

Rabbi Gurevich regularly conducted services in the Kiev Choral and Merchant Synagogues, where the wealthy Kievan Jews came for prayer. He was also a member of the board of the Jewish Free Loan Society "Gmilus Hesed" in the 1910s. Gurevich actively participated in the public life of Kiev. He was a member of the Kiev Public Assembly and of the Kiev Society of the Friends of Peace, which was the first pacifist society in the Russian Empire. It seems that he enjoyed his position as state rabbi.

But the events of the first Russian revolution demonstrated that his loyalty to the government was not without limit. On April 5, 1905, the police detained him at an illegal meeting of the members of the "All-Russian Jewish Union."[47] This meeting took place in the apartment of a Dr. Paul at 4 Bolshaia Vasilkovskaia Street. Twenty-seven Jewish medical doctors and lawyers participated in the meeting, including the Kievan lawyer Grigorii Grigor'evich Bogrov, father of Dmitrii Bogrov, the assassin of Stolypin.[48] However, the detention of Avram Gurevich did not have any negative consequences for his career and he was not punished. Many members of the intelligentsia participated in similar illegal meetings during the first Russian revolution. The authorities focused on fighting their main enemies, the radical revolutionaries, and the liberal intelligentsia who attended such meetings mostly escaped punishment.

Rabbi Gurevich had more serious trouble with the authorities a few years later. On October 2, 1908, police came with a search warrant to Rabbi Gurevich's apartment on 40 Pushkinskaia Street and arrested his nineteen-year-old son Boris, a student of Kiev St. Vladimir

---

46 Ibid.
47 Ibid., f.1423, op. 1, d. 9, l. 6.
48 Ibid.

University. According to the newspaper *Kievlianin*, Rabbi Gurevich demanded that the policemen who searched his apartment leave the room and "expressed his demand in a rude way."[49] As a result of the police report, Gurevich was called to court. The case was heard on October 28, 1908 in the absence of Rabbi Gurevich, who did not show up. The court found him guilty and sentenced him to four days of imprisonment or a twenty ruble fine.[50]

In spite of this trouble, Gurevich was reelected several times to the position of Kiev state rabbi of the first district. He kept the position until at least 1919. The Polish writer Jarosław Iwaszkiewicz wrote in his memoirs that Rabbi Gurevich performed the wedding ceremony of the writer Ilia Ehrenburg and Lubov Kozintseva in Kiev in 1919.[51] Gurevich probably emigrated with his family from Kiev in the early 1920s. He died in 1924.

Iakov Aronovich Aleshkovskii was elected as the rabbi of the second Kiev rabbinical district in 1906. He was born in Moscow in 1872. Aleshkovskii was the grandson of Rabbi Chaim Berlin on his mother's side.[52] He was educated in his grandfather's house and at the Volozhin Yeshiva. Aleshkovskii received rabbinic ordination in 1894.[53] But a Jewish education even from the most famous yeshiva was not enough to receive the position of state rabbi in the Russian Empire. At the turn of twentieth century, candidates for these positions were supposed to have a diploma from an eight-year gymnasium or a university. When Aleshkovskii attempted to receive the state rabbi position in Kiev for the first time in 1900, the authorities rejected him because he only had a certificate of graduation from a six-year gymnasium.[54]

---

49 *Kievlianin*, November 3, 1908.
50 Ibid.
51 Yaroslav Ivashkevich, "Vospominaniia ob Ehrenburge," *Voprosy literatury* 1 (1984): 200.
52 Chaim Berlin (b. 1832, Volozhin, Vilenskaia province; d. 1912, Jerusalem) was the rabbi in Moscow from 1865 to 1885 and in Elisavetgrad from 1892 to 1906. In 1889–1892, Berlin led the rabbinical court in Volozhin. He made his aliyah to Eretz-Israel in 1906. Chaim Berlin was the main rabbi of the Ashkenaz community in Jerusalem. *Rossiiskaia evreiskaia entsiklopedia*, s.v. "Berlin Khaim" 1: 122.
53 *Rossiiskaia evreiskaia entsiklopedia*, s.v. "Aleshkovskii Iakov," 1: 40.
54 Russian State Historical Archive, St. Petersburg (RGIA, St. Petersburg), f. 821, op. 8, d. 54, ll. 86–94.

Evidently, he soon received the necessary diploma because in 1903–1904, Aleshkovskii was the state rabbi in the city of Aleksandria, Kherson province. He then moved to Kiev where he held the position of state rabbi from 1906 to 1920. During these years, he also worked as inspector of Kiev Jewish community schools. Aleshkovskii studied law at the Kiev St. Vladimir University and received his doctorate in 1917.[55]

In his political views, Aleshkovskii was a religious Zionist. He was one of the leaders of the Zionist religious movement *Mizrahi* and later a member of the "Zionist Center of Ukraine." After the collapse of the monarchy in Russia and the creation of the independent Ukrainian People's Republic, Aleshkovskii was active in the new Jewish communal and national institutions. In 1917, Aleshkovskii became a member of the Technical Commission for the Organization of the Election of the Kiev Jewish Community Board. In 1917–1919, he became first a member and then vice president of the Jewish National Advisory Board of Ukraine. After the establishment of the Soviet regime in Ukraine, Aleshkovskii moved to Warsaw in 1921. There he became a leader of the movement *Mizrahi*. He was elected to the party's central ruling organs in Warsaw, and was the secretary of the world movement *Mizrahi* in Europe. In 1925, Aleshkovskii declined an offer to become the rabbi of Helsinki and moved to Eretz Israel where he became an educator. He settled in Tel Aviv, where he founded and became the principal of a Jewish girls' school, later the pedagogical seminary for girls *Talpiot*. Aleshkovskii was also the leader of the *Mizrahi* movement in Eretz Israel, and the chairman of the Tel Aviv branch of this movement. He died in Tel Aviv in 1946.[56]

Perhaps the most unusual fact in the biographies of Kiev State Rabbis Gurevich and Aleshkovskii was their meeting with Tsar Nicholas II. At the end of August and the beginning of September 1911, Nicholas II visited Kiev with Prime Minister Petr Stolypin as part of an official tour for the celebration of the fiftieth anniversary of the liberation of the serfs. Nicholas II was supposed to consecrate the monument to the tsar-liberator Alexander II in Kiev, which had been erected in honor of the anniversary.

---

55 *Rossiiskaia evreiskaia entsiklopedia*, s.v. "Aleshkovskii Iakov," 1: 40.
56 Ibid.

During the preparation for the tsar's visit to Kiev and the southwestern region of the Russian Empire, many delegations from a wide variety of organizations and groups asked to meet the tsar. One of these petitions was from representatives of the Jewish population of Kiev, which was submitted by Gurevich, who requested permission for "presentation to the tsar of a Jewish prayer book or Torah."[57] This petition was approved and the presentation was included in the official program of the tsar's visit.[58] Originally, the delegations requested permission to meet the tsar at the Kiev railway station, but because of security concerns this plan was not approved.[59] Instead, a reception was scheduled at the tsar's Kiev residence, Mariinskii Palace, on the first day of his visit, August 29, 1911, and meetings with the delegations on the second day of his visit. The printed program and detailed descriptions of the visit in newspapers make it possible to establish the chronology of events.

THE TSAR'S MEETING WITH THE JEWISH DELEGATION

Monday, August 29 at 4 pm was the scheduled time for the reception in the tsar's palace, which included representatives of the Orthodox clergy, military and civil administration, noblemen of the southwestern region, two professors of Kiev St. Vladimir University and Kiev Polytechnic Institute, representatives of the non-Orthodox clergy (including the rabbis), and foreign consuls. On the next day, at 2:30 pm, a parade was planned to take place in front of the tsar's palace in Kiev, including an introduction of the delegations: "1) from the peasants of the southwestern region with their syndics...with bread and salt from each province; 2) from the bridge builders of the city Kiev with bread and salt; 3) from city residents; 4) from two sects of Old Believers; and 5) from Jews—the rabbi, who will bring the Holy Torah to the tsar with two assistants."[60]

The meeting of the Jewish delegation with the tsar was described in the announcements section of the liberal Kiev newspaper *Kievskaia*

---

57 TsDIAK U, f. 442, op. 641, d. 35, part I, l. 909.
58 Ibid.
59 Ibid., 572.
60 Ibid., ll. 865–867.

Mysl' and the conservative *Kievlianin* on September 1, 1911. The texts of both of these publications are identical. The announcement said:

THE VISIT OF HIS IMPERIAL MAJESTY TO KIEV DEPUTATION FROM THE JEWISH POPULATION OF KIEV

On 30 August the three-person deputation from the Jewish population of Kiev consisting of State Rabbi A. B. Gurevich, Rabbi Ia. M. Aleshkovskii and barrister Goldenberg had the good fortune to be introduced to His Majesty the Emperor. State Rabbi A. B. Gurevich had the good fortune to appeal to His Majesty the Emperor with the following words: "Your Emperor Majesty, Most Gracious Sovereign, the Jewish population of Kiev has the infinite happiness to have the possibility in our person to throw ourselves to the feet of Your Imperial Majesty filled with our expression of infinitely loyal feelings, which inspires us together with all other nations of the great immense Russia. In each Jewish prayer-house, whether it be the beautiful choral synagogue in the lively capital or a modest holy cloister prayer-house in the depth of a country Jewish shtetl— we Jews each Saturday invariably send sincere prayers to Heaven, we appeal to God for the health, prosperity and well-being of Your Imperial Majesty and all the Royal Family. King Solomon bequeathed to us the wise words: 'Let us pray for the prosperity of the High Authority,' and the prophet Jeremiah in his epistle to his coreligionists wrote: '...let us take care for the peace of the country where we live and let us pray for its prosperity, because in its peace is your peace and its boon is your boon.'" Then Rabbi A. B. Gurevich had the good fortune to bring to the Tsar the scrolls of the Holy Torah and to add the following words: "Please give us the pleasure, Most Gracious Sovereign, of receiving from us the eternal witness of our prayers, the most holy, valuable and dear thing in our life—the Holy Torah." His Majesty the Emperor most graciously deigned to accept the Torah, and to thank the deputation, and ordered that His gratitude be conveyed to the Jewish population of Kiev for the expressions of their feelings and for the presented Torah.

Tsar Nicholas II came to Kiev during the Beilis affair, when Mendel' Beilis had already been imprisoned for more than a month. The city was in a pre-pogrom condition: the Black Hundreds were calling for revenge against the Jews for the ritual murder. However, neither Gurevich nor the other members of the Jewish deputation, Aleshkovskii and Gol'denberg, said a word about the serious problems facing the Kiev Jewish community. Gurevich's obsequious appeal to the tsar and presentation of the Torah scrolls angered many liberal and radical Jews in Kiev. Many Kievan Jews could not forget, and never forgave, the state rabbis. Six years later, in 1917, during the Convention of Jewish Organizations in Kiev, the delegation from Bund refused to stand in honor of the "Holy Torah Scrolls." David Zaslavskii, a Jewish publicist and member of the Central Committee of the Bund, explained the position of the Bund delegation in his pamphlet "The Response to Rabbis." He wrote:

> Why don't you bury *those* scrolls?...Because they are witnesses of your shame. If only those scrolls could speak—away from here! they would say. You sold us into shame, you made slaves of us...you fine Jews and guardians of religion—you bowed to the earthly god, to the idol of autocracy and you brought a sacrifice of your holy Torah scrolls....For pogroms—a Torah to the Tsar; for exiles—a Torah to the Tsar; for the Beilis trial—a Torah to the Tsar....With hatred in your hearts and a hypocritical smile on your lips you presented your Torahs to the Tsar...you trembled like slaves, like beaten dogs, and thereby profaned your own holiness...The people did not ask you to do this....Slaves you were and slaves you have remained.[61]

---

61 Zvi Y. Gitelman, *Jewish Nationality and Soviet Politics: The Jewish Sections of the CPSU, 1917-1930* (Princeton, NJ: Princeton University Press, 1972), 296. David Zaslavskii, who so stridently accused the Kiev rabbis, was not himself a person of immutable principles. Zaslavskii (1880-1965) changed his political views

Why did Gurevich initiate the meeting of the Jewish deputation with the tsar? Perhaps he thought that this meeting might show the local Black Hundreds that Jews are also loyal subjects of the Russian Empire, and that the highest authorities accepted the Jewish delegation. Perhaps he thought that after acceptance of the Jewish delegation by the tsar, the Black Hundreds would not dare to attack Jews in Kiev. An even more interesting question is why the authorities accepted Gurevich's request for a meeting of the Jewish deputation with the tsar. 1910 saw the beginning of a new rise of the revolutionary movement in Russia in which Jews participated significantly. Thus, the Stolypin government began to seek the support of the Jewish clergy, thinking that they could return radical Jewish youth back towards traditional Jewish values.

However, the state rabbis did not have any real authority or influence among Jews. The government intervened for a long time in the religious life of Jews, appointing state rabbis completely obedient to the authorities. The Jews therefore looked at state rabbis as government agents. Shtammer wrote in 1908 that "a state rabbi is something like a religious policeman and does not have any authority among Jews."[62] The anonymous author of an article in the Yiddish newspaper *Dos Folk*

---

many times during his life. He was a social-democrat from 1900, then a member of the Bund from 1903, and later a member of the Central Committee of the Bund. In 1922–1932, he wrote a number of articles on Jewish themes, which were published in the Soviet Jewish press. In 1924, he published in *Pravda* a letter expressing his complete solidarity with Bolshevik policies and began to write actively in the communist press. In 1934, he joined the Communist Party. He had journalistic talent and provided unwavering support for Soviet policies. These two qualities allowed him to become one of the most popular Soviet journalists in the 1930s–1950s. In his articles, Zaslavskii defamed the prominent Russian poets Osip Mandel'shtam and Leonid Pasternak when they were persecuted and repressed by the Soviet authorities. He blamed the Kiev rabbis for their compromise with the tsar. But he accepted far worst compromises with the Soviet regime. In the beginning of his journalist career, he called the Kiev rabbis "slaves." Thirty years later he did not dare to say anything about the tragedy of Jewish people during the Second World War, when he wrote articles about the cruelty of the Nazi regime on the occupied territory. In the 1950s, according to the shifting directions of Soviet policy, Zaslavskii furiously criticized the State of Israel. His faithfulness to the Soviet regime allowed Zaslavskii to avoid arrest and repression in the Stalin years.

62 Shtammer, *Na sud obshchestvennogo mneniia*, 20.

(The People) on December 22, 1906 provides an even sharper critique of the state rabbis. He called them "evil worms" and declared, "No respectable person would dirty his hands in this business, where consciences are bought and sold for a penny!"[63]

While the radical youth seems to have broken completely with Jewish religion and tradition at the end of the nineteenth century, there were still a significant number of religious Jews in Kiev. Who were their spiritual leaders?

As elsewhere in the Tsarist Empire, observant Kievan Jews were divided into Hasidim and Misnagdim. Kievan Hasidim belonged to many different sects. Many Kiev Hasidim were followers of the *tsaddikim* of the Twersky Hasidic dynasty who lived in various shtetls of the southwestern region.[64] According to Meir,

> There were also Polish and Lithuanian Hasidim of various stripes, the latter including Chabad or Lubavich Hasidim. Indeed, in 1866 *Kievlianin* reported that Kiev's Jewish leaders were attempting to install a grandson of the Hasidic leader Menahem Mendl of Lubavich as rabbi.[65]

The Chernobyl prayer house functioned in Kiev in the 1880s and "a cemetery consecration dispute between the Lithuanians and the Hasidim of Kiev" took place in 1892.[66]

However, according to the memoirs of Yekhezkel Kotik, who lived in Kiev from the late 1870s to the early 1880s, Kiev Hasidim did not strictly follow religious rules and were quite superstitious. Kotik recalled that his neighbor, "the wealthy Jew-Hasid sat with his guests-Hasidim on the porch on Saturday and smoked cigars."[67] But they talked about Hasidic rebbes and miracle-workers. When a Roma

---

63 *Dos Falk*, December 22, 1906, cited in Meir, *Kiev, Jewish Metropolis*, 284.
64 Meir, *Kiev, Jewish Metropolis*, 30.
65 Ibid., 31.
66 Ibid.
67 Yekhezkel Kotik, *Moi vospominaniia. Skitaias' i stranstvuia* (Moscow and Jerusalem: Mosty kul'tury. Gesharim, 2012), 200.

woman passed by they called her and asked her to predict their future.[68] Kotik came to conclusion that

> Most Kiev Hasidim were far from true Hasidism, they didn't know anything about Hasid and Hasidism, and did not travel to the rebbe...The only thing that tied Kiev Hasidim to Hasidism was their faith in miracles...they believed in magic, diablos, fortune-telling by cards and Gypsies, and other palm-readers, and so on.[69]

Sometimes travelling preachers, maggidim, came to Kiev. Kotik recalled that the Horodner Maggid from Minsk visited Kiev and stayed in his house.[70] He wrote that among various "Jewish groups in the city, the Lithuanians were the most stable and secure; they played an important role in Kiev, and had 'the best businesses, the finest synagogues, the most aristocratic Jews, and the most respectable rabbi.'"[71]

The division of Kiev Jews into Polish, Lithuanian, Chernobyl, and other groups showed that the majority of Jews in Kiev in the 1870s were newcomers who still identified themselves with their places of origin. Meir explains,

> No doubt for many Jewish migrants to Kiev, the prayer house served as a *landsmanshaft* (society of fellow townsmen), where the artisan or broker could take refuge from the anonymity and impersonality of the big city and mingle with like-minded people from the same town.[72]

Only by the turn of the twentieth century did the children of Jewish migrants in Kiev develop a strong Kievan identity and became quite proud of it.

---

68 Ibid., 199.
69 Ibid.
70 Ibid., 214.
71 Meir, *Kiev, Jewish Metropolis*, 31.
72 Ibid.

The most respected rabbis among Kievan Jews were the spiritual rabbis whom the Jews elected themselves. However, with the exception of the spiritual rabbi Shlomo (Solomon) Aronson, there is no information about them. The spiritual rabbis did not report to the authorities and Jews hid them by all possible means from the government. Such secrecy was necessary because the spiritual rabbis did not have the right of residence in Kiev. The number of Jewish clergy in Kiev was strictly restricted by the authorities and did not include the spiritual rabbis.[73] These rabbis either lived illegally in Kiev or had the right of residence in the city as merchants or artisans.

However, when Stolypin's government changed its attitude toward the Jewish clergy, seeing in them allies in the struggle against the revolutionary movement, Jews could finally legalize their spiritual rabbis. In 1906–1921, the Kiev spiritual rabbi was Shlomo (Solomon) Aronson (1862–1935). He was born in the town Krucha of Mogilev province into the family of the local rabbi Iakov Aronson. Shlomo received a traditional Jewish education, and at the age of fifteen he began to teach Talmud in the yeshiva of the town Liady, where his father was the *rosh-yeshiva* (Head of the yeshiva). In 1887 Shlomo Aronson became rabbi of the town Glukhov, in 1897 rabbi of the city Nezhin, and in 1906 the spiritual rabbi of Kiev.[74] In the late nineteenth and early twentieth century, even Orthodox Jews could not stay away from political movements. In his youth Aronson was a Palestinophile and "active in the *Hovevei Zion* movement, attending its conventions as a delegate."[75] Later, Aronson became a religious Zionist and joined the Mizrachi movement. Aronson published several articles in the Hebrew newspaper *Ha-Melits* (The Advocate) defending political Zionism against the attacks of its ultra-Orthodox opponents. Unlike the Kiev state rabbis, Aronson had a reputation as a defender of Jewish interests. He "frequently interceded with the Czarist authorities on behalf of the Jews."[76] Aronson and the Moscow rabbi Iakov Maze participated as

---

73 TsDIAK U, f.442, op. 532, d. 304, ll. 207–215.
74 *Rossiiskaia Evreiskaia Entsiklopedia*, s.v. "Aronson, Shlomo," 1: 63.
75 *Encyclopedia Judaica*, 2nd ed., s.v. "Aronson, Solomon," 2: 488.
76 Ibid.

religious consultants in the legal defense of Mendel' Beilis. Before the Beilis trial, Aronson and the lawyer Arnold Margolin met with the chairman of the Club of Russian Nationalists, Vasilii Chernov. They persuaded Chernov of the innocence of Beilis. Chernov together with Shul'gin co-edited the newspaper *Kievlianin* and they refused to publish any materials in support of the anti-Semitic campaign against Beilis.[77] Furthermore (as was described in chapter six), on the third day of the trial, September 27, 1913, Shul'gin published in the *Kievlianin* his article in defense of Beilis.[78]

During World War I Aronson worked for the relief of refugees from Galicia, who arrived in Kiev. After the February 1917 Revolution he established the nationalist-religious *Ahdut Israel* movement. In 1921 he immigrated to Berlin, where he served as rabbi of the Russian Jewish community. In 1923 he moved to Eretz Israel, where he was the chief Ashkenazic rabbi of Tel Aviv and Jaffa. He also took an active part in the Mizrachi movement and continued to help Russian Jewish immigrants, creating various welfare institutions for them.[79]

FATHERS AND SONS

The secularization and assimilation processes among Kievan Jews began as soon as the Jewish community was reestablished in the city in the 1860s. There were several factors that promoted these processes. Life itself in a large city required Jews to make some concessions in Jewish observance. Most of the businesses, plants, factories, and stores in Kiev belonged to Christians and operated six days a week, including Saturday. Poor Jews could not always find a job at Jewish enterprises and had to accept employment in businesses that worked on Saturdays. Kosher meat was available in Kiev, but it was more expensive as its price included the basket tax. Poor Jews, who could not afford to eat meat every day and whose children were often hungry, had to decide whether to pay extra for kosher meat.

---

77 Robert Berg, "Delo Beilisa splotilo evreev," http://www.jewish.ru/history/facts/2013/10/news994321376.php.
78 Victoria Khiterer, "Vasilii Shulgin and the Jewish Question: An Assessment of Shulgin's Anti-Semitism," *On the Jewish Street* 1, no. 2 (2011): 10.
79 *Encyclopedia Judaica*, 2nd ed., s.v. "Aronson, Solomon," 2: 489.

The well-to-do Jews had other temptations: there were many fancy cafés and restaurants in the city that were clearly not kosher. As already mentioned, acculturated Jewish youth often spent Saturday mornings in such cafés at the turn of the twentieth century.[80]

In addition to the financial pressures and temptations of the large city, the government assimilation policy had success at least among Jewish wealthy and educated circles. The ban on Jewish schools in the city forced the Kiev Jewish elite to send their children to Russian gymnasiums and universities. Many children from poor Jewish families remained without any education and were quite ignorant of Judaism and Jewish traditions. Before the early twentieth century, when the tsarist authorities finally realized that it was not the religious Jews but the radicals who were their real enemies, religious Jews were regularly targets for persecution by the police.

The Kiev police seem to have taken special Judeophobic pleasure in making round-ups of Jews on Saturdays. Izrail′ Beniaminovich Grinshtein wrote a petition on behalf of the Kiev Jewish community to the new Kiev, Podolia, and Volhynia governor-general, Mikhail Ivanovich Chertkov, on March 15, 1879 about the situation of Jews in Kiev under his predecessors.[81] Through this petition, he intended to draw the attention of the new governor-general to the precarious situation of Jews in Kiev. Grinshtein claimed in his note that the Kiev police particularly liked to make rounds-up of Jews on Saturdays. The police arrested hundreds of Jews in their places of rest and then escorted them to the local police station under the guard of Cossacks and soldiers. Because of the shortage of room in the police station, they were usually kept in the damp yard under guard all night.[82]

Only the next morning did the police decide who of those arrested were legal and who illegal. According to Grinshtein, the police arrested Jews so suddenly that they did not even have time to pick up their passports. The following morning, the wives and children of the arrested Jews brought their passports to the police station. The police then

---

80 Meir, *Kiev Jewish Metropolis*, 94.
81 TsDIAK U, f. 442, op. 829, d. 51, ll. 1–4.
82 Ibid.

released the legal Jewish residents and sent the illegal residents to prison. However, those illegal Jews who had money to bribe the police were released, while the others were expelled from the city.[83]

According to Grinshtein and Kotik, Governor-General Chertkov (September 1877–January 1881) was a kind man and was against round-ups of Jews.[84] Kotik wrote that Chertkov once was an eyewitness of a "procession" of arrested Jews escorted by police in Podol.

> There were old and young, women and children.
> The governor-general stopped the procession and asked the policemen, "Who are these arrested people?"
> "These are the Jews taken in the round-up, Your Excellency," the policeman answered.
> Chertkov winced.
> "Round-ups are for animals," he said with repugnance, and forbade round-ups [of Jews].[85]

However the governor-general's order did not stop the police, since the round-ups were a major source of income for the police as described earlier. However, during the Chertkov years, the police had to disguise these round-ups as searches for criminals. Grinshtein wrote in his note that the police, pretending they were searching for criminals, broke into Jewish houses and checked the documents of Jews, arresting illegal residents if they did not pay bribes.[86]

When Kotik arrived in Kiev in the late 1870s, he heard from local Jews that in a previous year the police had arrested "an entire synagogue of Jews" during the Kol Nidrei prayer on Yom Kippur.[87] Perhaps it was convenient for the police to arrest all the Jews gathered together in one place.

---

83 Ibid.
84 Ibid.; Kotik, *Moi vospominaniia*, 204.
85 Kotik, *Moi vospominaniia*, 204.
86 TsDIAK U, f. 442, op.829, d. 51, ll. 1–4.
87 Kotik, *Moi vospominaniia*, 188.

The Russian authorities, through their persecution of Jewish religious life, pushed Jews toward assimilation and secularization. In Kiev, it was much easier to break with Judaism than to follow the traditional religious way of life. Jews who broke with tradition had a better chance of finding a job in a Christian business, could avoid the burden of the basket tax, and were less likely to be arrested. At the turn of the twentieth century, many young Jews in Kiev—raised without Jewish education or knowledge of Judaism—broke with traditional ways of life.

While the Russian authorities could celebrate the success of their assimilation policy, they soon realized that they had created their own mortal enemies—Jewish radicals. Certainty, not all Jews who broke with Judaism joined the radical movement, but a significant number did. The first radical Jewish youth in Russia appeared in the 1860s and 1870s under the influence of populist and nihilist ideas of Russian radicals. Kotik described a few such Jewish radicals in his memoirs. One of them was the son of his wealthy Jewish neighbor, a fifteen-year-old student in the fifth grade of a Kiev gymnasium. He decided that his mission was "to save Russia."[88] A policeman, Mikhailov, received an order to detain the boy and bring him to the police station. However, Mikhailov accepted a bribe of 500 rubles from the boy's father, who said he could save the boy from imprisonment if the boy would denounce his radical views and tell the police that he no longer had any illegal literature. The boy refused to do so, saying he would state openly that "he is not satisfied with the current system of government."[89] The father then asked Kotik to persuade his son to reject his radical views. Mikhailov allowed two hours for him to do so. But all was in vain; the boy insisted upon his views: "the people are more important than individuals, and even if he would be executed or burned alive, he did not care, if this would be useful for the people."[90] The boy was therefore arrested and imprisoned for a significant period of time. His mother died from grief during his imprisonment. When the boy returned home from prison, he was so

---

88 Ibid., 206.
89 Ibid.
90 Ibid.

traumatized by his imprisonment and his mother's death that he became very depressed and never recovered.[91]

Kotik depicted in his memoirs the radical student Lipskii, who boarded in his house. Lipskii was the son of a Vilna *dayan* (religious judge). Because he wanted to receive a secular education, Lipskii fled from home. He went to Kiev to study at Kiev St. Vladimir University, but he also had to earn a living. During the day he worked as a loader at the Brodsky mill, while at night he prepared for the entrance exam.[92] One day Lazar Brodsky came to the mill and was surprised to see a Jewish loader. Lipskii described his meeting with Brodsky as follows:

> He found out that I am a Jew and was very surprised: how is it possible a Jewish young man is not afraid to carry the sacks together with the tramps! He called me and asked where I am from and if I don't have a better way to make the means for life than carry sacks with flour? A Jew is physically weak.[93]

Lipskii told Brodsky that he came to Kiev to study at the university. Brodsky took from his pocket fifty rubles and gave it to him. This was a significant sum, equal to four months' salary at the mill (where Lipskii made sixty kopeks a day). However, he refused to take the money, and instead of showing gratitude he insulted Brodsky, telling him that he wanted to earn money only by his own labor, and that he hates wealthy people and does not want any favors from them.[94]

Kotik wrote that Lipskii was one of the first socialists to appear on the Jewish street.[95] As a Jewish socialist, Lipskii decided to struggle against anti-Semitism in Kiev, but in this struggle he could not succeed without the help of the capitalist Brodsky. An anti-Semitic dramatic troupe came to Kiev and performed with great success a play insulting

---

91 Ibid.
92 Ibid., 210–211.
93 Ibid., 212.
94 Ibid.
95 Ibid., 213.

Jews to the laughter and applause of the audience. Lipskii, on Kotik's advice, asked for Brodsky's support to stop the play's performance at the Kiev theater. Brodsky purchased two thirds of the tickets and gave them for free to Jewish students on the condition that they would whistle and jeer at the play. As soon as the play began the following night, the Jews began to whistle and stamp their feet. Kiev's chief of police was in the theater and fearing a big scandal, he ordered the play to be stopped. Twenty Jewish students including Lipskii were arrested.

The next day, Lazar Brodsky and two other Jewish millionaires visited Governor-General Chertkov and told him that the troupe instigated hatred among different nations, setting one against the other. The governor-general sent for the director and ordered his troupe to leave Kiev within twenty-four hours. The arrested Jews were released.[96] Thus, the struggle with anti-Semitism sometimes united Kievan Jews who at other times were divided by religion and politics. Many years later, the Beilis affair united Kievan Jews again.

Being a socialist, Lipskii was "a big *apikoires* [atheist]," and Kotik decided to set up a debate between Lipskii and his other tenant, the Horodner Maggid. The debate turned out badly: Lipskii insulted the Maggid, screaming and laughing, and did not let him talk. "The Maggid became pale and could not find words…The end was completely disgusting. When the Maggid began to talk about miracles Lipskii leaped up, spat and impudently shouted: 'An Old Fool!'—and ran away from the room."[97]

After the debate the Maggid refused talk to Kotik and left his house the next day. Kotik concluded that it was not a great idea to organize such debates, since the two generations could not come to an agreement. The gap between generations grew even wider with time. The open violence against Jews on Kiev's streets during the pogroms of 1881 and 1905 as well as the Beilis affair demonstrated the total failure of the policy of *shtadlanut*. The Jewish communal and religious leaders who failed to protect their communities from violence and government persecution lost their authority in the eyes of the young generation.

---

96   Ibid., 212–213.
97   Ibid., 216.

Subsequently, young Jewish radicals flooded Jewish streets. Many older Jews who were accustomed to respecting state authorities were concerned that these young radicals might bring further troubles to the Jewish community. A group of such conservative Kiev Jews wrote an anonymous denunciation (they signed it "Jewish non-Zionists") to the chief of the Kiev province Gendarme Administration on October 1, 1903. They complained that in the Podol district and in the suburb Demievka there had appeared dangerous groups of socialists and Zionists who were seducing their children with anti-government propaganda. The denouncers provided the names and addresses of the members of these illegal groups and asked the chief of the Kiev province Gendarme Administration to take "the strictest measures" against them.[98]

Jewish radical youth actively participated in the Russian Revolution of 1905 and created self-defense detachments during the October 1905 pogrom in Kiev. The older generation of Kievan Jews, who worried about the consequences of Jewish self-defense actions, attempted in vain to stop their sons. During the pogrom, the Jewish self-defense units were helpless because, as illegal military units, they were fired on by the regular troops. The self-defense members soon gave up their positions and ran away. A violent crowd then attacked even more furiously the remaining Jewish population. In this way events developed in Demievka, where the young officer Vasilii Shul'gin came with his battalion. Shul'gin claimed that the "troops had to preserve 'neutrality,' and while saving the Jews we had to behave in such a way to give the Russian population no excuse to think 'the Yids bought off the officers.'"[99] Shul'gin stayed in the house of an old religious Jew in Demievka with whom he talked about the pogrom and Jewish self-defense. Shul'gin, as well as the Russian authorities, still believed that the older generation of religious Jews could persuade their youth to abandon the revolutionary movement. He told the old religious Jew that they, the elders, should stop their radical youth. The old man "jumped up" at Shul'gin's words and said:

---

98   YIVO, RG 80, folder 725, doc. 61870.
99   V. V. Shul'gin, *Days of the Russian Revolution: Memoirs From the Right*, ed. and trans. Bruce F. Adams (Gulf Breeze, Florida: Academic International Press, 1990), 34.

"Your honor! What can we do? You think they want to listen to us? Your honor! You know, it's a real misfortune. They come to my house. Who? The punks! They say 'Give!' And I have to give. They say 'self defense!' And we give for self defense. Well you know, your honor, what they did in Demievka, those scum?! 'Self defense!' How they can throw bombs! They're so smart! And when pogrom came, where was the self defense? Those lousy punks shot, shot and ran away. They ran away, and we stayed behind. They did the shooting and we got beaten. Lousy punks! 'Self defense!'"

"Nonetheless, you have to control your youth." [Shul'gin replied]

"Your honor, how can we control them! I am an old Jew. I go to synagogue. I know my Law. I have God in my heart. But these boys! They grab a bomb, go out and kill! There is your revolution! Your honor! Believe me, an old Jew. You say there aren't ten thousand of them [i.e., Jewish radicals]. Well then?! What's the problem?! Every one of the mangy scum, all of them, ought to be hanged like dogs! There's nothing else for it, your honor."

Since then, [Shul'gin wrote] whenever anyone asked me who is the worst Black Hundreder in Russia, I always remember that old Jew.[100]

Neither the persuasion of Jewish religious authorities, nor repression by the government, nor pogroms of the Black Hundreds could stop the Jewish radicals. The Kiev rabbis could not control even their own sons, who broke with the traditional religious lifestyle. The biography of Gurevich's son Boris was described in the previous chapter. The son of the Kiev state rabbi Lur'e, Iurii Larin (revolutionary pseudonym of Mikhail [Ikhil-Mikhl] Zalmanovich Lur'e, 1882–1932), became a prominent member of the social-democrat movement in Russia. The twenty-year-old Iurii Larin was arrested in 1903 for participation in the

---

100 Ibid., 35.

social-democratic movement and was sentenced to eight years of exile in Siberia. The next year, Larin fled from his exile to Switzerland, but during the first Russian revolution of 1905 he illegally returned to continue his revolutionary work in Kiev, St. Petersburg, and other cities. In 1913, Larin was arrested a second time for his revolutionary activities. He was soon released due to poor health, and lived in exile abroad. After the February 1917 Revolution, Larin returned to Russia, and from 1917 to 1921 he held some important administrative positions in the Soviet state: he was one of the creators of the State Planning Committee and member of its presidium, and a member of the presidium of the All-Union Economic People's Council. Larin also devoted attention to the difficult economic situation of Jews in the Soviet Union. He thought that the situation could be improved if Jews settled on the land. In 1923, Larin proposed the creation of Jewish agricultural settlements in Crimea, Ukraine, and Belorussia. Larin also wrote several books on the Jewish question in the Soviet Union, including *Evrei i antisemitism v SSSR* (The Jews and anti-Semitism in the USSR).[101]

The son of the Kiev spiritual rabbi Shlomo Aronson, Boris (Ber) Aronson (1898–1980), became a famous American stage designer. Boris was "one of ten children of the Grand Rabbi of Kiev [as the spiritual rabbi was known, to show his superiority over the state rabbis], he enjoyed the privilege, denied to Jews of less exalted status prior to 1917, of living in a relatively sophisticated city."[102] The Jews who lived in Kiev under the tsarist regime never forgot that they enjoyed a great privilege of living in this city. However, this privilege was not associated entirely with wealth, and the Grand Rabbi of Kiev was a man of modest means. Boris Aronson recalled that in his childhood he shared his bedroom with his three brothers. He wrote that his father was "a very educated man who knew Dostoevsky's and Tolstoy's writings very well, but had nothing to do with the visual arts."[103] The rabbi sent his

---

101 O. Sukhomlinova, *Iu. Larin* (Moscow: Istoki, 1989); A. L. Filonenko, *Vremia Iu. Larina* (St. Petersburg: Nestor, 1996); Iu. Larin, *Evrei i antisemitism v SSSR* (Moscow and Leningrad: Gosudarstvennoe izdatel'stvo, 1929).

102 Frank Rich with Lisa Aronson, *The Theatre Art of Boris Aronson* (New York: Alfred A. Knopf, 1987), 3.

103 Ibid., 4.

son to a traditional Jewish religious school, but the boy soon rebelled "against the orthodoxy of his father's way of life."[104]

> Boris chose his own nickname for himself—"the Outlaw"— and periodically ran away from home. Once, his father sent one of his brothers, Yanya, to find him. "It was known that he hung out at the Café Francois, an artists' haunt," Yanya recalled. "I found him there—expecting that he'd surely be in questionable company or imbibing hard stuff. But Boris was sitting by himself, drinking tea with milk. At the time I couldn't understand why he had run away when he could have had the same tea at home."[105]

Even Boris himself could not completely explain how he became obsessed with the theater, but it definitely happened under the influence of both Jewish and gentile cultural life in Kiev. Boris Aronson wrote,

> Perhaps it was the Purim plays I put on for my very large family—to get their holiday money. Perhaps it was the day I wandered into the Kiev Opera House and saw its magnificent curtain with a large peacock painted on it. I don't know if it was the curtain or the curiosity about what was behind it that made me run home and complain, "Here I am, ten years old, and I have not yet seen an opera!" This was where I belonged, that's all I knew, and I kept on crying.[106]

A few years later, Aronson enrolled at the Kiev art school, where he also obtained a general high school education. Under the influence of the Kiev artist Aleksandra Ekster, Aronson developed an interest in avant-garde art, especially constructivism. In 1921, Aronson moved to Moscow, where he met the directors of the Russian avant-garde theaters, Vsevolod

---
104 Ibid.
105 Ibid.
106 Ibid.

Meyerhold and Alexander Tairov, who also influenced him. He could have continued his artistic career in Moscow, but the young ambitious artist dreamt about America, which represented for him the pinnacle of the technological civilization that inspired his artistic creativity.

With false papers Aronson crossed the Russian border in 1922, stayed for a while in Poland and Berlin, and arrived in America in 1923.[107] He settled in New York and worked first as a scenic designer for Yiddish theaters and later for Broadway plays and musicals, including *The Diary of Anne Frank*, *Fiddler on the Roof*, *Cabaret*, and many others. He won the Drama Desk Award for Outstanding Set Design three times and the Tony Award for Scenic Design six times.

During his youth Aronson broke with the Orthodox Jewish way of life, but he never abandoned *Yiddishkeit*: images of Orthodox Jews and Jewish shtetls appeared in many of his avant-garde works. Critics continue to debate what most influenced Aronson: Jewish culture, Russian constructivism, or modern European Art? Elements of all are represented in his set designs. But there is no doubt that Aronson, as with many Kievan Jews of his generation, was first of all influenced by the urbanism and modernity that city life provided.

CONCLUSION

Nobody could stop modernity and its influence on new generations of Kievan Jews: not the state, spiritual rabbis, the government, or the Black Hundreds. In the early twentieth century, among young Kievan Jews the desire to live a modern life eclipsed the traditional religious values of their fathers. Kievan Jewish youth were interested in various aspects of modern life: some of them joined different political and national movements, while others became obsessed with modern art and technological innovations. And many of them considered the traditional lifestyle of their fathers to be an archaic obstacle blocking the way to the modern world.

The assimilation and secularization of Kiev Jews began in the second half of the nineteenth century. For a long time the government

---

107 Ibid., 8.

supported these processes as part of their struggle against "Jewish fanaticism and isolation." However, when the government realized that in place of "religious fanatics" arose Jewish radicals, they tried to change their policy toward the Jewish clergy. Stolypin, Shul'gin, and other Russian conservative nationalists naïvely hoped that the Jewish religious authorities could return the young generation to the traditional Jewish Orthodox way of life. However, this was a conservative utopia: the secularization processes among the Jewish youth had gone so far that nobody could make them revert.

The alliance between the conservative part of Jewish society and the government, which Stolypin proposed, did not last for long. On September 1, 1911, two days after the meeting of the Jewish delegation with Nicholas II in Kiev, the Jewish revolutionary Dmitrii Bogrov shot and mortally wounded Stolypin. This assassination symbolically ended the tsarist government's hopes that the Jewish religious authorities could persuade Jewish youth to abandon the revolutionary movement.

Conclusion

The Kiev Jewish community had many unique features compared to other Jewish urban communities in the Russian Empire. Nowhere else beyond the Pale did the Jewish population reach so high a percentage as in Kiev. The location of Kiev in the "heart of the Pale of Settlement" created a continuous influx of Jews to the city from the nearby shtetls and provincial towns. Local authorities continuously expelled illegal Jews from Kiev, and periodically some categories once legal were redefined as illegal. But, in spite of the authorities' restrictive measures and the frequent expulsions, the Jewish population grew, reaching 87,240 people or 15 percent of the city's total population in 1917.[1] In comparison, 34,995 Jews lived in St. Petersburg in 1910, comprising 1.8 percent of the total population.[2] The population of Moscow in 1912 included 15,353 Jews out of 1,617,157 residents—less than 1 percent of the total.

Jewish magnates, merchants, and brokers were very visible in Kiev and played an important role in the development of the city and its economy. The percentage of Jews among Kiev merchants and industrialists was significantly higher than the percentage of Jews in the total population. The high profile of the Jewish magnates, their luxurious lifestyle, the construction of two lavish synagogues in downtown Kiev, and the presence in the city of thousands of illegal Jewish residents caused anti-Semites to label Kiev a "Jewish city." Beginning in the 1860s when Jews were again allowed to settle in Kiev after their expulsion in 1835, Kiev Judeophobes became concerned that if all restrictions were lifted on Jewish residence in the city, the Jews would quickly outnumber the Christians.

Kiev was a Jewish city as well as a hostile place for Jews—Yehupets. While Jewish magnates were very visible, the Jewish middle class and poor Jews suffered from the high cost of living in Kiev, and thousands of illegal Jews trembled every night in attics and basements awaiting

---

1 *Kratkaia evreiskaia entsiklopediia*, s.v. "Kiev," 4: 771.
2 Iu. Snopov and A. Klempert, comps., *Evrei v Moskve. Sbornik materialov* (Moscow and Jerusalem: Gesharim, 2003), 378.

round-ups and eviction by the police. The illegal status of many Jews in Kiev caused the police to act in an arbitrary manner toward all Jews and encouraged widespread bribery among the authorities. The situation of Kiev Jews was more onerous than in other places of the Russian Empire due to state anti-Semitism mixed with the religious intolerance in this "holy Christian Orthodox city." But ultimately Kievan Jews suffered from the same system of state persecution as all Jews in the tsarist empire. According to Prime Minister Sergei Witte,

> Thus, the multitude of Jewish laws generate a mix of uncertainties with the possibility of a wide variety of interpretations. Therefore, on this basis, various arbitrary and contradictory interpretations have been created. The result is widespread bribery. The administration does not take from anybody else as many bribes as it receives from Jews. In some places a special bribery tax system has been created for Yids. Certainly, in this situation, all the pressure of the anti-Jewish measures are laid on the poorest class. The wealthier a Jew is, the more easily he makes the payoffs.[3]

However, Kievan Jews did not complain very much about the bribes. They were more afraid of authorities who did not take bribes, because this always meant the expulsion of thousands of illegal Jews from the city. During those periods when the authorities and police acted in connivance with the illegal Jewish residents, bribes helped many illegal Jews to stay in Kiev for a long time or even to legalize their status. Other times, when the high and local authorities took an uncompromising Judeophobic position, mass expulsions of Jews followed.

All Jews were expelled from Kiev by the order of Tsar Nicholas I in 1835. There were two partial expulsions of Jews from Kiev in 1886 and 1910, when several thousand Jewish families were evicted.[4] Jews

---
3   S. Iu. Witte, "Evreiskii vopros i russkaia revoliutsiia," in *Russkii antisemitism i evrei*, comp. A. Flegon and Yu. Naumov (London: Flegon Press, 1968), 36–37.
4   S. M. Dubnov, *History of the Jews* (South Brunswick, NJ: T. Yoseloff, 1973), 5: 553, 768.

were expelled during the reign of Nicholas I not only from Kiev but also from Nikolaev, Sevastopol', Kurland, and Lethland. The majority of Moscow Jews—almost twenty thousand of twenty-six thousand—were expelled in 1891.[5] But each time after such an expulsion, the economic life in Kiev and in other places deteriorated, prices rose, and the local gentile population expressed their dissatisfaction. The local authorities would then find an excuse to bring back, at least temporarily, Jewish merchants and artisans. During periods when the high officials were more tolerant toward Jews, the Kiev, Podolia, and Volhynia governors-general and Kiev governors stated openly that Jews were useful for the city economy, and that without them it was impossible to develop normal trade and industry.

After permission was granted for some categories of Jews to reside in Kiev in 1859–1861, which enabled the creation of a new Jewish community, Jewish merchants and industrialists contributed greatly to the modernization and development of the city's economy. Some of the companies established by Kiev Jews even had regional and country-wide economic significance, such as Brodsky's sugar corporation that produced in the 1890s one quarter of all the sugar in the Russian Empire, Margolin's shipping company on the Dnieper River, and Marshak's internationally recognized jewelry factory. Other Jewish enterprises were very important for the development of the city itself, including Lev Borisovich Ginzburg's construction company, which built the most fancy public buildings and the most fashionable elite residential apartments in Kiev at the turn of the twentieth century. Thousands of Jewish merchants and peddlers provided necessary goods for the city's population. At the end of the 1880s, Jewish industrialists produced one quarter of the gross revenue of all factories and plants in Kiev.[6] Jews contributed to the development of public transportation (Margolin's tram company) and free health care. The Kiev Jewish hospital, subsidized by the Jewish community, provided free treatment for both Jewish and gentile patients. Jewish investments in the economy and the work of Jewish

---

5   *Evreiskaia Entsiklopediia*, s.v. "Kiev," 9: 528.
6   Ibid., 9: 527–528.

companies supported the transformation of Kiev from a provincial town into a modern European city by the turn of the twentieth century.

Jewish entrepreneurs and merchants also received many benefits from life in Kiev. The city was the major commercial and industrial hub of the region. Businesses could be developed there with a high profile and merchants found in Kiev large markets for selling their goods. Bank loans allowed many businessmen to open their own enterprises. Their closeness to the local authorities helped wealthy Jewish entrepreneurs establish important business connections, and the most successful entrepreneurs became very rich in one or two generations. Kiev had a reputation as a city where it was possible to quickly make money. This attracted thousands of poor provincial Jews, who lived illegally in the city hoping to find financial success and happiness. However, the realities of life crushed the majority of these dreams. Many lived in Kiev below the poverty level and without legal status, a profession, or any regular income.

A number of Kiev Jewish philanthropic organizations attempted to help the poor Jewish population. They provided various kinds of financial aid and gave small loans to individual Jewish artisans for the establishment of businesses. However, these organizations were unable to overcome Jewish poverty in the city. Its roots were in the lawless status of many Jews and restrictions on the education of Jews. The resulting poor qualifications or absence of a profession was typical for many poor Jewish people.

Poor Jewish families were allowed to live in the districts Plosskii, Lybedskoi, and Podol, all far from downtown. This isolated their inhabitants from downtown businesses and enterprises, where they could potentially find a job. They lived too far to walk there and could not afford to spend money for a carriage. The poor Jewish families lived in horrible hygienic conditions, and tuberculosis was a common cause of death among them. However, in describing the misfortune of the poor Jewish population in Kiev, we should keep in mind that the Kiev Jewish community was one of the wealthiest in the Russian Empire, and the economic situation of Jews in many other communities was even worse than in Kiev.

The leaders of the Kiev Jewish community put a lot of effort and expense into improving the situation of poor Jews and protecting all Kievan Jews from further expulsions and persecution. The skillful *shtadlan* diplomacy of the leader of the Kiev Jewish community, Lazar Brodsky, was quite successful. During his presidency (1890s–1904), he was able to prevent major Jewish expulsions from the city and anti-Jewish violence. However, after his death, when his brother Leon became the leader of the Kiev Jewish community, state anti-Semitism and anti-Jewish violence increased both in Kiev and throughout the Russian Empire. Jewish community leaders then began their confrontation with the local anti-Semitic authorities and turned their efforts to the support of Jewish emigration from Imperial Russia.

In spite of the restrictions, persecutions, and anti-Semitism of the local administration and much of the gentile population, Kiev remained attractive to Jews, which is proved by the constantly growing number of Jews in the city up to the February 1917 Revolution. In Kiev, a Jew had a better chance than in an overcrowded shtetl to establish his own business, get a job, receive a gymnasium and university education, enter a profession, and enjoy all the benefits of city life with its recreation, concerts, clubs, and theaters. Wealthy Jews lived in Kiev in luxury, built mansions, synagogues, and clubs, and owned boats, trams, and dachas. But in the days of pogroms and anti-Jewish violence, all Kievan Jews shared the same fate: in those days, Yehupets overwhelmed the Jewish city. Wealthy and poor Jews had an equal chance of becoming victims of the rioters. The wealthy descendants of the Brodsky and Baron Ginsburg families were beaten in the streets of the elite Kiev district of Pechersk, as were poor Jews in the Podol and Galitskii market districts. The mansions of wealthy Jews were ransacked and vandalized, as were the humble houses and apartments of poor Jews.

The government policy of Russification and the prohibition of Jewish religious, educational, and cultural institutions in Kiev until the turn of the twentieth century promoted the assimilation and secularization of Kievan Jews. This policy affected the Jewish elite more than the common people. In 1881, the Russian authorities turned to a policy of state anti-Semitism with harsher persecution of Jews. This policy radicalized the Jewish youth, who actively participated in the national and revolutionary movements. When the tsarist government realized that they were creating enemies, there was a futile effort to reverse the policy and return the young generation of Jews to a traditional religious lifestyle. However, this conservative scheme could not be realized, not only because the state rabbi's authority had been undermined, but primarily because modern urban life had forever changed the lifestyle and mentality of the Jews.

However, in spite of all the persecutions of Kievan Jews during the tsarist regime, the city had not yet become "the inferno of Russian Israel," as Kiev was called by Simon Dubnov. From the perspective of the twenty-first century, after the Holocaust and the massacre of Jews at Babi Yar, all previous persecutions and misfortunes of Kiev Jews pale in comparison. Thus, the words of Dubnov were rather a prediction of the tragic fate of Kievan Jews, many of whom were murdered by the Nazis at Babi Yar in late September and early October 1941. No doubt, the long anti-Semitic tradition and the anti-Semitism of many local residents prepared fertile ground for the realization of Nazi plans for the extermination of Kievan Jewry.

APPENDIX

Dmitrii Bogrov and the Assassination of Stolypin

On September 1, 1911, the Jewish revolutionary and secret agent of the Okhranka,[1] Dmitrii (Mordko) Bogrov, mortally wounded the prime minister of the Russian Empire, Petr Arkad'evich Stolypin, in the Kiev City Theater (now the Kiev Opera Theater). Historians continue to debate Bogrov's motivation. The most common explanation, by historians Abraham Ascher and Anna Geifman, is that Bogrov killed Stolypin under pressure and even threats to his life by a revolutionary cabal.[2] According to this version of events, the revolutionaries, who discovered Bogrov's secret work for the Okhranka in the summer of 1911, demanded that he rehabilitate himself by assassinating a high Russian official. However, this theory cannot be reconciled with the fact that in June 1910 Bogrov proposed to assassinate Stolypin to a leader of the socialist revolutionaries (SR), Egor Lazarev. Lazarev tried to dissuade Bogrov, because he did not consider such an attempt feasible for a lone assassin.[3]

Another theory is that Bogrov, a naïve twenty-four-year-old anarchist, was just a simple dupe in the hands of the Okhranka, which

---

1 Okhranka, or Okhrana, abbreviation of *Otdelenie po Okhraneniu Obshchestvennoi Bezopasnosti i Poriadka* (Department for the Defense of Public Security and Order, 1881–1917): a prerevolutionary Russian secret-police organization that was founded to combat political terrorism and left-wing revolutionary activity. *Encyclopedia Britannica*, s.v. "Okhranka," http://www.britannica.com/topic/Okhranka.
2 Abraham Ascher, *P. A. Stolypin: The Search for Stability in Late Imperial Russia* (Stanford: Stanford University Press, 2001), 377–383; Anna Geifman, *Thou Shalt Kill: Revolutionary Terrorism in Russia, 1894–1917* (Princeton, NJ: Princeton University Press, 1993), 237–240.
3 Egor Lazarev, "Dmitrii Bogrov i ubiistvo Stolypina," *Volia Rossii* 6–7 (1926): 51–52.

used him to fulfill the tsar's secret desire to get rid of Stolypin.[4] According to this proposition, Nicholas II was jealous of Stolypin's popularity, which rivaled his own, and had encouraged the elimination of Stolypin. However, Nicholas II was in absolute control of the selection and firing of his ministers, so he did not need to kill Stolypin to remove him from political life.

The Russian historian S. A. Stepanov, who provides in his work various explanations of the Stolypin's assassination, also considers convincing a Jewish motivation and calls Bogrov an avenger from the Pale of Settlement.[5] In fact, Bogrov was a Jewish avenger from Kiev, the city where the government persecution of Jews was perhaps the most severe in the Russian Empire. I think that the assassination was an act of revenge for the persecution of Jews in Russia.

Many scholarly and popular works and memoirs have been written about the murder of Stolypin and his assassin. In spite of this, Dmitrii Bogrov's personality and reason for shooting Stolypin are still today a matter of debate among historians. According to Abraham Ascher, "Bogrov can be considered a Jew only if the Jewishness is defined in strictly racial terms."[6] Ascher and Geifman thought that Stolypin's assassination did not have any Jewish motivation.[7] But many people who personally knew Bogrov expressed the opposite opinion, claiming that Bogrov took revenge upon Stolypin for the persecution of Jews and government support for Jewish pogroms and the Black Hundreds.

Regarding Bogrov's religion there is incontestable evidence that he was, and considered himself to be, a Jew. This includes not only the statements of his brother and other people who knew Bogrov, but also his gymnasium diploma, which indicates his religion as Judaism. At his interrogation, Bogrov repeated several times, "I am of the

---

4 S. A. Stepanov, *Zagadki ubiistva Stolypina* (Moscow: Progress-Akademia, 1995), 112–133.
5 Ibid.
6 Ascher, *P. A. Stolypin*, 377.
7 Ibid.; Geifman, *Thou Shalt Kill*, 237–240.

Jewish religion."[8] Kiev State Rabbi Iakov Aleshkovskii was the religious representative at Bogrov's execution.[9]

Dmitrii Bogrov was born to a wealthy Jewish family in Kiev in 1887. His grandfather was the renowned Jewish writer and maskil Grigorii Isakovich Bogrov (Gersh Bekharav, 1825–1885), and his father Grigorii Grigor'evich Bogrov was a well-known Jewish lawyer. Grigorii Isakovich converted to Christianity just before his death due to his wish to marry a Christian woman. However, neither of his sons from the first marriage, who were already adults and had their own families, nor his grandchildren, followed his conversion. It appears that the conversion of Grigorii Isakovich Bogrov confused at least some historians, who assumed that his children and grandchildren were also converts.

Dmitrii Bogrov was a child of privilege: he had plenty of money, since his father was the owner of a five-story luxury mansion in downtown Kiev where the St. Petersburg hotel and restaurant are now located. In his youth, Dmitrii often travelled abroad with and without his parents. He graduated from the best gymnasium in Kiev and from the Kiev St. Vladimir University Law School.

But, as with many Jews of his generation, Dmitrii Bogrov felt terribly humiliated by the pogroms and anti-Jewish persecution. He wrote in a letter to his friend about his inclination to move away from Kiev after his graduation from law school because "the situation of a Jewish lawyer is better in St. Petersburg than in Kiev or Moscow."[10] For a brief period after his graduation, Bogrov worked as an assistant for a lawyer in St. Petersburg. Perhaps he was not satisfied with his situation there, because he soon returned to Kiev.

A. Mushin, author of the book *Dmitrii Bogrov i ubiistvo Stolypina* (Dmitrii Bogrov and the Assassination of Stolypin), wrote that Bogrov thought that Stolypin was the enemy since he was the main pillar of

---

8 Lazarev, "Dmitrii Bogrov i ubiistvo Stolypina," 76.
9 A. Serebrennikov, comp., *Ubiistvo Stolypina* (New York: Teleks, 1986), 22–23.
10 A. Ia. Avrekh, *P. A. Stolypin i sud'by reform v Rossii* (Moscow: Izdatel'stvo politicheskoi literatury, 1991), 216.

political reaction in Russia.[11] Bogrov's motivation for murdering Stolypin is best shown in his conversation with one of the leaders of the central committee of the Socialist Revolutionary Party (SR), Egor Lazarev, who published his memoir about Bogrov in the journal *Volia Rossii*[12] in 1926. According to Lazarev, Bogrov came to him in St. Petersburg in June 1910 (on the Orthodox Christian holiday of the Holy Trinity) to ask for the authorization of the Socialist Revolutionary Party to murder Stolypin. Bogrov described to Lazarev his motivation for killing Stolypin:

> I am a Jew and let me remind you that we are living thus far under the domination of the Black Hundreds' leaders. Jews never will forget the Krushevans, Dubrovins, Purishkeviches and other villains. Where is Gertsenshtein? Where is Iollos? Where are the hundreds and thousands of other Jews torn to pieces; Jewish men, women and children with ripped stomachs, with cut noses and ears? If people sometimes protest actively against such crimes, the little men are always blamed; the main culprits are never punished. The duty of the socialist parties and the intelligentsia is to point the masses to the real culprits. You know that the most powerful leader of the forthcoming political reaction is Stolypin. I came to you and said that I decided to eliminate him, and you recommend to me that instead of this I should do cultural, legal work...[13]

Political assassinations in the Russian Empire were committed by both sides: there were terrorist revolutionaries as well as hit men from the Black Hundreds. The thousands of Jewish victims of pogroms were not figments of Bogrov's imagination. According to Lazarev, Bogrov acknowledged his Jewish motivation for the assassination of Stolypin as revenge for anti-Jewish pogroms and political murders of Jewish deputies of the State Duma.

---

11 A. Mushin, *Dmitrii Bogrov i ubiistvo Stolypina* (Paris: Soiuz, 1914).
12 *Volia Rossii*, a monthly social-political and literature journal of Russian emigration (1924–1932), was published in Prague, then in Paris.
13 Lazarev, "Dmitrii Bogrov i ubiistvo Stolypina," 51–52.

Bogrov defined himself as an anarchist-individualist. He did not follow any political party in Russia. Bogrov joined an anarchist organization in Kiev in 1906, but in two months he was disappointed in its activity and became a secret agent of the Kiev Okhranka on his own initiative.[14] Historians continue to debate why Bogrov became an agent of the Okhranka. Some authors of memoirs about Bogrov wrote that he became a police agent to receive access to high-ranking authorities in order to murder one of them. Bogrov had been a secret agent of the Kiev Okhranka under the pseudonym Alensky in 1907–1910. Although the chief of the Kiev Okhranka, Nikolai Nikolaevich Kuliabko, confirmed in his report that Bogrov was a paid agent of the Kiev Okhranka, it has not been proved that anybody was arrested due to Bogrov's reports. According to Kuliabko, after his graduation from Kiev St. Vladimir University Law School, Bogrov moved to St. Petersburg in April 1910, and ceased his contact with the Kiev Okhranka.[15] In July 1910, Bogrov came to the chief of the St. Petersburg Okhranka, Mikhail von Kotten, and offered to become an agent. The offer was accepted and Bogrov became a secret agent under the name Nadezhdin. Bogrov explained his cooperation with the Okhranka during his interrogation as follows: "I decided to provide the St. Petersburg Okhranka and the Department of Police imaginary information, which I did for revolutionary purposes, so that I could make close contacts in these institutions and learn how they work."[16]

Von Kotten complained in his report that Bogrov was a lousy agent. He did not provide any valuable information. Von Kotten wrote that Bogrov always talked some nonsense (*nes okolesitsu*); still, the Okhranka paid him 150 rubles per month.[17] Bogrov left St. Petersburg for Nice, France in December 1910. He stayed in Nice for four months, then returned to Kiev in March 1911; however, he soon went to a dacha for

---

14 Russian State Military Historical Archive (RGVIA), f. 1769, op. 13, d. 11. ll. 114–116. Protocols of interrogation of Dmitrii Bogrov, from September 1, 1911. Cited in *Archivy Ukrainy* 3 (1990): 42–43.
15 Lazarev, "Dmitrii Bogrov i ubiistvo Stolypina," 69.
16 The State Archive of Russian Federation (GARF), f. 271, op. 1, d. 1. ll. 30–34. Protocols of interrogation of Dmitrii Bogrov, from September 2, 1911. Cited in *Arkhivy Ukrainy* 2 (1990): 44–47.
17 Lazarev, "Dmitrii Bogrov i ubiistvo Stolypina," *Volia Rossii* 6–7 (1926): 79.

the summer, returning to Kiev just a few weeks before the assassination of Stolypin.

When Bogrov returned to Kiev, he met with the chief of the Kiev Okhranka, Kuliabko, twice—on August 27 and 31, 1911. The first meeting, which was in Kuliabko's house, was also attended by the deputy director of the department of police of the Ministry of the Interior, Verigin, and the chief of the Secret Palace Police, Aleksandr Ivanovich Spiridonovich, who came to Kiev to provide security for the tsar's visit.[18] Bogrov told them that two revolutionaries, Nikolai Iakovlevich and Nina Aleksandrovna, were preparing to assassinate Stolypin and had already arrived in Kiev. Bogrov said that Nikolai Iakovlevich was staying in his apartment and was going to meet Nina Aleksandrovna, who was staying somewhere else, and that they had a bomb. The Okhranka gave Bogrov a ticket to the performance at the Kiev City Theater, which was to be attended by the tsar and Stolypin, because he promised to finger the potential assassins who would presumably also be in the theater. But instead, Bogrov himself calmly walked up to the front of the theater during the second intermission and shot Stolypin, mortally wounding him. It seems that the Okhranka did not use the young and "naïve" Bogrov, but on the contrary, Bogrov used the utterly incompetent chief of the Kiev Okhranka, Kuliabko, and the other top police officials to realize his plan. During his interrogation, Bogrov stated that Nikolai Iakovlevich and Nina Aleksandrovna did not exist; he had created the story to get a ticket for the performance attended by the tsar and Stolypin.[19] Thus, the assassination of Stolypin was an egregious failure of the Imperial Russian intelligence service.

Transcripts of Bogrov's interrogation show that Bogrov worried about his terrorist attack's consequences for Jews. Because of this, he did not dare kill the tsar. During his interrogation, Bogrov mentioned that he considered making an attempt on the life of Nicholas II, but he gave up this idea, because he was afraid of provoking a Jewish pogrom.

---

18 GARF, f. 271, op. 1, d. 1. ll. 38–39. Protocols of interrogation of Colonel A. I. Spiridonovich from September 3, 1911. Cited in *Arkhivy Ukrainy* 3 (1990): 46–47.
19 RGVIA, f. 1769, op. 13, d. 11. ll. 114–116. Protocols of interrogation of Dmitrii Bogrov, from September 1, 1911. Cited in *Arkhivy Ukrainy* 3 (1990): 42–43.

"He, as a Jew, did not have the right to do this, because this could have for Jews such dire consequences [i.e., a pogrom] and provoke further civil rights discrimination against them."[20] However, Bogrov categorically refused to sign this addendum to his statement, explaining his decision by saying that "if the government found out about this, they would prevent Jews from committing new terrorist attacks by threatening them with the organization of pogroms."[21]

Before his execution, Bogrov told Kiev the state rabbi, Iakov Aleshkovskii, "Please tell the Jews that I did not want to harm them in any way, on the contrary, I struggle for their good and for the happiness of the Jewish people."[22] Bogrov emphasized his Jewishness during his interrogation and said that he acted in the interests of the Jewish people as he understood them. He stated his Jewishness and Jewish motivation for the assassination of Stolypin several times: first to Egor Lazarev, then during his interrogation, and finally in a conversation on the way to the gallows with Rabbi Aleshkovskii.

The investigation of Stolypin's assassination slowed down somewhat the development of the Beilis case, since the investigators V. E. Fenenko and Lieutenant Colonel A. A. Ivanov conducted both inquiries.[23] During Bogrov's interrogation the prosecutor told him about the death of Stolypin, who died four days after the shooting. Bogrov met this news with great satisfaction; his life was not to be sacrificed in vain. Bogrov was executed on September 12, 1911, eleven days after attacking Stolypin. During Bogrov's execution the attendees included members of the Union of Russian People and other local Black Hundreds organizations who wanted to see for themselves the death of Stolypin's assassin.

After the shooting of Stolypin, the leaders of the Russian nationalists in Kiev again called for a pogrom against the Jews, but this time their initiative was not supported by the authorities. The tsar was still in the

---

20 GARF, f. 271, op. 1, d. 1, l. 24, http://www.doc20vek.ru/node/1673.
21 Ibid.
22 *Elektronnaia Evreiskaia Entsiklopediia*, s.v. "Bogrov Mordko (Dmitrii)," http://www.eleven.co.il/?mode=article&id=10689&query=БОГРОВ.
23 Stepanov, *Chernaia sotnia v Rossii*, 286.

city and in his presence the authorities would not allow Jews to be attacked.[24]

Hryhorii Hryhoriev wrote that to avoid the pogrom,

> the Kiev Jewish community, following the advice of [its president Leon] Brodsky, officially dissociated itself from Bogrov. The community deputies simultaneously asked for the permission of the authorities to hold a special service in a synagogue for the health of the tsar's family and that of the wounded Stolypin. This permission was granted. This tactic was proposed by Brodsky and, according to rumors, a significant payment [to the authorities] made it possible to avoid a pogrom.[25]

However, according to police reports, Jewish and Ukrainian radical youth showed their gratification with the assassination of Stolypin, who was the main government patron of the Russian nationalist and chauvinist forces.[26] After the execution of Bogrov, many Jewish students wore mourning clothes.[27]

The years of the Stolypin government were the years when the Black Hundreds flourished in Russia. Stolypin's promotion of Russian nationalist and chauvinist ideas, and suppression of national minorities, fit well with the ideology of Russian nationalistic organizations. The later disagreement between Stolypin and the leader of the Union of Russian People, Aleksandr Ivanovich Dubrovin, only regarded methods of suppressing revolutionary and national minorities' movements. While the government primarily preferred to use legal measures in the struggle against these movements, the Union of Russian People and other Black Hundreds organizations used methods of assassination and violence against their political enemies and Jews. With the assassination of Stolypin, who had patronized the Black Hundreds, the

---

24 Victoria Khiterer, *Dokumenty, sobrannye Evreiskoi istoriko-arkheograficheskoi komissiei Vseukrainskoi Akademii Nauk* (Jerusalem: Institut Iudaiki, Gesharim, 1999), 248–249.
25 Hryhorii Hryhoriev, *U staromu Kyievi* (Kiev: Radians'kyi pys'mennyk, 1961), 252.
26 TsDIAK U, f. 275, op. 1, d. 2528, ll. 21–27, 54, 124, 159, 187.
27 Solzhenitsyn, *Dvesti let vmeste*, 1: 442.

government subsidies to these organizations decreased and the movement declined.[28]

Starting in 1910, the revolutionary movement rose up again in Russia. Bogrov, by killing Stolypin, further destabilized the country's political situation, and accelerated the collapse of the tsarist regime. Bogrov's assassination of Stolypin was an act of retaliation for anti-Jewish pogroms, the murder of Jewish deputies of the State Duma, government support for the Black Hundreds, and the emerging Beilis affair. Thus Bogrov should be considered a Jewish avenger from Kiev, the city where Jews were persecuted and discriminated against worse than in any other place in the Russian Empire.

The anti-Semitic policies of Kiev's authorities created many such Jewish avengers. For example, a student of Kiev Polytechnic Institute, Pinkhas Dashevsky, made an attempt in June 1903 on the life of the instigator of the Kishinev 1903 pogrom, Pavel Krushevan.[29] In 1906, the nineteen-year-old Fanni Kaplan brought to Kiev a bomb with the purpose of killing Kiev, Podolia, and Volhynia Governor-General Vladimir Aleksandrovich Sukhomlinov (1905–1907), who was the head of the Kiev department of the Russian nationalist organization, the Russian Assembly, from the moment of its formation, and who authorized many persecutions of Jews in Kiev.[30] These two earlier terrorist attempts were unsuccessful, but they clearly show the desire of Jewish youth to avenge the pogroms and persecution of Jews in Russia. Simon Dubnov wrote that it was a vicious circle: the victims of the worst despotism in Russia, the Jews, joined in mass the liberation movement, for which the Black Hundreds took revenge against them with pogroms. These pogroms even more radicalized Jewish youth and pushed them further into revolution.[31]

---

28 Stepanov, *Zagadki ubiistva Stolypina*, 129; Stepanov, *Chernaia sotnia v Rossii*, 177–186, 284–285.
29 Pinkhas Dashevsky, *Elektronnaia Evreiskaia Entsiklopediia*, http://www.eleven.co.il/article/11378.
30 "The Explosion of the Bomb," *Kievlianin*, December 23, 1906.
31 S. I. Dubnov, *Noveishaia istoriia* (Berlin: Jüdischer Verlag, 1923), III: 394–395.

Bibliography

Archival Sources

The Central State Historical Archive of Ukraine in the City Kiev (TsDIAK U)
Fond 274 Kiev Province Gendarme Administration
Fond 275 Kiev Police Department
Fond 293 Kiev Censorship Committee
Fond 295 Kiev Temporary Censorship Committee
Fond 315 Chancellery of Military Prosecutor of Kiev Military District Court
Fond 316 Kiev Military District Court
Fond 317 Prosecutor of the Kiev Appellate Court
Fond 335 Chancery of the Provisional Odessa Governor-General
Fond 442 Chancellery of the Kiev, Podolia and Volhynia Governor-General
Fond 533 Chancellery of the Kiev Military Governor
Fond 707 Administration of the Kiev Educational District
Fond 838 Collection of leaflets
Fond 1004 Nisselovich L. N., Jewish Public and Political Figure
Fond 1010 Fridman N. M., Jewish Public and Political Figure
Fond 1220 Margolin A. D., Jurist, Jewish Public and Political Figure
Fond 1423 Collection of the documents gathered by the Jewish Historical-Archaeographical Commission of the All-Ukrainian Academy of Sciences

The Central State Archive of Film, Photo, Sound Documents of Ukraine (TsDA-KFFD U)
Collection of photo documents

The National Vernadsky Library of the Ukrainian Academy of Arts and Sciences
Fond 189 Sholom Aleichem, Jewish Writer
Fond 339 An-sky (Rappoport) S. A., Jewish Writer and Ethnographer

The State Archive of the City Kiev (DAMK)
Fond 1 Magistrate of the City Kiev
Fond 3 Kiev St. Sophia Cathedral
Fond 17 Kiev City Duma
Fond 153 Kiev Commercial Institute
Fond 163 Kiev Municipal Administration
Fond 186 The Kiev Dentistry School of Doctors L. Golovchiner, S. Lur'e and O. Pliner.
Fond 208 Kiev Jewish Hospital
Fond 253 Orphanage for Jewish Children Converted to Christianity

The State Archive of the Kiev Region (DAKO)
Fond 2 Chancellery of the Kiev Civil Governor
Fond 348 Kiev Department of the Society for Spreading Enlightenment Among Jews in Russia
Fond 444 Administration of the Jewish Emigration Society in Kiev
Fond 445 Committee of the Society for Aid to Jewish Victims of Military Action (KOPE), Kiev
Fond 864 Kiev Circuit Court

The Russian State Historical Archive, St. Petersburg (RGIA, St. Petersburg)
Fond 821 Department of Religious Affairs for Foreign Religions of the Ministry of the Interior.

YIVO Institute for Jewish Research, New York (YIVO)
Tcherikower Archive (RG 80-89)
David Edelstadt Archive (RG 517)

The Central Archives for the History of the Jewish People, Jerusalem (CAHJP)
Microfilms, microfiche and paper collections.

Periodicals
Annals of the Association of American Geographers
Arkhivy Ukrainy
Bessarabskaia zhizn'

Das Folk
Den'
East European Jewish Affairs
Evreiskaia starina
Evreiskii mir
Evreiskii student
Fakty
Folk Shtime
Gazeta po-kievski
Ha-tsofe u-mabit (later *Ha-tsofe*)
Illiustrirovannyi sionistskii al'manakh
The Illustrated London News
Interesnyi Kiev
Jewish Social Studies
The Journal of European Economic History
Kiever tagblat
Kiever wort
Kievlianin
Kievskaia gazeta
Kievskaia mysl'
Kievskaia pochta
Kievskaia starina
Kievskie eparkhial'nye vedomosti
Kievskie otkliki
Kievskoe slovo
Kievskie vesti
Korrespondent
Novoe vremia
Novyi voskhod
Odesskie novosti
Odesskii vestnik
Rech'
Revolutionary Russia
Russkaia volia
Smolenskii vestnik

Sovremennoe slovo
Tomskii obzor
Tovarishch'
Ukraina Moderna
Vestnik Evreiskogo Universiteta v Moskve
Volia Rossii
Yudishe naye leben
Zerkalo nedeli

Published Collections of Documentary Sources

Bisha, Robin, Jehanne M. Gheith, Christine Holden, and William G. Wagner, eds. *Russian Women, 1698–1917: Experience and Expression, An Anthology of Sources.* Bloomington: Indiana University Press, 2002.

Borovoi, S. Ia., ed. and trans. *Evreiskie khroniki XVII stoletiia (Epokha "khmel'nichiny").* Moscow: Gesharim, 1997.

Cologne, Linden A., ed. *Die Judenpogrome in Russland.* Leipzig: Jüdischer Verlag, 1910.

Gessen, G. V., ed. *Arkhiv russkoi revoliutsii.* 16 vols. Berlin: Slowo-Verlag, 1925.

Khiterer, Victoria. *Dokumenty, sobrannye Evreiskoi istoriko-arkheograficheskoi komissiei Vseukrainskoi Akademii Nauk.* Jerusalem: Institut Iudaiki, Gesharim, 1999.

Kolesnik, V. F., "Kotsur, A. P. and Teres, N. V., eds. *Istoriia Kyieva vid kniazhoi doby do suchasnosti: Zbirnyk dokumentiv i materialiv.* Kiev: Knyhy-XXI, 2005.

"Otchet o soveshchanii evreiskikh obshchestvennykh deiatelei, proiskhodivshem v Kovno 19–22 noiabria 1909 goda." *Evreiskii mir* (November–December 1909): 32–61.

Polnoe sobranie zakonov Rossiiskoi imperii (PSZ). 2nd ed. St. Petersburg: Tip. 2-go Otděleniiá Sobstvennoii Ego Imp. Velichestva Kantseliarii, 1825–1881; 3rd ed. St. Petersburg: Gosudarstvennaia tipografia, 1881–1913.

Portnova, N., comp. *Byt' evreem v Rossii. Materialy po istorii russkogo evreistva. 1880–1890.* Jerusalem: The Hebrew University of Jerusalem, 1999.

Rechi po pogromnym delam. Introduction by V. G. Korolenko. Kiev: S. G. Sliusarevskii Publishing House, 1908.

Serebrennikov, A., comp. *Soblazn Sotsializma: Revoliutsiia v Rossii i evrei.* Paris: YMCA-Press, Russkii Put', 1995.

———. *Ubiistvo Stolypina: Svidetel'stva i dokumenty.* New York: Teleks, 1986.

Verstiuk, V. F., Boiko, O. D., et al., comps. *Ukrains'ka Tsentral'na Rada. Dokumenty i materialy.* Kiev: Naukova dumka, 1997.

Vinogradov, V. K., ed. and comp. *Delo Fani Kaplan ili kto strelial v Lenina. Sbornik dokumentov.* Moscow: X-History, 2003.

Books and Articles

Abramson, Henry. *A Prayer for the Government: Ukrainians and Jews in Revolutionary Times, 1917–1920.* Cambridge: Harvard University Press, 1999.

Adler, Eliyana R. *In Her Hands: The Education of Jewish Girls in Tsarist Russia.* Detroit: Wayne State University Press, 2011.

Aksakov, Ivan. *Issledovanie o torgovle na ukrainskikh iarmarkakh.* St. Petersburg: Imperial Academy of Sciences Publishing House, 1858.

Andriievs'kyi, Oleksa. "Arkhivna dovidka pro sklad Kyivs'koho 'hromadianstva' u 1782–1798 rokakh." *Kyiv—Sviata zemlia. Khronika 2000* 49–50 (2002): 696–705.

Anisimov, Aleksandr. *Kiev i kievliane. Ia vyzovu liuboe iz stoletii…*2 vols. Kiev: Kurch', Telegraf, 2002–2003.

———. *Skorbnoe beschuvstvie.* Kiev: Tabachuk Ltd, 1992.

Ansky, S. *The Dybbuk and Other Writings.* Edited by David G. Roskies. New York: Schoken Books, 1992.

Aronson, I. M. "Geographical and Socio-economic Factors in the 1881 Anti-Jewish Pogroms in Russia." *Russian Review* 39 (1980): 18–31.

———. *Troubled Waters: The Origins of the 1881 Anti-Jewish Pogroms in Russia.* Pittsburgh: University of Pittsburgh Press, 1990.

Arustamian, Zhanna. "Ukrainskii Faberzhe." *Evreiskoe slovo* 20, no. 143 (May 21–27, 2003): 8.

Ascher, Abraham. *P. A. Stolypin: The Search for Stability in Late Imperial Russia.* Stanford, CA: Stanford University Press, 2001.

———. *The Revolution of 1905.* 2 vols. Stanford, CA: Stanford University Press, 1988–1992.

Assaf, David, ed. *Journey to a Nineteenth-Century Shtetl: The Memories of Yekhezkel Kotik.* Detroit and Tel Aviv: Wayne State University Press, 2002.

Avrekh, A. Ia. *P. A. Stolypin i sud'by reform v Rossii*. Moscow: Izdatel'stvo politicheskoi literatury, 1991.

Avrutin, Eugene M. "The Politics of Jewish Legibility: Documentation Practices and Reform During the Reign of Nicholas I." *Jewish Social Studies* 11, no. 2 (Winter 2005): 136–169.

Badanes, Gershon. [Gurevich, G. E.] *Evreiskie obshchestvennye dela v Kieve*. Kiev: Sliusarevskii Publishing House, 1910.

_____. "Kievskaia evreiskaia obshchina na Vserossiiskoi Vystavke 1913 g. v Kieve." *Vestnik evreiskoi obshchiny* 4 (October 1913): 18–25.

_____. "Kievskaia evreiskaia obshchina v 1913 g." *Vestnik evreiskoi obshchiny* 3 (March 1914): 34.

_____. *S odnogo vola tri shkury*. Kiev: I. M. Roset Publishing House, 1907.

Baratz, G. M. *O bibleisko-agadicheskom elemente v povestiakh i skazaniiakh nachal'noi russkoi letopisi*. Kiev: St. Vladimir University Publishing House, 1907.

_____. "Povesti i skazania drevnerusskoi pis'mennosti, imeiushchie otnoshenie k evreiam i evreistvu." *Kievskaia starina* (1906): 4–13.

_____. *Sobranie trudov po voprosu o evreiskom elemente v pamiatnikakh drevnerusskoi pis'mennosti*. I–II. Berlin and Paris: Impr. D'Art Voltaire, 1924–1927.

Baron, Salo W. *The Russian Jews Under Tsars and Soviets*. New York: Macmillan Publishing Co., 1976.

Beilis, Mendel. *The Story of My Sufferings*. New York: Mendel Beilis Publishing Co., 1926.

Beizer, Mikhail. *The Jews of St Petersburg: Excursions through a Noble Past*. Edited by Martin Gilbert. Philadelphia: The Jewish Publication Society, 1989.

Berg, Robert. "Delo Beilisa splotilo evreev," *Jewish.ru*, October 16, 2003, http://www.jewish.ru/history/facts/2013/10/news994321376.php.

Berk, Stephen M. "The Russian Revolutionary Movement and the Pogroms of 1881–1882." *Soviet Jewish Affairs* 7, no. 2 (1977): 22–39.

_____. *Year of Crisis, Year of Hope: Russian Jewry and the Pogroms of 1881–1882*. Westport, CT: Greenwood, 1986.

Berlyns'kyi, Maksym. *Istoriia mista Kyieva*. Kiev: Naukova Dumka, 1991.

Bershadskii, S. A. *Litovskie evrei*. St. Petersburg: Tipografiia M. M. Stasiulevicha, 1883.

Bogachek (Goldelman), Michael. "O diarkhii v drevnei Rusi." *Jews and Slavs* 3 (1995): 69-87.

Bohachevsky-Chomiak, Martha. *Feminists Despite Themselves: Women in Ukrainian Community Life, 1884-1939*. Edmonton: Canadian Institute of Ukrainian Studies University of Alberta, 1988.

Boichenko, V. O., ed. *Istoriia mist i sil Ukrains'koi RSR. Kyiv*. Kiev: Holovna Redaktsiia Ukrains'koi Radians'koi Entsyklopedii AN URSR, 1968.

Borovyi, S. "Nezdiisneni proekty utvoryty v Kyievi evreis'ku drukarniu (1836-1846)." *Bibliolohichni visti* 4 (1929): 30-33.

Bradley, Joseph. *Muzhik and Muscovite: Urbanization in Late Imperial Russia*. Berkeley and Los Angeles: University of California Press, 1985.

Briman, Sergei. "Evreiskii vopros v obshchem kontekste parlamentskikh diskussii Gosudarstvennoi Dumy." *Vestnik Evreiskogo Universiteta v Moskve* 2, no. 18 (1998): 63-71.

Brodsky, Alexandra Fanny. *Smoke Signals: From Eminence to Exile*. London: Radcliffe Press, 1997.

Brook, Kevin Alan. *The Jews of Khazaria*. 2nd ed. Lanham, MD: Rowman & Littlefield Publishing, Inc., 2006.

Brower, Daniel R. *The Russian City between Tradition and Modernity, 1850-1900*. Berkeley and Los Angeles: University of California Press, 1990.

Bulgakov, M. A. *Povesti, rasskazy, fel'etony*. Moscow: Sovetskii Pisatel', 1988.

Bushnell, John. *Mutiny amid Repression: Russian Soldiers in the Revolution of 1905-1906*. Bloomington: Indiana University Press, 1985.

Chemu nas uchit pokushenie Pinkhusa Dashevskogo? London: Izdanie "Molodogo Izrailia," [1903?].

Cherkaz'ianova, E. V. "Istoriia shkoly rossiiskikh nemtsev XIX-nachala XX veka v terminakh i poniatiiakh." *Vestnik Cheliabinskogo gosudarstvennogo universiteta* 18, no. 119, (2008): 39-46.

Darevskii, I. A. *K istorii evreev v Kieve*. Kiev: I. M. Roset Publishing House, 1907.

_____. *Le-korot ha-Yehudim be-Kiyov (melefanim behaiom)*. Berdichev: Publishing House of Y. G. Sheftel, 1902.

De-Ribas, Aleksandr. *Staraia Odessa. Istoricheskie ocherki i vospominaniia*. Moscow: Kraft, 2005.

Dubin, Lois C. *The Port Jews of Habsburg Trieste: Absolutist Politics and Enlightenment Culture*. Stanford, CA: Stanford University Press, 1999.

Dubnov, Simon. *History of the Jews*. 5 vols. South Brunswick, NJ: Thomas Yoseloff, 1973.

———. *Kniga zhizni. Vospominaniia i razmyshlenia. Materialy dlia istorii moego vremeni*. St. Petersburg: Peterburgskoe vostokovedenie, 1998.

Dubnow, S. M. *History of the Jews in Russia and Poland from the Earliest Times until the Present Day*. Translated by I. Friedlaender. Jersey City, NJ: Ktav Publishing House, Inc., 1975.

Dunlop, D. M. *The History of the Jewish Khazars*. New York: Schocken Books, 1967.

Eberhardt, Piotr. *Przemiany narodowościowe na Litwie*. Warsaw: Przeglad Wschodni, 1997.

Ehrenburg, Il'ia. *Liudi, gody, zhizn'*. Moscow: Tekst, 2005.

El'iashevich, Dmitrii. *Pravitel'stvennaia politika i evreiskaia pechat' v Rossii 1797–1917*. St. Petersburg: Gesharim, 1999.

Estraikh, Gennady. "From Yehupets Jargonists to Kiev Modernists: The Rise of a Yiddish Literary Centre, 1880s–1914." *East European Jewish Affairs* 30, no. 1 (2000): 17–38.

———. *In Harness: Yiddish Writers' Romance With Communism*. Syracuse, NY: Syracuse University Press, 2005.

Evreiskoe studenchestvo v Moskve. Po dannym ankety 1913 g. Moscow: n.p., 1913.

Fedor, Thomas Stanley. *Patterns of Urban Growth in the Russian Empire during the Nineteenth Century*. Chicago: University of Chicago Press, 1975.

Filonenko, A. L. *Vremia Iu. Larina*. St. Petersburg: Nestor, 1996.

Firsov, Sergei. "Simptomy bolezni "simfonicheskogo" gosudarstva: "delo" Beilisa i Pravoslavnaia Rossiiskaia Tserkov'." *Iudeisko-christianskie otnosheniia*. October 1, 2007, http://www.jcrelations.net/ru/?item =2875.

Frankel, Jonathan. *Prophecy and Politics: Socialism, Nationalism, and the Russian Jews, 1862–1917*. Cambridge: Cambridge University Press, 1981.

Freeze, ChaeRan Y. *Jewish Marriage and Divorce in Imperial Russia*. Hanover, NH: Brandeis University Press, 2002.

Friedmann, Eliezer Eliahu. *Sefer ha-zikhronot*. Tel-Aviv, n.p.: 1926.

Funduklei, Ivan. *Statisticheskoe opisanie Kievskoi gubernii*. St. Petersburg: Publishing House of Ministry of the Interior Affairs, 1852.

Galant, Illia. "K istorii kievskogo getto i tsenzury evreiskikh knig (1854-1855)." *Evreiskaia starina* 2 (1913): 264-278.

———. "Vyselennia zhydiv iz Kyieva roku 1835-ho." In *Zbirnyk prats' Ievreis'koi istorychno-arkheohrafichnoi komisii*, 2, edited by A. Ie. Kryms'kyi, 149-197. Kiev: Vseukrainskaiia Academiia Nauk, (1929).

Gassenschmidt, Christopher. *Jewish Liberal Politics in Tsarist Russia 1900-1914: The Modernization of Russian Jewry*. New York: Macmillan, 1995.

Geraci, Robert P. and Michael Khodarkovsky, eds. *Of Religion and Empire: Missions, Conversion, and Tolerance in Tsarist Russia*. Ithaca, NY: Cornell University Press, 2001.

Gessen, Iulii. "Graf N. P. Ignat'ev i 'Vremennye pravila' o evreiakh 3 maia 1882 goda." *Pravo* 30-31 (1908): 1631-1637 and 1878-1887.

———. *Istoriia evreiskogo naroda v Rossii*. Moscow: Gesharim, 1993.

Gitelman, Zvi. *Jewish Nationality and Soviet Politics. The Jewish Sections of the CPSU, 1917-1930*. Princeton, NJ: Princeton University Press, 1972.

———. "Native Land, Promised Land, Golden Land: Jewish Emigration from Russia and Ukraine." In *Cultures and Nations of Central and Eastern Europe: Essays in Honor of Roman Szporluk*, edited by Zvi Gitelman, Lubomyr Hajda, John-Paul Himka, and Roman Szporluk, 137-163. Cambridge, MA: Ukrainian Research Institute of Harvard University, 2000.

Glaser, Amelia. "Sholem Aleichem, Gogol Show Two Views of Shtetl Jews." *Jewish Journal*, March 10, 2009, http://www.jewishjournal.com/arts/article/sholem__aleichem__gogol__show__two__views__of__ shtetl __jews__20090311/.

Golb, Norman and Omeljan Pritsak. *Khazarian Hebrew Documents of the Tenth Century*. Ithaca, NY: Cornell University Press, 1982.

Graffman, Gary. *I Really Should Be Practicing*. Garden City, NY: Doubleday & Company, Inc., 1981.

Gruzenberg, O. O. *Ocherki i rechi*. New York: n.p., 1944.

Gurevich, B. A. *O voprosakh kul'turnoi zhizni evreev*. Kiev: Kievskoe obshchestvo druzei mira, 1911.

Hamm, Michael. *Kiev: A Portrait, 1800–1917*. Princeton: Princeton University Press, 1993.

_____, ed. *The City in Late Imperial Russia*. Bloomington: Indiana University Press, 1986.

Harkavy, Alexander. "Chapters from my Life." Translated by Jonathan D. Sarna. In *The East European Jewish Experience in America: A Century of Memories, 1882–1982*, edited by Uri D. Herscher, 52–73. Cincinnati: American Jewish Archives, 1983.

Herlihy, Patricia. *Odessa: A History 1794–1914*. Cambridge: Harvard University Press, 1986.

_____. "Odessa, Staple Trade and Urbanization in New Russia." *Jahrbücher für Geschichte Osteuropas* 21 (1973): 121–132.

Horowitz, Brian. *Empire Jews: Jewish Nationalism and Acculturation in 19th and Early 20th-Century Russia*. Bloomington: Slavica Publishers, Indiana University, 2009.

_____. *Jewish Philanthropy and Enlightenment in Late-Tsarist Russia*. Seattle and London: University of Washington Press, 2009.

Hryhoriev, Hryhorii. *U staromu Kyievi*. Kiev: Radians'kyi pys'mennyk, 1961.

Iampol'sky, P. *Pamiati doktora Maksa Emilievicha Mandel'shtama: Slovo, proiznesennoe v Kievskoi khoral'noi sinagoge v subbotu, 7-go aprelia 1912 goda, vo vremia panikhidy po pokoinom M. E. Mandel'shtame*. Kiev: n.p., 1912.

Iaron, S. G. *Kiev v vos'midesiatykh godakh: Vospominaniia starozhila*. Kiev: n.p., 1910.

Ikonnikov, V. S. *Kiev v 1654–1855 gg. Istoricheskii ocherk*. Kiev: Publishing House of the Emperor University of St. Vladimir, 1904.

Istoriia Kyieva, 1: *Starodavnii i seredn'ovichnyi Kyiv*, edited by I. I. Artemenko and H. Ia. Serhiienko; 2: *Kyiv periodu pizn'oho feodalizmu i kapitalizmu*, edited by V. H. Sarbei and P. V. Zamkovyi. Kiev: Naukova Dumka, 1986.

Ivanov, A. E. *Evreiskoe studenchestvo v Rossiiskoi imperii nachala XX veka*. Moscow: Novyi khronograph, 2007.

Ivashkevich, Yaroslav. "Vospominaniia ob Erenburge." *Voprosy literatury* 1 (1984): 200.

Ivshina, Larisa, ed. *Dve Rusi: Ukraina Incognita*. Kiev: Ukrainskaia press-gruppa, 2004.
Izraelitin, A. "Russko-evreiskie obshchedostupnye biblioteki." *Knizhki Voskhoda* (May 1905): 133–137.
Jabotinsky, Vladimir. *Fel'etony*. Berlin: S. D. Sal'tsman Verlag, 1922.
_____. *Izbrannoe*. Jerusalem and Petersburg: Biblioteka-Aliia, 1992.
_____. *Piatero*. Moscow: Nezavisimaia gazeta Publishing House, 2002.
_____. *Vybranni statti z natsional'nogo putannia*. Kyiv: Respublikans'ka asotsiatsiia ukrainoznavstva, 1991.
Judge, Edward H. *Easter in Kishinev: Anatomy of Pogrom*. New York: New York University Press, 1992.
K kharakteristike evreiskogo studenchestva (Po dannym ankety sredi evreiskogo studenchestva g. Kieva v noiabre 1910 goda). Kiev: n.p., 1913.
Kaganovich, Lazar'. *Pamiatnye zapiski: Moi 20 vek*. Moscow: Vagrius, 1996.
Kalnitsky, Mikhail. *Evreiskie adresa Kieva*. Kiev: Dukh i Litera, 2012.
_____. "Pravovoi status evreev Kieva (1859–1917)." *Ievreis'ka istoriia ta kul'tura v Ukraini. Materialy konferentsii*, Kyiv 8–9 hrudnia, 1994. Kiev: Oranta, 1995, 77–81.
_____. *Sinagoga Kievskoi iudeiskoi obshchiny, 5656–5756: Istoricheskii ocherk*. Kiev: Institut Iudaiki, 1996.
_____. "Zolotoe desiatiletie Gintsburga." *Art. City. Construction*. 1 (1995): 38–40.
Kantsedicas A. and I. Sergeeva. *The Jewish Artistic Heritage: Album by Semen An-sky*. Moscow: Mosty Kul'tury, 2001
Karamash. S. Iu. "Novi arkhivni dokumenty pro Kyivs'ku likarniu Zaitseva." *Likars'ka sprava* 7–9 (1996): 205–207.
Kasimenko, O. K., ed. *Istoriia Kieva*. 2 vols. Kiev: Publishing House of the Academy of Sciences of Ukrainian SSR, 1963.
Katsis, Leonid. *Krovavyi navet i russkaia mysl'. Istoriko-teologicheskoe issledovanie dela Beilisa*. Moscow and Jerusalem: Gesharim, 2006.
_____. *Osip Mandel'shtam: muskus iudeistva*. Moscow and Jerusalem: Gesharim, 2002.
Kaufman, A. E. *Druz'ia i vragi evreev: D. I. Pikhno*. St. Petersburg: Knigoizdatel'stvo Pravda, 1907.

Kazovsky, Hillel. *The Book Design of Kultur-Lige Artists*. Kiev: Dukh i Litera, 2011.

Kel'berin, E. P. *Desiatiletie Kievskogo evreiskogo khoral'nogo molitvennogo doma. 1898–1907*. Kiev: I. M. Roset Publishing House, 1909.

_____. *K istorii evreiskogo khoral'nogo molitvennogo doma v Kieve*. Kiev: I. M. Roset Publishing House, 1909.

_____. *Kievskoe evreiskoe uchilishche imeni S. I. Brodskogo*. Kiev: Lur'e and Co., 1905.

Khiterer, Victoria. "Arnold Davidovich Margolin: Ukrainian-Jewish Jurist, Statesman and Diplomat." *Revolutionary Russia* 18, no. 2 (December 2005): 145–167.

_____. "Arnol'd Davidovich Margolin—zashchitnik Beilisa." *Vestnik Evreiskogo Universiteta v Moskve* 3, no. 7 (1994): 156–162.

_____. *Dokumenty po evreiskoi istorii XVI–XX vekov v kievskikh arkhivakh*. Kiev: Gesharim, Institut Iudaiki, 2001.

_____. "Jewish Life in Kyiv at the Turn of the Twentieth Century." *Ukraina Moderna* 10 (2006): 74–94.

_____. "Max Mandelstamm, Palestinophile and Zionist Leader." *The American Association for Polish-Jewish Studies (AAPJS)*. New Views, http://www.aapjstudies.org/index.php?id=141.

_____. "The October 1905 Pogrom in Kiev." *East European Jewish Affairs* 22, no. 2 (1992): 21–37.

_____. "Vasilii Shul'gin and the Jewish Question: An Assessment of Shul'gin's Anti-Semitism." *On the Jewish Street* 1, no. 2 (2011): 1–25.

Khodorkovs'kyi, Iurii. *Ievreis'ki nekropoli Ukrainy*. Kiev: UTOPIK, 1998.

Kievskii i odesskii pogromy v otchetakh senatorov Turau i Kuzminskogo. St. Petersburg: Letopisets, 1907.

Kirkevich, Viktor. *Kiev i "Kievlianin."* Kiev: Varta, 2005.

Klausner, Joseph. *Historyah shel ha-sifrut ha-'ivrit ha-hadashah*. Jerusalem: Hevrah le-hotsaat-sefarim al yad ha-Universitah ha-Ivrit, 1958.

Klempert, Artur. "Palestinofil'stvo i sionizm v dorevolutsionnoi Moskve." *Rossiiskii sionizm: istoria i kul'tura. Materialy nauchnoi konferentsii*. Moscow: Sefer, 2002.

Klier, John Doyle. "The Concept of 'Jewish Emancipation' in a Russian Context." In *Civil Rights in Imperial Russia*, edited by O. Crisp and L. Edmondson, 121–144. Oxford: Clarendon Press, 1989.

———. *Imperial Russia's Jewish Question, 1855–1881*. Cambridge: Cambridge University Press, 1995.

———. "The Jewish *Den* and the Literary Mice, 1869–1871." *Russian History* 10, no. 1 (1983): 31–49.

———. "*Kievlianin* and Jews: A Decade of Disillusionment, 1864–1873." *Harvard Ukrainian Studies* 5, no. 1 (March 1981): 83–101.

———. "Krug Gintsburgov i politika shtadlanuta v imperatorskoi Rossii." *Vestnik Evreiskogo Universiteta v Moskve* 3, no. 10 (1995): 38–55.

———. *Russia Gathers her Jews: The Origins of the "Jewish Question" in Russia*. Dekalb: Northern Illinois University Press, 1986.

———. *Russian, Jews and the Pogroms of 1881–1882*. Cambridge: Cambridge University Press, 2011.

Klier, John Doyle and Shlomo Lambroza, eds. *Pogroms: Anti-Jewish Violence in Modern Russian History*. Cambridge: Cambridge University Press, 1992.

Kobchenko, Kateryna. *"Zhinochyi Universitet Sviatoi Ol'gy." Istoriia Kyivskykh vyshchykh zhinochykh kursiv*. Kyiv: Kyivs'kyi natsional'nyi universitet imeni Tarasa Shevchenka, 2007.

Kondufor, Iu. Iu., ed. *Istoriia Kieva*. 3 vols. Kiev: Naukova Dumka, 1986.

Koni, Anatolii Fedorovich. *Izbrannoe*. Moscow: Sovetskaia Rossiia, 1989.

———. *Sobranie sochinenii*. 5 vols. Moscow: Iuridicheskaia literatura, 1966–1969.

Kostomarov, N. I. *Russkaia istoriia v zhizneopisaniiakh ee glavneishikh deiatelei*. Moscow: Mysl', 1993.

Kotik, Yekhezkel. *Moi vospominaniia. Skitaias' i stranstvuia*. Moscow and Jerusalem: Mosty kul'tury, Gesharim, 2012.

Kotler, I. *Ocherki po istorii evreev Odessy*. Jerusalem: Noy, 1996.

Kovaleva, E. S. "Russkie philosophy-masony: predvaritel'nyi spisok personalii." *Sofiia: Rukopisnyi zhurnal Obschestva revnitelei russkoi filosofii* 7 (2005): 4.

Kovalinskii, V. V. *Kyivs'ki miniatiury*. Vols. 1–6. Kiev: Litopys, Kupola, 2002–2007.

_____. *Metsenaty Kieva*. Kiev: Kii, 1998.
Kulisher, M. "Evrei v Kieve. Istoricheskii ocherk." *Evreiskaia starina* 3 (1911): 351–366; 4 (1912): 417–438.
Kupernik, Avraham. *Le-Korot bnei Yisrael be-Kiyov*. Kiev: Defus Yaakov Sheptel, 1891.
Laqueur, Walter. *Black Hundred: The Rise of the Extreme Right in Russia*. New York: Harper Collins Publishers, 1993.
Lazarev, Egor. "Dmitrii Bogrov i ubiistvo Stolypina." *Volia Rossii* 6–7 (1926): 51–98.
Lederhendler, Eli. *The Road to Modern Jewish Politics: Political Tradition and Political Reconstruction in the Jewish Community of Tsarist Russia*. New York: Oxford University Press, 2001.
Leshchinskii, Iakov. *Gal'vestonskaia emigratsiia i emigratsionnaia politika*. Kiev: Rabotnik, 1912.
_____. "K psikhologii evreiskogo emigranta." *Evreiskiy mir* (November–December 1909): 40–50.
_____. *Vilenskaia evreiskaia obshchina. Ee uchrezhdeniia i finansy*. Kiev: Idisher Folksfarlag, n.d.
Levitats, Isaac. *The Jewish Community in Russia, 1772–1844*. New York: Octagon Books, 1970.
Lewis, Robert A. and Richard H. Rowland. "Urbanization in Russia and the USSR: 1897–1966." *Annals of the Association of American Geographers* 59, no. 4 (December 1969): 776–796.
Likhomanov, A. I. "Ia. Gurliand i evreiskii vopros v Rossii." *Vestnik Evreiskogo Universiteta v Moskve* 4 (1993): 142–152.
Lindenmeyer, Adele. *Poverty is Not A Vice: Charity, Society, and State in Imperial Russia*. Princeton: Princeton University Press, 1996.
Liubosh, S. *Poslednie Romanovy*. Leningrad: Petrograd Publishing House, 1924.
Lokshin, Aleksandr. "V poiskakh modus vivendi: Sionistskoe dvizhenie i tsarskoe pravitel'stvo v kontse XIX–nachale XX vekov." In *Rossiiskii sionizm: istoriia i kul'tura: Materialy nauchnoi konferentsii*. Moscow: Sefer, 2002.
Löwe, Heinz-Dietrich. *The Tsars and the Jews: Reform, Reaction, and Anti-Semitism in Imperial Russia, 1772–1917*. Chur: Harwood Academic Publishers, 1993.

Luchyts'kyi, Ivan. "Kyiv 1766 roku." *Kyiv—Sviata zemlia: Khronika 2000* 49–50 (2002): 637–695.

Lytvyn, V. M., ed. *Politychnyi teror i teroryzm v Ukraini XIX–XX st. Istorychni narysy*. Kiev: Naukova Dumka, 2002.

Magocsi, Paul Robert. *A History of Ukraine*. Seattle: University of Washington Press, 1998.

Malakov, Dmytro. *Arkhitektor Horodets'kyi*. Kiev: Kyi, 1999.

_____. *Tut buv Ievbaz, a potim ploshcha Peremohy: Istoryko-informatsiinyi fotoal'bom*. Kiev: Amadei, 2004.

Malyshevskii, Ivan. *Evrei v iuzhnoi Rusi i Kieve v X–XII vekakh*. Kiev: Publishing House of Davidenko, 1878.

Mandel'shtam, M. "Otkrytoe pis'mo." *Illiustrirovannyi sionistskii al'manakh* (1902–1903): 44–47.

_____. "Sushchnost' sionizma: Pis'mo sionista k docheri." In *Byt' evreem v Rossii: Materialy po istorii russkogo evreistva. 1880–1890*, compiled by Nelli Portnova, 272–274. Jerusalem: The Hebrew University of Jerusalem, 1999.

Marek, Pesakh. "Bor'ba dvukh vospitanii." *Evrei v Rossiiskoi imperii XVIII–XIX vekov. Sbornik trudov evreiskikh istorikov*. Moscow and Jerusalem: Jewish University in Moscow, Gesharim, 1995.

Marinbach, Bernard. *Galveston: Ellis Island of the West*. Albany: State University of New York Press, 1983.

Meir, Golda. *My Life*. New York: Dell Publishing Co., Inc., 1975.

Meir, Natan. "From Pork to Kapores: Transformations in Religious Practice among the Jews of Late Imperial Kiev." *Jewish Quarterly Review* 97, no. 4 (Fall 2007): 616–645.

_____. "Jews, Ukrainians, and Russians in Kiev: Intergroup Relations in Late Imperial Associational Life." *Slavic Review* 65, no. 3 (Fall 2006): 475–501.

_____. *Kiev, Jewish Metropolis: A History, 1859–1914*. Bloomington and Indianapolis: Indiana University Press, 2010.

Mironov, B. N. *Russkii gorod v 1740–1860-e gody: demograficheskoe, sotsial'noe i ekonomicheskoe razvitie*. Leningrad: Nauka, 1990.

Molchanov, A. N. "Iz Iugo-Zapadnogo kraia." *Novoe vremia*, no. 5270 (October 30, 1890).

Montgomery, James E. "Ibn Fadlan and the Rusiyyah." *Journal of Arabic and Islamic Studies* 3 (2000): 1–25.
Morozov, Yurii and Tatiana Derevianko. *Evreiskie kinematografisty Ukrainy, 1910–1945.* Kiev: Dukh i Litera, 2004.
Mowat, C. L., ed. *The New Cambridge Modern History.* 12. Cambridge: Cambridge University Press, 1968.
Murav′ev, Andrei Nikolaevich. "Zapiska o sokhranenii samobytnosti Kieva (Nachalo 1870-kh gg)." *Yehupets* 5 (1999): 259–267.
Mushin, A. *Dmitrii Bogrov i ubiistvo Stolypina.* Paris: Soiuz, 1914.
Nathans, Benjamin. *Beyond the Pale: The Jewish Encounter with Late Imperial Russia.* Berkeley and Los Angeles: University of California Press, 2002.
Neishtube, P. T. *Istoricheskaia zapiska v pamiat′ 50-letiia sushchestvovaniia Kievskoi evreiskoi bol′nitsy 1862–1912.* Kiev: n.p., 1912.
Novitskii, V. D. *Iz vospominanii zhandarma.* Moscow: Moscow University, 1991, reprint of 1929 edition.
Orshanskii, I. *Evrei v Rossii: Ocherki ekonomicheskogo i obshchestvennogo byta russkikh evreev.* St. Petersburg: O. I. Bakst Publishing House, 1877.
Pamiati Maksa Emilievicha Mandel′shtamma: rechi, stat′i i nekrologi. Kiev: K. Kruglianskii Publishing House, 1912.
Pataleev, O. V. *Staryi Kyiv. Zi spogadiv Starogo Grishnyka.* Kyiv: Lybid′, 2008.
Paustovskii, Konstantin. *Dalekie gody.* Moscow: Ast Astrel′, 2005.
Pavlenko, Iu. V. *Narys Istorii Kyieva.* Kiev: Feniks, 2003.
Penkalla, Adam. "The Socio-Cultural Integration of the Jewish Population in the Province of Radom, 1815–1862." *Polin* 3 (1988): 214–238.
Pereswetoff-Morath, Alexander. *A Grin without a Cat,* 1: *Adversus Iudaeos Texts in the Literature of Medieval Russia (988–1504);* 2: *Jews and Christians in Medieval Russia—Assessing the Sources.* Lund: Lund Slavonic Monographs, 2002.
Peretts, E. A. *Dnevnik E. A. Perettsa (1880–1883).* Moscow: Gosizdat, 1927.
Petrovsky, Y. "Abraham Harkavy or the Lost Chapter of Russian Judaica (Newly Discovered Documents from the Vernadsky Library, Kyiv)." *Jews and Slavs* 5 (1996): 157–168.
Philipponnat, Oliver and Patrick Lienhardt. *The Life of Irene Nemirovsky.* New York and Toronto: Alfred A. Knopf, 2010.

Pinkus, Benjamin. *The Jews of the Soviet Union: The History of a National Minority*. Cambridge: Cambridge University Press, 1988.
Pipes, Richard. *The Russian Revolution*. New York: Vintage Books, 1990.
Podraza, Antoni, ed. *Kraków-Kijów, szkice z dziejów stosunków polsko-ukraińskich*. Kraków: Wydawnictwo Literackie, 1969.
Poletika, N. P. *Vidennoe i perezhitoe (Iz vospominanii)*. Jerusalem: Biblioteka-Aliia, 1990.
Polonsky, Antony. *The Jews in Poland and Russia*. 3 vols. Oxford and Portland, OR: Littman Library, 2010–2012.
Potichnyj, Peter and Aster Howard, eds. *Ukrainian-Jewish Relations in Historical Perspective*. Edmonton: Canadian Institute of Ukrainian Studies, 1988.
Povist' mynulykh lit. Litopys. Kiev: Ukraina, 1996.
Pritsak, Omeljan. "The Pre-Ashkenazic Jews of Eastern Europe in Relation to the Khazars, the Rus' and the Lithuanians." In *Ukrainian-Jewish Relations in Historical Perspective*, edited by Peter J. Potichnyj and Howard Aster, 3–22. Edmonton: University of Alberta, 1988.
Raba, Joel. *Between Remembrance and Denial: The Fate of the Jews in the Wars of the Polish Commonwealth during the Mid-Seventeenth Century as Shown in Contemporary Writings and Historical Research*. New York: East European Monographs, 1995.
Rasputin, Grigorii. *Velikie dni torzhestva v Kieve! Poseshchenie Vysochaishei sem'i! Angel'skii privet!* St. Petersburg: M. P. Frolova Publishing House, 1911.
Régnier, Gérard (Clair, Jean). *The Great Parade: Portrait of the Great Artist as Clown*. New Haven: Yale University Press, 2004.
Riasanovsky, Nicholas V. *A History of Russia*. 7th ed. New York: Oxford University Press, 2005.
Rich, Frank with Lisa Aronson. *The Theatre Art of Boris Aronson*. New York: Alfred A. Knopf, 1987.
Rieber, Alfred J. *Merchants and Entrepreneurs in Imperial Russia*. Chapel Hill: University of North Carolina Press, 1982.
Rogger, Hans. *Jewish Policies and Right-Wing Politics in Imperial Russia*. Berkeley and Los Angeles: University of California Press, 1986.
Ro'i, Yaacov, ed. *Jews and Jewish Life in Russia and the Soviet Union*. Portland, OR: Frank Cass, 1995.

Roskies, David. *A Bridge of Longing: The Lost Art of Yiddish Storytelling.* Cambridge, MA: Harvard University Press, 1995.

Samoilenko, Elena. *Kievskaia gorodskaia politsiia v seredine XIX-nachale XX vekov.* Kiev: Khodak, 2000.

Samuel, Maurice. *Blood Accusation: The Strange History of the Beilis Case.* Philadelphia: Jewish Publication Society of America, 1966.

Sergeeva, I. and O. Gorshikhina. "Deiatel'nost' Kievskogo otdeleniia Obshchestva dlia rasprostraneniia prosveshcheniia mezhdu evreiami v Rossii v kontse XIX-nachale XX vv." In *Istoriia evreev v Rossii: problemy istochnikovedeniia i istoriografii: sbornik nauchnykh trudov,* edited by D. A. El'iashevich, 122-133. St. Petersburg: St. Petersburg Jewish University, Institute of Jewish Diaspora, 1993.

Shaginian, Marietta. *Taras Shevchenko.* Moscow: Khudozhestvennaia literatura, 1964.

Shandra, Valentyna. *Kyivs'ke general-gubernatorstvo (1832-1894): Istoriia stvorennia ta diial'nosti, arkhivnyi kompleks i ioho informatyvnyi potentsial.* Kiev: UDNDIASD, 1994.

Shchegolev, P. E., ed. *Padenie tsarskogo rezhima: stenograficheskie otchety doprosov i pokazanii dannykh v 1917 g. v Chrezvychainoi Sledstvennoi Komissii Vremennogo Pravitel'stva.* 7 vols. Moscow: Gosizdat, 1924-1927.

Sheinis, D. E. *Evreiskoe studenchestvo v tsifrakh (Po dannym perepisi 1909 goda v Kievskom universitete i Politekhnicheskom institute).* Kiev: Iosif Shefel'd Publishing House, 1911.

Shkandrij, Myroslav. *Russia and Ukraine: Literature and the Discourse of Empire from Napoleonic to Postcolonial Times.* Montreal: McGill-Queen's University Press, 2001.

Shkol'nik, Leonid. "Sholom Aleichem: 'Serdtse vlozhil ia v knigi svoi...'" *Evreiskii zhurnal* (February 3, 2009), http://www.jjew.ru/index.php?cnt=6194.

Shmakov, A. S. *Pogrom evreev v Kieve: Ocherk.* Moscow: Imperatorskii Moskovskii universitet, 1908.

Shnirelman, Victor. *The Myth of the Khazars and Intellectual Antisemitism in Russia, 1970s-1990s.* Jerusalem: The Vidal Sassoon International Center for the Study of Antisemitism, The Hebrew University of Jerusalem, 2002.

Sholem Aleichem. *The Bloody Hoax*. Bloomington: Indiana University Press, 1991.

_____. *The Further Adventures of Menachem-Mendl*. Translated by Aliza Shevrin. Syracuse, NY: Syracuse University Press, 2001.

Sholom Aleichem. *Krovavaia shutka*. Leningrad: Lira, 1990.

_____. *Sobranie sochinenii*. Moscow: Khudozhestvennaia literatura, 1988.

_____. *Sobranie sochinenii*. 6 vols. Moscow: Khudozhestvennaia literatura, 1974.

Shtammer, Lev. *Kto vinovat? K vyboram ravvina v Kieve*. Kiev: I. I. Gorbunov, 1897.

_____. *Na sud obshchestvennogo mneniia*. Kiev: n.p., 1908.

Shtif, Nokhem. *Di Eltere Yidishe Literatur, Literarishe Khrestomatye*. Kiev: Kultur-Lige, 1929.

Shul'gin, V. V. *Days of the Russian Revolution: Memoirs From the Right*. Edited and translated by Bruce F. Adams. Gulf Breeze, Florida: Academic International Press, 1990.

_____. *Gody-dni-1920*. Moscow: Novosti, 1990.

Siegelbaum, L. "The Odessa Grain Trade: A Case Study in Urban Growth and Development in Tsarist Russia." *Journal of European Economic History* 9 (1980): 113–151.

Sliozberg, G. B. *Dela minuvshikh dnei: Zapiski russkogo evreia*. 3 vols. Paris: Imprimerie Pascal, 1933–1934.

Snopov, Iu. and A. Klempert., comps. *Evrei v Moskve: Sbornik materialov*. Jerusalem: Gesharim, 2003.

Solzhenitsyn, Aleksandr. *Dvesti let vmeste*. 2 vols. Moscow: Russkii Put', 2001–2002.

Spiridovich, A. I. *Les Dernières Années de la cour de Tzarskoïé-Sélo*. 2 vols. Translated by M. Jeanson. Paris: Payot, 1928–1929.

Stampfer, Shaul. "Did the Khazars Convert to Judaism?" *Jewish Social Studies: History, Culture, Society* 19, no. 3 (Spring/Summer 2013): 1–72.

Stanislawski, Michael. *Tsar Nicholas I and the Jews: The Transformation of Jewish Society in Russia 1825–1855*. Philadelphia: The Jewish Publication Society of America, 1983.

_____. *Zionism and the Fin-de-Siècle: Cosmopolitanism and Nationalism from Nordau to Jabotinsky*. Berkeley and Los Angeles: University of California Press, 2001.

Stepanov, S. A. *Chernaia sotnia v Rossii 1905–1914*. Moscow: Rosvuznauka, 1992.

_____. *Zagadki ubiistva Stolypina*. Moscow: Progress-Akademiia, 1995.

Subbotin, A. P. *V cherte evreiskoi osedlosti: Otryvki iz ekonomicheskikh issledovanii v zapadnoi i iugozapadnoi Rossii za leto 1887 g.* 2 vols. St. Petersburg: "Ekonomicheskii zhurnal" Publishing House, n.d.

Subtelny, Orest. *Ukraine: A History*. 3rd ed. Toronto: University of Toronto Press, 2000.

Sukhomlinova, O. *Yu. Larin*. Moscow: Istoki, 1989.

Tager, A. *Tsarskaia Rossiia i delo Beilisa: Issledovaniia i materialy*. Moscow: Gesharim, 1995.

Taube, Moshe. "The Kievan Jew Zacharia and the Astronomical Works of the Judaizers." *Jews and Slavs* 3 (1995): 168–198.

Tolochko, Petr. *Drevniaia Rus': Ocherki sotsial'no-politicheskoi istorii*. Kiev: Naukova Dumka, 1987.

_____. *Istorychna topohrafiia starodavn'oho Kyieva*. Kiev: Naukova Dumka, 1972.

V. G. [the author signed the article only with his initials]. *Russkie gazety po otnosheniiu k nekotorym iz sovremennykh voprosov*, Part I, *"Kievlianin" po evreiskomu voprosu*. Kiev: n.p., 1880.

Veidlinger, Jeffrey. *Jewish Public Culture in the Late Russian Empire*. Bloomington: Indiana University Press, 2009.

Vernadsky, George. *A History of Russia*. 6th ed. New Haven: Yale University Press, 1969.

Vermel', S. "K istorii Aleksandrovsogo Remeslennogo Uchilishcha v Moskve." In *Evrei v Moskve. Sbornik Materialov*, compiled by Y. Snopov and A. Klempert, 262–268. Jerusalem and Moscow: Gesharim, 2003.

Vertinsky, Aleksandr. *Dorogoi Dlinnoiu*. Moscow: Pravda, 1990.

Vynohradova, Maryna and Mykhailo Kal'nyts'kyi. "Bezkoshtovna khirurhichna likarnia I. M. Zaitseva." *Zvit pamiatok istorii ta kul'tury Ukrainy* (1999): 188–189.

Waxman, Meyer. *A History of Jewish Literature*. New York: Yoseloff, 1960.

Weinberg, Robert. *Blood Libel in Late Imperial Russia: The Ritual Murder Trial of Mendel Beilis*. Bloomington: Indiana University Press, 2014.

_____. *The Revolution of 1905 in Odessa: Blood on the Steps*. Bloomington: Indiana University Press, 1993.

Weiss, Jonathan. *Irene Nemirovsky: Her Life and Works*. Stanford: Stanford University Press, 2007.

Westwood, J. N. *Endurance and Endeavour: Russian History 1812–1992*. 4th ed. Oxford: Oxford University Press, 1993.

Wisse, Ruth. *The Modern Jewish Canon*. New York: Free Press, 2000.

Witte. S. Iu. "Evreiskii vopros i russkaia revoliutsiia." In *Russkii antisemitizm i evrei*, compiled by A. Flegon and Iu. Naumov, 35–40. London: Flegon Press, 1968.

———. *Izbrannye vospominaniia, 1849–1911*. Moscow: Mysl', 1991.

Witte, Sergei. *The Memoirs of Count Witte*. Edited and translated by Sidney Harcave. Armonk, NY: M. E. Sharpe, Inc., 1990.

Wladeldo. "Kiev (Iz kul'turnoi zhizni mestnogo evreistva)." *Evreiskii mir* 7 (February 25, 1911): 19–20.

Zaionchkovskii, P. A. *Krizis samoderzhaviia na rubezhe 1870–1880-kh godov*. Moscow: Moskovskii universitet, 1964.

Zakrevskii, Nikolai. *Opisanie Kieva*. Moscow: Publishing House of V. Grachev and Co., 1868.

Zales'ka-Onyshkevich, Larysa. "Volodymyr Miiakovs'kyi." In *125 rokiv kyivs'koi ukrains'koi akademichnoi tradytsii 1861–1986: Zbirnyk*, edited by Marko Antonovych, 516–538. New York: The Ukrainian Academy of Arts and Sciences in the US, Inc., 1993.

Zhbankova, Ol'ga. "Mag i charodei farb," *Mystets'ka storinka*, http://storinka-m.kiev.ua/article.php?id=898

Zilberman, Iurii and Iuia Smilianskaia. *Kievskaia simfonia Vladimira Gorovitsa*. Kiev: Fond Volodymyra Gorovytsia, 2002.

———. "Kievskaia uvertiura Vladimira Gorovitsa." *Yehupets* 6 (2000): 277–283.

Zipperstein, Steven J. *Imagining Russian Jewry: Memory, History, Identity*. Seattle: University of Washington Press, 1999.

———. *The Jews of Odessa: A Cultural History, 1794–1881*. Stanford, CA: Stanford University Press, 1986.

———. "The Politics of Relief: The Transformation of Russian Jewish Communal Life during the First World War." In *Studies in Contemporary Jewry: An Annual*, vol. 4, *The Jews and the European Crisis 1914–1921*, edited by Jonathan Frankel, 22–40. New York: Oxford University Press, 1988.

———. "Remapping Odessa, Rewriting Cultural History." *Jewish Social Studies* 2, no. 2 (1996): 21–37.

Index

A

Abramovich, Tama Lezerov, 128–129
Acculturation of Jews, 157, 374–375, 411
Ahdut Israel movement, 410
Aisenberg, F., 75
Akkerman, 260
Aksakov, Ivan, 65, 67–68, 200
Aleichem, Sholom, xiv, 2, 19, 87,
    113–116, 131, 159, 161, 169, 251,
    334, 336–347, 363–364, 397
  The Bloody Hoax, 338
  Funem Yarid (From the Fair), 114, 159,
    169, 338, 363
  Menakhem-Mendl, 115, 338
  *Tevye der Milkhiger (Tevye the
    Milkman)*, 338
  The Wandering Stars, 344
Aleksandrovskii Sugar Refining
    Corporation, 142, 172
Aleshkovskii, Iakov Aronovich, 252,
    401–402, 404–405, 430, 434
Alexander I, Tsar, 54–55, 58
Alexander II, Tsar, 13, 17, 47, 73, 82, 84,
    87, 93, 112, 259–260, 283, 402
Alexander III, Tsar, 113, 259
Alexandrovskii Jewish artisan school, 292
All-Russian Exhibition of 1913 in Kiev,
    206, 258, 381–384
Al'tenburgskaia, Princess Elena, 225, 229
Am Olam movement, 270–271, 287, 350
America, 18, 176, 179–182, 190, 194,
    270–271, 287, 340, 344, 350, 352,
    368, 371, 380, 420
Annenkov, Nikolai Nikolaevich, 95, 154
Ansky, Solomon, 171
anti-Jewish pogroms/anti-Jewish violence,
    2, 6, 8–9, 12, 16–17, 33–34, 86,
    110, 113–114, 119, 137, 146, 152,
    161, 163–165, 172, 174, 176–177,
    182–183, 186–187, 190, 193–194,
    203, 208–210, 220, 222, 250,
    259–269, 271–279, 281–283, 287,
    306–307, 313, 316, 329, 337, 342,
    345–350, 352–353, 364–365, 383,
    385, 398, 405, 415–417, 426,
    429–431, 433–436
  of 1881–1882, 16, 86, 119, 161, 183,
    186–187, 250, 259–270,
    273, 287, 316, 345–350,
    364–365, 385, 415
  eyewitness account, 263–267
  October 1905, 8, 16, 114, 146, 165,
    174, 176, 183, 203,
    208–210, 222, 259,
    273–279, 282, 287–289,
    291, 306, 329, 337, 383,
    385, 398, 415–416
anti-Semitism, 1–2, 8–9, 12, 16–17, 19,
    113, 136–137, 147, 152, 160–163,
    165, 174, 195, 218, 220, 259, 273,
    279, 285, 287–288, 316, 329, 337,
    349, 354, 359–361, 385, 394, 398,
    414–415, 423, 426–427, 436
Aronson, Boris, 418–420
Aronson, Rabbi Iakov, 409
Aronson, Rabbi Shlomo (Solomon),
    409–410
Art Studio of Aleksandra Ekster, 367
Ashkenazi, Leon, 141, 299
assimilation of Jews, 86, 137, 176,
    181–182, 191, 314–316, 327–328,
    333, 349–350, 354, 374, 391,
    410–411, 413, 420, 426
Athens, 13, 354–355
Austria, 153

B

Babel, Isaac, 135, 322, 387
Babi Yar, 203, 427
Badanes, Gershon, 118, 143–144, 147,
    150–151, 166, 345, 348–349,
    382–384
Bakst, Leo, 162
Balta, 260

Baltimore, 179, 368
Baratz, Herman, 161, 361–366
Baron, Salo, 53
basket tax, 3, 142–143, 145–146, 153, 178, 240, 299–300, 306, 383, 396, 410, 413
Belaia Tserkov', 43, 231, 378
Beilis, Mendel, xvi, 9, 17, 149, 251, 279–282, 339–340, 361, 405, 410, 434
Beilis affair, ix, 12, 174, 259, 279, 280, 283, 287–288, 378, 380, 382–385, 405, 415, 436
Beilis trial, 9, 17, 115, 279–282, 338–341, 354, 361, 378, 405, 410
Beit-Hakneset, 388
Beit-Hamedrash, 388
Belorussia, 51, 68, 418
Benjamin of Tudela, 34
Berdichev, 50, 63, 66, 71, 75, 96, 98, 164, 267–268, 362, 391
Berdyaev, Nikolai, 354
Bergelson, David, 355
Berlin, 78, 214, 338–339, 376, 379, 384, 410, 420
Berlin University, 185, 193
Berlinskii, Maksim, 6, 36, 51
Bershadskii, Sergei, 39
Bessarabia, 273
Bessarabskii Market, xv, 160, 247, 265, 344
Bezak, Governor-General Aleksandr Pavlovich, 95, 112–113
Bialik, Hayim Nachman, 333, 346
Bibikov, Governor-General Dmitrii, 47, 63–64, 77–78, 80, 82, 201, 387–388
Black Death, 36
Black Hundreds, 16, 165, 178, 209, 276–277, 279–288, 361, 372, 380, 405–406, 417, 420, 429, 431, 434, 435–436
Bludov, Dmitrii, 58, 91, 93
Boarding House for Jewish Children, 382
Bobrinskii, Aleksei Alekseevich, 18, 153, 155
Bogachek, Michael, 26–27
Bogrov, Dmitrii (Mordko), ix, xvi, 253, 421, 428–436

Bogrov, Grigorii Grigor'evich, 400, 430
Bogrov, Grigorii Isakovich, 430
Bohachevsky-Chomiak, Martha, 226
Boston, 179, 368
Brazul-Brushkovskii, Stepan Ivanovich, 281–282
Brodskaia, A. F., 229, 235
Brodskaia, Berta, 299
Brodskaia, Eva, 299
Brodsky, Abram Markovich, 153–155, 315. *See also* Brodsky family
Brodsky, Alexander, 167, 177, 183–184
Brodsky, Alexandra Fanny, 136, 156, 158, 166–167, 180, 183
Brodsky, Gregory, 183
Brodsky, Isaac, 156
Brodsky, Israel, xv, 136, 141–142, 148, 153, 155–157, 245. *See also* Brodsky family
Brodsky, Joseph (Iosif), 156
Brodsky, Lazar, xv, 16, 19, 136–137, 140–141, 148, 157–158, 160–167, 169–170, 195, 198, 245, 304–305, 307–308, 389–390, 397, 414–415, 426. *See also* Brodsky family
Brodsky, Lev (Leon), xv, 18, 136, 141, 143, 146, 148, 152, 154, 157, 166–178, 180, 182–184, 198, 208, 235, 246, 275, 305–306, 374, 389, 435 *See also* Brodsky family
Brodsky, Michael, 182
Brodsky, Solomon (Zalman), 156, 246
Brodsky Artisan School, xvi-xvii, 223, 256, 275, 383–384
Brodsky Choral Synagogue, xv, 140, 142, 157–159, 211, 221, 247, 390–391, 395
Brodsky family, 16, 18, 136, 141, 148, 152–155, 166–167, 169, 180, 182, 184, 188, 195, 204–205, 217, 222, 261, 346, 369, 426
and conditions of work at Brodsky plants and factories, 167–169
construction of public buildings and synagogues, 157–160
cooperation among family relations, 167

financial assistance to the Provisional Government, 184
Galveston Project, 178–182
Jewish legal rights, negotiation of, 161–166, 173–178
philanthropy, 169, 171–172
recognitions, 169, 172
solving problems in communal life, 161–162
sugar refineries, 18, 142, 152–153, 155–157, 160, 169–170, 172, 183, 205, 424
Brodsky Jewish State School, 305–308, 312
Bronshtein, Wolf, 295–296
"Brotherhood of the Lovers of Zion" ("*Hovevei Zion*"), 188
Brower, Daniel R., 10, 46
Bulanzhe, Pavel Alexandrovich, 342
Bulgakov, Mikhail, 202, 332–333
Bykhovskii, G. B., 149

C

Catherine the Great, 45–46
Chernigov, 59, 273
Chernigov province, 59, 284
Chernoiarov, Lazar', 211
Chernov, Vasilii, 410
Chertkov, Vladimir, 342
Chicago, 215–216, 368
Chikhachev, Vice-Governor Nikolai Nikolaevich, 399
Chiniselli, Gaetano, 376
Chokolov, Nikolai Ivanovich, 18, 123
Christians
 in Kiev, 8, 13, 30–31, 33–35, 75, 90, 97
 efforts to convert Jews, 53–55
 guesthouses for Jews, 69–70, 72–73
 hiding of Jewish neighbors during pogroms, 209, 277
 house owners renting to Jews, 118–119
 Jewish merchants *vs*, 7–8, 33, 40, 53–55, 62, 86, 90, 94, 97, 107–108
 Jewish right of residence and, 99–102
 Judaized, 31, 37–38
 in Khazarian Kaganate, 24

night round-ups and expulsions of Jews, petitions against, 118–120, 133
Orthodox, 13, 37–38, 40–41, 44, 99, 107, 157, 189
pretexts used to expel Jews, 115–123
Committee to Aid the Victims of Pogroms, 187, 222
Conservatory, Kiev, 229, 230, 369
Constantine VII Porphyrogenitus, Emperor, 26
Contract Fairs, 7, 14, 52, 59–60, 65–69, 86
Conversion of Jews to Christianity/ converts, 13, 24–25, 30–31, 37–38, 42, 53–54, 56, 74, 97, 105, 186, 318, 327, 360, 365, 380, 387, 430
Crimea, 36, 418
Crimean salt trade, 32
Crimean War (1853–1856), 82

D

Daniil Romanovich, Prince, 35
Darevskii, Israel, 5, 40, 55, 101, 361
 Le-korot ha-Yehudim be-Kiyov (To the History of Jews in Kiev), 362
Das folk (The People), 357
Dashevsky, Pinkhas, 436
Demievka, 127, 265, 273, 394, 399, 416–417
Denikin, General Anton Ivanovich, 352
Der morgen shtern (The Morning Star), 358
Desiatiletie Kievskogo evreiskogo khoral'nogo molitvennogo doma (Ten Years of the Kiev Jewish Choral Synagogue), 140
Dmitrieva, Iu. A., 377
Dobrushin, Yekhezkel, 355
Dolgorukii, E. M., 52
Dondukov-Korsakov, Count Aleksandr Mikhailovich, 133, 161, 294–295, 297
Dorpat (Tartu) University, 185
Dragomirov, Mikhail, 147, 160, 174–175
Drentel'n, Governor-General Aleksandr Romanovich, 108, 110, 119–120, 261–263, 267–268, 297, 299

Dreyfus Affair, 164, 280
Dubnov, Simon, 6, 12, 14–15, 57, 132, 186–187, 261, 263, 349, 427, 436
Dubrovin, Alexander Ivanovich, 284, 431, 435
Durnovo, Ivan Nikolayevich, 388
Dutch revolt against Catholic Spain (1566–1648), 42
Dvortsovyi district of Kiev, 102

E

economic development of Kiev, role of Jews in, 91, 123, 198–203
   commercial life of city, 200–203
   entrepreneurs, 12, 14, 97, 207, 210, 217–218, 239, 371, 425
   Ginzburg's construction company, 158, 211–212, 424
   Jewish business elite, 204–218
   Jewish poverty in Kiev, 218–241, 261, 270, 315, 346, 384, 396, 425
Edelstadt, David, 350
education of Jews, 14, 19, 79, 83–85, 92, 93, 98, 105, 135, 144, 146, 150, 169, 170, 173, 174, 185, 193, 223, 227, 237, 290–331, 337, 356, 362, 366, 369, 391, 393, 401, 409, 411, 413, 414, 419, 425–426
   Jewish schools, 19, 74–75, 81, 85, 106, 137, 139, 150, 206, 291–313, 318, 330–331, 391, 411.
   Jewish students in general schools, 313–330
   language barrier, 293
   of national minorities in the Russian Empire, 290–292, 313
   pedagogical courses for Jewish teachers, 309
   Talmud-Torahs, 139, 206, 292, 294, 308, 330, 392
   heders, 173, 185, 215, 291, 301, 308, 309, 312, 330
   melameds, 292–294, 298, 300, 301, 308–309, 330
Ehrenburg, Ilia, 401
Eisman, Gustav, 108–110
Ekaterinoslav, 283
Ekaterinoslav province, 273
Ekster, Aleksandra, 419
Elizavetgrad, 260–261, 272
Epshtein, Mark, 367
Eretz Israel, 402, 410
Estraikh, Gennady, 355
Ettinger, Samuel, 26, 39

F

February 1917 Revolution, 3–4, 14, 16, 19, 50, 73, 98, 102, 130, 132, 134, 145, 184, 240, 282, 289, 327, 352, 361, 410, 418, 426
Fedorov, Vladimir (Tsvi-Hirsh Grinboim), 80
Feigin, Litman, 59–60
Fenenko, V. E., 434
Fen'sh, Andrei Mikhailovich, 54–55
Fine Jr., John V. A., 39
Finland, 333
Fishzon, Abram (Avraham), 371–373
Folk shtime (People's Voice), 357
France, 34, 217, 280, 368, 379, 432
Frankel, Jonathan, 161
Frenkel', Sergei Andreevich, 377–378
Frenkel', V. Iu., 235
Friedmann, Eliezer, 176
Funduklei, Ivan, 7–8, 56, 65–66, 212

G

Galant, Il'ia Vladimirovich, 55, 169, 361, 366
Galitskii (Jewish) market (*Evbaz*), 199–203, 426
Galicia, 32, 42, 153, 200, 410
Gal'perin, Iosif, 75
Gal'perin, M. B., 102, 275
Galveston, 18, 179, 181–182, 190
Galveston Project, 18, 179–182, 190
Gardenin, Nikolai, 390
Gelman, Yakov, 60
Germany, 3, 28, 30, 79, 134, 214, 287, 348, 352, 354, 376
Gesse, Governor Nikolai Pavlovich, 295, 297
Gesse, Lieutenant General Pavel, 89–91, 97, 133, 201, 268, 391
Gessen, Iulii, 92
ghetto, 73, 86, 95, 179, 192, 368

Ginsburg, Baron Evzel', 112–113, 133, 426
Ginsburg, Baron Vladimir Goratsievich, 173, 177, 221–222, 275, 366–367, 385
Ginsburg, Horace, 367
Gintsburg, Baroness Roza Sigizmundovna, 227
Gintsburg, Baron Goratsii Osipovich, 225, 227
Ginzburg, Alexander de, 183
Ginzburg, Lev Borisovich [Leiba Berkovich], 158, 204, 211–212, 217, 239, 241, 424
Gitelman, Zvi, 333
Glazov, Vladimir Gavrilovich, 325
Gliksberg, Teofil, 74
Gogol, Nikolai Vasilievich, 332, 337
Golb, Norman, 6, 22–23, 25
Gol'denberg, Avraam Moiseevich, 110, 142, 252, 396–397, 404–405
Gol'denberg, Mrs. Avraam Moiseevich, 110
Goldenberg, E. D., 229
Goldfaden, Abraham, 371
Gomel', 283, 342, 360
Gorin, Bernhard, 374
Gorodetskii, Vladislav, 211
Graffman, Gary, 204, 207, 208
Graffman, Nadia, 206, 208
Great Britain, 348, 368
Great Northern War (1700–1721), 48
Great Reforms, 18, 73, 84, 87, 91, 392
Grigor'eva, Ekaterina, 69–73
Grinshtein, Izrail' Beniaminovich, 293–294, 411–412
Gruzenberg, Oskar, 352
Guenzburg, Horace, 162
Gurevich, Rabbi Avram 252, 399–406, 417
Gurevich, Boris (Buzia) Avramovich, 24, 44, 350–354, 417
Gurevich, Grigorii E. (see Badanes, Gershon)
Gymnasium, First Kiev, 49–50, 255, 323
gymnasiums in Kiev, 14, 49–50, 76, 105, 144, 135, 185, 212, 228, 231, 255, 266, 269, 303, 309, 323
gymnasium, Vilna, 76, 185
gymnasiums, graduates of, 93
gymnasium, Kiev woman's, named after Ivan Fundiklei; 212,
women students, 228;
St. Petersburg Jewish women preparation, 228;
graduates, 231
gymnasiums, percentage norm (quota), 292, 301, 317, 320
gymnasiums, Jewish, 309, 312

H

ha-Kohen, Adam (Avraham Dov Lebensohn), 346
ha-Kohen, Zacharia ben Aharon, 37
Hamburg, 214
Hamm, Michael F., 9, 21, 40, 47, 49, 50, 283
Harkavy, Alexander, 270
Hasdai Ibn Shaprut, 31
Hasidism, 362–363, 408
Ha-tsofe (The Observer), 357
Hebrew, 6, 22–25, 27, 37, 77, 81, 116, 168, 176, 188, 227, 289, 293, 306, 309, 311–312, 328, 345–346, 355–357, 359, 362–363, 365, 391, 397, 409
Hebrew theater "Habima", 169
Herlihy, Patricia, 154
Herzl, Theodor, 188, 190, 345
Hetman, 3–4, 41
"Hibat Tsiyon" (Love of Zion) movement, 345, 347
Hirshbein, Peretz, 370
Historical-Archaeographical Commission of the Ukrainian Academy of Science, 10
Hofshtein, David, 334, 355
Holocaust, 427
Horowitz, Iohim, 369
Horowitz, Vladimir, 369
Hrushevs'kyi, Mikhailo, 42
Hryhoriev, Hryhorii, 277, 435

I

Iampol'skii, Rabbi Dr. Petr, 144, 186–187, 192, 395–396, 399
Iaron, S. G., 102–106, 205
Iaroslav, Prince, 29
Ibn Fadlan, 29

Ignat'ev, Governor-General Aleksei, 162, 206, 301, 389–390
Ignat'ev, Nikolai Pavlovich, 119, 162, 187, 269, 271
Ignatovka, 213
Imperial Military-Medical Academy, 395
Imperial Russian Music Society, 369
Israel, 11, 26, 187, 427
Italy, 340–341, 343, 368
Ivan III, Prince of Muscovy, 38
Ivanov, Lieutenant Colonel A. A., 434
Ivensen, Fedor, 391
Iziaslav, Prince, 31–32
Izraelitin, A., 311

J
Jabotinsky, Vladimir Ze'ev, 320, 334, 341, 356–357
Jagiello, Alexander, Grand Duke of Lithuania, 4, 39
Jaroszynski, 18, 153
Jerusalem, 23, 30, 100, 164, 331, 354–355
Jewish artisans, 6, 54–55, 58, 89, 93–94, 103–104, 108–112, 132, 137, 142–143, 214–215, 218, 220–224, 241, 273, 296–297, 300, 302, 358, 387, 393–394, 408–409, 424–425
Jewish State Artisan School (Solomon Brodsky Artisan School), 19, 172, 206, 223, 256, 275, 383–384
Jewish beggars, 151, 166
Jewish charitable and philanthropic organizations, 10, 15, 137, 139, 151, 172, 206, 212, 220–221, 225, 233, 239, 241, 292, 382, 425
Jewish Charity Organization of the Kiev City Administration, 382
Jewish Colonization Society (EKO), 15, 118, 181, 218
Jewish communal institutions, 8, 16, 18, 137–152, 194, 359, 402
Jewish communal life, democratization of, 16, 142–143, 172, 194, 221, 356
Jewish Community Board, 137, 139–143, 194, 402
Jewish culture in Kiev, 332–386
  acting and musical professions, 369–375
  circuses, 246, 375–377, 384
  high and popular culture, 368–381
  Jewish artists, 19, 213–215, 222, 367–368, 385, 419–420
  of Jewish elite, 333–336
  Jewish periodicals in Kiev, 357–361
  Jewish writers and intellectuals, 345–355
  literary works of Sholom Aleichem, 336–344
  national identity and, 332–336
  suppression of Jewish culture, 336
  Yiddish literature and language, 95–96, 113, 312, 328, 334, 340, 345, 347–348, 350, 355–359, 367, 369–374, 385
Jewish elite in Kiev, 5, 18–19, 138, 143, 167, 198, 317, 330, 333–337, 357, 366, 392, 397–399, 411, 426
  acculturated, 374–375
  business elite, 204–218, 396
  philanthropic activity, 151, 154–155, 166, 169, 172, 204, 206, 212, 217, 384
  Russified, 385
  women, 225, 233
Jewish Emigration Society, 18, 172, 178–182, 185, 191
Jewish funeral brotherhood (hevra kadisha), 52–53
Jewish guesthouses, 41, 68–73, 82–84, 85, 100, 114–115
Jewish Historical Ethnographic Society, 367
Jewish Inexpensive Dining, 382
Jewish merchants, 7–8, 14, 32, 34, 40, 51–52, 58–59, 63–64, 68, 73, 86, 90–92, 94, 96, 100, 102, 108, 124–126, 135–136, 153, 199, 241, 296, 302, 322, 368–369, 383, 385, 388, 393, 424
Jewish periodicals in Kiev, 357–361
Jewish population, 3, 14–16, 43, 88–98, 102–103, 106, 118, 133, 136, 140, 174–175, 218, 268, 330, 422
Jewish poverty in Kiev, 218–221
Jewish press in Kiev, 357–361
Jewish publications and their censorship, 73–85

Jewish religious life in Kiev
  assimilation and secularization, 410–420
  Chernobyl prayer house, 407–408
  prayer house, 34, 52, 61, 121, 139–140, 157–159, 387–393, 396–398, 404, 407–408
  prayer houses and synagogues, 34, 52, 61, 139, 387–393
  synagogue, 9–10, 14, 19, 33–34, 52, 61, 106, 137, 140, 142, 157–160, 172, 184, 207, 211, 221, 247, 264, 292, 330, 336, 361, 387–395, 397, 400, 404, 408, 412, 417, 422, 426, 435
  rabbis, 391–403
  Tsar's meeting with the Jewish delegation, 403–410
Jewish right of residence, 87–134
  periodic night raids and night round-ups of Jews, 115–123
  petition against persecution of Jews, 123–125
Jewish schools in Kiev, 292–313
  Brodsky family's contribution, 305–308
Jewish self-defense units, 276–277, 288, 416–417
Jewish students in general schools, 313–330
  classical education, 321
  enrollment for graduation and diplomas, 321–322
  externs, 320–321, 327
  government policy toward, 316–317
  in Russian gymnasiums and universities, 314–315
  system of percentage quota (*numerus clausus*), 105, 292–293, 301 303, 309, 313–314, 316–318, 320–327, 329–331, 366–367
  Women's higher courses, 319
Jewish Territorial Organization (ITO), 180, 182, 190
Jewish vocational training in Kiev, 144, 223, 241, 304, 306, 331

Jewish Welfare Committee, 140–143, 145, 150–151, 172, 194, 198, 202, 221
Jochelmann, Dr. David, 190
Joint-Stock Cinematograph Society, 378
Judaism, 9, 23–25, 37–38, 54, 79, 144, 178, 207, 293, 306, 309, 354, 366, 411, 413, 429
Judaizers sect, 31, 37–39
Judeophilia, 8, 315
Judeophobia, (also Judophobic) 2, 6, 8, 12, 17, 19, 58, 133, 162, 164, 259, 316, 411, 423
Judeophobe, 16, 96, 98–99, 107, 164, 261, 422
Justinian I, Emperor, 22

K

Kablukov, Sergei, 192–193
Kaganovich, Lazar, 168
kahal, Kiev, 51–52, 137–142, 194
Kalnitsky, Mikhail, xi–xii, 9, 212, 248–249
Kaminer, Isaak, 345
Kaplan, Feiga (Fanni, Fania) Khaimovna, 128–131, 436
Karamzin, Nikolai, 34, 37
Karavaevskii, Vasilii, 277
Kasso, Lev Aristidovich, 322
Kaufman, A. E., 163–164
Kaufman, Petr Mikhailovich, 325
Kazan', 319
Kazimierz, King Jan II, 43
Kazovsky, Hillel, 355, 367
Kel'berin, E. P., 140
Kel'berin, Izrail' P., 221
Khar'kov, 68, 226, 381
Kharitonenko, 18, 153
Kharitonov, Dmitrii Ivanovich, 381
Khazarian Jews, 4–6, 14, 23–27, 31, 44
Khazarian Kaganate, 24–26, 28–31
Kherson province, 260, 273, 402
Khorevitsa, 27
Khoriv, 22, 27–28
Khronika evreiskoi zhizni (Chronicle of Jewish Life), 173
Khronika Voskhoda (Chronicle of Dawn), 395
Kiev

expulsion of Jews from, 4, 14, 34, 39–40, 43, 51, 54–59, 61
foundation of city, 21–27
as a Jewish city, 2, 16, 44, 96–110, 422, 426
under Lithuanian and Polish rule (1320–1654), 3–4, 14, 35–44
mortality rate in poor districts, 234–235
Poles in, 41–44, 46–47, 49–50, 62, 65, 93, 96, 309, 313, 316
population (nineteenth century), 88, 90–91, 95–96
Varangian dynasty, 27–28
Kievan letter, 5–6, 22–24
Kievan Rus', 2–3, 5, 13–14, 25, 27–36, 44, 365–366
Kiev artisan school, 223
Kiev Art School, 367, 419
Kiev Cave Monastery (see Kiev-Pechersk Lavra)
Kiev Censorship Committee, 12, 74, 75–76, 78–80, 358
Kiev City Theater, xvi, 253, 428, 433
Kiev Commercial Institute, 322, 327, 365
Kiev Commissariat Commission, 59, 82–84
Kiev Contract Fairs, 65–69
Kiev Department of the Jewish Committee of Aid to the Victims of the War (EKOPO), 221, 239–240
Kiev Department of the Society for the Protection of the Health of the Jewish Population (OZE), 239
Kiev Jewish community, 135–195, 198, 210, 221, 224, 235, 239–240, 270, 294, 296–299, 299, 312–314, 330, 349, 383–384, 389–391, 395–396, 398, 402, 405, 411, 422, 425–426, 435
 budget of, 143–147, 150
 distribution of money for Jewish schools, 150–151
Kiev Jewish Department of the Society for the Protection of Women, 221–234, 241
Kiev Jewish hospital, 138, 144, 146–151, 154, 172, 194, 212, 216, 311, 383, 424

Kiev Jews, social and economic history
 primary sources of, 10–12
 published works, 5–10
Kiev province, 4, 7, 46, 49, 53, 57, 61, 63, 65, 71, 75, 77, 106, 108–109, 144, 151, 153, 185, 262, 273, 294, 308, 358, 380, 393, 416
Kiever tagblat (Kiev Daily Paper), 357
Kiever wort (Kiev Word), 357
Kievlianin (Kievan), 8, 17, 99–100, 116, 121, 127–130, 164–165, 170, 272, 316, 322, 331, 333, 361, 381, 401, 404, 407, 410
Kiev-Pechersk Lavra (Kiev Cave Monastery), 13, 22, 31, 48, 99, 365
Kiev police, 17, 59–60, 72, 101, 103, 117, 121–122, 145, 163, 189, 276, 279, 284, 294–295, 307, 342, 399, 411
Kiev Police Department, 12
Kiev Polytechnic Institute, 160, 169–170, 211, 254–255, 303, 324–325, 328, 403, 436
Kievskaia gazeta (Kiev Gazette), 278
Kievskaia Gosudarstvennaia Palata (Kiev State Chamber), 51
Kievskaia Mysl' (Kievan Thought), 341, 360, 403–404
Kievskaia starina (Kiev Olden Times), 366
Kievskie eparkhial'nye vedomosti (Kiev Diocese Herald), 96, 99
Kievskie novosti (Kiev News), 282
Kievskie otkliki (Kiev Review, Kiev Comments), 278, 360
Kievskie vesti (Kiev Herald), 116–117, 360
Kiev Society for the Care of Poor Jewish Artisans and Workers, 221–224, 240
 board of, 221–222
 funding for, 222
 goals of, 222–223
Kiev Society of the Friends of Peace, 400
Kiev St. Vladimir University, 49–50, 63, 86, 99, 105, 111, 140, 163, 170, 185–186, 254, 303, 314–315, 318–319, 321, 324, 328, 348, 350,

352, 362, 365, 399–400, 402–403, 414, 430, 432
Kii, Prince, 22, 28
Kiperman, Meier-Iakov Itskovich, 307
Kleigel, Governor-General Nikolai Vasilievich, 310
Klier, John Doyle, x, 8, 39
Kogan, Mark Osipovich, 297–298
Kokovtsev, V. N., 123
Komissarov, Abram, 121–122
Konashevych-Sahaidachnyi, Hetman Petro, 41
Kotik, Yekhezkel, 71, 407–408, 412–415
Kotten, Mikhail von, 432
Kovel', 343
Kovno, 15, 146, 172, 178
Kozintseva, Lubov, 401
Kreshchatik Street, 2, 88, 107, 166, 213, 242, 266, 275, 374
Krichevski, Fedor, 368
Ksenia, 209
Kulisher, Mikhail, 6, 40–41, 56, 63
Kupernik, Lev Abramovich, 360, 364
Kurland, 57, 85, 424
Kurlov, Governor P. G., 121–122
Kutaisov, Major General P. I., 268

L

Ladyzhnikov, E. P., 341
Lanskoi, Stepan Stepanovich, 91–93
Larin, Iurii, (Mikhail Zalmanovich Lur'e), 417–418
Lazarev, Egor, 431
leaders of Kiev Jewish Community, 135–194, 426. *See also* Brodsky family
Leshchinskii, Iakov, 179
Lettland, 57, 85
Levashov, Governor-General Vasilii, 56, 62–63, 97
Levenshtein, D. G., 239
Levin, Saul, 299
Levin, Yehudah Leib (see Yahalel)
Levinson, Vasilii, 81
Liatoshinskaia, Katerina, 323
Liberman, Aron, 348
Liberman, S. P., 102
Liberty Loan, 184
Linder, Max, 378

Linetskii, Yitskhok Yoel, 345, 347
Dos Poylishe Yingl (The Polish Boy), 347
Lips, Y., 75–76
Lipskii, 414–415
Lithuania, 3–4, 14, 35–36, 39, 95, 185
Litvakov, Moshe, 355
London, 21, 180, 368, 384
Lopukhin, Petr, 155
Loris-Melikov, Count Mikhail Tarielovich, 263
Lunacharsky, Anatolii Vasilievich, 368
Lur'e, Ia. S. (Jacob Luria), 38–39
Lur'e, Mikhail Zalmanovich (see Larin, Iurii)
Lur'e, Solomon Arkad'evich (Kalmanovich), 310–311, 396–398, 400
Lybedskoi district of Kiev, 69, 71, 73, 94, 97, 102, 103, 120–121, 125, 234, 236, 300, 374, 425
Lybid', 22, 28
Lybid', river, 61–62

M

Mabovitch, Moshe Yitzhak, 218
Magdeburg Law, 36, 40, 57
Makarov, Anatolii, 56
Malakov, Dmytro, 201
Malyshevskii, Ivan, 5, 31–33
Mandel'shtam, Osip, 192–193
Mandelstamm, Leon Iosifovich, 185, 189–190
Mandelstamm, Max Emilievich (Emmanuil), xv, 17–18, 141, 148, 172, 176, 178, 184–194, 248, 308, 349–350, 364
  development of ophthalmologic treatment in Russia, 186
  establishment of "Brotherhood of the Lovers of Zion" ("*Hovevei Zion*"), 188
  family, 185
  as ophthalmologist, 186
  Zionist movement, 188–189
Mandelstamm, Sofia, 299
Manevich, Abram, 19, 367–368
Margolin, Arnold, 177, 207–209, 251, 281–282, 410

Margolin, David Semenovich, xv, 138, 146, 177, 204–211, 217, 241, 249, 261, 308, 381, 385, 424
Margolina, Rozaliia Isaakovna (née Tsuker), 207, 229
Mariinskii Palace, 102, 403
Marshak, Iosif Abramovich, xv, xvi, 204, 212–217, 221, 223–224, 239, 241, 249–250, 308, 343, 424
Marshak's jewelry company, 212–217, 250
Maze, Rabbi Iakov, 409–410
Mazor, M.S., 239
Meir, Golda, 218–220, 271
Meir, Natan, vii–viii, xi, xviii, 8, 140, 145–146, 150, 172–173, 395, 407–408
Meisel, Nakhman, 355
Melenskii, Andrei, 52
Menakhem-Mendl, novel, 115, 338
Mendele Moicher Sforim (Sholem Abramovich), 333, 346
Meyerhold, Vsevolod, 379, 419–420
Miiakovs'kyi, Volodymyr, 323–324
Mikhoels, Solomon, 322
Milner, Moshe (Mikhail), 169
Minsk, 15, 98, 129, 226, 346, 408
Mizrachi movement, 409–410
modernization of Kiev, 197–198
Molchanov, A. N., 107–108, 139, 148, 160–161, 166
Moshe ben Yakov, Rabbi, 37
Moskalev, G., 209
Moscow, x, 6, 38, 57, 88, 134, 158, 197, 214–215, 266, 292, 298, 317, 319, 327–329, 332–333, 336, 354, 376, 379, 381, 384, 401, 409, 419–420, 422, 424, 430
Moscow University, 325
Mongols, 3, 34–36, 44
Montreal, 368
movies on Jewish themes
  Bog mesti (The God of Vengeance), 380
  censorship issues, 379–380
  David and Saul, 378
  Gore Sary (The Grief of Sara), 378, 380
  Kaznennyi zhizn'iu (Executed by Life), 378, 380

The Kiev Mystery or the Beilis Trial, 378–379
L'Haim (For Life), 380–381
Rakhil (Rachel), 378, 380
Tragediia evreiskoi kursistki (The Tragedy of the Jewess Student), 378, 380
Vera Chibiriak (Cheberiak), 378
Za okeanom (Beyond the Ocean), 380–381
Zhertvoprinoshenie Avraama (The Sacrifice of Abraham), 378
Zhidovka-vykrestka (The Converted Jewess), 380
Zhizn' evreev v Amerike (The Life of Jews in America), 380
Zhizn' evreev v Palestine (The Life of Jews in Palestine), 380
Zhizn' Moiseia (The Life of Moses), 378
Mstislavl', 367
Murashko, Aleksandr, 368
Murav'ev, Andrei Nikolaevich, 107
Mushin, A., 430

N

Narbut, Georgii, 368
Nathans, Benjamin, 17, 322
Nazi, 3, 11, 28, 53, 212. 287, 379, 427
Nemirovsky, Irene, xvii, 258, 334–336
Nemirovsky, Leonid, 336
Nervi, Italy, 340
Nestor, 22, 27–28, 30–31
New York, xiii, 11, 179, 270, 344, 350, 352, 368, 420
Nezhin, 366, 409
Nezhin Historical-Philological Society, 366
Nicholas I, Tsar, 14, 17, 46–47, 50–52, 54–58, 61–62, 71, 76, 79–80, 82, 84–86, 91, 95, 137, 423–424
Nicholas II, Tsar, xvi, 113, 252, 259, 281, 283, 285, 326, 329, 361, 369, 372, 402, 405, 421, 429, 433
Nikita, monk, 365–366
Nikitin, brothers, 376–377
Nikolaev, 57, 85, 94–95, 297, 424
Nikol'skaia Slobodka, 116, 127, 284
Nizhnii Novgorod, 260
Norov, Avraam, 81

Norsemen (Vikings, Normans), 3, 27
Novgorod, 27, 37–38, 366
Novitskii, Vasilii Dement′evich, 185, 262–263, 268
Novoe vremia, 107, 139, 148, 160, 330
numerus clausus for Jews, 317, 321, 325–326, 329

O

October 17 Manifesto, 17
Odessa, 15, 17, 19, 52, 66, 74–75, 88, 98, 128–129, 153–156, 158, 170, 187–188, 226, 260, 315–316, 333, 336–337, 347, 370, 376
Odessa City Duma, 154
Ol′denburgskaia, Evgeniia, 225
Olel′kovich, Prince Mikhailo, 37

P

Pale of Settlement, vi, xviii, 1, 3, 14, 17–19, 57, 68, 77, 85–86, 91, 95, 106, 111–112, 134, 136, 179, 227, 230, 233, 291–292, 299–300, 309, 314, 317, 322, 324, 329, 331, 367, 388, 422, 429
Palestine, 188–191, 270, 380
Palestinophile, 141, 184, 187, 345–347, 349, 395, 397, 409
Pantaleev, Aleksandr, 377
Paris, 21, 163, 174, 182, 214–217, 337–338, 348, 352, 365, 368, 379
Paul I, Tsar, 46, 54
Pavlenko, Iurii, 27
Pechersk, 48–49, 51–52, 61, 88, 102, 157, 275, 335, 399, 429
Peace Treaty of Belaia Tserkov′, 43
People′s Will, 259, 261, 348
Pereiaslav, 32, 43
Pereswetoff-Morath, Alexander, 365
 A Grin without a Cat, 365
Peter the Great, 46, 48
Petr Nikolaevich, Grand Prince, 206
Petrograd, 333, 367
Petrov, Nikolai Ivanovich, 265–266
Philadelphia, 179,
philanthropic organizations in Kiev, 137, 139, 172, 206, 212, 220–221, 239, 292, 383, 425
philo-Semitism, 273, 324

Pikhno, Dmitrii Ivanovich, 163–165, 176, 381
Pirogov, Nikolai Ivanovich, 315–316
Plekhanov, Georgii Valentinovich, 73, 341
Pleve, Viacheslav, 189
Plosskii district of Kiev, 69, 73, 94, 97, 102, 107, 120, 125, 127, 129, 234, 236, 265, 275, 294, 296, 300, 334, 374, 425
Podol, 22, 26, 32, 48–49, 51–52, 65–66, 69, 72–73, 76, 82, 91, 97, 102–103, 115, 120, 133, 149, 154, 157, 164, 174, 213, 231, 234, 243–244, 425
Podolia, 4, 42, 46, 66, 149, 164, 260, 273, 308, 362
pogrom, see anti-Jewish pogroms/anti-Jewish violence
Poland, 3–4, 9, 18, 35, 39–42, 46, 50–51, 95, 100, 233, 290, 333, 420
Poletika, Nikolai Pavlovich, 202–203
Polish-Lithuanian Commonwealth, 35, 95
Polish uprising of 1830–1831, 290
Polonsky, Antony, x, 9, 260, 273, 281
Poltava, 189
Poltava province, 273
Potemkin, Prince Grigorii, 155
Pritsak, Omeljan, 4, 6, 22, 25–26, 33
Proreznaia Street, 242, 275

R

Raba, Joel, 42
rabbis, 12, 58, 79, 141, 145–146, 159, 391–409
Rabinovich, Isaac, 367
Rabinovich, Rabbi Aron, 399
Raiskii, Zeilik, 121–122
Rasputin, Grigorii, 285–286
Razina, Ol′ga, 376
Representative Board for Jewish Welfare, 142
Revolution, 1905, 17, 142, 152, 166, 174, 178, 194–195
Riga, 226, 376
Rieber, Alfred J., 106, 169
Right Bank Ukraine, 51, 290
Rodionov, Nikolai Matveevich, 284
Roisen, Boruch, 391–392
Romanov, Aleksei, Tsar 43
Rostov-on-Don, 25, 226, 395

Rozenberg, Elka, 299
Rozenberg, Gabriel-Yakov, 390
Rozenberg, Maria, 299
Rubinchik, H.S., 239
Russian Society for the Protection of Women, 225–227, 233
Russification, 47, 85, 99, 290, 292, 309, 326, 330, 333, 336, 426
Russo-Turkish War of 1877–1878, 264, 395

S

Saksen-Al'tenburgskaia, Elena, 225
Salamonskii, Albert, 376–377
Schechter, Solomon, 6, 22–24
Sevastopol', 57, 85, 94–95, 226, 424
Shchek, 22, 28
Shcherbatov, Nikolai, 134, 239
Sheinis, D. E., 327
Shestov (Shvartsman), Lev, 354
    Afiny i Ierusalim (Athens and Jerusalem), 354
Shevchenko, Taras, 334
Shifer, Morits, 60
Shimanovich, 53
Shirinskii-Shikhmatov, Platon, 80
Shleifer, Georgii, 158
Shmakov, Aleksei, 177
Shohat, Azriel, 395
Sholom Aleichem (Sholom Yakov Rabinovich), xiv, xvi, 2, 87, 113–116, 131, 159, 161, 169, 251, 334, 336–347, 363–364, 397
Shor, Alexander-Chaim, 153
Shor, Meir, 152–153
Shtadlan/stadlanut, 16, 137, 152, 154–155, 161–162, 174, 195, 391–394, 415, 426
Shtammer, Lev, 147, 158, 395–398, 406
Shteinberg, Aron, 354
Shteinberg, Boruch Zelikovich (Boris Zacharovich), xvi, 255
Shtern, Lina, 377
shtetl, 1, 98, 104, 135, 153, 155, 179, 181, 213, 225, 231, 273, 320, 335–336, 346, 349, 355, 357, 364, 367–368, 371, 385, 404, 407, 420, 422, 426
Shul'gin, Vitalii Iakovlevich, 99–101, 123, 176

Shul'gin, Vasilii, 176, 274, 361, 410, 416–417, 421
Shvarts, Aleksandr Nikolaich, 317
Shvartsman, Osher, 355
Siedlce, 369
Sklovskii, Evgenii L'vovich, 343
slavery, 32, 36, 226
Sliozberg, Genrikh, 110, 160, 163, 192, 205–206
Slonimskii, Chaim Zelig, 397
Slutskii, Rabbi David, 54, 387
Society for Aid to Jewish Teachers and Melameds Living in Kiev and the Pale of Settlement, 308–309
Society for Spreading Enlightenment among Jews in Russia (OPE), 144, 150, 154, 172, 307–308, 311–313, 327
Society for the Protection of Women, 221, 224–234
Society for the Welfare of Poor Jews in Kiev, 220
Society to Maintain Summer Sanatorium Colonies for the Sick Children of the Poor Jewish Population in Kiev, xvii, 221, 234–239, 241, 257
    accomplishments of, 238–239
    selection of children for admission to, 236–237
Soifer, Iosif Abramovich, 378–379
Sokolow, Nahum, 193
Solov'ev, Sergei, 35
Solovtsov's Theater, 171, 211, 374–375, 379
southwestern region, 4, 7, 35, 46–47, 52, 67, 88, 93, 107, 124, 132, 139, 153, 156, 160, 164, 186, 206–207, 215–216, 260, 268, 370–373, 382, 403, 407
Soviet Union, 3, 168, 369, 379, 418
St. Bartholomew's Day Massacre (1572), 42
"St. Bartholomew's Night," 276
St. Petersburg, 7, 17–19, 55–57, 65, 75–76, 78, 81, 84, 88, 98, 107, 112, 123, 126, 133–134, 139, 158, 161–162, 169, 185, 187, 197, 207, 214–216, 225–230, 232, 268, 279–280, 286, 292, 298, 302, 317, 319, 333–334, 336, 358, 369–370, 372, 376, 381, 384, 393, 397, 418, 422, 430–432

St. Petersburg Jewish Department of the Society for the Protection of Women, 226–228
St. Sophia Cathedral, 13, 29
Stanislawski, Michael, 138, 291
Starokonstantinov, 392
State Jewish Theater (GOSET), 169, 322
Statute Concerning Jews of 1835, 64
Stites, Richard, 225
Stolypin, Petr A., ix, xvi, 123, 252, 284, 288, 325, 400, 402, 406, 409, 421, 428–436
Stroganov, A. G., 92–93
Struve, Petr, 333
Subbotin, A. P., 197, 199–201
Sukhomlinov, Governor-General Vladimir Aleksandrovich, 130, 306, 310–311, 325, 370–373, 375, 399, 436
Sviatopolk II, Prince, 32–33
Switzerland, 368, 418
Syrkin, Naum Solomonovich, 342

T

Tairov, Alexander, 420
Tatars, 3, 35–36
Tatishchev, Vasilii, 32–33
Tatz, 53
Tereshchenko, N. A., 153, 170
Thirty Years War (1618–1648), 42
Tolkachev, Zinovii, 367
Tolochko, Petr, 21, 26
Tolstoy, Count Ivan Ivanovich, 325–326
Tolstoy, Leo, 342, 418
Tomara, Governor Lev Pavlovich, 300
Tomashpol, 346
Toronto, 368
Trepov, Governor-General Fedor Fedorovich, 123, 158, 229, 394
Tritshel', K. G., 148, 399
tsaddiks, 140, 362, 407
Tsikhotskii, Viacheslav, 276, 279, 307
Tsukkerman, Rabbi Evsei, xv, 158–159, 161, 198, 221, 248, 295–296, 299, 363, 389, 392–395, 399
tuberculosis, 144, 234–237, 341, 350, 383, 425
Turau, Senator Evgenii Fedorovich, 274, 278–279, 306
Twersky Hasidic dynasty, 407

Tyshler, Aleksandr, 367

U

Uganda Plan, 190
Ukraine, 2, 3, 11, 42–43, 51, 65, 68, 156, 218, 251–253, 273, 290, 334, 336–337, 366–368, 379, 402, 418
Ukraine, civil war, 368
Ukrainian Academy of Arts and Science, 10, 368
Ukrainian Cossacks, 41–43
Ukrainian culture, 333–334, 386
Ukrainian Free Academy of Arts and Science, 207, 323
Ukrainian language, 291, 355
Ukrainian literature, 334
Ukrainian National Army, 2, 3
Ukrainian national movement, 47, 211, 291, 334
Ukrainian People's Republic, 207, 210, 402
Ukrainian war of liberation, 42
Union of Active Struggle with Revolution, 283–284
Union of Equality for Women (*Soiuz ravnopraviia zhenshchin*), 226
Uvarov, Sergei, 75, 77–80, 85

V

Vannovskii, Petr Semenovich, 263
Varangian dynasty, 27
Varshavskii, Mark, 345
Vashenboim, B.E., 239
Vasil'chikov, Governor-General Illarion Illarionovich, 82–84, 91, 93, 120, 133, 388
Veidlinger, Jeffrey, 369
Velizh affair, 58
Verednovich, 53
Veretnikov, Lieutenant General A. P., 121
Vertinsky, Alexander, 351–352
Dorogoi Dlinnoiu (On a Long Road), 351–352
Vestnik evreiskoi obshchiny (Jewish Community Herald), 359
Vetukhiv, Michael, 207
Vienna, 84, 162, 337, 384
Vilna, 15, 74, 76, 78, 80, 98, 185, 226, 239, 270, 369, 414

Vilna Censorship Committee, 74, 80
Vladimir, Prince, 13, 28, 30, 99
Vladimir Monomakh, 29, 32–33
vocational education for Jewish girls, 223
Volhynia, 4, 42, 46, 66, 343, 362, 392
Vol'tke, Grigorii, 73

W

Warsaw, 50, 60–61, 74, 88, 98, 146, 215, 339–340, 402
Weinberg, Robert, 9
Weiss, Jonathan, 335
Witte, Sergei Iul'evich, 156–157, 171, 286, 326, 423
World Exhibitions, 214–215

Y

Yalta, 94–95
Yehalel (Yehudah Leib Levin), 19, 168–169, 188, 345–347
Yehupets, 2, 16, 87, 110–132, 338, 422, 426
Yiddish literature and language, 77, 95–96, 113, 310–312, 328, 335, 340, 343, 347–348, 350 355–358, 367, 369–374, 385
Yiddish periodicals, 339, 358, 406
Yiddish troupes/theater, 369–371, 374, 420
Yudishe naye leben (New Jewish Life), 357–358

Z

Zaitsev, Iona, 142, 149, 389–390
Zaitsev, M. I., 102
Zaitsev, Mark, 149
Zaitsev Surgical Hospital, 144, 149, 383
Zak, A. I., 162
Zakrevskii, Nikolai, 6–7, 13, 31, 34, 40, 201
Zaks, M. R., 102
Zal'tsfish, Leon (Leiba), 60
Zangwill, Israel, 180, 182, 190
Zaria (Dawn), 360
Zaslavskii, David, 405–406
Zeiberling, Iosif, 73–86, 91
  Sefer Ein Yaakov, 80–81
Zeiger, Yakob, 60–61
Zheltukhin, P. F., Kiev military governor, 58
Zhitomir, 60, 75, 96, 347, 362
Zhitomir Publishing House, 75
Zhitomir Rabbinical Seminary, 392
Zhuravskii, D. P., 7–8
Zionism, 176, 188–189, 191–192, 409
Zionist movement, 141, 169, 188–189, 191–192, 346, 349, 359
Zipperstein, Steven, 151, 154
Zlatopol', 153, 155
Zygmunt I, King, 36
Zygmunt III, King, 41, 43, 55, 57

Victoria Khiterer is an Associate Professor of History and the Director of the Conference on the Holocaust and Genocide at Millersville University, PA. She is the author and editor of five books and over eighty articles in Russian and Eastern European Jewish History.

www.ingramcontent.com/pod-product-compliance
Lightning Source LLC
Chambersburg PA
CBHW052009290426
44112CB00014B/2175